CW00794288

St. Augustine's Abbey:

Report on Excavations, 1960–78

Painted Plaster, 1974.

COLOUR PLATE 2

Cornelian Intaglio of Ceres. In her left hand she holds two ears of corn and in her right hand a dish of fruit. (Fig. 62, no. 2).

COLOUR PLATE 3

Cloisonné Enamel Mount, originally fixed to a gold-plated silver object (Fig. 63, no. 1).

Monograph Series
of the
Kent Archaeological Society

(General Editor: A.P. Detsicas, B.A., M.A., D.Litt., F.S.A.)

No. IV

St. Augustine's Abbey: Report on Excavations, 1960–78

By

D. Sherlock, B.A., F.S.A., and H. Woods, B.A.

WITH A MAJOR CONTRIBUTION BY

L. Blackmore, B.A.

AND SHORTER CONTRIBUTIONS BY

F.W. Anderson; J. Bayley, B.Sc., M.Sc.; J. Blair, M.A., D.Phil., F.S.A.; D. Cook; E. Crowfoot; G. Edwards, B.A.; D.B. Harden, C.B.E, M.A., Ph.D, F.S.A.; M.E. Henig, M.A., D.Phil., F.S.A.; M.C. Horton, B.A.; M. Hutchinson, F.G.A.; B. Knight, B.A., M.Sc., D.Phil.; G. Lloyd-Morgan, B.A., Ph.D., F.S.A.; A. Locker; C. Miscampbell, M.A.; P. Northover; J. Ridgway; S.E. Rigold, M.A., F.S.A., F.R.Hist.S.; R.W. Sanderson, B.Sc.; A.D. Saunders, M.A., F.S.A.; J.C. Thorn; and R. Wyles.

EDITED BY

J. Geddes, M.A., Ph.D., F.S.A.

Published for the
Historic Buildings and Monuments Commission for England
by the
Kent Archaeological Society
Maidstone
1988

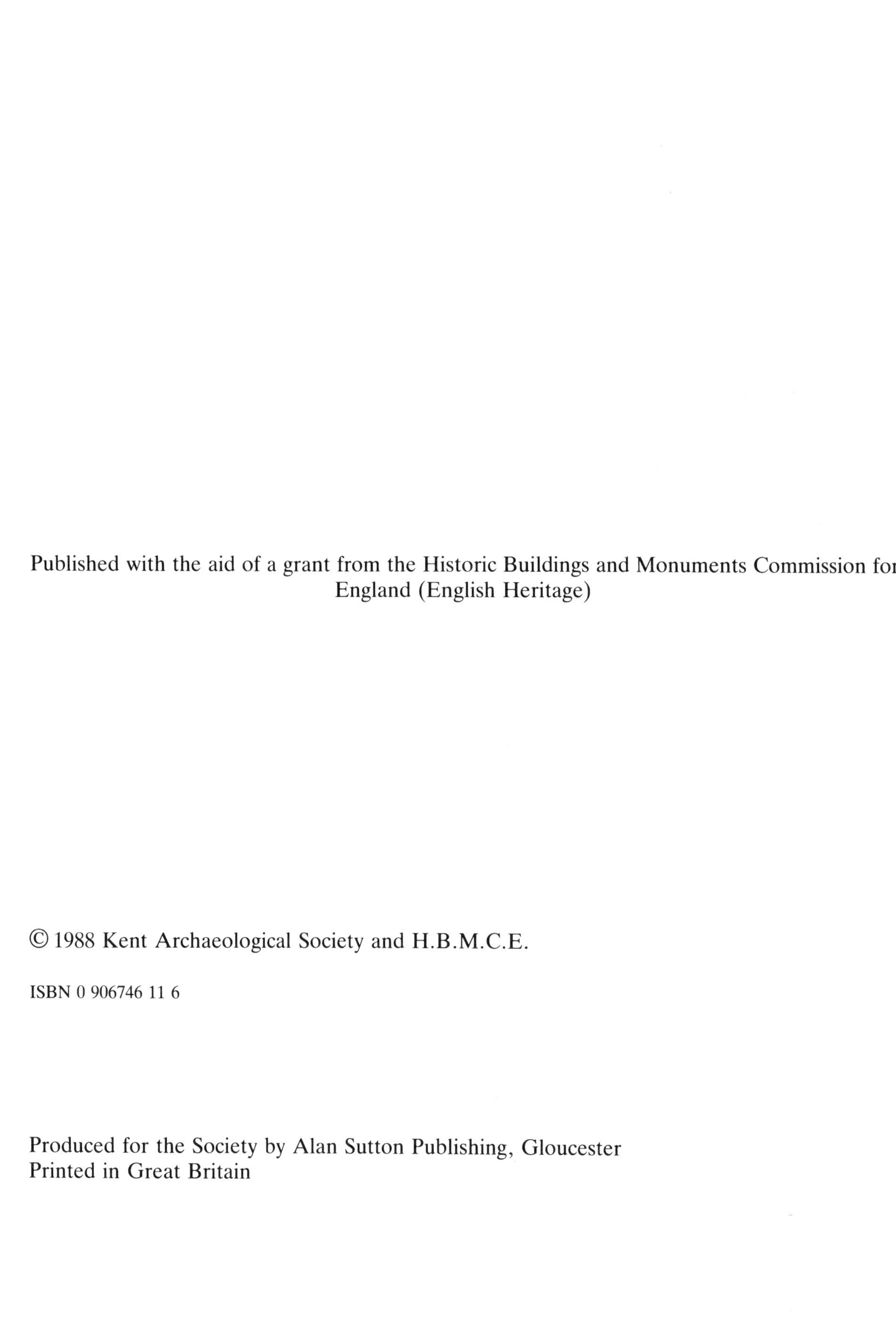

Published with the aid of a grant from the Historic Buildings and Monuments Commission for England (English Heritage)

ISBN 0 906746 11 6

Produced for the Society by Alan Sutton Publishing, Gloucester
Printed in Great Britain

CONTENTS

LIST OF FIGURES

LIST OF PLATES

ABBREVIATIONS

A.M.L.	Ancient Monuments Laboratory
Antiq. J.	*The Antiquaries Journal.*
Arch. Ael.	*Archaeologia Aeliana.*
Arch. Cant.	*Archaeologia Cantiana.*
Arch. J.	*The Archaeological Journal.*
B.A.R.	British Archaeological Reports.
Beds. Arch. J.	*Bedfordshire Archaeological Journal.*
Birmingham and Warks. Arch. Soc.	Birmingham and Warwickshire Archaeological Society.
C.B.A.	Council for British Archaeology.
Ches. Arch. Bull.	*Cheshire Archaeological Bulletin.*
D.o.E.	Department of the Environment
Dorset Nat. Hist. and Arch. Soc.	Dorset Natural History and Archaeological Society.
E. Anglian Arch. Reps.	*East Anglian Archaeological Reports.*
Glasgow Arch. J.	*Glasgow Archaeological Journal.*
H.B.M.C.	Historic Buildings and Monuments Commission
Herts. Arch.	*Hertfordshire Archaeology.*
J.B.A.A.	*The Journal of the British Archaeological Association.*
J. Brit. Soc. Master Glass Painters	*The Journal of the British Society of Master Glass Painters.*
Kent Arch. Rev.	*Kent Archaeological Review.*
Med. Arch.	*Medieval Archaeology.*
N.M.R.	National Monuments Record.
Northants. Mus. J.	*Northamptonshire Museum Journal.*
Pap. Brit. Sch. Rome	*Papers of the British School at Rome.*
Phil. Trans. Roy. Soc.	*Philosophical Transactions of the Royal Society.*
Post-Med. Arch.	*Post-Medieval Archaeology.*
Proc. Camb. Arch. Soc.	*Proceedings of the Cambridge Archaeological Society.*
Proc. Hants. F.C.	*Proceedings of the Hampshire Field Club.*
Proc. Harrow Archit. C.	*Proceedings of the Harrow Architectural Club.*
Proc. Soc. Ant. London	*Proceedings of the Society of Antiquaries of London.*
Proc. Soc. Ant. Scotland	*Proceedings of the Society of Antiquaries of Scotland.*
Proc. Suffolk Inst. Arch.	*Proceedings of the Suffolk Institute of Archaeology.*
Rec. Bucks.	*Records of Buckinghamshire.*
R.A.I.	The Royal Archaeological Institute.
R.C.H.M.	The Royal Commission on Historical Monuments.
Surrey Arch. Coll.	*Surrey Archaeological Collections.*
Sussex Arch. Coll.	*Sussex Archaeological Collections.*
Trans. London and Middx. Arch. Soc.	*Transactions of the London and Middlesex Archaeological Society.*
Trans. Mon. Brass Soc.	*Transactions of the Monumental Brass Society.*
Yorks. Arch. J.	*Yorkshire Archaeological Journal.*

BIBLIOGRAPHY

Addyman and Hill 1969 — P.V. Addyman and D.H. Hill, 'Saxon Southampton: A Review of the Evidence, pt. II. Industry, Trade and Everyday Life', *Proc. Hants. F. C.*, xxxvi (1969), 61–96.

Addyman and Priestley 1977 — P.V. Addyman and J. Priestley, 'Baile Hill, York: A Report on Excavations', *Arch. J.*, cxxxiv (1977), 115–56.

Aitkin 1970 — M. Aitkin, 'Dating by archaeomagnetic Methods', *Phil. Trans. Roy. Soc. London*, cclxix (1970), 77–88.

Ames 1978 — S. Ames, 'The Saxon Pottery' in Saunders 1978, 57–60.

A.M.L. Report 2175 — J. Bayley, *Six Skeletons from St. Augustine's Abbey, Canterbury*, 1977.

A.M.L. Report 2379 — D. Cook, *Wall-plaster from St. Augustine's Abbey, Canterbury*, 1977.

A.M.L. Report 2883 — J. Bayley, *St. Augustine's Abbey, Canterbury – The Charnel Deposits*, 1979.

A.M.L. Report 2884 — J. Bayley, *St. Augustine's Abbey, Canterbury – Burial 1056*, 1979.

A.M.L. Report 2901 — F. Powell, *St. Augustine's Human Bone Report*, 1979.

A.M.L. Report 4939 — J. Henderson, *The Skeleton from Trench D, F.16.*

Andrews 1977 — D. Andrews, 'Lo Scavo dell' Area Sud del Convento di S. Silvestro a Genova. Vetri, Metalli e Reperti Minori', *Archeologia medievale*, iv (1977), 162–207.

Anon *c.* 1800 — Anon, *The Canterbury Guide by an Inhabitant, c.* 1800.

Apted *et al.* 1977 — (Eds.) M.R. Apted, R. Gilyard-Beer and A.D. Saunders, *Ancient Monuments and their Interpretation, Essays presented to A.J. Taylor*, London, 1977.

Atkinson 1942 — D. Atkinson, *Report on the Excavations at Wroxeter in the County of Salop, 1923–7,* Oxford, 1942.

Barton 1965 — K.J. Barton, 'Medieval Pottery at Rouen', *Arch. J.*, cxxii (1965), 73–86.

Barton 1979 — K.J. Barton, *Medieval Sussex Pottery*, Chichester 1979.

Battiscombe 1956 — (Ed.) C.F. Battiscombe, *The Relics of St. Cuthbert at Durham*, 1956.

Beckmann 1974 — B. Beckmann, 'The main Types of the first four Periods of Siegburg Pottery', in Evison *et al.* 1974, 183–220.

Beeson 1977 — D.F.C. Beeson, *English Church Clocks, 1280–1850*, 1977.

Bennett 1978 — P. Bennett, 'Excavations at 16–21 North Lane, Canterbury', *Arch. Cant.*, xciv (1978), 165–91.

Bennett 1980a — P. Bennett, 'A Site found on the Line of the Canterbury By-Pass (N.G.R. TR 143561)' in Bennett *et al.* 1980, 267–89.

Bennett 1980b — P. Bennett, 'The Wincheap Cremations (N.G.R. TR 14155705)' in Bennett *et al.* 1980, 290–3.

Bennett 1980c — P. Bennett, 'Tyler Hill 1979 (N.G.R. TR 142264) in Bennett *et al.* 1980, 293–7.

Bennett *et al.* 1980 — P. Bennett, N. Macpherson-Grant, P. Blockley, 'Four minor Sites excavated by the Canterbury Archaeological Trust, 1978–9', *Arch. Cant.*, xcvi (1980), 267–304.

Bennett *et al.* 1982 — P. Bennett, S.S. Frere, S. Stow, *Excavations at Canterbury Castle*, The Archaeology of Canterbury, Vol. I.

Bennett 1984 — P. Bennett, 'The Outer Court of St. Augustine's Abbey', *Canterbury Archaeological Trust Annual Report*, 1983–4, 25–7.

Bennett *et al.*, forthcoming — P. Bennett, S. Campbell, *Excavations in the Cathedral Precincts 1: The 'Aula Nova', Almonry Chapel and Lanfranc's Dormitory*. The Archaeology of Canterbury, Vol. III.

Benson 1956 — H. Benson, 'Church Orientations and patronal Festivals', *Antiq. J.*, xxxvi (1956), 205–13.

Beresford 1977 — G. Beresford, 'The Excavation of a moated House at Wintringham in Huntingdonshire', *Arch. J.*, cxxxiv (1977), 194–286.

Berry 1974 — G. Berry, *Medieval English Jetons*, London, 1974.

Biddle 1961/2 — M. Biddle, 'The deserted medieval Village of Seacourt, Berkshire', *Oxoniensia*, xxvi–xxvii (1961/2), 70–201.

Biddle, Barfield and Millard 1959 — M. Biddle, L. Barfield, A. Millard, 'The Excavation of the Manor of the More, Rickmansworth, Hertfordshire', *Arch. J.*, xxvi (1959), 136–99.

Biddle and Kjølbye-Biddle 1984 — M. Biddle and B. Kjølbye-Biddle, 'Cat. No. 552, Floor-Tiles', in Arts Council of Great Britain, *English Romanesque Art 1055–1200*, Hayward Gallery, London 1984, 392 ff.

Bilson 1906 — J. Bilson, 'The eleventh-century East Ends of St. Augustine's, Canterbury, and St. Mary's, York', *Arch. J.*, liii (1906), 106 ff.

Blair 1981 — J. Blair, 'English Monumental Brasses before the Black Death' in Detsicas 1981, 256–72.

Blair, forthcoming — J. Blair, 'English Brasses before 1350; Types, Patterns and Workshops' in J. Blair, *The Earliest English Brasses*, Monumental Brass Society.

Bloice 1971 — B.J. Bloice, 'Norfolk House, Lambeth. Excavations of a Delftware Kiln Site, 1968', *Post-Med. Arch.*, v (1971), 99–159.

Blurton 1977 — T.R. Blurton, 'Excavations at Angel Court, Walbrook, 1974', *Trans. London and Middx. Arch. Soc.*, xxviii (1977), 14–101.

B.M.C. — H.A. Grueber and C.F. Keary, *A Catalogue of English Coins in the British Museum*, Anglo-Saxon Series II, London, 1893.

Bond 1910 — F. Bond, *Wood Carvings in English Churches: Misericords*, Oxford, 1910.

Brailsford 1962 — J.W. Brailsford, *Hod Hill: Antiquities from Hod Hill in the Durden Collection, British Museum*, 1962.

Brent 1864–65 — J. Brent, Note in *Proc. Soc. Antiq. London*, Second Series iii (1864–65), 55.

Brent 1879 — J. Brent, *Canterbury in Olden Times*, 1879.

British Arch. Assoc. Conf., 1982 — British Archaeological Association Conference Transactions, *Medieval Art and Architecture at Canterbury before 1220*, v (1979), 1982.

Brothwell 1972 — D.R. Brothwell, *Digging up Bones*, London, 1972.

Brownsword, forthcoming — R.A. Brownsword, 'Technical Aspects of Individual Brass Letters', in Blair, forthcoming.

Bulmer-Thomas 1979 — I. Bulmer-Thomas, 'Euclid and medieval Architecture', *Arch. J.*, cxxxvi (1979), 136–50.

Bushe-Fox 1949 — J.P. Bushe-Fox, *Richborough IV, Fourth Report on the Excavation of the Roman Fort at Richborough, Kent*, Soc. Antiq. London, Res. Rep. xxi, Oxford, 1949.

Cameron 1974 — H.K. Cameron, 'Technical Aspects of medieval monumental Brasses', *Arch. J.*, cxxi (1974), 215–37.

Cameron 1975 — H.K. Cameron, 'Some early Knights', *Trans. Monumental Brass Soc.*, xii (1975), i.

Caviness 1981 — M.H. Caviness, *The Windows of Christ Church Cathedral, Canterbury*, Oxford, 1981.

Charleston 1983 — R.J. Charleston, 'Vessel Glass' in Streeten 1983, 112–6.

Christie 1948 — A. Christie, *Samplers and Stitches*, 1948.

Christie and Coad 1980 — P.M. Christie and J.G. Coad, 'Excavations at Denny Abbey', *Arch. J.*, cxxxvii (1980), 138–279.

Clapham 1934 — A. Clapham, *English Romanesque Architecture after the Conquest*, Oxford, 1934.

Clapham 1955 — A. Clapham, *St. Augustine's Abbey*, Official Handbook, H.M.S.O. Minor revisions, 1975.

Clark and Leach 1982 — (Eds.) A. Clark and P. Leach, *The Archaeology of Kent to 1500*, C.B.A. Res. Rep. no. 48, 1982.

Clark and Carter 1977 — H. Clark and A. Carter, *Excavations in King's Lynn 1963–1970*, *Med. Arch.* Monograph no. 7, 1977.

Clarke 1975 — P.V. Clarke, 'The German Stoneware', in Schofield 1975, 206–11.

Colvin 1982 — (Ed.) H.M. Colvin, *History of the King's Works*, Vol. 4, H.M.S.O., 1982.

Cook 1978 — A.M. Cook, 'Catalogue of the Ango-Saxon Material', in Jackson and Ambrose 1978, 228–34.

Cook, Mynard and Rigold 1969 — A.M. Cook, D.C. Mynard and S.E. Rigold, 'Excavations at Dover Castle, principally in the Inner Bailey', *J.B.A.A.*, xxxii (1969), 54–104.

Cotton 1915 — C. Cotton, 'Ancient Walling at St. Augustine's', *Arch. Cant.*, xxxi (1915), 290–3.

Cotton 1939 — C. Cotton, 'St. Austin's Abbey, Canterbury, Treasurers' Accounts and others 1468–69', *Arch. Cant.*, li (1939), 66–107.

Cramp 1969 — G. Cramp, 'Report 2, University of Kent Archaeological Society. Medieval Pottery on the Campus', *Kent Arch. Rev.*, 16 (1969), 14.

Cramp 1970a — G. Cramp, 'Medieval Kiln', *Kent Arch. Rev.*, 19 (1970), 26–8.

Cramp 1970b — G. Cramp, 'Medieval Kiln, Part 2', *Kent Arch. Rev.*, 21 (1970), 11–12.

Crossley 1975 — D.W. Crossley, *The Bewl Valley Ironworks, Kent, c. 1300–1730*, R.A.I., 1975.

Crossley 1981 — (Ed.) D.W. Crossley, *Medieval Industry*, C.B.A. Res. Rep. no. 4, London, 1981.

Crowfoot 1981 — E. Crowfoot, 'The Textiles', in Thorn 1981, 81–2.

Cunliffe 1968 — (Ed.) B. Cunliffe, *Fifth Report on the Excavations of the Roman Fort at Richborough*, Soc. Antiq. Lond. Res. Rep. xxiii, Oxford, 1968.

Cunliffe 1977 — B. Cunliffe, *Excavations at Portchester Castle, III; Medieval, the Outer Bailey and its Defences*, Soc. Antiq. London, Res. Rep. xxxiv, London, 1977.

Davis 1934 — (Ed. and Trans.) A.H. Davis, *William Thorne's Chronicle*, Oxford, 1934.

Dawson 1979 — G.J. Dawson, *Excavations at Guy's Hospital, Southwark 1967*, Surrey Arch. Soc. Res. Vol. 7, (1979), 27–51.

Detsicas 1981 — (Ed.) A. Detsicas, *Collectanea Historica, Essays in Memory of Stuart Rigold*, Kent Archaeological Society, Maidstone, 1981.

Down 1974 — A. Down, *Chichester Excavations* 2, Chichester, 1974.

Drewett 1975 — P.L. Drewett, 'Excavations at Hadleigh Castle, Essex', 1971–2; *J.B.A.A.*, xxxviii (1975), 90–154.

Driver, Rady and Sparks, forthcoming — J. Driver, J. Rady, M. Sparks, *Excavations in the Cathedral Precincts 2: 'Meister Omers', Linacre Garden and St. Gabriel's Chapel*. The Archaeology of Canterbury, Vol. IV.

Drury 1974 — P.J. Drury, 'Chelmsford Dominican Priory: The Excavation of the Reredorter', *Essex Arch. and Hist.*, vi (1974), 40–81.

Drury 1981 — P.J. Drury, 'The Production of Brick and Tile in medieval England', in Crossley 1981, 126–42.

Drury and Norton 1985 — P.J. Drury and E.C. Norton, 'Twelfth-century Floor and Roof Tiles at Orford Castle', *Proc. Suffolk Inst. Arch.*, 36.1 (1985), 1–7.

Drury and Norton forthcoming — P.J. Drury and E.C. Norton, *The Medieval Floor Tiles of East Anglia*, The Census of Medieval Floor Tiles, London.

Drury and Pratt 1975 — P.J. Drury and G.D. Pratt, 'A late thirteenth- and early fourteenth-century Tile Factory at Danbury, Essex', *Med. Arch.*, xix (1975), 92–164.

Dunning 1942 — G.C. Dunning, 'The Pottery', in Spillet *et al.* 1942, 62.

Dunning 1951 — G.C. Dunning, 'Notes on medieval Pottery', in Murray-Threipland and Steer 1951, 143–9.

Dunning 1954 — G.C. Dunning, 'Imported French Pottery from Pit M15', in Frere 1954, 138–9.

Dunning 1955 — G.C. Dunning, 'Pottery and other Finds', in Rix and Dunning 1955, 138–52

Dunning 1957 — G.C. Dunning, 'Saxon and Medieval Pottery', in Murray-Threipland 1957, 36–7.

Dunning 1965 — G.C. Dunning, 'Heraldic and decorated Metalwork and other Finds from Rievaulx Abbey, Yorkshire', *Antiq. J.*, xiv (1965), 53–63.

Dunning 1970 — G.C. Dunning, 'Polychrome Jug' in Harrison and Flight 1970, 110–11.

Dunning 1972 — G.C. Dunning, 'The Costrel from the Biddenden Kiln', in Kelly 1972, 175–6.

Dunning 1975 — G.C. Dunning, 'The Stone Mortar in Little Baddow Church', in Drury and Pratt 1975, 161–3.

Durham 1977 — B. Durham, 'Archaeological Investigations in St. Aldate's, Oxford', *Oxoniensia*, xlii (1977), 83–203.

Eames 1975 — E.S. Eames, 'Medieval pseudo-mosaic Tiles', *J.B.A.A.*, xxxviii (1975), 81–9.

Eames 1980 — E.S. Eames, *Catalogue of Lead-Glazed Earthernware Tiles*, British Museum Publications, London, 1980.

Erdmann 1953 — K. Erdmann, *Arabische Schriftzeichen als Ornamente in der abendlichen Kunst des Mittelalters*, Akademie der Wissenschaften und Literatur Abhandlungen des Geistes und Sozialwissenschaftlichen, Klass 9, Jahrgang 1953.

Evans 1904 — S. Evans, Jun., 'Excavations at St. Augustine's Abbey, Canterbury. II. The Church of St. Peter and St. Paul, and some of the adjacent monastic Buildings', *Arch. Cant.*, xxvi (1904), 1–8.

Evans 1933 — J. Evans, 'Medieval Wheel-shaped Brooches', *Art Bulletin*, 15 (1933), 197–201.

Evans 1904 — S. Evans, 'Excavations at St. Augustine's Canterbury, II', *Arch. Cant.*, xxvi (1904), 1–8.

Evison, Hodges and Hurst 1974 — (Eds.) I. Evison, H. Hodges and J.G. Hurst, *Medieval Pottery from Excavations*, 1974.

Evison 1977 — V.I. Evison, 'An enamelled Disc Brooch from Great Saxham', *Proc. Suffolk Inst. Arch.*, xxxiv, pt. I (1977), 1–3.

Farley 1976 — M. Farley, '*Saxon and Medieval Walton, Aylesbury: Excavations 1973–4*', *Rec. Bucks.*, xx (1976), 153–290.

Farmer 1979 — P.G. Farmer, *An Introduction to Scarborough Ware and a Re-assessment of Knight Jugs*, private publication, 1979.

Fingerlin 1971 — I. Fingerlin, *Gürtel des Hochen und späten Mittelalter*, Berlin, 1971.

Fox 1909–13 — E. Fox and J. Shirley-Fox, in *British Numismatic Journal*, vi–x (1909–13).

Freestone, Johns and Potter 1982 — I. Freestone, C. Johns, T. Potter, *Current Research in Ceramics: Thin Section Studies*, London, British Museum Occ. Paper 32, 1982.

Freke and Craddock 1979 — D.J. Freke and J. Craddock, 'The Excavation of an early 16th-century Pottery Kiln at Lower Parrock, Hartfield, East Sussex 1977', *Post-Med. Arch.*, xiii (1979), 79–125.

Frere 1948 — S.S. Frere, 'Canterbury Excavations 1945 and 1946', *Arch. Cant.*, lxi (1948), 1–40.

Frere 1954 — S.S. Frere, 'Canterbury Excavations, Summer 1946: the Rose Lane Sites', *Arch. Cant.*, lxviii (1954), 101–43.

Frere 1966 — S.S. Frere, 'The End of Towns in Roman Britain', in Wacher 1966, 87–100.

Frere 1972 — S.S. Frere, *Verulamium Excavations* I, Soc. Antiq. Res. Rep. xxviii, Oxford, 1972.

Frere, forthcoming — S.S. Frere, 'Lanfranc's Dormitory', in Bennett *et al.*, forthcoming.

Frere, Blockley and Blockley, forthcoming — S.S. Frere, K. Blockley and P. Blockley, *Excavations in the Marlowe Car Park and associated Areas*, Archaeology of Canterbury, Vol. V.

Frere and Stow 1983 — S.S. Frere and S. Stow, *Excavations in the St. George's Street and Burgate Street Areas*, The Archaeology of Canterbury, Vol. VII, Maidstone, 1983.

Gaunt 1978 — J. Gaunt, 'The Excavation of a medieval Well at Worth', *Kent Arch. Rev.*, 54 (1978), 94–8.

Geddes 1983 — J. Geddes, 'Recently discovered Romanesque Sculpture in South-east England', in Thompson 1983a, 90–8.

Geddes 1985 — J. Geddes, 'The Small Finds', in Hare 1985, 147–7.

Gem 1982 — R. Gem, 'The Significance of the 11th-century Rebuilding of Christ Church and St. Augustine's, Canterbury, in the Development of Romanesque Architecture', in Brit. Arch. Assoc. Conf. (1982), 1–19.

Green 1974 — J.P. Green, 'Excavations at Norton Priory', *Ches. Arch. Bull.*, 2 (1974), 31–2.

Grierson 1956 — P. Grierson, 'The Salernitan Coinage of Gisulf II (1052–77) and Robert Guiscard (1077–85)', *Pap. Brit. Sch. Rome*, xxiv (1956), 37–59.

Grimme 1957 — E.G. Grimme, *Aachener Goldschmiedekunst im Mittelalter*, Cologne, 1957.

Grose *c.* 1797 — F. Grose, *Antiquities of England and Wales*

Hadcock 1952 — R.N. Hadcock, *Tynemouth Priory and Castle*, H.M.S.O., 1952.

Hagen 1973 — R. Hagen, 'Two Late Medieval Bronze Belt Chapes', *Beds. Arch. J.*, viii (1973), 119–22.

Hall 1973 — D.N. Hall, 'A thirteenth-century Windmill Site at Strixton, Northamptonshire', *Beds. Arch. J.*, viii (1973), 101–22.

Harden 1969 — D.B. Harden, 'Ancient Glass, I, Pre-Roman', *Arch. J.*, cxxv (1969), 46–72.

Hardwick 1858 — (Ed.) C. Hardwick, *Chronicles and Memorials*, Thomas of Elmham, Chronicle of the Abbey, Trinity Hall ms 1, Rolls Series, H.M.S.O., London, 1858.

Hare 1985 — J. Hare, *Battle Abbey: the Eastern Range and the Excavations of 1978–80*, 1985.

Harrington 1971 — D. Harrington, 'The Excavation of a medieval Kiln near Canterbury, 1971', *Kent Arch. Rev.*, 25 (1971), 149–51.

Harrison 1970 — A.C. Harrison 'Excavations in Rochester', *Arch. Cant.*, lxxxv (1970), 95–112.

Harrison 1972 — A.C. Harrison, 'Rochester East Gate, 1969', *Arch. Cant.*, lxxxvii (1972), 129–58.

Harvey 1984 — J. Harvey, *English Medieval Architects*, 1984.

Hasted 1799 — E. Hasted, *History of Kent*, (1st edn.), Vol. 4, 1799.

Hasted 1801 — E. Hasted, *History of Kent* (2nd edn., reprinted 1971), Vol. 12, 1801.

Hawkes and Hull 1947 — C.F.C. Hawkes and M.R. Hull, *Camulodunum. First Report on the Excavations at Colchester 1930–1939*, Soc. Antiq. London Res. Rep. xiv, Oxford, 1947.

Henig 1974 — M. Henig, 'Success as personified on a Roman Intaglio', *Glasgow Arch. J.*, iii (1974), 71–3.

Henig 1978 — M. Henig, *A Corpus of Roman Engraved Gemstones from British Sites*, B.A.R. 8(i) and (ii), 1978.

Henig 1983 — M. Henig, 'Archbishop Hubert Walter's Gems', *J.B.A.A.*, cxxxvi (1983), 56–61.

Henry 1970 — F. Henry, *Irish Art in the Romanesque Period*, London, 1970.

Hildebrand 1881 — B.E. Hildebrand, *Anglosachsiska Mynt*, Stockholm, 1881.

Hinton 1974 — D.A. Hinton, *A Catalogue of the Anglo-Saxon ornamental Metalwork 700–1100, in the Department of Antiquities, Ashmolean Museum*, Oxford, 1974.

Hinton 1980 — M. Hinton, 'Medieval Pottery from a Kiln Site at Kingston-upon-Thames', *The London Archaeologist*, vol. 3, no. 14 (1980), 377–83.

Hobley 1970 — B. Hobley, 'Excavations at the Cathedral and Benedictine Priory of St. Mary, Coventry', *Birmingham and Warks. Arch. Soc.*, lxxxiv (1970), 45–139.

Hope 1861 — A.J.B. Hope, 'Architectural Notes on St. Augustine's College, Canterbury', *Arch. Cant.*, iv (1861), 57–66.

Hope 1903 — W.H. St. J. Hope, 'Excavations at St. Austin's Abbey, Canterbury', *Arch. Cant.*, xxv (1903) 222–43.

Hope 1914 — W.H. St. J. Hope, 'Recent Discoveries in the Abbey Church at St. Austin's', *Archaeologia*, lxvi (1914), 377–400.

Hope 1917 — W.H. St. J. Hope, 'Recent Discoveries in the Abbey Church of St. Austin at Canterbury', *Arch. Cant.*, xxxii (1917), 1–26.

Horton 1978 — M.C. Horton, 'Medieval Floor-Tiles' in Tester 1978, 87–92.

Horton 1979 — M.C. Horton, 'The Floor-Tiles', in Smith 1979, 117–26.

Horton 1981 — M.C. Horton, 'A Group of sixteenth-century Flemish Tiles in England', in Detsicas 1981, 235–46.

Horton 1983 — M.C. Horton, 'Floor Tiles', in Streeten 1983, 70–87

Horton forthcoming — M.C. Horton, 'The Medieval Floor Tiles' in Tatton-Brown forthcoming.

Hurst 1962 — J.G. Hurst, 'Jugs with Bases thumbed underneath', *Med. Arch.*, viii (1962), 295–8.

Hurst 1968 — J.G. Hurst, 'The Post-Medieval Pottery', in Philp 1968, 57–69.

Hurst 1971 — J.G. Hurst, 'Cologne Stoneware', in Moorhouse 1971–6, 46–7.

Hurst 1972 — J.G. Hurst, 'A Wanfried Dish from Newcastle', *Arch. Ael.*, 4thh ser., l (1972), 259–62.

Hurst 1974 — J.G. Hurst, '16th and 17th Century Pottery from Saintonge', in Evison *et al.* 1974, 221–56.

Hurst 1977a — J.G. Hurst, 'Martincamp Flasks', in Neal 1977, 156–7

Hurst 1977b — J.G. Hurst, 'Langerwehe Stoneware of the fourteenth and fifteenth Centuries', in Apted *et al.* 1977, 219–38.

Hurst, Neal and van Beuningen 1975 — J.G. Hurst, D.S. Neal and H.J.E. van Beuningen, 'North Holland Slipware', *Rotterdam Papers*, 2 (1975), 47–65.

Hussey 1915 — A. Hussey, 'Further Notes from Kentish Wills, (c) References to the Abbey of St. Augustine', *Arch. Cant.*, xxxi (1915), 43–53.

Jackson and Ambrose 1978 — D.A. Jackson and T. Ambrose, 'Excavations at Wakerley, Northants., 1972–74', *Britannia*, ix (1978), 115–242.

Jarrett and Edwards 1961 — M.G. Jarrett and S.J.N. Edwards, 'Medieval and other Pottery from Finchale Priory, County Durham', *Arch. Ael.*, xxxix (1961), 229–78.

Jarvis 1983 — K.S. Jarvis, *Excavations at Christchurch 1969–1980*, Dorset Nat. Hist. and Arch. Soc. Monograph no. 5, Dorchester, 1983.

Jenkins 1950 — F. Jenkins, 'Excavations in Burgate St., Canterbury, 1946–8', *Arch. Cant.*, xliii (1950), 82–118.

Jenkins 1956 — F. Jenkins, 'A Roman Tilery and two Pottery Kilns at Durovernum (Canterbury)', *Antiq. J.*, xxxvi (1956), 40–56.

Jenkins, forthcoming — F. Jenkins, 'Excavations at St. Pancras', forthcoming.

Jennings 1981 — S. Jennings, 'Eighteen Centuries of Norwich Pottery', *E. Anglian Arch.*, 15 (1981).

Jope and Pantin 1958 — E.M. Jope and W.A. Pantin, 'The Clarendon Hotel, Oxford', *Oxoniensia*, xxiii (1958), 1–129.

Kelly 1972 — D.B. Kelly, 'An early Tudor Kiln at Hareplain, Biddenden', *Arch. Cant.*, lxxxvii (1972), 159–76.

Keen 1973 — L. Keen, 'Medieval Floor Tiles of the "Westminster Tiler", at Bengeo, Hertfordshire', *Herts. Arch.*, iii (1973), 90–3.

Knight 1983–4 — B. Knight, 'Researches in medieval Window Lead', *J. Brit. Soc. Master Glass Painters*, xviii (1983–4), 49–51.

Knowles 1951 — (Ed.) D. Knowles, *Decreti Lanfranci Monachis Cantuariensibus transmissa*, 1951.

Lambert 1921 — F. Lambert, 'Some recent Excavations in London', *Archaeologia*, lxxi (1921), 55–112.

Lambrick and Woods 1976 — G. Lambrick and H. Woods, 'Excavations on the second Site of the Dominican Priory, Oxford', *Oxoniensia*, xli (1976), 168–231.

Leeds 1923 — E.T. Leeds, 'A Saxon Village near Sutton Courtenay, Berkshire', *Archaeologia*, lxxiii (1923), 147–92.

Leland 1744 — J. Leland, *Collectanea* IV.

Lindsay 1964 — S. Lindsay, *Iron and Brass Implements of the English House*, London, 1964.

Lloyd-Morgan 1975 — G. Lloyd-Morgan, 'A Note on some Mirrors in the Museo Archeologico, Brescia', *Commentari dell' Ateneo di Brescia*, 174 (1975), 107–116.

Lloyd-Morgan 1981 — G. Lloyd-Morgan, *Description of the Collections in the Rijksmuseum G.M. Kam at Nijmegen IX: The Mirrors*, Nijmegen, 1981.

Lloyd-Morgan 1983 — G. Lloyd-Morgan, 'Some Mirrors from Roman Canterbury', *Arch. Cant.*, xcix (1983), 231–6.

Lloyd-Morgan with Reedie 1984 — G. Lloyd-Morgan with K. Reedie, 'A new Hand Mirror from Kent', *Arch. Cant.*, c (1984), 355–7.

L.M.M.C. 1940 — J.B. Ward-Perkins, *London Museum Medieval Catalogue*, H.M.S.O., London, 1940.

Long 1975 — C. Long, 'Excavations in the medieval City of Trondheim, Norway', *Med. Arch.*, xix (1975), 1–32.

L.R.B.C. — R.A.G. Carson, P.V. Hill and J.P.C. Kent, *Late Roman Bronze Coinage*, 1978.

Lyle 1965 — L. Lyle, 'The Stour Valley Research Group', *Kent Arch. Rev.*, 2 (1965), 34.

Mack 1975 — R.P. Mack, *The Coinage of Ancient Britain*, 1975.

Macpherson-Grant 1978 — N.C. Macpherson-Grant, 'The Pottery', in Bennett 1978, 174–90.

Macpherson-Grant 1980a — N.C. Macpherson-Grant, 'The Pottery' In Bennett 1980a, 274–89.

Macpherson-Grant 1980b — N.C. Macpherson-Grant, 'The Pottery' in Bennett 1980b, 292–3.

Macpherson-Grant 1980c — N.C. Macpherson-Grant, 'Chaff-tempered Ware. An unusual ?Belgic–early Roman product from Canterbury', *Kent Arch. Rev.*, 61 (1980), 2–4.

Macpherson-Grant 1980d — N.C. Macpherson-Grant, 'The Pottery' in Bennett 1980c, 294–7.

Macpherson-Grant 1980e — N.C. Macpherson-Grant, 'The Pottery', in Tatton-Brown 1980b, 47–52.

Macpherson-Grant 1981a — N.C. Macpherson-Grant, *Local and Imported Wares at Canterbury. Late Saxon, Saxo-Norman and Medieval: a provisional Guide*, Canterbury Archaeological Trust, March 1981.

Macpherson-Grant 1981b — N.C. Macpherson-Grant, *Saxo-Norman and Medieval Shell-on-surface*

Sandy Ware: an initial Form and Decoration Type Series, Canterbury Archaeological Trust, July 1981.

Macpherson-Grant 1982 — N.C. Macpherson-Grant, 'The Coarse Wares', in Bennett *et al.* 1982, 97–150, 165–8.

Macpherson-Grant 1983 — N.C. Macpherson-Grant, 'A Note on recent Pottery Finds', in Tatton-Brown *et al.* 1983, 130–1.

Macpherson-Grant 1984 — N.C. Macpherson-Grant, 'Summary of the Pottery', *Canterbury Archaeological Trust Report*, 1984, 28.

Macpherson-Grant, forthcoming — N.C. Macpherson-Grant, 'The Pottery' in Frere, Blockley and Blockley, forthcoming.

Macpherson-Grant and Green 1983 — N.C. Macpherson-Grant and M. Green, *Canterbury Ceramics*, Canterbury Archaeological Trust, 1983.

Mainman 1982 — A. Mainman, 'Studies in Anglo-Saxon Pottery', in Freestone *et al.*, 1982 93–100.

Mainman, forthcoming — A. Mainman, 'The Anglo-Saxon Pottery', in Frere, Blockley and Blockley, forthcoming.

Mair 1982 — R. Mair, 'The Choir Capitals of Canterbury Cathedral', in British Arch. Assoc. Conf. (1982), 56–66.

Manning 1972 — W.H. Manning, 'The Iron Objects', in Frere 1972, 163–5.

Mayes and Butler 1983 — P. Mayes and L. Butler, *Sandal Castle Excavations 1964–73*, Wakefield, 1983.

Mead 1977 — V.K. Mead, 'Evidence for the Manufacture of Amber Beads in London in the 14th and 15th Centuries', *Trans. London and Middx. Arch. Soc.*, xxviii (1977), 211–4.

Mellor and Pearce 1981 — J.E. Mellor and T. Pearce, *The Austin Friars, Leicester*, C.B.A. Res. Rep. no. 35, London, 1981.

Migne 1880 — (Ed.) Abbé Migne, Goscelin, *Historia Translationis S. Augustini Episcopi*, 13–46, *Patrologia Latina* 155, Paris, 1880.

Miles 1975 — D. Miles, 'Excavations at West St. Helen Street, Abingdon', *Oxoniensia*, xl (1975), 70–101.

Millard 1968 — L. Millard, 'Notes from Canterbury Museum', *Arch. Cant.*, lxxxiii (1968), 267–8.

Milne and Milne 1982 — G. Milne and C. Milne, 'Medieval Waterfront Developments at Trig Lane, London', *London and Middx. Arch. Soc.*, Special Paper no. 5, 1982.

Miscampbell 1981 — C.P. Miscampbell, 'A 12th-century Rebuilding at St. Augustine's Abbey', in Detsicas 1981, 63–5.

Moorhouse 1971a — S.A. Moorhouse, 'Finds from Basing House, Hampshire (*c.* 1640–1645): part 2', *Post-Med. Arch.*, v (1971), 35–76.

Moorhouse 1971b — S.A. Moorhouse, 'Two late and post-medieval Pottery Groups from Farnham Castle, Surrey', *Surrey Arch. Col.*, lxviii (1971), 39–55.

Moorhouse 1979 — S.A. Moorhouse, 'Tudor Green, some further Thoughts', *Medieval Ceramics*, 3 (1979), 53–61.

Murrray-Threipland 1957 — L. Murray-Threipland, 'Excavations in Dover', *Arch. Cant.*, lxxi (1957), 14–37.

Murray-Threipland and Steer, 1951 — L. Murray-Threipland and K. Steer, 'Excavations at Dover 1945–7', *Arch. Cant.*, lxiv (1951), 130–49.

Musty, Rogerson and Lloyd-Morgan 1973 — A. Musty, J. Rogerson and G. Lloyd-Morgan, 'A Mirror from the Romano-British Cemetery at Whitchurch, Salop', *Antiq. J.*, liii (1973), 278–81.

Mynard 1969 — D.C. Mynard, 'A Group of post-medieval Pottery from Dover Castle', *Post-Med. Arch.*, iii (1969), 31–46.

Mynard 1973 D.C. Mynard, 'Medieval Pottery from Dartford', *Arch. Cant.*, lxxxiii (1973), 187–99.

Myres and Green 1973 J.N.L. Myres and B. Green, *The Anglo-Saxon Cemeteries of Caistor-by-Norwich and Markshall, Norfolk*, Soc. Antiq. London Res. Rep. iii, Oxford, 1973.

Neal 1973 D.S. Neal, 'Excavations at the Palace and Priory at King's Langley, 1970', *Herts. Arch.*, iii (1973), 31–72.

Neal 1977 D.S. Neal, 'Excavations at the Palace of King's Langley, Hertfordshire, 1974–1976', *Med. Arch.*, xxi (1977), 124–65.

Norton 1976 E.C. Norton, 'The medieval Paving Tiles at Winchester College', *Proc. Hants. F.C. and Arch. Soc.*, xxxi (1976), 23–42.

Norton 1983a E.C. Norton, *A Study of the 12th- and 13th-century decorated Tile Pavements in France*, unpublished doctoral dissertation, Cambridge, 1983.

Norton 1983b E.C. Norton, 'Varietates pavimentorum: Contribution à l'étude de l'Art Cistercien en France', *Cahiers archéologiques*, (1983), 69–113.

Norton 1986a E.C. Norton, 'Early Cistercian Tile Pavements' in Norton and Park 1986, 228–55.

Norton 1986b E.C. Norton, 'The original two-colour Tiles in France and England', in (Ed.) D. Deroeux, *Terres cuites architecturales au Moyen Age*, Arras (Mem. Comité d'Histoire et d'Archéologie du Pas-de-Calais, tome XXII, 2), 1986, 256–93.

Norton forthcoming E.C. Norton, *Guidelines for recording Medieval Floor Tiles*, Medieval Pottery Research Group.

Norton and Horton 1981 E.C. Norton and M.C. Horton, 'A Parisian Workshop at Canterbury', *J.B.A.A.*, cxxxiv (1981), 58–80.

Norton and Park 1986 (Eds.) E.C. Norton and D.W. Park, *Cistercian Art and Architecture in the British Isles*, Cambridge, 1986.

Oman 1962 C. Oman, 'English Medieval Base Metal Church Plate', *Arch. J.*, xcix (1962), 195–207.

Oman 1974 C. Oman, *British Rings 800–1914*, London, 1970.

Orton 1977 C. Orton, 'Medieval Pottery', in Blurton 1977, 80–7.

Orton 1979a C. Orton, 'Medieval Pottery from a Kiln Site at Cheam: Part 1', *The London Archaeologist*, Vol. 3, no. 11 (1979), 300–7.

Orton 1979b C. Orton, 'Medieval Pottery from a Kiln Site at Cheam: Part 2', *The London Archaeologist*, Vol. 3, no. 13 (1979), 355–9.

Orton 1982a C. Orton, 'Pottery Evidence for the Dating of the Revetments', in Milne and Milne 1982, 92–9.

Orton 1982b C. Orton, 'The Excavation of a late medieval/transitional Pottery Kiln at Cheam', *Surrey Arch. Coll.*, lxxiii (1982), 25–92.

Page 1981 P. Page, 'Chalgrove-Harding's Field', C.B.A. Group 9 *Newsletter*, ii (1981), 150–3.

Parfitt 1976 J.H. Parfitt, 'A moated Site at Moat Farm, Leigh, Kent', *Arch. Cant.*, xcii (1976), 173–201.

Peacock 1977 D.P.S. Peacock, 'Ceramics in Roman and medieval Archaeology', in (Ed.) D.P.S. Peacock, *Pottery and Early Commerce*, London, 1977, 21–33.

Pevsner 1973 N. Pevsner, *London* I, Buildings of England, 3rd edn., Harmondsworth, 1973.

Phillips 1985 D. Phillips, *Excavations at York Minster*, Vol. 2, R.C.H.M., London, 1985.

Philp 1968 B.J. Philp, *Excavations at Faversham 1965: the Royal Abbey, Roman Villa and Belgic Farmstead*, Kent Arch. Res. Group Council, Res. Rep. 1, 1968.

Philp 1974 — B.J. Philp, 'A medieval Kiln Site at Tyler Hill, Canterbury', *Kent Arch. Rev.*, 36 (1974), 175–81.

Philp and Swale 1967 — B.J. Philp and J. Swale, 'Medieval Kiln Sites in Blean Forest', *Kent Arch. Rev.*, 10 (1967), 75–8.

Pitt-Rivers 1883 — A.L.F. Pitt-Rivers, 'Excavations at Caesar's Camp, near Folkestone', *Archaeologia*, xlvii (1883), 429–65.

Pitt-Rivers 1890 — A.L.F. Pitt-Rivers, *King John's House, Tollard Royal, Wilts.*, 1890.

Platt and Coleman-Smith 1975 — C.P. Platt and R. Coleman-Smith, *Excavations in medieval Southampton, 1953–1969*, Vol. II, Finds, Leicester 1975.

Plummer 1896 — (Ed.) C. Plummer, *Venerabilis Baedae Opera Historica*, Oxford, 1896.

Potts 1920 — R.U. Potts, 'St. Austin's Abbey, Canterbury', *Arch. Cant.*, xxxiv (1920), 139–47.

Potts 1921 — R.U. Potts, 'The latest Excavations at St. Augustine's Abbey', *Arch. Cant.*, xxxv (1921), 117–26.

Potts 1928 — R.U. Potts, 'A Note on the Plan of St. Augustine's Abbey Church', *Arch. Cant.*, xl (1928), 65–6.

Potts 1930 — R.U. Potts, 'Discoveries at St. Austin's Abbey, Canterbury', *Antiq. J.*, x (1930), 167–9.

Potts 1934 — R.U. Potts, 'The Plan of St Austin's Abbey', *Arch. Cant.*, xlvi (1934), 179–94, with Notes by A.H. Thompson, 183–91, and A.W. Clapham, 191–4.

Poulton and Woods 1984 — R. Poulton and H. Woods, *Excavations on the Site of the Dominican Priory at Guildford in 1974 and 1978*, Surrey Arch. Soc. Res. vol. 9, 1984.

Prior 1904 — E.S. Prior, 'Chichester Cathedral. A Table of the Styles of Masoncraft used from 1090 to *c.* 1450 with Extracts from Documents and other Notes', *Proc. Harrow Archit. Club*, i (1904), 25–32.

Pryor and Blockley 1978 — S. Pryor and K. Blockley, 'A 17th-century Kiln Site at Woolwich', *Post-Med. Arch.*, xii (1978), 30–85.

Rackham 1939 — B. Rackham, 'A Netherlands Maiolica Vase from the Tower of London', *Antiq. J.*, xix (1939), 285–90.

Rahtz 1969 — P. Rahtz, *Excavations at King John's Hunting Lodge, Writtle, Essex 1955–7*, London, 1969.

Rahtz and Hirst 1976 — P. Rahtz and S. Hirst, *Bordesley Abbey, Redditch, Worcestershire*, B.A.R. no. 23, 1976.

Reineking-von Bock 1971 — G. Reineking-von Bock, *Steinzeug. Kataloge des Kunstgewerbe Museums der Stadt Köln*, 1971.

Remnant 1969 — G. Remnant, *A Catalogue of Misericords in Great Britain*, Oxford, 1969.

R.I.C. — *Roman Imperial Coinage*, H. Mattingly *et al.* Coins of the Roman Empire in the British Museum, 1923–62.

Rigold 1962 — S.E. Rigold, 'Excavation of a moated Site at Pivington', *Arch. Cant.*, lxxvii (1962), 27–47.

Rigold 1964 — S.E. Rigold, 'Two Kentish Hospitals Re-examined', *Arch. Cant.*, lxxix (1964), 31–69.

Rigold 1967 — S.E. Rigold, 'Excavations at Dover Castle, 1964–66', *J.B.A.A.*, xxx (1967), 87–121.

Rigold 1968 — S.E. Rigold, 'Floor Tiles' and 'Medieval Pottery', in Philp 1968, 44–50; 54–6.

Rigold 1970 — S.E. Rigold, 'Six Copper-alloy Objects from St. Augustine's, Canterbury', *Antiq. J.*, l (1970), 345–7.

Rigold 1971 — S.E. Rigold, 'Eynsford Castle', *Arch. Cant.*, lxxxvi (1971), 109–71.

Rigold 1977	S.E. Rigold, 'A Mould for leaden Ventilators from Neath Abbey, South Wales', *Antiq. J.*, lvii (1977), 334–6.
Rigold 1978	S.E. Rigold, 'A medieval Coin-Balance from Roche Abbey', *Antiq. J.*, lviii (1978), 371–4.
Rigold 1979	S.E. Rigold, 'Painted Wall Plaster', in Smith 1979, 113–5.
Rix and Dunning 1955	M.M. Rix and G.C. Dunning, 'Excavations of a medieval Garderobe in Snargate Street, Dover, in 1945'. *Arch. Cant.*, lxix (1955), 132–58.
Rodwell 1976	K.A. Rodwell, 'Excavations on the Site of Banbury Castle, 1973–4', *Oxoniensia*, lxi (1976), 90–147.
Routledge 1882	C.F. Routledge, 'Roman Foundations at St. Pancras, Canterbury', *Arch. Cant.*, xiv (1882), 103–8.
Routledge 1902	C.F. Routledge, 'Excavations at St. Austin's Abbey, Canterbury. The Church of SS. Peter and Paul', *Arch. Cant.*, xxv (1902), 238–43.
Salzman 1967	L.F. Salzman, *Building in England down to 1540*, Oxford, 1967.
Sambon 1912	G. Sambon, *Repertorio generale delle Monete coniate in Italia e da Italiani all' Estero dal Secolo V^{o} al XX°*, Paris, 1912.
Saunders 1978	A.D. Saunders, 'Excavations in the Church of St. Augustine's Abbey, Canterbury, 1955–58', *Med. Arch.*, xxii (1978), 25–63.
Schaetzen 1949–50	P. de Schaetzen, 'La Tombe belgo-romaine de Riempst', *Bulletin de l'Institut archéologique Liégeois*, lxvii (1949–50).
Schofield 1975	J. Schofield, 'Excavations South of Edinburgh High Street, 1973–4', *Proc. Soc. Antiq. Scot.*, cxix (1975), 155–241.
Searle 1975	S. Searle, 'The Church points the Way', *New Scientist*, 61, 3 Jan. (1975), 10–13.
Sherlock 1982	D. Sherlock, 'A Sun Dial from St. Augustine's Abbey', *Arch. Cant.*, xcviii (1982), 19–26.
Sherlock 1983	D. Sherlock, 'The Account of George Nycholl for St. Augustine's 1552–1553', *Arch. Cant.*, xcix (1983), 25–46.
Sherlock, no date	D. Sherlock, *Medieval Floor Tiles in Suffolk Churches*, Suffolk Historic Churches Trust, Ipswich [1980].
Singer, Holmyard, Hall and Williams 1956	C. Singer, E.J. Holmyard, A.R. Hall, T. Williams, *A History of Technology*, Vol. 2, Oxford, 1956.
Smith 1979	G.H. Smith, 'The Excavation of the Hospital of St. Mary Ospringe, commonly called Maison Dieu', *Arch. Cant.*, xcv (1979), 81–185.
Somner 1703	W. Somner, *Antiquities of Canterbury*, 2nd edn. revised by N. Batteley, 1703.
Sotheby and Co. 1965	Sotheby and Co. *Catalogue of the well-known Collection of English Delftware, the Property of the late Professor F.H. Garner*, Part 2, Tuesday, 2 March, 1965.
Southern 1953	R.W. Southern, *The Making of the Middle Ages*, 1953.
Sparks 1984	M. Sparks, 'The Recovery and Excavation of the St. Augustine's Abbey Site, 1844–1947', *Arch. Cant.*, c (1984), 325–44.
Spillett, Stebbing and Dunning 1942	P.J. Spillett, W.P.D. Stebbing and G.C. Dunning, 'A Pottery Kiln Site at Tyler Hill, Canterbury', *Arch. Cant.*, lv (1942), 57–64.
Steane and Bryant 1971	J.M. Steane and G.F. Bryant, 'Excavations at the deserted medieval Settlement at Lyveden', *Northants. Mus. J.*, third interim, 9 (1971), 3–94.
Steane and Bryant 1975	J.M. Steane and G.F. Bryant, 'Excavations at the deserted medieval Settlement at Lyveden', *Northants. Mus. J.*, fourth interim, 12 (1975), 3–160.
Stephan 1981	H.G. Stephan, 'Werrakeramik und Weserware', *Keramik an Weser, Werra und Fulda*, 1981.
Stothard 1876	C.A. Stothard, *The Monumental Effigies of Great Britain*, London, 1876.

Stratford, Tudor-Craig and Muthesius 1982	N. Stratford, P. Tudor-Craig and A.M. Muthesius, 'Archbishop Hubert Walters' Tomb and its Furnishings', in Brit. Arch. Assoc. Conf. (1982), 71–93.
Streeten 1979	A.D.F. Streeten, 'Fabric Analysis and Distribution', in Freke and Craddock 1979, 114–6.
Streeten 1982a	A.D.F. Streeten, 'Potter's Kilns and Markets in medieval Kent: a preliminary Study', in Clark and Leach 1982, 87–95
Streeten 1982b	A.D.F. Streeten, 'Textural Analysis: an Approach to the Characterization of sand-tempered Ceramics', in Freestone *et al.* 1982, 123–33.
Streeten 1983	A.D.F. Streeten, *Bayham Abbey*, Sussex Arch. Soc. Monograph 2, 1983.
Streeten 1985	A.D.F. Streeten, 'Ceramic Building Materials', in Hare 1985, 79–102.
Streeten forthcoming	A.D.F. Streeten, 'Fabric Analysis and regional Comparisons', in Bennett *et al.* forthcoming.
Stubbs 1879	(Ed.) W. Stubbs, *The historical Works of Gervase of Canterbury*, Rolls Series 73, part i, 368 ff, 1880.
Taralon 1966	J. Taralon, *Treasures of the Churches of France*, London, 1966.
Tatton-Brown 1980a	T. Tatton-Brown, 'The Use of Quarr Stone in London and east Kent', *Med. Arch.*, xxiv (1980), 213—5.
Tatton-Brown 1980b	T. Tatton-Brown, 'Excavations at the 'Old Palace' Bekesbourne, near Canterbury', *Arch. Cant.*, xcvi (1980), 27–57.
Tatton-Brown 1983	T. Tatton-Brown, 'Medieval Kilns in the Tyler Hill Area', in Tatton-Brown *et al.* 1983, 127–30.
Tatton-Brown forthcoming	(Ed.) T. Tatton-Brown, *Excavations in the Cathedral Precints, part 2*, The Archaeology of Canterbury, Vol. IV, forthcoming.
Tatton-Brown forthcoming	(Ed.) T. Tatton-Brown, *Excavations in the Cathedral Precincts, part 2*, The Archaeology of Canterbury, Vol. IV, forthcoming.
Tatton-Brown with Bennett, Brown and Macpherson-Grant 1983	T. Tatton-Brown, P. Bennett, J. Brown and N. Macpherson-Grant, 'Recent Fieldwork around Canterbury', *Arch. Cant.*, xcix (1983), 115–31.
Tebbutt 1966	C.F. Tebbutt, 'St Neot's Priory', *Proc. Cambridge Antiq. Soc.*, lix (1966), 33–74.
Tester 1972	P.J. Tester, 'Medieval Pottery' in Harrison 1972, 142–50.
Tester 1973	P.J. Tester, 'Excavations at Boxley Abbey', *Arch. Cant.*, lxxxviii (1973), 129–58.
Tester 1978	P.J. Tester, 'Excavations on the Site of Leeds Priory, Part II', *Arch. Cant.*, xciv (1978), 75–98.
Thompson 1954	A.H. Thompson, *Roche Abbey*, official guidebook, H.M.S.O., London, 1954.
Thompson 1902	(Ed.) E.M. Thompson, *The Customary of St. Augustine's Abbey 1330–1340*, Corpus Christi College Ms 301, Henry Bradshaw Society 23, 1902.
Thompson 1904	(Ed.) E.M. Thompson, *The Customary of St. Augustine's Abbey 1330–1340*, Corpus Christi College Ms 301, Henry Bradshaw Society 28, 1904.
Thompson 1982	I. Thompson, *Grog-tempered Belgic Pottery of south-eastern England*, B.A.R. no. 108, i–iii, Oxford, 1982.
Thompson 1983	(Ed.) F.H. Thompson, *Studies in medieval Sculpture*, Soc. Antiq. London, Occ. Papers, N.S. 3, 1983.
Thorn 1979	J.C. Thorn, 'The Pottery', in Smith 1979, 154–83.
Thorn 1981	J.C. Thorn, 'The Burial of Abbot John Dygon', in Detsicas 1981, 74–84.
Thwaite 1973	A. Thwaite, 'The Chronology of the Bellarmine Jug', *The Connoisseur*, 255–62.
Urry 1953	W. Urry, 'The Notes on Guernes de Pont Sainte-Maxence, Vie de Saint Thomas', *Arch. Cant.*, lxvi (1953), 92–7.
Urry 1961	W. Urry, *Canterbury under the Angevins*. 1961.

Vidler 1932 — L.A. Vidler, 'Floor Tiles and Kilns near the Site of St. Bartholomew's Hospital, Rye', *Sussex Arch. Coll.*, lxxiii (1932), 83–101.

Vidler 1933 — L.A. Vidler, 'Medieval Pottery and Kilns found at Rye', *Sussex Arch. Coll.*, lxxiv (1933), 44–66.

Vince 1985 — A.G. Vince, 'Kingston-type Ware', *Popular Archaeology*, October 1985, 34–9.

Vogel 1781 — J.P.N.M. Vogel, *Collection de Pierres antiques dont la Chasse des SS. Trois Rois, Mages est enrichie dans l'Eglise métropolitaine à Cologne, Gravées après leurs Empreintes, avec un Discours historique analogue*, Bonn 1781.

Wacher 1966 — J. Wacher, *The Civitas Capitals of Roman Britain*, Leicester, 1966.

Ward-Perkins 1937 — J.B. Ward-Perkins, 'Late Medieval Flemish inlaid Tiles in England', *Antiq. J.*, xxii (1937), 442–443.

Webster and Cherry 1980 — L.E. Webster and J. Cherry, 'Medieval Britain in 1979', *Med. Arch.*, xxiv (1980), 218–64.

West 1963 — S.E. West, 'Excavations at Cox Lane (1958), and at the Town Defences, Shire Hall Yard, Ipswich (1959)', *Proc. Suffolk Inst. Arch.*, xxix (1963), 233–87.

Wheeler 1978 — A. Wheeler, *Key to the Fishes of northern Europe*, 1978.

Whittingham 1949 — A.B. Whittingham, 'The monastic Buildings of Norwich Cathedral', *Arch. J.*, cvi (1949), 86–7.

Whittingham 1951 — A.B. Whittingham, 'Bury St. Edmund's Abbey', *Arch. J.*, cvii (1951), 168–87.

Whittingham 1971 — A.B. Whittingham, *Bury St. Edmund's Abbey*, H.M.S.O. official guide-book, based on article in *Arch. J.*, cviii (1951), 168–87.

Whittingham 1980 — A.B. Whittingham, 'The Carnary College, Norwich', *Arch. J.*, cxxxvii (1980), 361–64.

Williams 1947 — A. Williams, 'Canterbury Excavations in 1945', *Arch. Cant.*, lxxvi (1947), 68–100.

Williams and Frere 1948 — A. Williams and S.S. Frere, 'Canterbury Excavations 1945 and 1946', *Arch. Cant.*, lxi (1948), 1–40.

Williams 1977 — F. Williams, *Pleshey Castle, Essex (XII–XVI Century): Excavations in the Bailey 1959–1963*, B.A.R. no. 42, Oxford, 1977.

Williams 1975 — J.H. Williams, 'Excavation at Gravel Walk, Canterbury, 1967', *Arch. Cant.*, xci (1975), 119–45.

Williams 1978 — J.H. Williams, 'Excavations at Greyfriars, Northampton 1972', *Northants. Arch.*, xiii (1978), 96–160.

Wilson 1964 — D.M. Wilson, *Anglo-Saxon Ornamental Metalwork 700–1100*, British Museum, London, 1964.

Wilson 1982 — M. Wilson, 'Description of the Pottery', in Bennett *et al.* 1982, 67–9.

Wilson 1983 — M. Wilson, 'The Pottery', in Frere and Stow 1983, 192–298

Woods 1980 — H. Woods, 'The Despoliation of the Abbey of Saints Peter and Paul and Saint Augustine between the Years 1542 and 1793', in (Ed.) M. Sparks, *The Parish of St. Martin and St. Paul, Canterbury* (1980), 76–81.

Woods 1982a — H. Woods, 'The Completion of the Abbey Church of SS. Peter, Paul and Augustine, Canterbury, by Abbots Wido and Hugh of Fleury', in Brit. Arch. Assoc. Conf. Trans. (1982), 120–4.

Woods 1982b — H. Woods, 'Excavations at Eltham Palace, 1975–79', *Trans. London and Middx. Arch. Soc.*, xxxiii (1982), 214–65.

Woodfield 1981 — C. Woodfield, 'Finds from the Free Grammar School at the Whitefriars Coventry *c.* 1545–*c.* 1557', *Post-Med. Arch.*, xv (1981), 81–159.

Zarnecki 1951 — G. Zarnecki, *English Romanesque Sculpture*, 1951.

PRIMARY SOURCES

Unpublished Manuscripts	
Rawlinson	Bodleian Library MS Rawlinson D 781 ff 170–178.
Tanner	Bodleian Library 868, 33 Hen. VIII, 22 April, 1541–21 April 1542.
	British Library, Royal MS 18 D11 f 148.
Maps	
Andrews	Joseph Andrews and Matthew Wren, *A Plan of the City of Canterbury*, 1768 (Copy in the Library of the Society of Antiquaries of London, red portfolio, Kent, 1, p. 43).
Doidge	W. and H. Doidge, *A Plan of the ancient City of Canterbury*, 1752.
Hollar	Hollar and Johnson, 1663.
Speed	John Speed, *Kent with her Cities*, 1610.
Engravings	
Buck	J. and N. Buck, 1735.
Godfrey	Godfrey, 1784.
Goldar	Goldar, undated.
Hassell	Hassell, undated.
Parkyns	Parkyns, 1792.
Thornton	Thornton, undated.
Stukeley	Stukeley, *Itinerarium curiosum* (1724; 2nd edn. 1776).

ACKNOWLEDGEMENTS

The authors would like to thank the many people who helped both on the excavations and during a decade and more of post-excavation work. In 1972, Tony Musty, then Assistant Inspector of Ancient Monuments, was assistant director of excavations and helped in the initial stages of writing up. In 1974, Christopher Miscampbell was assistant supervisor and in charge of finds in 1974–75. Pan Garrard, Louise Millard and Caroline Simpson also gave much assistance on the excavations. In 1975, Andrew Caldwell was assistant supervisor; Trevor Carbin, Pete Crane and Jeremy Nichols were site assistants. In 1976–78, Lyn Blackmore was responsible for the finds, Stuart Glen, Nick James, the late Neil McGavin, Sue Stallibrass and Jennifer Woods were responsible for most of the drawing and photography. To all these people we are very grateful.

We also thank numerous staff of the Ancient Monuments Branch of the Department of the Environment: Terry Bowyer, chargehand at St. Augustine's, and Len Colyer, superintendent from Dover Castle; Terry Ball, of the Drawing Office, for site survey work; members of the Illustrators' Office for drawing finds, especially Chris Boddington, Diane O'Carroll and James Thorn, who also drew plans and sections; members of the Laboratory, Eliza Lawler for photography, Marjorie Hutchinson and Barry Knight for conservation, Justine Bayley and Carole Keepax for analyses.

We are grateful to all those authors of specialist reports whose names appear in the text. We mention here especially Lyn Blackmore in recognition of her hard work in preparing the pottery reports, writing up Stuart Rigold's excavations and much other background work on various topics. For editorial work we thank first Richard Gem, and then Jane Geddes, both sometime Inspectors of Ancient Monuments, who had the difficult task of drawing together the results of three different excavations. Tim Tatton-Brown and Margaret Sparks provided helpful comments at proof stage. Mrs. E. Merrifield kindly compiled the general index.

We are also grateful to the Kent Archaeological Society for accepting this report for publication, and to the Society's honorary editor, Dr A.P. Detsicas, for his work on our behalf.

Finally, we wish to record our thanks to three men who have died since the excavations took place, whose advice, encouragement and friendship have meant a great deal to us and others involved in research on St. Augustine's. They are Jim Hobbs and Bill Urry, both of the University of Oxford and City of Canterbury, and Stuart Rigold, sometime Principal Inspector of Ancient Monuments for England, *quibus dona requiem*.

DAVID SHERLOCK and HUMPHREY WOODS
in festo S. Augustini MCMLXXXVI

INTRODUCTION

ANDREW SAUNDERS

St. Augustine's Abbey was sited to the east and beyond the walls of the city of Canterbury. The origins of the monastic foundation, a grant of land to the papal missionary St. Augustine, by King Aethelberht of Kent, is well recorded and elements of the first church of Sts. Peter and Paul, begun soon after 597, have been identified and are still visible. Following the Norman Conquest, the succession of Anglo-Saxon structures was systematically levelled in order to make way for the great monastic church and claustral buildings of the late eleventh- and twelfth-century St. Augustine's Abbey. After the Dissolution, parts of the monastic buildings were adapted as a royal residence on the route from Dover to London specifically for the arrival of Anne of Cleves, but it had a short life. The abbey buildings themselves were largely plundered for building materials intended for the defences of Calais, and during the next three centuries much of the site was divided into orchards, gardens and nurseries. The outer court was given over to the bowling green, skittle alley and brewery of a tavern beside the Fyndon Gate. In 1791, three acres to the south of the nave of the abbey church were sold for the erection of a General Hospital.

Margaret Sparks (1984, 325–44) has described the determination of Alexander James Beresford Hope who, in 1843, was first inspired to save the site; and, subsequently, how the Wardens and Fellows of St. Augustine's College, which was to be founded in 1844 and built on the site of the Outer Court, acquired painstakingly and piecemeal the various parcels of land into which the precinct had been divided. It was only in 1938 that the site of the monastic church, the chapel of St. Pancras to the east of it and the immediate area of the cloister were transferred by the College into the guardianship of the then Office of Works, and which are now in the care of the Historic Buildings and Monuments Commission for England. The General Hospital of 1791 was not acquired by the Trustees of the St. Augustine's Abbey Precinct Recovery Fund until 1939, but it was not until 1971 that the building, which encroached upon the south side of the Abbey church, was available for demolition. In 1969, however, the northern part of the precinct had been sold to the Church of England for the construction of Christ Church Teacher Training College.

The pattern of archaeological investigation of the abbey and its publication has been similarly piecemeal over a very long span of time. Again, Margaret Sparks has provided a list of thirty-three separate campaigns, large and small, beginning with William Butterfield's investigations in the undercroft of the abbot's hall preparatory to his building of the college library in 1843, and ending in 1983 with work in the base court by the Canterbury Archaeological Trust. The most substantial programmes of excavation were those carried out by Canon R.U. Potts of

St. Augustine's College between 1914 and 1931, initially with the help and advice of W. St. J. Hope, C.R. Peers and A.W. Clapham. These excavations examined the Saxon churches in detail, established the existence of late-Saxon claustral buildings and provided a plan of the precinct with most of the later abbey buildings defined. Subsequent excavation has been undertaken in response to, or as part of, the work of consolidating the exposed remains. This has led to the investigation of various points of detail: a re-examination and re-interpretation in 1955–57 of the pre-Conquest structures to the west of the original church of Sts. Peter and Paul (Saunders 1978, 25–63); and S.E. Rigold's work of 1960 and 1965, reported in this volume, which was also in response to necessary site works. The excavations of 1972–78, which form the major portion of this report, were a result of the demolition of the old hospital and the need to landscape its site along Longport. At first, exploratory trenches were needed to establish how far beyond the nave of the abbey church the area in the Department of the Environment's guardianship needed to be extended. In 1974 came the second objective, the uncovering of the south side of the abbey church in order to complete the display of its ruins. The abbey cemetery further south has been grassed and turned into public gardens, and the dream of the Trustees of the Precinct Recovery Fund has to that extent been fulfilled.

Historically, St. Augustine's Abbey is important as the birthplace of Christianity among the English. Its archaeological importance clearly lies in the material remains of that first monastic foundation and the development of the monastery through the pre-Conquest period, with its four separate churches on a single alignment from east to west. The analysis of the great Romanesque church of Abbots Scotland, Wido and Hugh of Fleury has only recently, and largely as a result of the 1972–78 excavations, been thoroughly considered (Gem 1982 and Woods 1982a). The only serious account of the subsequent changes and enlargement of the church and of the monastic buildings is that by Clapham (1955) in the official handbook to the monument. This is not surprising since little of its superstructure survives. The chief elements are the lady chapel, the crypt, the north wall of the nave and the north-west or Ethelbert Tower. The significance of the excavations of 1972–78 lies in the evidence they provide for the understanding of the phased construction of the west end of the first Norman church (Woods 1982a) and for the development of the later medieval church as revealed in the fragmentary remains of the south wall. The results of earlier excavations at the abbey lie chiefly in their contributions to knowledge of the plan of the buildings and, to some extent, their sequence. This latest report contains much detail for understanding the construction of the south nave wall, its component masonry and decorative detail.

There are still pieces of work by several hands awaiting publication. Perhaps the greatest lack, however, as Margaret Sparks identified (1984), is a synthesis and re-assessment of the near century and a half of investigation and excavation at St. Augustine's. The time for this may come when someone has re-excavated the pre-Conquest residential buildings from beneath the later cloister, so tantalisingly described by Clapham (1934) as 'amongst the earliest remains of a monastic cloister north of the Alps'. These could now be compared with the buildings south of the church of Bede's monastery of Jarrow excavated in the 1960s and 70s by Rosemary Cramp.

I. HISTORY AND TOPOGRAPHY OF THE SITE

D. SHERLOCK and H. WOODS

This chapter seeks to draw together documentary and topographical evidence for the development of the areas examined in the current excavations between the church and the southern boundary of the precinct, but does not attempt a complete account of the abbey buildings and precincts as a whole (for which see Tatton-Brown 1984, 171–86).

THE SOUTHERN BOUNDARY OF THE MONASTIC PRECINCT

It is obvious from the map (Fig. 1) that the length of road out of Canterbury to Sandwich known as Longport has been diverted at Cemetery Gate to pass round the southern boundary of the abbey precinct, though an earlier way through Cemetery Gate to St. Martin's Hill via a gateway (now blocked) in the south-east corner of the precinct wall existed at least until the Dissolution. Although Burgate Street, Church Street and the original Longport route are only roughly on the same alignment they probably originated as a Roman road. This is supported by excavations in Burgate Street in 1946 (Jenkins 1950, 90–1). Probable Roman burials in the area of the original road have been recorded by Leland (1774, 9). The 1972 excavations confirmed the existence of pagan Roman burials and of a Roman track (though on a slightly different alignment again). The date when Longport was diverted is not known.[1] Cemetery Gate was built *circa* 1390, but running east from its north-east corner, and ante-dating it constructionally, is a 300 m. length of wall, originally about 3.80 m. high, faced on its southern side with Roman bricks of an identical build to those re-used in St. Pancras' Chapel. It has been suggested (Cotton 1915) that this may have been part of the original precinct wall of St. Augustine's, which would agree with the spurious charter of 605, quoted in 1181, which gives the original southern boundary of the

1. It seems there were once at least two common footpaths running through or near the abbey precincts, one to the north and one to the south of the abbey buildings. Royal authority was obtained in 1320 to enclose the ground immediately to the north (Davis 1934, 435) and thus close one footpath. However, that the monks tried and failed to get authority to close the southern footpath can be gleaned from a no doubt ineffective remedy by Pope Clement IV (1342–52) that they could 'reconcile church and cemetery by blessed water' (Davis 1934, 559). Thorne also mentions (Davis 1934, 64) that the abbey was allowed to hold three fairs, two being granted from the early twelfth century. The right to hold one of these two was lost in Edward I's reign (1272–1307), partly owing to fights and quarrels in the cemetery. Because of this it seems possible that the fairs originally took place in the area of Longport and that, when the road was diverted, the traders were unwilling to move their market onto the newly created road. There is one thirteenth-century buttress surviving in the Longport wall.

precinct as 'the Burgate Way'. One possible date for the diversion of Longport is 1185 when Archbishop Baldwin consecrated two cemeteries, one for monks and one for the laity.[2] Even after Longport was diverted, the old way (the *via media*) continued to be mentioned in the wills of those wishing to be buried in the lay cemetery (Hussey 1915, 50) and was the basis for the famous jurisdictional agreement between the abbot and the citizens of Canterbury (Davis 1934, 250). It remained the boundary of jurisdiction between the city and the later county borough of Longport up until at least 1800 (Hasted 1801, 158). Charles Cotton who published a note on the boundary wall in 1915 'hoped that further excavations will be made in the grounds towards the east with a view to ascertaining whether the foundations of this wall extend in the direction of St. Martin's' (Cotton 1915, 293).

About a quarter mile to the east of Burgate, Longport by the late thirteenth century was crossed by the *Bordiche*, a bar providing an outer defence on the approach to the city (Urry 1961, 196) where the road ran between the precinct and the abbey barton.

THE PRE-CONQUEST ABBEY CHURCH

The present excavations did not impinge upon the area of the main complex of Anglo-Saxon churches, except near the south-west tower (cf. Saunders 1978, *passim*) where the structure already examined by Saunders was encountered again. This tower may perhaps be identified with that towards the construction of which Archbishop Eadsige gave 100 marks in 1047 (Davis 1934, 44–5; Saunders 1978, 63, note 12). The great post-Conquest church which replaced the Anglo-Saxon complex, however, was examined the whole way along its south side.

THE ROMANESQUE CHURCH

The demolition of the Anglo-Saxon churches of Sts. Peter and Paul and of St. Mary and their replacement by a single new church by the Norman Abbots Scotland and Wido, is described by a contemporary monk of the abbey, Goscelin, in his *Historia Translationis S. Augustini Episcopi* (Migne 1880, 13). In his prologue Goscelin refers to the period of about seven years that had elapsed between the translation of relics of 1091 and the composition of his work (*per hoc fere*

2. From an analysis of published wills (Hussey 1915, 43–53) it seems that the *via media* was not the dividing line between the monastic and lay cemeteries; but the wills are from the fifteenth and sixteenth centuries, so it is possible that there was such a division in 1185. In the customary of the abbey, *c.* 1330–40, it was for the sacrist to decide who should be buried *in magno cimiterio quod dicitur fraternitatis sepulturas seculirium*; he was also to make sure when a burial took place that no buried remains (*tecta*) were destroyed, either in the church or the south side of the chapter house or the adjacent cloister (Thompson 1902, 107), which would locate this cemetery to the north-east of the choir. Latterly, the common cemetery probably came right up to the south wall of the church while the monks' cemetery was around the north-east end of the church, separated from the common cemetery by the wall still stretching from the lady chapel to St. Pancras'. This wall, whose western end overlies the demolished south-east buttress of the lady chapel, and whose eastern end roughly aligns on the north wall of the porch of St. Pancras', would have also screened the monks from the view of the numerous pilgrims to St. Pancras'.

ab ipsa translatione septennium). He must have completed his *Historia*, therefore, about 1098. This places it before the death of Abbot Wido in 1099, which is significant in relation to the fact that the completion of the new building is not mentioned. The *Historia* is divided into two books. Book I describes the translation of relics itself during the abbacies of Scotland and Wido, and this was the central theme of the *Historia*. Book II describes events prior to this, and so Abbot Scotland's work is described in the last Chapter (XLI) of Book II and Chapters I and II of Book I. Wido's work is described from Chapter II onwards in Book I.

Abbot Scotland (1070–87) initiated the new work *c.* 1070–73 by demolishing the rotunda which Abbot Wulfric had started to build, in part of the monks' cemetery between the church of Sts. Peter and Paul and that of St. Mary, but which had been abandoned unfinished at his death in 1061. He then proceeded to construct the crypt of the new church, and above it the presbytery. The choir also was completed (on the site of Wulfric's rotunda) and the monks moved into the new building.

Scotland then proceeded to the western half of the new church. The first stage was the removal of the burials from the church of Sts. Peter and Paul and its south porticus of St. Martin; but, either on account of his own reservations or because he did not have the requisite permission, he did not translate the main relics of the abbey from the north porticus of St. Gregory. He then continued the new construction 'right up to the porticus' of St. Gregory (which stood on the site of the third bay of the north aisle westward from the crossing and must have constituted a major obstacle to the progress of the work). At this stage of the work Scotland died.

Abbot Wido (1087–99), before turning his attention to the nave, first completed the construction of a tower over the crossing (the infrastructure of which, together with the transepts had been built already by Scotland). Then in 1091, impatient with the delay to the nave, he demolished the porticus of St. Gregory without having the relics translated from it first. Following the demolition, the relics were extracted from their tombs among the debris and translated to new shrines in the ambulatory and radiating chapels of the east arm. It is to be presumed that the construction continued immediately thereafter, but Goscelin does not give a date for the completion of the nave and west end of the church. This could be either because it was not germane to his story or because work was still in progress when he finished his *Historia* in 1098.

The *Chronicle of St. Augustine's* by William Thorne, a monk of the abbey in the fourteenth century, gives the date of the completion of the abbey church as 1091 under Abbot Wido: 'In A.D. 1091 he completed the church which his predecessor Scotland had been unable, owing to death preventing it, to finish completely, and brought to a successful end the work of translating the saints' (Davis 1934, 59). But clearly this is no more than a misunderstanding by Thorne of Goscelin's narrative. There is thus no documentary evidence for the date of completion of the Romanesque church.

WORKS TO THE CHURCH IN THE LATE TWELFTH AND THIRTEENTH CENTURIES

There are no documentary references to major works on the church again until the last third of the twelfth century. But then in 1168 'the church was in great part burnt; in this fire many ancient documents perished, and moreover the very shrine of St. Augustine and many saints of the place were woefully damaged' (Davis 1934, 94). In this fire the eastern part of the church must have been affected: the last radiating chapel where St. Augustine's shrine stood and perhaps the north transept for the scriptorium existed next to this in the fourteenth century (Clapham 1955, 21) and, possibly, ancient documents may also have been kept there in the twelfth century. However, 'books sent by Gregory to St. Augustine' apparently survived the fire and are shown above the high altar in the drawing in Thomas of Elmham's *Chronicle* (Plate I).

The restoration that must have followed the fire is difficult to date precisely (Miscampbell 1981, 63–5). It may have started already in the 1160s but dragged on for a variety of reasons. Papal bulls were issued by Alexander III (1159–84) to St. Augustine's about this time and one is specifically concerned with 'the repair of the church which has been burnt' (Hardwick 1858, 429). The completion of the work may be connected with the coming of Archbishop Hubert to the abbey on 7th November, 1193, to celebrate mass (Stubbs 1879, 523). There is, anyway, no record of a formal rededication of the church at this juncture.

A new phase of work in the second quarter of the thirteenth century may be indicated by isolated references. In 1221 the prior, John, perhaps inspired by the translation of St. Thomas at the cathedral the previous year, decided to open the shrine of St. Augustine and examine the contents. This was duly done and the relics then re-enshrined (Davis 1934, 189). Nothing is said of any building work associated with this, but it may well be that the examination was preparatory to a remodelling of the shrine chapel and other parts of the east end, for in 1240 there took place a rededication of the high altar of the church and of the altars of St. Augustine and of St. Adrian (Hardwick 1858, 45). St. Adrian's shrine stood in the south radiating chapel (that of Sts. Stephen, Lawrence and Vincent; with St. Thomas' altar in the crypt) which formed part of the area of the current excavations.

A similar remodelling of the north radiating chapel may have taken place twenty years later. In 1262, Abbot Roger II opened the shrine of St. Mildred in the north radiating chapel and then re-enshrined the relics (Davis 1934, 243). Eight years later, in 1270, this was followed by a rededication of the altar of St. Mildred (Davis 1934, 254). 1262 was also the year of the canonisation of St. Richard of Chichester, and the altar of St. Richard in the crypt of the same radiating chapel may also have been rededicated in 1270.

FROM THE FOURTEENTH CENTURY TO THE DISSOLUTION

The process of remodelling chapels, probably involving the insertion of new windows, and perhaps vaults, without disturbing otherwise the existing shell of the structure, is likely to have continued from the thirteenth century through to the Dissolution, but documentary evidence for it is only scattered.

In 1300, the shrine of St. Augustine was again opened, this time by Abbot Thomas, and a new sculptured stone monument constructed before the relics were re-enshrined (Davis 1934, 344). Other work of uncertain extent must have led on from this period to a rededication of the high altar of the church in 1325 (Davis 1934, 439). At the same time as the high altar there were rededicated the altars of St. John the Baptist in the south transept and St. Mary in the crypt (Davis 1934, 439). The second of these may provide a date for the known remodelling of the crypt.

Subsequent to 1325 there is little documentary evidence for alterations to the church except in relation to chantry chapels and to the bell tower(s), which are discussed below.

THE BELL TOWER(S)

The bell tower or towers of the abbey form a complex problem which it is difficult to unravel wholly satisfactorily on the basis of the available documentary and archaeological evidence.

As noted above, there was a tower under construction for the abbey in 1047, and Abbot Wido had built a tower over the crossing between 1087 and 1091. Probably quite apart from these, and first referred to as already in existence in the late thirteenth century, is the bell tower which stood at one end of the *Bordiche* between the abbey precinct and the barton (see p. 4). This bell tower must have been a detached structure towards the south-east corner of the precinct along Longport, and may have stood on the site of the mound to the south of St. Pancras. Christ Church also had a detached bell tower.

In 1391, Thomas Ickham, a former sacrist of the abbey, left in his will 174 marks to buy two large bells for the campanile in addition to 60 marks for 2 bells 'in the tower at the end of the church' (Davis 1934, 672–3). The *c.* 1130–40 customary of the abbey (Thompson 1904, 291), seems to distinguish in fact three places in which bells were hung. There are six bells that formed one ring and which hung '*in turri*' (three greater bells, Big Absalon, Matthew and Big Richard) and three lesser bells (un-named) which hung '*in ordine ante gradus*': the *gradus* is presumably the *gradus chori*, in which case the bells must have been located in the crossing tower. These four bells could not all be rung together because they made the tower shake, and so they must be distinguished from four other bells which could be rung together and which were located '*in campanili*'. That the four in the campanile were not merely part of the ring in the tower already referred to is suggested by the fact that one of the bells in the campanile was called Big Bubantus, a name not belonging to the six. Another bell (whose location is uncertain) was called Wulfric, and could perhaps have been an Anglo-Saxon survival. Thomas Ickham's bequest in 1391 would have brought the number of bells in the campanile up to six, and in the tower at the end of the church up to eight (assuming that the campanile and the tower referred to in the two documents are the same).

It should not be assumed, however, that where later sources refer singly to either a tower or a bell tower they necessarily relate to the tower at the west end of the church on the one hand or to the detached bell tower on the other. Both these structures were towers and in both bells were hung; both, therefore, could be referred to as a tower or bell tower without misdescription – as could the crossing tower. It is important to remember this when taking into account the evidence from wills in the years between 1461 and 1516, which left money to the work of rebuilding the bell tower or steeple of the monastery. The references in these wills have been gathered together by Hussey (1915, 43–53):

1. To the re-building of the Bell Tower of the Monastery of St. Augustine £10. – Richard Bernes of St. Paul's parish, 1461.
2. To be buried in the cemetery of St. Augustine. That seven acres of land at Westgate in the Isle of Thanet be sold by my son John, and half the money among the Convent of St. Augustine and the other half to their new Bell Tower. – Walter Martin of St. Michael's parish, 1462.

3. To the work of the Bell Tower of St. Augustine at Canterbury £3 6*s*. 8*d*. – John Hersing of Littlebourne, 1468.
4. To the Tower of the church of the Monastery of St. Augustine, for two years, 40*s*. – James Brooke of St. Mary, Northgate, 1472.
5. To the work of the Bell Tower of St. Augustine 6*s*. 8*d*. – John Chambleyn of St. Paul's parish, 1475.
6. To be buried in the cemetery of St. Augustine; and to the work of the Bell Tower 6*s*. 8*d*. – William Letherar, dwelling within the Hospital of St. John the Baptist, outside the walls of Canterbury, 1475.
7. To the work of the new Tower of the Monastery of St. Augustine 20*s*., to be paid within three years of my death. – William Browne (or York) of St. Mary Magdalene parish, 1478.
8. To the new Bell Tower of St. Augustine 20*s*., whereof they have in their hands of my stipend 6*s*. 8*d*. – Simon Flegard, clerk of St. Paul's parish 1483.
9. To be buried in the cemetery of St. Augustine; and to the new Bell Tower there 20*s*. – William Bisshope, browderer, of St. Paul's parish, 1491.
10. To be buried in the churchyard of St. Augustine outside the walls of Canterbury. To the making of the new Steeple there twenty parcels of 46*s*. 8*d*. in the hands of Mr Dygon, late the debts of John Symon, on consideration that I be rung in at the time of my burying. – Anne Whythe, now the wife of Edmund Mynot, late of the parish of St. Andrew, 1492.
11. To be buried in the cemetery of St. Augustine, and to the making of the new Bell Tower of that Monastery 6*s*. 8*d*. – Henry Parker, draper, of St. Mary Magdalene parish, 1497.
13. Towards the making of the new Steeple of St. Austen's 3*s*. 4*d*. – Thomas Goldsmethe of St. Mary Bredman parish, 1498.
14. To be buried in the churchyard of St. Augustine, near the grave of my son Adrian. To the reparation of the Bell Tower 20*d*. – Richard Cooke, tailor, of St. Andrew's parish, 1499.
15. To be buried in the churchyard of St. Austen's. To the Steeple 40*s*., so that the Abbot and Convent make me a brother and my wife a sister of their Chapter House, and that we may be rung in as a brother and sister there. – John Russhelyn of St. Mary Magdalene parish, 1501.
16. To the making of the new Steeple of St. Augustine 13*s*. 4*d*. – John Whitlock of St. Alphege parish, 1503.
17. To be buried in the cemetery of St. Augustine, nigh unto the grave of Bennett my wife; and to the building of the Steeple of the Monastery 13*s*. 4*d*., whereof Dom. Matthew Browning received 6*s*. 8*d*. during my life. – Thomas Sparowe of St. Michael's parish, 1516.
18. To be buried in the cemetery of St. Augustine; and to the building of the new Steeple of the same church 40*s*. – William Thompson of St. Mary Bredman parish, 1516.

Whereas it may seem quite likely that the bell tower, the tower and the steeple referred to in these wills may be one and the same structure, it cannot be taken for granted. Moreover, these documents do not themselves allow the structure or structures in question to be located. What is clear, however, is that some major building project was in hand during the late fifteenth and early sixteenth centuries.

In connection with this project it may be significant that one of the benefactors to St. Augustine's in the early sixteenth century was Robert Vertue, whose will reads:

> 'To be buried within the Church and Monastery of St. Augustine without the walls of Canterbury, or else in such place where it shall please God. To Dom Simeon Vertue, a goblet with a cover parcel gilt – Robert Vertue, citizen and Freeman of London, 1506'.

John Harvey (1984, 306) has suggested that Robert Vertue may have been responsible for the bell tower. He had worked as a mason at Westminster Abbey, becoming the King's Master Mason in 1487. Subsequently, he worked at Greenwich Palace and the Tower of London, and designed Bath Abbey Church and Henry VII's Chapel at Westminster Abbey. Harvey argues that Vertue's direction that he should be buried in the church of St. Augustine's Abbey suggests that he was master mason there.

THE CEMETERY, THE CHARNEL CHAPEL AND THE HUNTINGDON CHANTRY

Goscelin had referred to the monks' cemetery that until the time of Abbot Wulfric had lain in the area of the crossing of the later great church (*supra* p. 5), but it is not until 1185 that there is clear reference to the existence of the two cemeteries (dedicated by Archbishop Baldwin – *supra* p. 4) one of which must have been the lay cemetery on the south side of the church.

The heavy use of the lay cemetery is suggested by the need felt, less than a century after the dedications, to construct a charnel chapel, presumably for storing the remains disturbed by new burials. The fabric of the chapel was completed in 1287 (Davis 1934, 291), but apparently it was not dedicated until 1299 (Davis 1934, 303) – on the feast of St. Cuthbert. The charnel chapel is referred to subsequently a number of times. In 1468/9, £2 was paid to the brethren celebrating mass in the charnel house (Cotton 1939, 87). In 1477, William Stephen asked to be buried in the porch (*in portico*) of the chapel of St. Mary in the cemetery; this could be the charnel chapel, whose dedication is otherwise unknown. In 1503, Richard Down of St. Andrew's parish asked to be buried 'beside the charnel house beside the image of Our Lady'. (There was another image of St. Mary at St. Pancras', before which William Kynton of St. George's parish asked to be buried in his will of 1502). In 1451, Edward Septvans asked to be buried 'against the Hawthorn near the Charnel' and, in 1516, Michael Welles of St. Paul's asked to be buried 'beside the tomb of St. Austin and next to my father-in-law on the charnel side'.

Other structures also are referred to in connection with burials in the cemetery. Thus, in 1475, John Chamberlain of St. Paul's parish asked to be buried in the cemetery 'before the water conduit there'. While in 1469 there is a reference to a burial on the south side of the *via media*. Other wills are less specific or simply ask to be buried near existing burials (see Hussey 1915, *passim*).

Some lay burials took place not strictly in the cemetery itself but in chantry chapels grafted onto the south aisle of the nave and intruding into the area of the cemetery. Among these must be accounted the chantry of Juliana de Leyborne, Countess of Huntingdon. Her will, referring to the chapel in question reads (*Arch. Cant.*, i (1858), 8):

> 'In the name of God. Amen.
>
> 'On Saturday, the 30th day of October, in the year of our Lord, 1367, I, Juliana de Leyborne, Countess of Huntyngdon, make my testament after this manner:
>
> "Of sound mind. First, I bequeath my soul to God, and the blessed Virgin, and all His Saints; and my body to be buried in the Church of the Monastery of St. Augustine of Kent, in the new Chapel, on the south side of the church. Item, I leave all my goods and chattels, moveable and immoveable, to the disposal of Sir Alexander Wayte, Canon of Wyngham, Sir John Amublee, Rector of the Church of Harrietsham, and John de Middleton, appointing the same executors of this my testament, that they may dispose, for my soul, in rewards of my servants, and other works of charity, as to them may seem most expedient.
>
> "Item, I appoint the Lord Thomas, the Abbot of the Monastery of the aforesaid Church of St. Augustine's, supervisor of this my testament.
>
> "Done the day and year as above.
>
> "In whitness whereof, to this my testament my seal is appended'.

This chantry has always been identified as that found by earlier excavators in the angle between the south aisle and the south transept: however, the excavation of the second chantry projecting beyond the south aisle further west may cause this identification to be questioned (*vide infra*).

The only further documentary evidence that may point towards the position of the chapel is provided by Thorne (Davis 1934, 483) who says that it lay opposite Abbot Ralph's grave. The location of Abbot Ralph's grave itself is known, but the sense in which the chapel was 'opposite' this grave is uncertain. It may seem likely that the abbot's burial was in a more easterly (i.e. more important) than westerly position in the church, and hence that the Huntingdon chantry was the more easterly of the two excavated. Against this must be set the fact that Abbot Hugh III (*d.* 1224) was buried five bays west from the crossing. His grave slab is still *in situ*. The argument is therefore not conclusive.

THE DISSOLUTION AND THE SIXTEENTH-CENTURY DEMOLITION OF THE ABBEY BUILDINGS

The abbey was suppressed by Henry VIII in 1538 and the following year the king instructed his Surveyor, James Nedeham, to convert part of the complex of buildings (the abbot's palace) into a royal residence (Colvin 1982, 59). However, it was not until 1541 that orders were given for the church itself to be unroofed and for the demolition to proceed so that the timbers and stone could be transported to Calais for the king's military works there (Colvin 1982, 61). Nedeham's account books (Oxford, Bodley MS Rawlinson D 781, ff 170–178) contain, among other things, important evidence relating to 'the chapel of the charnel house' and to 'the great steeple and the two great buttresses that stood before the same steeple', and this evidence is quoted here in full from Woods 1980:

f.172 Anno Regni Regis Henrici viiji xxxiijo [1541–42]
The Kynges Maner off Sent Austens
Paymentes made And payde by me Jamys Nedam Clerke and Surveiour of our souerayngne ye Kinges wurkes . . . frome Sondaye ye xxvi ti daye of februarij Inclusyve unto Sondaye ye xix th daye of Marche exclusyve by ye space of iij Weykes.
Bryklayers

f.172b Working Aswelle in makyng new And settyng up a waille to close in ye Kynges Garden yt was brokyn downe with ye fawyll of ye great stepul to ye East syd of ye Churche. As Also makyng and settyng up of ye walle to Close in y Kynges garden of ye sought syd next ye Chur[ch] yarde yt was brokyn downe with ye fawylle of ye Chapelle of ye Charnelle-howse.

f.174 Laborers to the Bryklayers and also Comen Laborers Laborying not only in beryng of water slakyng of Lyme and Makyng of mortar serving ye bryklayers With stone flynt and morter with gevyng Attendance to ye bryklayers nothing be lakyng to them to ye furtheryng And spedy settyng up of ye walle. But Allso dygyng owte of grett stones yt fylle from ye stepulle in to ye Kynges garden with beryng of them in handbarows to ye stone hepes. Ryddyng and trying with Clensyng away of ye Rubbryshe and beryng oute of ye same from ye Kynges garden. Brekyng of grett Rookes yt wer undermynyd of ye ij great butterassys and ye great stepulle yt felle over in to ye Kynges garden and upon ye waylle of ye same garden With beryng awaye ye Rubbryshe of ye same. Makyng and trying oute awaye to sett up a scaffolde for ye bryke layers to worke upon to sett up ye same waylle to close in ye garden with Doyng alle other labores nidfulle to be done.

f.175 Anno Regni Regis Henrici viiji xxxiijo
The Kynes Manour off Sent Austens
Paymentes Made And payd by me Jamys Nedam Clerke [etc] . . . from Sonday ye xxvi ti daye of Marche unto Sondaye ye xxiij ti day of Aprylle by ye space of on Monethe.
Bryklayers

Workyng nott only in Makyng new And settyng vp A stone waylle to Cloese in ye Kynges Garden. Which was broken downe with ye fawlle of ye grett stepulle. But also makyng and settyng vp of ye waylle next ye Charnell Howse in lyke manner which was brokwn downe as ys aforsayd with ye greatt stepulle with hewyng of koyn stonys for ye Corners of ye sam waylle And mendyng other Reparacions abowtt in ye sayd manour.

f.175b Comen Laborers

Laboryng nott only in brekyng of great and hard Rookes or grett peces falyn from ye grett stepulle And ye ijth grett butterassis yt stode befor ye sam stepulle beyng fallen down in to ye Keyng[s] Garden and upon the waylle of ye sam garden with dygyng out of Great stone lying upon ye sayd waylle and on Every syde of ye same beyng Croshyd And bettyn down with ye fawlle And ye ij butterassis But also beryng out of ye same Garden alle of ye stons. With makyng Cleyn A rom or A waye on Every syd of ye walle yt ye bryklayers may sett vp scaffoldes on Every syd to mak up ye same waylle Ageyne. And beryng out of ye Rubbryshe in baskettes from ye wurkmen as they Worke with doyng all other labors as ye tym Requirid.

f.177 Anno Regni Regis Henrici viiji xxxiiijo [1542]

The Kynges Manor off Sent Austens

Payments Mad And payd by me Jamys Nedam Clerke [etc] . . . from Sonday the xxiijth day of apprylle vnto Sondaye the xxjth daye of May by the space of fower Wekys.

Bryklayers

Workyng not only in Contynuyng in makyng newe And settyng vp of a Stone waylle abowt ye Kynges garden beyng broken down with ye fawlle of ye grett stepulle And ye ijth grett butterassis. But also hewyng and workyng of quyn or Corner stons for ye Corner of ye wallys with doyng other thinges ther.

f.178 Anno Regni Regis Henrici viiji xxxiiijo [1542]

The Kynges Manor off Sent Austens

Paymentes Mad And payd by me Jamys Nedam Clerke [etc] . . . from Sondaye ye xxjth daye off Maij vnto Sondaye ye xjth Daye of Juyn by ye space of iij Weykes.

Bryklayers

Workyng nott only in Makyng of ye New Waylle Abowt ye Kynges Garden to close yt from ye Churche yard. But also makyng And End And fynysshyng of ye same with Muryng vp of ye great Churche west Dore Joynyng to ye forsayd Garden.

The king's garden is stated to have lain adjoining the great west door of the church and can only be supposed to have occupied the area marked 19 on Fig. 1. This being so, it is difficult to see how the collapse of a tower to the east of the church could have damaged the wall about this garden: 'East syd' on f.172b, therefore, must be a mistake for west side. This emendation is borne out by another account of October of the same year (Colvin 1982, 61), which refers to 'digging out stone from the great steeple thrown down that stood at the west end of St. Austen's Church'. The great steeple and its two great buttresses, therefore, must have been the south-west tower of the church which, with the Ethelbert tower, flanked the west front. That the great steeple is also that which was under construction *c.* 1461 x 1515 (*vide supra*) is likely but not conclusively demonstrable.

The charnel house by its fall is said to have damaged the south wall of the king's garden, and this wall is likely to be that running eastward from Cemetery Gate to return northward on a line with the west front of the church.

That the salvage of material from the demolition of the church was still continuing ten years later is shown by the accounts of George Nycholl (assistant to Sir Thomas Moyle, general surveyor to the Court of Augmentations) made in connection with repairs to the king's house (St. Augustine's College MS 11676). Most of the salvaged material was sold to the burgesses of Canterbury. These accounts have been published in full (Sherlock 1983) but the following extracts immediately relevant to the south-west tower may be cited here:

f.1v Anno R E Vi vi^{to} [1552/3]
The Kings pales of Sent Austens without the walls of Canterbury
The accompte of George Nycholl of ye pshe of Sent Paull without ye walls of Canterbury as well of all manner of sales of assheler Cayn stone with other grett broken Cayn stons, flynt, hard broken stonis and chalke stons Commyng of the buyldyngs defaced wthin ye site or precynct of ye late monestery of sent Austens wthout ye mured walls of Canterbury forsayd As also of payments of ye money comming therof, And also certyn redye money mor receavyd of my master Sr Thomas Moyll knyght as yt apperyth after in the accompte of my Receyts payd and layd out for the new Repayryng, buyldyng and mendyng of the Kyngs maiesties grett hall The gret chamber called the wardroobe Chamber The dresser kychyn with certeyn other nedfull places as yt followyth after partycularly, Mad and done by the commanndment and appoyntment of ye aforsayd Syr Thomas Moyll knyght, on of ye generall Surveyrs of the Kyngs maiesties lands. From the xxix daye of Apryll in the vj yer of the Reine of our soverayng lord Kyng Edward the Syxte unto ye natyvytie and byrthe of our lord Jehus Cryst In the first yer of our soverayng ladye Queyn Mary next ensuyng as after particularly ys contayned and declared.

f.2r Furst Sold and Recevyd of mother Chapman of Sent Paulls parshe for ij Court loode of flynt and rubyshe stone dygyd from ye mase hep and Rubyshe of ye old stepyll and other placs at vid lood xxid [there follow 43 other items of sale].

f.4r Ao R Marie 1 [1553]
[38 sales are itemized including the following]
Recs of Mr Thornhest forsayd for xxxix lood of assheler cayn stone dygyd som out of ye undercroft and from the walls of ye old church and stepul walls. And from ye walls of the south yeld of ye church at iiijs 1od. vijli xvjs.

Also worth noting here is a reference to the salvage of marble and tiles:

f.2r Rec of Lenard Strenger of Chyllam for iiii small rownd pyller marbull stones at vi d a pece – iis.
f.3r Rec of Mr Quylter of Sent Dunstons for i C of small pavyng tyll – xiid.
f.3v Rec of Thomas Wylliams of Fordych for ii rownd marbull pyllers stons – xiid.

THE SITE BETWEEN THE DEMOLITION AND 1793

The king's house itself did not impinge upon the area of the excavations and so its subsequent history need only be noted briefly. It ceased to be a royal residence under James I and in 1612 was granted to the Wooton family, from whom it passed to the Hales; the house itself fell into ruin in the course of the eighteenth century (Colvin 1982, 63).

Part at least of the lay cemetery occupying the area between the demolished abbey church and Longport continued in use, presumably serving some of those Canterbury churches that had no burial ground of their own – as it had done before the Dissolution. However, in 1591, St. Paul's church bought its own cemetery on the south side of Longport (Hasted 1799, 641–2) and must have ceased using St. Augustine's thereafter.

For the general topography of the site and for the fate of the surviving fragments of the abbey buildings some of the best evidence in this period is provided by topographical views and maps. The earliest view, indeed may be one that precedes the Dissolution: this is a late fifteenth-century illumination in BL Royal MS 18D. 11, f.148, which shows a group of Canterbury pilgrims outside the walls of a city with a large church behind them (Plate II). The twin west towers of St. Augustine's may be represented here.

The earliest post-Dissolution prints and plans show no buildings between Longport and the former abbey church. In Braun and Hoggenburg's map of the city of *c.* 1560 (Plate III) the abbey buildings appear to have been rotated through 90°, making east, south, etc., so as to fit on the map. A picturesque map in colour of about twenty years later (Plate IV)[3] shows the royal apartments that were built at the Dissolution dominated by the converted abbey kitchen, with four ruined arches running eastwards, presumably those of the nave. There is no representation of St. Pancras'. The precinct gates have been reduced to two: one massive gate flanked by circular towers in the centre of the west wall, and one smaller though hardly less imposing on the site of the eastern exit onto Longport. Another map of *c.* 1620 (Plate V) shows Ethelbert's Tower and the great hall between Cemetery and Fyndon gates enclosed by a wall with a small archway on the north side and two houses on Longport. Further away on the bend in Longport, the eastern gate is shown in the outer precinct wall which by then surrounds an area of formal gardens and orchards, extending up as far as St. Martin's (i.e. including the later area of nos. 11, 12 and 14 on Fig. 1). In Hollar and Johnson's map of 1663 (Plate VI) based on Speed's map of 1610, the abbey church is represented by a rectangular ruin of five bays. To the east of the church is represented a free-standing square tower with pyramidal roof which 'ground plott' might be the detached campanile. The tower is not shown, however, in *c.* 1640 when Daniel King published his engraving of Thomas Johnson's view of St. Augustine's (Plate VII), but to the south of the church is another building partly obscured by bushes, which he numbered 4 and called *ruinae aliquot sive quaedam cenobii reliquiae*. These are most probably remains of the fallen south-west tower of the church.

The same structure seems to be shown in the views of Stukeley and Harris (1722), and N. Buck (1735) and Stukeley and I.V. der Gucht (undated)[4], and here confirmation that it did indeed belong to the south-west tower is provided by Stukeley's description of it in his *Itinerarium Curiosum* (1724, 2nd edition 1776):

> 'At the west end of this church, as I conjecture, were two great towers half of one is still remaining, called Ethelbert's Tower: all the whole stones and pillars about it are skinned off as far as they can reach; and every year a buttress, a side of an arch, or the like, passes *sub hasta*. There is part of the other standing, if it can be so said, that is only not fallen; I call it *muro torto*: it is a vast angular piece of the tower, about thirty foot high, which has been undermined by digging away a course at the bottom, in order to be thrown down, but it happened only to disjoint itself from the foundation, and leaping, as it were, a little space, lodged itself in the ground in that inclining state, to the wonderment of the vulgar, who do not discern the meaning of it, though the foundation it came from is sufficiently visible: thus happening to be equally poized, it is a sight somewhat dreadful, and forbids a too near approach on any side, with the apprehension of its falling that way.'

The 1752 map of Canterbury by W. and H. Doidge is among the most reliable of the period (Plate VIII): it shows south-east of Ethelbert's tower, no. 23, 'Ruins of a Tower' which must be again the south-west tower. The same map is also of importance because, together with Andrews and Wren's map of 1768, it shows for the first time a mound situated to the south of St. Pancras'. This mound, therefore, cannot be made entirely of spoil from the construction of the hospital in 1791 as has sometimes been supposed.

The ruins of the south-west tower are shown again by Godfrey (drawn 1759, published 1784), Parkyns (1772) and by Thornton in his undated plan (Plate IX). On Thornton's plan, the tower, item K, is described as 'a large mass of leaning ruin, supposed to have been part of a steeple.'

3. For the advice on the date of this and the following map, we are grateful to Miss Anne Oakley, Cathedral Librarian.
4. In the collection of the Royal Museum, Canterbury. Another undated view in the same collection is by Goldar, while one by Hassell is in a private collection.

The boundary wall between the abbey nave and St. Pancras', with its pronounced three-sided bend by-passing the south transept, is approximately on the line of the wall that was only demolished in 1972. 'E, The inside of the church' is really the adjacent abbot's chapel, the only chapel not demolished at the Dissolution. 'II, St. Pancreas' Chapel' is really two buildings, the western one a small dwelling shown on an engraving by Hooper of 1784 (Maidstone Record Office). The remainder of the 27-acre (11 hectares) abbey precinct is variously shown as garden, hop ground and orchards.

Francis Grose, in his *Antiquities of England and Wales* (*c*. 1797) devotes only a sentence to the south-west tower: 'to the left of Ethelbert's Tower is a large inclining mass, or shapeless lump of stones: This is conjectured to have been part of a Tower'. He is informative, though, on the robbing of the Ethelbert Tower and other buildings: 'These venerable remains have suffered almost as much from the depredations of its different owners and occupiers, as from the ravages of Time. It is at present lett for a Public-house. The ruins of the Church have been converted into a Tennis-Court; the Great Gate into a Cock-pit; and in 1765, workmen were set to pull down the Tower for the sake of materials. They accordingly began at the top, but Time have rendered the cement almost as hard as stone, the workmen proceeded slowly, as to make the price of their labour exceed the value of the stones taken down: wherefore it was thought proper to desist. At the same time other workmen were employed about the foundations of the fallen buildings; when many pillars, capitals, and ornaments were discovered buried together in a heap; as also divers stone coffins, in which pieces of woollen garments and hair were found. But this subterranean work answering no better than that commenced aloft, the holes digged were filled up, and the ground levelled. Some, indeed, attribute the relinquishing of this undertaking to the interposition of persons abroad, who represented to the proprietor the barbarism of destroying so venerable a ruin, and the indecency of disturbing the bones of the dead, which was undoubtedly done without his knowledge'.

The surviving fragment of the south-west tower was finally demolished, and there is a graphic account of this in *The Gentleman's Magazine* for July 1793 (Being the First Number of Vol. LXIII Part II), p. 667: 'The huge fragment of antiquity in Canterbury, situated to the left of Ethelbert's Tower, and within the precinct of St. Augustine's monastery now part of the inclosure of the new county hospital, which had withstood the shocks of the elements, and the corroding hand of Time, in a very *inclined position*, for many ages, was a few days ago pulled down; but so strong was the cement of the materials it consisted of, that the united efforts of 20 men were scarcely sufficient to accomplish it. When it fell, its weight was so immense that the ground shook for a considerable distance round. It is composed of chalk and flint in irregular layers, cemented so firmly, as to be nearly as hard as solid rock. Three private men belonging to the Surrey militia, now in barracks there, contracted to remove it for the value of the materials, which they have sold for one shilling the cart-load, for mending the highway. It is supposed there are not less than 500 loads, exclusive of the rubbish'.

The occasion for the demolition was the building of the Kent and Canterbury Hospital begun in 1791 (Plate X), one of the earliest of its kind in England, on part of the site of the former cemetery (which presumably by this time had fallen largely into disuse).[5] Hasted (1801, 165)

5. Though some of the nurses who died while working at the hospital were buried here. Information from Dr F.M. Hall of the Kent Postgraduate Medical Centre (*in lit*. 23rd September, 1980).

describes burials that must have been disturbed by the building works, when he records the finding 'a few years ago . . . of a stone coffin of one block with a cover having a ridge along the middle. . . Other coffins composed of several stones set edgeways and cemented together with mortar were found . . . at a depth of about 7 ft. and fronting the east. . . Great quantities of human bones, of different sizes and at different depths were dug up likewise. . . All these were turned into the ground again at random'.

Hasted also describes (1801, XII, 221) both Ethelbert's Tower and the recently demolished remains of the south-west tower:

'When we enter the site of the monastery, the first object is Ethelbert's Tower, whose beauty, though much defaced, especially by sacrilegious hands of late years, will witness to succeeding ages, the magnificence of the whole, when all stood compleat in their glory together. . . . There are but small remains of the ancient abbey church; the above tower, a wall of one of the isles on the southern side, and the east end of another, or at least of a chancel, with the stone case or frame of a pointed Gothic window belonging to it, are all that are left of it; so that what the dimensions of it were, can hardly be traced with any degree of certainty. The west side, however, of Ethelbert's Tower being adorned with small pilastres from the top almost to the bottom of it, seems to show that there were never any cross isles, nor any part of the church continued westward from it. This tower seems to have stood either in the centre of the west front of the church, or perhaps towards the southern part of it (*Note.* Mr Somner supposes, that Ethelbert's Tower was sometime a steeple or bell tower, annexed and contiguous to St. Augustine's church, standing by the north side of the west end thereof, and opening on the south side or quarter of it, as it is a square piece, into the nave or body of the church, as on the east into the north isle thereof, even just as that we call Arundel steeple in Christ Church doth, from which it differs but a little in the work. Of certain, this and the church when standing, were contiguous; and there are those that remember that north isle standing in their time, entire and undemolished. Batterley's Somner, p. 32); about fifty-six feet southward from it, was, till lately, a very massive ruin, composed of flint and rubble stone, of an extraordinary thickness, seemingly a part of the two sides of a hollow square tower, having to all appearance been one a companile or belfry, but whether separate from the building of the church itself, or contiguous, can only be conjectured; an effort has been made, many years past, to undermine it, by which means it had been thrown very much out of its perpendicular, and hung tremendous to the view in a very inclined position. (*Note.* It was composed of chalk, flints, and mortar, in regular layers, cemented so firmly, as to be nearly as hard as a solid rock, appearing to have been once faced with ashlar stone. It measured 32 ft in height, and in the part where it had separated, more than 20 in breadth, and had every appearance of having formed the angle, or corner of a square building, the walls of which, exclusive of dilapidations, were more than 10 ft thick; the solidity of it, and its very shallow foundation, seemed to shew its antiquity). This huge fragment was taken down in June 1793, having been undermined by the united efforts of near 200 men, and with the assistance of jacks and ropes, was, not without great difficulty, thrown down, its immense weight seemingly shaking the ground to some distance. In its fall it separated into three parts; the materials of it were supposed to amount, exclusive of the rubbish, to near 500 cart loads.')

The anonymous author of *The Canterbury Guide by An Inhabitant* (*c.* 1800), refers to 'the other part' of the south-west tower being pulled down, but in other respects follows Hasted:

'In the common cemetery, which adjoins to the church southward, about sixty feet from it, there stood till lately a large massive ruin, composed of flint and rubble stone, of an extraordinary thickness, having been to all appearance, to sides of a campanile or bell tower. It seemed some efforts had been made many years ago, when the other part of it was pulled down, to undermine this part likewise, by which means it had thrown out much of its perpendicular. It was taken down in 1793, by the united efforts of near two hundred men, the materials, exclusive of the rubbish, amounting to near 500 cart loads.'.

FROM 1793 TO 1971

In the nineteenth century the greater part of the former precinct of St. Augustine's Abbey passed into the possession of the Corporate Body of St. Augustine's Missionary College which was founded in 1848 on much of the site of the king's house; and in the same decade arrangements were first made for part of the remains of the abbey to be preserved. Archaeological excavations were subsequently carried out and have continued intermittently into this century, directed by St. John Hope, Clapham, Peers, Potts and others, until 1938 when the remains of the abbey church and cloister eastward from the west walk, together with St. Pancras' Chapel, were placed in the guardianship of what is now the Department of the Environment (Sparks 1984, 341). The boundary, however, remained between this area and that where the hospital had been erected to the south of the former abbey church.

The hospital was modernised in this century and various ancillary buildings were added up to 1937 when the hospital moved to a new site and its buildings were taken over and further extended (Plate XI) by the Technical High School for Boys. Two coffins were exposed and covered up again in 1937 when the former hospital basement was deepened. One was of limestone and one lead.[6] The Technical College in turn closed down and moved in 1971. All the buildings were then pulled down by Dover Demolition Co. in 1972, except for the former hospital mortuary (which was retained as an archaeological finds store for the excavation which began in that year).

FROM 1972 TO 1981

Following the closure of the Technical College, which stood on land leased from the St. Augustine's College Trustees, the latter generously offered the Department of the Environment the opportunity of taking into guardianship extra land between the south side of the former abbey church and Longport. Excavations were therefore undertaken; first, to explore how much extra land should be taken into guardianship and, then, to uncover the strip of land along the south side of the Department's existing boundary which had always and evidently been too close for the proper display of the abbey ruins (the boundary wall overlay the south side of the church in several places; Plate XII). With this first objective, trial trenches were dug across the site in 1972 (trench I by Frank Jenkins (Jenkins, forthcoming), trenches II and III by David Sherlock and Anthony Musty). Subsequently, the whole area between the church and St. Pancras' and Longport was scheduled under the Ancient Monuments Acts and the Department of the Environment took into guardianship a strip of land averaging 6 m. wide, from the east end of St. Pancras' to the south transept of the main church and an area of land from the nave to the Longport boundary wall (see Fig. 6). The addition to the guardianship area means that the area of the probable charnel chapel discovered in Trench III is available for future excavation and display; also that the greater part of the medieval and later cemetery is available for study as well as the earlier periods beneath. Levels taken in 1972 on the line of the new north–south

6. Information from Dr T.A. Clarke of the Kent Postgraduate Medical Centre (*in lit.* 24th March, 1980).

boundary show that some Saxon and earlier levels still probably lie undisturbed beneath the cellar floor of the old hospital (Fig. 8).

With the second objective, that of uncovering the south side of the abbey church for the proper display of its ruins, further excavation began in 1974. In that and the subsequent year areas were excavated by David Sherlock from the south-east corner of the lady chapel, along the presbytery, round the south transept and up to the third bay of the nave. Then, between 1976 and 1978 further areas were dug by Humphrey Woods from the west end of the fourth bay of the nave up to the west end of the church where part of the south-west tower had already been uncovered by Andrew Saunders between 1955 and 1957 (Saunders 1978). All finds from the excavations are now (1982) being stored at Dover Castle pending the provision of a proper museum on site.

Meanwhile, after the new guardianship area had been agreed, the City took over the southern part of the site from the Trustees of St. Augustine's College and created formal public gardens. The ground was levelled up by re-using the excavated topsoil and turfed. A 20 m. length of the old boundary wall east of the lady chapel has been left standing because it contains early masonry[2] (Plate XIII). The entrance to the guardianship monument via the north side of St. Augustine's College has been closed and visitors are admitted from Longport. This allows visitors to enter the church more appropriately near the original doorway in the south-west tower, instead of arriving via the monks' cloister and north transept. Since 1984 the monument has been in the care of the Historic Buildings and Monuments Commission for England.

II. EXCAVATIONS BY S.E RIGOLD TO THE NORTH AND EAST OF THE NORTH TRANSEPT, CRYPT AND LADY CHAPEL, 1960

LYN BLACKMORE

SUMMARY

Excavations to the east of the north transept revealed a possible Roman layer, the construction trench of the eleventh-century crypt, a fourteenth- or fifteenth-century deposit, and features associated with the demolition of the abbey and subsequent landscaping. To the north and east of the chapel of St. Richard was a cemetery. One grave was fully excavated, and evidence for five other possible graves was recorded.

INTRODUCTION

In October 1959 permission was granted by St. Augustine's College for the boundary dividing the north-east side of the abbey church from the College playing field to be repositioned in order to improve the access to the chapel of St. Pancras and to facilitate repairs to the east wall of the cloister. The restricted area enclosed by the former boundary is shown in Fig. 2; the new boundary lies between 1.80–2.70 m. to the north, and continues eastwards on a straight line up to the chapel of St. Pancras. The opportunity was thus taken to re-expose the wall and staircase between the north transept and the slype, which since 1902 had been hidden beneath the grass bank which ran inside the line of the old boundary, and to investigate by means of trial trenches the areas to the east of the chapel of St. John in the north transept, and to the north of the crypt and lady chapel. The work was supervised in 1960 by the late S.E. Rigold, who was at that time the Assistant Inspector of Ancient Monuments responsible for the abbey.

EARLIER EXCAVATIONS

The eastern side of the north transept and the small apsidal chapel of St. John the Evangelist[7]

7. Dr Gem has suggested that this may have originally been the chapel of St. Gregory completed by 1091 (Gem 1982, 8).

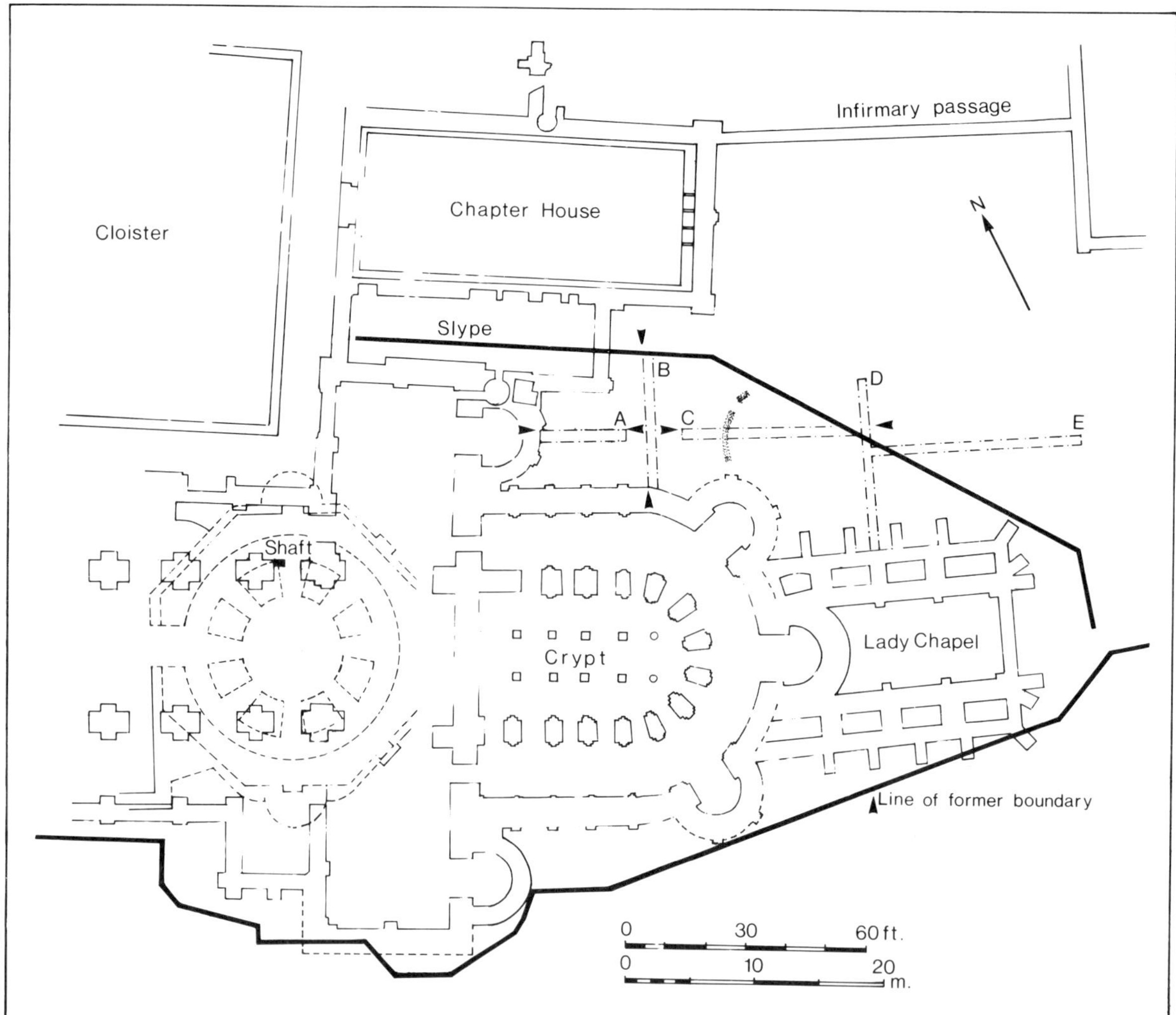

Fig. 2. Plan of the Eastern Part of the Church showing the Location of the Trenches (1960) and Shaft (1965).

were first excavated in 1902 by Evans (1904, 5), who found that only 1.20 m. of the walls survived above ground level, and that only a small part of the outer face of dressed (Caen?) stone remained *in situ*. The bulk of the worked stone found inside the chapel was of post-Romanesque date, and this prompted the suggestion that the chapel was probably damaged in the great fire of 1168, and remodelled in the late twelfth century. Without further excavation, however, the possibility that this masonry was derived from later internal embellishments to the original fabric of the chapel cannot be discounted. No evidence for damage by fire was found in the sections of wall examined in the 1960 or the 1974–75 excavations. This point was also made by Geddes (1983, 95), who noted that, due to ill-feeling between the abbey and Henry II between 1161 and 1173, it is unlikely that any major rebuilding took place during these years.

Within the north transept a curious feature was discovered *c.* 1950 in the western pier of the crossing. Here a niche was found which contained two stone blocks hollowed out as receptacles for heart canisters, and covered by a stone slab. No plans or other records of the discovery survive other than five photographs (D.o.E./H.B.M.C. nos. A940/4–940/8).

The crypt was originally excavated in 1901 (Routledge 1902, 238–43), when the northern apsidal chapel was found to contain a coffin with a skeleton thought to be that of Abbot Wido, the successor of Abbot Scotland, who completed the building of the church in 1091 and died in 1099.

THE 1960 EXCAVATIONS

The layout of the excavation was largely predetermined by the linear nature of the site, and apparently consisted of five trenches: Trenches A, B and C (probably excavated in March) in the area between the north transept and the crypt; Trenches D and E (probably excavated in May), forming a 'T' in the area to the north of the lady chapel. In addition, the area around and between these trenches was watched as the bank was cut back and the site cleared. The work of exposing and consolidating the outer face of the east wall of the cloister and the consolidation of the staircase connecting the north transept and the slype were also observed and photographed.

It is to be regretted that the excavator was never able to complete his report on the site, for the surviving records are sadly incomplete. Section drawings for Trenches A, B and C are shown in Fig. 3, but there are no section drawings of Trenches D and E. The main features discovered in Trench D were recorded on a plan (Fig. 4) and to some extent photographically, but there is no record of Trench E other than an outline on an architect's plan of the site dated May 1960 and some ambiguous photographs which may relate to either Trench C or Trench E. The finds pose a particular problem since the layers excavated were not numbered. Correlations of the original locations given for the pottery and the layers excavated are presented in Table 4. Virtually no finds are specifically recorded as coming from trenches in the area of the lady chapel, and it is tempting to assume that these trenches produced little material; the quantity of pottery from the western part of the site, however, leaves this open to doubt, and it is possible that many finds labelled 'east of north transept' derive from Trenches D or E. The find-spot of the Limoges figurine (Fig. 53, no. 1), quoted as 'east of north transept, extreme east end, level with end of lady chapel' is debateable since it is not clear whether the description refers to the west end (Trench C) or east end of the chapel (Trench E). A number of small finds are described as deriving from a 'metal cache' east of the north transept; the nature and post-medieval date of the finds, however, which include a seventeenth/eighteenth-century window catch, do not suggest any real intent to conceal, and these items probably derive from pit F4 (Fig. 3a).

In the absence of any written site records, layer and feature numbers have been invented for the purposes of this report, and much of the text is perforce based on photographic evidence, the finds, or conjecture, a poor substitute for the scholarly account that the excavator, with his remarkable memory, would certainly have produced.

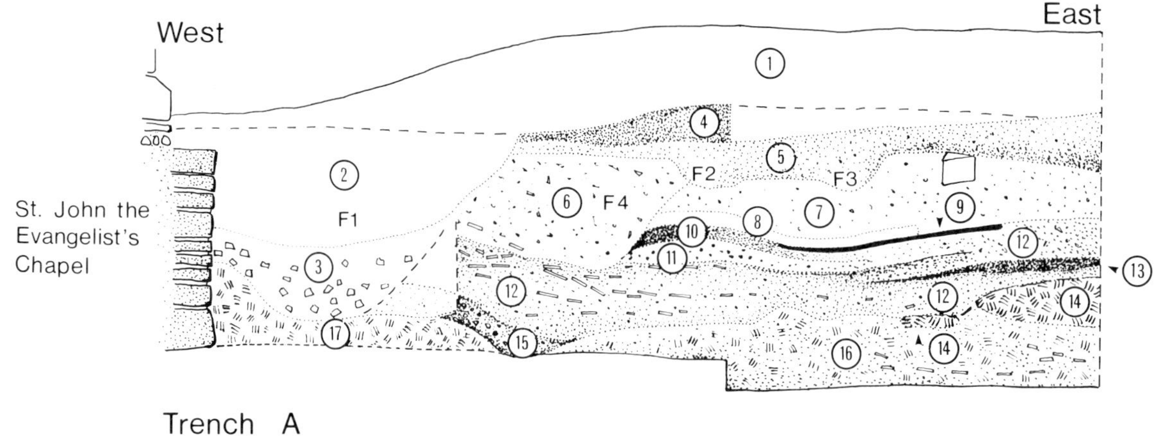

Fig. 3a. Section of Trench A, North Side (1960).

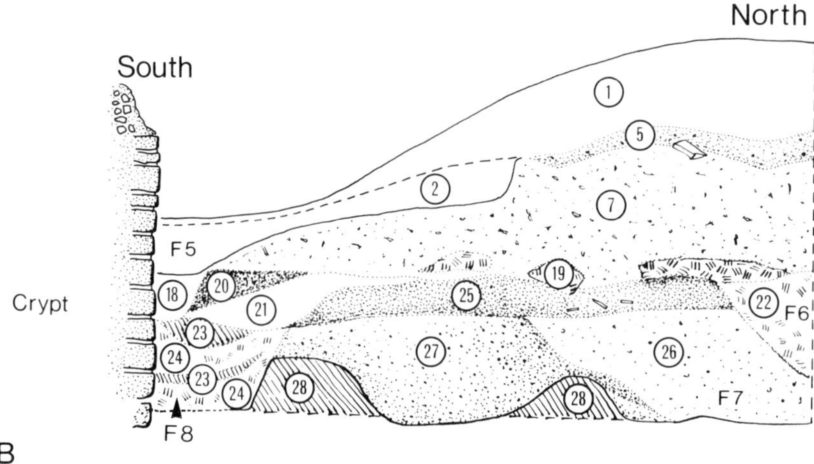

Fig. 3b. Section of Trench B, West Side (1960).

Trench A (Fig. 3a).

Trench A was placed just to the south of the northern buttress of the chapel of St. John the Evangelist in the north transept, and extended eastwards for 6.17 m. The trench was 0.99 m. wide and reached a maximum depth of 1.75 m. below the 1960 ground surface (1), which sloped gently down toward the chapel. At the west end of the trench the medieval and post-medieval layers had apparently been removed to a depth of 1.52 m. by earlier excavations (F1). The lower

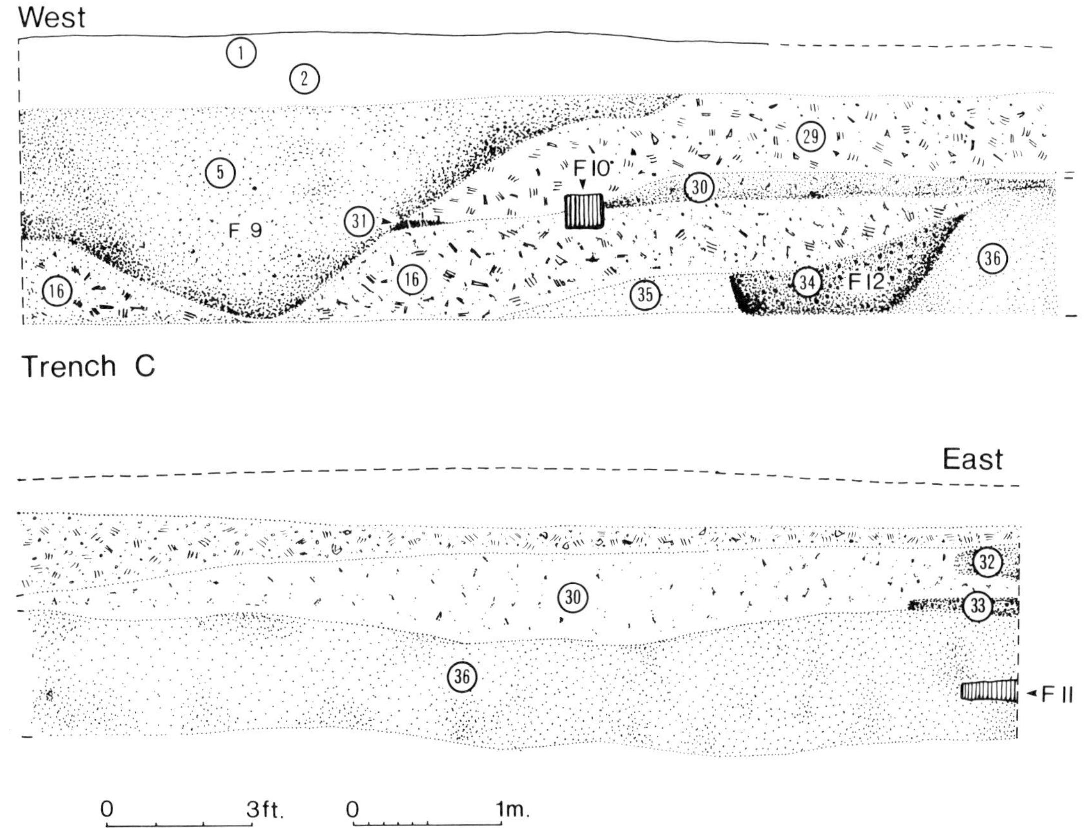

Fig. 3c. Section of Trench C, North Side (1960).

Key to layers shown in Figs. 3a, b and c: after S. E. Rigold. **1**. Topsoil. (A, B, C). **2**. Backfill from earlier excavations. (A, B, C).**3**. Rubble. (A). **4**. Decayed mortar. (A). **5**. Mortar. (A, B, C). **6**. Building debris, some tile. (A). **7**. Gravel and building debris. (A, B). **8**. Clay. (A). **9**. Charcoal. (A). **10**. Dark soil. (A). **11**. Mortar and gravel. (A). **12**. Loose gravel, tiles and building debris. (A). **13**. Mortar. (A). **14**. Clean clay. (A). **15**. Rubble (A). **16**. Disturbed clay with tiles (A, C). **17**. Dark clay. (A). **18**. Lime mortar. (B). **19**. Clay. (B). **20**. Decayed lime. (B). **21**. Red clay and gravel. (B). **22**. Clay fill of pit F6. (B). **23**. Red clay. **24**. Dark clay. (A). **25**. Disturbed dark soil and tiles. (B). **26** Fill of pit F7. (B). **27**. Dark soil. (B). **28**. Red clay. (B). **29**. Clay with gravel and building debris. (C). **30**. Unspecified. (C). **31**. Clay. (C). **32**. Yellow clay. (C). **33** Gravel. (C). **34** ?Grave fill in F12. (C). **35**. Unspecified (?as 36). (C). **36**. ?Dark soil with mortar (C).

edge of F1, however, is not clear, and the alternatives recorded by the excavator are therefore reproduced in Fig. 3a. To the east of this, the first layers encountered were two mortar deposits (4 and 5), the upper of which (seen at the approximate centre of the trench) was described as a 'decayed floor'. The lower deposit, which was only partly sealed by the 'floor', was not described. Sealed by the mortar layers were two slight depressions (F2, F3) and a large post-medieval pit (F4), the eastern edge of which was just clipped by F2. F4 contained building debris (6), fragments of vessel glass, tile (probably roof-tile) and sixteenth/seventeenth-century pottery, much of which joins with sherds in the adjacent demolition deposits (Fig. 78, nos. 9, 12; Fig. 79, nos. 13–15, 17–18, 20, 22, 25), notably a Raeren anthropomorphic jug (Fig. 81, no. 38). It is also possible that a number of small finds (Fig. 53, no. 2; Figs. 54–5, nos. 7, 9, 10, 13–15, 21, 22, 23) derive from F4.

F2, F3, and F4 were cut into an uneven demolition deposit (7) of gravel and building debris with a maximum depth of *c.* 0.45 m. This overlay a number of lenses of clay (8), charcoal (9), dark soil (10), mortary gravel (11), mortar (13), and tile fragments which interleaved with a second thicker deposit of gravel and building debris (12). Layers 7 and 12 in trenches A and B together contained a quantity of pottery and fifteenth/sixteenth-century coins (nos. 4, 5) and jettons (nos. 3–7). Towards the south end of the trench the gravel was looser and contained a quantity of roof-tiles. Below this were a thin layer of rubble (15) and patches of clean clay (14), colour unknown, possibly as (17) or (19) in Trench B. Layers 12, 14 and 15 directly overlay a thick but uneven layer of disturbed clay (16) containing a few sherds of thirteenth/fifteenth-century pottery (Fig. 78, nos. 1–4). Layer 15 overlay both (16) and a deposit of dark clay (17).

At the west end of the trench the footings of the chapel of St. John the Evangelist were exposed to a depth of 1.21 m. (Plate XIV), but no evidence of a construction trench for the chapel was found. The footings consisted of nine courses of roughly hewn blocks of varying thickness. Above them and set back was a levelling course of flints and smaller stones to support the first dressed and chamfered stones of the ashlar wall face. Above this the wall survives to three or four courses of ashlar.

Trench B (Fig. 3b).

This trench was placed just to the east of the fourth buttress of the crypt and approximately 2.28 m. to the west of the northern apsidal chapels dedicated to St. Richard of Chichester (below) and the Holy Innocents (above). Trench B was 0.76 m. wide and extended north from the north wall of the crypt for a distance of 4.57 m., reaching a maximum depth of 2.43 m. below the 1960 ground level. To the north of this (but not recorded in section by Rigold) the trench continued for a further 5.64 m. and to a depth of 0.91 m. into the bank, from which medieval (Fig. 78, no. 8) and post-medieval pottery and a Roman coin (no. 1) were recovered; a late Saxon penny (no. 1) was also found in the spoil of the earlier excavations. The build-up of the later deposits in Trench B shows a general similarity to that seen in Trench A. Removal of the topsoil (1) revealed a mortar deposit (5) and mortar and rubble debris (7) containing fragments of roof-tile and sixteenth/seventeenth-century pottery. At the south end of the trench layer 7 sealed an area of decayed lime mortar (20). These layers were cut by the earlier excavation trench (F5), which contained lime mortar (18). Sealed by (7), and also by a few isolated wedges of clay (19), colour unknown, possibly as (8) or (14)), was a disturbed fourteenth/fifteenth-century deposit of disturbed clay with (probably roof-) tiles (25) similar to that seen in Trench A (16). At the south end of the trench layer 25 was cut by tips of red clay and gravel (21) and lime mortar (20). At the north end of the trench (25) was cut by a late medieval pit (F6) filled with clay (22) which contained fifteenth-century pottery, two fifteenth-century coins (nos. 3, 4) and a few scraps of bronze. F6, which was partly sealed by a wedge of clay (21), was cut into a large, possibly Roman pit (F7) which in turn cut into an uneven layer of dark soil (27). The fill of F7

(26) is not recorded, although shells are noted on the section drawing at the interfaces of (22/26) and (26/27). Pit F7 contained four sherds of Belgic cooking-pot and 26 sherds of Roman pottery, including four of samian. Layer 27 produced 38 sherds of Belgic and 85 sherds of Roman pottery, including twelve of samian, but also eleven sherds of medieval and two sherds of fifteenth-century pottery, which leave the date of the deposit open to doubt. Two large fragments of oak charcoal (*Quercus* sp.) were also recovered from (27). Sealed by the dark soil was an irregular layer of red clay (28), possibly natural or redeposited natural. At the south end of the trench both the red clay and the dark soil were cut by the foundation trench for the footings of the crypt (F8), which was filled with lenses of dark clay and red clay (23 and 24). Layer 24 contained one sherd of early medieval shell-tempered ware and two sherds of Roman pottery. The level from which this trench was cut appears to have been destroyed by a late-medieval/early post-medieval feature (25).

The footings of the crypt (Plate XV), like those of the chapel in the north transept, were constructed of irregular, roughly-cut blocks of undressed stone. In all, seven courses of approximately the same thickness were revealed below the modern ground surface. Above these was a single string course of thinner blocks, and then a thicker course; no chamfered offset was apparent at this point. Only two more uneven courses survived above this, although the flint rubble core remains to a height of *c.* 0.60 m. above the present ground level. The excavated portion of the construction trench for the footings produced three sherds of Roman pottery and one sherd of early medieval shell-tempered ware.

Near the north end of the trench the removal of the bank revealed the south-east buttress of the slype, of which three courses of dressed stone were exposed to a depth of 0.91 m. (illus. N.M.R. neg. A5475/4A).

Trench C (Fig. 3c)

This trench was placed *c.* 1.22 m. to the east of Trench B, and apparently ran east–west on the same alignment as Trench A for a distance of 13.10 m. The earliest feature consisted of a few horizontal stone slabs (F11), possibly the cover of a grave. These were found in the medieval graveyard ((36), possibly also (35)), at a depth of *c.* 1.52 m. from the 1960 ground surface. At the east end of the trench (36) was sealed by a layer of gravel (33). Toward the centre of the trench the words 'grave soil' (F12, layer 34) are apparently written in pencil on the original section drawing, with an area of shading. This could be a hurried note for 'gravel and soil', but may refer to grave F13 (see below). The 'grave' was cut away from the west and was sealed by a layer of clay with (probably roof-) tile fragments (16). Resting on (16) was the flint core of a flimsy north–south wall (F10). Only two sherds of Roman and one sherd of possible early medieval pottery were found beneath this wall, and its date is thus uncertain. To the east of F10 was a thin deposit of clay (31), possibly the same as (8) or (14) in Trench A. To the west of F10 there extended a deposit (30, nature unknown), which at the east end of the trench contained a wedge of yellow clay (32). Layers 16 and 30 were sealed by a thick layer of clay and gravel (29) with building debris, probably the same as (7), which extended obliquely across the site. Cutting (29), (31), and (16) was a large ditch-like feature (F9) approximately 1.21 m. deep, filled with mortar (5). On the north side of the trench this mortar was seen to the west in Trench A, but rapidly disappeared to the east; on the south side it continued obliquely at a high level for a further 5.48 m. or so, apparently levelling up the site.

The Cemetery Area (Fig. 4)

Following the excavation of Trench C, stripping of the topsoil to the north and east of the crypt (Plate XVI) further exposed the flimsy wall (F10), which ran in an arc towards (but stopping short of) an apparent grave (F13). Only the rubble core of the wall survived, the dressed facing apparently having been robbed out, and the structure was only exposed to a maximum depth of *c.* 0.30 m. It is thus impossible to know the exact date, length or function of the feature, or its relationship to F13. The grave, which measured approximately 1.52 m. by 0.76 m. was apparently cut from a mortary level *c.* 0.90–1.20 m. below the modern topsoil; it was not sealed by a grave slab. There is no sign in the photographs of this area that the grave was disturbed by the construction of the wall, nor does the wall appear in the section to the north of the grave. It would appear, therefore, that the grave post-dates the wall, but both may be of post-medieval date.

Trench D (Fig. 4)

This trench was placed between the second and third buttresses of the late medieval lady chapel. The trench, which was 0.91 m. wide, seems to have reached a depth of approximately 1.80 m. for most of its length. In the absence of any section drawing or site notes the following is based on an architect's plan and some photographs showing the bottom and west face of the trench.

The earliest feature appears to be a possible wall (F14), represented by a rough alignment of dressed clunch blocks, running on an east–west alignment approximately 7.60 m. to the north of the lady chapel. No construction trench for this feature is visible on the photograph. The wall would appear to have been demolished in antiquity, since the dressed stones are displaced and do not clearly represent either the inner or the outer face of the structure. To the south of the wall, cutting into the dark soil at the base of the trench (39), and possibly contemporary with the wall, was a three-sided arrangement of stone blocks (F15), which may represent the head of a coffin. To either side of the wall was a low bank of rubble (40) possibly derived from the levelled core of F14, which was sealed by a dark layer *c.* 0.30–0.60 m. thick (41). This in turn was sealed by a thin, even, layer of mortar (42) which extended from 1.52 m. to the north of the lady chapel to the end of the trench, but was interrupted in the area just to the north of the wall by the cut for a grave (F16). The burial consisted of an individual placed with the head to the west in a stone coffin made of four rectangular slabs on either side, one slab across the east end, two half slabs at the west end on either side of the head, and three small slabs around the head (Plates XVII, a and b). There is no record as to whether the grave was also covered by horizontal slabs. The original trench revealed only the head and upper half of the coffin, but was extended eastwards to allow the full excavation of the feature. Unfortunately, only the skull, arms and trunk as far as the pelvis were located for study (see Table 15 ; a full report on the remains is available in AML 4939). The remaining fill of the grave (43) consisted of numerous compacted

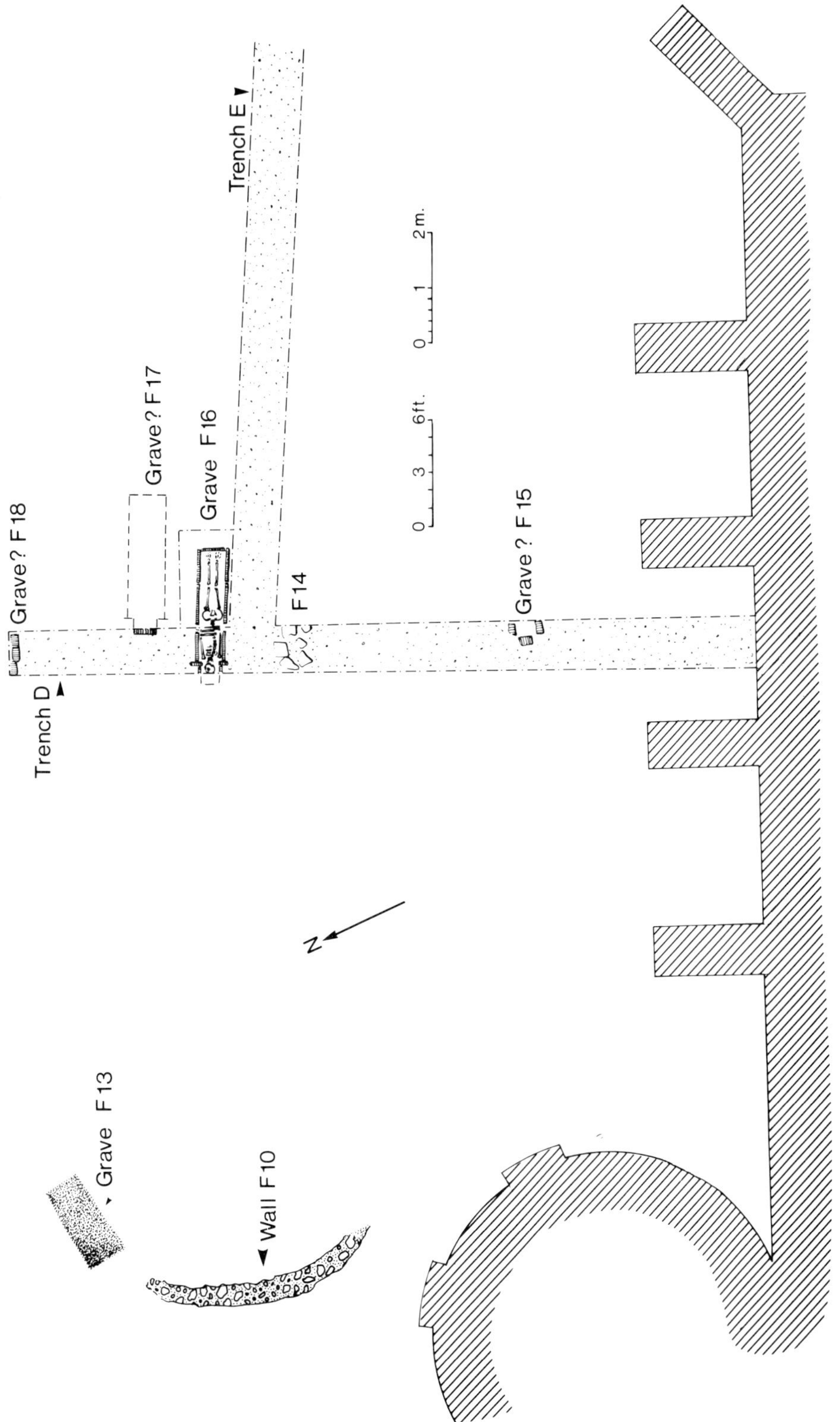

Fig. 4. Plan of the Area to the North of the Lady Chapel, showing the location of features in trenches D and E (1960).

lenses of clay and earth flecked with mortar, but was truncated at approximately 0.30 m. above the top of the vertical stone slabs (F18). Virtually no dating evidence was found in the grave, but one sherd of late medieval fine ware would, if from this feature and not from F12, suggest a date in the early/mid fifteenth century. To the north of the excavated grave the head of another coffin (F17) was visible in the eastern section of the trench; vertical slabs (F18) at the north end of the trench may represent the side of a third burial in this trench. The level from which these other graves were cut is not known (and possibly did not survive), but the similarity in style suggests that they may all be roughly contemporary. The layers above the mortar deposit are not clear but would appear to comprise three main elements: a dark soil (44), superimposed at the south end of the trench by a 'bank' of slightly lighter soil (45), and at the middle and north end of the trench by a wedge-shaped deposit of light soil containing building debris (46), which increased in depth toward the north end of the trench. The footings of the lady chapel were apparently not investigated.

Trench E

The location of this trench is uncertain. It was apparently placed at right angles to Trench D, but its relationship with the extension for the grave (F16) is not clear. The architect's plan, which was drawn before the full excavation of the grave, shows Trench E just to the south of the grave (Fig. 4). The trench does not, however, figure in the photograph of the fully excavated grave (Plate XVIIb), or in any other photographs of Trench D. It is possible that either the line of Trench E was adjusted to continue that of the grave extension, and that the section and some photographs ascribed to Trench C in fact relate to Trench E, or that the trench was intended, but was never excavated.

DISCUSSION

Trenches A, B and C

The crypt and north transept were constructed as part of the new Norman church begun by Abbot Scotland. Since building began in *c.* 1070 at the east end of the church and proceeded westwards, the date of the crypt and transepts should be placed at *c.* 1070–80, and the method of construction may be expected to be the same as that employed for the nave, the foundations of which were also probably laid by Scotland (see p. 5). In Trench B, Rigold thought that the red clay (layer 28) found at the base of the trench represented the site natural, and that the dark soil (27) and the pit (F6) were of Roman date, since these produced predominantly Belgic and Roman pottery. Natural red clay was found to lie at 2.94 m. below the 1974 ground surface on the south side of the lady chapel, and the natural ground surface is known to slope down from north to south. If the presence of medieval pottery in (27) and the absence of Roman deposits in Trenches A and C are ascribed to the subsequent disturbance of the Roman and medieval layers in these trenches, then it is possible that (26) and (27) were indeed of Roman date. The trench for the footings of the quire (F8, layers 23, 24) contained only three sherds of Roman and early medieval pottery, but given the extremely solid rammed foundations which are known to underlie the nave at the west end of St. Augustine's and the crypt of the cathedral (1096–1110) it seems unlikely that the construction trench for the quire was fully excavated. Recent excavations in St. Gabriel's Chapel in Anselm's extension to the cathedral (Driver *et al.*, forthcoming) showed that the walls of the cathedral were built up as an inner skin of dressed stone with poured and rammed gravel and mortar filling the void between this facing and the natural into which the crypt was inserted. The walls rested on rammed gravel and mortar foundations, and were capped by external footings constructed over the rammed mortar and bonded to the inner face with a rubble core. The crypt wall at St. Augustine's, which on the inner face continues to a depth of some 4.57 m. below the present ground surface, should likewise rest on solid foundations below the floor of the crypt in order to support the vaults of both the crypt and quire. Rammed mortar or a similar aggregate should also be present behind the inner face of the wall and below the outer footings. No evidence for any such mortar deposit is present either in the section drawing or in the photographs of Trench B, while the construction trench and early medieval levels had apparently been truncated in the late medieval or early post-medieval period. The trench for the construction of the north transept was apparently not reached. A full understanding of the construction techniques must therefore await the results of further excavation.

Layers 35 and 36 in Trench C probably represent the medieval graveyard soil, and although only one possible grave (F13) was noted, the lack of layers recorded in this area suggests that either the soil had been thoroughly disturbed, or that the section was hastily recorded. In either case features other than F11 and F12 probably went unnoticed in this layer. The deposits of disturbed clay (16), (22), (25) contained no imported stoneware, which was common in the subsequent levels, but local wares include a few sherds of fifteenth-century date. It is possible that these deposits relate to the remodelling of the chapter house in 1324–32 (Davis 1934, 437, 439), but more likely that they are associated with the construction of the lady chapel or sixteenth-century disturbance prior to the actual demolition of the abbey. The earlier medieval levels had clearly been removed before or during this activity. If layers 16 and 22 are the same then pit F6 is in fact quite a large feature which appears to have disturbed the grave F12. This in itself suggests a late date for the deposit. The curving wall in Trench C (F10) is enigmatic. It was sealed by demolition debris and is therefore possibly of late fifteenth/sixteenth-century date; it may have been associated with a feature or features removed by F9, perhaps a flimsy structure similar to that found in 1976–78 (p. 87), thrown up for use during the demolition of the abbey, or an ornamental feature associated with the garden of the king's palace (see Plate V).

The deposits (7) and (12) above (16), (22), (25), and (36) contained a range of late-medieval and post-medieval pottery, with many joining sherds in different groups, window and vessel glass, and an assortment of medieval and later small finds, the latest of which was a small silver propelling pencil (probably nineteenth-century); these layers are all associated with the demolition of the abbey and subsequent landscaping. F2 and F3 may represent the vestiges of scaffold bases; the large feature F9, however, appears to have been dug purely for the disposal of mortar and rubble. The various mortar and rubble deposits, which continue as a thinner spread to the west in Trench A and to the south in Trenches B and C, would seem to be essentially the same as those seen to the south of the church in the excavations of 1972–78.

Trenches D and E

As above, the interpretation of this area is hindered by the incomplete nature of the evidence. It would appear that there was a burial ground of unknown dimensions, to which the infirmary or infirmary passage would have given access. The level from which the graves were cut having been removed, the date of the excavated burial relies on the date of the first mortar deposit in Trench D. If this is associated with the construction of the lady chapel then the stone coffin should date to the mid-fifteenth century or later. The one sherd of late-medieval pottery, if from this grave, and not from F12, would agree with this. The style of the coffin (F16) is similar to a late-medieval coffin discovered in earlier excavations in the south walk of the cloister (D.o.E. photograph A5481/14).

AN EXCAVATION BY S.E. RIGOLD OF A SHAFT IN THE NAVE, 1965

D. SHERLOCK

Early in 1965 a shaft was discovered in the transept of the church beside the north-east corner of the second Norman pier on the north side. It had been sunk into one corner of a former pier of Abbot Wulfric's octagon (Fig. 2). Its excavation was recorded in photographs by S.E. Rigold who also collected the finds, while a plan and section were drawn by the then Ministry's draughtsman, M.F. Kilburn (Fig. 5). In March 1965, the rim of the shaft was consolidated and fitted with a metal grill. There is no record of how the shaft came to be discovered.

The section shows that the shaft was just over 3 m. deep, its bottom some 1.20 m. below the grassed level within the former octagon. It had been back-filled with six layers of mortar, flint and chalk in varying combinations. The seventh layer contained earth and rubbish which had presumably accumulated while the shaft was open. Besides a quantity of pottery (Fig. 82), the shaft contained at the bottom an unusual collection of eight lead weights and numerous fragments of lead and copper alloy (see below, p. 184). On the ceramic evidence the shaft would appear to have been backfilled in the early to mid-fourteenth century.

The purpose of the shaft is conjectural but the presence of the weights suggested to Rigold in 1965 that it was to accommodate the weights of a mechanical clock. There was a clock in the care of the sub-sacrist in the fourteenth century (Thompson 1904, 374), and it is quite possible there was one hereabouts, judging from other monasteries. Dunstable, for example, had a clock *supra pulpitum* in 1283; Ely had one near the crossing by 1291; and Canterbury Cathedral had a new clock (distinct from the water clock) in 1292. Wells Cathedral had a fourteenth-century clock in its north transept (Beeson 1977, 6 and 9). Against the possibility of a clock it must be said that no comparable shafts are known and that surviving early clock weights are much heavier. For example the two in the Cotehele (Cornwall) clock of 1490 weigh 90 lbs. each. The St. Augustine's weights look like those that are made to slide along the top of a steelyard, but they are unmarked and appear to be in random units of weight.

Alternatively, the shaft and weights may have been a counter-poise system for the raising of sacred images on the pulpitum or the elevation of the lid of the pyx during the veneration of the Host. The copper alloy fragments found with the weights may have been part of such a

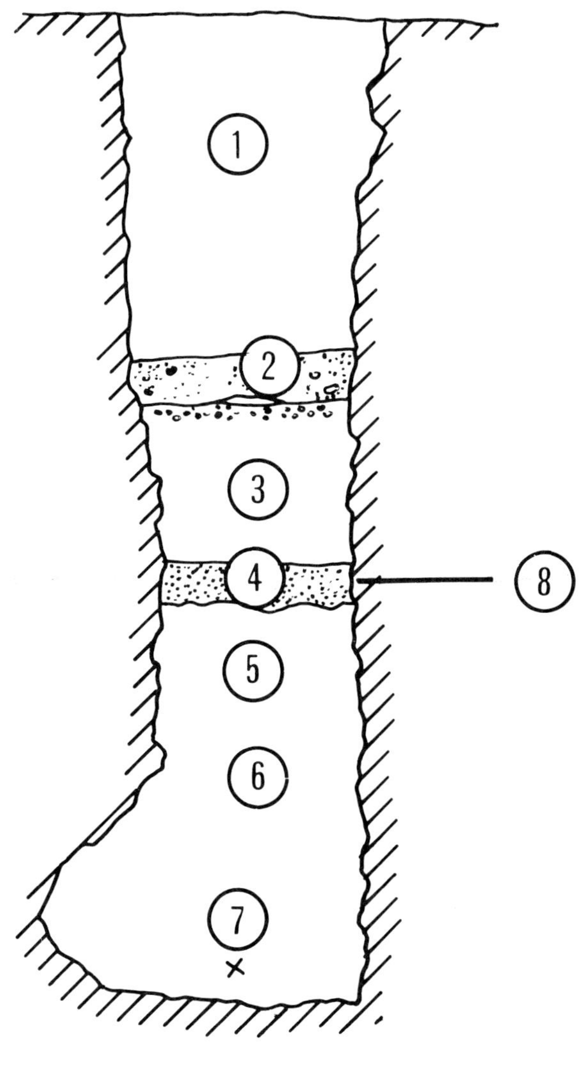

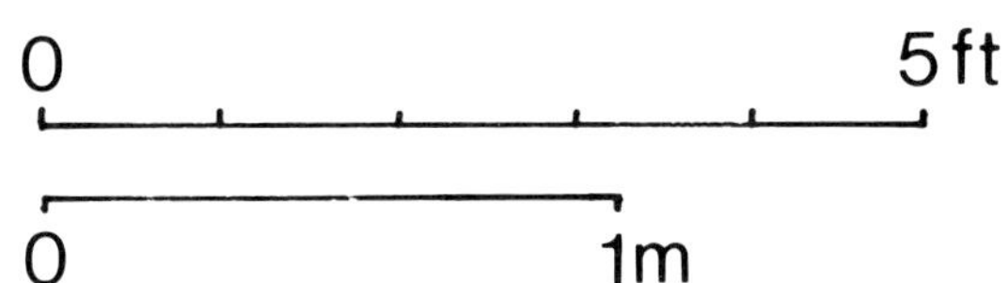

Fig. 5. West–east Section through the Shaft (1965).
Key to Layers: **1**. Mortar layer or floor on flint infill interspersed with larger stones. **2**. Mortar. **3**. Flint with chalk infill. **4**. Chalk. **5**. Small flints in chalk. **6**. Larger flints in chalk. **7**. Earth, shells, flint, chalk and bones. **8**. Grass level in octagon.

mechanism. Some idea of the appearance of a pulpitum in the late fourteenth century may be gained from Thomas Elmham's drawing (Plate I), although we must remember that the shaft may have been filled in by his day. The above suggestions for clock or counter-poise both assume that the shaft and weights are related. The third possibility is that the shaft was simply a well, such as existed beneath the present choir of York Minster (Phillips 1985, 50).

Besides pottery and metalwork the bottom of the shaft also yielded human, animal and fish bones (for the latter see below, p. 309), fragments of glass and coloured marble *tesserae* (see below 135).

III. EXCAVATIONS BY DAVID SHERLOCK, 1972–1975

TRIAL TRENCH III, 1972

LYN BLACKMORE

SUMMARY

Excavation produced three masonry structures. At the south end the hearth of a post-medieval building had been constructed against the Longport Wall. At the north end there was a rough medieval structure perhaps part of a tomb. In the centre of the trench were two clasping buttresses of a large medieval building. The only other features of note were a possible bank and a medieval road surface which overlay an earlier roadway, possibly Roman.

Trench III, to the west of the main excavations is here published before Trench II which became part of the Area 2 excavations of 1975 (see below p. 53). Trench I was excavated by Dr Frank Jenkins (see above p. 16).

EXCAVATION (Figs. 6, 7, 8)

Outline sections of Trenches III and II are shown in Fig. 8, together with a profile (A–A) across the site on the line of the Department of the Environment's new boundary. It can be seen from these that the construction of the hospital basement would appear to have disturbed very little of the Norman and earlier levels. Trial Trench III was machine-dug to the depth of layer 12 (Fig. 7), the major rubble layer about 1 m. below ground level. Thereafter it was hand-dug. The trench was not fully excavated to natural. (Numbers in brackets hereafter refer to the layers and features in Fig. 7). The trench lay partly in an area formerly occupied by a building (2, 3, 4) which was part of the hospital complex (Fig. 6; Plates XVIII and XIX). Between this building and the Longport wall lay a refuse tip (1) belonging to the hospital period. The site was also cut by service trenches for the pipes (7) and a large brick-lined sewer (11). The last turf surface (8) was, therefore, quite deeply buried. This overlay another ground surface (9), from which some robbing of earlier features had taken place (17). The whole trench was covered by the rubble and mortar layer 12 which would appear to equate with layer 35 in the 1974–75 excavations and which may derive from the final destruction of the flint building (19), or the seventeenth-century landscaping. Layer 12 contained a quantity of Roman, medieval and post-medieval pottery (see pottery report, Tables 8–9, and Fig. 83) and other finds of these periods (see below p. 275 and finds reports p. 187).

The large medieval flint building (19) only appeared in the trench as the corners of two

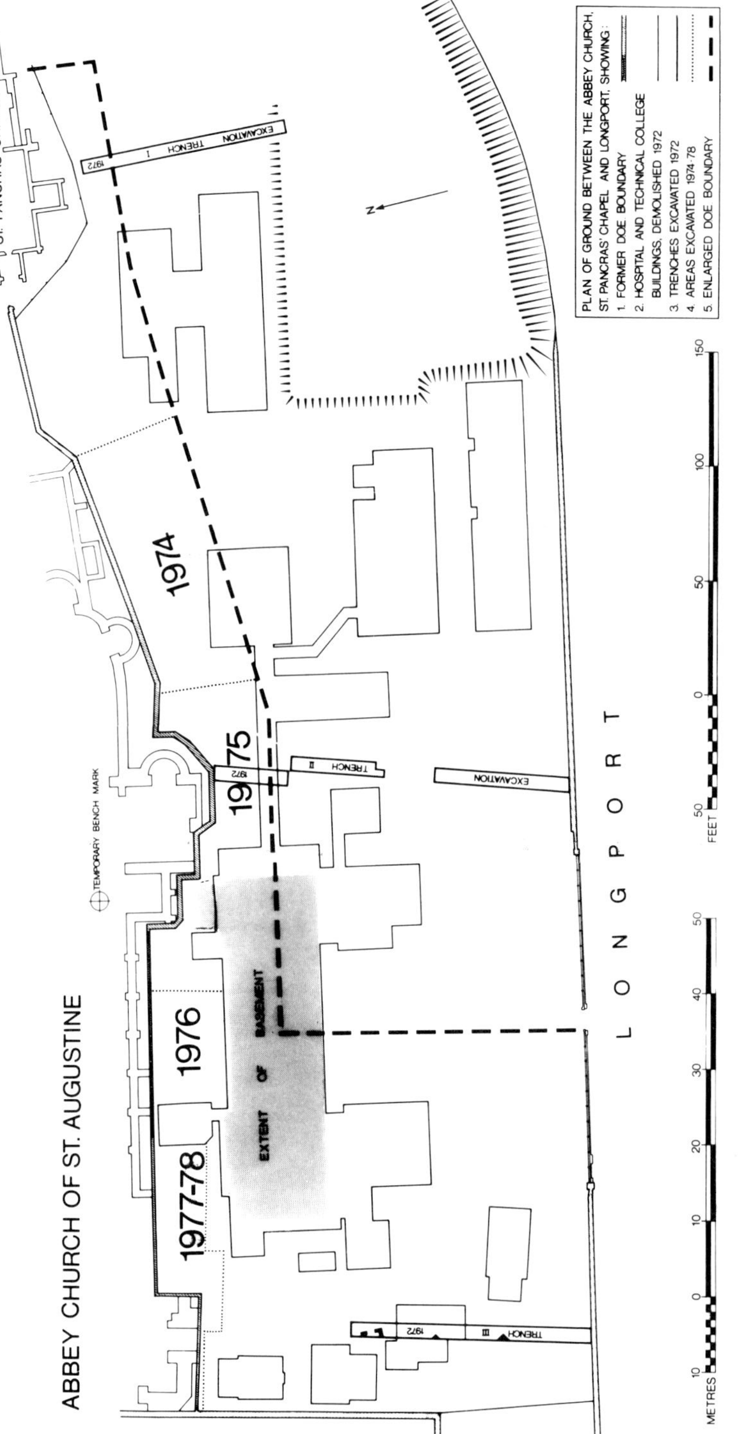

Fig. 6. Plan of Ground between the Abbey Church, Longport and St. Pancras' showing modern Buildings and Boundaries and Extent of Excavations 1972–78.

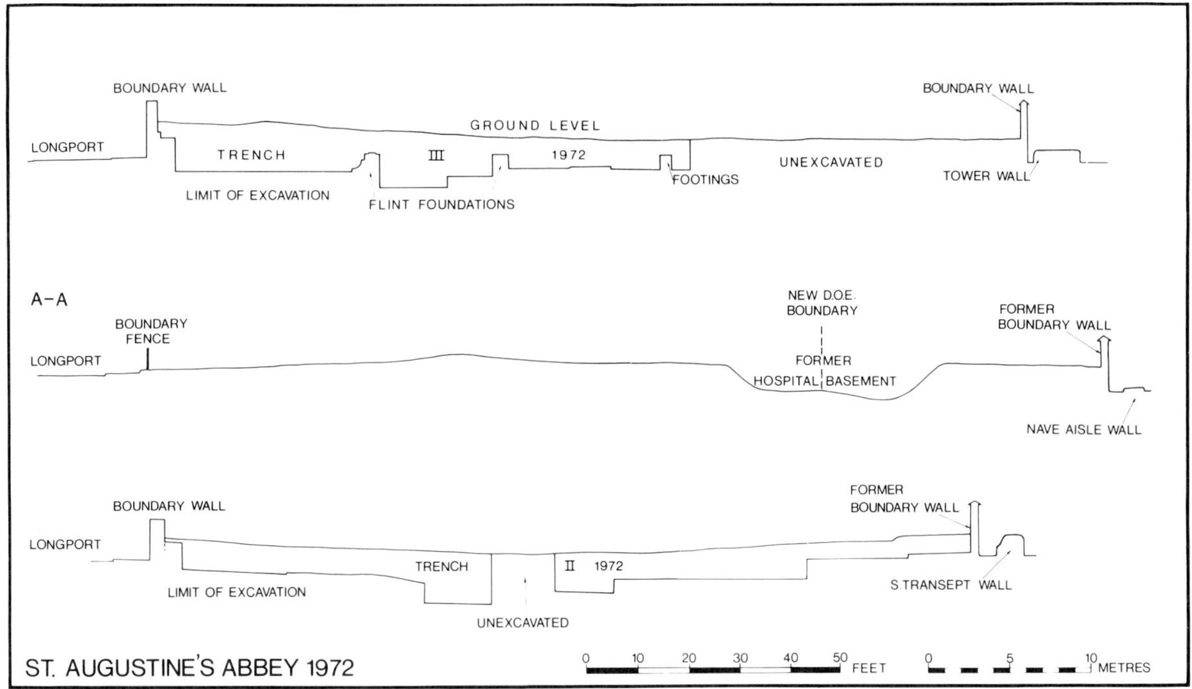

Fig. 8. Profiles North-South across former Hospital Grounds, taken 1972.

diagonal clasping buttresses each over 2 m. high (Plates XX, a and b). These buttresses were well and strongly built with roughly-coarsed flints bedded in a hard yellow mortar, the top of which showed the imprint of the first course of the ashlar superstructure.

The northern buttress had a single off-set course and a foundation trench (24). On the north side of this trench a deposit of dark shelly soil sealing the road surface was cut from layer 30. On the south side the stratigraphy was disturbed by the post-medieval drain (11 and 28) which had stained the soil. The shadow of the first ashlar course was visible on top of the surviving stump of this buttress. The southern, more substantial buttress apparently had a series of offsets, although the method of construction is not clear in view of the ambiguous nature of layers 27, 26, 23 and 22 to the south of this buttress, and layer 40, which lay between the two buttresses. If layers 27 and 40 may be taken as the contemporary ground surface, then the southern buttress, unlike its northern counterpart, occupied the full width of the construction trench at this height. Equally layer 27 may represent the spoil displaced from the construction trench, and 40 the subsequent levelling between the two buttresses. Layers 26, 23 and 22 may either be associated with the construction of 19 or with later demolition activity. In view of the similarity of layers 26 and 42, it is possible that layer 26 represents the soil displaced from the lower levels of the construction trenches for 19 but layers 23 and 22 may equally represent the backfilling of a construction trench or a robber trench, and layer 21 the masons' trample, or, as found in the

1976–77 excavations, the washing of mortar from the ashlar blocks dismantled at the time of the Dissolution (p. 67). In either case it would appear from the pottery (Fig. 83, nos. 8 and 9) and other finds in layers 27, 40 and 30 that structure 19 is earlier than the late medieval period. The structure was apparently demolished and the buttresses partially robbed in the late sixteenth or early seventeenth century, and the area levelled with a substantial deposit of dark soil (18), which extended for almost the entire length of Trench III sealing the southern buttress, and probably the northern one, although this area was found disturbed. Layer 18, which produced a quantity of late and post-medieval pottery (Fig. 83, nos. 14–17) including two sherds of stoneware (nos. 15 and 16), would appear to equate with layer 4 in the 1974–75 excavations, and may represent landscaping in the seventeenth century. The full depth of the buttresses was not established although the high proportion of redeposited Roman sherds in layers 26 and 24 suggests that their foundations must penetrate deeply into the underlying Roman deposits. Layer 24, the construction trench for the northern buttress, produced only Belgic and Roman material, including a samian stamp of A.D. 155–190.

Layers 33, 42, 43 and 44 produced a quantity of Saxo-Norman pottery (see pottery report and Fig. 83, nos. 1–7) showing that these deposits were all of early post-Conquest date. The way that these layers fell is suggestive of a bank or *vallum* running parallel to the Longport road (31) with the southern buttress being dug deeply into it to provide a proper footing. Given the narrowness of the trench, however, this could equally reflect an oblique view of an overlarge foundation trench for structure 19. The ambiguous layer 27 has already been discussed. Layer 46 produced no finds but would appear to be contemporary with layer 27.

To the north of structure 19, and sealed by layer 30, was a cobbled road surface (31) with two ruts in it (45; see Plate XXII). No finds were recovered from (31) or the major underlying road surface (39) so that it is impossible to date or estimate the duration of these features. It is suggested, however, that if not in themselves Roman, they follow the line of the Roman road leading east from Burgate, although positive evidence for this cannot be given from Trench III as time did not allow for a section to be cut through the road surface. As (31) was sealed by layer 30, however, this last road surface would appear on both ceramic and stratigraphic evidence, to have gone out of use in the thirteenth century, before, or at the time of the construction of the massive flint footings (19). Unfortunately, the northern edge of layer 30 and thus the relationship between this layer and masonry footings at the north end of the trench (20) had been disturbed and destroyed, probably in the eighteenth century, by a pit (17) which had also removed part of their southern wall.

All that survived of structure 20 were two masonry corners of poor build but containing some good quality re-used masonry (Plate XXI). This, together with the ceramic evidence from layer 34, would suggest a fourteenth- or even fifteenth-century date for this structure. (It may also be contemporary with the tombs excavated to the north in 1976–77). Layer 34 also produced a quantity of Roman pottery, possibly derived from graves 47 and 48. The walling of (20), which had much mortar and rubble infill, was laid on a bed of broken roof tiles (35). These may indicate the original floor level, whilst the mortar layer (33), over the dark soil layer (34), perhaps indicates a later floor level. No trace of plaster could be seen on the surviving walling. Beneath the building was a layer of puddled chalk (37) of a similar shape to the area occupied by the walls but not contingent to them. This puddled chalk surface was not related to (20), which had its footings some 20 cm. higher. However, it may represent an earlier building on the site although no structural evidence was found. This chalk layer lay over a thin band of soil on the road surface (39). A gilt bronze pin came from layer 38 (Fig. 60, 26).

At the southern end of the trench a hearth (13) had been built against the Longport wall (Plate XXIII). This wall had a rammed chalk footing and then a chalk block footing below the offset to the rough ashlar surface of the present wall. On the offset was a hearth of edge-laid tile with a chamfered stone surround. This hearth overlay an earlier surface of edge-laid tile which was associated with the sandy mortar surface (10). In the narrow trench excavated no sign could be found of the structure to which this hearth belonged. The surface seals layer 12; therefore, the building is post-medieval.

DISCUSSION AND INTERPRETATION D. Sherlock

The flint foundations or buttresses (19) encountered in the west face of Trench III near the southern end must have belonged to a substantial building. Pending the full excavation of this building, which is unlikely to happen for some years, it is justifiable to speculate on what it may have been.

From stratigraphy it has been shown to be medieval rather than Roman; and it is unlikely to have survived the Dissolution. There are only two substantial buildings known to have lain to the south of the abbey church, namely a bell tower and a charnel chapel. Evidence for the bell tower is discussed above, p. 7. Sturcture 19 may perhaps be identified with the latter. The charnel chapel was previously thought to be the small appendage mid-way along the south side

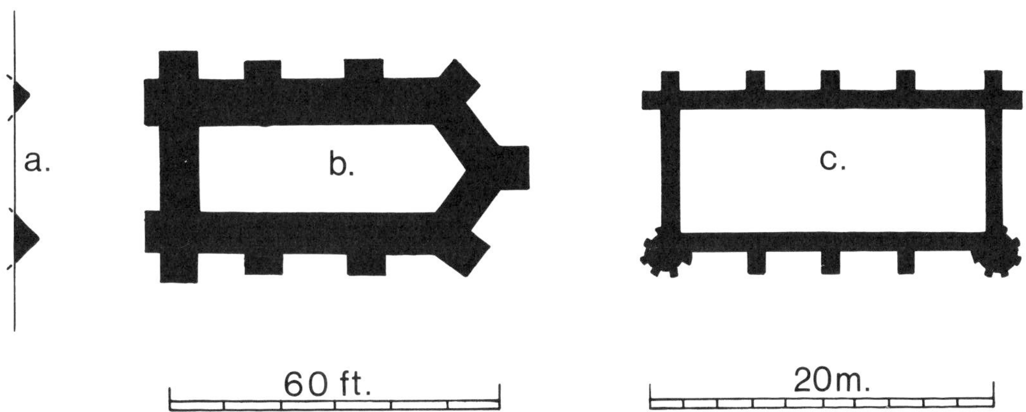

Fig. 9, *a*. Foundations revealed in Trench III. *b*. Charnel Chapel, Bury St. Edmund's Abbey. *c*. Chapel of the Carnary, Norwich Cathedral (after plans in Whittingham 1951 and 1949).

of the nave of the church (Clapham 1955, 23, and plan) but the excavations there in 1976–77 now make this most unlikely. It is, however, possible that the two flint buttresses in Trench III are part of the east end of the charnel chapel. A number of factors point to this interpretation: first, the location of the charnel chapel whose collapse necessitated the repair of the king's garden wall in 1542 (see above, p. 11) cannot be that to the chapel in the south wall of the nave. Secondly, the foundations lie about 65 m. south of the centre of the west end of the abbey church in almost exactly the same location as the charnel chapel of Bury St. Edmund's Abbey. Thirdly, the two buttresses are not quite identical, one being larger and slightly forward of the other (Fig. 9a). The St. Edmund's charnel chapel had a pointed and buttressed east end (Fig. 9b) which would allow a similar plan to be reconstructed from the surviving remains at St. Augustine's. Last, the Bury St. Edmund's and St. Augustine's charnel chapels were not only similar in plan and location (in both abbeys the cloister was on the less-usual north side), but they were also similar in date. That at Bury St. Edmund's was built by Abbot John of Northwold (1279–1301) and described as 'recently built' in 1300 (Whittingham 1951, 182–3) while that at St. Augustine's was finished in 1287–88 and consecrated in 1299. Both these great Benedictine abbeys presumably required charnel chapels when their lay cemeteries became overcrowded after three or more centuries of burials. Both were conveniently situated near a gateway into the town, that at St. Augustine's being still known as Cemetery Gate. This was again the case at Norwich and Ely Cathedrals where remains of charnels also survive. The Norwich charnel (Fig. 9c), which was founded by Bishop Salmon in 1316 (Whittingham 1980, 361) and subsequently conveyed to the city for the use of the city's dead, and the St. Edmund's charnel both had thick buttressed walls to support a vaulted first-floor chapel where masses were offered for the souls of those whose remains lay below. If, as seems probable, the great flint buttresses were part of the abbey charnel chapel built in 1287–88, only further excavation can prove it. The pottery from associated layers agrees with a later thirteenth-century construction date but there are no small finds to support the interpretation with the exception of some fragments of stone with mouldings which might be contemporary with its construction and which came from general demolition layers (See p. 90).

The bank into which the southern buttress of the chapel cut might be a section of the *fossatum* in Longport called *Bordiche*. The road surface would appear to be lying too far north to be a section of the *via media* but the surface beneath it is roughly on the alignment of the Roman road from Burgate (Jenkins 1950, 90).

The foundations near the northern end of the trench are probably the footings of a large tomb or monument in the cemetery. The hearth remains at the southern end may belong to one of the houses shown on the map of *c.* 1620 (Plate V). They are too late to have been part of the sacrist's house which, it has been suggested, occupied this area (Tatton-Brown 1984, 182, fig. 5).

The finds from Trench III are discussed in the various finds reports below. They comprise fragments of architectural stone (see catalogue), floor-tiles and window glass, three medieval coins (one from layer 8), three Roman coins in good condition from layers 18 and 27 and the samian stamps from layers 12 and 24. The following are numbered and described in the Small Finds report: 25 stud, 32 scales pan, 33 letter E, 34 pin, 60 shears blade, 68 spindle whorl, 70 bead, 74 sculpture fragment, 77 hone and 80 a cresset. From layers 8 and 34 came fragments of waste *speculum* metal (i.e. with a high tin content) from casting (p. 196, no. 58).

TRIAL TRENCH II, 1972

SUMMARY

No structural remains were found, except for a chalk wall abutting the modern wall on Longport. Burials throughout were mainly disturbed. Some fallen masonry from the abbey church was found near the north end. Natural ground was located at a depth of about 2.80 m. near the centre of the trench. Because of the similarity with Trench III and the absence of structures, no detailed plan or section are published here.

EXCAVATION (Figs. 6, 8, 10)

Trench II ran from the south-east corner of the south transept of the abbey church in a southerly direction to the modern boundary wall on Longport (Fig. 6). To avoid the concrete foundations of the old hospital it was necessary to shift the trench eastwards after the first 10 m., and, to allow vehicular access to the eastern part of the old hospital grounds, it was necessary to leave a gap in the trench about half-way along. Like Trench III, it was 2 m. wide and dug partly by machine and partly by hand. It was densely disturbed to a depth of 0.50–1 m., particularly in the northern part, by modern drains, services and foundations connected with the old hospital. Undisturbed natural clay was found at a depth of 2.80 m. in a trial trench near the centre of Trench II, but the rest of the trench was not excavated below about half that depth.

No structures were encountered in Trench II, except for a chalk-block wall similar to that in Trench III, which lay against the north face of the modern brick wall on Longport (Plate XXIV). This was 1.15 m. wide just below ground level where it was encountered and was 1.50 m. high at the limit of the depth excavated. There was slight evidence in the eastern section of Trench II that the wall had been built in a trench cut vertically into a bank immediately to its north. At the northern end of Trench II (Fig. 10) there were three small areas of ashlar that had fallen face downwards, evidently from the adjacent wall of the south transept of the abbey church (Plate XXV). Their furthest limit was approximately 4.80 m. south of the south-east corner of the transept. Each comprised about a dozen blocks of Caen stone set in decayed yellowish mortar. These stones were left and lifted as part of the area excavation in 1975 (see below).

South of the areas of fallen masonry and at a depth of between 1.00 m. and 1.50 m. there was a heavy concentration of burials, some of which had evidently been cut into by later burials. Upper levels had been much disturbed by post-monastic activity on the site. Between 26 m. and 29 m. north of the south face of the chalk wall on Longport, a pebbled surface was found. It could have been a trackway or road, but it had no definable north or south edge. It was approximately on the same line as the later road encountered in Trench III but both were about 7 m. north of the old route out of the city on the line of Church Street and Burgate. The dating of this feature is uncertain, but it would appear to be early as neither the pebbled surface nor the layer above it produced pottery later than the late twelfth or early thirteenth century and both layers were sealed by approximately 0.50 m. of burials.

The pebbled surface 26–29 m. north of Longport produced only three sherds of Belgic and

Roman pottery, two sherds of early Norman pottery and one sherd of probably late twelfth- or early thirteenth-century Tyler Hill ware. The layer, which immediately overlay this surface, contained only two sherds of Roman pottery and one sherd from a roughly hand-made cooking-pot in a reduced sandy fabric laced with coarsely crushed shell, probably made locally at Tyler Hill in the early twelfth century. A trial hole was dug in Trench II between 13.50 m. and 17.50 m. north of Longport to establish the depth of natural ground. This trial hole cut through a black peaty layer about 15 cm. thick and an 80 cm. layer of dark soil, neither of which produced any finds, until hard orange undisturbed natural clay was revealed at 2.80 m. below ground level, i.e. 50 cm. below the level of the pavement on Longport, or 13.015 mm. Cut into this clay but only partly visible because of the confines of the trench were two adult burials aligned north-west and south-east. It was not possible to examine these properly and they were back-filled, but it is possible that they are pagan Roman burials.

DISCUSSION

For further discussion of the area of Trench II see below p. 53 (Excavations 1974–75). Finds from Trench II, in addition to the fallen stones mentioned, included floor-tiles, window glass and lead, and pottery of all periods. With the possible exception of finds associated with the pebbled surface described above, these and a number of valuable small finds were all in disturbed contexts. See Finds Report below p. 187, 1 and 2 (Roman brooch and knife handle), 17 and 19 (strap end), 21 (buckle) and 52 (implement).

AREAS 1 AND 2, 1974–75

SUMMARY

The lady chapel was partly excavated and shown to be of two periods, both before *c.* 1509. A substantial part of the fallen south wall of the presbytery, mostly of the late twelfth century, was found and provides important evidence for the eleventh- to thirteenth-century church. There was no evidence of how the wall collapsed. The south end of the transept had been greatly damaged. Information was gained regarding the insertion of the chantry between the transept and the nave. In the footings of the south aisle wall of the nave there was slight evidence for two periods of construction. The ground to the south of the church had been used for burials.

EXCAVATION AND INTERPRETATION (Figs. 6, 10, 13, 16)

After the 1972 trial trenches, which had helped to determine the Department of the Environment's new site boundary, excavations began again in April 1974 at the south-east corner of the lady chapel and continued westwards along the south side of the abbey church to just beyond the transept (Fig. 6). The purpose of the excavations was, firstly, to uncover and investigate those parts of the abbey which had hitherto been protected by the old boundary wall; and secondly, to take down the adjacent ground to the level of the ruins already displayed. By the end of the summer of 1974 an area *c.* 15 x 30 m., as far west as the section of the fallen wall

(Fig. 13), had been cleared (Area 1). The fallen wall and ground westwards (Area 2, including parts of the 1972 Trench II) were excavated in July and August 1975 (see below pp. 47–55).

The east and west boundaries (Fig. 6) between the abbey ruins and the Technical College, F43, appear from old maps to have altered little at least since the building of the Hospital, begun in 1791. The bend in the boundary wall round the site of the south transept can already be seen on Doidges' plan of 1752 (Plate VIII).

Because of hospital and later occupation no serious archaeological investigation had previously taken place south of the boundary wall. The wall actually overlay part of the lady chapel, St. Thomas's Chapel, the south transept and the chapel attached to the south aisle of the nave. The ground was found in 1974–75, however, to have been much disturbed by hospital foundations, service trenches, gardening, tree roots, etc. The method of excavation, therefore, was to remove disturbed ground by mechanical means and then proceed by hand. The great principle not to excavate below late-monastic levels has meant that the greater part of the cemetery remains for future excavation. Natural ground encountered in the centre of Trench II in 1972 lay approximately 2.80 m. below ground level and there is no reason to suppose that it was exceptionally deep at that point. Work began each year by dismantling the length of former boundary wall along Areas 1 and 2. The cement mortar used in the wall suggests a construction date for it early in this century. It was found to contain much re-used building material, especially Roman bricks, medieval floor-tiles and fragments of Romanesque and later carved stones. The better-preserved pieces were saved and some are published here in the finds section. A mechanical excavator then removed the disturbed topsoil, modern foundations, drains, etc., which covered the whole site to a depth varying from 0.50 to 1 m. There was a general slope down from south to north.

Area 1

Following the removal of top soil Area 1 was cleaned by hand trowel. The first layer encountered (layer 1) produced some further foundations and disturbance from old Hospital and Technical College buildings but, generally, it consisted of dark brown earth littered with disturbed human bones. This layer must represent the levelling of the site for the building of the hospital in 1791. No significant conclusions could be deduced from the finds from Area 1. Two residual coins, an Edward I or II farthing (lost *c.* 1320) and a Nuremburg jeton of *c.* 1530–40 were found near the north-east corner in layer 1. Another jeton of *c.* 1500 came from layer 4 in the same area. Because of the eighteenth-century building and disturbance, when the cemetery was ransacked for stone coffins and great quantities of human bones were dug up (Hasted 1801, 165), little information could be gained by either a study of the pottery or the bones. The pottery (Fig. 87, nos. 42, 43, 48, 50 and 55) is discussed below (p. 279); the bones were re-buried in the 'water bottle' or well situated near the south side of Area 2 (Fig. 10). In the south-east corner of Area 1, a small trench (1 x 2.40 m.) was dug to test the medieval burial level. Bones were encountered to a further depth of 1.60 m. where the soil was clayey and possibly natural with burials cut into it. One sherd of samian ware was found in the trench and some Roman bricks. To avoid the lengthy and specialised task of excavating an almost entire medieval cemetery, it was decided not to go deeper elsewhere in Areas 1 or 2 unless there were indications of buildings or other structures.

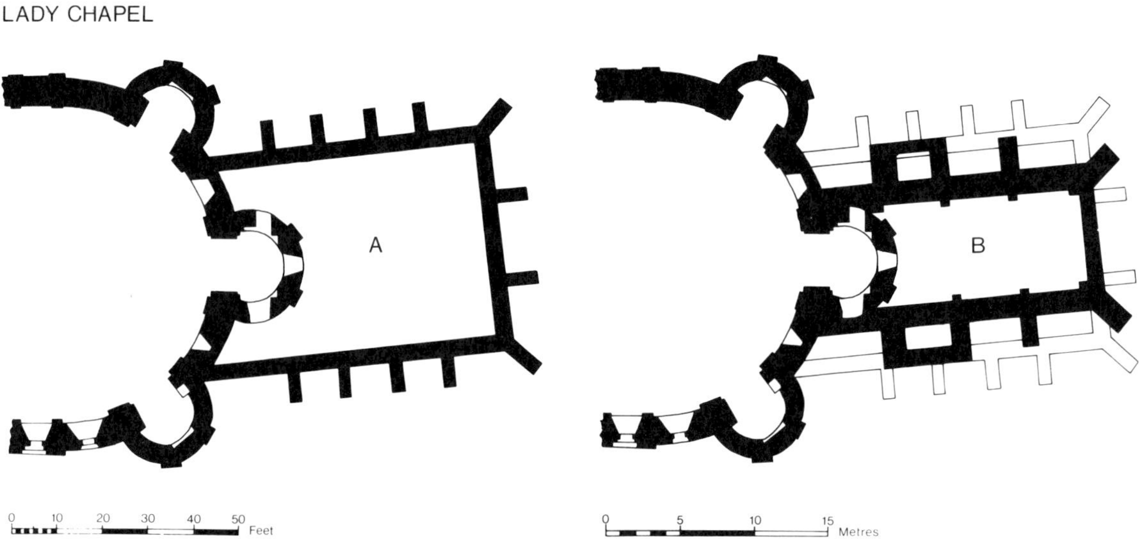

Fig. 11. The Lady Chapel, showing earlier and later Plans.

The South Side of the Lady Chapel

The rectangular building added in a secondary phase onto the east end of the Romanesque church is not identified by any documentary references, nor are there prints or pictures to show it before demolition: it is, however, in the classic location for the lady chapels that were subsequently added to many of the greater monastic churches (see below p. 59 and Fig. 12) and linked with the choir in Nedeham's demolition accounts of 1542 (Bodleian Library, Rawlinson MS D781, 175r).[8]

The lady chapel was first excavated by C.F. Routledge who published his results in 1902 (Routledge 1902, 238–43). He was puzzled by the double lengths of walling on the north and south sides of the chapel, but thought that it was built some time in the fourteenth century and then enlarged 'about the close of the fifteenth century, perhaps by Abbot Dygon himself' whose tomb was found within it.[9] At the time of its enlargement the inner walls would, he thought, have been replaced by arcades, the 'boxes' between the walls then becoming separate chapels (Routledge 1902, 242). This explanation has been generally accepted, though Canon Potts thought there was only one build and that the chapel was erected at the beginning of the sixteenth century with flying buttresses (Potts 1934, 182).

8. Against this interpretation Dr Gem suggests the chapel could simply be a rebuilding of the Trinity Chapel (belatedly rivalling the great chapel at the cathedral) to provide a more dignified setting for the shrines of the saints.
9. Abbot Dygon died on 10th May, 1509, the day after he attended Henry VII's state funeral, but his own funeral plate gives the year 1510 (see Thorn 1981).

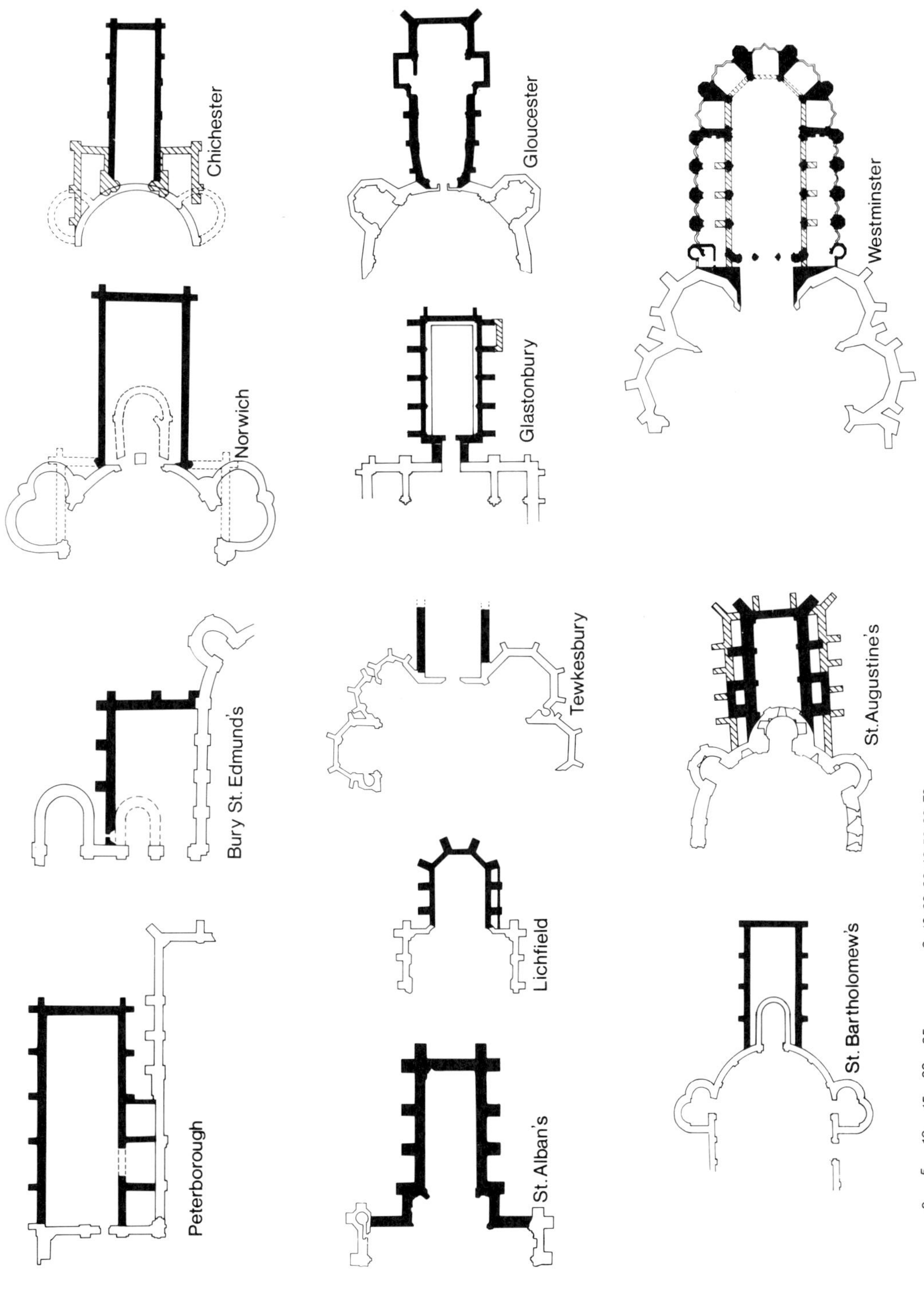

Fig. 12. Comparative Plans of eastern Lady Chapels in England.

When the hospital boundary wall on the south side of the chapel was pulled down in 1974, it was found that the inner buttresses and western 'box' lay over the outer wall footings and were of a different build, showing that the chapel must have been reduced in width, not enlarged (Fig. 11). The other buttresses survived up to three courses of 55 cm. high. They were built of knapped flint with ashlar quoins on out-spreading flint-and-mortar foundations. The inner buttress and 'box' wall was wider and built of smaller Caen stone ashlars with fewer flints, but the inner south-east angle buttress was built of large close-fitting blocks of grey limestone which continue round to form the east face of the chapel.

The widths of the outer and inner buttresses are 0.80 m. and 1.50 m., respectively. The later, narrower chapel thus had more substantial walls and buttresses, presumably to support the outward thrust of the floor over the chapel crypt. The bays of the crypt correspond with the position of the later buttresses and 'box' walls. The eastern crypt wall and the inner southern buttress encountered a hard mortar surface approximately 0.20 m. below the present top of the walls, but the whole area had been greatly disturbed in post-medieval and modern (presumably Routledge's) times. It was not excavated below the level of the mortar. Fragments of Delft-type porcelain (Fig. 87, no. 57), clay pipes and modern glass were recovered. There were also signs of the robbing of the ashlar face on the inside of the outer wall. This presumably took place when the wall was superseded by the inner wall. The crypt measures 6.5 x approx. 13 m., a double square. The internal dimensions of the earlier chapel are 12.5 m. (nearly twice as wide) by about 18 m.

There is now no way of knowing why the chapel was narrowed or whether the first chapel was ever completed. The walls are not so dissimilar as to preclude a change of plan during construction. Possibly the first plan was too ambitious and the money was not forthcoming. It is known from contemporary documents that the abbey was in debt in the late fifteenth century (Cotton 1939, 67); possibly unstable ground, a change in architectural fashion, the need for a crypt, or the death and burial wishes of Abbot Dygon made it necessary or desirable to narrow the building. It will be observed that the outer buttresses on the north side of the chapel still survive about twice as high as those excavated on the south side, but subsequent re-pointing of the remains exposed by Routledge now makes it impossible to examine the fabric of the north walls for evidence of building periods, etc. The two phases are shown separated in Fig. 11.

The discovery that the chapel was narrowed still leaves the north and south 'boxes' unaccounted for. These compartments may have been side chantries, not pierced by arches in the main wall as Routledge suggested, but entered by doorways. A threshold to the north compartment can still be observed three courses above the floor, but there was no corresponding threshold in the southern compartment because the wall is higher there. Alternatively, the compartments may have been charnel chapels or 'boneholes' without permanent access, for re-interring burials, perhaps those disturbed when the crypt was dug. West of both compartments there may have been two more 'boneholes' utilising the earlier outer walls. The northern one is in the form of a stone-lined pit, blocking the Norman crypt window and with no evident means of entry, but on the south side of the chapel there is now no trace of the earlier outer wall which would have formed a second southern compartment. The south-east window of the Norman crypt was too ruined to show whether it was subsequently blocked, but the core-work of the surviving southern wall appeared to continue westwards, and later acted possibly as a buttress because the ground falls steeply here to the Norman crypt window. The southern wall must have been destroyed by the time the brick gulley (described below) was laid.

In the area to the south of the lady chapel were random scatters of mortar extending some 15 m. south between the east end of the chapel and St. Thomas' Chapel. Two distinct types of mortar were recognised here, layers 2 and 3, which doubtless reflect the different building periods of the lady chapel and St. Thomas' Chapel. Layer 2, the mortar deposit opposite the lady chapel, was much darker than layer 3 and included flints and other debris. Layer 3, which lay opposite St. Thomas' Chapel, was much cleaner and lighter in colour than layer 2, and contained a quantity of painted stonework and wall-plaster (see Finds report, p. 122). No dressed stonework that could be attributed to the chapel itself was found except for one piece carved with a Tudor rose (see stone report Cat. no. 153, p. 110). This absence of stonework may reflect the fact that the chapel was built of the newest and therefore most re-usable stone. Embodying a form of worship that was objectionable to the new Reformation, the lady chapel may have been one of the first buildings after the Dissolution to catch the zealous eyes of the king's demolition men (Colvin 1982, 61). The pottery from these layers (Fig. 87, nos. 49, 51 and 55) is discussed below.

The South Side of the Presbytery Aisle and of St. Thomas' Chapel

The presbytery and south transept are essentially the work of Abbot Scotland (1070–87), though it is uncertain what work may have been carried out after the fire of 1168 or the dedications of 1240 and 1325. The remains of the crypt show eleventh- and twelfth-century mouldings, with enlarged windows in Perpendicular style. The date when these windows were inserted is not known, but it is possible that they are contemporary with Abbot Dygon's lady chapel. The surviving mouldings are in the same fine-grained Portland stone that faces the east wall of the lady chapel. What is left of the dressed stone of the transept looks Norman, except in the chapel which was inserted in the angle between the transept and the nave. Sealed by layers 2 and 3 in Area 1 was layer 4, a fairly smooth dark soil flecked with chalk. This must represent the build-up of the ground surface during and following the demolition *c.* 1540–50, as it produced sherds of late fifteenth- and sixteenth-century pottery (see Pottery, p. 279, Fig. 86, nos. 28, 29, 37, and 39), and was sealed by the mortar and rubble deposits described above. Below layer 4 in the angle between the lady chapel and the presbytery, a rough soakaway, which had already been exposed by previous excavations (see p. 42), was found (Fig. 10, 3). This consisted of a channel made of small stone flags leading into a brick gulley *c.* 3.50 m. long. At the southern end there was slight evidence that this brick gulley was originally joined by another brick gulley at an angle of 45° from the north-west (see Fig. 10). These gulleys, the bricks of which were arranged widthways, fed into a trench which followed the curvature of the presbytery wall, and thence into a bell-shaped hollow (Fig. 10, 4) to the south-east of St. Thomas' (the south-east radiating chapel was dedicated to St. Thomas at crypt level, and to Sts. Stephen, Lawrence and Vincent at the upper level). To the south-west of the chapel this curved drainage trench opened out into a second bulbous hollow (excavated in 1975), which was sealed by the fallen wall (see below p. 47). The drainage trench then disappeared, but may well have continued to follow the south side of the church around the south transept.

The brick gullies appear to have been designed to carry rainwater from the confluence of the gutters of the roofs above St. Thomas' Chapel and the eastern radiating chapel later extended by Abbot Dygon's Chapel. In their latest form they must date, therefore, from the completion of the lady chapel in *c.* 1509. The dating of the curved and bulbous hollows must remain conjectural as the ground surface from which they were cut was not excavated. It is possible that these features are contemporary with the enlarging of the crypt windows. There was some evidence that the curved trench continued under the lady chapel, but the nature of the silts and the pottery recovered from the western hollow (see below) would suggest that, even if this were the case, the drainage system can only antedate the lady chapel by a few years, and that the hollows rapidly filled with debris at the time of the mid sixteenth-century demolition. Both the curved trench, and the eastern hollow were sealed by layer 4. The western hollow was sealed by the fallen wall.

The eastern hollow was not fully excavated, but a narrow trench dug to a depth of approximately 20 cm. along the centre of the depression encountered a mortar deposit, layer 5, under which was layer 6, a layer of dark soil similar to layer 4. Of these two, layer 5, which contained fragments of Roman and medieval brick tile, two twelfth- and fourteenth-century moulded stones, medieval pottery (Fig. 85, nos. 21 and 22) and five sherds of Langerwehe and Raeren pottery (not illustrated) datable to *c.* 1475–1575, was clearly a demolition deposit. Layer 6 was not excavated.

To the west of this hollow (Fig. 10, 4) a second exploratory trench measuring 8 m. long and 1 m. wide, was dug into the medieval drainage trench opposite St. Thomas' Chapel, to a depth of 80 cm. below the bottom of layer 4. This revealed a series of clay and mortar tips, layers 10, 11, 12, 13 and 14, against the massive footings for the outer wall of the presbytery, but the level of the construction trench itself was not reached. Fragments of fifteenth- to sixteenth-century brick, possibly from the gulley described above, found in layers 11, 12 and 13 would suggest that these tips all date to the mid sixteenth-century demolition. Layer 14 yielded a quantity of Roman pottery, and a few sherds of thirteenth- and fourteenth-century pottery (Fig. 85, no. 23).

The western hollow, which was fully excavated in 1975 after the removal of the fallen wall (see below p. 49) appeared to be cut from a height of approximately 13.81 m. O.D. on the north side. To the south it was cut into layer 72, a deposit of dark brown clayey soil with flecks of charcoal, chalk and some yellow mortar, not unlike layer 54, to the west of the south transept (see below p. 54). At its lowest point, 13.08 m. O.D., the hollow was approximately 75 cm. deep. It appeared to have had a limited life-span, with only two probable and two possible silts. The probable silts consisted of layer 74, a rainwashed deposit of fairly yellow-brown sand, more prominent on the north side of the hollow, and layer 75, a deposit of brown sandy soil containing much mortar. Layer 76, which consisted of a brown soil with flecks of chalk and shell, seen on the south side of the pit only, and layer 77, a stoney layer at the centre of the hollow may represent further silts, but the similarity both of the deposits themselves and the pottery they contained suggest that layers 76 and 77 are contemporary with layers 71, 68 and 69, and that these are all tips of layer 4 and demolition material. Of the upper tips layer 71 consisted of a brown soil similar to layer 69, but with fewer white flecks; fragments of yellow mortar were noted at the interface of layers 71 and 72. This was sealed by layer 68, a stoney layer which occupied the centre of the hollow, and layer 69, a brown soil densely flecked with fragments of chalk, shell and some mortar. This sloped down from the north and was found around the edges of the hollow over layer 68, which protruded at the centre of the hollow. On the eastern side of the soakaway layer 4 merged with layers 68 and 69. This overspill was designated layer 4/69.

Layers 68, 69 and 4/69 were all sealed by a substantial dump of rubble and mortar, layer 63, and the 'fallen wall' (see below), which was partly embedded in layer 69 and, to the south, in layer 4. Layers 68, 4/69 and 63 all produced joining sherds of sixteenth-century earthenware (see pottery report and Fig. 84, nos. 6, 7; and Fig. 85, no. 17), and Raeren and Cologne stoneware (Fig. 87, nos. 61, 62 and 65), indicating that the backfilling of the soakaway and the demolition of the south aisle wall all took place within a short space of time. Layer 69 produced a Nuremburg jeton of the 1520s or 1530s and layer 4, another of the 1500s.

The Tumble (Area 1)

The most significant discovery of the 1974 excavation was the mass of building debris ('the tumble') which forms the bulk of the finds section in this report (Fig. 10, 5–7). This appeared to be immediately on top of and to the south of the late medieval drainage system, mainly opposite and to the west of St. Thomas' Chapel. Because of the scant records of earlier excavations this is the first large quantity of carved stone from St. Augustine's of which the original location is known. Some 400 dressed stones or fragments of stones were recovered from the area south of the presbytery. Lying in a large heap some 1.50 m. thick were fragments of walling, both facing and core-work, packed in bright yellow mortar which had freshly preserved both mouldings and the painted plaster. Except for some length of parapet (totalling *c.* 3 m. long) and probably some of the squared ashlar, the dressed stone appeared to have come mainly from the inside of the presbytery. It included parts of Caen-stone vaulting ribs with dog-tooth moulding, Kentish rag 'marble' shafts, Perpendicular window jambs, and one stiff-leaf capital fortunately preserved unharmed in a bed of old mortar (Plate L, a). The method of excavation was to clear away the mortar, flints and other core-work to look for stones still in juxtaposition, then to photograph and lift them. In this way it was possible to retrieve two almost complete arches which lay in the drainage trench just to the west of St. Thomas' Chapel, and a large number of fragments of painted plaster some still adhering to mortar. Five half drums from an attached column were found a few metres south of these arches. Generally, the mortar appeared to have come away from the stones on impact with the ground and then to have settled and re-hardened somewhat in the course of time. Besides masonry, one large piece of parapet lead-work, some minor pieces of tracery with decomposed glass and some iron dowels were also recovered.

The Fallen Wall (Area 2)

Excavation continued westwards in this fashion down to the level of the medieval soakaway until it became apparent that an entire section of outer walling had fallen outwards rather than downwards in a tumble (see Fig. 13). This wall, which proved to be parts of two pilaster buttresses either side of a window, was excavated in 1975. The remainder of the 1974 work was devoted to stripping the topsoil off this fallen wall and to defining its extent in preparation for the following year. About 50 cm. of topsoil was removed by mechanical excavator and the same amount of loose rubble and mortar, mixed with earth, layer 19, was removed by shovel down to where the core of the wall became hard-packed. Layer 19 produced five sherds of stoneware (see Table 11b) including two sherds of Raeren joining with sherds from layers 4 and 63 (Fig. 87, no. 63). The upper face of the wall (i.e. the inside when it was standing) had been completely robbed leaving no evidence for its original thickness. The only surviving feature was a small area of plaster *c.* 45 x 20 cm. on a level with the chamfered offset, which was once part of the splay. The main pilaster of the window that was adjacent to the west side of the fallen wall lay 1.10 m. above (i.e. in from) the (outer) wall face. Clearance of the rubble and mortar on the rising ground to the south of the fallen wall showed up the impression of the continuation of the main pilaster buttress of the outer face of the wall robbed of all but two of its stones but leaving white plaster adhering to the soil beneath. The main pilaster could be seen to have been *c.* 1.10 m. wide with two 16 cm. offsets either side. Its furthest point, 9.30 m. away from the church, gives a rough idea of the original height of the presbytery aisle wall; but near the apse in the transept evidence of the fallen wall extended only some 3.75 m. southwards.

There appeared to be three main areas of the lower (i.e. outer) face of the wall, which had not broken up on falling: at the north and south ends, and at the north-west end (Fig. 10). These were fairly hard, substantial lumps of masonry compared with the loose rubble core in the centre. Once its extent had been defined the method of excavating the wall in 1975 was as follows: a two-metre square grid frame was placed over the fallen wall to enable all the worked or otherwise significant stones apparent at that height to be plotted. They were then numbered and lifted. The smaller rubble and the mortar in which they lay was then cleaned down some 15 or 25 cm. until another layer of stones considered worth plotting lay exposed. This operation of plotting and removing the core-work was repeated four times until the inside faces of the ashlar blocks of the outer wall-face lay exposed (Plate XXVIII). This system made it possible to look for signs of building or re-building methods and to know what kind of stones were used or re-used in the construction of the core-work. The final stage was to photograph, number and plot the outer face as it lay in the ground (Plate XXVII). Arrows were painted on problematical stones to indicate the direction in which they were orientated.

It would have been possible to remove all the facing stones and store them in a pile pending a decision on when and where to re-erect them. However, because of the risk of not being able to re-assemble them correctly at a later date and partly in order to be able to study the only surviving substantial piece of external masonry of the church east of the nave, it was decided to re-assemble the stones face upwards nearby. The method of doing this was as follows: the final plan of the wall with numbered ashlars was reversed by tracing it onto another sheet of paper and righting the numbers to facilitate reading (cf. Fig. 14a). Then, working from south to north, the stones were lifted, numbered and transported one or two courses at a time to where they could be re-set face up on a bed which was prepared by sifting old mortar and small stones from the previously excavated core-work. This ready-made bed was especially necessary since it was known from the end of the 1974 excavation that the wall contained several offsets. In the event, for the outer stones of the fallen wall to rest on the ground it was necessary to build the new inner core of the wall up to about one metre. The fragments of wall thus re-created consisted of a main pilaster buttress about 5.50 m. × 1.20 m. with chamfered string-course, two offsets and jambs for windows either side. A final plan of the wall was drawn as it lay reconstructed, showing the gap in the wall mended at the point where it had broken in falling (See Plate XXIX and Fig. 14b; compare with break in section shown in Fig. 13).

After removal of the face stones, the rubble underlying the wall, layer 63, was excavated.

Again all dressed stone was planned and numbered before lifting, using numbers upwards of 20,000 in order to make a clear distinction from the stones in or above the fallen wall face. The profile of the medieval drainage trench discussed above was then recorded along the western limit of the 1974 excavation (section Fig. 13). There was no evidence of how the wall collapsed or whether it was done deliberately. It was probably undermined by the removal of the lower stones on its outer face and then pulled over. There were no remains of timber or charcoal to suggest the setting fire of temporary shoring with resulting collapse. The fact that the inner face had been thoroughly robbed suggests deliberate felling.

Description of the Fallen Wall

(a) Core

The core-work of the wall itself was found to contain:

1. Sections of black 'marble' shafts;
2. Small squared blocks of Caen-stone ashlar;
3. Large and small chunks of roughly hewn greenstone;
4. A few fragments of Roman brick;
5. Some moulded Caen-stone;
6. Large and very large flints, some of them oblong;
7. Bright sand-coloured mortar;
8. White plaster, often adhering to the face of Caen-stone and sometimes overlying paintwork;
9. Lumps of mortar with white plaster and paintwork, one with fragments of black lettering;
10. A few fragments of lead window cames; and
11. A few pieces of iron spikes up to about 0.20 m. long.

See also Geology Report, below p. 121.

The section (Fig. 13) shows that the core-work, where it had not broken up on impact with the ground, had been built in courses like the face-work, the greenstone forming the bulk of the core. There was no sign of layers in the core-work which might have indicated pauses in the original building of the wall. The only internal feature was a surface of plaster indicating the window splay already mentioned.

(b) Face

The piece of wall uncovered is of a plain pilaster relieved only by a horizontal string course and flanked on either side by offsets. The side towards the window opening (i.e. the west side) has three offsets, the outer unchamfered, the other two chamfered. On the east side of the pilaster there is at least one unchamfered offset, maybe two. There is no window opening on this side

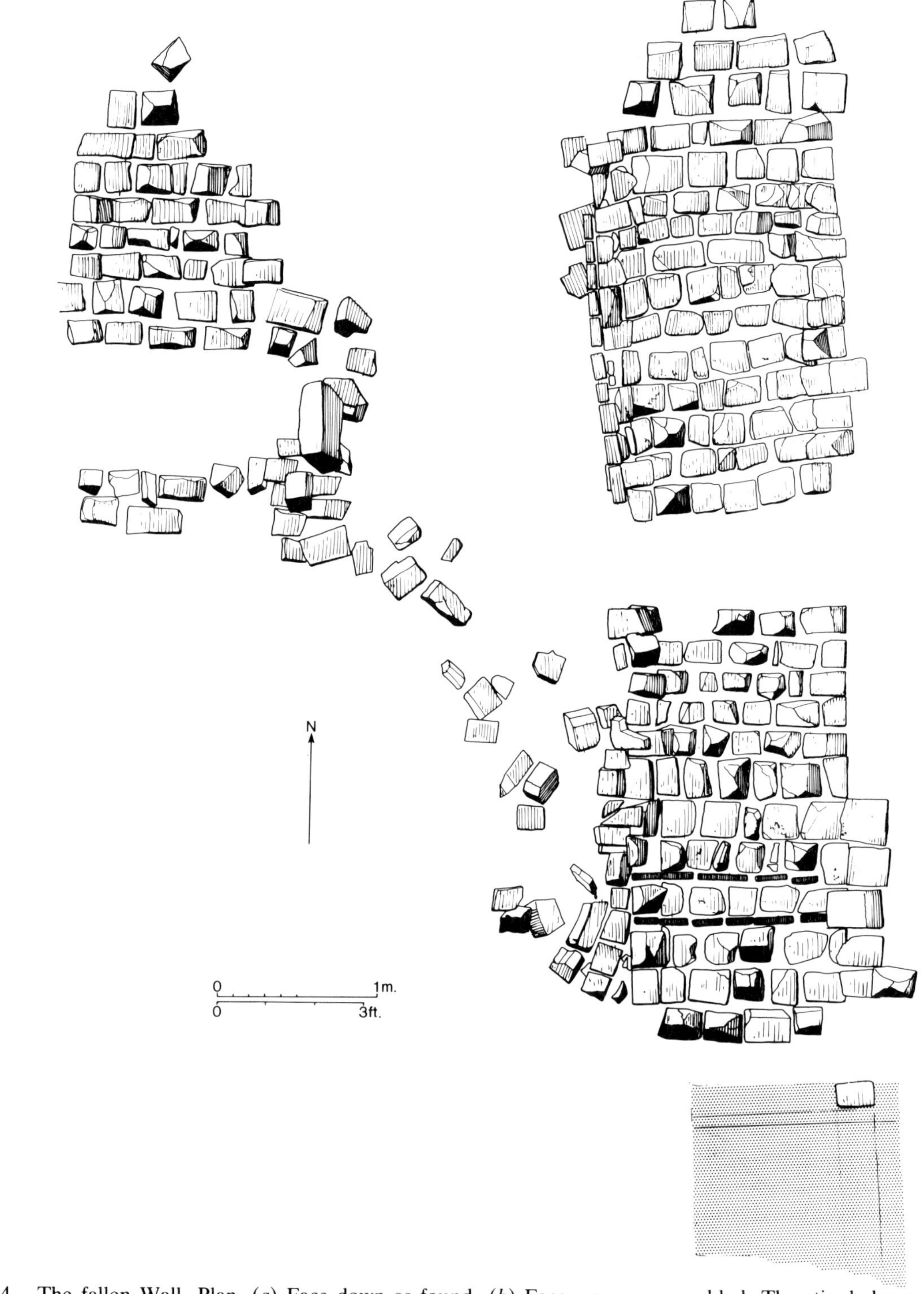

Fig. 14. The fallen Wall, Plan. (*a*) Face down as found, (*b*) Face up as reassembled. The stippled area in (a) represents the impression in the ground of the robbed wall.

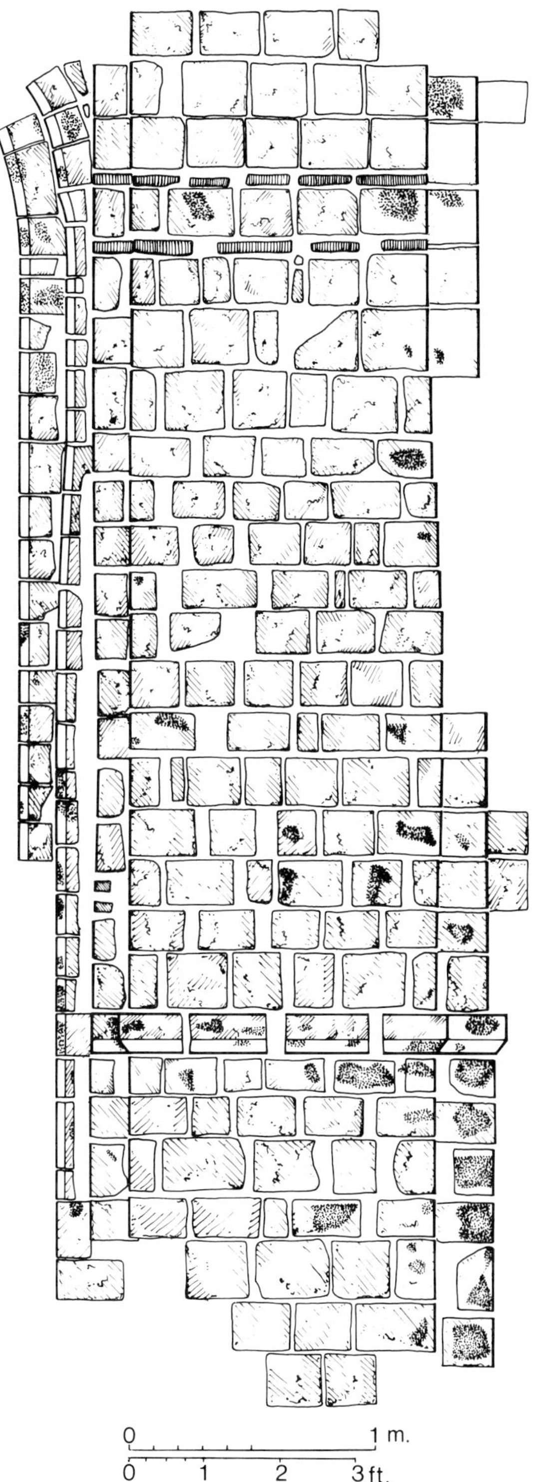

(*b*)

since the church wall is turning in towards the apse and the offset is probably in place to indicate this turn and make the pilaster stand out.

The piece of wall as re-assembled is 27 courses (i.e. *c.* 5.55 m.) high (excluding two courses of Roman brick), and in width has an average of just over five stones per course excluding offsets (Fig. 14b). The wall rose a further five courses to a second string course which would have originally stood about 9.50 m. high. The evidence for this comes from further stones that fell to the ground and left their imprint but were subsequently robbed. The width of the fallen wall as reconstructed on the ground (*c.* 1.25 m.) is wider than the assumed original width of the bay of the choir from which the wall came, which is only *c.* 1.10 m. wide. Both measurements exclude the offsets of the wall. This is probably accounted for by the slight spreading of the falling wall on impact with the ground. There are seven courses below the string course. The bottom three courses are fragmentary, possibly disturbed when the boundary wall was built. A further two courses (not reconstructed or drawn) lay under the boundary wall (Fig. 13). The bottom two courses are both 19 cm. high, then the next course is 23 cm. high. Above that there are two courses (*c.* 13 cm. high) sandwiching two taller courses. The string course is 15 cm. high and then a course of big stones 21 cm. high is above it. Then come two smaller layers (*c.* 14 cm. high) sandwiching three larger ones (*c.* 18 cm.). There is then a course (*c.* 18 cm. high) of almost square blocks followed by five courses of stones, which although some are as tall as the courses before them, nevertheless look smaller and distinctive as if they were all built in separate seasons. Above these courses are seven layers of stones averaging 20 cm. in height. In between the third and fourth, and fourth and fifth courses are the courses of Roman bricks, *c.* 5 cm. high and up to 30 cm. wide. This analysis may have significance for determining how many seasons it took the masons to build up to the full height of the church.[10]

The offsets on either side of the pilaster appear to have been built with the courses alternately wide-short. On the window side this is interrupted at the eighth course which is short instead of wide. However, this stone was interpolated in the excavators' reconstruction. On the other side (i.e. the east side) the regular pattern stops at the 22nd course where the rest of the courses are wide (the 27th course must be short but is missing). Throughout the pilaster there is an attempt at placing the stones alternately in wide and short courses, something that follows naturally from the placing of the offsets. This is given up from courses 22 to 26. Roman bricks are used sparingly. There are two courses with six in each. They continue westward to the Norman offset, but for some unknown reason do not continue eastward to where the apse begins. There are four other Roman bricks used upright in the wall. They are not, however, used for the jambs of the later window opening. Three of them could be blockings of put-log holes. The other brick is broken in half and used as an offset to the Norman window.

Evidence that the main window in the excavated piece of wall was a secondary insertion is provided by the fact that the chamfer on the western return of the string course has been cut off. It is possible that the bottom of the window was found (see pp. 108–9, nos. 131 and 135). Three courses below the string-course, the chamfer on the middle offset came to an end. The outer chamfered offset may have met the sill of the window on the course immediately below.

10. In 1487, the masons at Helmingham Church, Suffolk, were ordered to build a 60 ft. tower in 10 years, i.e. 6 ft. a year (Salzman 1967, 547).

However, against this is the fact that all the inner offsets below the string-course are now in surmised positions so the windows may have continued further down the wall.

All the facework of the wall is of Normandy limestone, imported probably from Caen (see geology report, p. 121). It was covered with an even layer of gritty white plaster 2–4 mm. thick.

The plain character of the pilaster and string-course would be consistent with an eleventh-century date for the original construction of the wall. The pointed window must be considerably later, therefore, since it clearly belongs to the late twelfth or early thirteenth century.

THE SOUTH SIDE OF THE TRANSEPT

Excavation continued to the west of the fallen wall in order to expose the outer faces of the south transept and of the chantry chapel between the transept and nave. At the same time it was intended to explore the relationship of these two structures and to expose any other features in the area formerly occupied by the hospital, which had not been destroyed by the latter's foundations and basements. The area of excavation extended as far as the third bay of the south aisle of the nave and, for the most part, halted at the late-medieval ground surface, represented by layer 4 in the area of the south transept and layer 37 in the area to the west of the chantry chapel.

The paucity of building stone from this area was in marked contrast to the amount recovered from the area to the south of the presbytery, which is evidence for the thoroughness of the demolition work carried out by George Nycholl's men in the 1540s and 1550s (see above p. 11). Two of the three small patches of fallen masonry which were encountered in Trench II in 1972 (see above p. 39 and Plate XXV) hardly extended into the 1975 area. When examined and lifted the stones were found to be slightly smaller (average 20 x 18 cm.) than those in the fallen wall south of the presbytery, but they were more square and uniform, matching in character those still surviving in the north aisle wall. They had diagonal tooling and their face was plastered. One stone in the southern of the two areas was inset, suggesting that there was some pilaster or other vertical moulding on or near the south-east corner of the south transept.

A large part of the south face of the transept was unfortunately incorporated in or damaged by the hospital boundary wall, while the south-east corner was also cut by a brick-lined well which was contemporary with the hospital. The removal of the boundary wall exposed a pit of mortar and rubble, F46, which occupied a central position immediately to the south of the south wall of the transept (see Fig. 10). This pit, which produced no dating evidence, was also cut by a drain-pipe trench which bifurcated into trenches running south and approximately south-east. To the east of this pipe-trench layer 4 was relatively undisturbed; it produced a wide range of medieval pottery and other finds consistent with that from the rest of Areas 1 and 2 (see Fig. 86, nos. 27, 31, 36 and 38). To the west of the north–south pipe trench, however, the whole area was found to be much disturbed by hospital buildings and service trenches, including a brick-lined storage well or cistern, which lay approximately 5 m. to the south of the south transept. To the north-west of this feature much of the area in the angle of the south transept and the chantry chapel had been almost completely destroyed by hospital foundations, to the extent that only a narrow strip approximately 1.70 m. wide survived between the west face of the south transept and the area occupied by the hospital basement (see Fig. 6). This had been disturbed by two intersecting late or post-medieval graves or reburials, F52 and F83, but against the west wall of the south transept between 14.55 and 14.09 m. O.D. was found a sequence of clay and mortar deposits, layers 51, 53, 54, 55 and 56, not unlike those found in the soakaway to the south of the presbytery. Of these, layer 53 produced no finds, while layers 51 and 54 contained only Roman material. Layer 56, however, the lowest deposit, which consisted of dark brown clayey soil with animal bones, contained fragments of medieval floor-tiles and two sherds of fifteenth- or sixteenth-century pottery, one of which joins with a sherd from layer 4, showing that these layers are demolition deposits, which may have accumulated in the hollow of a former soakaway. Layer 56, which varied greatly in depth from 3.50 cm. to 13 cm., was sealed by layer 55, a light grey mortary soil approximately 5 cm. thick. This in turn was sealed by layer 54, a hard compact layer of brown clayey soil with lumps of orange clay, a few small stones and fragments of Roman brick, very similar to layer 72, which would appear to represent the ground surface *c.* 1540. Over this deposit, which was approximately 12 cm. thick, was layer 53, a spread of greensand chippings resting on a thin layer of white mortar, together averaging 3 cm. thick, which presumably represents the debris resulting from the robbing of the faced stones from the west wall of the south transept. Layer 53 was sealed by layer 51, a mortary yellow-grey brown stoney soil, approximately 12 cm. deep. These layers were all banked against the west wall of the transept, sloping away to the west at an angle of approximately 15°.

The removal of these clay and mortar deposits showed that the lower parts of walls of the south transept, like those of the south aisle (see below p. 70) and the cloister consisted of two very different methods of construction, divided by an offset of chamfered blocks with greenstone quoins. The upper portion was constructed of finely dressed ashlar. Below the chamfer, however, at approximately 14.55 m. O.D., the face of the wall became much less even, with pockets of earth and mortar between the larger, more roughly-cut stones. The chamfered course was set at approximately 15.30 m. O.D. on the exterior and 15.20 m. O.D. on the interior, although a certain amount of variation was noted, particularly on the east side, where the level of greenstone blocks fell from north to south: on the outer wall the greenstone block to the north of the apse was set at 15.65 m. O.D., whereas that at the south-east corner stood at 15.31 m. O.D. On the inside the greenstone block to the north of the apse stood at 15.26 m. O.D., compared with 15.23 m. for the corresponding block to the south. On the west side the levels were more consistent, dropping by only 5 mm. from the north-west to the south-west corner where the greenstone quoin was set at 15.32 m. O.D. The internal chamfer on the west wall survived at 15.25 m. O.D., but that on the outer wall was rather damaged. The third block from the south-west corner survived, but that to the south had lost its dressed face. Towards the junction with the south wall of the chantry chapel there were signs that the outer wall of the transept had been refaced with smaller chamfered blocks set back approximately 30 cm. from the face of the foundations. It is possible that this was effected when the chantry chapel was built, to act as a form of keying but, as these mouldings bear a strong resemblance to those on the inner face, it is not possible to assign a date to this operation. The height of the chamfer at this point was 15.37 m. O.D.

The 1975 excavation was halted at 14.00 m. O.D. at which point no foundation trench for the south transept was apparent. If, however, this transept is comparable with the south aisle wall excavated further west (see below p. 70), then the footings may rest on a lower expanded footing and ultimately on a raft of rammed mortar. At the west end of the church the foundation trench for the south aisle wall was found to be cut from a level of approximately 13.51 m. O.D. It seems reasonable, therefore, to suppose that the foundation trench for the west wall of the transept, unless disturbed, survives for future study approximately 50 cm. below the limit of the 1975 excavation.

THE CHANTRY CHAPEL

In the angle formed by the transept and south aisle of the nave is a small later chapel which has been identified by Potts who excavated it (Potts 1921, 123) and all subsequent writers as the chapel of St. Anne where Juliana de Leyborne, Countess of Huntingdon, was buried in 1367. When it was first excavated a quantity of good-quality painted and gilded tabernacle work was found and was thought to have come from her tomb. The chapel had an altar inserted into the transept wall and measures internally 4.88 × 3.65 m. Its own wall was buttressed on the south side and at the south-west corner; there was a crude buttress stone at foundation level only in the south-east corner. They were built of ashlar, with a flint core, and a flint offset bonded with yellow mortar, resting on a chalk foundation. The ashlar blocks had been robbed but enough of the core-work survived to show that the average thickness of the wall was approximately 80 cm. thinner than the adjacent Norman walls. At the highest point, on the western buttress, the chantry chapel wall survived to a height of 15.70 m. O.D. or 10 cm. above the floor level inside. The flint offset varied in width, being approximately 50 cm. wide in the angle of the buttress at the south-west corner and 10 cm. wide along the south and west walls. The height of this offset was approximately 15.56 m. O.D.

Excavation showed that the foundations for the west wall of the chantry were built directly against the outer face of the south aisle wall, while those of the south wall abutted the west wall of the south transept. At the south-west corner of the chapel, the chalk foundation for the westernmost buttress had cut through that of a flint-built table tomb (Fig. 10, no. 10). As noted above, there were signs that the chamfered course on the outer wall of the transept has been set back by approximately 30 cm. at the junction of this wall with that of the chantry chapel, while the eastern edge of the flint facing for the tomb had been cut back by approximately 10 cm. in order to accommodate the ashlar blocks of the chapel wall. The chalk foundations for the south wall of the chapel were trench-built in two phases. In the lower levels, the chalk occupied the full width of the trench, widening as it proceeded westwards (presumably lighter foundations were considered adequate by the massive transept wall); but in the upper levels, only the vestiges of the foundation trench were visible in section beside the central buttress on the south side of the chapel. This trench unfortunately produced no finds. Over this lower foundation and apparently sealing part of the foundation trench was an expanded chalk footing of visibly separate, obviously contemporary, construction. No construction trench was visible here, suggesting that unless it was destroyed when excavated in 1920, the footing of the wall either occupied the full width of the cut, or was constructed over the original ground surface; but the presence of the boundary wall, which butted against this footing, prevents further interpretation here.

A small trench excavated within the chantry chapel to establish the nature and width of the chalk foundation for the south wall showed that this was neither even in width nor perfectly aligned with the ashlar superstructure. The highest point of the foundation on the inside of the chapel was approximately 20 cm. lower than that on the outside, i.e. approximately 14.90 m. O.D., while the height of the outer face varied from 15.31 m. O.D. at the south-west corner to 15.14 m. O.D. at the centre point of both the south and west walls. The foundation for the south wall also increased in width from approximately 1.68 to 1.88 m. towards its western end. The reason for this is not clear, unless perhaps disturbance by earlier burials there caused the ground to be more soft.

Compared with the quantity of fine fourteenth-century moulded stone recovered from outside the chapel (Potts 1921, 123), the finds from the area to the south and west of the chapel were disappointingly few except for the pottery (see p. 279).

THE SOUTH SIDE OF THE NAVE

The removal of the north–south leg of the hospital wall immediately to the west of the chapel enabled a section to be drawn (Fig. 16) to show the build-up *c.* 1540–50 of layer 37 over the late medieval ground surface sealing the foundation of Tomb 10, which itself may have remained exposed until the time of the Dissolution. To the south of Tomb 10 the late-medieval ground surface was represented by layer 42, a deposit of grey-brown soil very similar to layer 37, but blacker, being more densely flecked with charcoal. Two features were noted in this: layer 40, a square post-setting, which presumably dates from the demolition of the chantry chapel, and a possible grave, distinguished by a lighter coloured soil, which was not excavated. To the north of Tomb 10 the late-medieval ground surface was represented by layer 38, which was also very similar to layer 37, but rather more grey in colour. In both cases the division between layers 37/42 and 37/38 was virtually indistinguishable, but on the basis of the distribution of the demolition debris, appeared to be at approximately 15.20 m. O.D. to the south of Tomb 10, and approximately 15.00 m. O.D. in the area between the tombs and the south aisle wall. It would appear, therefore, that this area was lowered in the mid-sixteenth century in order to facilitate the demolition of the chantry and south aisle wall at this point. (Similar removal and redeposition of the graveyard levels was noted in the 1976 excavation to the west of this area – see below p. 72). Layer 37, which contained pottery similar to that found in layer 4, was obviously contemporary with that layer, but differed greatly in character. Whereas layer 4 consisted of a relatively smooth dark soil, layer 37, being a mixture of layers 38, 42 and other graveyard deposits, was medium grey-brown in colour, and contained fragments of flint, stone, brick, chalk, mortar, and a great quantity of human bone, resembling layers 515 and 763–766 in the 1976–78 excavations. Layer 37 was sealed by layers 36 and 35, which would appear to be the equivalent of layers 2 and 3 to the south of the lady chapel, and to have been subsequently cut and contaminated by a number of pipe-trenches for the hospital, and the foundation trench for the hospital boundary wall. The pottery from these demolition deposits is discussed below.

The other main features revealed in the area to the west of the chantry chapel and to the south of the nave were the four table tombs, nos. 10, 11, 12 and 13. The remainder of the ground was not excavated below about 15.00 m. O.D. to avoid disturbing burials, though it was clear from the level already reached that the ground had been used as a cemetery for a long period, causing much disturbance and the redepositing of human bones.

TOMB MONUMENTS (Fig. 10, 8–13)

The other excavated features which remain to be described are six tomb monuments all lying approximately on a level with the nave floor. They were too fragmentary to be consolidated and displayed, so have now been backfilled and turfed over by the Department. The burials they are presumed to have commemorated were not investigated. They were all presumably ransacked for grave slabs in the eighteenth century. They will be described from east to west (see numbers on Fig. 10).

8. South-east of the lady chapel was a rectangular chalk foundation approximately 1 × 2 m. built over a roughly mortared arch (Plate XXXI, a). Excavation on the north side of the arch showed the space underneath had been backfilled with disturbed bones and that both the arch and outer buttress of the lady chapel had disturbed earlier burials when they were constructed, though it was not possible to say which of them was the later. The top of the chalk was on a level with the top of the outer buttress which could indicate a late date. The foundations of the chalk went down at least 30 cm. below the mortar spread around the foot of the buttress.

9. Near the southern end of the fallen wall was a similar rectangular chalk foundation, 2.20 × 1.50 m. standing 48 cm. above the top of the level of the medieval burials (layer 4). Its surface had a crushed appearance which could have been the result of masonry from the church having fallen on top of it. Embedded on top of it were two small pieces of Purbeck marble with a hollow-chamfered edge, all that remained of the grave slab.

10. Foundations for the western buttress of the fourteenth-century chantry chapel had cut into the chalk foundations of another altar tomb, the surviving dimensions of which measured 1.22 m. × 2.05 m. It was built of flint on chalk. The top of part of its east end (east of the section in Fig. 16) had been lowered 10 cm. to facilitate the setting of the first course of facing stones on the west buttress of the chapel. The tomb, therefore, antedates the chapel but is likely to be late medieval because of the build-up of the ground-level around there.

11. 2.80 m. due west of Tomb 10 were the fragmentary foundations of a tomb, *c.* 1.60 m. × 60 cm., composed of re-used Caen-stone ashlars (layer 49) *c.* 20 cm. × 15 cm. high.

12. A rough chalk-block foundation, *c.* 2.40 × 1.20 m., lying 4 m. south south-west of 11. A number of thirteenth- and fourteenth-century potsherds (including Fig. 86, no. 24) were recovered from the area of this tomb, possibly derived from the soil displaced by its construction.

13. (F48) Chalk blocks and re-used roof-tiles formed a rectangular box structure *c.* 1.25 × 2.50 m. lying 1 m. south of Tomb 12. The interior which measures 2.40 m. × 34 cm. had been robbed (Plate XXXI, b).

RECONSTRUCTED ELEVATIONS OF THE PRESBYTERY (Fig. 15)

J.C. THORN

Exterior Evidence of Pilasters

None of the exterior ashlar connected with the presbytery and crypt has survived above the present ground level *in situ*. The exterior face of the north transept chapel of St. John the

Evangelist shows only the lower portion of the original facing *in situ* (Fig. 3a). It has a continuous chamfered plinth with courses of ashlar above, and pilasters placed at regular intervals.

The discovery of the fallen wall (Figs. 13, 14, 15) proved that pilasters identical to those on the chapel had extended around the presbytery (Fig. 15). However, no chamfered plinth was found in the debris, suggesting that this part of the wall had remained *in situ*, and had subsequently disappeared. This missing part has been included in the reconstruction at crypt level, based on a comparable example from the chapel (5). The corresponding north transept chapel plinth had been rebedded when the late fourteenth-century windows were inserted into the crypt (8 and 10).

The fallen wall was found in close proximity to the crypt (Fig. 10) and consisted of a main and intermediate pilaster (Fig. 15, 1 and 2). Their original position was established by correlation with the known bay width between the crypt pilasters (11), and the space between them indicated the span of the windows. The main pilaster has a simple chamfered string-course in the body of the ashlar. This is identical to the string-course surviving *in situ* on the north aisle wall, from which the level of the southern string-course may be deduced. The overall height of the wall was indicated by an impression of the corbel table (3) in the soil beyond the fallen wall.

Evidence of Windows

The fallen wall (Fig. 14, b) includes the eastern reveal of a large ambulatory window with an arch springer belonging to a lancet opening. This shows that the ambulatory windows of the presbytery had been radically altered to the Early English style. However, the voussoirs of an original Romanesque window were found in the tumble nearby (see p. 99). They can be compared with the contemporary windows still in the north aisle wall of the nave. These suggest that the presbytery windows originally had a smaller opening, with the outer sill level with the chamfered string-course (4). On the interior, the splays may have been half a bay wide and probably reached the soffit of the ambulatory vault (20). Restricted by the height of the vault above and the string-course below, the Romanesque windows would have been about one third the height of the later lancets.

The surviving mouldings (Fig. 14, b) show that the inserted lancets occupied the entire space between the pilasters both on the exterior (6) and on the interior splay (7), and that they cut the string-course (4). The outermost order of the window consisted of small pieces of chamfered ashlar tucked behind, and not bonded like quoins to the pilaster body. The remains of another lancet window were found further east of the fallen wall (see p. 101). In the nearby debris were several pieces of carved Purbeck marble relating to some embellishment in the presbytery. These consisted of a bell capital (p. 105, no. 94), shaft ring (p. 105, no. 93) and numerous long segments of connecting shafts (p. 105) supporting an arch with three rolls (no. 143). Miscampbell has suggested that these form the inner surround of the splayed window. It is very likely that they replaced part of the bay columns (16) by removing the quarter-round shafts and tucking the shaft-rings into the body of the splay (14). Below the lancet window, on the interior, there was evidence for a string-course (17). There may have been a Romanesque blind arcade below the window, later dismantled and re-used in the lancet windows.

Of the original crypt windows only the sills and reveals survive, on the north side of the church, and they are extremely small. By contrast, the southern windows were completely removed and the openings enlarged to form two-light windows (8) in the late fourteenth century. This alteration removed the chamfered plinth between the external pilasters (5) and lowered the ground surface. The reveals of these new windows extended to the crypt pilasters (11), and a re-used string-course was placed on their sills (9).

One of these two-light windows had been forced through the wall thickness in what was originally a blind bay (10). This would have removed the base of a main pilaster, bringing the adjacent windows very close together, and substantially weakening the wall above.

Crypt and Presbytery Supports

The wall pilasters around the crypt ambulatory survive to their full height (11), and must have been matched by the surviving pier base (12). The inner group of column bases (13) remains, and early twentieth-century photographs (National Monument Record, BB 51/930) show they had cushion capitals which have since disappeared (19). At presbytery level no piers or pilasters have survived *in situ*, and it is only from the debris found that any indications are given (see p. 111). Half- and quarter-round shafts were found, suggesting that the ambulatory may have had a wall articulation similar in appearance to the north aisle of the nave. It is also possible that the outside of the wall would have been articulated by half-round shafts further east, by the south-east chapel.

Floor Levels

No floor levels have survived on the surrounding walls of the presbytery. It is only the crypt vault springer (18) above the wall pilaster (11) which indicates that the presbytery floor was higher in level than that of the nave. The remains of the north aisle wall arcading in the nave show the level of the capitals, and this is projected through to the presbytery (15), making allowances for the raised presbytery floor. The only feature to survive at gallery level is the pilaster base over the north aisle arcading against Ethelbert's Tower (Fig. 24). From this the level of the nave gallery can be established. The suggested position of the presbytery vault (20) and gallery floor (21) is based on the respective levels found in the north aisle of the nave. In the presbytery, the gallery floor and vault below must have been removed when the lancet windows were inserted.

THE LADY CHAPEL

CHRISTOPHER MISCAMPBELL and DAVID SHERLOCK

PLAN AND ELEVATION (Figs. 11, 12)

In England lady chapels were often located at the east end of Benedictine and other churches, and a number were built or re-built in this position at the end of the thirteenth century following a revival of the cult of St. Mary (see table 2, Fig. 12). Bury St. Edmund's, whose Abbot Anselm (1121–48) seems to have re-introduced the cult (Southern 1953, 239), built one after a fire of 1275, but it was sited to the east of the north transept (Fig. 12). At Chichester Cathedral the late twelfth-century lady chapel to the east of the high altar, opening off the ambulatory, was re-built *c.* 1300. There was a similarly sited lady chapel at St. Alban's completed *c.* 1310. Bishop Chisul's lady chapel in St. Paul's Cathedral was consecrated in 1314, but its situation is unknown. In view of the rivalry among the greater religious houses, it is perhaps surprising that St. Augustine's did not add a lady chapel to its east end in the thirteenth century, but then neither did Christchurch Cathedral (where the great Trinity Chapel already provided a monumental termination to the church). St. Augustine's (like Christchurch) had a chapel dedicated to the Blessed Virgin Mary in the north aisle of the nave as well as in the crypt.[11] The former at any rate continued as a lady chapel after the building of Dygon's eastern chapel at the beginning of the sixteenth century (Table 1). It is interesting that the two nearest major Benedictine houses, Canterbury Cathedral and Rochester Cathedral, built new lady chapels in the mid-fifteenth century and at the beginning of the sixteenth century, respectively. In Kent such chapels were perhaps a late development in the cult of the Virgin Mary. Neither Christchurch nor St. Andrew's, Rochester, however, built their lady chapels at the east end of the church but added them onto one of the main transepts: in placing a lady chapel at the east end, therefore, St. Augustine's might have been reviving an earlier tradition. Winchester Cathedral indeed had an eastern lady chapel by *c.* 1220, which was almost totally remodelled in the Perpendicular style (with a crypt) by Bishop Courtenay (1486–92). But it is doubtful whether the plan in the first period at St. Augustine's is as early as 1220. In elevation, the lady chapel would, no doubt, have been similar to those in Christchurch and in Rochester Cathedral which in turn probably looked to the royal chapels for inspiration as did Abbot Bere's King Edgar Chapel at Glastonbury. All these buildings are tall and unaisled with long windows between deep-stepped buttresses and low-pitched roofs.

We can only speculate on the arrangements connecting the presbytery and the lady chapel. A comparison of presumed floor levels suggests that there would have been steps down from the level of the ambulatory into the new lady chapel; however, the eastern apsidal chapel appears to have been left intact, with its ground-floor level becoming an entrance lobby for the lady chapel and the crypt level remaining in use as a chapel. On the other hand, it does seem strange that the builders of the new chapel did not destroy the old eastern apsidal chapel in order to achieve a straight-ended connection with the choir, and it remains a possibility that in fact the main level of the old chapel *was* pulled down while only the crypt was left intact, for the present evidence is confused by the alterations carried out in this area earlier this century for the use of the chapel by St. Augustine's College. Whatever precisely happened, the access to the new chapel at this point must have disrupted the arrangements associated with the shrines of St. Augustine and St.

11. Clapham (1955, 6). In the treasurer's account of 1468–69 there are recorded payments made to the 'warden of the chapel of Blessed Mary in the nave of the church' and to 'the warden of the chapel of Blessed Mary in the crypt' (Cotton 1939). The existence of these two chapels in 1468/9 is good evidence for the first eastern lady chapel not having yet been begun. The crypt chapel was re-dedicated in 1325 (Davis 1934, 439). An eastern crypt chapel dedicated to the Virgin was customary. It occurred *inter alia* beneath the high altar at Canterbury Cathedral from 1130. The cathedral also had an altar dedicated to the Virgin at the east end of the north aisle of the nave (Stubbs 1880).

Mellitus, and it may be that they were transferred from the old eastern chapel into the new.[12] Fragments of Perpendicular canopy work have certainly been found in the building debris (see stone report, p. 114, Fig. 29, no. 153). However, only the grave of Abbot John Dygon has been found in the chapel. It is just possible, judging from the inscription found in his grave (Potts 1920, 146–7) that this chapel was founded as a memorial chapel to that abbot in the same way that the nearly contemporary lady chapel at Westminster Abbey was a memorial to Henry VII and the Tudor family. As for the architect of the later chapel, it may have been Robert Vertue (*fl.* 1475; *d.* 1506) who also worked on Henry VII's chapel at Westminster, Bath Abbey and elsewhere and whose will directed that he should be buried at St. Augustine's (Harvey 1984, 306; see also above, p. 8).

ALIGNMENT

Finally, something must be said about the most striking feature of the plan, its deviation from the main alignment of the abbey church by some 5° to the north. There is no obvious topographical reason for this, such as unstable ground or an earlier building in the way, so it is tempting to speculate that it may be to do with the changing position of either magnetic north or sunrise at the time when the foundations were set out. Either or both explanations could have a bearing on the date and although they may each lead to circular arguments they are worth investigating briefly. More research could be done on both of these in the light of recent archaeological work on churches at Wells and elsewhere.[13]

Magnetic North

Various readings were taken with a prismatic compass in July 1977 and calculations made to compare magnetic north now with various positions of magnetic north on the known declination-inclination date-curve. In theory, if the main church and the lady chapel were both set out due east of magnetic north at the time of their foundations, then their axes indicate they would have been built in *c.* 1280 and *c.* 1360, respectively. A similar curve based solely on known foundation dates of churches, mainly in the Sussex area, gives dates of 1200 and 1500, respectively. For St. Augustine's the first obvious inference from these dates is that the late eleventh-century church was *not* set out by compass. But in the case of the lady chapel, if there is any truth in the 1360 date, then Abbot Dygon was indeed re-modelling an earlier building.[14]

12. Routledge 1902, 243. At Tynemouth Priory the shrine of St. Oswin may have been transferred to the fourteenth-century lady chapel on the north side of the church because it was so popular with visitors that it disturbed the services (Hadcock 1952, 12).
13. See for example the plan of the late Anglo-Saxon lady chapel and later developments in Wells Cathedral (*Current Archaeology*, 73 (1980), 80); also 'skew chancels' in Bulmer-Thomas 1979, 142–4.
14. For discussion on magnetic north, we are grateful to Dr A.J. Clark, formerly Geophysics Section, Ancient Monuments Laboratory, and Miss Jane Fox, Oxford Research Laboratory for Archaeology. See Aitken 1970, 77–78 and Searle 1975, 10–13.

Sunrise

It has been suggested that some medieval churches and chapels were laid out on certain saints' days according to the position of the sunrise. As the earth's axis alters there might be a possibility of dating them by sunrise. But there are even more difficulties here than with magnetic north since the axis moved only slightly and local horizons have to be taken into account. Results here were very inconclusive for either the day or year of the setting out of the lady chapel.[15]

TABLE 1

Documentary References to Lady Chapels and Altars at St. Augustine's

Year	*Chapel/Altar*	*Reference*
618	St. Mary's Chapel, built by King Eadbald, later swallowed up by Abbot Scotland's crypt; located on west side of Rotunda.	Plommer 1896 II, 6.
1325	Peter, Bishop of Hungary, dedicated the altar of St. John the Evangelist to the Blessed Virgin Mary; also the altar of the Blessed Virgin Mary in the crypt to the same virgin; also the altar of St. Mary in the infirmary.	Davis 1934, 439.
1463	'To painting the image of our Lady where the abbot lieth, 20*s*.'	Hussey 1915, 44.
1468/9	Payments to 'the warden of the chapel of Blessed Mary in the nave of the church and to the warden of the chapel of Blessed Mary in the crypt'.	Cotton 1939, 84.
1477	Burial in the porch of the chapel of St. Mary within the cemetery. Presumably the charnel chapel whose dedication is unknown.	Hussey 1915, 48.
1524	Burial 'in the body of the church as nigh to the chapel of St. Mary there as it may please my Lord Abbot . . . '	Hussey 1915, 45.

15. See Benson 1956, 205–213. For calculations of sun-rise at Canterbury on various festivals in various years, we are grateful to Ann Philox, H.M. Nautical Almanac Office, Herstmonceux.

TABLE 2

Selected List of English Lady Chapels with Dates

West	
1184–86	Glastonbury Abbey, on site of *vetusta ecclesia*
Free-standing North-East	
1271–86	Peterborough Cathedral
North-East	
1275-	Bury St. Edmund's Abbey
1450–55	Canterbury Cathedral (north-east of western transept)
South	
ante c. 1512	Rochester Cathedral (south-east of western transept)
East	
ante 1187	Chichester Cathedral, lengthened 1290–1300
c. 1220-	Winchester Cathedral with crypt (replaced 1493–1500)
1245–57	Norwich Cathedral (no longer extant)
1290–1300	Chichester Cathedral, replacing one of *ante* 1187
1300–37	Lichfield Cathedral
1310-	St. Alban's Abbey
1314-	St. Paul's Cathedral (no longer extant; position unknown)
1325	St. Augustine's Abbey, in the crypt (Davis 1934, 439)
c. 1330	St. Bartholomew's Priory, Smithfield
1350–1400	Tewkesbury Abbey (now lost)
1457–83	Gloucester Cathedral, replacing one of 1224
1497–1510	St. Augustine's Abbey, with crypt, replacing one of 1325
1493–1500	Winchester Cathedral, replacing one of *c.* 1220
1503–12	Westminster Abbey replacing one of 1220
Note also East	
1493–1525	Glastonbury Abbey, Edgar chapel on site of earlier chapel

IV. EXCAVATIONS BY HUMPHREY WOODS, 1976–78

H. WOODS

EXCAVATIONS

Excavations on the south side of the abbey church between the areas excavated by David Sherlock (1974–75) and Andrew Saunders (1955–57) were carried out during July 1976, July 1977 and July and August 1978.

For the purposes of the excavation and recording the total area was divided over the three seasons into six units: Areas I, II, III, IV, V and VIII (see Figs. 6 and 10). All features, layers and finds were given a series of numbers. Area I was allotted numbers 1 to 499; Area II numbers 500 to 699; Area IV numbers 700 to 999; Area III numbers 1000 onwards; Area V numbers 5000 onwards, and Area VIII numbers 8000 onwards. Although the arbitrary divisions of the total area, made before excavation commenced, were to disappear as excavation progressed and temporary baulks and sections were removed, the original system of numbering has been retained both in this report and in the permanent site archive. Areas I, II and III were commenced in 1976; the first two were finished in 1977, and Area III in 1978. Area IV was begun in 1977 and completed in 1978, and Areas V and VIII were excavated in 1978.

At the beginning of the 1976 season Areas I and II as initially numbered (that is, comprising the whole of Areas I, II and III as definitively numbered) were divided by a baulk 1 m. wide whose eastern face was 7 m. west of the eastern limit of excavation. The total area that year measured 23 m. from east to west and 8.80 m. from north to south. The northern limit of excavation was formed by the consolidated rubble core-work of the south aisle wall of the abbey church.

Post-Dissolution ground build-up to an average depth of 20 cm. was trowelled off before any structures were encountered. Once this had been removed, it became apparent that the area of excavation contained two buildings: a chapel, facing the sixth bay of the nave west of the crossing (Plates XXXIII and XXXV) and, juxtaposed to it, a rectangular building opposite the seventh and eighth bays (Plate XXXII). To the west of this was a large buttress. It was decided, therefore, to remove the baulk and sub-divide the excavation into three open areas: area III, to embrace the chapel; I, the area to its east; and II, the area to its west.

Area I

The latest feature was F31, a trench draining the area from north-east to south-west. It respected and skirted the southern buttress of the chapel (Plate XXXV). The looseness of its fill suggested that this trench represented the robbing of a medieval feature, probably one of the lead pipes of the abbey waterworks whose conduit head still survives on St. Martin's Hill. A conduit in the cemetery itself was referred to in a will of 1475 (see above p. 9).

The foundation trench for the chapel wall (1061) was solidly packed with several layers of clay, rubble and pebbles, none producing any dating evidence. The trench was sealed by the flint base for a tomb (67) (Plate XXXV). This was not removed as it had already been consolidated for display. The graves and other tomb bases from this area are listed in Table 15.

Area II

Building X was formed by walls 520, 530, 514A and 569 (Plate XXXII). Part of its northern wall (569) had been cut away by the boundary wall of the Kent and Canterbury Hospital in 1791 and only its north-east corner survived to any height (top 15.78 m. O.D., base 14.96 m. O.D.). The building materials used were chalk, ragstone, flint and Caen-stone and the footings were loosely bonded with a rough, crumbly pink mortar.

The west wall of building X was contiguous to buttress F519, which projected from the south aisle wall of the church (Plate XXXII). A robbing cut for the buttress had partially cut away footing 520 of building X, indicating that the latter had already been demolished when the buttress was robbed down to its present level (15.315 m. O.D.) (Plate XXXII). Despite the presence of two medieval sherds in the robbing cut, it is impossible to guess the date at which buttress 519 was reduced, since buttresses were often left standing when the walls to which they lent support had been entirely robbed away. The west wall of the abbey dormitory is an example of this: although the wall has vanished, two of its buttresses still survive to their full height. Buttress 519 was not primary. The primary buttress projecting only 60 cm. from the face of the aisle wall, survived in the form of two large blocks of ragstone chamfered on the eastern and southern edges. The secondary buttress, 519, had been butt-jointed onto this. It was composed of courses of flints with knapped faces carefully laid and bonded with an extremely hard, yellow mortar. Impressions of the ashlar blocks forming the southern face survived, showing this to have been 2.75 m. south of the original face.

Building X was slightly cut into ground surface 552 from which graves 549, 560, 574, 581, 589, 592, 595, 603 were cut (see Table 15). Its west wall partly covered graves 574, 595, 560 and 577. In grave 581 a bronze shroud pin was found lying on the left scapula. From grave 549 a halfpenny of Edward III was recovered. This was probably not lost before the 1350s. Grave 574 yielded a pewter six-pointed star, probably a pilgrim's badge (Fig. 69, no. 72).

Three more graves (see Table 15, 557, 577, 580) were dug into a layer of chalk and mortar (582). This layer yielded a cut halfpenny of Henry III, probably lost around 1260, but in any case by 1280. A layer of demolition material (553) overlay 514A, and the southern buttress of the adjacent chapel. This would indicate that both buildings were demolished simultaneously. 553 contained large quantities of tile, including decorated floor-tile and fragments of ashlar. The walls of the south aisle were still being taken down in 1553 (see p. 12) and, as the chapel is attached to the south aisle, this was probably taken down at the same time. Building X seals the final phase of burials in the lay cemetery, which would suggest it is a post-monastic structure

(Plate XXXII). If it were put up when the abbey was dissolved in 1538 and demolished in 1553, it would have had a life of only fifteen years. The most likely explanation for it would seem to be that it was a temporary workshop for the men engaged upon the task of dismantling the abbey. Its temporary nature would account for the shoddiness of its method of construction, so evident in its surviving footings.

Several layers of soil had accumulated in the gap between building X and the west wall of the chapel. These were eventually cut by a scaffold base (541) against wall 514A and a trench (573) against wall 512. A scaffold-post pipe (579) was accommodated within scaffold base 541, and the trench 573 would probably have supported a series of scaffolding posts. The scaffolding would have been used for taking down the chapel.

No foundation trench was found to the west of footing 512A such as was found in Area I for the east wall of the chapel, so it must be presumed that footing 512A occupied the full width of its foundation trench.

Area III

As in Area I, the latest feature was the trench running from north-east to south-west, in this area numbered 1027 (Plate XXXV). This cut through the demolition layers. At the bottom of the feature an articulated skeleton was partly exposed, lying in a moist black graveyard soil. This was not excavated.

The width of the interior of the chapel was covered by a series of post-demolition deposits. It appeared that loads of materials were dumped more or less simultaneously to fill the interior of the chapel and spilled over the area immediately to the south. A wide range of small finds was recovered from one of these deposits (layer 513) including two Nuremburg jetons of the sixteenth century. In other layers were fragments of a hollow chamfered memorial slab and one arm of a Purbeck marble cross (Fig. 37, no. 39, pp. 113, 130).

To the south of the chapel was a series of deposits of mortar, one upon another. The extreme hardness of these deposits suggested that the area had been used for washing mortar off ashlar stone after it had been taken down from the chapel and before resale as building material. Its deposition in a very wet state would account for its having dried to such a consistency. The mortar contained very little dating evidence, but a few sherds of pottery were recovered. A single scaffold base was cut through the mortar layer. It must have been associated with the taking down of the chapel. It was partly cut by the robber trench 1027 so there would probably have been more scaffold bases in the area occupied by the trench.

The south wall of the chapel had been completely robbed (Plate XXXIII, XXXV). This had clearly occurred while the rest of the building was being taken down, for large quantities of the building materials of the chapel were found in robber trench 1007. The trench contained many blocks of chalk ashlar with deep V-shaped chisel marks on the backs, for keying in. In addition there were quantities of Caen-stone ashlar, Caen-stone mouldings, a piece of upper greensand with a groove cut into one face, probably part of a window frame, one piece of moulded Purbeck marble and a number of nails and earthenware roof-tiles (see Figs. 36 and 37, nos. 18, 27, 28, 30, 32). A group of pottery was recovered, very similar to that in the demolition layers above. Robber trench 1007 was sealed by the demolition layers. The Caen-stone would have

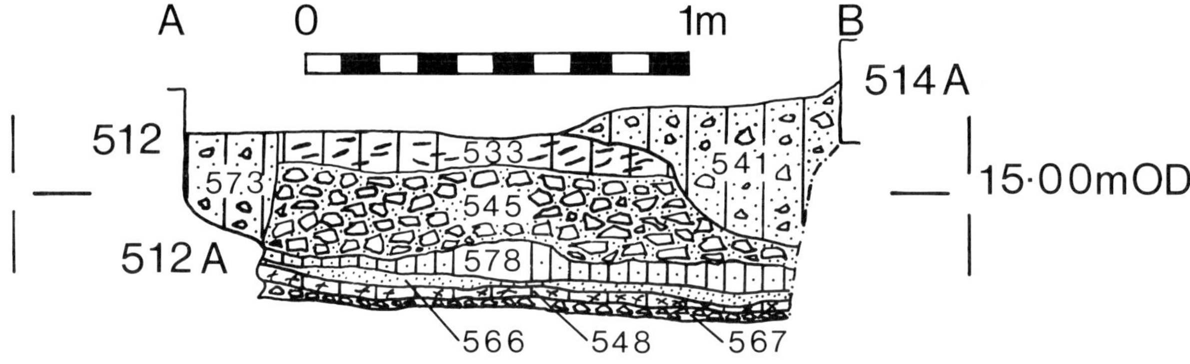

Fig. 17. Section A–B on Fig. 10.

come from the external and internal facings of the chapel. Caen-stone was used extensively for this purpose at St. Augustine's. The chalk, being a light stone, probably came from the vault of the chapel roof. Chalk is the material used in the surviving tunnel vault supporting the abbot's chapel in the west cloister range.

The removal of the fill of trench 1007 exposed immediately to the south a burial vault (1051) built of brick and chalk. The bottom of the trench reached a layer of moist black graveyard soil identical to that under ditch 1027. Much loose human bone was exposed but no articulated skeletons. On the northern side of the robber trench a cut for a grave was visible, sealed by the floor of the chapel.

The removal of all the demolition layers and robber material revealed the overall picture of the chapel (Plate XXXV). It was clearly not primary as the chamfered offset of its east wall, 1061, was butt-jointed onto the south aisle wall at a point above the chamfered offset of the latter. It had two buttresses at each of its exterior corners.

The mortar bedding for six grave slabs survived within the chapel (Plate XXXIII). The impressions of the slabs were side by side in a north–south line down the middle of the floor, and were bordered to east and west by a floor surface of re-used Roman tiles (Plate XXXIII). The chapel had every appearance of having been the chantry of a single family. To the south of the robbed south wall was the vault already mentioned and three sepulchral slabs (Plate XXXV, p. 130). It could be assumed that the graves covered by these slabs, and those contained in the vault, were members of the family for whom there was no burial space left within the chantry.

The core-work of the walls and buttresses was of flint bonded with a very hard yellow mortar. The lowest course of dressing survived on both faces of the eastern wall, F 1061. On the outside it consisted of chamfered blocks of greensand, with a single chamfered block of re-used oolite from the Roman town. At the point where tomb base 67 was butt-jointed onto wall 1061, a single stone of the first course above the chamfer survived. This was of Caen stone. The interior dressing was all of Caen-stone except at the point opposite buttress 1062 where there was a feature, F1065, which appeared to be a pier base, dressed with greensand. The pier was supported on a flint footing, 1066, protruding 1.04 m. from the west face of wall 1061. 1066 was in turn supported on layers of rammed hoggin cut in to the underlying black graveyard soil. A similar flint footing, feature 1067, supported on a hoggin foundation protruded from the west wall of the chapel, F512, in a corresponding position to F1066. There were several large settlement cracks in 1066 and the footing was pulling away from wall 1061, as a result of the robbing of the south wall.

An 80 cm. stretch of the internal facing of wall 512 survived at the point where this was butt-jointed onto the south aisle wall. This facing was of Caen-stone. Elsewhere on the inside face of this wall clear impressions in the mortar showed where the ashlar had been robbed. On the west face of the wall a 2.06 m. stretch of the facing survived where it ran south to meet buttress 531. This facing was all of Caen-stone with the exception of one large block of Purbeck marble. Purbeck marble was the material used to dress the outer faces of buttresses 531 and 1064, except on the north-west corner of buttress 531, where the dressing was of Caen-stone. This use of Purbeck marble on the exterior of the chapel points to a late date for the chapel, as Purbeck was used only for interiors in the period when it was first introduced.

The tiled surface bordering the impressions of the sepulchral slabs was of re-used Roman tiles (Plate XXXIII). None was complete and they had been laid almost like crazy paving. The edges almost met the flint footings of the east and west walls but were 10 cm. distant from the faces of the walls, which would suggest that the Roman tiles merely served as the matrix for the floor of the chapel. There was some mortar in their bedding. On the east side of the chapel the surfaces of many of the tiles had been mortared over and there were fragments of decorated medieval tiles in the demolition layer directly above the Roman tiles. Presumably, the floor of decorated tiles would have been carried up to the ashlar faces of the east and west walls.

The mortar bedding for the tomb slabs contained some interesting finds. Layer 1009 had gouge marks indicating the use of a crowbar to prise up the tomb slab which had lain on it. Layer 1010 was the bedding for a Purbeck tomb slab, one fragment of which was still *in situ* (SF 190, Plate XXXIII). Three other fragments from the same slab had already been recovered from the demolition layer above (Fig. 37, no. 39, p. 130). In layer 1011 part of a plain Purbeck slab survived.

In the bedding for another slab, layer 1012, a number of painted architectural fragments had been used to build up a flat surface. To its west, more painted mouldings were found in layer 1004, used (like the Roman floor-tiles), as a matrix for the floor, their moulded surfaces being turned face downwards and their flat backs uppermost. The fact that these mouldings were painted and, in one case, had mortar adhering, shows they were not masons' waste but had been used.

At the time when the chapel was being built, therefore, some part of the abbey was being torn down or repaired. The two voussoirs (Fig. 36, no. 16, p. 128) could have come from the aisle window, which went out of use when the chantry chapel was built.

Layer 1013 appeared to be the last burial within the chapel. Some slivers of Purbeck marble from its tomb slab adhered to its surface. It was, therefore, decided to excavate this as a sample of the six graves within the chapel (Plate XXXV). The skeleton was in a wooden coffin 50 cm. wide at the head and 27 cm. wide at the foot (see Table 15). The wood was well preserved in the moist grave fill and has been identified as elm. The coffin nails were all *in situ*. The lid had collapsed and the remnants were found lying over the skeleton.

Of the graves to the south of the chapel, only vault 1051 had been disturbed. It must originally have had a cover but this had been removed and an accumulation of deposits was found covering it. The vault was constructed of chalk ashlar, brick and flint. In the backfill of the vault a lead-alloy *méreau* (p. 245) was found. Near the bottom was a well-preserved skeleton which had been in a wooden coffin, and below that was an earlier burial in a lead coffin (see Table 15, 1054, 1056). The top of the lead coffin was very corroded in the area underlying the stomach and intestines of the burial above it, presumably as a result of fluids draining through, but the rest of the coffin was in an excellent state of preservation, as was the individual inside it, who was a woman aged between 18 and 25. Nails were found around the coffin showing that the lead coffin had been contained within a wooden coffin. Some fragments of the outer coffin survived and were identified as probably of oak. The coffin was tailored around the body to fit exactly and the lead sheet was drawn up over the face in such a way as to indicate its shape (Plate XXXIV). When the coffin was opened many fragments of a woollen shroud were found. The head was wrapped in a woollen bandage, the hair and organic matter surviving within this wrapping (see p. 235). In the walls of the vault to the north and south of the head-piece of the coffin, grooves had been cut for the passage of ropes used in lowering the coffin into the vault which was 1.12 m. deep (Plate XXXIV). The coffin was 48 cm. wide at the shoulders but only 24 cm. wide at the feet so no rope grooves were needed at the foot end.

When the coffin was lifted, many more nails were found under it on a surface of compacted sandy clay loam flecked with mortar, which served as the base of the vault. Below the vault was moist black graveyard soil, identical to that under ditch 1027 and robber trench 1007. Loose charnel in this layer probably represented the late Anglo-Saxon graveyard level (see p. 81).

Three sepulchral slabs were also found to the south of the chapel (Cat. No. 40, p. 130, SF405, 406, 407; Plate XXXV). The vault 1051 had partially cut away grave 1059 on its southern side, so clearly slab 406, approximately over the grave, had been moved slightly southwards to allow for the construction of the vault. Slab 405, to the east of 406, was not lifted due to shortage of time. Slab 407, to the south of 405 was lifted and a grave found lying directly underneath it (1060, see Table 15).

Area IV

Area IV was the westward continuation of Area II up to the point where the north boundary wall of the Kent and Canterbury Hospital returned south at a right angle. The western and northern limits of the area were defined by structures 702 and 741. The removal of the hospital wall exposed the remainder of structure 702, which, to its west and north, had been partially examined by Saunders during his excavations between 1955 and 1957 (Saunders 1978, 33, 35). The lowest course of facing stone survived along the whole of the east side of 702 and also at its south-east corner (Plate XXXVI). The facing was of rag and Caen-stone, toothed deeply into the flint core-work. The mortar impressions of the second course survived, showing it to have been set back 6 cm. from the face of the lowest course (Plate XXXVI). The pink mortar bonding the facing stones was in marked contrast to the yellow mortar of the core-work, showing that the structure had been refaced. To the east of 702, below nineteenth- and twentieth-century layers were robber trenches containing an eighteenth-century clay pipe. These trenches cut a spread of mortary layers (719), which had been laid while wet and had set on the ground like those in Area III. They gave the appearance of having been washed-off ashlar blocks, which had been taken from the abbey walls for resale as building material. Layer 726 contained three blocks of Caen-stone ashlar laid end to end, each bearing an identical mason's mark (Fig. 37, no. 35). Sealed below layers 719 and 726 were two trenches containing four stone-lined scaffold holes. The wide variety of stones used had been taken from the abbey. They included two quarter-round Caen-stone column drums, a fragment of banded shaft and part of a Caen-stone capital (Fig. 35, no. 4). The unworked stones included Portland, rag, greensand, Caen, oolitic limestone, chalk and flint, together with one piece of Roman tile.

The second structure exposed by the removal of the 1791 hospital wall was a buttress (740). It was opposite the ninth pier base (westward from the crossing) of the arcade dividing the nave from the south aisle (Plate XL). The graves from this area (758, 773, 775, 787) are tabulated (Table 15).

Between 702 and 740 a series of tips dating from the immediately post-Dissolution period to the eighteenth century were cleared away. Their removal exposed the top of the footing of structure 702 and the full dimensions of buttress 740. 702 was built on a footing of flint bonded with yellow mortar. The eastern face of the footing was not parallel with the face of the superstructure. To the north, the footing extended 12 cm. beyond the face, and to the south 1.16 m. (Plate XL). The excavated length of buttress 740 was 2.40 m. Its southern limit corresponded to the mortar impressions of the southern face of buttress 519 in Area II. Like buttress 519 it would, therefore, have extended 3.35 m. south from the face of the south aisle wall and, although nothing survives of the aisle wall or its primary buttresses at this point, it must be presumed that feature 740, like 519, was of secondary build.

Above ground the aisle wall is absent from the eighth bay west of the crossing, though below ground the north side of its footings was excavated by Saunders (1978, 36–8). A cutting was laid across the turf immediately east of Saunders' trench VII in order to establish the line of the southern face of the wall and examine the relationship of structure 702 to the south aisle wall.

The first feature encountered below ground was a stretch of masonry (741), which was the southern face of the foundation for the south aisle wall. It was built of ragstone, roughly faced on the south and laid in courses bonded with a loose mortar mix of sand and small ballast. The backs of the stones had not been dressed. The layer (747) covering the foundation contained eighteenth-century finds including pottery, clay-pipe stems and one clay pipe bowl. The fact that the ragstone facing of the foundation had been left when the core of the wall was robbed would suggest that the core-work was of a different material, and that the robbers only wanted this particular material. Flint is found as core material in all the walls of the abbey surviving above ground, so it seems likely that it would also have been used in the core of the foundation. A layer of extremely hard rammed mortar and rubble (750) supported the south aisle foundation and also ran under structure 702 (Plate XXXVII).

In order to examine more fully the relationship of structure 702 and buttress 740 to the south aisle foundations, Area IV was continued to the natural brickearth in an area measuring 4.20 m. north and south and 3.76 m. east and west at its southern limit. The northern limit was defined by structures 702, 740 and 741 and measured 4.40 m. east–west (Plate XL).

Along the line of feature 741 the turf was stripped off to see if masonry 741 survived at the junction with buttress 740. Under the turf, robber backfill, layer 778, was encountered consisting of yellow crushed mortar and loose brown loam with small gravel pebbles. The removal of robber fill 778 exposed more of masonry 741. Its highest surviving point was at

14.729 m. O.D., but at the junction with buttress 740 it had been robbed as low as 14.311 m. O.D. Buttress 740 was butt-jointed onto masonry 741 (Plate XXXVIII).

Under the sixteenth- to eighteenth-century deposits between 702 and 741 were demolition layers containing red earthenware roof-tiles, many with round peg-holes surviving, occasional small fragments of glazed tile, fragments of burnt Caen-stone and many twisted pieces of lead window cames. Below the demolition debris was the ground surface at the time of the Dissolution of the abbey containing various lumps of chalk, Caen-stone chippings, some animal bone and quantities of human charnel. Dug into the old ground level were two stone-lined scaffold bases. Since they were sealed by the demolition debris, they must represent an early stage in the dismantling of the buildings. Cut through the ground level just south of buttress 740 was a grave (787) which had been dug to respect the buttress. There was no trace of a coffin and the skeleton was in very poor condition.

At the foot of 741 was a 16 cm. offset, 741A, on the south aisle foundation (Plate XXXVIII). Tipped down against the offset was a layer containing a cut halfpenny of King Edward the Confessor (790) sealed well below the Dissolution ground level 784. Beside it were several large blocks of Kentish rag in layers 793 and 797. The blocks were not dressed, but they gave the appearance of having been heaped up ready for masons to dress them for incorporation into the foundations of the south aisle wall. This stock must have proved surplus to requirements, and was subsequently covered with a series of tips and dumped layers. Sealed by layer 797 was layer 794, which yielded a coin from south Italy, of Robert Guiscard as Duke of Apulia (1076/7). Sealed by layer 794 was the foundation trench, F 796, for the south wall footing, and layers 795, 798 and 799. Layer 798 yielded a shallow bowl of the eleventh century. The foundation trench was cut from layer 795 (Plate XXXVIII). Trench 796 was filled with mixed brickearth, loam and gravel. Against the foundation 741A droppings of mortar were encountered in the backfill at the base of each course of stone. In addition, the brickearth backfill occupied the interstices between each course of stone. This interleaving of mortar droppings and brickearth showed that the construction trench had been backfilled in a continuous controlled operation as the foundation was built up from its base.

The bottom of the foundation trench for the south aisle wall was made up of compacted rubble 801 (Fig. 18). This rubble was excavated as far as was physically possible (82 cm.). Along the south edge of 801 was a layer of grey-brown clay loam which was cut by structure 702. Under the loam 807/809 was clean natural brickearth. What must have happened was that the construction trench for the south aisle wall was dug into the natural brickearth, but a short space of time elapsed before the rubble 801 was poured in. This interval was long enough for soils from the deposits overlying the brickearth (see below) to collapse down the side of the trench, perhaps as the result of rain.

At the eastern end of the foundation trench (796) the rammed hoggin foundation for buttress 740 was partly visible. The hoggin was above a bed of flint bonded with yellow mortar, very like the footing of structure 702. Sealed by layer 799 was the late Anglo-Saxon graveyard (803). It had been cut by foundation trench 796. A total of twelve individuals were represented among the bones (see table 15); all the graves were so intersected that no complete skeleton survived (Plate XXXIX). The skull of 803C rested on a cushion of flints, a practice which evidently survived at St. Augustine's until immediately before the Conquest, for layer 803 was below the dump of charnel (790) containing the coin of Edward the Confessor (see above). A total of 47 individuals were represented in the charnel. These bones must derive from skeletons from the cemetery to the south and south-west of the Anglo-Saxon Church of Sts. Peter, Paul and Augustine.

Much of this cemetery would have been destroyed by the digging of the construction trenches for the south aisle and south-west corner of the Romanesque abbey church, the resultant charnel being employed to help raise the ground level to the south of the new church.

Three more layers (804, 805 and 806) were found below the Anglo-Saxon graveyard (803) before natural brickearth was reached. They contained exclusively Belgic and Roman pottery and must represent midden carted out of the Roman town along the road to Richborough and dumped along the roadside (see p. 80). Layers 804, 805 and 806 had collapsed down the side of the south aisle construction trench (796) to form 807/809 (Fig. 18). A coin of Constantine II was found in layer 809.

Of the three structures examined in the part of Area IV taken down to natural, namely structures 702, 740 and 741, structure 741 was the earliest, being cut from layer 795, which was sealed by layer 794 containing the coin of Robert Guiscard of Apulia (1076/7). The other two were later and probably contemporary, being cut from 784, the Dissolution ground level. 702 and 740 cut all the layers sealed below 784, with the exception of layer 801. The foundation for buttress 740 rested on layer 801 (see above). Structure 702 did not reach 801, nor did it reach natural brickearth; it terminated in 806 (Fig. 18).

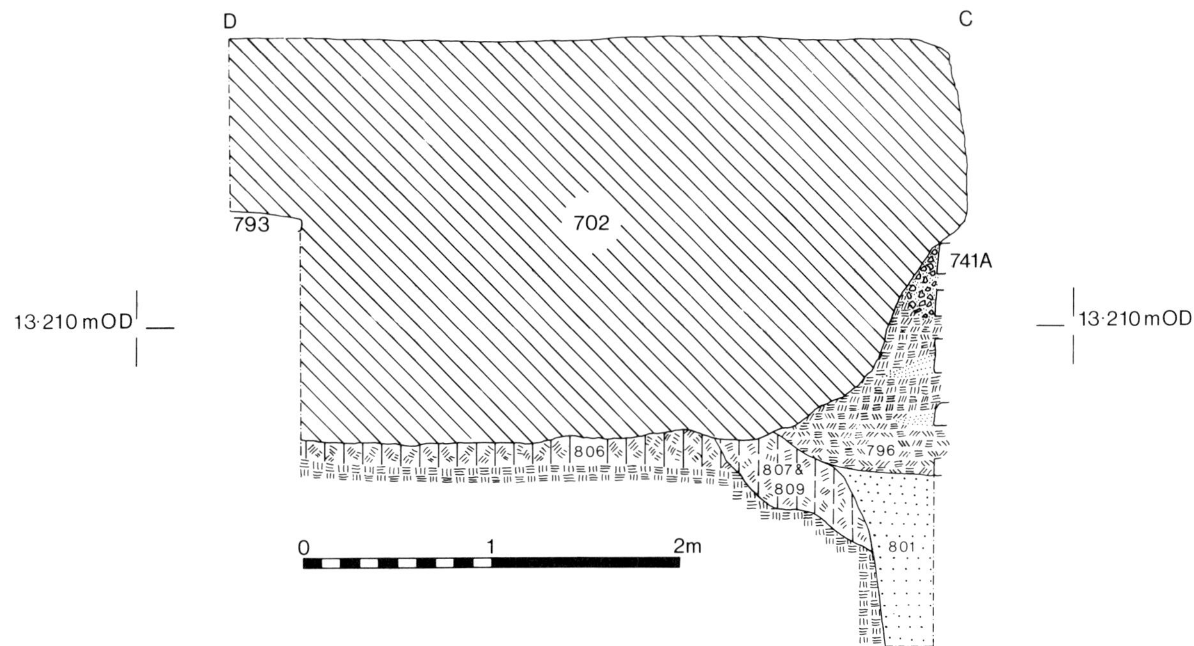

Fig. 18. Section C–D, on Fig. 10.

Area V

Area V was to the south and west of the structure numbered 702 in Area IV (Plate XL). Area V also embraced the ground between the west side of the structure and the late Anglo-Saxon tower excavated by Saunders (1978, 32–5), extending slightly south of the old hospital boundary wall. When the hospital wall was removed, a number of moulded stones from the abbey buildings were found in it. A selection of these is illustrated below (Figs. 35 and 36, nos. 2, 3, 17). Northwards, area V went as far as the chalk wall in Trench IIA of Saunders' excavation.

Area V was important because it revealed the relationships and function of several structures at the west end of the abbey. To the south of the buildings, the Anglo-Saxon and later medieval graveyard continued, with a certain amount of sixteenth- to nineteenth-century debris on top. Excavation started at the level of modern turf (14.69 m. O.D.) where Saunders had excavated and at the level of twentieth-century tarmac (16.29 m. O.D.) in the area which had, until 1978, been enclosed by the hospital boundary wall. The surface of the Anglo-Saxon graveyard was reached at 13.77 m. O.D.

The latest feature was a pit partially cutting into the core-work of the structure numbered 702 in Area IV and 5140 in Area V. Its fill included nineteenth-century bottles and ceramics, not discussed in the pottery report but recorded in the archive. The pit was itself cut into layers containing further nineteenth-century ceramics.

The graves in the area south of the buildings are discussed in Table 15. Within this area, built up over the Anglo-Saxon cemetery, only the features relating to the buildings will be discussed below.

Various bases for scaffold poles were found (5057, 5058, 5084, 5085, 5086, 5079, 5081, 5082, 5093, 5096, 5097, 5100, 5118). Many were lined with stone from the abbey buildings including a voussoir and the base of an angle shaft from 5085 (Fig. 36, no. 12), a quarter-round column drum with a mason's mark, a piece of twelfth-century 'barley sugar' column (Fig. 36, no. 8) and a large fragment of a column with multiple shafting, all from 5081.

There was a substantial trench (5078) dug parallel to 5140. It measured 8.36 m. east and west, was 42 cm. wide at the western end and 1.22 m. wide at the eastern end, and had a maximum depth of 29 cm. It was full of mortar, large flints and stones. This trench must represent the work of undermining in 1793. A similar trench (5129) was found to the east of wall 5130, which ran south from the late Anglo-Saxon tower excavated by Saunders. The trench was probably dug to accommodate scaffolding for dismantling wall 5130 although no scaffold bases were visible in the 83 cm. length of the trench which was exposed. Wall 5130 was butt-jointed onto the Anglo-Saxon tower (5105), so was clearly later. It had been trench-poured and was bonded with pink mortar.

Layers 5071, 5074, 5087, 5088 and 5089 were the equivalent of layers 754 to 766 in Area IV. Although all the pottery from these layers in Area V was residual medieval, late sixteenth- and seventeenth-century pottery was recovered from layers 754 to 766, so the equivalent layers in Area V must also represent made ground of the late sixteenth and seventeenth century. Layer 5089 sealed a trench of semicircular profile (5120) running north and south, placed centrally between structures 5105 and 5108. It was 52 cm. deep. Its position suggested that it might have originally accommodated a lead pipe, perhaps to take rainwater away from the roof.

A construction surface (5158/5159) of dark brown soil mixed with many small pieces of chalk, some flints and a few pebbles spread between 5105 and footing 5107A, and to the south of 5140. Layers 5158/5159 were sealed by very dark brown soil with some large flints, a few Roman bricks and a large quantity of human charnel (5156/5157). These layers had clearly been dug up from the Anglo-Saxon graveyard (5160/5161) which lay immediately below layers 5158/5159. The graveyard had been disturbed by the digging of the foundations of the south-west corner of the Norman church and its contents dumped over the construction surface. This closely reflects the sequence of layers 790, 793, 797 and 794 in Area IV, which accumulated when the Norman south aisle footing was constructed.

The graveyard (5160/5161) was the equivalent to layer 803 in Area IV. Shortage of time and money prevented the excavation of this part of the graveyard, although the trowelling off of the top 36 cm. exposed four articulated skeletons (5160 A, B, C, D; see Table 15). There were no discernible grave cuts for any of these. Burial 5160C was chopped at the ankles by footing 5107A. Its skull was supported on a pillow of Roman tiles and chalk. The left leg of 5160D had been destroyed below the knee by structure 5105 and from the sixth lumbar vertebra upwards by wall 5130. Skeleton 5160D was not lifted but the other three were, and are discussed below (p. 311).

Layer 5160 was cut by a rubble footing (5165) which supported the chalk wall (5106), exposed in Trench IIA of Saunders' excavation (Plate XLI). A hole had been cut into the east face of structure 5105 and rubble footing 5165 keyed into it. At the point where 5165 was keyed in, there was a vertical settlement crack in 5105 and the structure had canted over slightly to the north. The footing 5165 was cut by footing 5107A, which was butted up against wall 5106. Footing 5165 was not excavated in Area V, but the corresponding layer in Area VIII, 8001, was excavated and is described below.

The top of layer 5160 was at 13.77 m. O.D., whereas the top of layer 803 in Area IV was 13.35 m. O.D. The late Anglo-Saxon ground surface was, therefore, on a gentle gradient, the ground rising to the south of the churches. This gradient was reflected in all the later layers superimposed above the Anglo-Saxon ground surface.

The construction trench (5104) for footings 5107 and 5107A had been emptied in earlier excavations and was found to contain recent backfill. The offset footing 5107A, which occupied the inside width of the trench, was cut from layer 5147 right down and into the Anglo-Saxon graveyard 5160.

Footing 5140 (Figs. 22, 23) cut layers 5115, 5134, 5136, 5143, 5144, 5149, 5151, 5153, 5157, 5159 and 5161 and graves 5139 and 5148. Footing 5140 was essentially the same as 702, being of flint rubble bonded with yellow mortar, trench-poured from layer 5115 at 14.36 m. O.D. At a distance of 4.28 m. west of the east face of 702, footing 5140 kinked in by 10 cm., suggesting that the structure might have been built in two stages, the eastern arm in one and the southern arm in another (Plate XL). Two blocks of the ragstone facing of 5140 survived, 36 cm. north of the edge of the footing (Plate XL). As in Area IV this facing was bonded with pink mortar, in marked contrast to the yellow mortar of the core-work, indicating that the facing was not primary. Running westwards from the surviving facing stones was a line of pink mortar indicating the position of the remainder of the facing.

Footing 5107 was of quite different nature from 5140 and 702, though similar to the refacing of these footings. It was of ragstone blocks, bonded with pink mortar. The same was true of 5107A (Plate XLI). At the junction of 5140 and 5107 was a structure, feature 5108, which gave the appearance of being the base of a newel stair (Plate XL). Feature 5108 projected 64 cm. west of the face of 5107 and 36 cm. south of the face of 5140. It was only one course deep, and its highest surviving point was 14.77 m. O.D. Like 5107 it was constructed of ragstone bonded with pink mortar. Its bottom was at 14.57 m. O.D., and rested on layer 5103 (see above). Resting on 5108 were dressed ragstone blocks, feature 5141, which must have been the lowest treads of the stair (Plate XL). The top of these was at 14.93 m. O.D. Like 5107 and 5108 they were bonded with pink mortar, and the mortar between 5141 and 5108 was packed with oyster shells. This method of preventing mortar from falling out of freshly bonded stonework was quite commonly employed in the late Middle Ages.

Wall 5106 was of chalk (Plate XLI). The top of the footing was of dressed blocks, below which were pieces of chalk which had been dressed only very roughly, the whole footing being supported on layer 5165. The highest surviving point was at 14.63 m. O.D. It had been robbed at the junction with structure 5105, so its relationship to 5105 could not be determined, though layer 5165 was demonstrably later than 5105, as has already been described, and footings 5107 and 5107A were later than both 5106 and 5165: 5107 and 5107A were butted up against 5106, 5107A curving in to meet it, and in addition 5107A cut layer 5165 (Plate XLI).

Area VIII

Area VIII measured 5.60 m. east and west and 5.82 m. north and south. Its east boundary was parallel to the west boundary of the cutting laid across the south aisle footing in Area IV, and was 1.95 m. west of this. It ran from feature 702 to the line of the north face of the south aisle footing, extrapolated from the surviving stonework to the east. The west section ran from the north face of wall 5106 (see above under Area V) to a footing, feature 8014, which runs north and south between the south aisle footing and the sleeper wall supporting the arcade between the nave and south aisle (Plate XLII). Area VIII was defined to the north by the line of the north face of the south aisle footing, and to the south by structure 702 and 5140 of Area V. Features 702, 5140 and 5106 in this area were not renumbered with numbers in the 8000 series. Moreover, 5140 is here referred to as the southern arm of 702. Saunders had trenched Area VIII of the current excavations down to the level of the rammed mortar and rubble which, in Area IV of the current excavations, had been found to support the surviving stonework of the south aisle footing. The backfill of Saunders' trench VII was isolated and emptied (Saunders 1978, Fig. 6). The removal of this backfill showed that down to the level of the rammed mortar and rubble, layer 8001, most of Area VIII consisted of eighteenth-century robber material. This layer, of mortar, small fragments of flint and rubble mixed with earth and dust, corresponded to layer 747 in Area IV. A number of clay pipe-stems and sherds of the eighteenth century were recovered from it. Some fragments of structure had survived the robbing. Abutted by structure 8014 was a single ragstone, feature 8017, which had previously been exposed in Saunders' Trench VII. To the west of this was feature 8015, which consisted of two more ragstones, one on top of another, and abutting structure 8014. The level on the top of the upper one was 13.96 m. O.D. (Plate XLII).

In the angle formed by the east face of footing 5107 and the north face of the southern arm of 702 was a group of very large blocks of worked ragstone, feature 8013 (Plates XLII, XLIII).

One of them was chamfered like the ragstone bases of the buttresses of the church, of which one was encountered in the primary phase of feature 519 (Area II), and of which several survive on the north side of the church and on the exterior of the apse projecting from the north transept. All the other stones were worked and moulded, but the purpose for which they were originally worked could not have been ascertained without taking the feature to pieces. All that can be said as a general comment is that they were typical of the stones at the bases of buttresses, piers, and internal pilasters of the building period spanned by the abbacies of Scotland and Wido. The level on the top stone was 14.66 m. O.D. East of feature 8013 were two further pieces of ragstone, feature 8016, one of which was a large dressed block abutting 702 (Plate XLII). Its top was at 13.93 m. O.D. Features 8013, 8015, 8016 and 8017 all rested on layer 8001 (Plate XLII).

A section was laid north–south across 8001 (Fig. 20; Plate XLIV) and the eastern half of the area excavated. Layer 8001, which was 15 cm. thick, was found to consist of loose beige mortar, flint chippings and small fragments of chalk (Plate XLIV). The upper part yielded prolific quantities of Roman tile and brick, and some coloured window glass. This probably came from the destroyed Anglo-Saxon church of Sts. Peter, Paul and Augustine (see p. 135).

The removal of layer 8001 exposed a line of ragstone blocks, feature 8018, the highest of which was at 13.52 m. O.D. (Fig. 19). These lined up with feature 741A in Area IV. They were apparently employed as a revetment to the core of the south aisle footing, layer 8019, which was of mortar rubble, with occasional flints and pieces of ragstone. To the south of feature 8018 was the construction trench for the south aisle foundation, feature 8002 (Plate XLVI). This corresponded to trench 796 in Area IV. As in trench 796, below each course of ragstone revetting, the mortar forming the core of the foundation was found to have spilt into trench 8002 and interleaved with the brickearth backfill of 8002, demonstrating that as each course of revetting was laid and the mortar rubble core rammed down, brickearth backfill was simultaneously shovelled into the vacant part of the construction trench to fill this up to the same level, and prevent the rubble footing and its revetment from falling over. Also as in 796, the brickearth backfill of 8002 occupied the interstices between the revetting stones.

Layer 8001, and trench 8002 with feature 8018 and layer 8019, represented two quite separate phases of foundation work. A third phase was represented by feature 8010, which was sealed by 8001 and cut 8002, 8018 and 8019 (Fig. 20, Plate XLV). Feature 8010 was cut from 13.47 m. O.D. From the north, the cut for it removed feature 8018 and layer 8019 to a depth of 1.34 m. To the east 8010 cut feature 8002 and layers 8007, 8008, 8003, 8004, 8005, 8006, 8009 and 8012 (see below). To the south it cut layers 8003, 8004, 8005 and 8006.

The total depth of feature 8010 was 2.74 m. of which the final 1.74 m. was cut into natural brickearth (Plate XLV). A number of nails were recovered from the sides of 8010, suggesting that they had been shored with planks to prevent collapse until the foundations were laid. This may have been done because, when the foundation trenches for the south aisle footing had been dug, the sides had partially fallen in, as evidenced by layers 807 and 809 in Area IV and layers 8009 and 8012 in Area VIII (see below). The uppermost 1.52 m. of 8010 consisted of alternating layers of laid flint and extremely hard, rammed orange mortar and rubble. Each course of flints was closely tessellated. The flints were a mixture of the fresh irregular shapes which are found as a natural deposit in the Kentish chalk beds, and heavily rounded boulders which must have come from a beach. They varied in size from 16 to 20 cm. long. The rubble in the mortar layers between the flint courses consisted of Roman brick, ragstone, fragments of flint and gravel. The

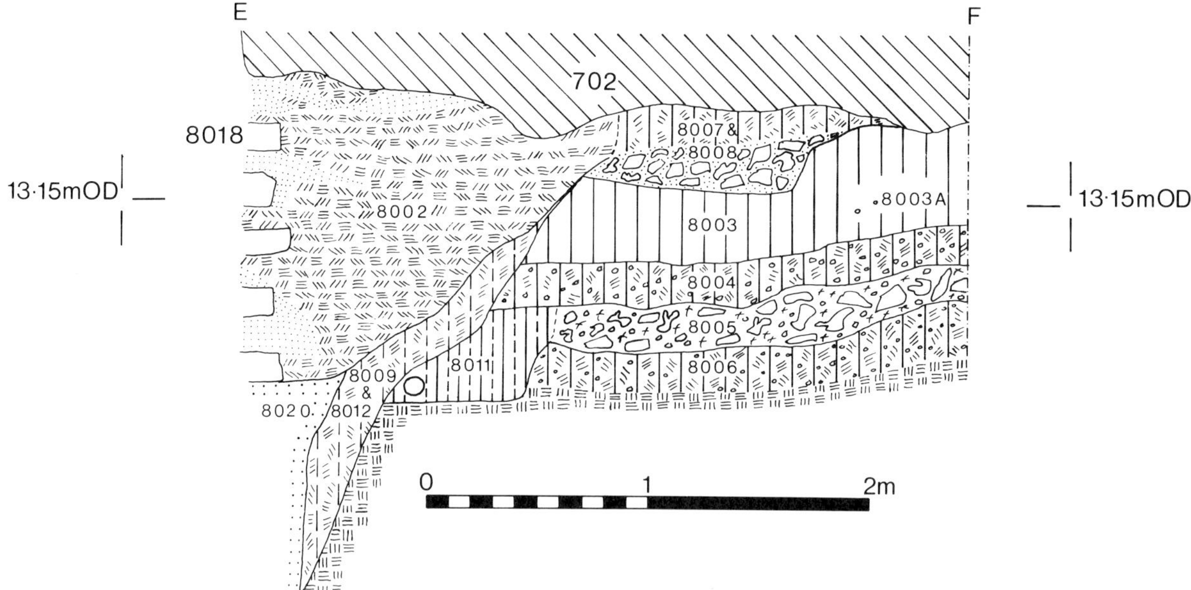

Fig. 19. Section E–F on Fig. 10.

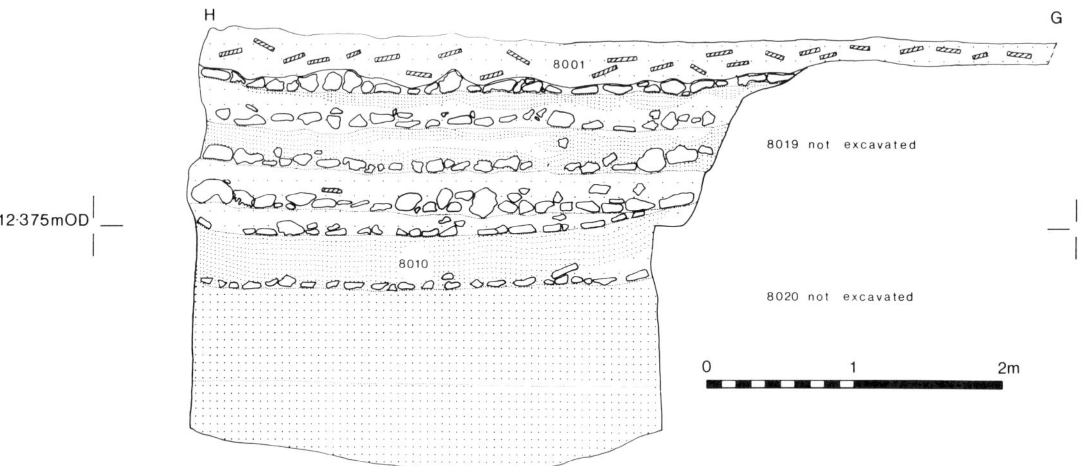

Fig. 20. Section G–H on Fig. 10.

lower 1.22 m. of the fill was of poured rubble. This had been poured in two separate stages, as there was a composition surface 59 cm. from the bottom of the cut indicating that the operation had been temporarily halted while the first tip was pounded down as hard as possible before the rest was poured in.

The bottom of feature 8010 was at 10.73 m. O.D. The nature of this foundation gave the impression that it was intended to support a superstructure of great weight and, by implication, of great height.

The removal of the fill of 8010 exposed a section through trench 8002, layers 8007, 8008, 8003, 8004, 8005, 8009 and 8012 (Fig. 19).

The fill of 8002 was very mixed tan to dark grey-brown sandy clay loam with gravel, and some flints and human bone, interleaved with lenses of mortar spilling through from 8019, as described above. The human bone would have come from the Anglo-Saxon cemetery disturbed by the digging of the south aisle foundation. Trench 8002 was cut by 702. Layers 8009 and 8012 were equivalent to layers 807 and 809 in Area IV, representing a collapse of the deposits through which 8002 was cut, down the side of the trench in the interval between its being dug and the foundation work being laid in it. Layer 8009 was fine grey-brown silty clay loam with chalk flecks; this overlay 8012, which was mid tan brown clay loam. These two layers were contained in a 17 cm. wide gap between the natural brickearth and the lowest layer of foundation work for the south aisle, layer 8020, which was the equivalent to layer 801 in Area IV. Layer 8020 was of poured rubble occupying the full width of the construction trench. Its top was at 12.41 m. O.D. and its base at 11.02 m. O.D. Feature 8018 and layer 8019 were superimposed on it (Plate XLVI).

Trench 8002 cut layers 8007, 8008, 8003, 8004, 8005 and 8006, and feature 8011. These survived to a maximum width of 32 cm. between 8010 and structure 702. Layers 8007 and 8008 were contained in a pit 82 cm. deep cut into layer 8003. Layer 8007 was dark brown clay loam with gravel; 8008 was a mixture of crushed Caen-stone, light olive-brown sandy loam, very compacted yellow mortar and large flint and ragstone rubble. An oolite moulding (Fig. 35, no. 1) was recovered from the rubble, and probably came from the destroyed Anglo-Saxon church.

Layer 8003 was fine dark grey-brown clay loam with occasional gravel pebbles, and a large quantity of human charnel. This was the Anglo-Saxon graveyard, equivalent to layer 803 in Area IV and layers 5160/5161 in Area V. A single articulated burial, feature 8003A, was exposed, though no grave cut was visible in the uniform cemetery soil. The skull was cushioned on a nest of flints and two fragments of Roman brick, like burials 803C and 5160C (Plate XLVII).

Layers 8004/8005/8006 were the equivalent of layers 804/805/806 in Area IV, and represented dumps of midden of the Roman period. Like layers 804/805/806, layers 8004/8005/8006 yielded large quantities of Roman and Belgic pottery. It was these layers and layer 8003 that had partially collapsed down the side of the south aisle construction trench, feature 8002, to form layers 8009 and 8012.

Sealed by layer 8004, cutting layers 8005 and 8006 and partially eroded by layer 8009 was feature 8011, a burial. The fill was of very mixed tan to dark grey-brown sandy clay loam with gravel and flints. The skeleton was orientated east and west.

Natural brickearth was encountered below layer 8006 at 12.49 m. O.D. The eastern arm of structure 702 cut 8002, 8003 and 8007. The southern arm cut 8001 and 8003.

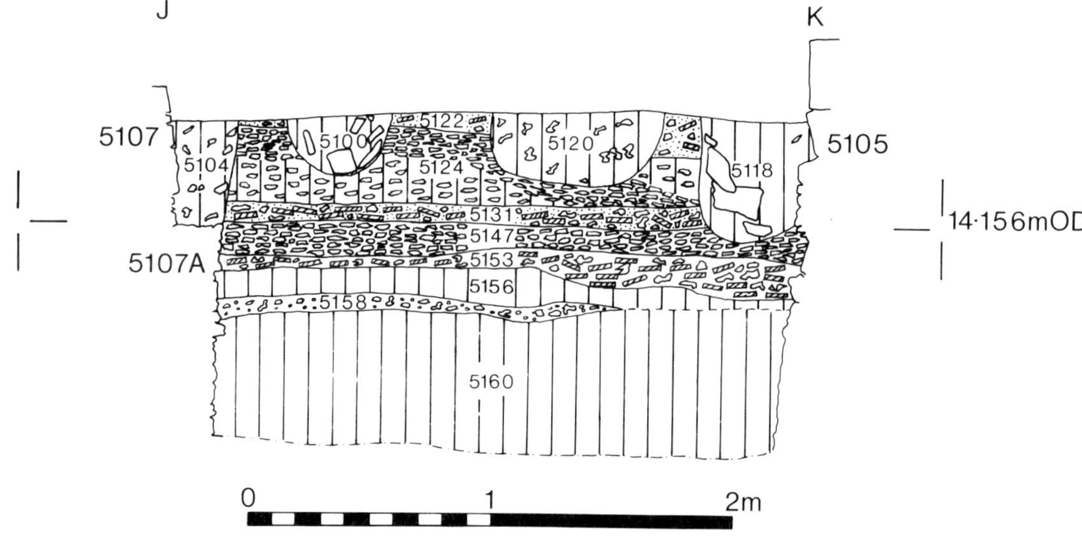

Fig. 21. Section J–K on Fig. 10.

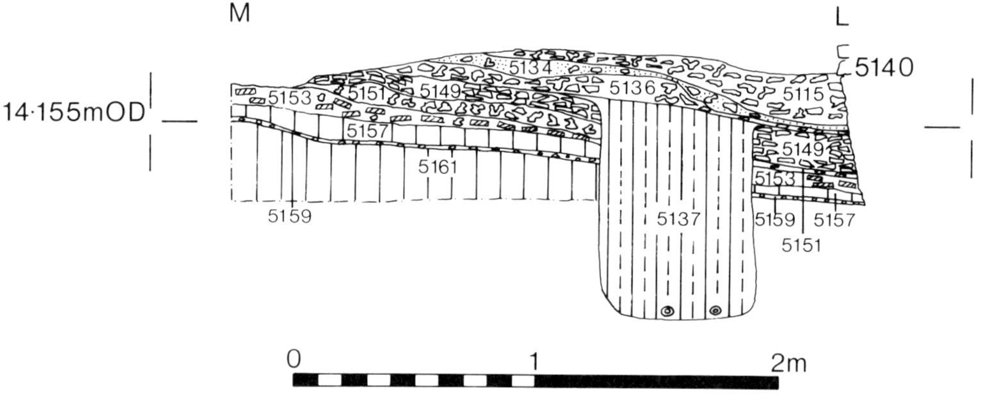

Fig. 22. Section L–M on Fig. 10.

DISCUSSION AND INTERPRETATION

THE ROMAN AND IMMEDIATE POST-ROMAN PERIODS

Throughout the site of St. Augustine's Abbey, excavations have demonstrated that this area to the east of *Durovernum* was used as an extra-mural rubbish dump. Rubbish would have been carted along the road to *Rutupiae* (Richborough) and tipped to either side. The earliest coin from these layers of rubbish (found in 1960) was of Dubnovellaunus, minted *c.* 5 B.C. and fairly soon lost. The latest was of Valens, minted A.D. 364–375 and soon lost. The pottery came from

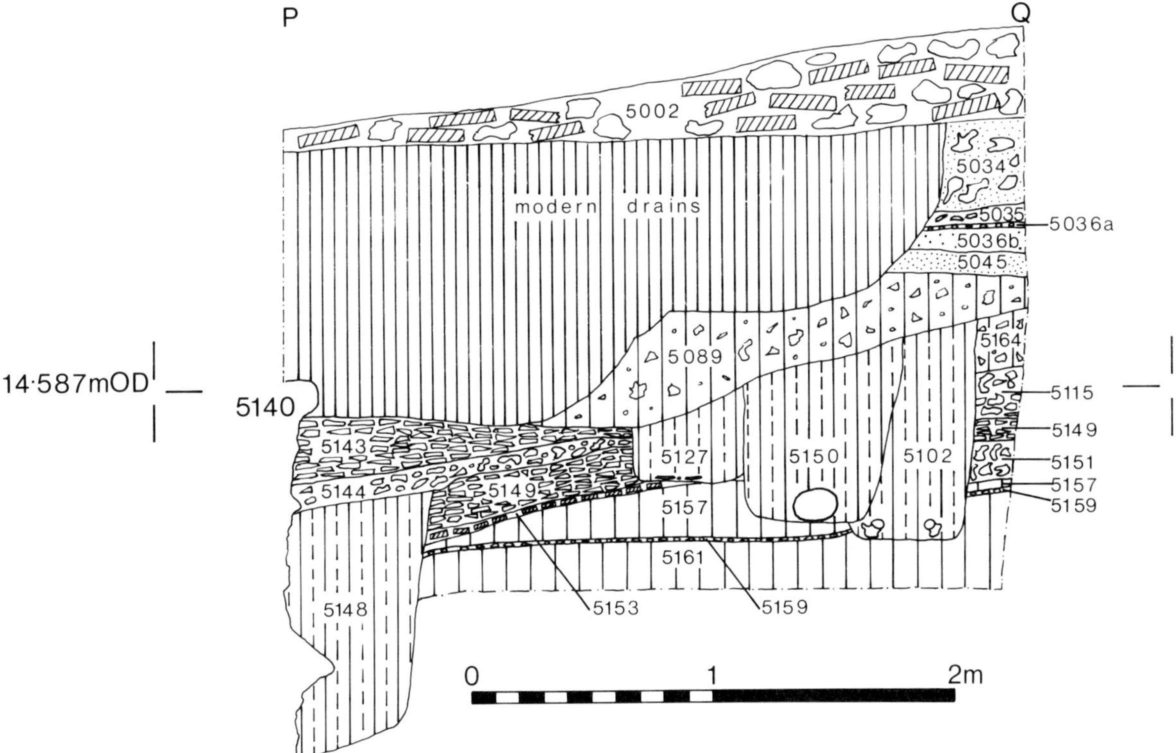

Fig. 23. Section P–Q on Fig. 10.

all periods within this numismatic date-range, and earlier. In addition to being a rubbish dump the area served as a burial ground (see above p. 40). A single Roman burial, F 8011, was encountered in the 1976–78 excavations. This was aligned east and west, which fact, unless it merely reflects the alignment of the road, suggests that the burial may have been Christian.

No evidence was found of any use of the site between the fifth century and the foundation of the abbey of Sts. Peter and Paul by Augustine at the end of the sixth century. Layers 803, 8003, 5160 and 5161, which represent the Anglo-Saxon cemetery, were found directly to overlie layer 8004, the latest deposit of Roman midden. The cessation in use of the Roman cemetery and the absence of Germanic graves with grave goods are significant for any discussion of continuity of settlement in Canterbury.

THE ANGLO-SAXON PERIOD

The Cemetery

The Anglo-Saxon cemetery was encountered in Areas III, IV, V and VIII. In Area III it was represented by the (un-numbered) layers of moist black soil under robber trench 1007 and trench 1027, and layer 1058 under vault 1051. The excavation of robber trench 1007 revealed much loose human bone in the soil, and the excavation of trench 1027 exposed a single articulated skeleton. The excavation and removal of vault 1051 exposed layer 1058 in which again much loose human bone was evident. This pattern of loose bone associated with articulated skeletons was also found in Areas IV, V and VIII. It was the result of continuous intersecting of graves, which were clearly dug without respecting the positions of previous interments. This would indicate that no grave markers were used in the Anglo-Saxon cemetery, with the result that the positions of earlier graves were not known. Certainly no grave markers were found, although quite a large area of the cemetery was excavated.

All the graves were very shallow, and a total of nine coffin nails was recovered, seven in association with burial 803F, and two loose in layer 5160. With only one certain exception, then, the occupants of the Anglo-Saxon graves were buried without coffins. The practice of burial without coffins was retained by the Benedictine monks of Lanfranc's era (Knowles 1951, 124), presumably because it was the norm. The skulls of three of the skeletons, numbers 803C, 8003A and 5160C, were supported on 'cushions' of flints and pieces of Roman brick (Plate XLVII). Males, females, juveniles and infants were represented, so this was not the monks' cemetery.

Two items which must have been buried as grave goods were recovered, a sixth- or seventh-century kidney-shaped buckle, and an eighth-century scramasax. These taken in conjunction with the enamelled polychrome bead found in Saunders' excavation (Saunders 1978, 32), indicate that the Christian missionaries were not, for two centuries, successful in stamping out pagan burial customs.

Architectural Fragments and Window Glass

Three architectural fragments from the Anglo-Saxon church, and a number of pieces of window glass, were recovered during the excavation. One architectural fragment lay in a shallow pit in the top level of the Anglo-Saxon cemetery. This doubtless fell from the old church when it was being demolished by Abbot Scotland in 1070 (Fig. 35, no. 1). It is difficult to date. The other two fragments (Fig. 35, nos. 2 and 3), are late Anglo-Saxon. No. 2 is part of a Corinthian capital probably of the tenth or eleventh century. No. 3 is a baluster probably of the eleventh century.

Of the fragments of window glass from layer 8001 (Fig. 41), one is of soda, and coloured sky-blue (no. 1), the others of potash. Of the potash fragments, two are neatly grozed into shapes, one triangular (no. 3) and one circular (no. 2). The potash pieces are so weathered that it is not possible to determine what their colour was. The glass cannot be dated easily (see p. 135).

The West Tower, Structure 5105

Of the structures excavated, only one, 5105, belonged to the pre-Conquest period (Plates XL, XLI), and this had been examined already by Saunders (Saunders 1978). That it was pre-Conquest seemed to be confirmed in the present excavations by the fact that a cut had been made into its eastern face, and the foundation raft, 5165, for the Norman south-west tower had been keyed into it (Plate XLI). This, however, is not in itself conclusive. The current excavations have shown there to be three phases in the design and construction of the Norman west end, and 5165 belongs to the third phase. It is thus clear that structure 5105 precedes the final design of the Norman west end, but it is not precluded that it might be a primary Norman structure. On the other hand, the foundations of structure 5105 (as examined by Saunders) seem of clearly different character from 8018, 8019 and 8020 (as also from 741A and 801) and it is unlikely, therefore, that 5105 is in fact Scotland's work: a pre-Conquest date is most probable.

It can perhaps be identified with the tower towards the construction of which Archbishop Eadsige gave 100 marks in 1047. After the Conquest, Abbot Scotland demolished all the Anglo-Saxon structures except the porticus of St. Gregory, the church of St. Pancras and, so it seems, this tower. The tower may be that western tower of the monastery into which Scotland moved the burials from St. Mary's Church.

THE ROMANESQUE BUILDING SEQUENCE

The building of the Romanesque church was carried out by three abbots, Scotland, Wido and Hugh of Fleury. Scotland ruled from 1070 to 1087 and, as related by Goscelin, built the crypt and presbytery, the crossing, and the two bays of the nave westwards from the crossing up to the Anglo-Saxon porticus of St. Gregory, wherein were the shrines of the saints, which he was afraid to demolish. Goscelin's text makes it clear that Scotland did everything he could towards the construction of the nave short of knocking down the porticus, and this suggests that he may have cut the foundation trenches for the north and south walls of the nave. The north wall was clear of the porticus, and so the cutting of the trenches and laying of the foundations would not have involved disturbing the latter.

The archaeological evidence supports this interpretation. As described above, three phases of foundation work were identified in Areas IV and VIII. The first phase was represented by: in Area IV, construction trench 796, foundation 741A and, below these, layer 801 (Plate XXXVIII), and in Area VIII, construction trench 8002, layer 8019 and its stone revetment 8018, and, below these, layer 8020 (Plate XLVI): these would be the foundation laid out by Scotland. It would appear that this was intended to continue westwards and meet up with structure 5105. The nave as envisaged by Scotland, then, would not have had towers at its west end, but merely turrets, as later at Rochester Cathedral, and he intended to rework the Anglo-Saxon tower to this function.

Wido, who succeeded as abbot in 1087, spent his first four years on completing the crossing tower, then in 1091 he demolished the porticus of St. Gregory so that he could complete the nave.

From the archaeological evidence it is clear that Wido scrapped Scotland's plan for the west front and decided upon a twin-towered design. Layer 8010, which partly cuts away the earlier foundation work 8018 and 8019, is the foundation for the south-west tower (Plates XLIV, XLV). It is 29 cm. deeper than Scotland's foundation. When 8010 had been laid in the ground, a raft of compacted rubble, layer 8001 (Plate XLII), was laid over 8018 and 8019 to support the stonework of the footings.

The footing of the tower in Area VIII is represented by features 8013, 8015, 8016 and 8017

(Plate XLII). The excavated footing for the south wall of the church was feature 741 in Area IV (Plate XXXVIII). The footings were carried up 1.27 m. above the Saxo-Norman ground surface before ashlar walling with a chamfered offset at its base was commenced. This pattern is repeated on the cloister side of the church, and it is difficult to see why Wido decided to have the floor and walls of the church so much higher than the ground outside. The footings would have been visible. These were rather roughly dressed and cannot have been very pleasing to the eye.

Like Scotland, Wido decided to retain the Saxon tower, but for a different purpose. He cut away two sides of it so that it could serve as a clasping buttress to the new tower. Nothing survives above floor level of the south-west tower, but the north-west tower stood until 1822, when most of it was blown down in a storm. There are several engravings of this tower and they show its architecture to be of the period of Hugh of Fleury's abbacy (1099–1124). Many architectural details still survive at ground level, and column bases survive in one corner at gallery level (Fig. 24).

It is clear, therefore, that although it was Wido who planned the towers, laid the foundations and built the footings for them, the actual superstructure at least of the north tower was not completed until after his death. The work of Hugh of Fleury marks the end of the Norman period of building.

LATER MEDIEVAL PHASES

Footings of uncertain Date

Two footings are of uncertain date, footing 5106 (Plate XLI) and footing 5130. A trench had been dug by an unknown previous excavator south of footing 5106 removing the deposits through which it must have been cut. No section drawing of this trench survives. The footing must, however, be earlier than footing 5107, which over-rides it, and footing 5107 is of the fourteenth century rebuilt in the fifteenth (see below). 5106 cannot have been inserted until the ground outside the church had built up 1.27 m. (see above) because it is constructed of chalk and would not have been capable of withstanding any weathering. Its function is uncertain, but it could have been the sill of a door into the tower.

Footing 5130 was discovered when the twentieth-century perimeter wall of the Kent and Canterbury Hospital was removed, but only a short stretch of it was exposed because of the proximity of the still-standing hospital mortuary. No diagnostic ceramic evidence was recovered from layers 5134, 5156 and 5158, through which it was cut. It was butt-jointed onto the Saxon tower. It may have been a wall dividing the cemetery from the outer curia, joining up with the standing length of wall running east from the Cemetery Gate. If this interpretation were correct it would add support to the idea of 5106 being the sill of a door into the tower from the cemetery.

Fourteenth-century Structures

By the fourteenth century, the Norman south-west tower and the south aisle wall near it would

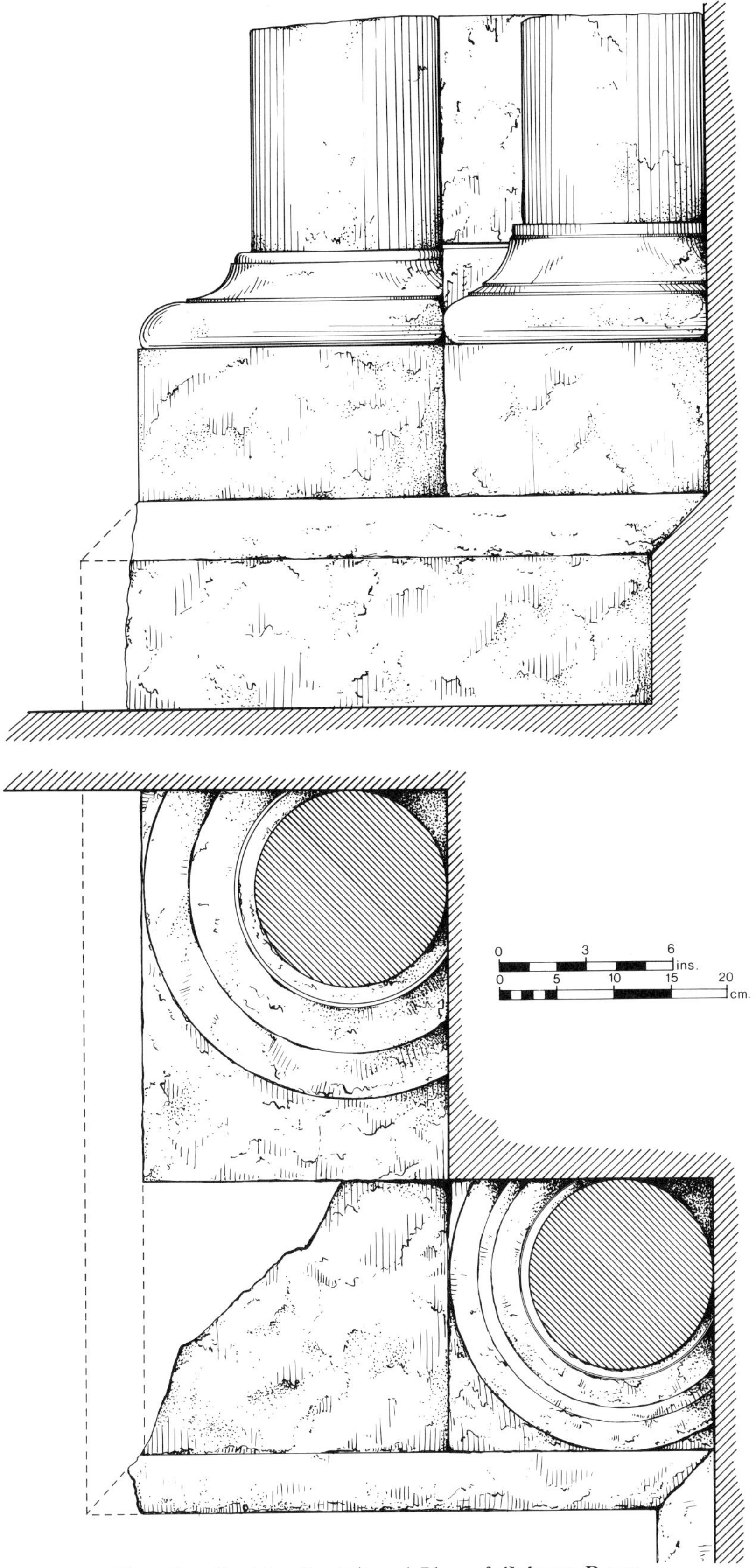

Fig. 24. Elevation (looking South) and Plan of Column Bases surviving at Gallery Level, in the South-west Corner of the North-west Tower.

appear to have developed a weakness, for a massive clasping buttress, structure 702/5140, was added at the south-east corner of the tower to match the existing clasping buttress, structure 5105, at the south-west corner (Plate XL). At the same time buttresses 740 and 519 were butted onto the south wall of the church (Plates XXXVIII, XXXII). Two of the layers cut by structure 702/5140 yielded medieval pottery, layers 786 and 5149. From layer 786 came a sherd of the early to mid-thirteenth century, but from layer 5149 came a sherd dated to between 1300 and 1325. Buttresses 519 and 740 were cut from the same level as buttress 702/5140, and the three structures represent a strengthening operation for the south-west corner of the church, now two centuries old. Later a complete re-working of the west end had to be undertaken (see below).

A similar or slightly later date is indicated by ceramic evidence for the building of the chantry chapel in Area III (Plates XXXV, XXXIII). The layers antedating it contained pottery deposited between 1300 and 1320, but a sherd of Scarborough ware of a type in production in 1250–1350 was recovered from layer 594.

Layer 594, which was under the sixteenth-century workshop (see below), was equivalent to layer 578 in the area between walls 512 and 514A (see section A–B). Layer 578 was cut by the footing, feature 512A, for the west wall of the chapel.

Evidence for the length of use of the chapel for its primary function (for burials) is suggested by the dating of the last two burials in or connected with the chantry, those contained in vault 1051 (Plate XXXIV). Layer 1053, the backfill over the second burial, yielded a lead *méreau* which could be of the fifteenth century. Two sherds of 'Tudor Green' pottery were found in layer 1045, a cut for the re-bedding of grave slab 406, which had to be moved slightly when vault 1051 was constructed. Although this type of pottery can date as early as 1430–1440, it became more widespread in the late fifteenth century (see p. 297).

Fifteenth- and early sixteenth-century Structures

The final phase of building within the life of the monastery took place in the fifteenth and sixteenth centuries, when the whole west end of the church was remodelled. Evidence for this could be seen above ground before the current excavations took place, for on the north-west tower the Romanesque façade had been skinned over with a new façade in the fifteenth-century idiom (since the abbey ruins were placed in the guardianship of the Department of the Environment, parts of the fifteenth-century work have been removed to expose the Romanesque detail encased within it). In the area excavated, the fifteenth-century work was represented by the refacing of structures 5105 and 702/5140, the rebuilding of footing 5107 and the construction of a stair, feature 5108, at the south-west corner of structure 702/5140 (Plate XL). At the same time the probable door represented by sill 5106 was blocked up and a drain-pipe placed centrally between footing 5105 and 5108 (Fig. 10). The position of this pipe was indicated by robber trench 5120. Visual examination of the mortar used in the refacing of structure 702/5140 and in footings 5107 and 5108 suggested that they were the same mix. The mortar was pink, in marked contrast to the yellow mortar of the core-work of 702/5140. Subsequent chemical analysis of the mortar confirmed the visual impression. Feature 8014, whose southern face was exposed in the area of excavation, was more fully excavated by Saunders and dated by him to the fifteenth century (Plate XL). It would seem to belong to the same phase of work.

If a major re-building of the south-west tower took place in the fifteenth and sixteenth centuries, this should probably be identified with the series of wills between 1461 and 1516 (Hussey 1915, 43–53), for the making of 'the new steeple' (see p. 7). With this phase of building we come to the end of the architectural sequence within the lifetime of the monastery.

POST-DISSOLUTION PHASES

Sixteenth-century Structures and Demolitions

Two final structures remain to be dealt with, one standing, the other excavated. The first is King Henry VIII's garden wall, described in the pay books of James Nedeham, Surveyor of the King's works (see above p. 10), which was damaged when 'the great steeple and the two great buttresses that stood before the same steeple' fell across it as they were being demolished in 1541. The 'steeple and the two buttresses' it is here suggested may be identified with the south-west tower as rebuilt in the fifteenth and sixteenth centuries, represented by the remodelling of structures 5105 and 702/5140. The wall enclosing the garden (the garden must have been the former abbots' outer curia), must have been built between 1538, when Abbot Foche surrendered the abbey to the Crown, and 1542.

The second structure is building X (Plate XXXII). It was obviously built while the chantry chapel and buttress 519 were still standing, because it respected them (Plate XXXV). It sealed the final phase of burials in the monastic cemetery, and chemical analysis of the mortar bonding the footings showed this to be entirely different to any of the mortars in the medieval footings. It must, therefore, be post-Dissolution. A layer of demolition material, layer 553, overlay wall 514A and the western wall of the chantry chapel, wall 512. This would suggest that both building were demolised simultaneouly. The accounts of George Nycholl (see p. 11) show that the south aisle was still being dismantled in the first year of the reign of Mary (1553). As the chantry chapel was attached to the south aisle it seems reasonable to assume that the chapel was taken down at the same time as the aisle. Building X can best be interpreted as a temporary workshop for the men engaged upon the task of dismantling the church buildings. When the taking down of the south aisle and chapel had been completed, their workshop was taken down also, as it was not longer needed.

Later Cemetery

The subsequent history of the site is well recorded in the documentary sources given above, and will not be included in this discussion, which has been confined to archaeological evidence recovered from the ground. There is one point, however, which is not covered fully by the seventeenth- and eighteenth-century documents. After the Dissolution of the monastery, the lay cemetery was retained by the City of Canterbury as a common cemetery for those parish churches whose graveyards were full. The site of St. Augustine's Abbey cemetery continued to exercise this function until 1791, when it was sold, and the Kent and Canterbury Hospital built upon it two years later.

V. BUILDING MATERIALS

1. STONEWORK FROM EXCAVATIONS 1972–75. Christopher Miscampbell

The stone described and illustrated here is all from the south side of the abbey church, except where similar stones from other provenanced areas in the abbey are used for comparison. Surviving mouldings *in situ* from the south crypt windows are mentioned for comparison but are not described. Most of the worked stone from the excavations is described, duplicate pieces being noted under a representative stone. The dressed ashlar, however, mostly coming from the fallen wall, is discussed under that heading. It is all Caen-stone unless otherwise stated. All the greensand is Kentish rag. These and other types of stones have been identified by F.W. Anderson whose report follows the catalogue (p. 121).

The arrangement of the catalogue is in areas, and within these areas the stones are described as far as possible in chronological order. The arrangement of the areas is as follows:

1. From Trenches II and III;
2. From the demolished modern boundary wall;
3. From the 'tumble' south of St. Thomas' Chapel (Area 1);
4. From the 'fallen wall' (Area 2):
   (a) Area above fallen wall (layer 1 and unstratified).
   (b) Area above fallen wall (layer 19).
   (c) Area beneath fallen wall (layer 63);
5. From elsewhere (Areas 1 and 2).

Abbreviations

d:	diameter	m:	minimum measurement of a broken piece
h:	height	w:	width
l:	length	s:	section
D:	Drawing shown in Figs. 25–29	M:	Moulding shown in Figs. 31–33

Where two measurements are given, the first is the length of the piece. Dimensions are not given where the fragments are so small that measurements would be meaningless.

CATALOGUE

1. *Moulded Stones from Trenches II and III (1972)*				
No.	*Description*	*Dimensions in cm.*	*Other Information*	*Figure*
	Trench II, layer 1			
1.	Stone reddened by fire, Diagonal tooling. Quarry-tooled. Two incised crossed, mason's mark.		Romanesque. Two other pieces of this reddened by fire from Trench III.	
2.	Fragment of stone with chevron (?) decoration.			
3.	Voussoir. Moulding of hollow, bead and roll.		cf. no. 119 (fallen wall)	
4.	Fragment of stone with cusp. Blind arcading?			
	Trench III, layer 12			
5.	Fragment of window (?) jamb. Double ogee roll with large fillet.		Fourteenth century.	
6.	Fragment of moulding. Single roll, incised line on one face.			
7.	Fragment of base. Chamfer, hollow roll and hollow.			
8.	Fragment of moulding. Hollow, chamfer and ogee roll.			
9.	Fragment of moulding. Hollow, two chamfers at different angles. Kentish.			
10.	Fragment of string-course (?). Moulding on string; chamfer, hollow and sunken hollow.			25
	Trench III, layer 18			
11.	Fragment of stone with chevron decoration.			D 25
	Trench III, layer 34			
12.	Fragment of stone with crochets from canopy.			D 25
	Trench III, layer 43			
13.	Section of Bethersden marble shaft.			
2. *Stones from the demolished Boundary Wall*				
14.	Base, one large roll, one smaller roll. Some diagonal and horizontal tooling. Circular setting-out line on the top.	h:19 d:20	Romanesque, pre-Abbot Scotland?	30

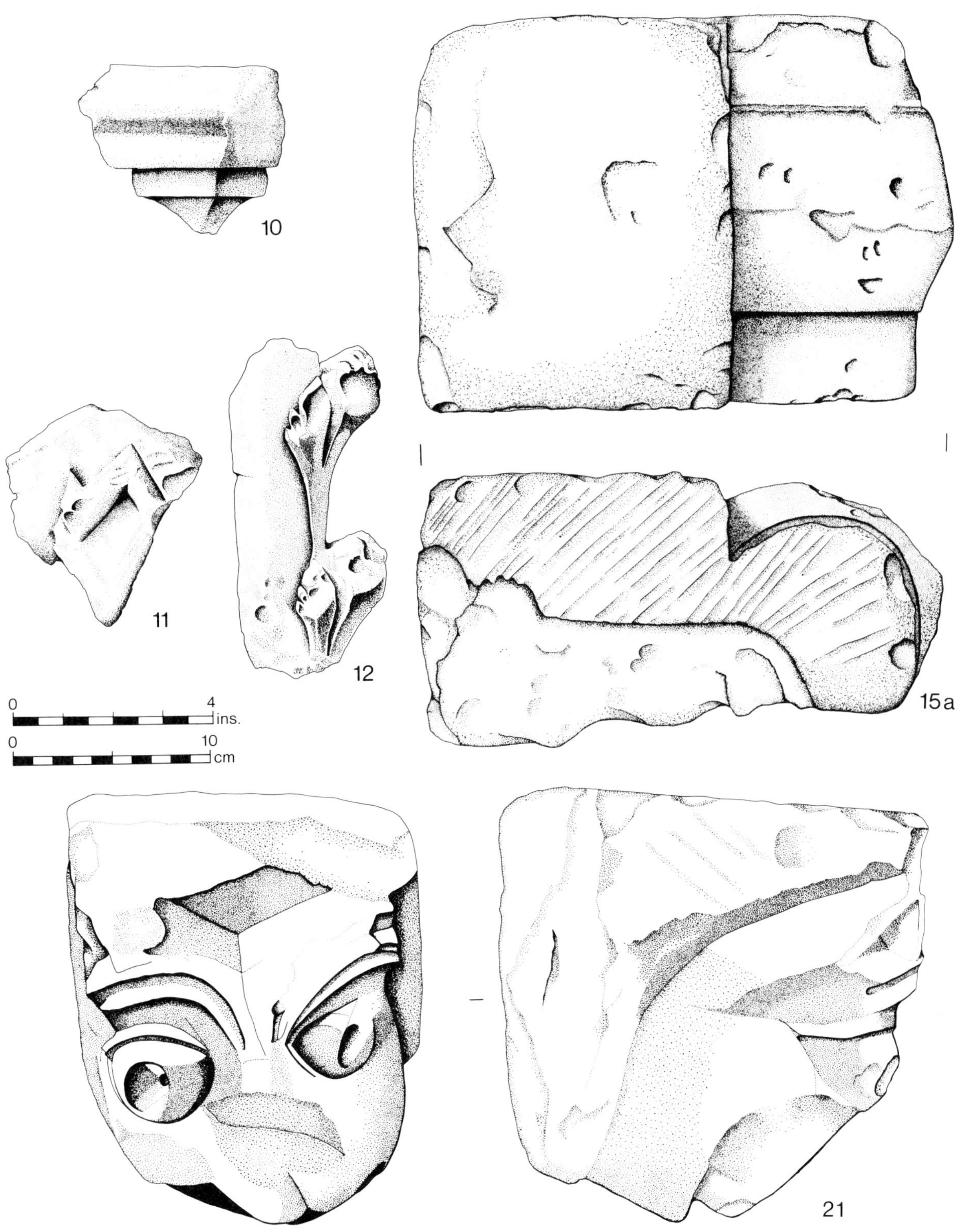

Fig. 25. Worked Stone, 1972–74.

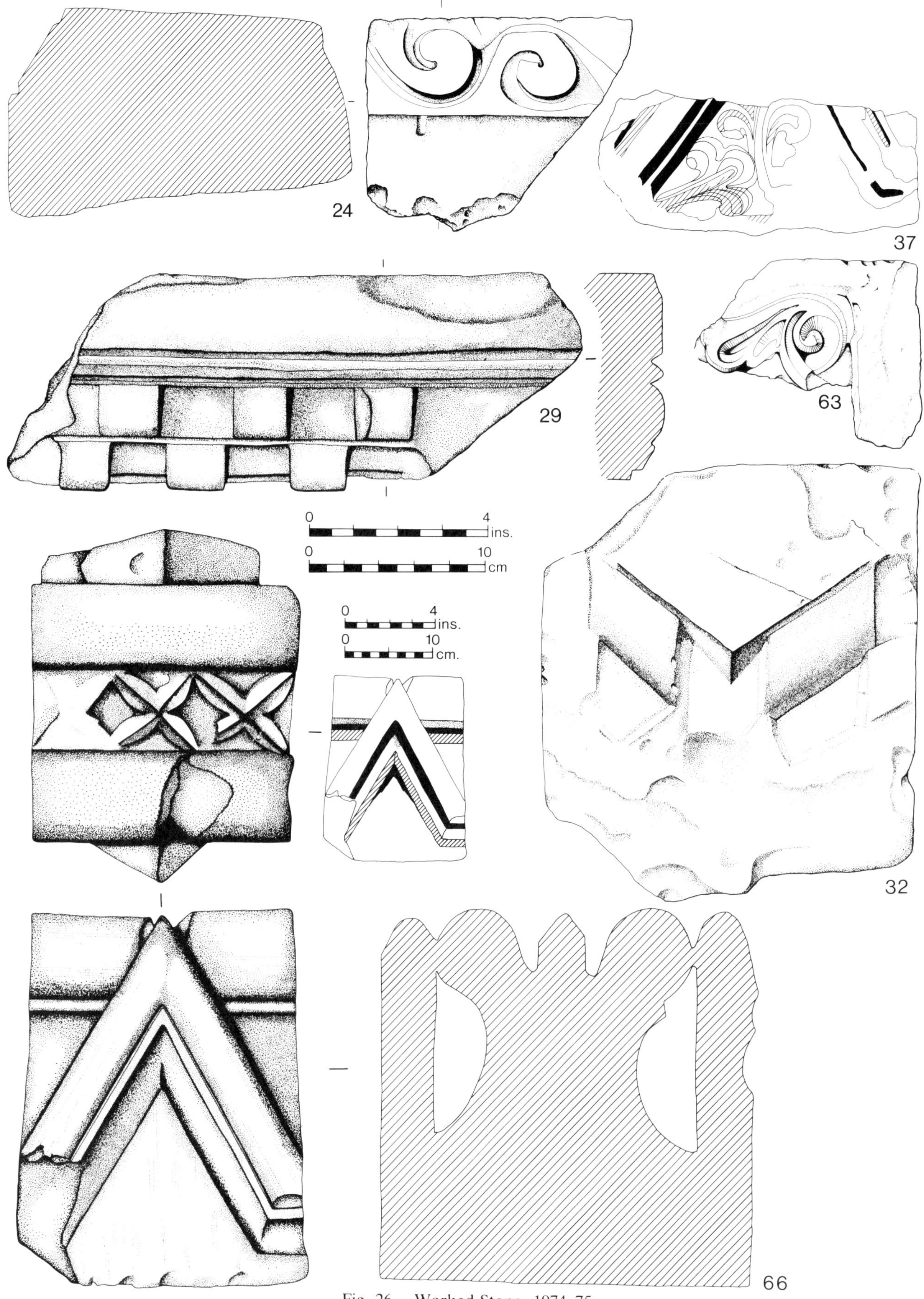

Fig. 26. Worked Stone, 1974–75.

No.	*Description*	*Dimensions in cm.*	*Other Information*	*Figure*
15.	Attached base, roll hollow and roll.	h:13.3 d:*c.* 18	Eleventh century.	
15a.	Annulet on attached shaft.	h:17.5 d:9	One other piece SA 394.	D 25
16.	Fragment of capital (?); one small roll, one larger roll.	h:17.5 d:*c.* 12		
17.	Quoin of chamfered plinth or string-course. Chamfer slightly undercut. Diagonal tooling small quarry mark.	h:17.5	Abbot Scotland, *post* 1070. Not the same as no. 126 (below).	3. 4
18.	Return of quoin of chamfered string-course. Diagonal tooling.	h:15	Similar to no. 17 (above).	
19.	Return of chamfered string-course.	1:20 x 21	Cf. no. 126 (below).	
20.	Fragment of piscina or font. Meeting of sill and jamb on rounded wall.			
21.	Corbel carved with grotesque face.			D 25
22.	Fragment of capital with two hollows, the lower hollow possibly undercut. Some diagonal tooling. Hole on top of capital (*c.* 15.5 cm. deep) for keying.	h:m:19.5		
23.	Cushion capital. Pronounced vertical tooling on cushion. Square abacus.	h:15.5 d:18	Cf. no. 62 (Tumble).	
24.	Section of chamfered impost block with scroll design. Red paint in hollows of scroll.	1:15		D 25
25.	Section of diaper-work frieze, decoration of sunken triangles.	17.5 x 17.5	Four other pieces, two being of a trapezoid section.	
26.	Section of diaper-work frieze, decoration of four sunken petals within a circle. Quarr limestone.	33 x 17	Three other pieces, total length 107.	
27.	Section of diaper-work frieze, decoration of sunken rectangular panels. Quarr limestone.	30 x 19.8		
28.	Fragment of billet frieze.	*c.* 16.5 x 13.5		
29.	Section of string-course with billet.	32.8 x 12		D 25
30.	Section of string-course with billet. Quarr limestone.	37.4 x 15.2	One other piece. Total length 69.	
31.	Voussoir with billet.	27 x 18		
32.	Section of zig-zag billet frieze. Slot for dowel (?) in its side.	21 x 21		D 25
33.	Voussoir with chevron decoration.	h:*c.* 117	One other piece; cf. no. 129 (below).	
34.	Voussoir with raised chevron decoration.	h:*c.* 23		
35.	Section of curved attached roll. Oolitic limestone. (Lincolnshire limestone: Weldon type).		Romanesque?	M 31
36.	Fragment of attached base, roll and hollow.	h:8 d:*c.* 20	Late Romanesque.	
37.	Voussoir with dog-tooth on soffit of voussoir between two rolls. Chevrons	1:18.3	Cf. no. 66 (below). Late twelfth century. See footnote	

No.	*Description*	*Dimensions in cm.*	*Other Information*	*Figure*
	overlapping the rolls. Shallow foliated motif on one chevron. Red paint on the foliage.		21 (p. 113).	
38.	Jamb with hollow and chamfer moulding one side; naturalistic leaf-carving going up the stone the other side.	h:15		
39.	Springer of blind arcading. Lincolnshire limestone, Weldon type.	h:32 w:32		
40.	Jamb of arch; three rolls with fillets and hollows.	h:17.5	Thirteenth century	M 31
41.	Fragment of vaulting boss with naturalistic foliage springing from three slim filleted ribs.	width of rib: 8	Another similar fragment (same no.)	
42.	Fragment of jamb, three hollows and two rolls. Fine tooling.	h:m:19 w:25.5		
43.	Fragment of double-chamfered window sill with glazing groove and ogee roll beneath sill on the opposite side. Setting-out line.	h:6.5 l:m:28		
44.	Lincolnshire limestone. Weldon type. Section of string-course, chamfer, hollow and bead. 90° return to wall. Mason's mark.	h:10 l:32.8		
45.	Section of string-course chamfers, hollow and bead. 45° return to wall re-cut to receive glazing bar? Heavy incised marks in bedding surface for mortar.	l:10.5 9.5 on return	Bedding marks similar to no. 48.	
46.	Section of string-course, chamfer, reverse chamfer and hollow.	l:33.2 h:15		
47.	Section of blind cusped arcading. Highly finished surface.	l:24.5		
48.	Fragment of cusped tracery. Different 'orders' on either side. Arrow-like bedding marks.	h:21	Bedding marks similar to no. 100.	
49.	Fragment of window mullion with glazing grooves on both sides.	h:10	Central mullion for no. 99, window series.	
50.	Section of corbel (table) two hollows, roll, chamfer and sunk chamfer. Unfinished? Fine comb tooling.	l:7.6		
51.	Section of arch hood-moulding chamfer, reverse chamfer, ogee hollow and reverse chamfer.	w:8	Similar ogee to nos. 99 and 103.	
52.	Fragment of arch hood-moulding: scroll and bead. Heavy diagonal bedding marks on underside.	h:8.5 l:28		
53.	Section of parapet weathering roll, double chamfer, roll with fillet and hollow. Slope	l:31.8	Cf. no. 109.	M 31

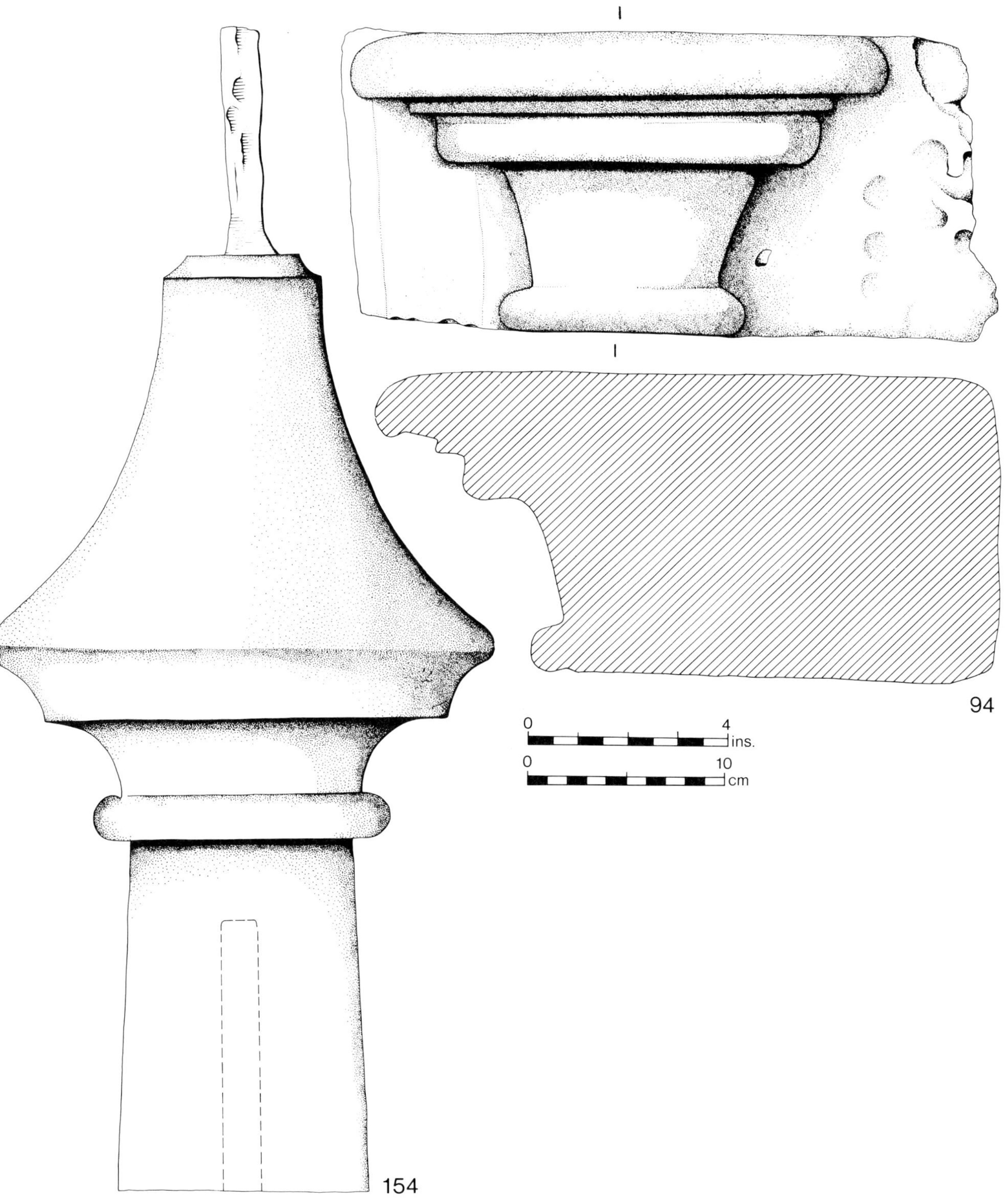

Fig. 27 Worked Stone, 1974–75.

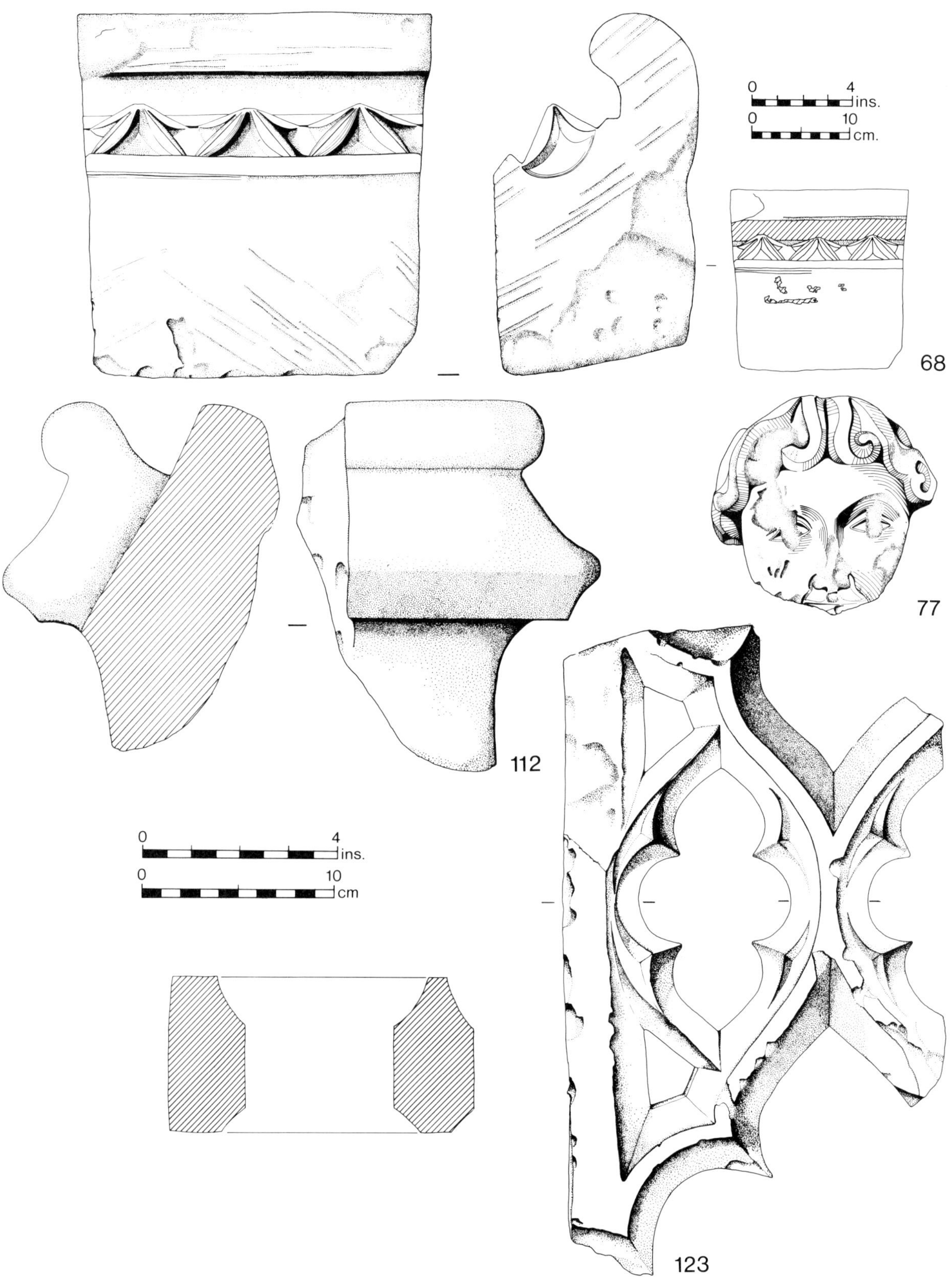

Fig. 28. Worked Stone, 1974–75.

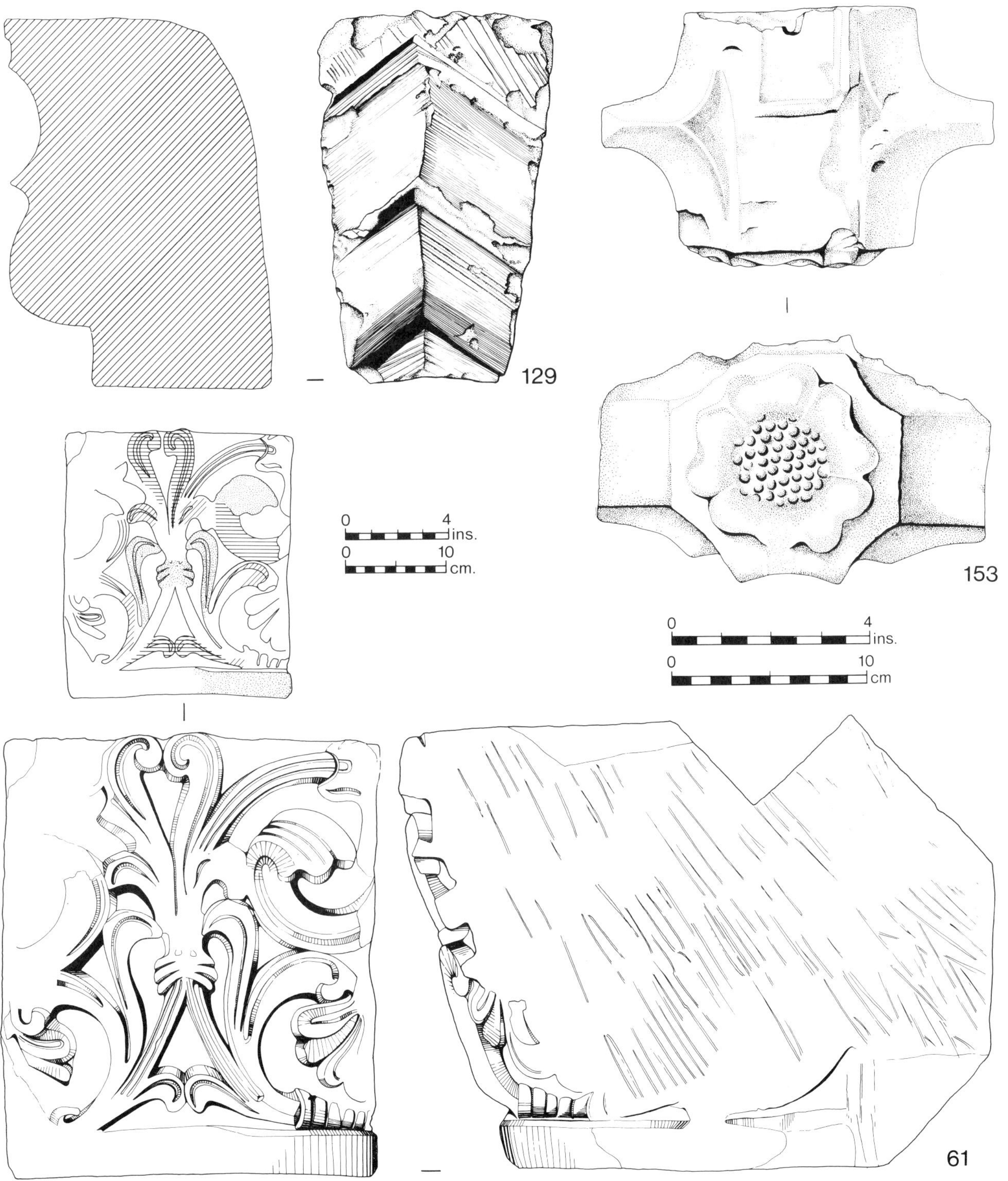

Fig. 29. Worked Stone, 1974–75.

No.	*Description*	*Dimensions in cm.*	*Other Information*	*Figure*
	on one side indicating end of this length of parapet.			
54.	Rainwater head.	h:11.5 24.7 x 19.5	Cf. no. 20.	
	3. *From 'Tumble' south of St. Thomas' Chapel* Area 1, Layer 3			
55.	Fragment of attached base, single roll. Coarsely tooled. Circular setting-out line on top, horizontal setting-out line on back.	h:18	Romanesque.	
56.	Section of half-round respond, keyed.	h:15.2	One other piece, h:17.8. One piece: keyed at one end, h:165.	

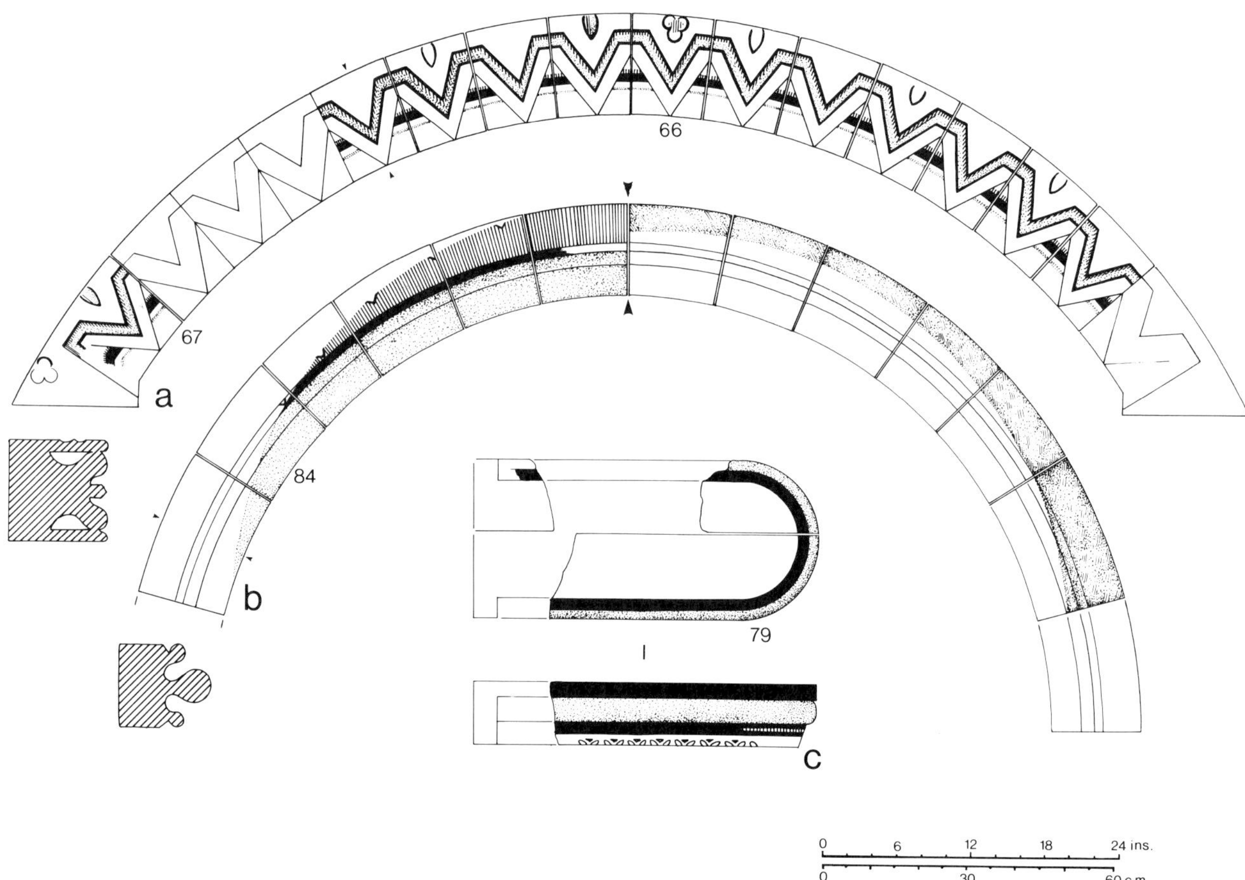

Fig. 30. Decorated Stonework from the Tumble, *reconstructed by J.C. Thorn* (Cat. nos. 66, 67, 79, 84).

No.	*Description*	*Dimensions in cm.*	*Other Information*	*Figure*
57.	Section of quarter-round respond.	h:19	One other piece, making up a half-round respond.	
58.	Section of half-round respond. Lincolnshire limestone, ? Barnack.	h:21.5 d:28.5		
59.	Section of half-round respond. Very eroded face. Very coarse white plaster on face.	h:16.5	12 other stones, 11 of oolitic Lincolnshire limestone. Of those 6 of Ketton variety, 1 of Barnack and 1 of Portland. One fine-grained brown sandstone, probably Pulborough variety. One with mason's mark. Total height about 4.57 m.	
60.	Section of half-round respond. Pronounced vertical tooling.	h:16	Caen-stone.	
61.	Pilaster capital, decorated with acanthus leaves. Dark brown background; leaves in sky blue and pink. Re-cut as jamb with chamfer and rebate.		Date: early twelfth century, re-cut in early thirteenth century. See footnote 20.	29 (also Geddes 1983, Pl. 34, *a*).
62.	Cushion capital fitted into internal angle of wall. Roll at base of capital. Diagonal tooling on chamfer. Coarse white plaster.			M
63.	Fragment of scroll-work from capital. Setting-out line on top. Blue, ochre, dark purple and pink paint on scroll-work.	w:4.5	Colour analysis by A.M. Laboratory was inconclusive.	D 25
64.	Section of shaft. Coarse vertical tooling.	h:42.7 d:15.2	Four other pieces. Total length; m:137.6.	
65.	Section of bowtell, keyed. Window arch? Curved. Coarse horizontal tooling.	l:28 d:14.2	Nine other pieces, varying from 13 to 24 cm. in length. All curved.	
66.	Section of voussoir with dog-tooth on soffit of arch between two rolls and chevrons overlapping the rolls. Setting-out lines. Black, orange, dark red paint on white ground, whitewashed over.	l:17.2 w of block 20.5 height to dog-tooth l:20	Late twelfth century. Ten other pieces, all of the same length, most with setting-out lines, six pieces of the same recovered from Chapter House (now in Dover Castle store).	D 26, 30 Also in Geddes 1983, Pl. 34, *b*.
67.	Spring to the above voussoirs. A window arch.	l:34.2 width of block 20.5		30
68.	South of arch hood-moulding with dog-tooth, roll, chamfer, reverse chamfer, dog-tooth and chamfer. Orange paint on roll, purple on underside, yellow on chamfer and reverse chamfer, purple on underside of hood-mould, (purple decoration?), paint on chalky white ground. Horizontal tooling on roll.	l:77	Two other pieces, lengths 19 and 22 cm. One other piece from the Chapter House (in Dover Castle store).	D 28

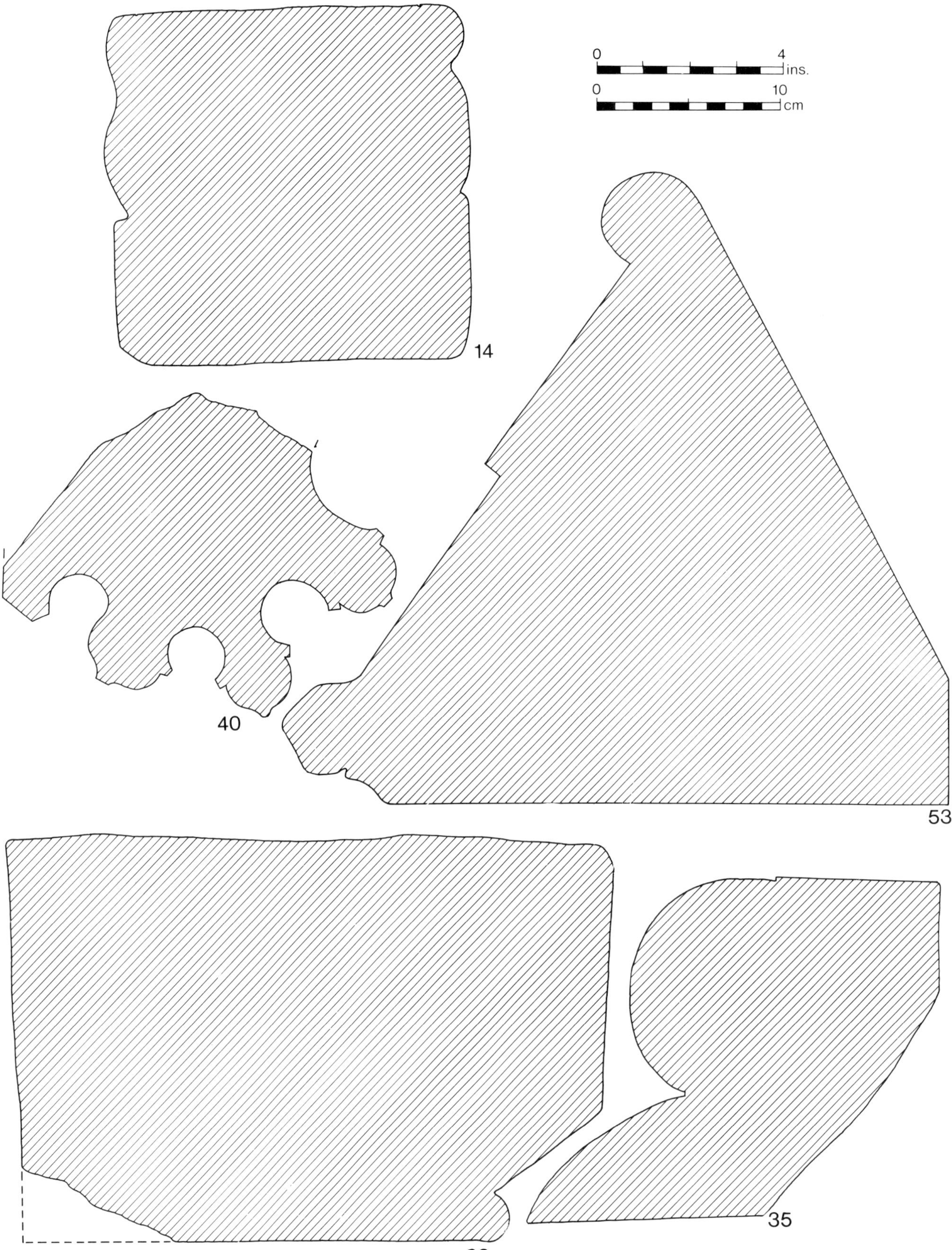

Fig. 31. Stone Mouldings, 1974–75.

No.	*Description*	*Dimensions in cm.*	*Other Information*	*Figure*
69.	Section of jamb. Three faces. Chamfered central face has red paint. Other two faces black paint over white chalky ground. Pronounced vertical tooling.	l:14.2	Early thirteenth century (?). Four other pieces, lengths 17, 17, 17.7 and 15 cm., one has its side cut back as if to receive the back of an arch. One piece partially white-washed. One piece, central face has orange paint.	
70.	Section of jamb. Four faces. Double chamfer. Pronounced vertical tooling. Purple paint on one face, white plaster on the other three, paint and plaster over white chalky ground.	l:16.4	Two other pieces, lengths 17 and 15 cm. One has white plaster on all faces, two thin coats on one face.	
71.	Section of jamb. Four faces. Double chamfer, 'outer' chamfer orange paint, 'inner' two faces black? 'Inner' chamfer white plaster. Paint and plaster over white chalky ground. 'Outer' chamfered face contains hole *c.* 2.5 cm. wide blocked with plaster, Kentish rag.	l:24	Nos. 69, 70 and 71 are similar in tooling and detail.	
72.	Section of jamb. Three faces with 90° rebate and ? internal chamfer.	l:19	One other piece with three painted faces only.	
73.	Section of edge moulding with snub-nosed roll. Plaster adhering showing downward continuation of wall. Remains of slot for glazing bar 6.5 cm. deep. Signs of burning especially on bottom side of moulding. Setting-out lines on edges and bottom.	l:29.5	Two other pieces. One l:23.3 has a very slight curve, traces of red paint on the upper part of the mould, and signs of burning, especially on bottom side. Mason's marks. The other l:16.7 has burning marks, plaster showing the downward continuation of the wall, remains of a slot for glazing bar 6.1 cm. deep, and setting-out lines.	34
74.	Fragment of corbel (?). Roll and cavetto moulding. Some horizontal tooling. Slot for nail on outside, filled with paint later? Orange paint on roll, black paint on cavetto. Paint on plaster. Two, possibly three coats of whitewash over paint.	l:14 m. w: 18.6		
75.	Fragment of corbel or hood-moulding stop, scalloped. Orange paint on white ground.	l:m:13		
76.	Fragment of wall bracket? Roll and cavetto moulding. Horizontal tooling. Five sides painted orange on roll, black on cavetto	l:22.5 h:10.5		M 32

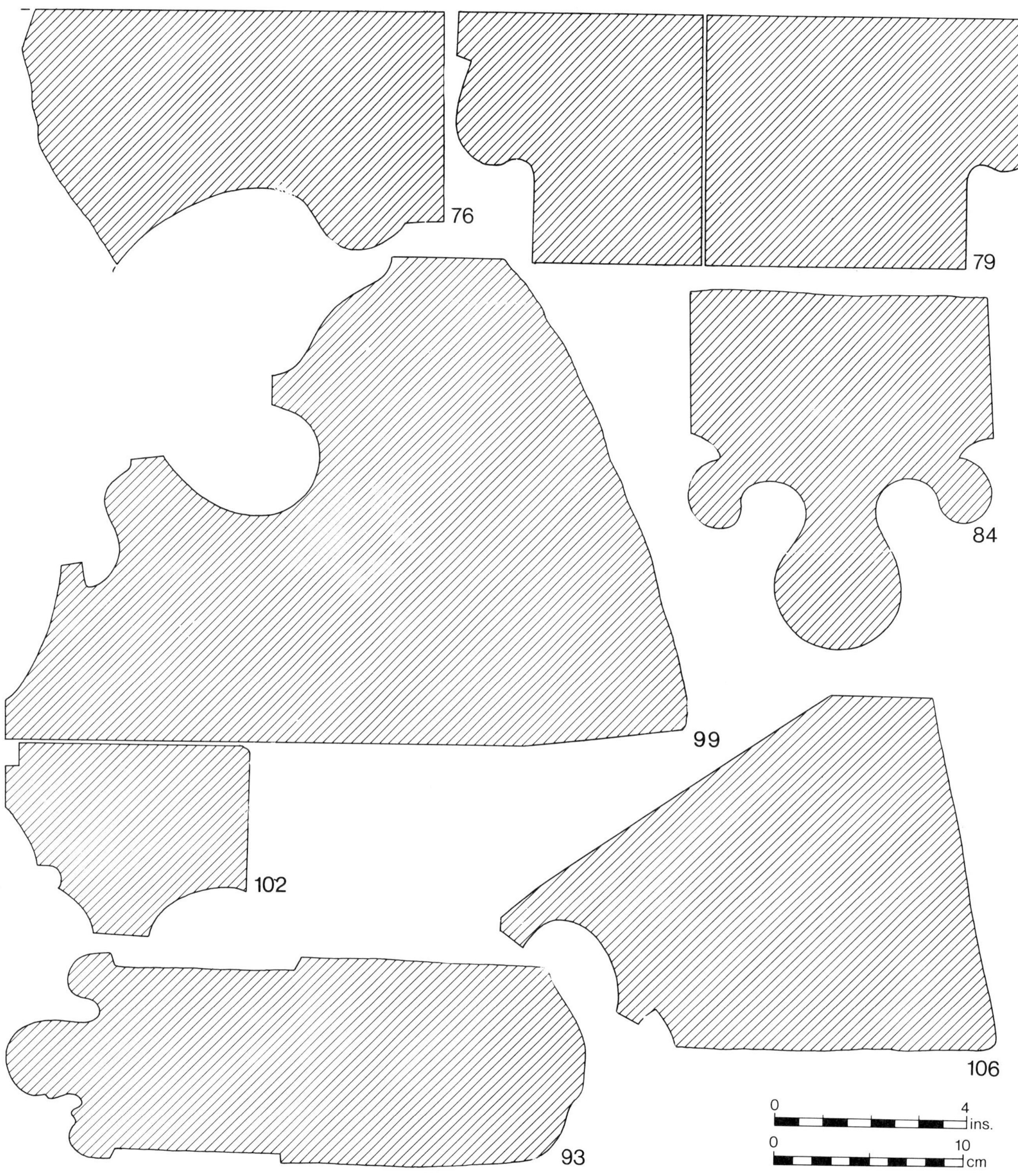

Fig. 32. Stone Mouldings, 1974–75.

No.	*Description*	*Dimensions in cm.*	*Other Information*	*Figure*
	purple? on top. Green on one side. White on the other. Paint on plaster, two coats of whitewash over. Setting-out line on bottom.			
77.	Fragment of head, painted with yellow and pink hair, bright red lips, pink face.		Paint analysis by A.M. Laboratory inconclusive.	D 28
78.	Fragment of stop to moulded capital: chamfer, hollow and keeled roll. Two leaves of rose petal? decoration, purple on white background on chamfer. Two coats of whitewash over.	h:12.4 w:14		
79.	Section of moulded attached capital with round abacus. Chamfer, hollow, keeled roll and dog-tooth. Painted as no. 68.	h:13 l:27	Two other pieces making three-quarters of one capital. Length of two pieces: 55 cm.	M 30C
80.	Section of arch hood-moulding, one side cut steeply away. Chamfer, straight, reverse chamfer, roll and hollow. Horizontal tooling on roll. Purple paint on straight, orange on roll, black on half the hollow, white with purple decoration on the other half. White plaster covered by painted plaster covered by one coat of whitewash.	l:14.3 w:c 8.8	Two other pieces, lengths 25 and 21 cm.	
81.	Section of springer (?) of transverse vaulting rib. One large roll, one small roll. Vertical tooling on rolls, horizontal on inside of springer. Three layers of whitewash. Kentish rag.	l:16	One other piece, 1:7.	
82.	Fragment of voussoir showing springing of two arches. Two hollows and rolls on one arch. Other arch too fragmentary. Orange paint on rolls, black in hollows for one arch; purple in hollows for other. Paint on plaster, whitewashed. Kentish rag.	l:21		
83.	Section of voussoir, two rolls, one large, one small, three hollows. Orange paint on rolls, black in central hollow, purple on outer hollows. Paint on thick white ground. Two coats of whitewash over. Kentish rag.	l:26	One piece. 1.24. Line of whitewash, etc., on underside of voussoir goes diagonally across it. Two fragmentary rolls and a small keystone? roll.	
84.	Section of vaulting rib. One large central roll, two small side rolls, two hollows, undercut. Horizontal tooling on rolls, vertical on one side. Brick-red paint on plaster on rolls. Black in hollows. Purple on one side of the rib. Part of black lozenge decoration visible. Greensand.	l:20 w of block *c.* 15.5	Five other pieces all found as part of the same rib. The paint continues along the rib, the amount of paint reducing gradually to fit the web of the vault. One piece has three small crosses. One large	Plate XLVIII, 30, 32

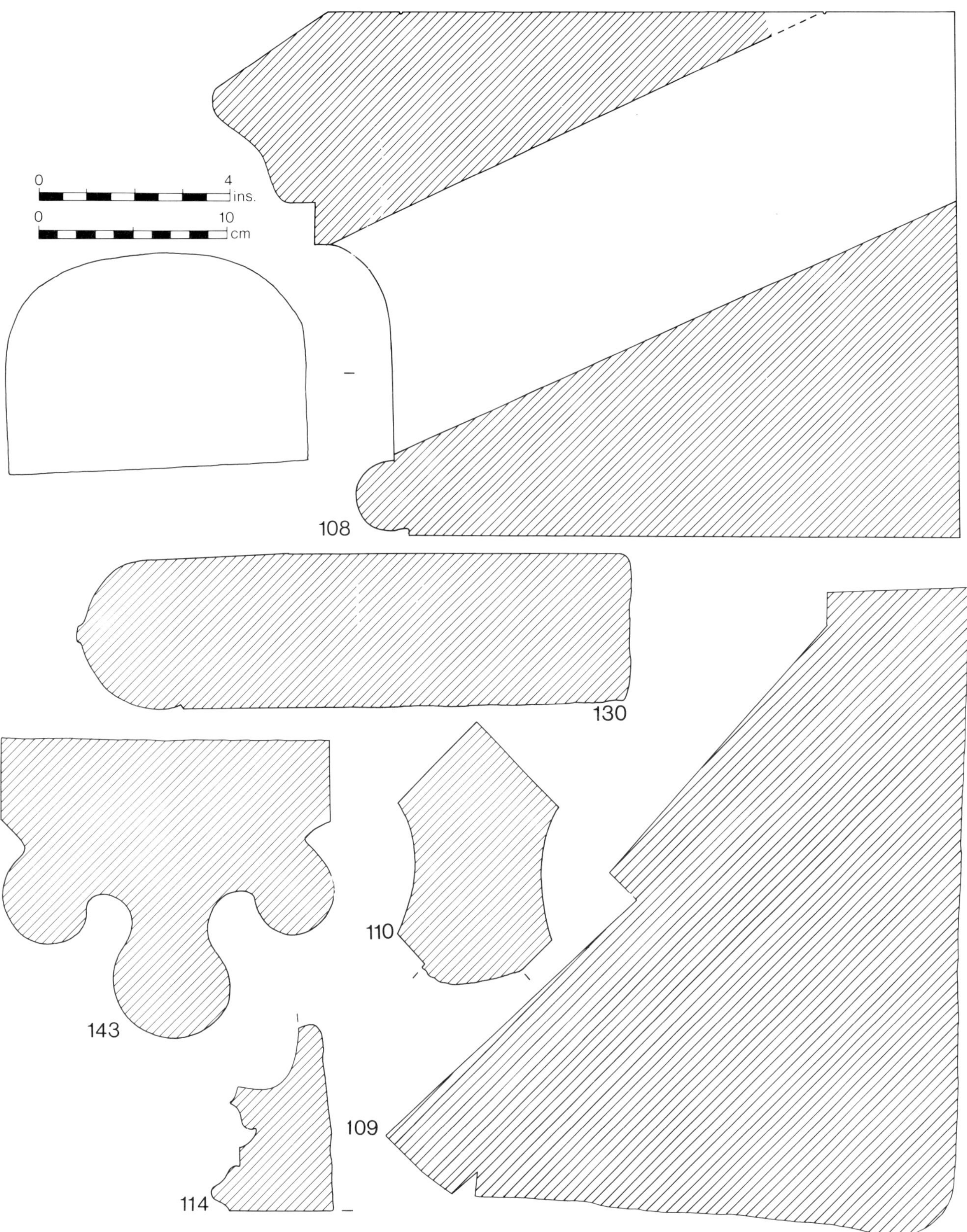

Fig. 33. Stone Mouldings, 1974–75.

No.	*Description*	*Dimensions in cm.*	*Other Information*	*Figure*
			incised cross. Another a large incised cross and a small one on the same side. Two others an incised cross each. These are presumably setting out marks. One piece from the chapter house. Another piece (no. 145) from the garden wall.	
85.	Junction of chamfered and rebated blocks with sill. Setting-out line for rebate. Ragged groove on one side.	l:19.2		
86.	Chamfered and rebated sill, continuation of no. 85. Square hole (2.3 cm.) on top of sill, part of hole (4 x 2 cm.) on side of chamfer, centre 9 cm. from edge of rebate. Both glazing bar holes. Same ragged groove as above.	l:18.8	One other piece; it has the same ragged groove but no glazing bar holes.	
87.	Chamfered sill, no rebate.	l:16.2		
88.	Jamb with chamfer, 90° rebate and reverse chamfer. Pronounced vertical tooling. Coarse thick plaster.	h:21.2	Four other pieces, total section 1:7.22. One has part of a slot for large window bar.	
89.	Part of put-log hole with stone blocking.		Possibly one other piece.	
90.	Fragment of rim of Bethersden marble base.			
91.	Fragment of rim of Purbeck marble.			
92.	Section of marble shaft. One end blank, in the other an iron dowel 1:3.8. One thin coat of whitewash. Kentish rag.	h:69.5 d:8.3	Seven other pieces. All diam. 8.3; three broken. Total section h:m 3.85 (=13 ft. 9 in.). One has iron dowel one end. Four have holes for dowels. Two have creamy mortar at one end.	
93.	Shaft-ring, or knop. Purple paint one side, red on chamfer, two thin coats of whitewash. Bethersden marble.	h:8.5 to fit shaft *c.* 8.5	One other piece, without chamfered jamb, h:9.4 to fit shaft 8.5.	M 32
94.	Attached bell-capital with chamfered jamb cut away so as to allow the marble shafting to be fitted into it. Diagonal and circular setting-out lines on top. Pale red paint on chamfer, white plaster or ground underneath. Purple and black paint on the other side of capital, very light purple paint over, thick plaster underneath.	h:14.4; to fit shaft *c.* 9.2		D 27
95.	Voussoir with chamfer and 90° rebate. Pronounced horizontal tooling. Thick coarse white plaster.		Twenty-one other pieces. Some have fragments of spikes in their sides. One has	

No.	*Description*	*Dimensions in cm.*	*Other Information*	*Figure*
			a half-circular hole in the back. Two have half-slots for window bars.	
96.	Voussoir, external reveal.	l:15	Five other pieces, together with lead sheeting. See p. 140	Plate XLIX
97.	Stiff-leaf capital, complete. Round abacus. Setting-out lines on the top. Coated with thick white plaster.	w of base: 13.5 w of top: 22	The style is classic for *c.* 1220 and close to the Lincoln Cathedral stiff-leaf work of that date. Cf. also Becket's shrine and Bishop's Palace, Chichester, also of that date.	Plate L,a
98.	Fragment of attached respond.	h:m:23	Early fourteenth century.	
99.	Window jamb with ogee rolls and hollows. Rebate at back for insertion into window opening. Glazing groove. Whitewashed. Remains of lead in slot for glazing bar. Unintelligible mason's mark.	h:28 groove 1.4 wide, 1 cm. deep.	Four other pieces total section h:153.9. All are whitewashed and have glazing grooves except one (h:242). One has a hole on the top at the back for a key or bar. See also no. 102.	M 34
100.	Fragment of cusped window jamb with glazing groove. Whitewashed. Distinctive 'cartwheel' bedding marks. A continuation of no. 99, from higher up the wall.	h:m 29.5	Two other pieces, f:h:21.5 and 34.5. One has the same bedding marks as no. 100, the other a deeply incised X on the base. A large fragment now stored in Dover Castle has similar markings.	
101.	Fragment of window mullion with glazing grooves both sides, cusped. Whitewashed. Incised cross on the base.	h:12.2 w:14	One other piece, f:h:10. Part of central mullion tracery belonging to no. 99.	
102.	Part of a jamb with hollows. Glazing rebate. Lead sunk into rebate for glazing bar.	h:24.2	Continuation of no. 99 inside of window probably on same level as window jamb without glazing groove. It is the same height, as no. 122.	M 32
103.	Jamb with ogee wave, fillet and hollow. Whitewashed.	h:26	Continuation of no. 99, probably on same height as no. 100.	
104.	Keystone or springer to arch, continuation of no. 103. Whitewashed.			
105.	Window jamb, two hollows. Gritty coarse plaster on outer face.	h:m:23	Five other pieces. One has wedge-shaped slot for keying. Another a curved slot, length 14 cm., width 2.5 cm., possibly for a glazing bar. One has mason's marks.	34
106.	Hood mould with two hollows, similar but	h:49.5		M 32

No.	*Description*	*Dimensions in cm.*	*Other Information*	*Figure*
	not identical to no. 105 above. Rebate at back tapering away.			
107.	Window jamb, two hollows, three-quarter circle, glazing groove and hollow. Wedge-shaped slot in base for keying. One face left wrought. Gritty coarse plaster on outer face.	h:20		
108.	Section of string-course below parapet with aperture for (?)water spout.	h:24.2 l:90.5	Three other pieces, one fragmentary. Combined l:269.8.	M 33
109.	Section of weathering above parapet, two chamfers at different angles.	l:64		M 33
110.	Section of window mullion, hollows and chamfers.	h:12.3		M 33
111.	Fragment of corner of pedestal, roll with fillet, hollow and bead. Purple-red paint on upper part of roll and bead. Mid-green paint in hollow. Round hole in hollow 2.5 deep.	l:13.2 x 12.8		
112.	Corner of pinnacle with string moulding. Fine comb tooling.	l:13 (string: 13)	One other piece, smaller and broken.	D 28
113.	Fragment of pinnacle, chamfer, string-course, two reverse hollows, fillet, two hollows. Hole in base, diam. 12.7, for iron spike. Mortar still adhering to sides of hole.	h:4.9	One other piece.	
114.	Fragment of moulding, string-course on 45° turn, or fragment of capital? for octagonal pier. Very fine tooling.	l:m19 2.5 on return.	Fifteenth century.	M 33
115.	Corner fragment of rectangular shallow bowl (a holy water stoop?) in smooth Purbeck marble. A hollow moulding outside.	l:11.5 x 7.8 h:5	From Area 1, layer 5.	
116.	Corner fragment of bowl? Complex of mouldings outside. Fine tooling.	l:9 x 3.2	From Area 1, layer 5.	
	4. *From 'fallen Wall': Area 2.* (a) Area above fallen wall: layer 1, and unstratified.			
117.	Fragment of Anglo-Saxon interlace. Weathered.			
118.	Fragment of base of minor shaft. Hollow?, double chamfer. Deeply incised line underneath.	h:m:7.6	Romanesque.	
119.	Section of voussoir. Hollow, bead and roll. Weathered.	l:11	Thirteenth century; cf. no. 3 (Trench II).	
120.	Section of window mullion.	l:32.5		

No.	*Description*	*Dimensions in cm.*	*Other Information*	*Figure*
121.	Fragment of window mullion. Hollows and chamfers. Finely tooled.	l:m:21	Two other pieces, one from tumble: l:12.3; and one from fallen wall: l:32.	
122.	Fragment of window jamb.	l:m:13	Continuation of no. 99 (tumble).	
123.	Fragment of openwork balustrade; cusped tracery, quatrefoil patterns. Very fine tooling but rough tooling on top, with two diagonal parallel lines.	l:m 29.7 2:7.6		D 28
124.	Fragment of moulding, complex of rolls and hollows. Fine tooling.	l:m:6 w:9.5		
(b) The rubble above the wall: Layer 19. Also one moulded stone re-used in the core-work (no. 129) and the string-course facing stones from the third bay west of the transept.				
125.	Double hollow base. Re-used as chamfered and rebated jamb, probably part of window formed by no. 136, etc. Part of a slot for large window bar. Diagonal tooling in hollows.	1 of re-used base: 18 dimensions of base; 18.8 x 14.5	Date: about 1070s.	
126.	Return of chamfered string-course. Diagonal tooling.	25.5 x 11.5 h:15	Eleventh century. Five other pieces, one return. All making up the string-course for the third bay east of the transept.	
127.	Probably a continuation of return of no. 126 above.		One other piece for other side of a pilaster.	
128.	Section of bowtell, keyed.	l:12.8	One other piece l:11.3. Similar to, but smaller than no. 64 (tumble)	
129.	Voussoir with chevron decoration. Re-used in core-work.	w:10.5		D 29
130.	Section of edge-moulding, roll with fillet, undercut on lower side. Setting-out lines. Pronounced horizontal tooling. Whitewashed, two coats. Three crosses incised on the lower surface (not illustrated).	l:11.6 h:8	Three other pieces, total l:81.9	M 33
131.	Section of edge-moulding, same as above except there is a chamfered sill with ? glazing groove on the other side. Also a lead slot for glazing bar. Mason's mark.	l:32		34
132.	Kentish rag marble shaft, one end blank; from the other end an iron dowel protruding 1.8 cm. Whitewashed, one thin coat.	h:78.5 d:8.8	Three other pieces, d. slightly wider. Total m:l:37.7, two have holes for dowels.	

No.	*Description*	*Dimensions in cm.*	*Other Information*	*Figure*
133a. 133b.	Caen-stone internal reveal, cut for the insertion of 133b, a fragment of Kentish rag marble shaft ring. Setting out mark. Pronounced vertical tooling.	h: of shaft ring 8.8, fitting exactly into recess in reveal. Reveal h:18.7.	Found close to no. 132 which fits onto it. Possibly the choir aisle windows were shafted internally.	
134.	Fragment of small Purbeck marble shaft or column base.			
135.	Jamb or sill with slight chamfer. Whitewashed with two thin coats.	l or h: 15.5	Five other pieces, total l or h: 97.6.	
136.	Jamb with chamfer and acute rebate. Pronounced vertical tooling. Thick coarse white plaster.	h:21.5	Twelve other pieces. Four have a slot for a large window bar. One has no rebate but must be equivalent to another piece on the other side of the window.	
137.	Jamb with chamfer and small 90° rebate.	h:28	One other piece, total h:58.	
138.	Jamb with 45° chamfer. Pronounced vertical tooling. Thick coarse white plaster.	h:13.6	Seven other pieces. Two with pronounced vertical tooling, the others have a smooth finish. One has mason's doodles.	
139.	Fragment or corbel. 'Corinthianesque'.		Late twelfth century.	
140.	Voussoir with chamfer and acute rebate. Pronounced vertical tooling. Thick coarse white plaster. Mason's mark.	l:16.3	Thirteen other pieces. One has the remains of three spikes to wedge the iron frame into the rebate(?); one has part of a slot.	34 42, no. 4 (iron).
141.	Chamfered voussoir, no rebate.		Ten other pieces.	
142.	Voussoir; external reveal. Diagonal tooling.	l:13	Possibly nine other pieces.	
143.	Voussoir with one large and two small rolls. Pronounced vertical tooling. Whitewashed.	l:32.5	Fourteen other pieces. Most are white-washed. Most have a mason's mark or setting-out line, sometimes one, sometimes both sides, which is in all cases a cross. (Not illustrated).	M 33
	(c) The Rubble beneath the Fallen Wall			
144.	Section of external reveal. Mason's mark.			34
145.	Roll to vaulting rib. Red paint.	l:13.5	Cf. no. 84 (tumble).	
146.	Irregular tufa block, plastered and painted. Linear, zig-zag and circular decoration. Black, white and purple paint over chalky white plaster.			

No.	*Description*	*Dimensions in cm.*	*Other Information*	*Figure*
147.	Jamb with 45° chamfer. Pronounced vertical tooling.		Cf. no. 138.	
148.	Chamfered voussoir. Pronounced vertical tooling. Coarse white plaster.		One ? other piece. It has diagonal tooling.	
149.	Section of half-round respond. Incised diagonal intersecting lines at back with dots in spaces. Fine surface, possibly used as a gaming board or abacus.	l:19.2 width of attached side: 9 cm.	See below p. 119 (graffiti)	34
150.	Section of springer of respond of arch (?). Diagonal intersecting lines at back and side of section; mason's mark.	width of base 7 x 6		34
151.	Fragment of base of pinnacle.	l:11.2	Similar to no. 112 (tumble).	
152.	Fragment of pinnacle. Roll moulding. Finely finished.	l:11.3	Similar to no. 151.	
	5. *Moulded Stones from elsewhere on the Site, 1974–75.*			
153.	Vaulting pendant with Tudor rose, blank panelling on two sides, cusping on the other two.		From south of lady chapel.	D 29
154.	Pinnacle. Iron spike (diam. 1.5) protruding 10.2 cm. from the top of the pinnacle for purpose of holding a cross or other finial. Spike socketed in lead.	h:30	Found by wall of south transept.	D 27
155.	Fragment of half-round respond.	h:19	From Area 2, layer 37 (see above p. 56); cf. no. 58.	
156.	Fragment of moulding on 45° turn. Roll and fillet. Fine comb tooling. Mason's mark.	l:6 3 on turn	From Area 2, layer 66 (disturbance in connection with building of modern boundary wall.)	34
157.	Fragment of moulding. Hollow and chamfered roll.	l:m:12	As above.	
158.	Fragment of jamb or window mullion.	h:17	From Area 2, layer 67 (Dissolution/demolition layer).	

DISCUSSION C. Miscampbell

Pre-Conquest

Much Anglo-Saxon building-stone must have been available for re-use in the post-Conquest building. However, an examination of the core-work above the fallen wall showed that the south wall of the presbytery aisle had been totally built of new stone. Roman bricks had been used in two courses, and occasionally elsewhere on the fallen wall, but otherwise pre-Conquest worked stone had only been re-used in the modern boundary wall: this was presumably stone that had been used as core-work for the post-Conquest church.[16]

Romanesque

All the dressed ashlar found in the tumble, on the outer face of the fallen wall and in several smaller areas south of the south transept (including Trench II) was Caen-stone, diagonally tooled. As there is no record of a re-building of the Romanesque church, it is reasonable to suppose that this was the stone from Abbot Scotland's church. Indicative of the early date of the presbytery were the thickness of mortar in the joints of the ashlar masonry in the fallen wall (sometimes as much as 6 cm.), the profile of the string-course of the fallen wall (a flat upper edge and a simple chamfer beneath), and the re-use of Roman brick as a building material. A number of diagonally tooled ashlar blocks was uncovered in Trench II and must have come from the south wall of the south transept. One off-set stone was found in the pile of debris suggesting that the south transept wall was articulated by at least one pilaster.

It seems likely that the shafts found in the tumble (Cat. no. 64) along with the roll mouldings (Cat. no. 65) are all part of one window opening in the presbytery. They all had coarse vertical tooling. The roll mouldings were all keyed. It is possible that a base found in the same area (Cat. no. 55), with a single roll moulding would have been the base to these shafts and one of their capitals would have been the cushion capital recovered from the tumble (Cat. no. 62).[17] Two roll mouldings were recovered from the collapsed window area of the fallen wall (Cat. no. 128). Both were keyed, and in tooling and shape they were similar, but the fallen wall mouldings had a smaller diameter. The stones could not have come from the presbytery windows since they were altered later (see below). It could be that the smaller mouldings were used in the south presbytery gallery but, perhaps because of careless construction, they were not of the same diameter as the larger mouldings (Cat. no. 55), which may have come from the upper storey of the radiating chapel, assuming it had one (see below), or from the main window opening to the radiating chapel.

Further east in the tumble was found part of the internal and external reveals of an arch (Cat. no. 96) and a long length of lead sheeting (see p. 140, no. 19 and Plate XLIX). The distance between the inner and outer reveals was just under 1 m. and was filled by plaster and rubble. There was a stone at one end of the arch which formed an offset. The diagonal tooling and wide gaps for mortar between the stones indicated that this arch was part of the late eleventh-century church. There was no obvious indication where this arch might fit in the church, but it seems most likely that it was part of the gallery storey, and perhaps the innermost order of the window either to the radiating chapel or to the gallery west of the chapel. The lead sheet would probably have been used as flashing to prevent stone erosion, as it was found behind and below the arch.

The twenty sections of half-columns and the two sections of quarter columns (Cat. nos. 56, 57, 58 and 60) found in the tumble may have been attached to the flat pilasters shown on Fig. 10,

16. The boundary wall was built in 1910. The area between this wall and the church was then excavated for stones and used for mixing mortar. It seems reasonable to suppose that most of the stones used in the boundary wall came from the southern walls of the abbey church, either from the core or the facing stones.
17. But see Gloucester Cathedral north apsidal chapel where the surviving Norman triforium window has continuous shafting uninterrupted by capitals.

on either side of the radiating chapel window opening.[18] Evidence for this suggestion comes from a group of five of these half-columns, together with a single offset stone, found together face downwards in a position slightly south-west of the window opening, which are shown on Fig. 10. Further east, just beyond the bell-shaped depression projecting from the chapel was a shallower and smaller depression, which looked to be the imprint of robbed-out half-columns. When the chapel was destroyed it would appear to have split apart in the centre and this would account for the distance between the five half-columns and the depression further to the east. All except six of the half-columns showed coarse vertical tooling when the white plaster was removed. These six (see Cat. no. 60) were of roughly uniform height and showed finer vertical tooling, of the same type as the stones from the enlarged presbytery aisle windows. The difference between the half-columns could be explained by the heightening of the radiating chapel and the tooling of the necessary half-columns in the current manner. One of the half-columns was found juxtaposed with a piece of parapet string-course (Cat. no. 108) which, however, had a fourteenth-century moulding.

Apart from the Romanesque bases and capitals already mentioned, a few others were recovered, both from the modern boundary wall and from the tumble. A double hollow-chamfer base had been re-used as a chamfered and rebated jamb in the fallen wall window (Cat. no. 125). It had been cut down for re-use but can only have been the base of a minor shaft, perhaps in a wall arcade in Abbot Scotland's church. Its crude profile indicates a date in the 1070s.[19] A large cushion capital, found in the tumble (Cat. no. 62), was on a return similar to the angle of return between the semi-circle of the radiating chapel and the curving wall of the ambulatory, so it may have come from there. Also found in the tumble were a fragment of scrollwork (Cat. no. 63) and a pilaster capital (Cat. no. 61) carved with acanthus leaves, subsequently re-used as a chamfered and rebated jamb, which may be dated by the fine necking on the bottom of the capital to the early twelfth century.[20] A small cushion capital (Cat. no. 23) and a capital with two hollows (Cat. no. 22) were discovered in the boundary wall and were both possibly part of a Romanesque wall arcade, as may have been also a section of a chamfered impost block carved with continuous scroll-work (Cat. no. 24).

A chevron voussoir (Cat. no. 125) had been re-used as a chamfered and rebated block in the fallen wall window. Several pieces of chevron decoration, probably voussoirs, were recovered from the boundary wall (Cat. nos. 33 and 34). It is generally accepted that chevron decoration made its appearance in England in the early twelfth century (Clapham 1934, 128) and at St. Augustine's Abbey it is first noticed on Ethelbert's Tower (erected in the first quarter of the twelfth century). Its use in the eastern arm may be connected with alterations to the shrines.

18. In view of the smallness of the chapel, it seems likely that it was lighted by one window only on the ground floor. Side windows would have weakened the structure and possibly made it unsuitable for there to be a vault, which undoubtedly did exist later on. Compare the south transept eastern apsidal chapel of Christchurch Priory, Dorset, where a variation of such a scheme occurred in the original building *c.* 1110.

19. Clapham 1934, 119. Note also its use at Mont St. Michel Abbey (*ibid.*, 17, n.2).

20. S.E. Rigold, pers. comm. Similar necking on capitals appears in Ernulf's crypt at Canterbury and at Southwell Cathedral. The evidence of this and other fine capitals now in the museum suggests that the shrine area of the choir was re-done in the 1120s (or possibly after 1130, following the consecration of Ernulf's work at Canterbury Cathedral), survived the fire of 1168 and was destroyed in 1221 when, as Thorne records, 'the altar and the whole stone work on which the shrine stood was broken up to be repaired and decorated' (Davis 1934, 189).

Other Norman decoration found re-used in the boundary wall consisted of billet (Cat. nos. 28, 29, 30, 31 and 32) and various kinds of diaper work (Cat. nos. 25, 26 and 27). Some of the billet work and all the diaper was of Quarr-stone, a favourite building stone in Hampshire and West Sussex but exhausted by the mid-fourteenth century. This appears to be its earliest appearance in Kent to date (see p. 121) and here its use is restricted to friezes marking horizontal distinctions and also over doorway arches.

Late twelfth Century, Transitional

There were no indications that any major alterations were made to the Romanesque eastern arm between its building and the fire of 1168. However, if actual evidence is sought for the 1168 fire, it must be admitted that there were virtually no signs of burning on any of the excavated stones; the only burning that was noticeable probably belonging to sixteenth-century demolition works (Cat. no. 73). Nor does the internal face of the wall of the north aisle of the nave appear to have suffered.

The most important stones of the late twelfth century from the excavations were the dog-tooth and overlapping chevron voussoirs, identical to the internal window voussoirs in the Corona and Trinity Chapel in Canterbury Cathedral, and found in the tumble in a broken arch (see Cat. no. 66). There were 11 pieces (Cat. no. 66) together with the springing stone to the arch (Cat. no. 67). Also found in the tumble were three sections of an arch with dog-tooth (see Cat. no. 68), which looked as if they were part of the hood-moulding to the above arch (i.e. Cat. no. 66). Cat. no. 75, which was scalloped and painted orange, may have been the stop to this hood-moulding, or alternatively a corbel to a vaulting rib-shaft. The position of this arch was something of a puzzle. It was found slightly south-east of the central window of the radiating chapel but its diameter is too wide to span that window. A possible alternative is the arch opening between the ambulatory and the radiating chapel, probably looking towards the chapel, since the voussoirs are plainly meant to be seen only from one side. They are only painted on one side and the chevron on that side has two 'V' carvings on it. This would mean that the round arch there would have to be cut back to receive a depressed Gothic arch. The arch was certainly not the transverse arch nor the wall arch of the ambulatory vault, since it is not wide enough.

There was a single voussoir found in the boundary wall (Cat. no. 37) of similar type to Cat. no. 66, except that it had a shallow foliated motif cut into the chevron.[21] Six other pieces of overlapping chevron voussoirs (now stored in Dover Castle) came from earlier excavations. They are said to have been found in the chapter house but are really unprovenanced (S.E. Rigold, pers. comm.). It is possible that they came from the radiating chapel on the north side of the presbytery. The half-columns already mentioned (Cat. no. 56) may be of this date as additions to an outside flat pilastered wall. No trace was found of a capital supporting the chevron arch unless it was the fragment of scroll-work of a capital found in the tumble (Cat. no. 63) or, possibly, the bell-capital (Cat. no. 94) found there. Two shaft-rings (see Cat. No. 93), possibly the fragment of a base (Cat. no. 90) and eight sections of marble shafts were

21. Compare the north aisle nave wall arcade at New Shoreham, Sussex, which is late twelfth-century, where there are similar voussoirs.

also found in the tumble suggesting an internal elevation in the south radiating chapel of a marble-shafted window with shaft-rings supported by a chevron arch. The 'marble' shafts of the windows were of a Kentish rag (see geology report below) which, when polished, turns a very dark blue. The shaft-rings, capital and fragment of base were all of Sussex marble, of similar colour, except for the shaft-ring found above the fallen wall which was of the same local rag as the 'marble' shafts. The only moulding which seemed out of place was the bell-capital since it is generally accepted that bell-capitals did not arrive in England until the early thirteenth century.[22] An explanation for its presence is that the capitals may have been renewed at the time of the alteration of the south ambulatory windows when the radiating chapel windows may have been lengthened and an opportunity taken to insert new capitals beside new marble shafts to fit in with the recent work. There are, however, slight traces of purple paint on the capital which suggests that it was put in the church at the time of the Transitional rebuilding. Fragments remained of Purbeck marble shafts (Cat. no. 91), and it is possible that the entrance to the radiating chapel was decorated with these. Three pieces of edge moulding were found in the tumble (see Cat. no. 73) with a total length of 702 mm. and these may have been part of a continuous external string-course around the chapel. The profile was that of a crudely executed keel indicating a late twelfth-century date.

Nine chamfered jambs were excavated from the tumble (Cat. nos. 69 and 70). They were painted and had been whitewashed (though the whitewash had flaked off some of the jambs). Four were double-chamfered and five single-chamfered. All looked as if they were inner reveals of an arch, probably of the radiating chapel window. It was interesting that one of the jambs (Cat. no. 71) was of Kentish ragstone while all the others were of Caen-stone suggesting, perhaps, that the rebuilding needed to be done in a hurry and that the builders could not wait for the next shipment of Caen-stone. The same might be said of the variety of stone types used in the half-columns.

A large number of vaulting ribs were found in the tumble together with a quantity of vaulting plaster painted with stars on a dark blue background and only a fragment of a rib (Cat. no. 145) in the fallen wall area. It is suggested that the south-eastern radiating chapel would have been a three-storey chapel (as at Bury St. Edmund's Abbey) and that the rib-voussoirs excavated with the large mass of painted plaster would have been part of the ground-storey vaulting, the idea being, perhaps, to fire-proof the building after the disaster of 1168. They were all of greensand stone and also painted. Two types of rib were excavated, the first with one large and two small rolls (Cat. no. 84); the second with one large and one small roll (Cat. nos. 81, 82 and 83). Six pieces of the former were uncovered lying face down in the form of part of an arch (Plate XLVIII). It could be seen that the stones had been placed near the top of the arch since on both sides of the ribs the area of paint became smaller and smaller and then began to become larger. From this is seems that the arch was round-headed, deeply undercut and with hollow-chamfered edges when the outer walls met the outside of the stones. It spans about 2 m. which is approximately the width of the radiating chapel window opening shown in Fig. 10. If it was an internal arch for this window (rather than part of a vaulting rib) then it is possible that it

22. But compare the moulded capitals in the Trinity Chapel in the cathedral crypt, built in 1179–81 by William the Englishman; also the Purbeck marble moulded capitals in the choir of Portsmouth Cathedral, part consecrated by 1188.

was supported by the marble columns and capitals mentioned below (Cat. nos. 90, 93, 94 and 79). The one small fragment (of a roll from an arch similar to Cat. nos. 83 or 84) found under the fallen wall and not from the tumble (Cat. no. 145) was probably a splinter from the radiating chapel though it is possible that it indicated that the south ambulatory was rib-vaulted in the same way as the radiating chapel and at the same time.[23] Three pieces of an internal hood-moulding (Cat. no. 80) in the tumble would have probably fitted over the internal window arch of the radiating chapel.

Thirteenth Century (pre-1240), Early English

(See pp. 57–9 and Fig. 15 for the reconstruction of internal and external elevations of the presbytery south aisle wall).

The Early English alterations to the eastern arm have been identified partly by the tooling on the stones, which is either horizontal or vertical and is always pronounced, partly by the lack of paint on the stones, and partly by the mouldings themselves. However, it must be admitted that pronounced tooling occurs on the rolls of the dog-tooth and chevron voussoirs, that the marble shafting has been painted in red ochre and that the bell-capital mentioned above could be of either period. These indications, then, are not proof but seem to give a reasonable explanation for the position of most of the worked stone.

Although the Early English work is 'whitewashed' and not painted, examination of the earlier carved stone has shown that it, too, was whitewashed eventually. It is unlikely that methods of whitewashing stone would have changed significantly in a hundred years. It is, therefore, impossible to say whether the radiating chapel was painted because it was ritually significant; or because the builders, starting from the east end, changed their minds and whitewashed the wall east of the chapel; or, more possibly, because when the presbytery aisle windows came to be altered in the thirteenth century it was necessary to take out the old painted stones and it was then thought sufficient to whitewash the wall, the radiating chapel being later whitewashed to conform. The only guide is that fragments of a black-letter inscription were found by the fallen wall and they are believed to be of the fourteenth century (see p. 122). So there may have been several periods of whitewashing in the church.

On the south side of the church, that is, in the ambulatory, rebuilding work did not affect the shell of Scotland's church.[24] Instead, the eleventh-century windows were enlarged and lengthened. The external Romanesque string-course, showing the sill of the original window, was cut back on its first offset and two continuous orders of chamfered jambs inserted to flank the new rebated window. As has been remarked in the discussion on the eleventh-century church, the fallen wall window did not seem to have been heightened; rather the new chamfered voussoirs were mortared against the recessed voussoirs (Cat. no. 142) of the eleventh-century

23. The crypt aisles were groin vaulted, as was the north aisle of the nave (Bilson 1906, 108–9). Presumably, the ambulatory aisles were vaulted in a similar manner at first, although there is no evidence to prove it.
24. The position of the fallen wall window bears out Bilson's suggestion (1906, 110) that the choir of the church had as many bays as the crypt. The spacing of these bays must have been very cramped.

window. The bottom of the fallen wall window was probably not found (though see the discussion of the fallen wall, p. 52). However, a piece of the junction between a chamfered and rebated jamb with the sill was found (Cat. no. 85) in the tumble, as well as two pieces of the continuation of the rebated sill (Cat. no. 86). These must have come from the window east of the fallen wall window showing that it, too, was enlarged at that time. The window west of the fallen wall window was probably a lancet as well since the eleventh-century string-course looked as if it had been cut back in the same way as the fallen wall to receive the thirteenth-century window. Ten chamfered and rebated jambs were excavated from the tumble (Cat. no. 88). They did not have the same mouldings as the jambs from the fallen wall (Cat. no. 136), which had chamfers and acute rebates. Five of the jambs from the tumble had chamfers, 90° rebates and reverse chamfers, five had chamfers and 90° rebates only. These jambs may have all come from the same window, i.e. the window east of the fallen wall window or possibly from both that window and the central window in the radiating chapel. Evidence that they all were part of the same arch came from the fact that they were found with twenty-two voussoirs of similar tooling (Cat. no. 95), which fitted to make part of one arch, and that arch would probably have fitted over the window east of the fallen wall window. If it is accepted that these jambs and voussoirs formed one window then we must assume that the radiating chapel outer jambs were robbed because no other outer jambs survive. So it would be impossible to say what the outside of the radiating chapel main window looked like.

From the stones excavated, it seems that the enlarged ambulatory windows would have had interior arches shafted in marble, with marble bases, capitals and shaft-rings, and supporting an arch with three rolls (Cat. no. 143). A shaft-ring of the same period was found inserted into an interior reveal having an angle of about 10° (Cat. nos. 132 and 133 a and b), suggesting that the marble shafts, with shaft-rings, stood proud of the wall as indicated on the reconstruction drawing (Fig. 15). A fragment of the internal window splay, of plaster, was found in the fallen wall 0.67 to 0.86 m. from the outer facing stones (above p. 48). There was no paint on the plaster, it being whitewashed only. Also found above the fallen wall was another fragment of whitewashed plaster with a black-letter inscription on it. This was in contrast to a large irregular block of tufa (Cat. no. 146) found underneath the fallen wall, which was painted and did not seem to have been whitewashed over. It is possible though that the whitewash had flaked off the stone. Six chamfered pieces with two thin coats of whitewash (Cat. no. 135) looked as if they were jambs of a locker in the south ambulatory wall (similar to the locker in the crypt of the south-east radiating chapel).

Work after 1240 and before 1325

The stiff-leaf capital (Cat. no. 97) in the tumble was in perfect condition but no fragments of any other similar capital were discovered. It may have been inserted into an existing window, perhaps that west of the radiating chapel, to replace a bell-capital. It would be tempting to associate it with the moving of the shrines (Plate I) before the dedication of 1240, i.e. supposing that the marble shafts and capitals had been taken out and replaced by a capital with a short marble shaft beneath it which would act as a stop to the internal arch. This would allow a shrine to be built against the wall of the church.

The next major alterations to the south wall of the presbytery appear to come with the insertion of new crypt windows and the addition of a parapet. All the evidence for this comes from the tumble. Five jambs were discovered (Cat. nos. 99 and 100), whose mouldings were roughly similar to the surviving mouldings *in situ* in the south crypt windows. The windows had glazing grooves and were cusped. The beginning of the cusp (Cat. no. 100) and its continuation piece (Cat. no. 103) appeared to form an internal arch, the keystone or springer of which was also discovered (Cat. no. 104). A piece of the hood-mould to this arch was also discovered (Cat. no. 106). Another section of hood-mould, of similar date and style was taken from the boundary wall. One of the tall jambs had no glazing groove (Cat. no. 99) but appeared to be related to a smaller piece (Cat. no. 102), in such a way that the two pieces together created a rebate at the back of the stone and a glazing groove. A number of pieces (Cat. nos. 103, 104, 105 and 107) were found, also in the tumble, with similar mouldings to the above and presumably part of the crypt windows. Their rough outer plastered face indicated that they ought to have been on the outside (but so far it has proved impossible to work out their exact position).

Four pieces of the string course below the parapet were uncovered, totalling 2.70 m. in length (Cat. no. 108). One had an aperture for a water spout. Above the string-course there could have been two or three courses of plain ashlar stones and then the weathering (Cat. no. 109) or the weathering might have been immediately above the string-course. As there was no curving on these stones they must have come from the south ambulatory wall. This parapet would have been that of the aisle wall, rather than a possible central parapet above the clerestory.[25] Evidence for an earlier parapet came from Cat. no. 53, which was a piece of weathering at the turn of a wall of the church; double-chamfered with a roll and fillet, found in the dismantled boundary wall. Two pinnacles, one in the tumble (Cat. no. 113) and one by the fallen wall (Cat. no. 154) were excavated as well as small fragments of pedestals to pinnacles (Cat. nos. 111, 112, 151, 152). These may have emphasised the vertical distinction between the bays of the windows. It is probable that all this work was done before the re-dedication in 1325.

There seemed to be no evidence for a re-building of the inside of the church at this time. A section of a string-course of this date (Cat. no. 46), coming from the boundary wall, may have been internal or external.

Little incidental interior stonework of this date was excavated. Two corner fragments of bowls or piscinae, one of Purbeck marble, were found in the tumble (Cat. nos. 115 and 116) and may have come from the radiating chapel. A double-cresset lamp (p. 199, Cat. no. 81) was uncovered from beneath the fallen wall. The very fine piece of openwork (Cat. no. 123) with cusped mouldings from the fallen wall area may have been part of an open-work screen around a shrine. The fragment of cusped blind panelling (Cat. no. 47) was also of workmanship fine enough to have come from a screen in the church.

Late Medieval

Only one carved stone of any importance from a later date was uncovered and that some 11 m. south of the lady chapel. It was a fragment of a pendant in Kentish ragstone with a Tudor rose

25. Compare the parapet of Winchelsea Church, East Sussex, which is very similar and seems to have been completed by the early fourteenth century.

design on the end (Cat. no. 153). Too small to have hung from the roof of the lady chapel, its most likely provenance would have been the vault of a tomb canopy or chantry in the lady chapel.

EVIDENCE FOR BUILDING AND GLAZING METHODS

Windows

It was impossible to tell how the Romanesque church was fenestrated. Only the shafts of the gallery stage opening were recovered (Cat. no. 64). One piece of sill with a glazing groove was found in the boundary wall (Cat. no. 43). It was of oolite stone which, when compared with other pieces excavated, seems to indicate a date before the thirteenth century. The arrangements for the thirteenth-century window could be more easily reconstructed from the fallen wall. The innermost chamfered order was rebated, probably for glass. Small quantities of *grisaille* glass were found in the fallen wall and tumble as well as the possible corner piece of an iron frame (Fig. 42, no. 2) supporting the glass and fitting into the rebate. The frame itself appears to have been secured into the rebate by means of tapering spikes hammered in between the jambs and voussoirs of the rebated blocks. Traces of the spikes were discovered in six of the jambs and voussoirs, driven into the stones not more than 5 cm., in ones, twos and in one case threes (Fig. 42, no. 4). The iron frame may have been supported at intervals by large iron bars running across the window. Holes for these bars occurred in the fallen rebated jambs between courses eight and nine, and ten and eleven above the Norman string-course, the holes being slightly less than 10 cm. high and about 3–4 cm. deep. Similar holes were noted from rebated jambs in the tumble. None of the voussoirs had such holes. A part of the chamfered and rebated sill was uncovered in the tumble (Cat. no. 86), having a slot down the side at the chamfer and a smaller square hole on the flat top above the chamfer. The former slot could have held a vertical bar running up the full length of the window as part of an iron grid to protect the window. The latter hole seems too small for such a purpose, though it could have held a subsidiary bar. Several 'squares' of lead were excavated which could have fitted into the iron frame (p. 138, Fig. 42, no. 2), which had two holes inside into which the lead could have been inserted to hold the squares in position. The crypt windows had glazed grooves, 1 cm. wide and 1.5 cm. deep. One window jamb (Cat. no. 102) had a lead matrix sunk into the groove to hold an iron window bar, the purpose being to prevent the iron corroding and splitting the stone.

Two of the jambs with hollows, part of the same crypt window series (Cat. no. 107) had wedge-shape slots, possibly for cramping to the stone above: they were not cramped to each other. Another of these jambs (Cat. no. 105) had a curved slot 2.5 cm. deep and about 14 cm. long by the side of its glazing groove. If its purpose was to hold a strengthening bar, then the lead matrix needed to surround it has been robbed. Also, there would have been difficulties in fashioning a matrix which could have surrounded such a bar. An alternative purpose for the slot could be for cramping.

Bedding and Mortar Marks

Those on the Norman ashlar masonry are very slight. There are heavy incisions in some of the inserted thirteenth-century window jambs, especially in the voussoirs to the internal wall arch. The cusped fourteenth-century jambs to the crypt windows (Cat. no. 101) have deep patterned incisions, similar to the 'cart-wheel' bedding marks.

Tooling on the Stone

The tooling is one of the most important factors here used for distinguishing building periods. Of the dressed ashlar blocks 99 per cent had diagonal axe tooling, suggesting a date before the end of the twelfth century for the building of the shell of the church. Of the carved Romanesque stones, the double hollow chamfer base (Cat. no. 125) was diagonally tooled in the hollows whereas the chevron voussoirs (Cat. nos. 33, 129), of later date, were tooled horizontally along the hollows. There was no tooling visible from the Quarr-stone sections of friezes and string-courses (Cat. nos. 26, 27, 30). The half-columns (Cat. nos. 56, etc.) had very coarse vertical tooling, as did the gallery shafts and arch voussoirs (Cat. nos. 64, etc.). On the latter the tooling occurred only on one side suggesting that it had been done once the stones had been fixed into position. These half-columns must be earlier than the six (Cat. no. 60) found in the tumble, which have sharp and pronounced vertical tooling.[26]

The chisel tooling is noticeable on all work done between the fire of 1168 and the dedication of 1240. However, on the dog-tooth arch (Cat. no. 66) it only exists on the minor rolls clasped by the chevrons. On the moulded capital (Cat. no. 79) it is only evident on the top of the capital. Elsewhere on these stones the tooling is fine, probably done with a stone abrasive. The vaulting ribs (Cat. nos. 81, 82, 83, 84) are tooled in this manner. It is the inserted thirteenth-century window jambs (Cat. nos. 136, 137, 138) that are most strongly tooled vertically or horizontally as are the voussoirs of the internal arch of the ambulatory wall (Cat. no. 143), the lines being 2.5 mm. apart, though probably tooled by a 1 cm. chisel.

Later work, i.e. between 1240 and 1325, can be identified by the use of a claw chisel on flat surfaces, where the indication is usually shallow, and an abrasive stone in the hollows. The string-course (Cat. no. 108) with its weathering (Cat. no. 109) and the pinnacles from the tumble (Cat. nos. 113, 154) are finished purely by an abrasive stone.

MASONS' MARKS AND OTHER GRAFFITI D. Sherlock

A selection of these is published in Fig. 34. The majority of them appear to be simple mason's marks on thirteenth-century stonework. No. 149 is part of a counting board: there is a very

26. Compare Chichester Cathedral; the internal refacing of nave and choir and the vaulting after the fire of 1186 where Prior (1904) notes the use of fine, diagonal axe tooling and claw chisel tooling (six notches to the inch). He also mentioned that St. Hugh's choir at Lincoln Cathedral (late twelfth-century) has the same mixture of tooling.

similar example on the south-east pier of the nave of St. Alban's Abbey. The lines in no. 150 may represent the numbers 30 and 35. No. 156 probably includes the name Robert.

Cat. no. 17	On chamfered plinth.
Cat. no. 73	On top of edge mould.
Cat. no. 73	On base of roll on edge mould.
Cat. no. 73	On side.
Cat. no. 99	On decorated window jamb.
Cat. no. 105	On back of window jamb.
Cat. no. 105	On back of window jamb.
Cat. no. 105	On back of window jamb.
Cat. no. 131	On roll.
Cat. no. 140	On voussoir.
Cat. no. 144	On ashlar block from fallen wall.
Cat. no. 149	On ashlar respond from the fallen wall.
Cat. no. 150	On base of respond from the fallen wall arch.
Cat. no. 150	On base of respond from the fallen wall arch.
Cat. no. 156	On roll with fillet moulding.
Cat. no. 156	On roll with fillet moulding.

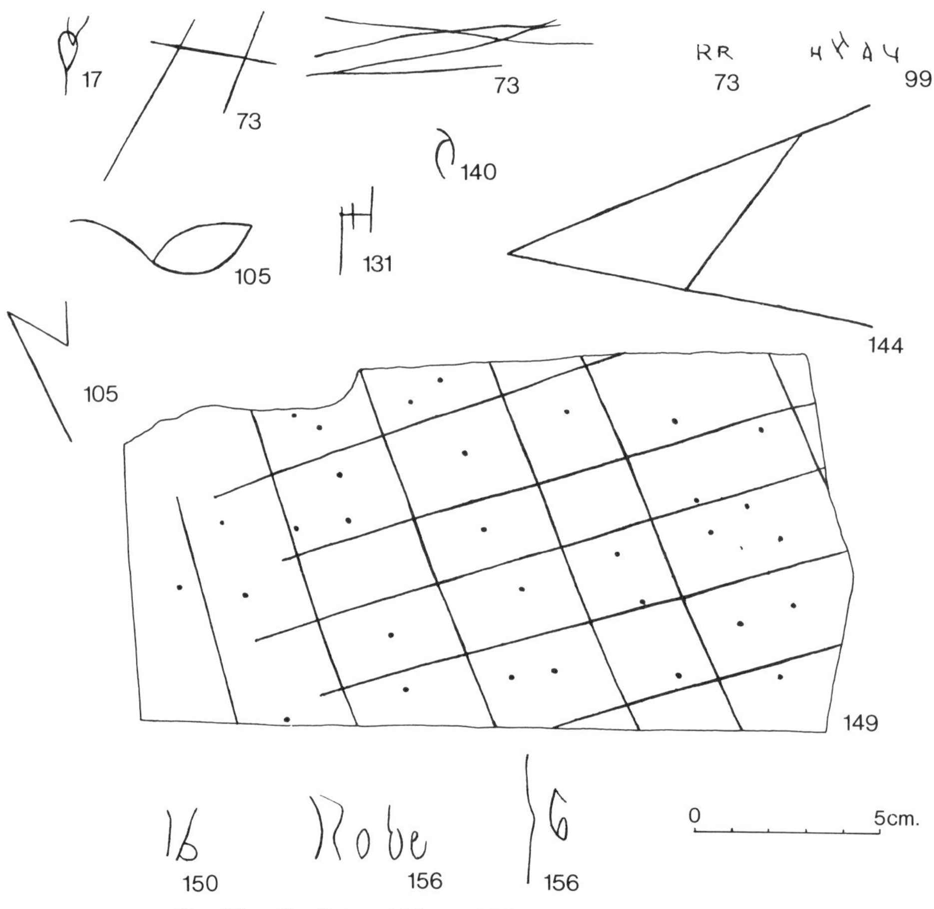

Fig. 34. Graffiti and Masons' Marks on Stones, 1972–75.

GEOLOGICAL REPORT ON STONEWORK FROM EXCAVATIONS, 1972–75. F.W. Anderson

Following an examination of the excavated stones now stored in Dover Castle the following nine types of stone were identified:

1. Caen Limestone, a Jurassic limestone principally from the Calvados province of Normandy, but there are many quarries also in the provinces of Vienne, Yonne and Meuse. First imported after the Conquest, probably by Archbishop Lanfranc for his new cathedral begun *c.* 1070; also used at St. Alban's and St. Paul's in the eleventh century. Also found at Canterbury in door jambs of St. John's Hospital (founded by Lanfranc), with flint at St. Martin's, and in bonding at the castle. As over 83 per cent of the stone recovered from St. Augustine's is Caen-stone, it seems likely that this was the principal building material used in the late eleventh and early twelfth centuries.

2. Kentish Rag, Hythe beds of the Lower Greensand, mainly from the Maidstone area. In medieval time there were quarries at Boughton. It was used in the foundations of old St. Paul's Cathedral, in Rochester Castle and the Tower of London keep. In Kent it was widely used, mostly in coastal area, for example at Hythe, where the chancel was re-built in the early thirteenth century with prolific marble shafting. For Canterbury it was probably brought by way of river transport and/or the Roman road. There it was used by the Romans for the jambs of the Quenin Gate and a base re-used at St. Augustine's, in the tenth century at St. Augustine's for Abbot Wulfrid's rotunda, in the West Gate (1375–81) and Christchurch Gate (1517). The peak use of this greyish stone was in the fourteenth century, after which it dropped out of favour until the nineteenth century. The harder shelly seams of Kentish rag were black and capable of polish. Shafts of this stone, like Bethersden marble (see below), were found at St. Augustine's in the fallen wall area.

3. Lincolnshire Limestone (including varieties from Ketton, Weldon, Barnack, Ancaster, Clipsham, etc.), a Jurassic limestone. This was used by the Romans and later builders although in medieval times it was little used except locally, as in Stamford. It was much used in Cambridge in the seventeenth and eighteenth centuries. Most sites are in Northamptonshire and East Anglia. In Kent it was used in columns in Roman Canterbury and at Reculver. At St. Augustine's it was used in Romanesque decorative stones (diaper work).

4. Quarr. This was a shell bank in the Bembridge Limestone (Oligocene) found near Ryde, Isle of Wight. It was first exploited by the Romans (Portchester) and much used by Anglo-Saxon builders for quoins and door and window frames throughout Hampshire, the Isle of Wight and Sussex. In the eleventh to thirteenth century it was used extensively in Hampshire and West Sussex (Winchester Cathedral, Southampton wall, etc.), but the supply was exhausted by the middle of the fourteenth century. The use of Quarr in London and east Kent has been examined by Tatton-Brown (1980a), who has shown that it was confined to the period *c.* 1070 to 1120.

5. Sandstone, probably Pulborough (West Sussex) stone, a hard sandstone in the Hythe Beds of the Lower Greensand. It has been worked since Roman times. One example from St. Augustine's, a section of a large Romanesque half-column from the tumble, an oddity in a dozen such stones all otherwise from Caen or Lincolnshire (Cat. no. 59).

6. Portland Stone, from the Upper Jurassic of Dorset. Rarely used except locally before the

seventeenth century. Its occurrence at St. Augustine's is an oddity like the last. I have no other record of its use in Kent before 1723.

7. Bethersden Marble, a hard blue-black shelly limestone from the Weald of Kent. Not strictly a building stone and used only for small shafts, tombs, fonts, etc. Not known to have been used outside Kent and Sussex. A very similar marble could be obtained from Kentish Rag beds (see 2 above).

8. Purbeck Marble, a blackish shelly limestone from the Upper Jurassic of Dorset. Strictly not a building stone, nevertheless extensively used for the shaft of nave arcades, etc. It has been used at all periods for tombs and, especially in the twelfth and thirteenth centuries, for fonts which have a wide distribution in southern England, except where other similar marble such as Alwalton (Hunts.) or Bethersden were locally available. It was used with striking originality for string-courses as well as shafts in Canterbury Cathedral by William of Sens after 1174.

9. Tufa, a deposit of calcium carbonate also known as Travertine, generally formed by springs in limestone areas. This material was much in demand in Roman times for bath linings and, because of its lightness, for vaulting in the medieval period. It was used in Eynsford Castle as a dressed stone, *c.* 1100. Only one piece was recovered from St. Augustine's (Cat. no. 146).

PAINTING ON PLASTER AND STONE FROM EXCAVATIONS 1974–5. D. Sherlock

Painting and gilding were found on both plaster and stone in the fallen wall (Area 1, p. 47), i.e. on what were once the internal surfaces of the south wall of the ambulatory and St. Thomas's Chapel. Painting on both was, in the first period, of a rich and unified scheme of decoration, which belongs stylistically to approximately the same date as that of the architecture. Some of the surfaces of plaster fragments were sufficiently curved to show that the decoration extended up into the vaulting. At a later date it was all white-washed over.

The painting on the plaster (Colour Plate 1) is exceptionally rich in colour, in intensity and in the number of pigments. The cinquefoil flower (pattern 5; see below) is typical of the thirteenth century, except that it is blue instead of red. The quatrefoil ornament (pattern 4) may well represent a morse of vestment fastener, going with the gilt strips, which are in imitation of jewelled borders of such garments. These strips (pattern 6) are too small, narrow and richly decorated to have merely come from the border of whole scenes. The small fragments of imitation ashlaring (pattern 7) are a common scheme of decoration throughout the thirteenth century. Compare for example that from Maison Dieu, Ospringe (Rigold, 1979, 114, Fig. 12, no. 3). The black Gothic lettering (pattern 1) appears to go with the brightly-coloured paintwork. There are other fragments of lettering (not analysed), black on a white ground with no red, which differ from those of pattern 1 in that they are more cruciform. They are probably fifteenth-century and may be part of the fashion for a return to the more austere whitewashed decoration of that period. The surviving letters seem to be . . . *munio Sc* . . . perhaps for *communio sanctorum*.

On the stonework the most important painting was on the chevron and dog-tooth arch (Cat. no. 66) and consisted of a dark red strip between two black strips with trefoils or petals of red, with a black border in the chevrons. There were also red and black stripes in the mouldings behind the chevron but the dog-tooth itself was only limewashed. The voussoirs of this arch are shown reconstructed in Fig. 30. The greensand arch (Cat. no. 84) was painted with dark red on the rolls and black in the hollows. The edge of the dark red showed first, how the stones were set out and secondly, that the dark red continued onto the vaulting itself. The hood mould stone (Cat. no. 68) had a stripe of orange and a stripe of red, both on a white ground.

Paint was also found on a number of other stones in the tumble, which are described in the catalogue.

Examination of the paint David Cook, Marjorie Hutchinson and Barry Knight (Ancient Monuments Laboratory), and S.R. Wyles (Laboratory of the Government Chemist); with Josie Ridgeway and Glynis Edwards (Ancient Monuments Laboratory) (A.M.L. report no. 2379).

Close examination and exposure of the various paint layers was followed by analysis of samples by X-ray diffraction (XRD), where necessary supplemented by X-ray fluorescence (XRF) and microchemical tests.

All the painting has been whitewashed over. This whitewash consists of two layers of even and almost equal thickness, together making a layer between ¼ and ½ mm. thick, which had to be removed to reveal the painting. Samples of the whitewash from six different pieces of plaster were examined and all show consistently the same two layers. They are of the same date (presumably two to give a good cover): this is certain because they are intimately bound and the interfaces are brilliant white; there is no dirt between them.

The structure of the plaster layer is as follows: coarse lime-based rendering, thick layer of lime plaster, thin coat of lime plaster, paint. Both the whitewash covering the paint and the white ground to which the paint had been applied consist essentially of calcite (i.e. the painted surface is lime plaster and not a sulphate *gesso*).

The painting is elaborate, though perhaps crude in places. The decoration is multi-coloured, eight different colours being apparent. They are black, deep blue, dark red, orange-pink, white, pink, orange and orange under gilding. Some pieces exhibit a subtle effect where, e.g. a thin translucent coat of a light colour, white or pink, has been painted over a darker colour to lighten and change the darker colour. Yet again, some pieces show shading of one colour into another, for instance orange into dark red.

The painting appears to have been done with a free-hand brush, the strokes being clearly visible in most cases. The only exceptions to this appear to be the two fleurs-de-lys. Whether the two tracings are similar enough for both fleurs to have been done with the same stencil is a matter for conjecture; certainly even a stencil does not produce exactly identical copies. In addition, it is observed that neither fleur-de-lys shows brush-strokes, which suggests that each may have been stippled through a stencil.

CATALOGUE

Plaster

Pattern 1. A black-letter inscription on white, the white painted over dark red, the dark red exposed on the adjacent area which has black lines and blue on it. On one piece the inscription is divided from the dark red adjacent area by a black line, on another piece there is no dividing line. Five pieces – the dark red paint showed no XRD pattern but gave a strong XRF signal for iron suggesting the pigment was amorphous haematite (Fe_2O_3).

Pattern 2. White chevrons outlined in black, with a lower border of white edged with black; under the chevrons black fleurs-de-lys stencilled on an orange ground. Two pieces – the white is calcite and the orange (-pink) minimum or red oxide of lead (Pb_3O_4).

Pattern 3. Gilt strips with black detailing *over* the gilt – where this has been done, even though some of the black is missing, the gilt is better preserved; the detailing is alternate circles and lozenges, and a black line on both sides of the strip. These strips probably relate to the two large joined pieces, both with gilding. Eleven pieces – the black shows no XRD pattern and is probably carbon. The orange paints – in the background to the gilt lozenges and under the gilding – now contain red lead and calcite in varying proportions; originally, they may have been the same.

Pattern 4. A black and white stylised quatrefoil flower shape, appearing to cover the joints of orange lines, the whole over a dark red field. Three pieces.

Pattern 5. Cinquefoil flower shape with white centre and blue petals on a dark red ground. One piece – the white is cerussite ($PbCO_3$) – as distinct from white lead, which is hydrocerussite – and the blue, azurite (2 $CuCO_3.Cu(OH)_2$).

Pattern 6. Black, orange, white, a blue strip; outlined black and black lozenges, the latter filled in orange and this orange further detailed with a white lozenge and a central dot. The spaces between the lozenges in some pieces filled with blue, the whole on a dark red ground, which has orange shading on two pieces. Five pieces – the (pink/orange,) again, contains red lead and calcite (cf. Pattern 3).

Pattern 7. Other odd pieces, six in all: including one possibly of Pattern type 1, one which looks like part of an elaborate design but is unidentifiable on its own, one has a black 'comb' on blue with some dark red, and one with dark red lines imitating ashlar.

Stonework

Type 1. Section of vaulting rib of Kentish Rag (cf. Cat. no. 84; samples taken from A.M.L. 775760). The white underlay showed a strong XRD pattern for calcite with a trace of quartz. Weaker and less distinct patterns of these were also present in other samples. The black is probably carbon black. The brick-red/orange pigment could be minium(?) and the dark red/purple due to haematite (?), but if so they are insufficiently crystalline and/or concentrated in these samples (cf. Type 2 below).

Type 2. Section of arch hood mould (Cat. no. 80, A.M.L. 775782). The orange-pink is minium, the dark-red/purple haematite, from the XRD patterns. No colorant was indicated by XRD or XRF in the grey/black which is probably carbon black.

Type 3. Section of voussoir with dog-tooth on soffit or arch, and chevrons (cf. Cat. no. 66; samples from 'keystone', Cat. no. 67, A.M.L. 775770). The brick/dark red shows strong XRD patterns for cinnabar (HgS – hexagonal) with some minium, the orange only minium.

Note All samples, on both plaster and stonework, showed more or less well developed patterns for lead metaborate hydrate ($Pb(BO_2)_2.H_2O$). This is interpreted as contamination from lead pipe-work in the rubble overlying the excavated levels, due to demolition of modern hospital and technical college buildings.

See also shell with pigment (p. 200, no. 84).

2. STONEWORK FROM EXCAVATIONS, 1976–78. H. Woods

No.	*Description*	*Dimensions in cm.*	*Location and other information*	*Figure*
	Pre-Conquest			
1.	Oolite moulding with two bevelled faces and a narrow band running across these two faces. The top of the stone is broken.	h:18.5 l:10.5 w:10	Pit 8008 sf 586	35
2.	Part of Corinthian capital.	h:23	Similar capitals have been recovered from earlier excavation of the Anglo-Saxon church. Another similar capital in crypt of Christ Church (1096-1110). Wall 5000.	35 Pl. Lb
3.	Baluster encircled by abraded band and two narrow bands above and below this. Dressed at top, bottom broken off. Probably a mid-wall window shaft.	d:3.2	Eleventh century or earlier. Wall 5000.	35
	Post-Conquest			
4.	Capital of Caen-stone decorated with foliate motif, bearing traces of red paint. The stone is dressed top and bottom.	h:11 w:16 l:16	Scaffold base 745 s.f. 486.	35
5.	Fragment of worked Purbeck marble from bell capital.	circum: 13.5	Layer 513.	36
6.	Fragment of moulded abacus.	surviving circum: 9	Layer 701	36
7.	Volute or hood stop in Reigate stone.		Layer 766.	36
8.	Fragment of attached twisted nook shaft.		Twelfth century, from scaffold base 5081.	36
9.	Fragment of shaft in Caen-stone.		Layer 763.	36
10.	Column fragment in Reigate stone. Broken at both ends.	ml:8.5	Layer 500.	36
11.	Rear of nook shaft, front broken off. Caen-stone.	ml:17.5	Layer 733	36
12.	Base of angle shaft (partly reconstructed), probably from a window.		Similar very simple bases are *in situ* in the two bays west of the crossing which date to Scotland's abbacy 1070–87.	36

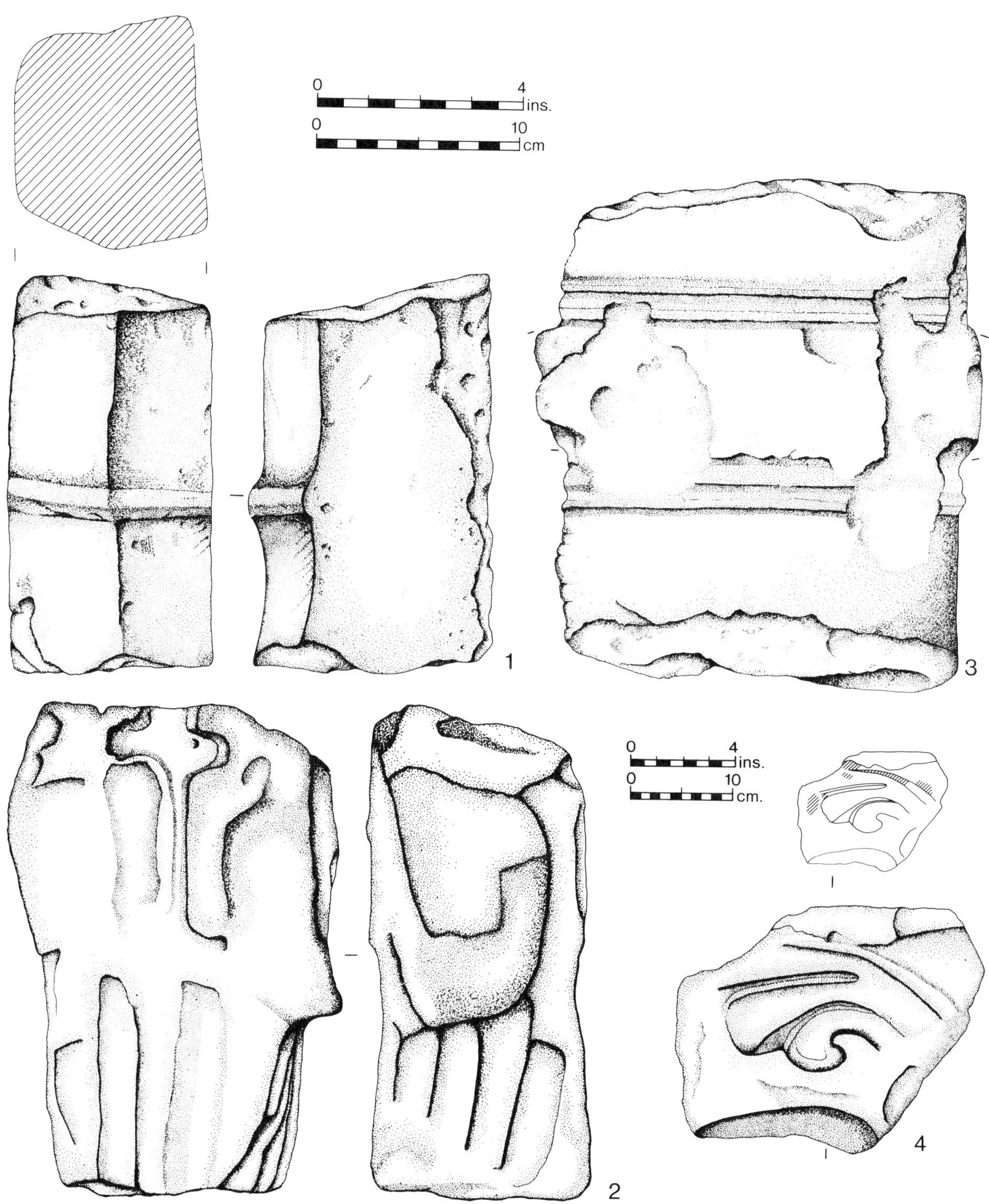

Fig. 35. Worked Stone, 1976–78.

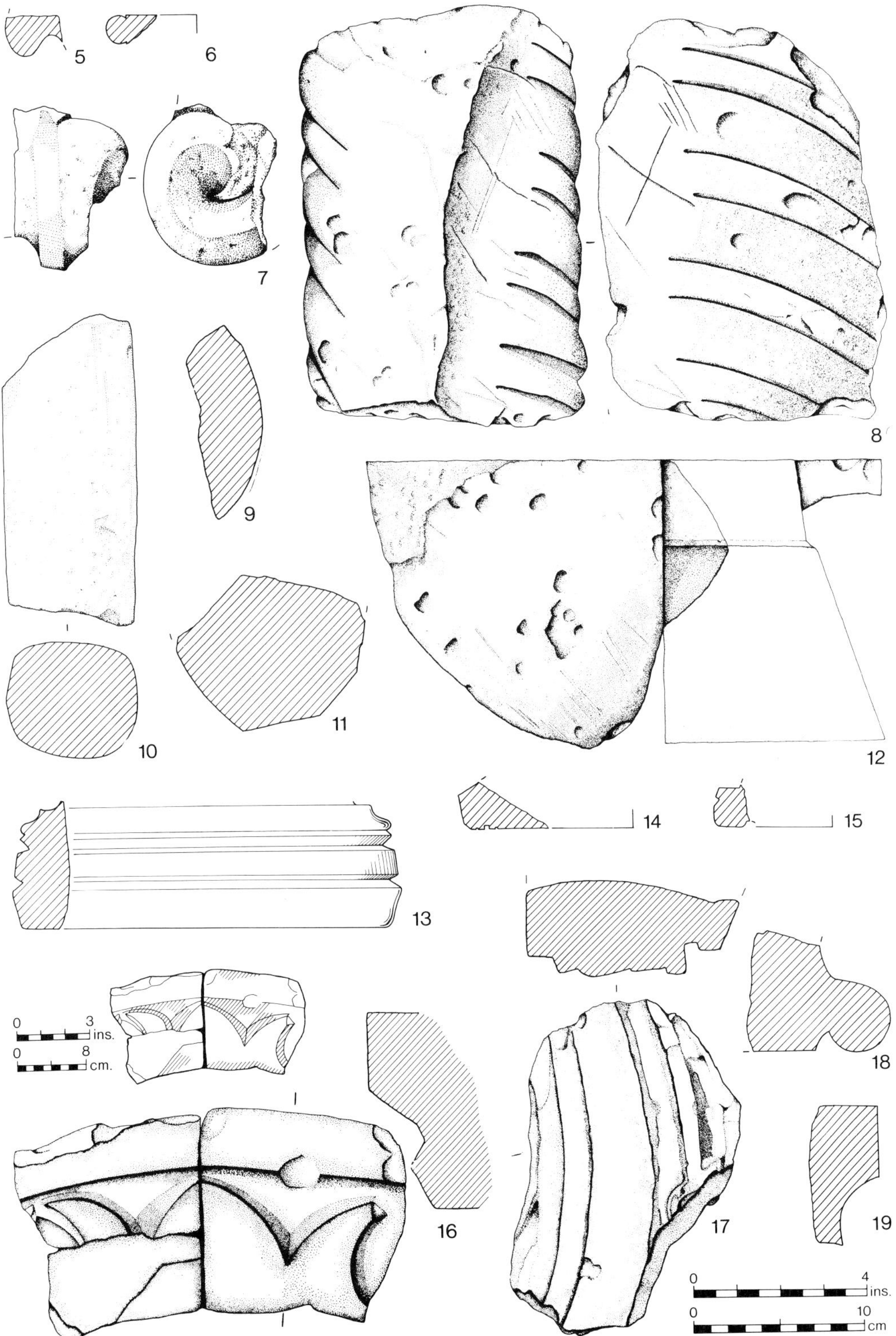

Fig. 36. Worked Stone, 1976–78.

No.	*Description*	*Dimensions in cm.*	*Location and other information*	*Figure*
			Late eleventh century. From scaffold base 5085.	
13.	Fragment of column base in three orders. Traces of red paint.		Layer 3	36
14.	Fragment of column base in Caen-stone with incisions in the base, parallel to the outer edge of the base.	surviving circum:10	Layer 763	36
15.	Fragment of column base in Caen-stone.	surviving circum:6	Layer 763	36
16.	Two voussoirs (one broken in two) from an arch or window surround. Concave outer edge. Plain border containing decoration of a single V-shaped cut on each stone, emphasised with red paint.	h:12 h:11	Layer 1004. S.f. 255, 256/257	36
17.	Tracery from blind arcading, much abraded.		Wall 5000.	36
18.	Fragment of string-course.	ml:13	Robber trench 1007	36
19.	Fragment of string-course.	ml:9.8	Layer 701.	36
20.	Crocket in Caen-stone.		Layer 5055.	37
21.	Fragment of roll moulding in Caen-stone.	ml:23.5	Layer 701.	37
22.	Fragment of plain roll. Broken at both ends.	ml:5.2	Layer 503.	37
23.	Fragment of plain roll.	l:8	Layer 1001.	37
24.	Fragment of plain roll in Caen-stone. Part of circumference broken. Broken at both ends.	ml:7	Layer 763.	37
25.	Fragment of plain roll. Part of circumference broken off.	ml:8	Layer 1012. S.f. 418.	37
26.	Fragment of plain roll.	ml:10	Layer 513.	37
27.	Fragment of filleted roll in Caen-stone.	ml:13	Robber trench 1007	37
28.	Fragment of filleted roll with fillet snapped off.	ml:4	Robber trench 1007.	37
29.	Fragment of double-filleted roll, one broad fillet (snapped off), one narrower. Broken at both ends.	ml:8	Layer 513.	37
30.	Fragment of filleted half roll with ogee moulding, perhaps part of a string-course.	ml:7	Robber trench 1007.	37
31.	Fragment of Purbeck marble, rounded at one end. Uncertain purpose.	l:5	Layer 540.	37
32.	Corner fragment with recess for seating of a square or rectangular piece above. Rounded kerb on one side only.		Robber trench 1007.	37
33.	Fragment of Caen-stone ashlar with mass dial on face. From demolition layer inside chapel, so perhaps it was originally on exterior of this chapel.		Layer 1002	37
34.	Graffito of a cross and flag (cf. medieval representations of Christ as the Lamb carrying a flag), surmounting a heart. This			

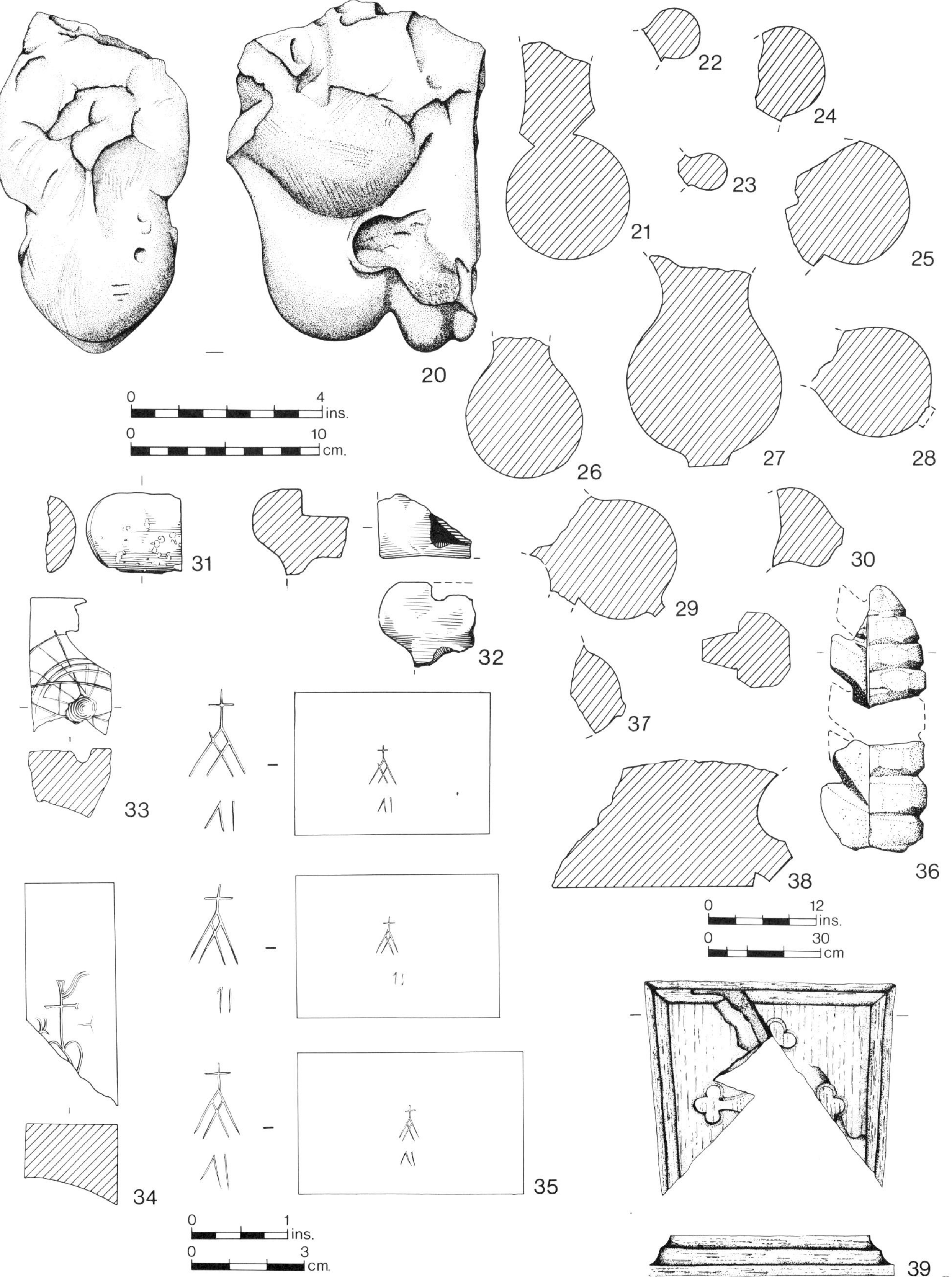

Fig. 37. Worked Stone, 1976–78.

No.	Description	Dimensions in cm.	Location and other information	Figure
	could be a precursor of latter-day representations of the Sacred Heart of Jesus.			
35.	Mason's mark of a gable with a cross finial. Underneath, but upside down, the Roman numeral IV. The three ashlar blocks were recovered lying together. The numeral perhaps refers to a course in the wall.		Layer 726. S.f. 480, 481, 482.	37
	The Sepulchral Monuments			
36.	Two fragments of a finial from a tomb canopy.		Layer 513	37
37.	Fragment of Purbeck marble decoration from a table tomb.	ml:8	Layer 709	37
38.	Fragment of table tomb.	ml:15.5	Layer 1002	37
39.	Composite drawing of s.f. 187, 188, 189, 190. The head end of a Purbeck marble sepulchral slab with double hollow chamfer bearing a cross in slight relief. Trefoil terminals to the arms. The slab tapers towards the foot end. The cross indicates that this was originally intended for a priest, but it was used upside down in the chapel for a lay burial.		Similar slab is in the crypt of Christ Church. Layers 1005 and 1010	37
40.	Three sepulchral slabs. Top left s.f. 406. Top right s.f. 405 has a double hollow chamfer cf. no. 39 above. This and slab 406 taper towards the foot end. Bottom right, s.f. 407. All of Purbeck marble.		Immediately south of the chapel	Plate XXXV

A PIETA. H. Woods

During the course of the excavations my attention was drawn by my wife to a graffito (Fig. 38) on the exterior of the north wall of the north aisle, in the grounds of St. Augustine's College. The graffito has been much damaged by ivy and general corrosion of the stone, so it seems appropriate to publish it before it decays away completely.

The graffito is clearly visible on three blocks of Caen-stone ashlar and, although there are further incisions on adjacent blocks which must represent more of the composition, these adjacent stones are so weathered as to make it impossible to decipher the remainder of the composition.

The three stones illustrated seem to represent a *Pietà*. The Virgin Mary cradles the dead Christ on her breast, while a weeping man, presumably St. John, is on the left. Long cuts from the eyes and cheeks represent his tears.

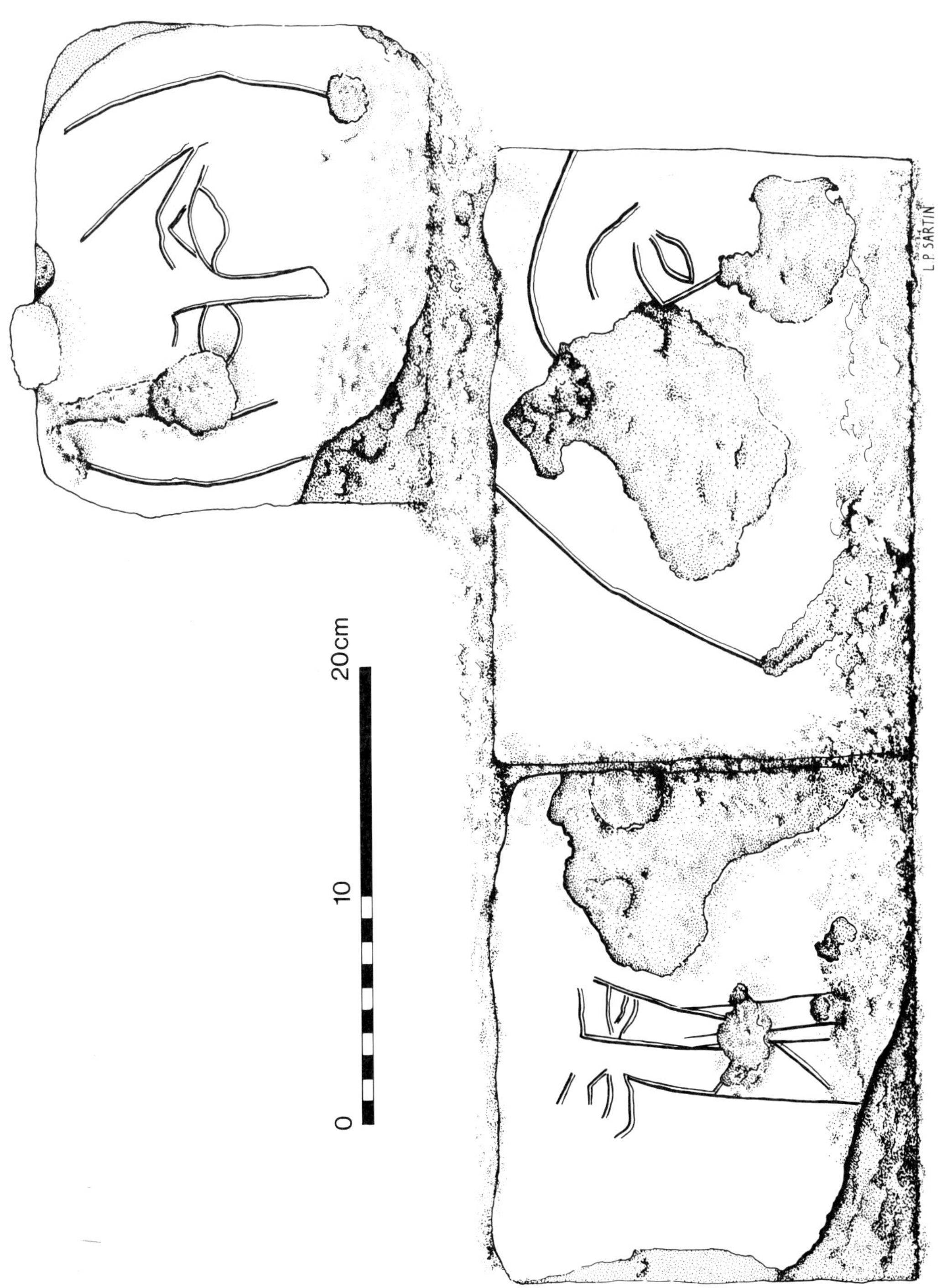

Fig. 38. Graffito, 1976–78.

This convention, as also the method of delineating the eyes and noses on all three faces, mark this out as medieval, and probably quite early in the post-Conquest period. The graffiti in the crypt of St. Andrew's Cathedral, Rochester, are the closest parallel.

The head of St. John is on the same level as that of Christ. If it is presumed that the dead Christ is recumbent in the lap of the seated Virgin, St. John must be kneeling.

The abbot's lodgings were in the west cloister range, which returned north from the north aisle of the church. The east gable of the abbot's chapel still survives immediately to the east of the graffito, supported upon a tunnel vault. The graffito would, therefore, have been on the south wall of the vaulted chamber beneath this chapel. This chamber may have been an outer parlour, by analogy with the arrangement at Westminster Abbey.

3. WINDOW GLASS 1960 and 1965 David Sherlock

Some thirty pieces of window glass were recovered by S.E. Rigold in 1960, of which the majority are too decomposed or fragmentary to be studied. The three most important pieces are illustrated in Fig. 39.

1. Pale blue painted glass, grozed all round. 45 mm. thick. Twelfth–thirteenth century. From Trench B, medieval rubbish pit at north end of trench, 2.13 m. below surface. A.M.L. 78203256.
2. Blue painted curved strip 24 mm. wide; 2.5 mm. thick. Twelfth–thirteenth century. From Trench A/B(?). Dissolution building debris. A.M.L. 78203258.
3. Fragment of green painted glass in good condition depicting drapery. 2 mm. thick. Fourteenth century. Same provenance and Lab. no. as last.

General Remarks

All the pieces show considerable exterior corrosion, showing that they had been in windows for some time. The quality of the grozing varies according to the thickness of the glass. Surviving

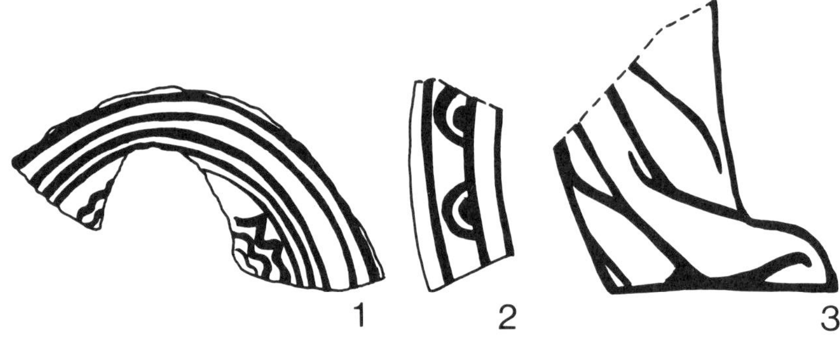

Fig. 39. Medieval Window Glass, 1960. (Scale: ½)

colours range from blue, green, ruby (i.e. flash red) and white, but some of the pieces that are now opaque may represent other lost colours. The absence of window lead found with the glass suggests that it was salvaged. The date-range of the glass is all late twelfth to fourteenth century. Amongst the designs represented there were no heads, hands, etc., to give an idea of the scale of the glazing, though the few drapery fragments show that there was some figured glass. There were also some fragments of thirteenth century geometric *grisaille* glass. Like the fragments found in the later excavations, there is insufficient glass to allow comparison with glass in Canterbury Cathedral.

TWELFTH CENTURY AND LATER WINDOW GLASS FROM EXCAVATIONS 1972–75 (Fig. 40)
D. Sherlock

Over a hundred pieces of window glass were recovered from the three seasons of excavations. Most of them were too fragmentary or decomposed to be drawn or even studied; a predictable result of their burial in wet, acid ground but disappointing when they are compared with the riches that survive in the cathedral, one of the major centres of medieval window glass in

Fig. 40. Medieval Window Glass, 1972.

western Christendom. Nevertheless, one or two of the pieces do show that the abbey could have rivalled the cathedral in its glass as well as its stonework. Many of the pieces have evidence of heavy corrosion on their exterior, which must have taken place before burial and therefore shows that they were up in position for a long time. As well as clear glass there was a range of four discernible colours: highly durable soda blue, a darker, poorly durable blue, a flashed ruby and a green, the last two characteristically fourteenth-century. The paint varied in tone from a dark red/brown (thirteenth century) to all-brown (fourteenth-century). There were no black or grey washes. The bulk of the designs discernible are in thirteenth-century *grisaille*, being formal or geometric and presumably go with the new lancet windows in the presbytery. There were no fragments of human features, heraldry or inscriptions and nothing was identifiable iconographically. The glass was unfortunately not included in the Canterbury volume of the *Corpus Vitrearum Medii Aevi*, where other glass probably from St. Augustine's but now in the cathedral is discussed (Caviness 1981).

Of those illustrated in Fig. 40, no. 1 is the most important piece (A.M.L. 743661). It is from a twelfth-century border (?) design. The design is painted on a highly durable blue glass still in excellent condition and comparable with work from such major centres of production as at the cathedral, York or Chartres. It was found in Trench III and must have fallen from the nave or south-west tower of the church or, less likely, the presumed charnel chapel, if indeed that had glazed windows. It is 4 mm. thick. The grozing has been done clumsily. Nos. 2–4 are also from Trench III. The design in no. 3 may be for pictorial background; drapery or hair seems less likely. Nos. 5, 7, 9, 11, 14 and 16 came from immediately beneath the boundary wall in Area 2 and the remainder from Dissolution levels in Area 1, no. 6 coming from the tumble near the south radiating chapel. No. 5 is a fragment in stiff leaf style comparable with the stiff leaf stone capital from the presbytery (Cat. no. 97, A.M.L. 743661) and perhaps also with the style of the glass in one of the east windows of the cathedral (*c.* 1200). No. 8 is part of the extremity of a foliate boss design. No. 10 probably represents the bottom end of a fold of drapery with cusps and cinquefoils below or less likely, the other way up, a Lombardic capital letter. The design is picked out in a matt wash. No. 11 shows a fragment of drapery, late thirteenth- or early fourteenth-century. The glass was originally green but is now corroded and opaque. No. 12 is about a century earlier, depicting blue hook fold drapery on a thick matt background. No. 13, another fragment of drapery, early fourteenth-century, came from opposite the window to the west of the fallen wall. Nos. 14 and 15 are fourteenth-century border designs picked out in a matt wash on clear glass. There was a number of other unpainted pieces from window borders. Two complete pieces of clear glass measured 25 x 75 x 3 mm. One piece of red border glass was 20 mm. wide, another blue, 14 mm. wide. One would expect a strip of border glass to survive more easily because it is the most difficult part of a window to remove. The windows themselves would have been taken out for the value of their lead and iron, examples of which were also found and are described next.

ANGLO-SAXON WINDOW AND VESSEL GLASS FROM EXCAVATIONS, 1976–78. H. Woods

1. Fragment of sky-blue soda window glass.
   Layer 8001.
   A.M.L. 782325.

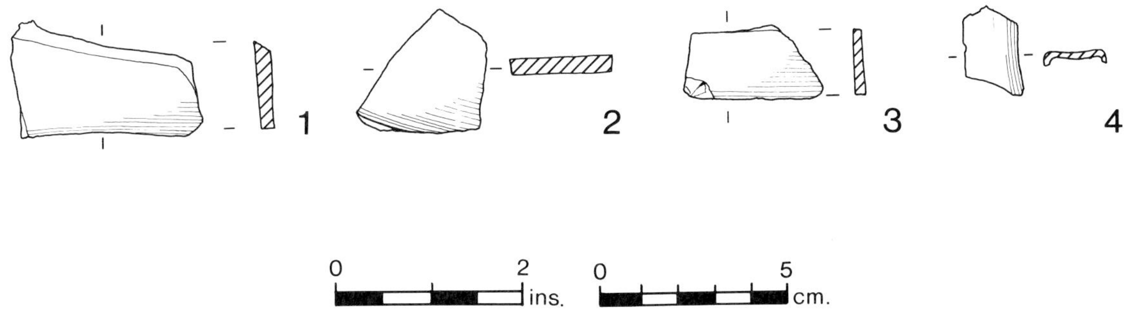

Fig. 41. Anglo-Saxon Window and Vessel Glass: **1**. Blue soda fragment. **2**. Potash roundel. **3**. Potash corner. **4**. Yellow soda vessel fragment.

2. Fragment of a grozed roundel of potash window glass.
   Layer 8001.
   A.M.L. 782325.
3. Part of a grozed triangular quarry of potash window glass.
   Layer 8001.
   A.M.L. 782325.
4. Fragment of yellow vessel glass.
   Layer 8001.
   A.M.L. 782324.

4. STONE AND GLASS MOSAIC, 1965 D. Sherlock

Twenty-nine pieces of Cosmatesque mosaic work, made probably by visiting Roman or Parisian craftsmen are recorded as having come from the shaft in the nave. This type of work, made up of composite marble ground with inlays of *tesserae*, including blue and gilded glass and geometric sections of '*verde antico*' and '*rosso antico*', was applied to shrines, tombs, etc., and on a larger scale to floors. Late thirteenth-century examples are to be found in Westminster Abbey (Pevsner 1973, 422, 424) and in the shrine area of Canterbury Cathedral (Norton and Horton 1981). About sixty other unprovenanced pieces also survive from St. Augustine's, and 106 pieces which are said to have come from the abbey church (A.M.L. 78203037 and 3038; S.A.M. 284). For the following reports on the 1965 stone and glass pieces, I am grateful to R.W. Sanderson of the British Geological Survey and D.B. Harden:

Stone

Sample 1. Two pieces of green altered porphyritic basalt or andesite. These are very similar to samples of the *porfyro verde antico* from Marathonisi, southern Greece. This rock was much used in Roman times for architectural decoration.

Sample 2. Two pieces of very fine even-grained white limestone. It was hard to determine whether this is a piece of indurated chalk of local origin or possibly one of the French limestones.

Sample 3. A fibrous white limestone. The small size of this fragment makes identification uncertain; the material has a fibrous texture, which suggests that it is a piece of calcite veining or perhaps a sheared marble.

Samples 4 and 5. Dark grey fine-grained limestone containing finely comminuted fossil fragments. These pieces appear to be examples of a Carboniferous limestone. Similar material may be found in England (Somerset–Gloucester or the Pennine region) and on the Continent (e.g. northern France and Belgium).

Sample 6. A fine grained white marble. This is almost certainly from the Mediterranean area.

Sample 7. Two fragments of pink and white sheared limestone *breccia*.

Sample 8. A fragment of fine-grained pink recrystallised limestone with small (*c*. 2–3 mm.) irregularly elongate bodies of grey calcite spar. Samples 7 and 8 are pieces of limestone *breccia* probably from Italy or the Pyrenées. The smallness of the pieces makes it impossible to be more definite.

All the samples are of foreign, i.e. non-Kentish origin, about half almost certainly from the Mediterranean area.

Glass

Sample 9. Eleven pieces of blue semi-opaque glass.

Sample 10. Two fragments of opaque turquoise coloured glass.

Sample 11. Two pieces of translucent bottle green glass, one with a gilded facet overlaid with a thin (1 mm.) layer of clear colourless glass.

Sample 12. Two pieces of opaque white glass.

Sample 13. A fragment of reddish-brown streaked dark grey glass. One surface of this sample is gilded, the gilding again being overlaid with a very thin layer of clear colourless glass.

The turquoise, dark blue and white examples could be, and perhaps are, normal Roman *tesserae* such as occur in both wall and floor mosaics in Roman times for specific purposes (e.g. to provide more correct colouring for details of faces, etc., than *tesserae* of natural stone or pottery could produce). The two gilt *tesserae* and the parallel plain green one are probably post-Roman and for more sophisticated use than that to which the Roman-style *tesserae* were put.

The gilt ones are carefully made in a technique first used in Hellenistic times for making plain *tesserae* that are scattered amongst patterned ones in Hellenistic cast mosaic glass vessels. There are examples from the third century B.C. in the Canosa group in the British Museum (Harden 1969, 62, Pl. IX, B), where all the *tesserae* appearing white in the illustration either have a gold-leaf layer between colourless layers or are of opaque yellow glass, usually sandwiched with colourless on one or both sides. To make mosaic *tesserae* of this type it was necessary to cast them in flat moulds with a background layer covered with gold leaf and which itself was covered with a colourless layer to protect it during manufacture and afterwards. It seems that all gilt mosaic *tesserae* are made in this way and the colourless glass surface layer is never absent (any more than it is even today on the gilded *tesserae* used by Italian mosaicists).

The Canterbury *tesserae* reviewed below are divided into two groups according to their probable dates:

Group 1 (samples 9, 10 and 12) are all plain, cuboid *tesserae* of glass roughly chipped from specially made cast-glass cakes. R.W. Sanderson distinguishes those in sample 9 (which he calls semi-opaque) from those in sample 10 and 12 (which he calls opaque). This distinction is not necessary: all are in essence equally opaque or semi-opaque – whichever is preferred – and any apparent difference in opacity, such as even occurs among those in 9, is due either to weathering or to ingrained dirt or lime. This group, as indicated above, could be of any date within the Roman period and is unlikely to be later than the demise of all Roman influence, which must have occurred in the Kentish area by about A.D. 600 at the latest.

Group 2 (samples 11 and 13). The pieces in this group, especially the two gilded *tesserae*, are more sophisticated and, in my view, are no longer 'late Roman' but are better thought of as being within the early medieval orbit, i.e. not earlier than *c*. 750–1000. The two gilded ones do not seem to be cut out of rounded mosaic 'cakes', but rather from flat mosaic plaques, the upper and under surfaces of which are in parallel planes, while their under surfaces also retain the pock-marking, which they would acquire from the metal or other surface they came into contact with during the casting process. On the third, ungilded, piece there are no pairs of opposing planes in parallel; but there is one flat surface, which shows some similarity with the under surface of the gilded *tesserae* of similar green glass, and it, too, could therefore have come from a flat mosaic plaque. Besides, both these green translucent *tesserae* differ considerably in translucency and finish from all the *tesserae* in group 1. The other gilded *tessera* is a far more carefully-made piece than any of the others. However much it may be erroneous to date the two pieces in sample 11 as not before *c*. 750–1000, there can be no doubt that this well-made *tessera* with its fine gilding, made from a batch of streaky reddish-brown and dark grey opaque glass and neatly cast in a flat mould, is not earlier than Carolingian and might well be later than the Norman conquest. It seems to resemble gilt mosaic *tesserae* in Cosmati work which was flourishing during the thirteenth century, for example, in the pavement of the feretory (chapel of Edward the Confessor) and on the shrine of Edward the Confessor in Westminster Abbey, both *c*. 1270, as well as on other neighbouring monuments. In sum, group 1 would seem to date from the fourth to the early sixth century A.D. and group 2 from the Carolingian period up to some time after 1066.

5. STRUCTURAL LEAD AND IRONWORK FROM EXCAVATIONS, 1972–75 D. Sherlock and B. Knight

It is appropriate to consider lead and ironwork from the structure of the building under one heading because the two were used together in several ways, namely in roofing, where lead sheeting was fixed with iron nails; in windows where iron was used for framing and fixing leaded lights, as well as for glazing bars; and in iron clamps and dowels set in masonry sockets filled with lead. Iron rods used for joining sections of marble shafting are described above in the stone report (p. 105).

It is clear from the scraps of lead that remain, and from the way that they have been cut, that leadwork from roofs and windows was systematically robbed. There is no evidence in the form of slag or melted globules to say exactly where it was melted down, but this was often done on Dissolution sites near the source of supply.[27] About a hundred small fragments and one large piece of lead were recovered. Ironwork seems also to have been removed deliberately, since no really substantial pieces such as glazing bars survive although there was evidence for them in holes in the masonry, which in some cases still had lead fillings. Nearly 700 pieces of iron were recovered from the three seasons of excavations, but most of them are nails and in a very poor state of preservation.

Roofing lead was removed either by ripping it off and leaving the nails behind, or by cutting round the areas where it was nailed to the timber behind pieces roughly 10 cm. square with two or three nails in them. The timber itself was also salvaged as we know from Nedeham's accounts and Henry VIII's orders in 1541 (see above p. 10), but it is not clear how the nails now surviving became detached from the wood they were driven into. There is no sign of them having been prized out. Possibly the pieces of wood with them in were sawn off and discarded and have later rotted away in the ground.

The larger pieces of ironwork, like the window lead, came mainly from the tumble and fallen wall areas and must have been used for securing the windows. If this is so, both iron and lead must date from the enlarging of the choir windows in the first quarter of the thirteenth century. The quantity of iron recovered from opposite the lady chapel was very small, consisting almost entirely of 2–7 cm. long nails. Elsewhere coffin nails were the most common iron finds, due to the presence of the monastic cemetery extending close up to the south wall of the abbey church.

Selected List of Finds (* denotes illustration in Fig. 42)

* 1. Iron implement, possibly a window latch, with two bolts on the plate for attaching it to the window surround. Length 15 cm.
Unstratified and possibly post-Dissolution.
Length 15 cm. A.M.L. 795437.

* 2. L-shaped strip of iron with three holes, 17.5 x 6 x 3 cm. thick. Possibly from a window frame.
From Area 1, layer 3.
A.M.L. 795434.

3. U-shaped piece of iron, 4 x 3.5 cm. It seems too small to have been a stone clamp; perhaps for clamping strips of lead. Two similar pieces from the same context, one with an L-shaped end.
From Area 1 layer 14.
S.A. 74, 1346.

27. At Roche Abbey, Yorks., for example, timber from the choir stalls was burnt to melt the roof lead (Thompson 1954, 4).

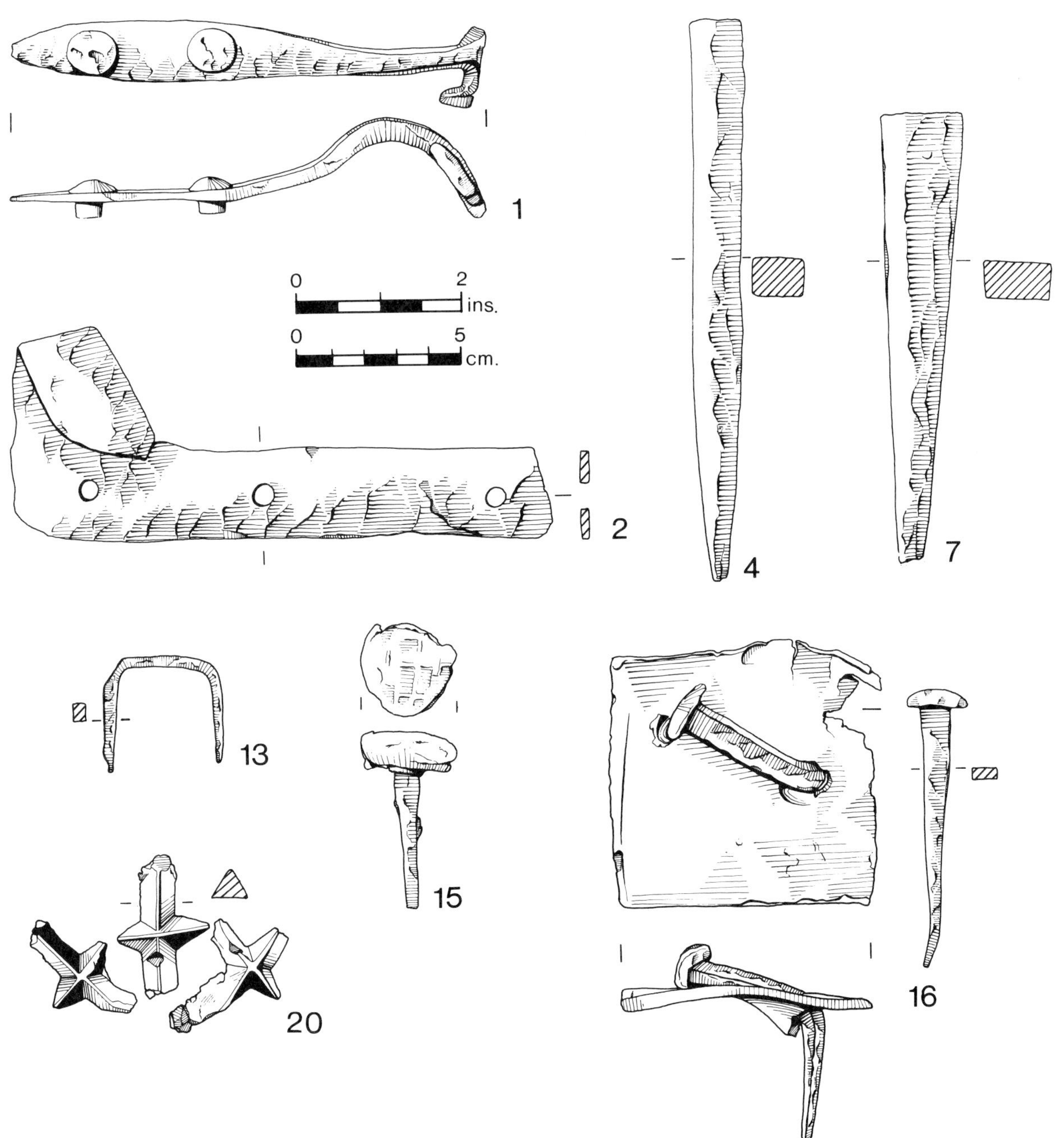

Fig. 42. Structural Lead and Ironwork, 1972–75.

* 4. Fragments of thin blade-like spikes or tongues. Several of these were found wedged, often in trees, in between voussoirs from both the tumble and the fallen wall (e.g. Stone Cat. no. 140). Their purpose is not known.
A.M.L. 795435.

5. L-shaped piece, slightly twisted, found between voussoirs 1494 and 1950 near the springing of the fallen wall arch. Purpose unknown; possibly the same function as no. 4. Length 9.1 + 4.5 cm.
S.A. 75, 2608.
There were at least three other types of spikes in addition to the above, almost all found in Area 1 layer 3 or Area 2 layer 19.

6. Chisel-like spikes, round in section one end becoming rectangular. Length from 17 to 19 cm.

* 7. Spikes, rectangular in section but tapering only a little on the wider sides. Lengths varying from 5 to 20 cm.

8. Spikes tapering evenly in both dimensions, so they could have been used like nails though they have no sign of a head. Lengths about 11–14 cm. long. Some of the different types were clenched.

Nails can be categorised into at least seven different groups but, because of their high state of corrosion, it is difficult to say much about them. A great many now have points that have got bent to make them look like hooks or have ends curved up to form loops. This presumably occurred when the point of the nail hit something hard in the wood or on the other side of the wood. It also means probably that the wood must have perished with the nail in it because it would have been almost impossible to extract the nail in that shape unless the wood was very rotten.

9. Large round-headed nails 8–10 cm. long, common in the fallen wall, and tumble areas.

10. Nails with 'figure of eight' head excavated from the same area as the last.

11. Simple long, square-sectioned nails with small heads, less common than the last two types. Examples from Area 2, layer 19 and unstratified contexts.

12. Very short nails with clout heads, common over the whole excavation.

*13. Staple.
A.M.L. 795431.

14. Nail with oval head. Only one example.

*15. Nail with head encased in lead. Only one example.
A.M.L. 795427.

*16. Typical square-cut piece of roof lead 3 mm. thick, with two iron nails, 8.5 cm. long. 10 other similar pieces each with two or three nails.

17. Circular lead dowel, *c.* 9 cm., with remains of iron. Probably a hinge pivot.
A.M.L. 795430.

18. Lead socket with remains of iron (?); 2.5 cm. square and 3 cm. deep. Compare with p. 189, no. 11.
S.A. 75 2526

19. Large strip of lead with a double fold weighing approximately 15 kg. Length 1.84 m. width unfolded approximately 25.5 cm. thickness 3 mm. Found with the voussoirs of the

arch (Cat. no. 96, p. 106) in the fallen wall and so perhaps a piece of window flashing (See Plate XLIX).
S.A. 74 1175

*20. Three small fragments of a cast lead window ventilator. Complete but smaller examples of such ventilators have come from Battle Abbey (Geddes 1985, Fig. 48.1), Bayham Abbey (Streeten 1983, 111, Fig. 49.6), and a mould for casting them was found at Neath Abbey (Rigold 1977, Pl. LXIb).
From Area 2, layer 3.
A.M.L. 791801.

Window Lead

Most of the lead that survived was window lead, being small torn pieces of cames weighing generally only about one ounce, a tiny percentage of what must have been systematically removed. The widths of the cames average 3–4 mm. Four fragments of cames showed the shapes of missing lights and one has some coloured glass still in position but the shapes are not unusual or worth illustrating.

What little window lead survives is mostly in the form of small unused offcuts, possibly from construction phases, and twisted fragments dropped at the time the windows were destroyed. One fragment still contains some glass and another piece of tracery is sufficiently complete to enable the size of the glass it contained to be deduced, but nothing can be said about the glazing as a whole. The fragments found are all medieval types A, B and C, as would be expected. One definite and one possible tie for attaching glazed panels to the ferramenta were found. Three fragments were found, which appear to come from the hinge end of the moulds in which cames were cast. These parts would be unsuitable for use in glazing and were therefore cut off and discarded – this would have happened during periods of construction or reglazing.

Descriptions

1. Fragment of tracery which would have enclosed a trapezoidal piece of glass approx. 37 x 23 x 40 x 23 mm. Type B, width of flanges approx. 4 mm., width of groove approx. 3 mm., overall depth approx. 7 mm. Reinforced in one place with another piece of came soldered parallel to the first; remains of tie soldered to the back face, apparently a piece of type B split in the web.
A.M.L. 743719.
2. Incomplete fragment of tracery which would have enclosed a right-angled triangular piece of glass approx. 37 x 50 x 62 mm. Fragments of glass still *in situ* but too corroded to guess original colour. Type B, width of flanges approx. 4.5 mm., width of groove approx. 3 mm., overall depth approx. 7 mm. Reinforced along shortest edge with another piece of came soldered parallel to the first.
A.M.L. 743720.
3. Includes one tie roughly cut from sheet lead approx. 6 mm. wide and 3 mm. thick, soldered

to remains of came and twisted round a bar approx. 16 mm. wide. Also an unused piece of type A apparently from the hinge end of the mould, 88 mm. long, width of flanges approx. 3.5 mm., width of groove approx. 3.5 mm., overall depth approx. 10 mm. The two halves of the mould were misaligned so that the flanges do not line up on opposite sides of the web, and on one side the height of the flanges decreases towards the end so that on that side the came becomes an ungrooved bar.

S.A. 2858.

4. Offcut of type A from hinged end of mould, 45 mm. long, width of flanges approx. 4 mm., width of groove approx. 3 mm., overall depth approx. 8 mm. On both sides the flanges gradually diminish to nothing so that the end of the piece is just a thin sheet of the same thickness as the web.

   S.A. '74 (no number).

5. Three small offcuts of lead 23, 35 and 40 mm. long. Two of these are discarded but unused lengths of window came, types A and C. From Area 2, layer 71.

   A.M.L. 756278.

For details of the terminology and typology of window lead, see Knight 1983–4, 49–51.

VI. CERAMIC BUILDING MATERIALS

BRICKS AND ROOF-TILES, 1972–1975 D. Sherlock

Roman Bricks and Tiles

Some seventy-five bricks or fragments of bricks were recovered in 1972–75, from either the demolished boundary wall, or the fallen wall of the church, or other excavation areas in late contexts. They may be assigned to five categories with complete examples only in the first two. Bricks re-used in the fallen wall are described above with the fallen wall. There were no stamps or graffiti on any of the fragments.

1. Large bricks similar to those re-used in the fabric of St. Pancras. S.A. 74, 431, is the largest, measuring 33 cm. square and 3.5 cm. thick, and comes from the demolished boundary wall opposite the lady chapel. Some other fragments were up to 5 cm. thick.
2. Smaller square bricks, roughly 16.5 cm. square and 4 cm. thick. These appear to be *pila* tiles, for supporting the floor of a hypocaust.
3. *Tegulae*. Five fragments, two with signs of burning from various late-medieval or disturbed contents.
4. Some forty fragments of box-tiles with characteristic combing marks for keying mortar. One has a ventilation hole.
5. One small cube of about 1.5 cm. is possibly a *tessera* from a pavement.
   From Area 2, layer 4.
   S.A. 75, 1559.

Medieval and later Bricks

In the 1972–75 excavations there was an absence of any brick which could be said to be medieval. The reason for this is presumably the availability of Roman brick where stone and flint were not required. St. Pancras's Church is almost entirely built of Roman brick, and Roman bricks were also found re-used in the fallen wall of the abbey church.

One fragment of brick (S.A. 75, 2606) may be sixteenth-century since it was found in the rubble immediately beneath the fallen wall. It is approximately 6 cm. thick but its other dimensions are unknown. It is well-fired good clay of rose-red colour. It has a hard white mortar adhering.

Other fragments are of hard evenly-fired purple-red which may be ascribed to the hospital period (eighteenth-century or later).

Medieval Roof-Tiles

About 150 fragments of roof peg-tiles were recovered from the 1972–75 excavations. They came from all areas in no particular concentrations. This small quantity would suggest that at the Dissolution roof-tiles, on those buildings that had them, were deliberately taken down and removed, rather than allowed to fall off and break, and this is confirmed by surviving orders for unroofing and dismantling the abbey church in 1541 and 1552 (Colvin 1982, 61).

The fragments were such that it was not possible to give the overall dimensions of any of the tiles. Only one tile survived with its complete width. This tile (1972, 272, Trench III) measured 20.5 cm. across and averaged 1.40 cm. thick. Judging by the wear from the tile that would have overlapped it, this tile must have been about 40 cm. long. Ten small curved fragments survived of what appeared to have been ridge-tiles.

Most of the fragments could be seen to come from either the upper or lower part of the tiles, not only because of the presence or absence of holes for the pegs but also because the tiles were all only partially glazed and glazing was always absent from the fragments with the peg-holes, i.e. from the parts that were overlapped. The glazes were either brown or dark green like those on floor-tiles and occurred in roughly equal proportions on about half the total number of fragments. Some tiles, however, were probably completed unglazed. The holes for the pegs were about 1 cm. in diameter and placed 2 cm. from the top of the tile. All the tiles appear to have been rectangular, rather than pointed, at their lower end.

The date of the fragments appears to be late medieval. In 1468/9 £1.0.0 was paid to Nicholas Alleyn for the purchase of 6,000 tiles (Cotton 1939, 95) and there were doubtless many other purchases at other times now unrecorded.

MEDIEVAL FLOOR-TILES 1972–78 AND EARLIER M.C. Horton

Introduction

Excavations since 1845 at the site of St. Augustine's Abbey have recovered quantities of medieval floor-tiles (Sparks 1984). Some areas of pavement have been reburied, others left exposed, while many tiles and fragments came from destruction levels. Most of the loose tiles are on permanent loan to the Historic Buildings and Monuments Commission and others have been reset at the abbey itself. Very little of the paving remains *in situ* and open to view; the most important areas are at the west end of the nave, and in the crypt chapels of St. Richard of Chichester and St. Thomas the Apostle.

The present collections form only a proportion of the tiles excavated from the abbey. In the early days, it would appear that only good examples of complete tiles were retained, and very few fragments survive from this work. A number of the surplus tiles have found their way into museum collections, while others undoubtedly remain in private hands. The British Museum (Eames 1980, Cat. nos. 1763, 2146, 11554–11559), Maidstone Museum and the Royal Canterbury Museum have tiles from the abbey. Many of the tiles reset in the refectory of Canterbury Blackfriars are reputed to have come from St. Augustine's, through the collecting of an antique dealer, Mr Powell, the owner of the Blackfriars during the interwar years.

The excavations of 1972 to 1978, the principal concern of this report, produced many tiles and fragments. These have greatly amplified the range of types and designs known from the abbey. These modern excavations were of particular importance, because they provided, for the first time, tiles from stratified contexts. Although none were found *in situ*, and most came from disturbed and Dissolution contexts, this new material provides clearer evidence of the chronology, typology and location of the floor-tiles than was available from the earlier excavations. (The excavations of S.E. Rigold in 1960 and A. Saunders from 1957 to 1960 did not find any floor-tiles).

A comprehensive study of the medieval floor-tiles from St. Augustine's Abbey has been attempted, to include both the finds from these modern excavations and those that survive from the earlier work. This approach was felt justified as some of the pieces from the modern excavations were incomplete or very worn, and could only be understood with reference to comparable examples from the earlier finds. However, two aspects have been excluded from the present study. A square tile, in a soft orange fabric, with a sun-dial scratched on an upper surface has recently been published elsewhere (Sherlock 1982, 19–26). Also excluded are the fragments of *opus alexandrinum* stone pavement in the collections probably excavated from the crypt where 'bits of porphyry and serpentine mosaic' were found (Routledge 1903, 243).

The floor-tiles from the abbey have been divided into groups on the basis of their fabric, shape and size, the nature of decoration and glazes used. The tiles retaining their decoration have been listed within each group as separate design numbers. The terminology used in description is derived from Peacock (1977) for fabric, and Drury and Pratt (1975), Eames (1980) and Norton (forthcoming) for tile design and technology. Table 3 provides a summary of

TABLE 3

Total Counts of Medieval Floor-Tiles from St. Augustine's Abbey

Group	Monument	Loose	St. Pancras	1972	1973/4	1975	1976	1977	1978	TOTAL
A	7	11			1	3	76	49	24	171
B1	246	58	5	6	19	31	87	34	8	494
B2	13	37	3	5	8	48	25	8	1	148
B3	57	20		2	2	1	50	39	3	174
C	1	3			1		3	8	1	17
D	17	2				1	7	2		29
E	1	4	1		1		1	1	3	12
F	2	6	2		5	15	29	85	3	147
G		2								2
H		1					1			2
I		1								1
J										–
K		2		1			1			4
L		1								1
M		11		1	3	1	1	3	1	21
N		10			4		6	5		25
TOTAL	324	169	11	15	44	100	287	234	44	1248

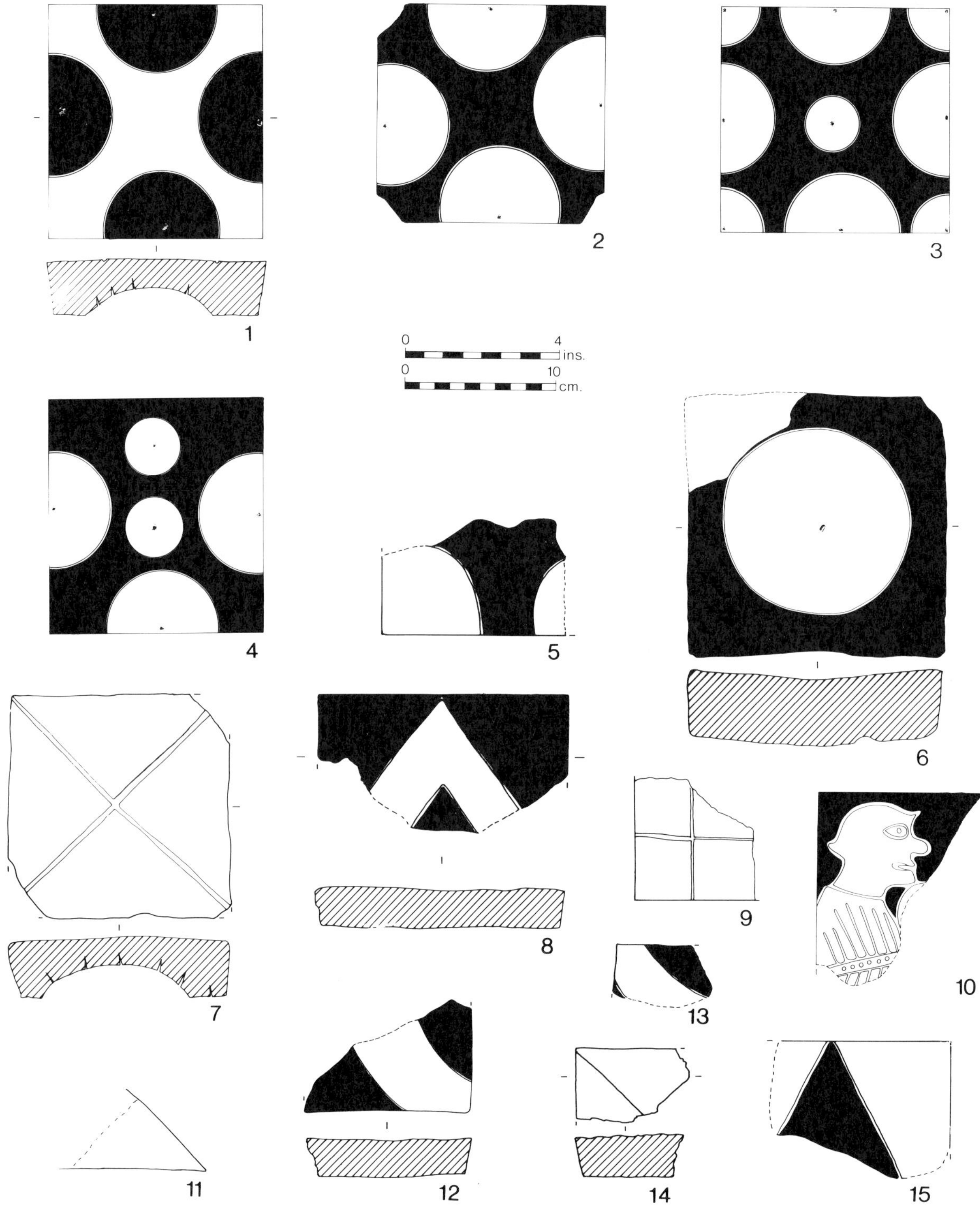

Fig. 43. Medieval Floor-Tiles, with inscribed lines and slip clay decoration. Group A. (Scale: ¼)

distribution of tile groups from the abbey, both in the collections and from the modern excavations. Details of exact provenance, layer and trench number are lodged in the archive. The number of examples of each design recorded from the abbey is given in brackets in the catalogue below. A total of 1248 tiles and fragments were available for study.

The Tiles (Map of all sites mentioned, Fig. 52, b)

Group A. *Clowes Wood Inscribed Tiles* (Fig. 43)

Square tiles, with sides of between 140 mm. and 150 mm. long and 24 mm. to 34 mm. thick. The paste is hard, pink maroon in colour, with abundant fine and medium sized quartz temper; occasional larger inclusions are sand- and silt-stone fragments and gravel. There are few air holes, a grey core and margins. The fracture is rough and lumpy, and numerous cracks occur on the surface. The tile was moulded into shape, with the sides flattened; the top face of the tile is often irregular, and the base is unsanded. The sides have a slight to medium bevel. If keying were employed, (normally on the thicker tiles only), two methods were used. In one, the tile was repeatedly stabbed with a pointed instrument, 3 mm. in diameter. Up to 200 holes may occur on the back of a single tile. These holes occur in pairs, suggesting that a pair of closed dividers (used to decorate the upper surface) made these marks. The stabs were made when the tile was still in its mould, as in some cases, the holes penetrate the edges. The function of these holes seems to have been to let out the water vapour during drying and firing from the body of the tile. The second type of keying was the more usual scoop key, a flattened cone, 80 mm. in diameter and 20 mm. deep, gouged out by a broad knife.

The decoration of the tile was set out using hand-scoring onto the wet clay. An edge was used to guide the straight lines, while compasses were used for the circles. For the latter, the central compass hole is clearly visible. White slip was hand-painted onto the tiles, normally on only one side of the inscribed line. The tile was thereafter glazed with a greenish yellow lead glaze.

Two slightly different types of tile occur. One (nos. 1–7) is mainly with keys, between 37 and 32 mm. thick, the second (8–18) is without keys, and only 26 mm. thick. But in all other respects, such as fabric, glaze and decoration, the tiles are identical.

1. Four inscribed half circles; scoop and stab keys (1).
2. Four inscribed half circles, slipped in reverse (1).
3. Four inscribed half circles, centre circle and corner quarter circles (1).
4. Three inscribed half circles, two smaller centre circles (1).
5. Four inscribed quarter circles (2).
6. Centre inscribed full circle, no keys (3).
7. Diagonal lines, but no slip survives, scoop and stab keys (1).
8. Inscribed chevron, no keys (7).
9. Inscribed lines, four by four chequer, but no slip left (1).
10. Inscribed human face and upper torso, with tunic and pelletted belt, no keys (1).
11. Triangular mosaic fragment, slipped, no keys (1).
12. Curving ribbon, producing large circle across sixteen tiles (1).
13. Design as 12, but from another area of panel (1).

14. Single scored line, total slip cover (1).
15. Incribed triangle, no keys (1).

In 1967, tile wasters were found in Clowes Wood, near Canterbury, during the construction of a field drain (Millard 1968). Extensive patches of burning in the vicinity, indicated the close proximity of a kiln site. The wasters were of the same fabric as this group, and were decorated with white slip and inscribed lines. Clowes Wood lies within the Tyler Hill area, an important production centre of roof-tiles and pottery from the twelfth century onwards (Norton and Horton 1981, 78). The tiles from St. Augustine's were most probably made at the Clowes Wood kiln, or nearby.

The tiles set out to copy the effect of mosaic paving while retaining the more convenient square shape, easier both to fire and lay. The differential application of white slip on either side of the inscribed lines highlighted the simple geometric, or in one case (no. 10) the anthropomorphic decoration. This type of tile has been called pseudo-mosaic (Eames 1975), but this is now thought to be a rather inappropriate term as it covered several different techniques for producing mosaic effect. Significantly in this group one fragment of true mosaic (no. 11) was also recorded, suggesting that part of the pavement may have been composed of triangular as well as rectangular tiles.

Great difficulties surround the dating of these tiles. The general absence of diagnostic designs has led to a variety of suggested dates. Mrs. Eames (1975; 1980, 63) places them in the late thirteenth or early fourteenth century, on the basis of general similarity to other pseudo-mosaic tiles from Bedfordshire. These tiles are, however, quite different in both design and style. S.E. Rigold (1968, 44) compared them to the local mosaic tiles of the early thirteenth century. These mosaic tiles, now termed the Medway Mosaic (Horton 1983, 72) are now re-dated to around 1260. They are found at the Benedictine Rochester Cathedral and at Cistercian and Premonstratensian foundations, but do not occur at Faversham Abbey, Canterbury Cathedral or at St. Augustine's. The inscribed tiles are quite different to these mosaic tiles, and their crude appearance suggests a date prior to the Cistercian sponsored innovations in tile production.

Dr Norton (1983a, 97; 1986b, 268–9) considers that slip decoration on two-colour tiles was introduced to England from France in the mid-thirteenth century, and suggests that the St. Augustine's tiles must belong around or after 1240. He compares them to the tiles from Saint-Benoît-sur-Loire, where there is a group of *sgraffiato* tiles laid perhaps just before 1250. These tiles are quite different in technique, made by cutting away the body clay. They do, however, show geometric as well as zoomorphic figures and foliate designs.

Better parallels are the hand-incised tiles, but without white slip, produced by the Cistercian order in the late twelfth century. Examples are from Cîteaux itself (around 1195), Saint-Benigne, Dijon and Fontenay (Norton 1983b, 73, 84, 89). Particularly close parallels for the mosaic designs, such as no. 5 are found at Saint-Quentin (France), and the Cistercian foundations at Pilis (Hungary) and Thoronet (France) dated to the end of the twelfth century (Norton 1983b, 89, 90). Very early Cistercian tiles of the counter-relief type were made in Kent in the twelfth century and have been reported at Boxley Abbey (Tester 1973, Fig. 6, no. 2; Norton 1983b, 103; 1986, 237, Fig. 30c). An inscribed tile of the type found on the Continent was, however, found at the site of the Cistercian abbey of Sawley (Yorks.). But St. Augustine's Abbey was not a Cistercian foundation and the inscribed tiles with these Continental parallels have not been found at Boxley or the other Cistercian houses in southern England.

One technological feature, which suggests an early date for the St. Augustine's tiles, is the use of moulding rather than knife cutting for shaping the tile. Virtually all two-colour tiles are cut to shape using a square template, from a prepared slabe of clay. Usually this group appears to have been shaped, in the manner of bricks, within a prepared mould, although sometimes the shape was finished off with a knife. Moulds were used to shape the high relief decorated tiles, now believed to date largely from the twelfth rather than the thirteenth century. The best recorded and dated group comes from the chapter house of St. Alban's Abbey, of around 1160, (Biddle and Kjølbye-Biddle 1984). Other evidence suggests that the Clowes Wood inscribed tiles may also belong to the twelfth century.

No inscribed tiles have been reported *in situ* at St. Augustine's Abbey, and all the fragments found could be ascribed to either Dissolution contexts, or ground surfaces dating from 1250 to 1350 (p. 86). Especially large numbers of fragments were found in the area outside the nave on its south side during the 1976 excavations. This may indicate that these tiles were originally situated in this general area of the nave and were robbed out at the Dissolution. Other areas of the church were certainly paved with these tiles but no fragments were retained, and only a small number of whole tiles survive from the excavations in the transepts and east end of the church.

The nave was built about 1080 (p. 5) and this group of tiles may have been laid at this date, but this would be most unlikely as ceramic floor-tiles are unknown from early post-Conquest buildings except one possible fragment from the cathedral precinct (Horton forthcoming). A better context might be provided by the refurbishment of the church, especially the nave, after the great fire of 1168 (Miscampbell 1981, 64). The tiles may have been part of this scheme, which seems to have concentrated upon the insertion of vaults and the remodelling of capitals. The date of completion of the work is not know, and the tiles would have been laid in the final stages. A date between 1174 and 1193 has been suggested (p. 6).

A tile of the inscribed type has also been found at the cathedral (Eames 1980, Cat. no. 7782), almost identical in design to no. 7 from St. Augustine's. Its provenance from within the cathedral is unknown but, if it belonged to the same period, a context might be the extensive rebuilding after the great fire of 1174. Close similarities have been shown in the very innovative work of this decade at both St. Augustine's and the cathedral (Miscampbell 1981; Mair 1982). The tiles could have formed part of this movement. Ceramic floor-tiles were extremely rare at this date.

Inscribed tiles of the same group were also found at Faversham Abbey. The collection of 564 fragments from robber trenches, destruction levels, pits, and two small areas *in situ* (but heavily disturbed) in the nave and north aisle provided a similar range to that found at St. Augustine's. The quantity and distribution of these tiles suggest that much of Faversham Abbey was paved with these inscribed tiles. The excavator at Faversham was unable to resolve whether the tiles belonged to the period I work (probably completed around 1154), the 'repairs' of 1178, or the drastic reconstruction of period II, around 1220, (Philp 1968, 41). One inconclusive piece of evidence was that the tiles were found in concentration outside the shortened east end of the period II work, but within the longer royal chapel of period I (Philp 1968, 17, 18), suggesting that they may predate the period II construction of 1220.

An inscribed tile, said to have been dug up at the site of Canterbury Blackfriars is in the British Museum (Cat. no. 2214). It shows a human face and torso, similar in style to St. Augustine's no. 10. The Blackfriars was founded in 1237 and the church was completed around

1256. This evidence would suggest a very much later date for this group, but the tiles from Blackfriars have a dubious provenance. None were collected from excavation, but from unrecorded digging in the area of the church. In addition, many were brought together in a private collection, mixing together tiles from the Blackfrairs and from many different sites, including St. Augustine's Abbey itself. Reset on the refectory floor are more examples of the inscribed group whose provenance must be treated with suspicion. The tile in the British Museum may also have a suspect origin.

In Suffolk, inscribed tiles without the use of slip, are known from Orford Castle (Sherlock n.d., design no. 140; Norton 1983a, 128; Drury and Norton 1985). The circle motif is used in single- and multiple-tile designs, very similar to both the St. Augustine's tiles and the Cistercian parallels cited above. The tiles are of the same size and thickness as the Kent group, the main difference being that they are without slip. Some of the Orford Castle tiles were found to have been used to build a fireplace, which formed part of the primary construction of the castle keep, placed on documentary evidence *c.* 1165–67. Dr Norton believes that these tiles were derived from French models which are now lost (1983a, 129).

A tile of unknown provenance, but probably from the same group, now in the British Museum (Cat. no. 2727), is also of the same shape with inscribed decoration on the upper surface. It shows a praying figure, beneath an arcade of round-headed arches, with Transitional capitals broadly similar to those associated with the post-fire reconstructions of the 1170s at St. Augustine's and in the cathedral.

Two possible dates can be suggested for these inscribed tiles: *c.* 1170 or *c.* 1240. In favour of the earlier date, it is now believed that floor-tiles were becoming a feature of some major churches in the latter part of the twelfth century in southern England. The high relief tiles at St. Alban's and its dependencies, the Cistercian tiles from Boxley Abbey and the inscribed tiles from Orford Castle suggest at least three separate traditions, with probable Continental origins. Unglazed floor-tiles of this date have also been reported from Battle Abbey and South Mimms Castle in Hertfordshire (Streeten 1985, 84–85). The building works during the 1170s at Canterbury and Faversham would provide a context for similar innovations in Kent. The tiles themselves, from the point of view of design, can be readily accommodated at this date, both by comparison to Cistercian tiles of the 1180s and 1190s, and the Orford Castle tiles of *c.* 1170. There are several objections to this hypothesis. One, that the inscribed tiles were found at the Canterbury Blackfriars, founded in 1237, can be dismissed in view of the known contamination of the tiles from this site. More serious is the technological argument that the St. Augustine's tiles use white slip in their decoration. The Continental inscribed tiles, as well as those from Orford Castle, do not use white slip; indeed, the first Continental parallels for white slip to be used in this way occur in the early thirteenth century (Norton 1986b, 268–9). Two-colour stamped tiles date to the mid-thirteenth century on both sides of the English Channel. In this respect the St. Augustine's inscribed tiles would be fifty years ahead of their time.

A date around 1240 is equally difficult to accept. While this would corroborate the Blackfriars dating, it does not seem to coincide with any major building programmes at any of the abbeys. Faversham and St. Augustine's were in poor financial shape, while major rebuilding had been completed at the east end of the cathedral only a few decades earlier. Further, extremely competent mosaic pavements were now being made in northern France. Canterbury, with its Continental tastes, would have been aware of these, as it was with the tiles produced in the

Parisian Basin in the 1280s (Norton and Horton 1981). Nobody would have been satisfied with the very crude and archaic inscribed tiles, even with their slip embellishment.

Very few twelfth-century tiles are known, and it may be that the model for the St. Augustine's inscribed tiles has not yet been found on the Continent. White slip was used on mosaic tiles to produce a polychrome effect in non-Cistercian contexts in the twelfth century, but it seems that this polychrome effect was thought initially inappropriate at the early Cistercian foundations, from where most of the inscribed tiles have hitherto been found. Two-colour inscribed tiles may have existed in the churches of other foundations but have not survived.

Alternatively, the Kent inscribed tiles may be a local development from these Cistercian tiles. This would suggest slip decoration of two-colour tiles had its origin here, and not on the Continent, as has hitherto been claimed (Norton 1986b, 268–9). Close connections with French craftsmen have been shown in the rebuilding of St. Augustine's and the cathedral and the tiles could form part of this movement. Craftsmen adapted designs and techniques from France, to suit local requirements. A ceramic industry already existed in the area of Tyler Hill; both roof-tiles and pottery made there have been found stratified in twelfth-century contexts in Canterbury. Clowes Wood lies very close to the Tyler Hill pottery kilns, and some local innovation could easily have occurred there.

On balance, a date of about 1170 would seem most probable. Faversham Abbey and Orford Castle were both royal works, and it is possible that a royal commission introduced these tiles to England. Alternatively, Faversham Abbey may have been tiled after the Canterbury orders, which would therefore have been responsible for their introduction as part of the post-fire rebuilding schemes. At the same time some of the tiles, or tilers, reached the other royal works at Orford Castle. All five foundations had major building works going on in the decade of 1168–78. By 1180, the Clowes Wood workshop had probably ceased production. When floor-tile making was revived a century later at Tyler Hill, the products were made and decorated in a totally different way, using stamps and mosaic work. At present, the Clowes Wood tile workshop can be claimed to be one of the earliest to use white slip on floor-tiles in Europe. But it seems to have been an isolated precursor and not the prototype of the two-colour tiles of the thirteenth century.

Group B. *Tyler Hill Products*

This group forms the bulk of tiles found at the abbey, with a total of 816 examples. The fabric of the Tyler Hill products is uniform and distinctive. The body is bright red, sometimes red margins with a grey core, with a well-sorted fine sand and quartz temper. The fracture is clean, and in well-fired examples, almost shiny. There are sometimes gravel inclusions. The tiles are generally well-made, hard, dense and show little sign of wear. Knife shaping is always used, the sides have a slight to medium bevel, and the bases are unsanded. There are no nail holes or keys. The lead glazes used in this group are dark yellow, although occasionally, especially on the plain tiles, green glazes are employed.

A variety of decorative techniques is used on these tiles, which occur in a number of different shapes and sizes. Thus, both curvilinear and rectilinear mosaic occurs in addition to the more usual square tiles. Slip decoration is applied using both the stamp-on slip and slip-over impression methods. On the basis of technique and size, three sub-groups have been defined for

Fig. 44. Medieval Floor-Tiles. Two-colour, slip-decorated tiles, from Tyler Hill workshops. Gloup B1. (Scale: ¼)

this large range of products, which may relate to separate workshops within the Tyler Hill complex.

Group B1. (Figs. 44, 45)

Square tiles which are 118 mm. in length, and 23 mm. thick. Slip decoration is applied generally by the slip-over impression technique, with a dark yellow glaze.

Rectilinear mosaic tiles form part of this group. They are fired as square tiles, generally 120 mm. x 23 mm. thick, with score lines on their upper surface. Subsequently, they were broken along these lines into the required shapes. The mosaic work employed both plain and slip-decorated tiles. Two examples of slip-decorated mosaic (nos. 35 and 36) used the slightly smaller unit of 104

Fig. 45. Medieval Floor-Tiles. Two-colour, slip-decorated and mosaic tiles from Tyler Hill workshops. Group B1. (Scale: ¼)

mm. The mosaic pieces were probably broken into their pieces at the abbey, rather than the kiln. An interesting group of such pieces of mosaic, partly broken from their parent tiles, is in the British Museum, brought from the site of the abbey (Cat. nos. 11, 554–11, 559).

16. Single pattern fleur-de-lys, set diagonally, (44).
17. Single pattern, daisy with six petals, in double border, with corner trefoils, (31).
18. Single pattern, intersecting branches, in double cusped border, (3).
19. Continuous pattern, double circle segments, rectangular dots, central quatrefoil, (15).
20. Continuous pattern, using circle segments, corner trefoils, and centre four-petalled flower, (2).
21. Continuous pattern, circle segments and floral decoration, (4).
22. Continuous pattern, intersecting chevrons, four-petalled daisies, star and suns, (2).
23. Four-tile pattern, triple arcs, sun, moon and stars, (4).
24. Four-tile pattern, multiple arcs, with daisies, (1).

25. Four-tile/continuous pattern, cusped arcs, fleur-de-lys, addorsed animals, (5).
26. Four-tile/continuous pattern, double quarter circle, four-petalled flowers, tree, (20).
27. Four-tile/continuous pattern, double arcs, lozenges and stiff leaf, (9).
28. Sixteen-tile pattern, grotesque animals, eight-petalled daisies within circle, between double arcs, (3).
29. Sixteen-tile pattern, border as 28, with corner dragon, (1).
30. Sixteen-tile pattern, centre panel, winged monsters, daisies in circles, (1).
31. Sixteen-tiles pattern, corner 'upside down' face, floral, between arcs, (2).
32. Sixteen-tile pattern, floral between arcs, (3).
33. Sixteen-tile/continuous pattern, arcs, four- and six-petalled daisies, (1).
34. Sixteen-tile/continuous pattern, variant of 33, (12).
35. Mosaic, slip-decorated, with four elements (floral cross in cusped borner), intended to be broken into four pieces; 104 mm. square, (1).
36. Mosaic, slip-decorated, four elements, (castle, daisy, fleur-de-lys, dancette), intended to be broken into four pieces; 104 mm. square, (1).
37. Mosaic, slip-decorated, from a four-element tile, similar to 36, but of the larger size of 118 mm., (1).
38. Mosaic, slip-decorated, labyrinth quarter tile, from tile 118 mm. square, (1).
39. Mosaic, slip-decorated, lion passant guardant, on quarter tile, from tile 118 mm. square, (1).
40. Mosaic tiles, either slipped and clear/yellow glazed, or clear glazed, without slip, broken off from tile 120 mm. square. Square mosaic pieces, b and e; triangular pieces, a, c, d, and f, (27). Similar tiles also in the British Museum (Eames 1980, Cat. nos. 11,555–11,559).
41. Mosaic tiles, either slipped and clear/yellow glazed, or clear glazed without slip, broken from tile 120 mm. square. Square mosaic pieces, g and i, triangular pieces, h, (5).

Not illustrated: Plain tiles, without slip, covered in dark brown glaze, (25).
Plain tiles, with slip, mottled green glaze, (29).

Two pavements of this sub-group survive in Kent and provide a clear idea of the manner of arrangement. In the chancel of Brook Church, only the square tiles are found, employed in continuous, four- and sixteen-tile designs. A number of designs are missing from the St. Augustine's assemblage: thus, nos. 28, 29, 30 belong together, but the fourth tile to complete the panel (left-hand border tile) is not present, in this sixteen-tile panel. The other panel is represented by nos. 31 and 32, the right-hand border tile is missing. The centre is made up with four-tile designs, sometimes as no. 26. Possible reconstructions of these panels have been published elsewhere (Horton 1979, 124, Fig. 17). How the mosaic tiles were arranged can be established from the surviving pavement at the Corona Chapel of Canterbury Cathedral (Norton and Horton 1981, 67, Fig. 3). A similar range of shapes was represented from tiles 120 mm. square, broken into segments. The St. Augustine's tiles were, however, divided into very much smaller pieces than we have recorded from the Corona pavement. On the other hand the Corona pavement has a 'Maltese cross' mosaic absent from St. Augustine's. Other differences are that only the red fabric was used at the abbey whereas the Corona Chapel pavement employed a pale cream as well as a red fabric, thus achieving a three-colour effect. The range of shapes in the British Museum from St. Augustine's is somewhat larger and includes rectangles, triangles, and lozenges (Eames 1980, designs S 2, 9, 13, 39, 44, 45, 48). But at both sites the mosaic tiles were made from a parent tile of 120 mm., rather than the more usual 118 mm. size employed on the decorated tiles.

We have argued elsewhere (Norton and Horton 1981, 77) that the slip-decorated mosaic tiles (nos. 36, 37, 38 and 39) were intended as borders to the plain mosaic panels, or to be used within the panels. No. 36, with its smaller size, had the tiles set diagonally, as was found at St. Germain-des-Prés (Norton and Horton 1981, 70, Fig. 4.4). The other tiles, with their larger size (nos. 37, 39), were probably used as borders, or set square within panels. The labyrinth tile (no. 38) would produce an attractive continuous border. All the mosaic designs, except the last, were also reproduced on the full size 118 mm. tiles.

Group B2. (Figs. 46, 47)

Square tiles, of sides 116–118 mm. long and 16 mm. thick. These tiles have only a slight bevel, and the base is unsanded with occasional patches of glaze and vegetation imprints. The thinness of the tile causes warping in some cases. The fabric is characteristic of Tyler Hill products, bright red to orange in colour. Slip decoration was applied by the stamp-on slip method; the glaze is dark yellow, sometimes pale green.

42. Single-tile pattern, fleur-de-lys set diagonally, (3).
43. Single-tile pattern, six-petalled daisy within circle, (2).
44. Single-tile pattern, six-petalled daisy within double circle, (1).
45. Continuous pattern, dancette, (1).
46. Continuous pattern, interlacing circles, square pelletting, (2).
47. Continuous pattern, eight-petalled daisies within squares and circles, (2).
48. Single-tile pattern, floral design, (1).
49. Single-tile pattern, floral, within cusped border, (3).
50. Continuous pattern, lion rampant in cusped border, (1).
51. Border pattern, bush within droplet border, (1).
52. Single-tile pattern, lion statant, in square frame, (4).
53. Single-tile pattern, beast in square frame, (1).
54. Single-tile pattern, gryphon passant, within square frame, (5).
55. Single-tile pattern, hunting scene, showing two dogs jumping over a tree, within square frame, (2).
56. Single-tile pattern, lion passant, in square frame, (1).
57. Border pattern, beast, showing head end, (3).
58. Single-tile pattern, lion passant guardant, upraised paw, (2).
59. Single-tile pattern, beast within square frame, (1).
60. Single-tile pattern, dog leaping over tree, (2).
61. Four-tile pattern, foetal animals in cusped border, (10).
62. Four-tile pattern, green man, in double border, (3).
63. Four-tile pattern, face and monsters within arcs, (2).
64. Four-tile pattern, double circle, lozenges, with tree and monsters, (5).
65. Four-tile pattern, two lions addorsed regardant within arc, (2).
66. Four-tile pattern, addorsed birds, within cusped border, (1).

Fig. 46. Medieval Floor-Tiles. Two-colour, slip-decorated tiles from Tyler Hill workshops. Group B2. (Scale: ¼)

67. Four-tile/continuous pattern, daisies within interlacing arcs, (1).
68. Four-tile pattern, fleur-de-lys, (1).
69. Border pattern, floral, 195 mm. x 72 mm., (7).
70–80. Fragments, (11).

Not illustrated: Plain tiles, unslipped, with dark brown glaze, (68).

This sub-group provides a less complex range of patterns than the previous group. Mosaic tiles do not form part of the scheme, while the border tiles are simple floral designs. No sixteen-tile panel is recorded, while four-tile designs are rare. The majority of subjects chosen are sub-heraldic, showing beasts within square frames (nos. 52–59). These would no doubt have been interspersed by plain tiles, of which a large number of pieces were found.

Fig. 47. Medieval Floor-Tiles. Two-colour, slip-decorated tiles from Tyler Hill workshops. Group B2. (Scale: ¼)

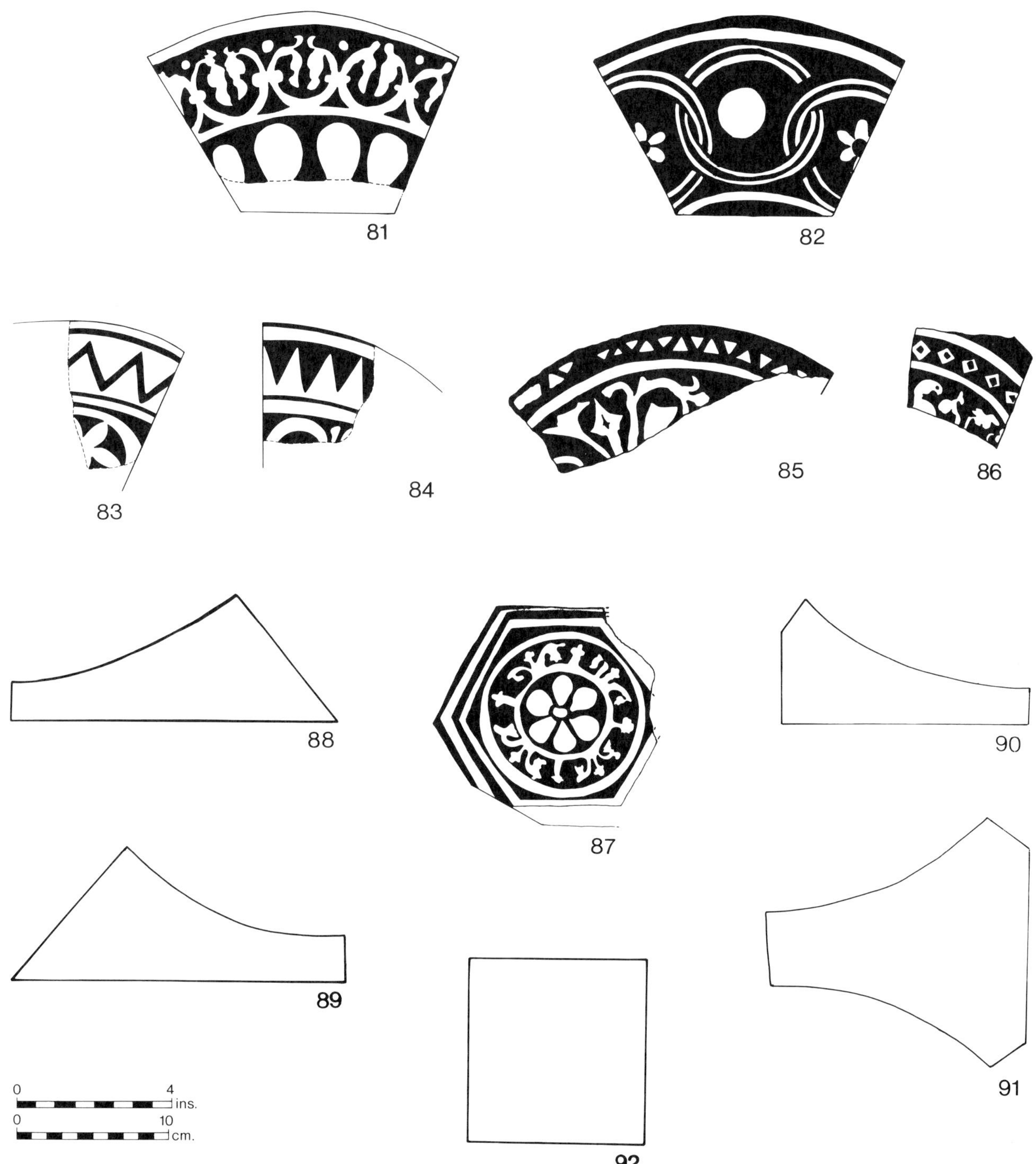

Fig. 48. Medieval Floor-Tiles. Two-colour, slip-decorated segmental mosaic from Tyler Hill workshops. Plain tiles are green glazed. Group B3. (Scale: ¼)

However, the tiles are closely related to group B1, not only in fabric but also in the detailing of the floral decoration, the use of lozenges and square pellets, and in the design of the four-tile patterns. This sub-group would appear to be slightly later, and derivative from the earlier and original range of designs.

Group B3. (Fig. 48)

Mosaic tiles, using curvilinear shapes, and segmental roundels within a square frame. The tiles are 24 mm. thick, but sometimes up to 35 mm. thick. The fabric is similar to the previous group B tiles, bright red in colour, with well-sorted sand temper, air holes and some traces of lamination, but generally well-fired. The slip decoration applied to the roundels is by the slip-over impression method, while the mosaic frames are unslipped with a mottled dark green or green brown glaze. The tiles have no keys or nail holes, and are all individually shaped by knife-cut edges.

81. Segmental tile from roundel, decorated with floral arcade and daisy leaves, (7).
82. Segmental tile from roundel, interlocked circles, (15).
83. Segmental tile from roundel, fragment, (11).
84. Segmental tile from roundel, fragment, (4).
85. Segmental tile from roundel, tree design, (1).
86. Segmental tile, from roundel, fragment. Given to Maidstone Museum, from St. Augustine's Abbey in 1919.
87. Hexagonal tile, forming centre of roundel, petal design, with floral border. Now in Canterbury Museum, originally from St. Augustine's Abbey.
88. Plain mosaic tile, roundel frame edge tile, (3).
89. Plain mosaic tile, roundel frame edge tile, (5).
90. Plain mosaic tile, roundel frame corner tile, (2).
91. Plain mosaic tile, roundel frame, centre tile, (21).
92. Plain square tile, 118 mm., used in mosaic, (104).

A fragment of pavement of this group remains *in situ* (but reset in concrete), at the west end of the nave, on the south side (Plate LII). From this a clear picture emerges of how the mosaic elements fitted together (Fig. 52, a). Only the roundels were decorated and these comprised six segmental tiles which, when fitted together, comprised a circle of 400 mm. Each roundel had a different design, and at least six are known from the abbey (nos. 81–86). Inside the roundel was set a hexagonal tile. In the nave pavement these are too damaged to study and the only hexagonal tile surviving is in Canterbury Museum, from the abbey (no. 87). This design fitted with no. 81 to form the complete roundel.

The roundels were set within a plain frame of green glazed tiles. A number of types were recorded; those needed to edge out the pavement, and those linking roundels. These pieces (nos. 88–91) were set around a plain square tile (no. 92) very similar to the plain tiles of groups B1 and B2 but with a green rather than brown glaze.

The large numbers of these plain square tiles (no. 92), found in the 1976 and 1977 excavations, without the associated roundels and frames are hard to explain. These excavations were adjacent to the nave and the decorated roundels may have formed only a small element of paving comprising mainly square green-glazed tiles.

These mosaic tiles compare closely to the other two sub-groups. The fabric is the same, and there are close similarities in the style of decoration, (e.g. nos. 64, 69, 85). Furthermore, B1 tiles, such as no. 26, are incorporated within the border of the *in situ* area of mosaic paving, suggesting contemporaneity. However, the two types of mosaic must be carefully distinguished. Those found in group B1 (nos. 35–41) are derived from square tiles, scored and broken after firing, while in the curvilinear mosaic here, each individual tile is prepared prior to firing.

Discussion

These group B tiles throw considerable light upon the origins and development of tile production at Tyler Hill, near Canterbury. They were made from the brickearth found in this area of the Forest of Blean. Kiln sites have been located with surface scatters of floor- and roof-tile waste material (Norton and Horton 1981, 78; Philp 1974). The decorated tiles comprise designs from both groups B1 and B2. Where excavation has taken place, as during the construction of the University of Kent (Harrington 1971), the kilns were found to have a bottle-shaped plan, with two or three chambers. An archaeomagnetic date of 1300±25 years was obtained from one kiln site. From the waste material, floor-tiles seem only to have been one part of the extensive Tyler Hill industry. Pottery and roof-tiles were made here much earlier and two-colour tile-making was apparently incorporated within existing production.

Elsewhere, it has been shown that the Tyler Hill floor-tiles were produced under clear French, probably Parisian, influence around 1285–90 (Norton and Horton 1981). Particularly characteristic is the use of rectilinear mosaic and slip-decorated quarter tiles. Tilers may have been brought over to assist in the re-paving of the cathedral. At the completion of this work, they successfully marketed their products, dropping to mosaic element, to other Kentish abbeys such as Faversham (Rigold 1968), and to over fifty parish churches (Drury 1981, 134, Fig. 96).

The earliest tiles, and those closest to the Parisian models, are the two fabric mosaic tiles from the Corona Chapel. Associated with these, but not *in situ*, were tiles identical to the B1 group. St. Augustine's Abbey is the only other site with rectilinear Tyler Hill mosaic work, and it may well be that the Parisian workshop produced both for the abbey and the cathedral, simultaneously. But the two-fabric mosaic tiles are absent from the St. Augustine's assemblage, and only tiles of the more usual red fabric are found. Thus, the St. Augustine's B1 group may be slightly later in date than the Corona pavement; the more complex features of the mosaic panel having already been dropped.

The B2 tiles derive closely from the Parisian workshop, but differ in design and complexity. The wasters at Tyler Hill show that they were made in adjacent or nearby kilns. Parallels to this group are generally found in a range of parish churches quite separate from the B1 tiles. Thus, B1 tiles occur at Brook, Adisham, Snargate and Smeeth, but from St. Clement's Sandwich and Gillingham the tiles are all of the B2 type. They can be considered later perhaps made about 1300.

The B3 tiles are more complex. The use of slip-over impression suggests affinity with the B1 tiles, as do some of the designs used. Curvilinear mosaic is otherwise unknown in the Tyler Hill products and the tiles show clear affinities with other segmental tiles not in a Tyler Hill fabric,

Fig. 49. Medieval Floor-Tiles. Two-colour, slip-decorated tiles. Upper tiles are 'Westminster tiler' (Group C). Lower tiles are 'Lewes group' (Group D). (Scale: ¼)

from Essex at Leez Priory, Coggeshall and Little Waltham (Drury and Norton forthcoming) and with a small group of tiles from Delft Street, Sandwich. A plain hexagonal tile has been reported from Leeds Priory in Kent (Horton 1978, 91). Segmental tile mosaics were present in southern England, particularly from Clarendon Palace, and the technique may have been adopted by the Tyler Hill factories. But a more likely source of influence comes from northern France, for example in the segmental pavement formally at Saint-Omer.

Group C. *The 'Westminster Tiler'* (Fig. 49)

Square tiles, with sides of 114 mm. long and 24–26 mm. thick. The fabric is bright orange red, with a fine well-sorted sand temper, sparse gravel inclusions, and a characteristic orange grog. The fracture is rough, with some laminations and air holes, red margins and sometimes a grey core. The base is unsanded, the sides generally have no bevel, but are knife-cut. The decoration is applied by the slip-over impression method, and glazed with a dark yellow, or greeny-yellow glaze. Sometimes, the tiles are broken off into triangular pieces, along score lines.

93. Continuous pattern, dancette, (8).
94. Single-tile pattern, floral cross, (1).
95. Continuous pattern, vair, (2).
96. Single tile, mounted knight, (1).
97. Single tile, fleur-de-lys, in British Museum (Cat. no. 2146, design no. 2147).
98. Single tile, animal fragment, (1).
99–102. Fragments (4).

The chief characteristic of this group is the inclusion of grog in the temper. The tiles are also very crudely made, with poor glazing and firing. Similar tiles have been recognised *in situ*, on the floor of the Pyx Chamber, Westminster Abbey (Eames 1980, 207), hence the name generally given to these tiles. The same range of designs, with 'what appears to be a grog of crushed red tile' is known from sites in Hertfordshire, Buckinghamshire, Bedfordshire, London, as well as the south Midland counties of Leicestershire and Warwickshire (Keen 1973; Eames 1980, 208–9). Recently, products of this school have been found east of London, in Essex at Waltham Abbey and Pleshey Castle, while in Kent they are known from Lesnes Abbey, Canterbury Cathedral, Temple Manor, Strood, St. Clement, Sandwich and Faversham Abbey. It is not clear whether all these collections, so widely spread, belong to the same production centre, or whether multiple itinerant centres were established. No kiln sites have yet been found. The study of the designs used indicates some regional variation. In Kent, the tiles have a Thames/Medway distribution, suggesting an up-river origin, perhaps London, or even beyond.

Mrs. Eames has set out the dating of these tiles (1980, 208), and concludes that they belong to the period 1290–1350. At St. Augustine's Abbey two fragments came from stratified contexts associated with the chapel ground surface dated to 1260–1350, and may perhaps have formed part of the chapel floor, built in the early to mid-fourteenth century (p. 69).

Group D. *The 'Lewes Group'* (Fig. 49)

Square tiles, with sides 111 mm. long and 19 mm. thick. The fabric is distinctive, pale pink orange margins and core, with a fine well sorted sand temper, and occasional inclusions of darker red grog, from crushed tile. The fracture is generally smooth, a little lamination, and some air holes. The base is unsanded, the edges are knife-cut, with a slight to medium bevel; there are no keys or nail holes. The decoration is applied by stamp-on slip, and the tiles are glazed with a yellow glaze, which leaves a very characteristic 'pine-apple' colour to the surface.

103. Continuous pattern, fleur-de-lys, in frame, (6).
104. Single-tile pattern, fleur-de-lys and tree, (3).
105. Continuous pattern, six-petal daisy in interwoven arcs, (2).
106. Continuous pattern, geometrical, (11).
107. Four-tile pattern, floral, (3).
108. Sixteen-tile pattern, leaf within border, (1).
109. Sixteen-/four-tile design, intersecting arc with bird in corner, (2).
110. Four-tile design, fragment, (1).

These tiles, with their very distinctive fabric and glaze have a widespread distribution within south-east England, with outlying examples as far north as St. Mary's Abbey, York, as far west as Eynsham, near Oxford, and Muchelney Abbey in Somerset. A large group of these tiles were excavated from the site of St. Alban's Abbey chapter house. Others are known from London, (L.M.M.C. 1940, 237, no. 7), but the greatest concentration lies in Sussex and Kent. Examples survive in the churches of Horstead Keynes, Poynings, Woodnesbourgh, and stray finds and excavated collections from Whitefriars Sandwich, Pivington, Langdon Abbey, Shulbrede Abbey, Lewes Priory (whence the name of the group), Angmering, Stonar and St. Thomas' Winchelsea.

The dating of these tiles can be established with some certainty. Their presence at both Winchelsea (established 1280) and Stonar (abandoned 1385) suggests that they date to the fourteenth century. Poynings Church was completely rebuilt in 1368, and the tiles seem to have been part of this scheme, suggesting a date-range 1365 to 1385; a reasonable date on stylistic grounds.

No kiln site has been found for this group. The distribution suggests a coastal and river based trade, reaching parish churches in south-east England, but only the major abbeys further afield. The rather un-English style led Ward-Perkins (1937) to suggest that these tiles were Flemish imports. In a survey of the Low Countries I have been unable to identify any examples of this group. However, in Upper Normandy, Dr E.C. Norton has noted tiles with very similar designs and fabric. Trade between northern France and the Cinque Ports on the south coast could well result in such a distribution pattern. While it is not yet proven that the tiles were made in northern France, similarity to other French tiles suggests that this was the most probable origin.

Fig. 50. Medieval Floor-Tiles. Two-colour, slip-decorated tiles. Upper tiles are the 'geometric group' (Group E). Lower tiles are products of the central Kent industries (Group F). (Scale: ¼)

Group E. *Geometric Tiles* (Fig. 50)

Square tiles, 114 mm. in length and 29 mm. thick. The fabric is pale pink red in colour, extremely mixed, with many cracks and air holes. While the core is not grey, there are many grey streaks in the fired tile. The temper is largely ill-sorted sand, with many coarse inclusions of gravel and sandstone. In a number of cases the tiles have cracked and broken along very irregular fractures. The sides are knife-cut, with a medium bevel, no keys or nail holes. The base is sanded with the same material used in the temper with numerous small holes.

The tiles are decorated using stamp on slip (where it is possible to tell) and are glazed with a thick rich yellow glaze.

111. Continuous pattern, interlacing arcs, (2).
112. Continuous pattern, circle and disc, (3).
113. Continuous pattern, quartrefoil and discs, (1).
114. Continuous/border pattern, interlocking double circles, (2).
115. Continuous/border pattern, interlocking squares, (1).

In colour, this fabric seems to be related to Tyler Hill, although there are clear differences in the preparation of the clay and the temper. This small group of tiles is little known in Kent. A tile similar to no. 114 was found at Ospringe, although apparently in a Tyler Hill fabric, (Horton 1979, Fig. 118 e), while the idea of the intersecting double circles is followed in no. 82, another Tyler Hill product. There are sufficient differences to distinguish this group, at least as it appears at St. Augustine's, from the Tyler Hill products. Perhaps these tiles are from a later concern in the Blean area.

Group F. *Central Kent Industries* (Fig. 50)

Square tiles, 121 mm. in length and around 20 mm. thick. The fabric is orange red or, when heavily fired, darker red with many air holes, porous and very sandy in feel. The temper is sand, with characteristic black flecks, probably flint, and occasional pieces of grog. Larger inclusions are sandstone and gravel. The fracture is slightly laminated. The tile always fires red throughout, but with an occasional grey upper margin. The tiles have knife-cut sides, and only a slight bevel and no keys or nail holes. The bases are unsanded.

The tiles are decorated by stamp-on slip (nos. 116–125) or slip-over impression (nos. 126–128), and are especially characterised by their greeny glazes, both on the surface and often on the underside.

116. Four-tile pattern, floral arcading and tree, (1).
117. Four-tile pattern, two lions rampant, within arcs, (3).
118. Single-tile pattern octafoil in circle, corner dots, (1).
119–125. Fragments (9).
126. Single-tile pattern, showing knight on horseback with helm, heraldic dressage and upraised sword, (3).

127. Four-tile pattern, crude floral design in double circle, (2).
128–131. Fragments (6).

Not illustrated: Plain tiles, slipped with a clear glaze, giving yellow green surface, (12).
Plain tiles, unslipped with green glaze, (94).
Plain triangular mosaic, by scoring tiles above, (11).

These somewhat rough and sandy tiles, with their dark glazes differ from the superior Tyler Hill products. However, they can be shown to have a similar but more limited distribution and would appear to be approximately contemporary. A group of these central Kent tiles have been published from Ospringe (Horton 1979, 121), although there is no duplication between the sites in the range of designs. The largest group is in the treasury of Canterbury Cathedral (relaid) as well as a useful group from the recently excavated Poor Priests' Hospital, in Canterbury. St. Augustine's designs also occur at Lesnes Abbey, Preston by Faversham, Doddington and St. Clement's Church, Sandwich, Eastry, and Davington Priory. On the basis of this distribution, a kiln site would be expected near Faversham, close to the line of Watling Street. There are some similarities with some of the wasters from the Rye kilns (Vidler 1932, 93, no. I.6), but none of these central Kent tiles are found in the south of the county, or in Sussex.

The tile showing a knight on horseback is of some interest (no. 126) and appears to be a rather sophisticated product in comparison with the other tiles of this group. The fabric and surface treatment are nevertheless very similar, except that the tile is rather harder fired. The design occurs elsewhere only at Blackfriars, Canterbury, but this may have come from St. Augustine's originally. The portrayal of a knight on horseback is a design taken from designs on Clarendon tiles (Eames 1980, 193), sometimes believed to represent the scene of Richard and Saladin; the crusader context is also suggested on these tiles by the heraldic cross on the shield. But in the St. Augustine's tile only a battle scene seemed intended. The dressage is heraldic and no tile showing an opposing warrior is known. Tiles of this sort were the model for the crude derivatives produced by the Westminster School (Group C), such as no. 96.

The large number of plain tiles found close to the chapel on the south side of the nave (p. 000) suggests that this building was paved with tiles of the central Kent industries. A late thirteenth-century date was previously suggested for these tiles (Horton 1979, 121), but an association with this chapel would suggest a fourteenth-century date.

Group G. (Fig. 51)

Square tiles, 121 mm. in length, and 22 mm. thick. The fabric is orange red, with much well-sorted sand and flint temper. The tiles have a rough fracture, and laminated air holes. The base is unsanded, and the sides are knife-cut, with a slight bevel. There are no nail holes or keys, and the design is applied by the slip-over impression method, then glazed with a green yellow glaze.

132. Sixteen-tile pattern, corner tile, stiff leaf foliage, daisy within border, (1).
133. Sixteen-tile pattern, side tile, double border, daisies and monster animal, (1).

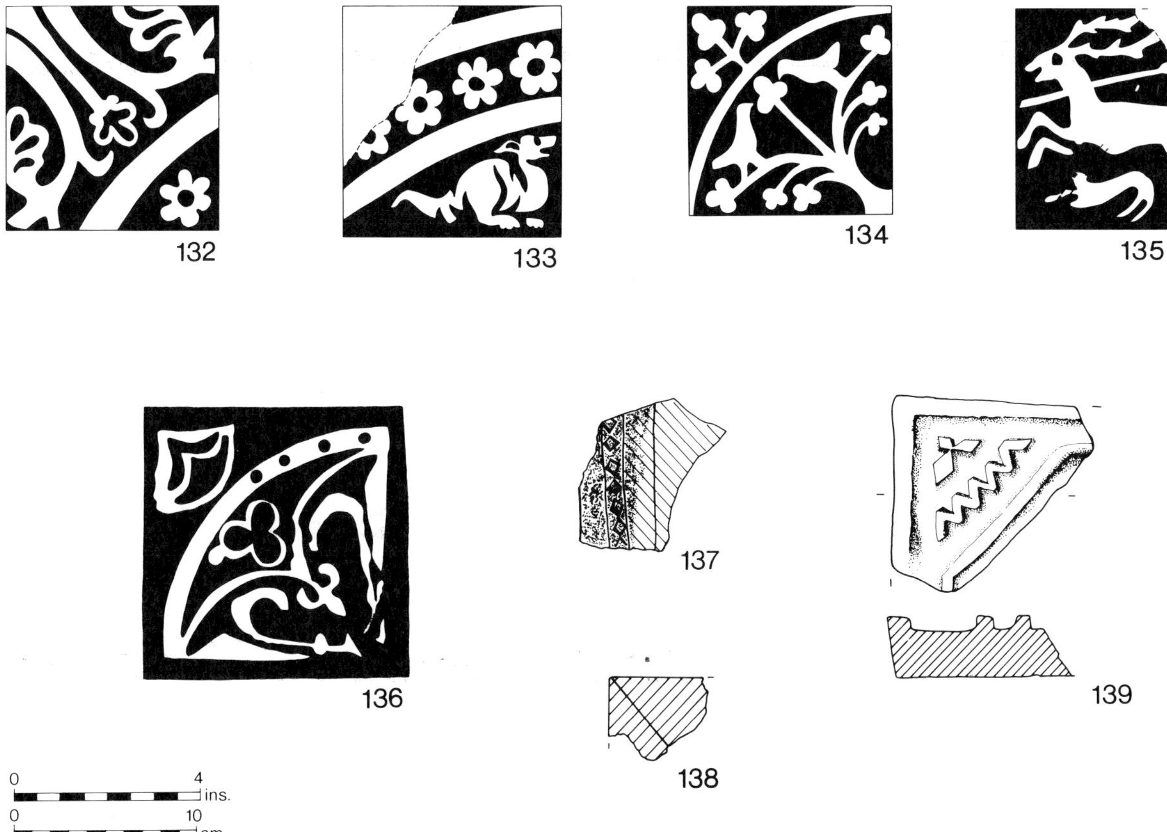

Fig. 51. Medieval Floor-Tiles. Two-colour, slip-decorated, Groups G, H, and I, stamped and line impressed Group K and high relief Group L. The stipple on no. 137 represents areas of white slip, the hatched area green glaze. (Scale: ¼)

A tile identical to no. 132 is known from Canterbury Cathedral (British Museum Cat. no. 266), but otherwise this group is unknown. The sixteen-tile arrangement is similar to certain Tyler Hill products (e.g. nos. 28, 29) but the fabric is very different. It could be a copy of the Tyler Hill series and would thus belong to the early fourteenth century.

Group H. (Fig. 51)

Square tiles, 110 mm. in length, and 20 mm. thick, with a bland pink-orange fabric and a fairly harsh texture, very badly mixed, with chunky fracture and laminations. The temper is sparse ill-sorted sand and there are white flecks and streaks, possibly caused by chalk. The tiles were shaped by a knife-cut, have an unsanded base with vegetation marks and a large bevel. There are no nail holes or keys, and the stamp-on slip decoration is covered with a yellow glaze.

134. Four-tile design, two birds in a tree, (2).

This tile is known from only two other sites in Kent: Faversham Abbey (Rigold 1968, 49, no. 98) and Cranbrook Parish Church (in Maidstone Museum, 1948. 5001/G). At Faversham the tile was believed to be part of the Tyler Hill series, but there are clear differences in shape, such as the large bevel and the fabric. The characteristic 'bland' appearance found on this tile, with weathering to a pinkish colour, is a feature of tiles from southern Kent and East Sussex (Horton 1983, 75, group D). A kiln site has not been found, but there are suggestions that production was linked to the Rye kilns (Vidler 1932, 93). The Rye tiles do not have the characteristic strong bevel found here (Streeten 1986, 87). The unusual design of the St. Augustine's tile is reminiscent of Bayham Abbey no. 28, which seems to date to the late thirteenth or early fourteenth century.

Group I. (Fig. 51)

Square tile, 114 mm. in length, and 18 mm. thick, with a dull red fabric, firing to a grey core. There is a well-sorted sand and flint temper, the tile is well fired, with a slightly laminated fracture. Knife-cut edges, with a slight bevel, an unsanded base, no keys or nail holes. The decoration is by slip-over impression, with a yellow, slightly splotchy glaze.

135. Single tile pattern showing a hunting scene; a deer, with an arrow through its neck, is chased by a dog, (1).

This design can be compared to an identical tile from Eastry Church, and another, reset in the eastern crypt at Canterbury Cathedral. Recently, this design has also been found at the Poor Priests' Hospital excavations in Canterbury, with its pair showing the huntsman behind a tree having just shot his arrow. The fabric of these tiles is similar to group F above, with black specks in the temper, but the size and quantity of sand used in the tile are different. While probably related to the central Kent industries, on the present evidence this particular tile seems to be quite distinct and would belong to the fourteenth century.

Group J. (Fig. 51)

Square tile, 142 mm. in length, and 24 mm. thick. Pale orange red fabric, with some well-sorted sand temper, and small gravel inclusions. Smooth, but slightly laminated fracture, unsanded base, knife-cut edges, slight bevel, and unusually four scoop keys on reverse. The decoration is slip-over impression, with a yellow glaze.

136. Four-tile pattern, floral design within circular border with pelletting. British Museum Cat. no. 1763 bought on April 12th, 1926, from Mrs. Theobald, of Folkestone, who dug the tile up forty years previously from St. Augustine's Abbey.

This design cannot be directly paralleled. The size is unusual for Kent, as is the use of keys. A tile with keys perhaps of the same group is known from Preston-by-Faversham (Maidstone Museum, 1933, 21) and of the right size and general style without keys at Newington, All Saints', Maidstone and Doddington.

Group K. (Fig. 51)

Fragments, 26 mm. thick. The fabric is dull red to dark red-brown, with a very sandy, ill-sorted temper. A smooth laminated fracture, the tile is fairly hard, with knife-cut edges, an unsanded base, and slight bevel. On the base are broad knife marks, which seem to have been intended as keys.

White slip has been applied to the outside edge of the tile, the centre of the tile is unslipped. Scored lines have been applied to the upper surface, together with a repeating lozenge stamp, providing a partial '*sgraffito*' effect. Another tile in the same fabric has a white slip coat and a single scored line. The yellow green glaze gives a polychrome pattern across the slipped and unslipped surfaces.

137. Tile with line impressed and stamped decoration, (3).
138. Plain tile, slipped with scored line, (1).

No. 137 is an unusual piece is without direct parallel. Line-impressed tiles are common in East Anglia but, with this exception, do not reach Kent. One possibility is that it is an example of figure mosaic as has been reported from Old Warden, Prior Crauden's Chapel in Ely and Norton Priory (Eames 1980, 38). These date to the middle of the fourteenth century. The fragment could represent part of an ecclesiastical stole. Its edge is very slightly curved confirming that it might fit in as part of a figure mosaic, but with such a small fragment it is difficult to be certain. The fabric is different to the East Anglian or Cheshire tiles; its origin remains unknown. Stamps on tiles, of a somewhat different type are known from Boxley Abbey (Tester 1973), but again the fabric is very different.

Group L. (Fig. 51)

Square tile fragment, probably 250 mm. in length and 32 mm. thick. The fabric is dull, pinkish red orange, with a well sorted sand temper, a rough uneven fracture and few air holes. The tile has been moulded into shape with straight sides, and a flat, unsanded base. The decoration is in high relief, perhaps caused by pressure moulding, with the decoration upstanding up to 9 mm. The glaze is dark red to chocolate brown in colour, and thickly applied.

139. High relief tile, with simple geometric decoration, (1).

Relief decorated tiles are among the earliest types found in England, now recognised to belong to the twelfth as well as the thirteenth centuries (Biddle and Kjølbye-Biddle, 1984). But this tile from St. Augustine's with its dark glaze and very bold relief does not seem to be part of this early tradition. A better comparison would be with high relief heraldic tiles, known from the Midlands, of fifteenth-century date (e.g. Eames 1980, 116 and design no. 310). This tile is not part of a shield, but an octagonal panel, of unusually large size for a decorated floor-tile.

Group M.

Plain square tiles, occurring in three sizes: 248 mm. square × 40 mm. thick; 202 mm. square × 30 mm. thick and 183 mm. square × 26 mm. thick. The fabric is a uniform pale pink orange with occasional streaks of yellow. The sand temper is well sorted, and there are occasional air holes; inclusions comprise small pieces of gravel, and grog from crushed tile. The fracture is smooth, the core and margins are red, and there is little lamination. The edges are knife-cut, with a medium to slight bevel. The base is sanded. On each tile there are up to twelve nail holes (normally one in each corner, and two on each side) although sometimes only four are found. Three types of surface are found; slipped with a clear glaze giving a yellow effect, unslipped with a clear glaze giving a red effect, and unslipped with a dark green glaze, leaving a dark green or brown surface colour. A total of 31 fragments were recorded.

These tiles are characteristic of the fifteenth century and were used in paving large areas of the abbey, such as the cloister walk (Plate LI) and the eastern end of the crypt. The nail holes on the upper surface, used to hold the tile in position during cutting, are a particular feature of these plain tiles, imported from the Low Countries. English tiles of this period do not generally have these characteristic holes, although tiles from Battle Abbey with nail holes have recently been suggested as being of local manufacture (Streeten 1985, 86). However, when there is documentary evidence for the import of the Flemish tiles, they can be correlated with plain square tiles with nail holes (for Winchester College, see Norton 1976). Certainly, the import of plain tiles, possibly as ballast, was on a large scale from the fifteenth century and many churches and abbeys were paved with them (Horton 1981, 245). The Flemish tiles continued to be imported in the sixteenth century, as they were found at the palace at Bekesbourne, near Canterbury.

Group N.

Plain square tiles, 28 mm. in size and 32 mm. thick. The bright orange-red fabric has well-sorted sand temper, and inclusions of red ironstone and gravel. The fracture is smooth, with little lamination, and few air holes. The base is unsanded, with a slight bevel, but no nail holes. Two types of surface are found: slip painted, often very thinly, with a clear glaze, and unslipped with a green glaze. A total of 26 tiles or fragments were found.

These tiles are similar to the previous group, but the absence of nail holes suggests that they were locally made in imitation of the Flemish tiles. The abbey employed tilers in 1442, and while they may have been making roof-tiles they could have produced floor-tiles as well. The fabric is comparable with Tyler Hill products. Tiles of similar type are reported from Higham Priory, Leeds Priory, Ospringe, Malling Abbey, and Bayham Abbey (Horton 1983, 82, group H9). A kiln, producing comparable plain tiles, without nail holes, was excavated at Radwinter in Essex, also dating to the fifteenth century (Webster and Cherry 1980, 262).

The famous sun-dial tile from St. Augustine's Abbey was apparently made in the fabric of this group (Sherlock 1982, 23). If the floor-tiles were locally made, specially for the abbey, then the sun-dial may also have been a special commission.

The Tiling of St. Augustine's Abbey

The quantity of medieval floor-tiles found both during the present and past excavations demonstrates how extensively paved were the abbey and the precinct buildings. Many of these tiles were taken from destruction levels overlying the floors while only a very few areas of paving remained intact. At the Dissolution many tiles were taken up and re-used elsewhere. From accounts of the sixteenth-century robbing of the abbey, building material littered the site, much of which was sold, packed into carts and taken away. In 1553, Mr Quylter paid 12*d.* for one hundred 'small paving tiles' (Nycholl MS f.3r; see p. 12).

All the pavements excavated at St. Augustine's were found during the early excavations at the church, cloisters, and at St. Pancras's. Most were reburied without adequate record and only a limited number of photographs and plans survive. The recent excavations did not recover any tiles *in situ*, but large numbers of fragments were found which give some indication of the range of tiles used in particular areas. Combining what is known from the surviving tiles, the evidence from the early excavations, and the modern work, some reconstruction can be attempted of the original floor scheme.

Virtually the first discovery by excavation at St. Augustine's was of a tile pavement. In the clearing of the undercroft of the abbot's hall in 1845 'fragments of an interesting encaustic tile pavement including a pattern of a bird pecking at berries' were found (Hope 1861, 63). These tiles were latter copied by Mintons, and the encaustic copies were laid in the ambulatory of the students' buildings at St. Augustine's College. It appears design no. 138 formed part of this pavement which is now lost. The next excavations at the abbey between 1867 and 1868 (Sparks 1984) did not record any tile discoveries even though the north walk of the cloister, the frater and the kitchen were partly uncovered.

The Abbey Church

In the subsequent excavations at the eastern end of the abbey church undertaken by Canon Routledge and Mr Sebastian Evans, considerable quantities of both loose and *in situ* tiles were found. In the crypt, the floor comprised large black and yellow tiles (Evans 1904, 3) presumably plain tiles described above in groups M and N. Decorated tiles were found in the north apsidal chapel (St. Richard of Chichester) where the altar rested on 'painted tiles', but the photograph of the excavation shows tiles only *in situ*, against the north-east wall (Hope 1903). Today fourteen of these tiles survive in position. They are all of group M, 250 mm. square, some with a black brown glaze and others clear glazed with a yellow slip. Elsewhere in the chapel are many relaid tiles, plain tiles of group N, and decorated tiles of group C (no. 98). The floors of the lady

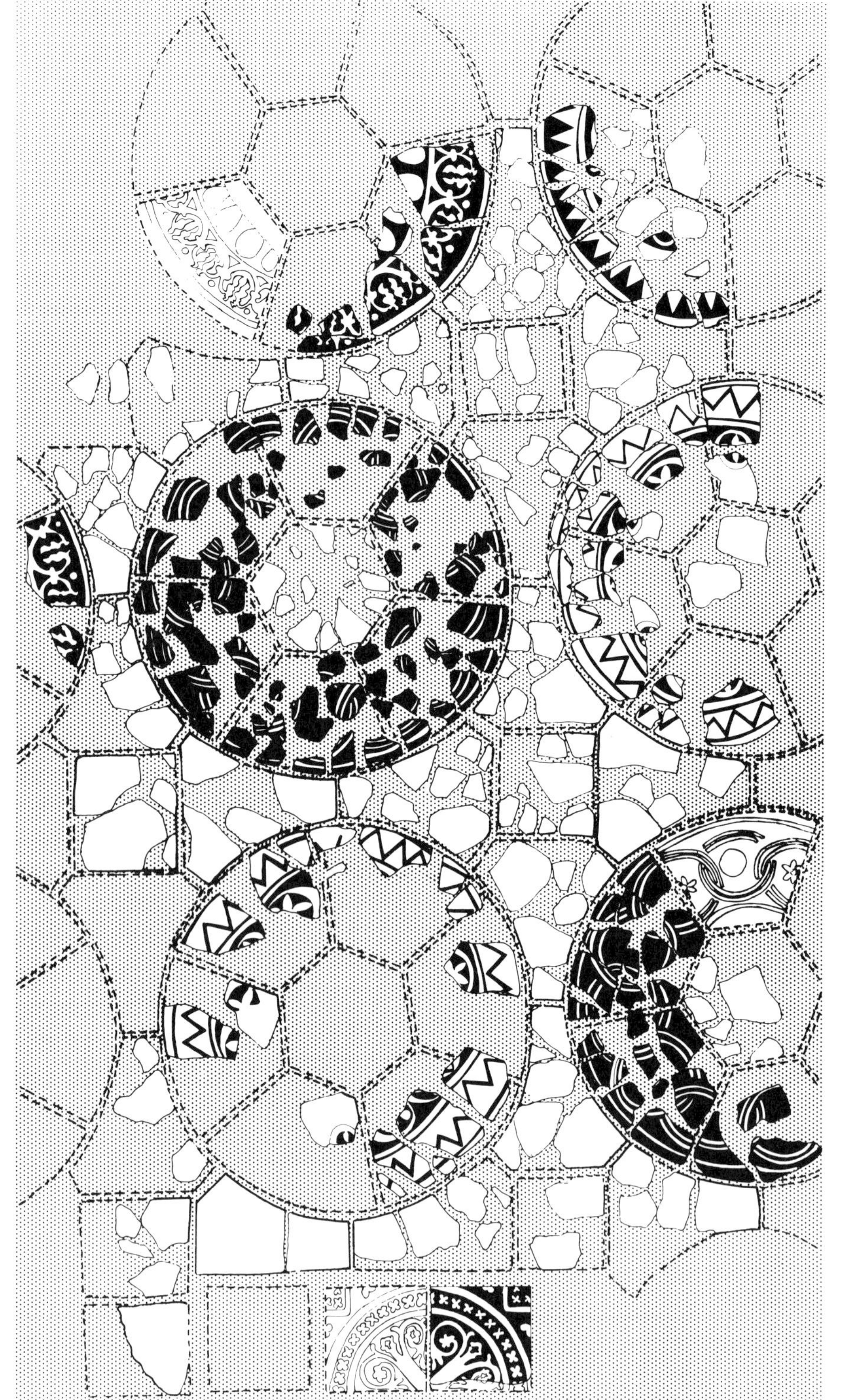

Fig. 52a. Medieval Pavement, remaining at the western End of the Nave, South Side, using Tiles of Groups B1 and B3. Two stray fragments of no. 117 (Group F) are also set into the pavement.

chapel and the central crypt chapel were destroyed at the Dissolution, and the tiles now relaid in front of the altar of St. Mary and the Angels seem to have been brought from elsewhere in the abbey. They are presently set in concrete.

Routledge found a tiled floor around the altar in the south apsidal chapel (St. Thomas the Apostle). It remains today, but seems to have been reset, perhaps in medieval times. 232 tiles are set in a diagonal fashion, across an area of 2.25 × 2.20 m. The tiles respect the line of a Purbeck marble step in front of the altar and may be a medieval resetting of used tiles. The tiles which are very worn (eleven different designs were recognised) belonged to group B1, with a single exception from group A. Around this patch of pavement many fragments of plain and decorated tiles have been reset as crazy paving in recent times. The excavations in the north transept discovered that 'all traces of flooring had gone' at the eastern end (Evans 1904, 5). Some tiles are exposed here today, and are probably reset. On the south side, is a patch of fourteen plain tiles, 238 mm. in size, of group N set with their alternate colours.In the altar niche of St. Benedict are four tiles of group A and six tiles of group B with their designs showing clearly.

Excavation of the south transept and the nave was undertaken after the Great War, under the direction of Canon R.U. Potts. There is no record of tiles in the south transept, but a small area does survive today, relaid, but probably in its original position. The tiles are found in the recess of the east wall, in the lobby for the stair, leading (probably) into the central tower. They are all plain tiles of group B1, two have yellow slip, and a green brown glaze, the remainder have only a brown glaze. There is a total of twenty-seven complete tiles, seven half tiles and three fragments.

The Nave Pavements (Fig. 52, a)

An important mosaic pavement was found between the pillars of the westernmost bay on the south side of the nave, during Canon Potts' excavations in the nave. It is shown on a published plan (Potts 1934) and photographs (Plate LII) of its discovery survive (now kept with the H.B.M.C.). The tiles have been consolidated in position, but are now very much damaged through frost action. Remains of seven roundels are still visible, of group B3, using designs nos. 81–84, contained in plain mosaic frames. On the north side, the mosaic work came to a straight edge, and the pavement continued using square tiles, of group B1. One tile still in position (no. 26) lay next to one of the same design, (shown in the contemporary photograph, but now lost), forming a four-tile design. This is important evidence to show that tiles of groups B1 and B3 were laid together within a single scheme and must have been contemporary. Two fragments of another tile (no. 117, group F) have been reset into the pavement, and are clearly not in an original position. They do not appear on the original photograph of the pavement when it was discovered.

The discovery of large numbers of plain tile fragments of group B3 outside this area of the nave in 1977 shows that plain tiles also formed part of this pavement inside the nave and south aisle. Canon Potts found an extensive area of diagonal tile paving, in the south aisle, opposite the ninth bay from the east (Potts 1934, plan) which was probably plain and of this type. In the seventh bay, not marked by Potts but still in position, are some plain tiles of group B3 type with a very dark green glaze. The paving is still visible though virtually destroyed. On the north side of the nave this plain group B3 paving continued. A small patch survives at the eighth bay. There are eight plain tiles set diagonally, with one decorated tile (from group B1) at the edge (no. 19). In conclusion, it seems that most of the western end of the nave and the aisles were paved with Tyler Hill products. Much of the area was covered with plain tiles, set presumably in a diagonal geometric fashion, but there were also small areas of slip-decorated tiles and segmental mosaic.

Few tiles remain in position at the east end of the nave and there are no documented discoveries. However, on the north side, in a passage leading between the transept and aisle, there are four tiles in position, of group N, with yellow and brown colours. These tiles may have been placed here during the refurbishment of the cloister in the fifteenth century. On the south side there is no record of the type of floor. Fragments of group A were found outside the nave in the 1975–78 excavations, and probably the east end of the nave was once paved with these, perhaps ending at the pulpitum.

Other tiles found in the area of the chapel south of the nave during the 1977 excavations can be identified with the original flooring of this structure. In particular tiles of groups C and F were found to be concentrated in this area, but always in levels above the construction of the chapel. Both these groups of tiles are believed to date from the early to mid-fourteenth century. Unglazed Roman tiles were found on the floor of this chapel, probably laid as a bedding for a glazed tile floor above.

The Precinct Buildings

Outside the abbey church considerable areas of tile pavement have been discovered in the past, but all were covered up. In 1900, tiles were found in the slype between the north transept and the chapter house 'shewing small square and triangular red and blue tiles worked into a star pattern' (Evans 1904, 6). These may have been tile mosaic of group B1. In the cathedral Corona pavement, quite elaborate designs were attempted, including a panel of Maltese crosses; star patterns could well form part of this group (Norton and Horton 1981). Unusually, tiles were not found in the adjacent chapter house. The cloister walk, as was normal, was paved with large plain tiles. These were found extensively *in situ*, along the east walk, and are recorded in a photograph (Plate LI). The tiles are either of group M or N, and would date to the fifteenth century. Another patch of tiles was found by Canon Potts (1934, 187) north of the dorter, but nothing is known about it.

Tiles were also found in four areas of the infirmary, but it can probably be assumed that they were plain, similar to those in the cloisters. They were found in the room to the west of the infirmary hall, on the south side of the hall, outside the infirmary chapel, and in the kitchen (Potts 1934, 188–90, plan). In the infirmary bath-house, the fireplace was lined with 'Flanders tile'. This was most probably brick.

Fig. 52, b. Sites in southern England mentioned in Connection with medieval Tiles.

Chapel of St. Pancras

Finally, a number of tiles are known from the chapel of St. Pancras. In 1882, Canon Routledge reported a few coloured tiles from the south side of the church, as well as a pavement 14 in. below the surface 'consisting of coloured and patterned tiles' (1882, 104). In 1900, St. John Hope (1903, 232) found tiles in the south porticus, at the east end, and against the north wall of the church, which formed 'a pavement of tile pavers 4½ in. square, alternately yellow, and black or dark green, portions of which remain here and there'. Between the western porch and the north western wall, on the floor of the fifteenth century chapel, were 9½ in. tiles, presumably of group N. The excavations of Dr Frank Jenkins produced a small number of fragments from the chapel, none in position. Of the eleven recognisable fragments, five were of group B1, four of group B2 and two of group F. It seems likely, therefore, that the tiles found in the earlier excavations were mostly of the Tyler Hill type.

Conclusions

This survey has shown that by the sixteenth century, most of the floors of the abbey were paved with floor-tiles. Although the survival of these floors has been fragmentary, and their recognition by excavation somewhat patchy in the early years, the impression emerges of an abbey richly furnished with many decorated floors. Over several hundred years, the abbey must have been a major consumer of tiles, and an important influence upon the tile industry.

The tiles from St. Augustine's Abbey are the most important and diverse assemblage known from the region. The range of designs and types is greater than survives in either Rochester or Canterbury Cathedrals, or from any of the other abbeys such as Boxley, Bayham, or Leeds. This is partly due to over a hundred years of sustained excavation on the site; no other abbey in the region has been so completely exposed. But the large number of tile groups is also significant, covering a period from the late twelfth until the sixteenth century. The abbey seems to have been constantly purchasing tiles, both for the church and conventual buildings, not necessarily related to major building works. These tiles came from a wide geographical area: from Tyler Hill and, when these were unavailable, from the southern and western parts of the county as well as London. The quality of the tiles used in the abbey was never very good. The fine tiles found at Bayham and Battle Abbeys, for example, did not reach St. Augustine's, perhaps surprisingly for a foundation of such wealth.

One particular absence from the abbey is the late Anglo-Saxon polychrome relief tiles. These distinctive tiles have been found at many of the major late-Saxon foundations (Bury, Winchester, St. Alban's, York), as well as in the cathedral precincts at Canterbury (Horton, forthcoming). It is curious that none were found at St. Augustine's. An explanation may be that during the early excavations only complete tiles were kept, and that no undamaged Saxon polychrome tiles were found.

VII. SMALL FINDS

SMALL FINDS FROM EXCAVATIONS, 1960–65 Martin Henig (Figs. 53–57)

* denotes find illustrated

Ecclesiastical Ornament – Copper Alloy

*1. *Champlevé* enamelled figure of a saint from a reliquary; cast and gilded. Eyes of blue glass inserted. Two rivet holes in body for attachment. Length 67 mm. Justine Bayley writes that 'the base metal was copper and gilding, mercury gilding (X-ray fluorescence). The four fields running the length of the figure contained blue enamel, the lowest of the triangular fields red, and the other two triangular fields pale turquoise. The small horizontal field just below the neck was empty'.

Rigold (1970, 345–6, Fig. 1, no. 2) identified this piece as Limoges work of the thirteenth century, like the Centaur below, and cited a reliquary in the Victoria and Albert Museum (Inv. M. 572–1910) and a single figure from Stoke Newington (*L.M.M.C.*, 288, Pl. LXXXI, 3). Other examples include three in the Ashmolean: from Woodeaton, Oxfordshire (Inv. 1958, 624); Fairford, Gloucestershire (Inv. 1927. 6413) and Bury St. Edmund's, Suffolk (Inv. 1927. 6414); one in Ashwell Museum, Hertfordshire, and one from Chalgrove, Oxfordshire (Page 1981, 153, Fig. 48). These figures are evidently very common.

From uppersoil and building debris, east end of Trench E.

A.M.L. 7716144.

*2. *Champlevé* enamelled plaque, 89 mm. in diameter, depicting a male Centaur shooting with a bow. One-half only remains, the plate having snapped in two, fortunately leaving the most interesting part. The sunk areas of the plate are roughened to take enamel. Justine Bayley writes 'The base metal was copper with traces of lead and probably arsenic. The gilding was mercury gilding (X-ray fluorescence). Only traces of enamel survive; the colour, where it could be determined, was blue. The gilding appears to have been applied before the enamel'. The late G.C. Dunning described the plaque as follows:

> 'The design shows the figure of a Sagittarius, a composite being with the head and trunk of a man and the body and legs of a horse (i.e. a Centaur). Details of the head and dress are indicated by incised lines. The hair is long and curly, and falls down to the neck. Dress is shown by paired lines down the trunk, ending in a fringe round the waist. The left arm is outstretched and the hand grasps a bow, of which the string and an arrow are pulled by the right hand.
>
> The lower part of the body shows the right foreleg stretched out horizontally; fortunately, the foot is preserved bent back behind the plate at the end of the large hole. The foot of the left hind leg is present, close to the

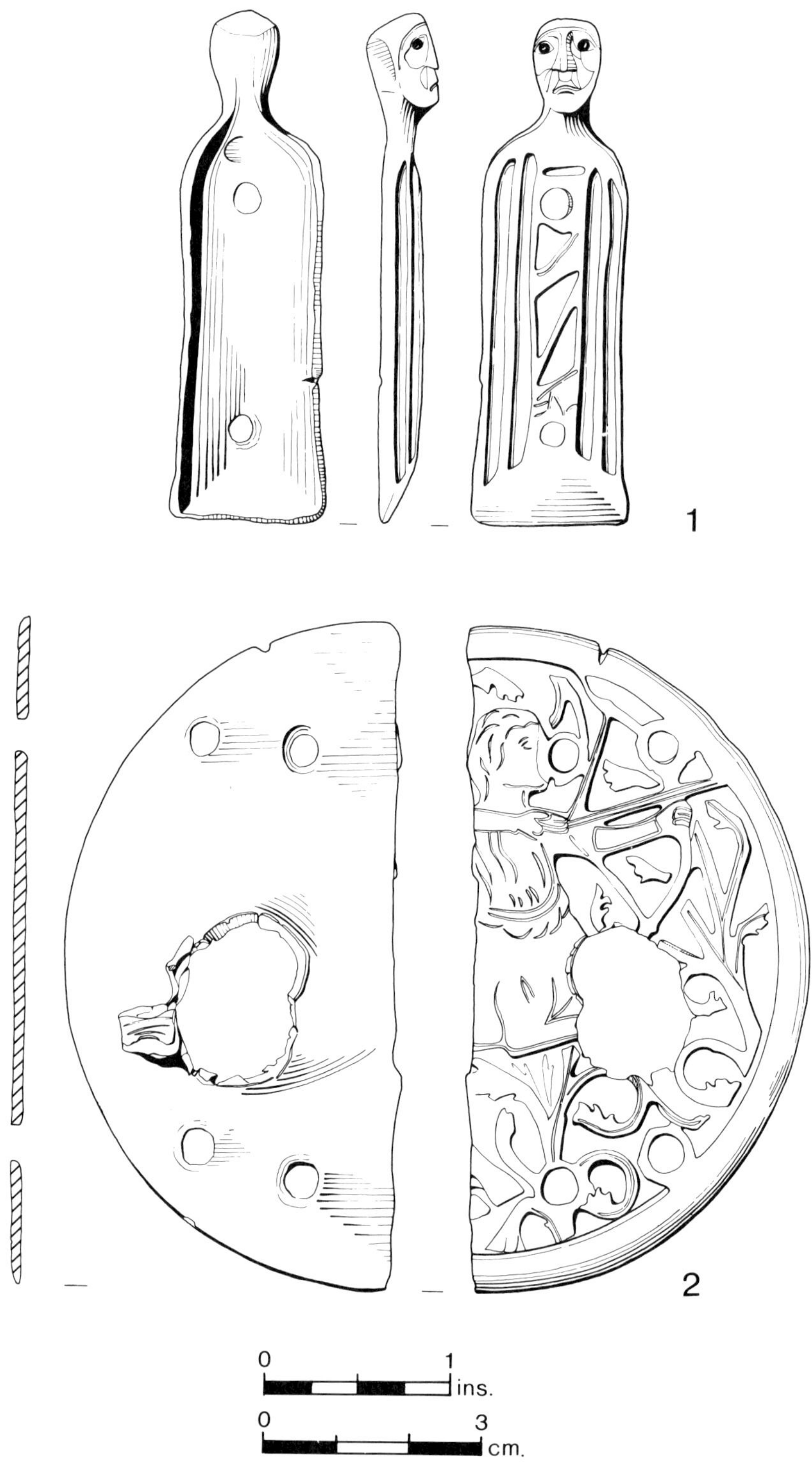

Fig. 53. Small Finds, 1960.

broken edge at the bottom of the plate. The field is occupied by branching trees, one in front of the figure and another below it, and a small frond is behind the head. The branches of the trees end in leaves serrated on one side only. The hind quarters of the figure would occupy the other half of the plate and there would be space for more trees round the margin.'

Medieval enamels usually represent religious subjects rather than secular or mythical scenes or figures. The plate found at Canterbury is, therefore, a welcome addition to the repertory. The Sagittarius is represented rather infrequently in medieval art, but occurs in sculpture engaged in a fight with a sea monster on a twelfth-century capital at Winchester Cathedral (Zarnecki 1951, 38 and Pl. 73) and as a sign of the Zodiac on a font of similar date at Hook Norton (*ibid.*, 31, Pl. 36).

It is occasionally carved in wood on misericords (Bond 1910, 14, Pl. p. 13, Exeter). M.D. Anderson (in Remnant 1969, p. xxxvi) explains this as 'symbolising the soul of Christ departing to deliver souls from Hell'. In illuminated manuscripts the figure usually has astronomical significance. The plaque may be identified as Limoges work rather than English. Thirteenth century.

Found with no. 18 and copper alloy scraps below mortar deposit, probably Trench A.
A.M.L. 7716159.

*3. Book clasp, with splay at one end and hook at the other. Upper plate ornamented with concentric circles near hook and engraved feather-like motifs at splay; attached to lower plate by means of three rivets length 55 mm. Cf. no. 23 p. 193, below; also finds from Whitefriars, Coventry (Woodfield 1981, 94, nos. 48–9), Sandal Castle, Yorks. (Mayes and Butler 1983, 235–6, no. 113). A very common type, continuing into the sixteenth century. The Coventry examples are said to be associated with the post-Reformation grammar school.
Below mortar deposit, probably Trench A.
A.M.L. 7716156A.

*4. Cresting, pierced by nine quatrefoils; crenellations or soldering along top. There is a line of tinning along one side above quatrefoils, and on both side below quatrefoils. Length 66 mm.; width 11 mm. For openwork quatrefoils on a box fitting see Rahtz (1969, 87 and Fig. 49, no. 103). Cf. also no. 6, p. 189, below.
From below mortar deposit, probably Trench A.
A.M.L. 7716158B.

*5. Strip of binding, ornamented *en repoussé* with wreath or rosette-like figures. Pierced by three rivet holes. Length *c.* 108 mm.; width 9 mm. Cf. finds from the Maison Dieu at Ospringe (Smith 1979, 137–8, Fig. 24, nos. 123–7, especially no. 124 with eight-petalled flowers).
From below mortar deposit, probably Trench A.
A.M.L. 7716157.

*6. A pair of compasses; arms of copper alloy; iron pin at pivot. The upper part of one arm neatly slots into the other arm. Below this point a moulding is visible on both arms. Length 110 mm. Cf. an example from The Marsh, Finsbury Circus, but without moulding (Lambert 1921, 99). Compasses were used by architects and craftsmen (Singer *et al.*, 1956, 383 and 391, Pl. 31 and Fig. 356) but, in view of the small size of this pair, it is tempting to see them as belonging to the important St. Augustine's *scriptorium*.
Unstratified.
A.M.L. 7716146.

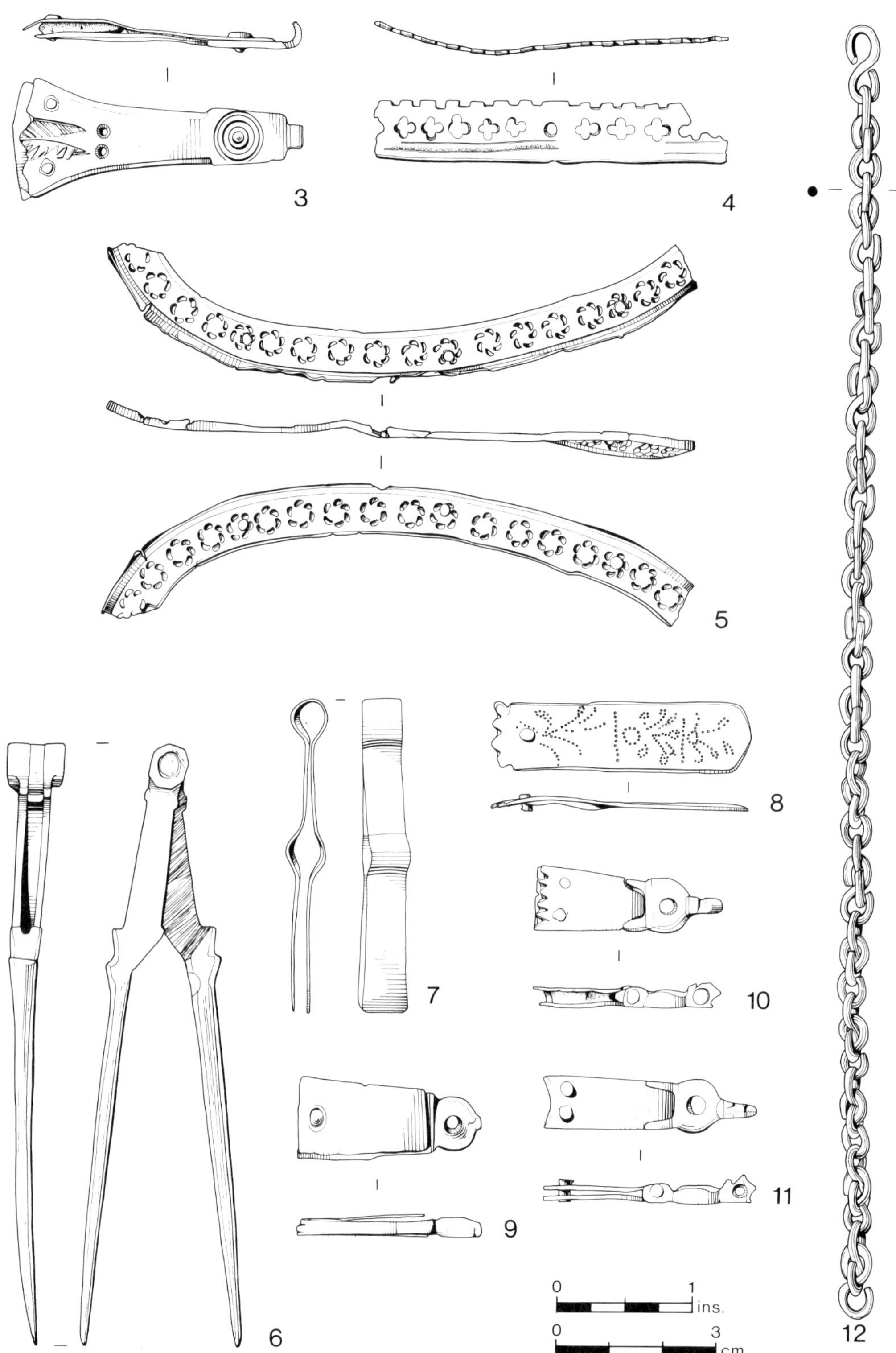

Fig. 54. Small Finds, 1960.

Other Metalwork – Copper Alloy

*7. Pair of tweezers, composed of strip of sheeting, bent over on itself. At the centre point the metal bulges outwards to provide a grip. Length 57 mm.
From 'cache' east of north transept, probably Trench A, F4.
A.M.L. 7716148.

*8. Strap-end; top plate pierced by rivet hole; floral ornament delicately pricked out upon it. Length 49 mm. Cf. examples from Blackfriars, Oxford (Lambrick and Woods 1976, 214–5, Fig. 11, no. 6) and Portchester, Hants. (Cunliffe 1977, 204, and Fig. 10, no. 73). Perhaps fourteenth century.
From below mortar deposit, probably Trench A.
A.M.L. 7716158C.

*9. Two plates riveted together with forked middle. Possibly book-fastening. The central (thicker) plate projects as a pierced circular extension. Simplified version of 10 and 11 below. Length 34 mm.
From 'cache' east of north transept, probably Trench A, F4.
A.M.L. 7716151A.

*10. Hinged strap-end; probably fastening of book but perhaps a belt-end. Clasp consists of a plate and a sheet of copper alloy bent over on itself and secured (through the leather of the strap) with two rivets. Notches are cut along the top edge. The front part is circular and pierced vertically (? for attachment to book cover); there is a further extension, laterally pierced. Length 35 mm. Cf. an example from the Austin Friars, Leicester (Mellor and Pearce 1981, 133, no. 28, Fig. 48).
From 'cache' east of north transept, probably Trench A, F4.
A.M.L. 7716149.

*11. Hinged clasp; type as last. Length 39 mm.
From below mortar deposit, probably Trench A.
A.M.L. 7716156B.

*12. Length of chain with S-shaped links. Length 233 mm. Compare Fig. 60, 50, p. 196, below.
From below mortar deposit, probably Trench A.
A.M.L. 7716153.

*13. Buckle, D-shaped. Plate missing. Length 22 mm. Cf. an example from the Austin Friars, Leicester (Mellor and Pearce 1981, 133, Fig. 48, nos. 25 and 26).
From 'cache' east of north transept, probably Trench A, F4.
A.M.L. 7716151B.

*14. Buckle, D-shaped (loop broken); was joined to belt by rectangular opening within bar. Width 36 mm. Type as Fingerlin 1971, 191–2, esp. Fig. 323, an iron example from Eger, dated fifteenth/sixteenth century.
From 'cache' east of north transept, probably Trench A, F4.
A.M.L. 7716151C.

*15. Rivet, through square plate; point bent. Length 20 mm.
From 'cache' east of north transept, probably Trench A, F4.
A.M.L. 7716151D.

*16. Dagger-chape, tinned, with U-shaped depression at top. Made by folding over sheet metal. Length 37 mm. For examples of similar manufacture, see *L.M.M.C.* (287, no. 6 from Fetter Lane, London) and Mayes and Butler (1983, 232–3, Fig. 1, no. 75, from Sandal Castle, Yorkshire, but without U-shaped depression).
From trench north-east of north transept, probably Trench B.
A.M.L. 78203347.

*17. Mount from upper part of scabbard. Ornamented with engraving in two panels, the lower one an ornamental motif, but above Kufic or pseudo-Kufic letters. Length 54 mm., width 40 mm. For Arab inscriptions in the West, see Erdmann (1953, 467–513). They are also cited by Muthesius in a discussion of the silks in Archbishop Hubert Walter's tomb, the chasuble of which was decorated with pseudo-Kufic letters. (Stratford *et al.* 1982, 82–3, P1. XXXIA).
Unstratified.
A.M.L. 777671.

18. Simple finger-ring. D-shaped section. Terminals hammered together. Diameter 23 mm.
From below mortar deposit, probably Trench A.
A.M.L. 7716155.

19. Four pins with drawn stems; heads of coiled wire. Lengths 25, 26, 38 and 39 mm.
Below mortar deposit, probably Trench A.
A.M.L. 7716154.

20. Ten lace-tags, lengths 18, 19, 22, 24, 24, 25, 28, 29, 34 mm. Type as no. 91 p. 220, below.
From below mortar deposit, probably Trench A.
A.M.L. 7716145.

21. Upper arm of pair of scissors, broken at fulcrum. Finger-hole is egg-shaped. Length 82 mm. Lambert (1921, 99, Fig. 22, 7) shows as example from Finsbury Circus, London, with finger-holes similarly shaped but constructed not by solid casting but by bending the metal into a loop.
From 'cache' east of north transept, probably Trench A.
A.M.L. 7716151E.

22. Two functional copper alloy rings: (a) with rectangular cross section. Diameter 24 mm. (b) similar, but break at one point. Diameter 24 mm. Cf. examples from the Maison Dieu, Ospringe (Smith 1979, 144–5, Fig. 28, nos. 174, 175).
From 'cache' east of north transept, probably Trench A, F4.
A.M.L. 7716150.

23. Pin. Heavy dress pin, head missing. Shank in two parts lengths 53 mm. and 65 mm.
From 'cache' east of north transept, probably Trench A.
A.M.L. 7716145.

24. Button, pyramidal form. Height 7 mm.; width 12 mm. Cf. Woodfield (1981, 94, Fig. 5, no. 41).
From east end of trench east of north transept 0.9–1.2 m. below clay layer.
A.M.L. 78203266.

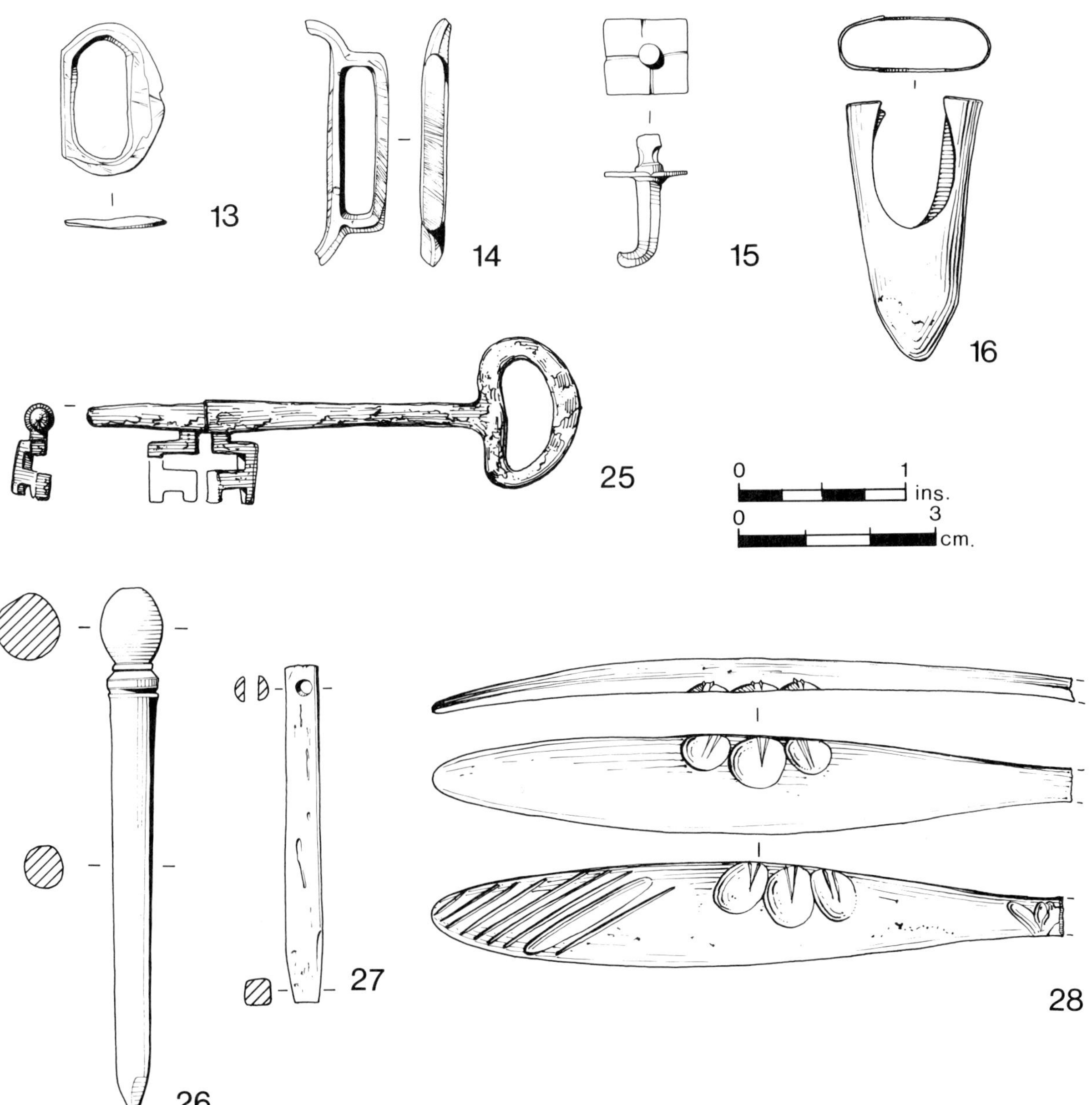

Fig. 55. Small Finds, 1960.

Iron

25. Iron key with kidney-shaped bow; length 146 mm. For type see *L.M.M.C.* (Fig. 42 and pp. 141–3. Type VII B) and Lambrick and Woods (1976, 218 and Fig. 12, no. 41) Blackfriars, Oxford.
From below mortar deposit, Trench A.
A.M.L. 78203277.

Bone

*26. Bone bodkin or parchment tracer, ovoid head with moulding between it and the shank, the other end of which has been sharpened to a point. Length 76 mm. Cf. Jarvis (1983, 77 and Fig. 33, no. 44) Christchurch Priory, Dorset.
From Dissolution debris, probably Trench A or B.
A.M.L. 7716162.

*27. Bone peg from musical instrument, length 49 mm. Rectangular head, circular shaft (pierced). From a harp or fiddle-type instrument. Cf. examples from St. Aldate's, Oxford (Durham 1977, 163–6, nos. 9–11).
From Dissolution debris, probably Trench A.
A.M.L. 7716163.

*28. Bone tooth-brush handle narrowing at end and towards brush where it has snapped. Ornamented with grooves on upper surface and semicircular depressions towards one side on both upper and lower surface. Post medieval. Length 95 mm.
From below mortar deposits, Trench A.
A.M.L. 78203767.

29. Side-plate from knife-handle pierced by three copper alloy rivets. Post medieval. Length 65 mm.
From below mortar deposit, Trench A.
A.M.L. 78203264.

Metal Finds from the Shaft

* illustrated in Fig. 57

Lead

1. Eight penannular lead weights, total weight 32.75 kg. 2 illustrated*. Their approximate weights are as follows: 6.5 kg. (14 lb. 5 oz.), 6 kg. (13 lb. 4 oz.), 4.25 kg. (9 lb. 7 oz.), 4 kg. (8 lb. 13 oz.), 2 of 3.25 kg. (7 lb. 2 oz.), 3 kg. (6 lb. 10 oz.) and 2.5 kg. (5 lb. 8 oz.).
A.M.L. 78203085, 78203084, 791285.
2. Annular lead weight of 4 kg. (8 lb. 13 oz.).
A.M.L. 791285.

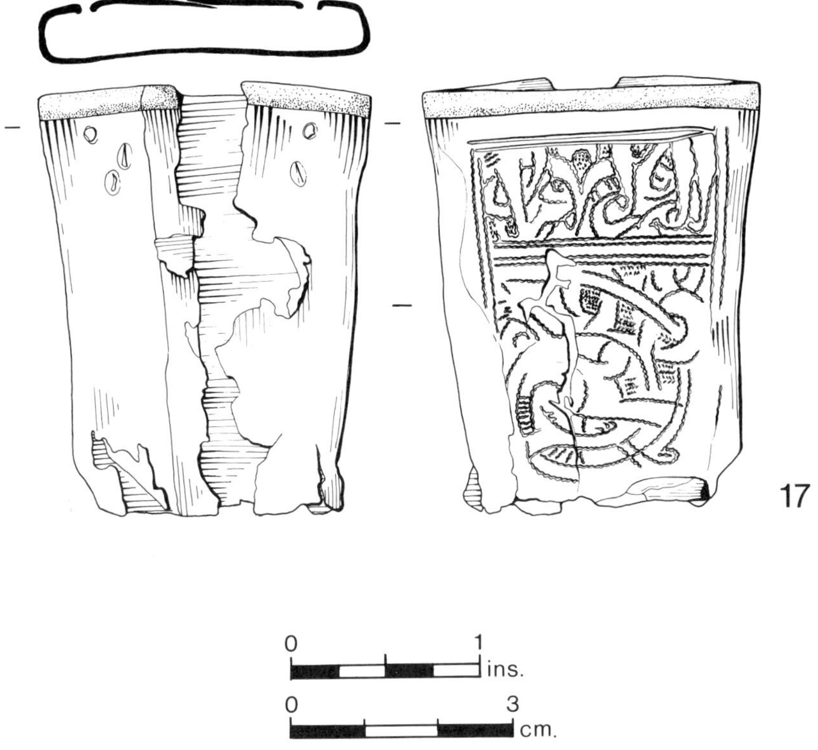

Fig. 56. Small Find, 1960.

3. Miscellaneous small pieces weighing altogether 5.25 kg (11 lb. 10 oz.). They are mainly off-cuts of sheet lead, the purpose of which is unknown.

Copper Alloy A.M.L. 78203261

*4. Rounded and tapering rod, broken at either end, max. diam. 9 mm., length 92 mm.; this is one arm of a folding balance. Cf. examples from a mid-thirteenth-century context at Trondheim (Long 1975, 28, Fig. 10, p) and the fifteenth century at Roche Abbey (Rigold 1978, 372, Fig. 6).

*5. Flat-sectioned right-angled staple, the ends pierced with rectangular loops; 20 mm. across, the ends 15 mm. long. Eight other examples.

*6. Similar staple made of a wider strip of metal and rather longer. Four other examples.

*7. Strip, 30 mm. wide, 217 mm. long with a slot 10 x 105 mm. cut out of the centre.

*8. Smaller strip (broken and incomplete) 23 x 135 mm. with a slot 8 x 65 mm.

*9. Solid triangular lump with remains of holes either side, approx. 10 x 15 mm. A cog?

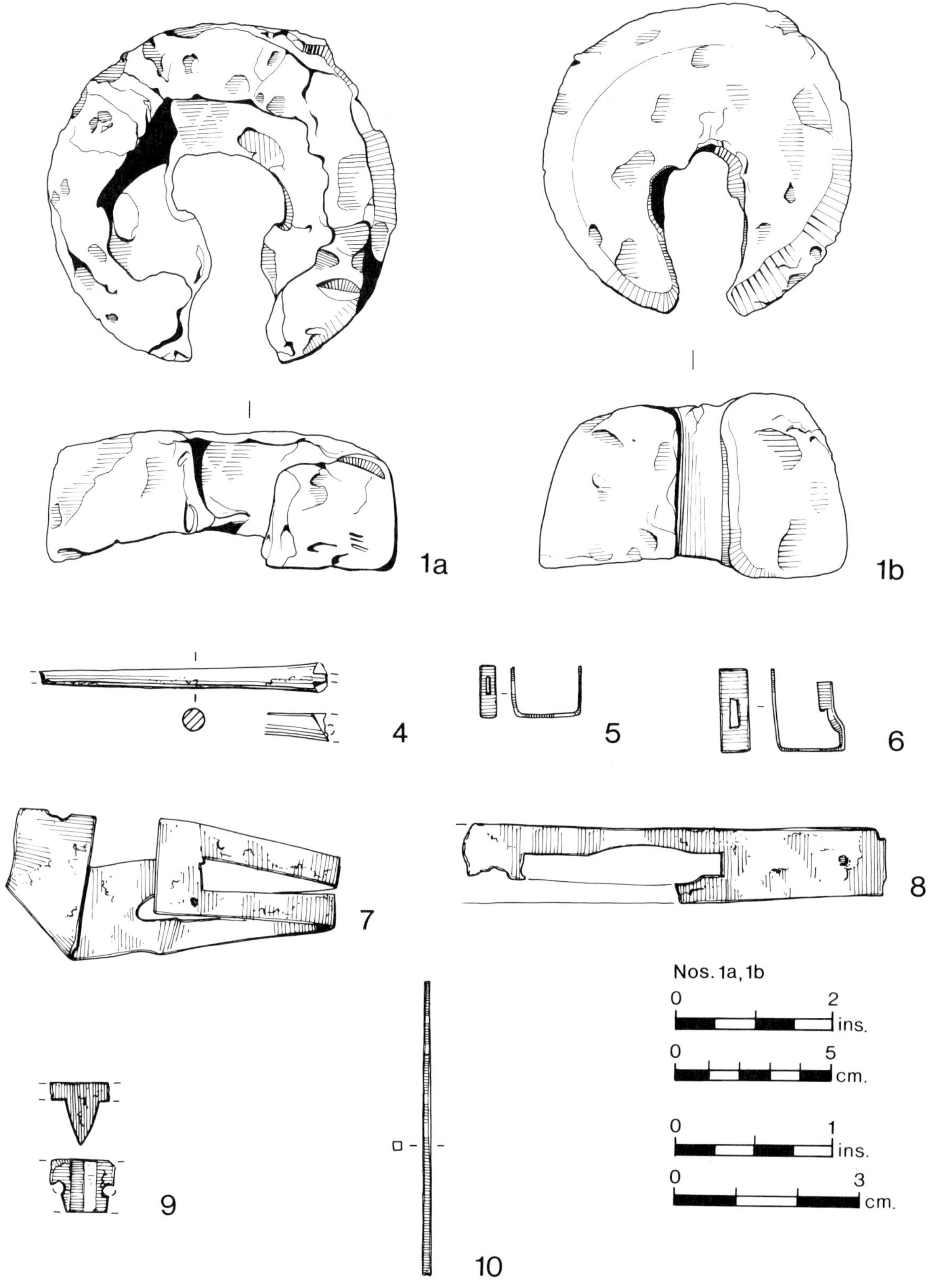

Fig. 57. Small Finds, 1965.

*10. Fragment of copper alloy rod, broken at either end, 3 mm. square, 92 mm. long. Another shorter fragment 4 mm. square, 47 mm. long.
11. 14 small fragments of strips like those described above, and other flat pieces, some of them holed for nails.

VESSEL GLASS, 1960 David Sherlock

Fragments of some twenty glass vessels were also recovered. From the sealed pit (Trench A, F4) came fragments of the bases of two urinals and a flask, and the fragment of a larger bottle, all Wealden glass of the fifteenth or early sixteenth century. Fragments of about nine other urinals came from other later and post-Dissolution layers in Rigold's trenches, all of which may be compared with Wealden glass urinals from Bayham Abbey where they were also found in roughly similar locations near the north transept (Charleston 1983). Other Wealden glass sherds were from bottles and flasks of a similar date and style. There was also one sherd of a seventeenth-century beaker. The remainder were sherds of seventeenth- to nineteenth-century bottle glass.

SMALL FINDS FROM EXCAVATIONS, 1972–75 Martin Henig and David Sherlock

* denotes illustrated in Figs. 58–61.

Roman
(See also architectural finds and pottery and coin reports, pp. 143, 249, 236, 238, 240.

*1. Copper alloy brooch, simple 'Nauheim' type with four-turn spring; catch plate incomplete. 35 mm. Hawkes and Hull (1947, 312, Type VII: Pl. XCII, 55–58); Brailsford (1962, 7, Fig. 7, C18, C19, C21).
From Trench II, layer 4.
A.M.L. 743697.
*2. Bone plate, from knife-handle, ornamented with ring-and-dot pattern. Length 56 mm. Less possibly medieval. Compare Cunliffe (1968, Pl. LXII).
From Trench II, layers 1 or 2.
A.M.L. 743702.
3. Rim of bowl in amber-coloured glass. Late first or second century.
From Area 2, layer 35. S.A. 75 2871.
(No A.M.L. no.)
4. Funnel-shaped rim of a flask or flagon in blue-green glass, late first to third century. See also nos. 28 and 56 below.
From Area 2, layer 69. S.A. 75 3157.
(No A.M.L. no.).

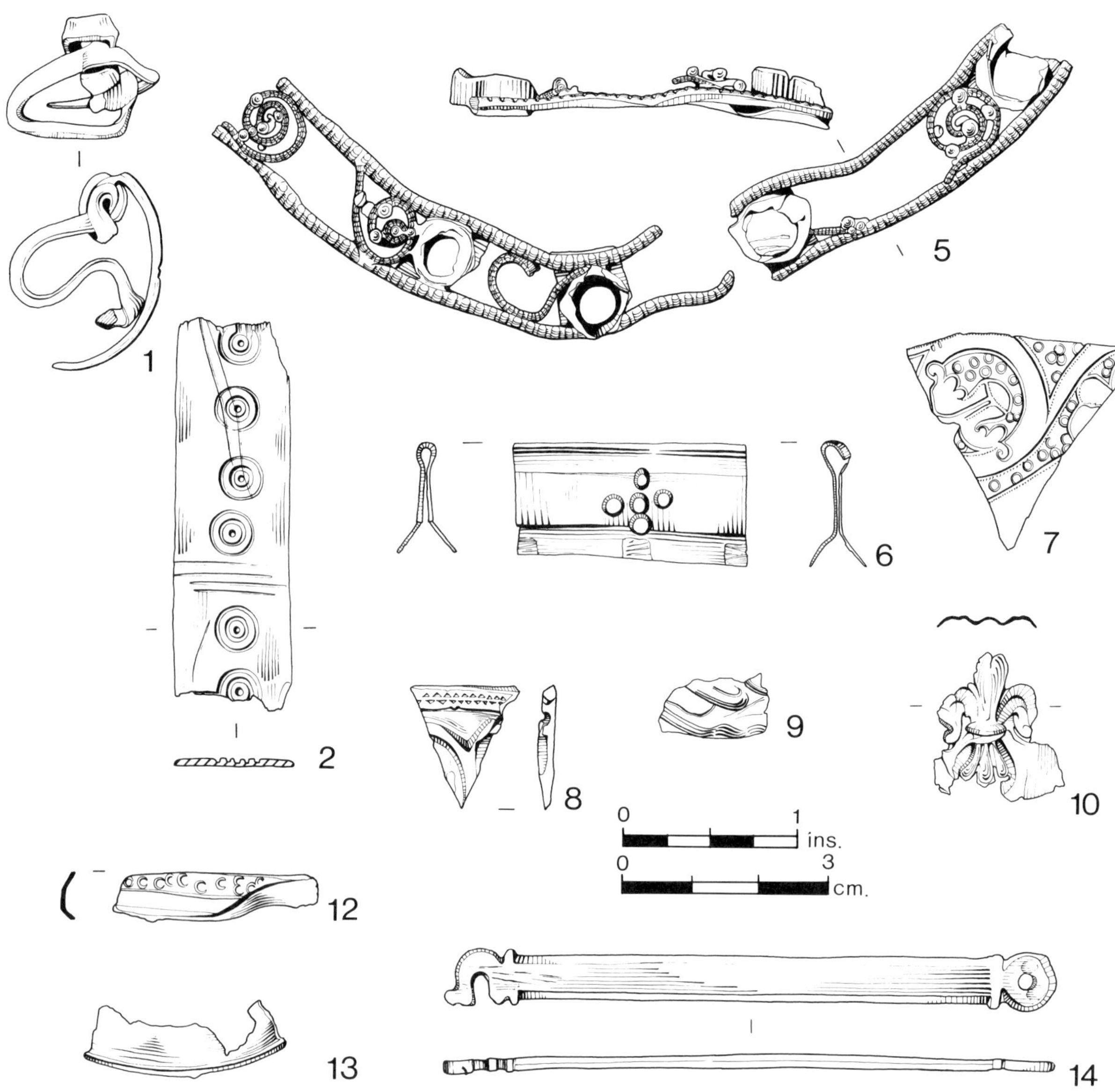

Fig. 58. Small Finds, 1972–75.

Medieval and Later

Copper Alloy

Religious Ornament

*5. Gilt-copper alloy ornamented strip, probably from a tomb, reliquary or shrine. The decoration consists of scrolls in imitation filigree with attached globules. There are mounts for jewels, one now empty, two containing a white powder (an adhesive?) and one still holding an imitation gem in blue glass. Two pieces of the strip remain. Lengths 80 and 54 mm. Compare filigree decoration on the King's School, Canterbury, brooch (Wilson 1964, 124, no. 10) which is late Anglo-Saxon but the mode of ornamentation continues. For decoration on reliquaries and shrines compare those at Aachen (Grimme 1957, 11, 19f) and those depicted in Elmham's chronicle (reproduced here in Plate I). The closest parallel is on the head of the effigy of William of Valence (*d*. 1296) in Westminster Abbey (Stothard 1876, P1. opp. p. 76). See also no. 2, p. 204, below.
From Area 1, layer 4.
A.M.L. 743654.

*6. Cresting, pierced by five holes, with flanges tinned at three places on each side. Length 33 mm.; height 17.5 mm. Compare cresting from mid-fourteenth-century chrismatory from St. Martin's Church, Canterbury (Oman 1962, 204 and P1. XXVI A) and above, p. 179, no. 4.
From Area 1, layer 76.
A.M.L. 756300.

*7. Gilt-copper alloy plate, perhaps part of shrine, decorated on the front with punched and incised decoration, mercury gilded. The decoration is a scroll containing a fleur-de-lys type device, a typical late twelfth-century motif. 32 mm. Found with no. 13, which may be part of it.
From Area 1, layer 4.
A.M.L. 743658.

*8. Small triangular piece of metal with incised and gilded ornament. 17 mm.
From Area 2, layer 75.
A.M.L. 756302.

*9. Small piece of metal with simple leaf design, moulded in relief; gilded. 14 mm.
From Area 1, layer 4.
A.M.L. 743662.

*10. Fleur-de-lys on thin plate. A trace of gilding survives on the back. 20 mm.
From Area 2, unstratified.
A.M.L. 756294.

11. Lead dowel with remains of copper alloy rod (diam. 5 mm.) set in it, perhaps for a statuette. See also architectural lead no. 18 (p. 140, above).
From Area 2, layer 35.
A.M.L. 794512.

*12. Strip of copper alloy with ornamentation of impressed circles, gilded. 29 mm.
From Area 2, layer 37.
A.M.L. 756295.

*13. Plate, with sharp carination at one point, decorated with curved, intersecting lines in relief. 20 mm. Found with no. 7.
From Area 1, layer 4.
A.M.L. 743658.

*14. Copper alloy catch with hole for attachment at one end and hook at the other; bevelled sides. Probably from a casket. 89 mm.
From infill of south-east 'box' of lady chapel.
A.M.L. 775158.

*15. Gilt copper alloy ring. The bezel consists of a central mount which contains a *cabochon* of glass, backed by a glass plate and a thin foil of gilt silver laid on a fragment of textile for reflecting. This is held in place by four claws of metal. Surrounding the mouth were eight little cones each topped by a *cabochon* of green glass, six of which now remain. E. Crowfoot comments: 'On the textile the spinning is Z,Z, its appearance suggests flax, but it is too deteriorated for weave or count to be certain. Diam. 21 mm. The hoop is a simple strap of metal affixed to the bezel through its underside. Diam. 22 mm.' A hole on the far side of the bezel seems to militate against the ring having been used as an ordinary finger-ring.
A virtually identical object (Thorn 1981, 80) comes from the tomb of Abbot Dygon (*d*. 1510) and the hole may best be explained as a means of attachment to the finger of a glove worn by the corpse. Gilded and with its jewel-like insets, the ring would have appeared to be of some magnificence for the corpse's lying in state. The style is related to that of certain fourteenth- and fifteenth-century wheel-shaped brooches like one from Edworth, Beds. (Evans 1933, 197f, Figs. 4 and 6). See also no. 12a, p. 207, below.
From Area 1, layer 6.
A.M.L. 743661.

*16. Gilded, copper alloy mount, probably intended for a jewel; ovoid. 16 × 12 mm; height 8 mm.
From Area 2 layer 4.
A.M.L. 743656.

Dress

*17. Strap-end, decorated with criss-cross pattern. Two rivets at top, one of which survives. 31 mm. For the form compare Durham (1977, 148 and Fig. 30, no. 26) St. Aldate's, Oxford.
From Trench II, layer 1.
A.M.L. 743698.

*18. Copper alloy strap-end buckle, trapezoidal form with sides overlapping the plate which is tinned and still contains leather. Buckle 17 mm; plate 23 mm. Compare *L.M.M.C.*, 272 and P1. LXXV, 8; Steane and Bryant (1975, 108 ff., Fig. 42, no. 19) Lyveden; no. 23, p. 210, below. Unstratified.
A.M.L. 756279.

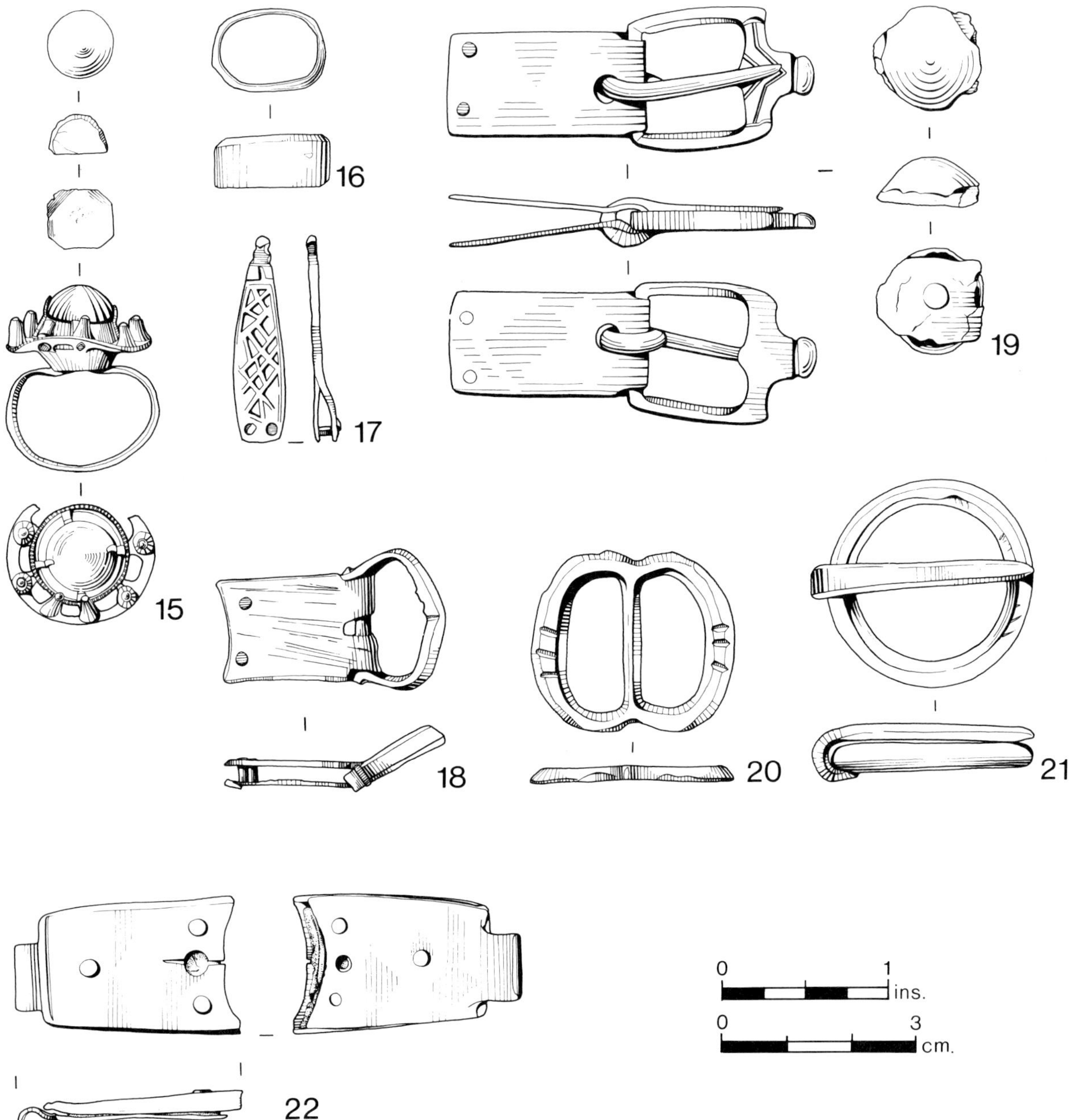

Fig. 59. Small Finds, 1972–75.

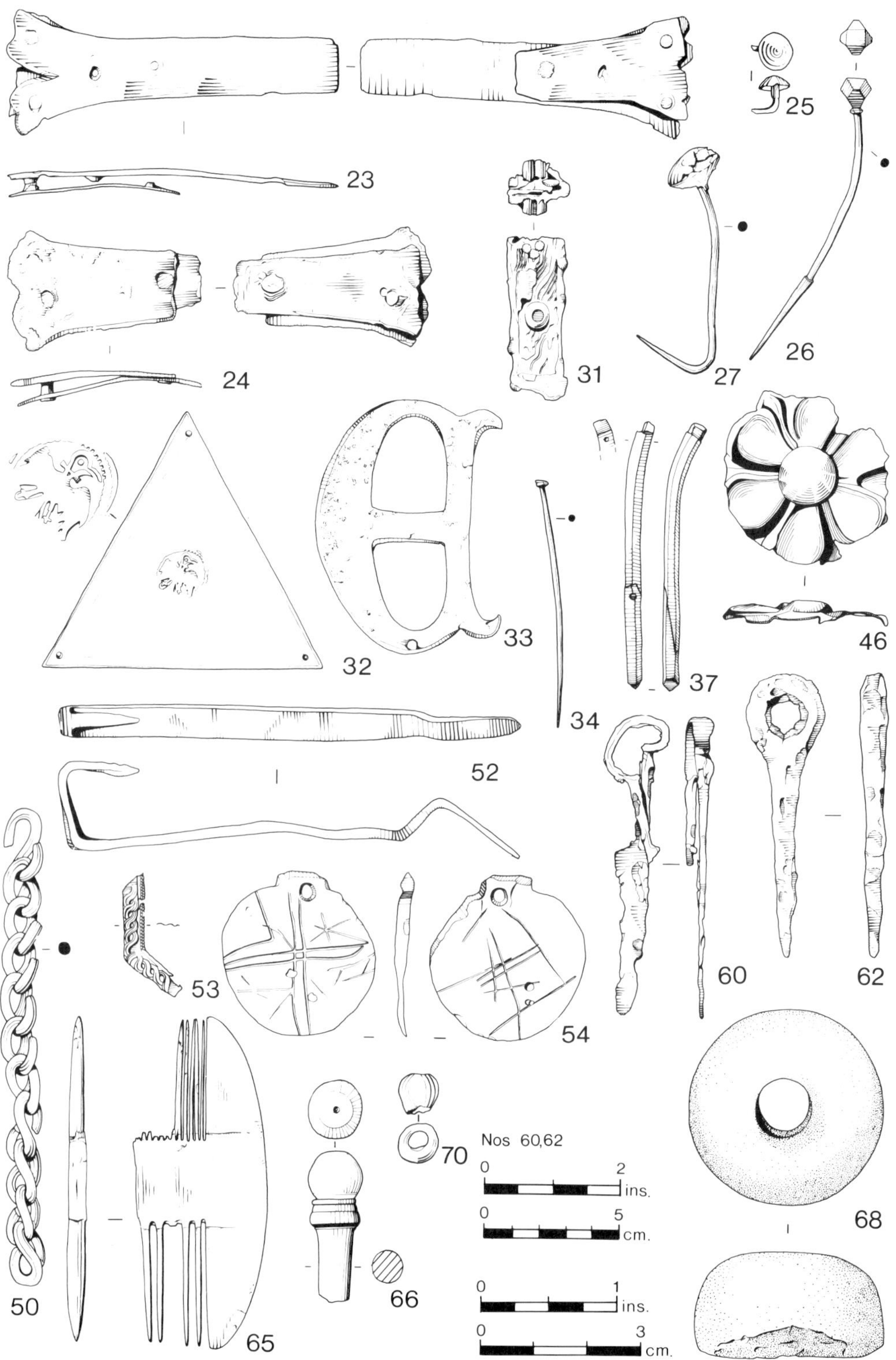

Fig. 60. Small Finds, 1972–75.

*19. Copper alloy strap-end buckle, rectangular form with central prong; plate retains leather and fabric. Associated with this buckle is a simple stud from the belt. E. Crowfoot comments on the textile: 'On the front of the buckle is a piece of leather belt over the ring, and on the pin and plate deteriorated remains of replaced textile, spinning Z, Z, lying in the folds, surface crushed on the plate, but clear on the ring. One the back are replaced fragments of textile, on *c.* 12 × 13mm. Z, Z, tabby weave, 16/15 threads per cm. The appearance suggests flax. Probably all the replacements come from the same fabric'. Buckle 26mm.; plate 30 mm.; stud 15 mm. diameter. See also no. 23, p. 210, below.
From Trench IIc, layer 1.
A.M.L. 721300.

*20. Spectacle buckle with notched sides. 32 mm. Compare Lambrick and Woods (1976, 214 and Fig. 11, no. 5) Oxford Blackfriars.
From Area 1, layer 1.
A.M.L. 743650.

*21. Penannular buckle. Diam. 34 mm. Compare *L.M.M.C.* 275, Pl. LXXVII, 1 and 2; Clarke and Carter (1977, 287ff, Fig. 130 no. 5); Platt and Coleman-Smith (1975, 260, Fig. 242, no. 1776); Steane and Bryant (1975, 112, no. 40, Fig. 42) Lyveden.
Trench II. Unstratified.
A.M.L. 743683.

*22. Strap-end, with hook-like projection in front. At the back it is curved, with three rivet holes, the central one replaced by a larger opening on the lower plate. Some leather remains. 32 mm.
From Area 2, layer 37.
A.M.L. 756297.

*23. Book-mount with bifurcated end. Gilt copper alloy. Both upper and lower plates remain. 63 mm. Compare Williams (1977, 189 ff, Fig. 43, no. 22); Moorhouse (1971a, 59 and Fig. 25, no. 162) and above, p. 179, no. 3.
Unstratified.
A.M.L. 775157.

*24. Strap-mount with swallow-tail end. Upper and lower plates remain. Similar to last. 7 mm.
From Area 2, layer 37.
A.M.L. 756296.

*25. Stud with domed head, gilt. Diam. 6 mm.
From Trench III, layer 38.
A.M.L. 743685.

*26. Gilt copper alloy pin with facetted head, below which is a simple moulding. 58 mm. Compare late Anglo-Saxon pin (Addyman and Hill 1969, 67 ff, Fig. 26, 5).
From Area 1, layer 3/4.
A.M.L. 743716.

*27. Pin with lentoid head which is hollow and filled with lead. 60 mm. Compare Platt and Coleman-Smith (1975, 260, Fig. 243, nos. 1788, 1790); also no. 85, p. 220, below.
From Area 2, layer 35.
A.M.L. 756288.

Miscellaneous

28. Bronze unguent spoon, simple shank (incomplete) and small ovoid end. Possibly Roman. Length 28 mm.
From Area 1, unstratified.
A.M.L. 775156.
29. Small bronze ring; simple form. Diam. 12 mm.
From Area 1, layer 35.
A.M.L. 756287.
30. Bronze ring with slightly flattened hoop. External diameter 23 mm.; 3 mm. thick.
From Area 1, layer 6.
A.M.L. 743663.
*31. Knife-handle of wood, with iron blade now largely missing. On each side is a bronze rivet with washer and a group of three bronze studs for decoration. 30 mm.
From Area 1, layer 1.
A.M.L. 743659.
*32. Copper alloy scale pan in the form of an equilateral triangle with a hole in each corner for suspension. In the centre of the upper side is a punched roundel with beaded border containing a bird as a device. 53 mm.
For a similar scale pan from Tollard Royal, compare Pitt Rivers (1890, 20 and Pl. XIX, 17); also Rigold (1978, 371–4). For a sixteenth-century representation of a balance with one round and one triangular pan, see Singer *et al.* (1956, 746, Fig. 678). For a central device, compare the bronze plate found in the abbey cloister garth (Potts 1930, 168, Fig. 2).
From Trench III, layer 12.
A.M.L. 743696.
*33. Copper alloy Lombardic letter E. John Blair comments that this letter is abnormal in being well under the standard 2 mm. thickness and almost (though not quite) identical to one at Tilsworth, Beds. Date *c.* 1300–50. See also below, p. 232.
From Trench III, layer 12.
A.M.L. 743695.
*34. Copper alloy pin with head of coiled wire. Length 46 mm.
From Trench III, layer 18.
A.M.L. 743692.
35. Pin similar to last. Length 54 mm. 118 others, mostly simpler and shorter, from this part of site: many show traces of tinning or silvering, perhaps shroud pins. Biddle *et al.* (1959, 182 and Pl. XXIB); Clarke and Carter (1977, 289, Fig. 230, no. 19); Hobley (1970, 119 and Fig. 16, 6); Rahtz and Hirst (1976, 203 and Fig. 38, 16, 18 and 19); Andrews (1977, 194 and Pl. XL, 39–40). See also no. 88, p. 220, below.
From Area 2, layer 35.
(No A.M.L. nos.)
36. Strip of copper alloy, bent and facetted. 50 mm.
From Area 2, layer 3/4.

A.M.L. 743714.

*37. Fragment of copper alloy bar with scarfed and riveted joint, and notch one end. Length 50 mm.
From Area 2, layer 50.
A.M.L. 794513.

38. Length of copper alloy wire. 23 mm. Also 9 other pieces.
From Area 2, layer 3.
A.M.L. 743717.

39. Loop of twisted copper alloy wire. 10 mm. Also three others. Compare Drury (1974, 56, Fig. 8, 19); Biddle *et al.* (1959, Pl. XXIB); Platt and Coleman-Smith (1975, 264 and Fig. 244, nos. 1817–1820, dated 1550–1650).
From Area 2, unstratified.
A.M.L. 756281.

40. 'Boot-lace tag'- containing remains of leather. 28 mm. Also 37 others. Biddle *et al.* (1959, 184, no. 16, Pl. XXIB); Lambrick and Woods (1976, 216, Fig. 11, no. 15); Rodwell (1976, 136 and Fig. 17, 18–20); Hobley (1970, 119 and Fig. 16, 3–5). See also no. 91, p. 220, below.
A.M.L. 756284.

41. Two pieces of sheet metal, rivetted together (2 rivets). 71 mm.
From Area 2, unstratified.
A.M.L. 776281.

42. Pieces of sheet metal with 2 rivet holes at one end. 87 mm.
From Area 2, unstratified.
A.M.L. 776282.

43. Fragment of metal sheet. 27 mm. Six other pieces.
From Area 2, layer 69.
A.M.L. 756299.

44. Fragment of curved metal sheet with four rivet holes. 53 mm.
From Area 1, layer 5.
A.M.L. 743660.

45. Tack with a domed head. 10 mm. Three others.
Unstratified.
A.M.L. 776283.

*46. Stud in thin metal with six-petalled flower design. 34 mm.
Area 2, unstratified.
A.M.L. 794514.

47. Tube made by rolling metal sheet, similar to a tag-end but much longer, 57 mm.
From Area 2, layer 3/4.
A.M.L. 743715.

48. S-shaped copper alloy hook. 21 mm.
From Area 1, layer 14.
S.A. 74, 1054. (No. A.M.L. no.).

49. S-shaped copper alloy hook. 10 mm.
From Area 2, layer 4.
S.A. 75, 2826. (No A.M.L. no.).

*50. Chain of ten links, S-shaped hook at one end. 86 mm. Found with no. 62.
From Area 1, layer 3.
A.M.L. 743725B.

51. Needle with flattened eye. The lower half is triangular in section. 82 mm.
Unstratified. S.A. 75, 2288.
(No A.M.L. no.).

*52. Bent implement. Length 92 mm.
From Trench II, layer 1.
A.M.L. 734699.

*53. Thin, angled strip with impressed cable pattern design. 24 mm.
A.M.L. 743655.

Lead and Speculum

*54. Simple disk with suspension tag; on one side is a crudely incised cross; diam. 28 mm.
Compare Lambrick and Woods (1976, 216 and Fig. 12, 33), Oxford Blackfriars.
From Area 2, layer 37.
A.M.L. 750391.

55. Lead disk. Diameter 14 mm.
From Area 2, layer 35.
A.M.L. 756289.

56. Triangular fragment of *speculum* mirror. Possibly Roman. See no. 1, p. 201, below.
From Area 2, layer 35.
A.M.L. 750390.

57. Fragment of *speculum* metal (i.e., with high tin content). Length 33 mm.
From Area 2, layer 37.
A.M.L. 756292.

58. Lump of waste *speculum* metal from casting (bell metal?). 44 mm. Another fragment, S.A. 72, 30, from layer 8, 29 mm.
From Trench III, layer 34.
A.M.L. 743688.

59. Thin lead disc with faint heart-shaped impression. Diam. 10 mm.
From Area 2, unstratified.
A.M.L. 750387.

Iron

*60. Shears, one blade missing. 109 mm. Type *L.M.M.C.*, 155 ff. Pl. XXXII, 8 and 10 (Type III); Cunliffe (1977, 198 and Fig. 106 no. 38); Beresford (1977, 257 and Fig. 43, no. 16).
From Trench III, layer 12.
A.M.L. 743681.

61. Ferrule. Above the point are two flat plates each with three rivets for attachment into a wooden haft. 260 mm.
From Area 1, layer 3.
A.M.L. 743726.

*62. Spike, square in section widening at blunt end which is pierced. 102 mm. Compare Beresford (1977, 257 and Fig. 45, 59 'a support loop possibly set in a wall'). Found with the bronze chain (above, no. 50).
From Area 1, layer 3.
A.M.L. 743725A.

63. Buckle. A simple D-shaped type of harness buckle, width 38 mm., tongue missing. Steane and Bryant (1975, 129 and Fig. 48, no. 126) Lyveden.
From Area 1, layer 3.
A.M.L. 743724.

64. Key with kidney-shaped bow. 64 mm. *L.M.M.C.*, 141, Type VII (Pl. XXVI, 49, for shape of bow); Rodwell (1976, 138 and Fig. 18, no. 2) Banbury Castle.
From Area 2, layer 4.
A.M.L. 756273.

Bone

*65. Comb, teeth cut on two modules, curved end plate. Much of it is missing. Width 60 mm.; surviving length 24 mm. Tebbutt (1966, 51, Fig. 4c) St. Neot's Priory.
From Area 1, unstratified.
A.M.L. 775160.

*66. Head of a pin or stylus with baluster mouldings. Surviving length 28 mm.; diam. 6 mm.
From Area 1, unstratified.
A.M.L. 794509.

67. Fragment of shaft of pin. Length 31 mm.; diameter 2.5 mm.
From Area 1, unstratified. S.A. 75, 1587.
(No A.M.L. no.).

Ceramic

*68. Spindle whorl. Diam. 35 mm.; piercing 10 mm.
From Trench III, layer 18.
A.M.L. 743664.

*69. Fragment of clay tobacco pipe bowl with reeded design. Fragments of four other pipes were found in 1972 and 39 in 1975. Of these, eleven came from bowls and the remainder from stems. None of the fragments has maker's initials or stamps. All the other bowls are undecorated except for a single roulette around the tip of four. The bases of the bowls are all flat and without 'feet'. They may be dated by their typology to roughly the second and third quarters of the seventeenth century. The stem fragments were entirely plain,

averaging from 6 to 12 mm. in diameter. There were pipemakers in Canterbury in the seventeenth century and there is no reason to suppose that any of these fragments were made other than locally.
From Trench II, top soil S.A. 72, 62.
(No A.M.L. no.).

Glass

*70. Green glass bead. 7 mm.
From Trench III, layer 40.
A.M.L. 743666.

71. Part of 'hemmed' foot of eighteenth-century wine glass.
From Area 1, layer 5. S.A. 74, 1021.
(No A.M.L. no.).

72. Part of base of vessel in medieval Wealden glass with remains of pontil mark.
From Area 2, layer 63.
A.M.L. 756317.

73. Fragment of Wealden 'forest glass'. Fifteenth–sixteenth century.
From Area 2, layer 4. S.A. 75, 2720.
(No A.M.L. no.).

Stone

*74. Fragment of Caen-stone carved with drapery; fourteenth-century, possibly from a reredos. Length 221 mm.
From Trench III, layer 18.
S.A. 72, 214. (No A.M.L. no.).

75. Fragment of oblong triangular bead in violet amethyst. Surviving length 28 mm.
From Area 2, layer 63.
A.M.L. 794510.

*76. Stone (Caen?) with a hole, possibly a weight.
From Area 2, unstratified.
A.M.L. 791795.

77. Piece of reddish sandstone with quartz crystals, approximately 100 × 70 × 150 mm., showing signs of having been used as a hone for sharpening an instrument with a blade approximately 6 mm. wide.
Area 1, unstratified.
S.A. 74, 987. (No A.M.L. no.).

78. Fragment of micaceous schist hone. 55 × 9 × 15 mm.
From Trench III, layer 34.
S.A. 72, 271. (No A.M.L. no.).

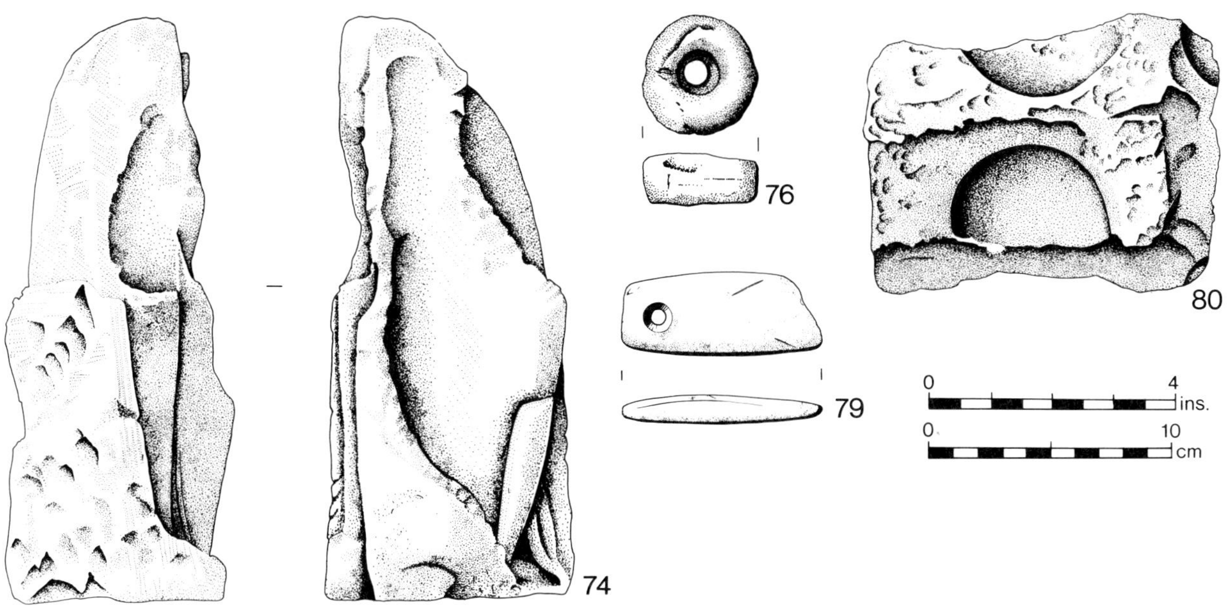

Fig. 61. Small Finds, 1972–75.

*79. Hone-stone with hour-glass piercing at top. Total length 41 mm. Compare *L.M.M.C.*, Pl. XCIV, 3.
From south of chapel on west side of transept, unstratified.
S.A. 75, 2781. (No A.M.L. no.).

*80. Part of a Caen-stone cresset with cuts surviving for four circular bowls, each 80 mm. in diameter and 58 mm. deep.
From Trench III, layer 18.
S.A. 72, 269. (No A.M.L. no.).

81. Fragment of a Caen-stone cresset with two rectangular recesses in it. On the back a simple hollow. Reddened by fire.
From Area 2, layer 63 (rubble beneath fallen wall).
S.A. 75 2061. (No A.M.L. no.).

82. Circular stone shot. Diam. 50 mm.
From Area 2, Dissolution layer.
S.A. 74, 1417. (No A.M.L. no.).

83. Two small fragments of white 'marble' veneer, 3 and 6 mm. thick. Possibly Cosmatesque tile mosaic like some pieces discovered during the pre-war excavations (see above p. 135). The 'marble' has been identified by the Natural History Museum as fragments of fossil shell from the Cretaceous bivalve *Inoceramus*.
From Area 2, beneath demolished boundary wall.
A.M.L. 791796.

Shell

84. Oyster shell containing pigment.
From Area 1, layer 1.
A.M.L. 776280.

Dr. Barry Knight reports: 'At first sight this object appeared to be an ordinary oyster shell. However, the earth fill fell out as it dried, to reveal that the inside of the shell was covered with bright blue pigment. On closer examination, bright red specks were seen dispersed on the inner surface of the fill, and a dull greenish buff encrustation was also visible on the inner surface of the shell. It was clear that the shell had been used several times for the different colours. The lowest layer was green, followed by blue, green and red.

The three pigments were sampled and examined by X-ray fluorescence and X-ray diffraction with the following results:

Blue

XRF: Copper detected strongly
XRD: Azurite [$2CuCO_3.Cu(OH)_2$]

Red

XRF: Mercury detected strongly
XRD: Cinnabar [HgS]

Green

XRF: Copper and lead detected strongly, tin weakly
XRD: White lead [$2PbCO_3.Pb(OH)_2$] and lead-tin yellow [Pb_2SnO_4].
Additional very faint lines: unidentified component.

No tests were made for organic binders.

The presence of azurite and cinnabar is unremarkable as they are both familiar pigments of the Middle Ages. Lead-tin yellow is also a common pigment, but when mixed with white lead one would expect the colour to be pale yellow. The unidentified third component is presumably a green copper-containing pigment, which gives the greenish tinge to the mixture.

It is impossible to say what the palette might have been used for. However, given the small quantities of paint involved it was more probably a small-scale usage such as manuscript painting, rather than for large-scale decorative work such as wall painting. There is, of course, ample evidence for both these activities at St. Augustine's. Similar oyster shells with pigments have come from Mount Grace Priory, Yorks. (unpublished), Glastonbury Abbey, Som. (site museum) and Faversham Abbey (Philp 1968, 51).'

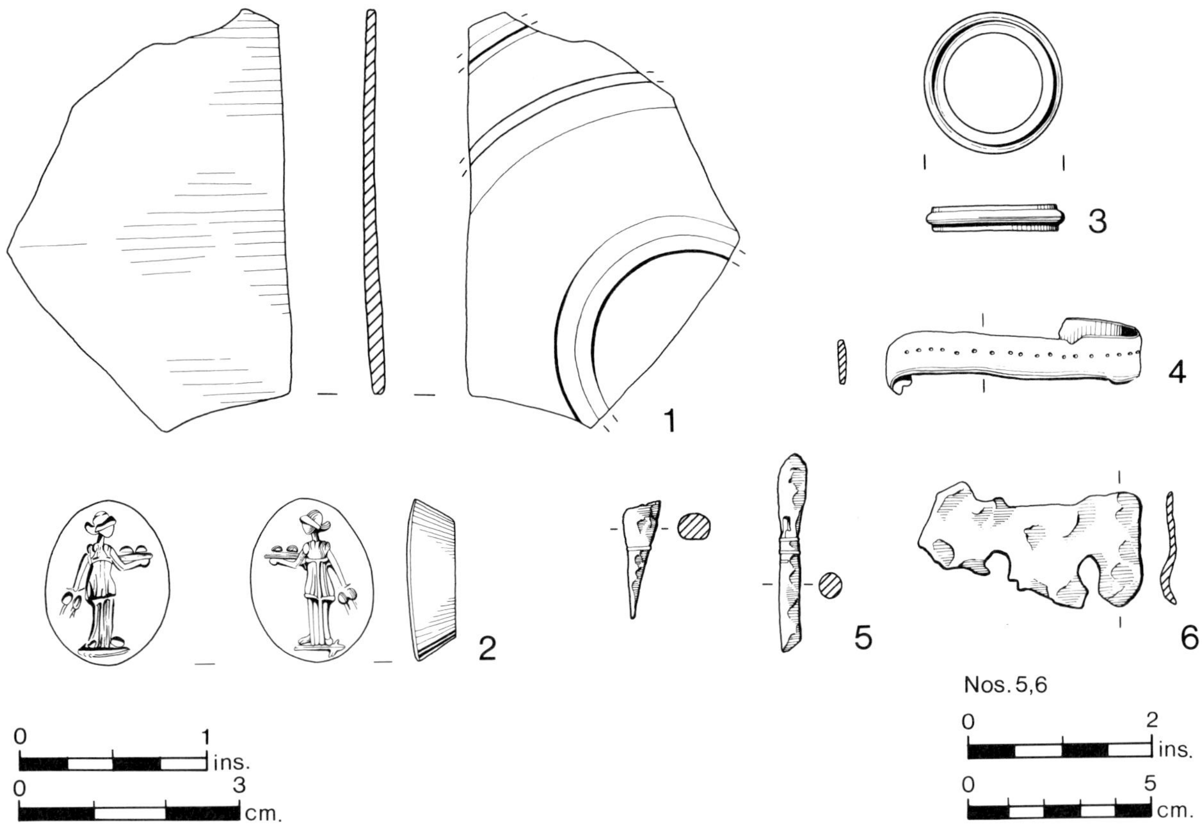

Fig. 62. Small Finds, 1976–78, Roman.

SMALL FINDS FROM EXCAVATIONS 1976–1978 Martin Henig and Humphrey Woods

Roman (Fig. 62)

1. *Speculum* mirror, fragment. G. Lloyd-Morgan writes: 'The mirror is a fragment of a mirror disc measuring 4.9 x 4.7 cm. with a minimum original diameter of about 10 cm. The reflecting side is plain, and the back is turned with two series of concentric circles at the edge, and a further series around the centre. The mirror would have been completed with a simple handle, having either a baluster or loop-shaped grip. It is interesting to note that John Brent mentions finds of handles from Castle Street, and from a sarcophagus burial near St. Edmund's Church in 1864 (Brent 1864–5, 55, no. 3; Brent 1879, 49; Lloyd-Morgan 1983, 231–6). Unfortunately, in neither case are the pieces illustrated or described in detail.

   More than eight examples of this type of hand mirror have now been found in Britain

(Lloyd-Morgan 1981, 44–8, Group H). One small fragment comes from Richborough, and a near complete mirror disc from Deal is now in the British Museum (No. 83, 10–24, 1). Another example in the British Museum (No. 1854, 12–27, 75) was found in London in 1837 and there are further examples at York (unnumbered) and Colchester (Joslin Collection, no. 528, and possibly no. IV from the West Lodge Cemetery area). In 1983, some fragments in the Royal Museum Canterbury (No. RM 113) were recognised as an incomplete mirror belonging to the same group (Lloyd-Morgan with Reedie 1984, 335–7, Fig. 1). Some of the most beautifully preserved complete examples, now in the Landesmuseum Ioanneum, Graz, are from Poetovio, now Ptuj, Yugoslavia (Nos. 7448, 7599, 7725), with a similar piece, ex colln. Herman Wolff in the Römaische-Germanische Museum, Cologne (No. 837).

The group is closely related to the very popular hand mirrors of Group K decorated with a series of circular holes bored through around the edge, and found in most provinces of the Roman Empire (Lloyd-Morgan 1981, 49–56, Group K). Just over 5 per cent of the total of known examples come from Britain, including ones from Richborough, London, Verulamium and Colchester. Like the simpler Canterbury mirror and the group it belongs to, they seem to have been produced in some quantity in the first century A.D., probably in the workshops of North Italy (Musty, Rogerson, Lloyd-Morgan 1973, 278–281, Fig. 3, Pl. LVb; Lloyd-Morgan 1975, 107–116, cf. 110–114, Fig. 7–10).

The discovery of another hand mirror in Canterbury is therefore welcome, not only for the light it sheds on earlier reports, but also as a useful addition to the series of Roman mirrors found in Kent.

The writer is most grateful to Mr. K.G.H. Reedie of the Royal Museum Art Gallery Canterbury, and his staff for help in her researches and encouragement to publish the mirrors in the old collections.'

Layer 25.
A.M.L. 765738.

2. Cornelian intaglio. (Fig. 62; Col. Plate 2). The intaglio depicts Ceres, standing to the front and facing left. In her left hand, she hold two ears of corn and in her right hand a dish of fruit. The type is common on gems, although on other examples from Britain the goddess faces right and the attributes are reversed (cf. Henig 1974, 71–73; Henig 1978, 39–41, nos. 259–274, P1s. IX, XXXIII, XXXIV. Note no. 264 in a Migration-period setting from Lyminge and no. 268, a paste from Richborough). Most examples can be dated to the second century A.D. In the case of the St. Augustine's gem, as it is not from a Roman layer, there is a possibility that it was employed with other plain stones in ornamenting a shrine, book-cover, etc. (cf. Vogel 1781; Henig 1978, 162–3 and 1983, 56–61).
   Layer 25.
   A.M.L. 765663.
3. Bronze ring; convex inner section and moulding running around outer edge. Probably a harness ring. Diam. 18.5 mm.
   Layer 806.
   A.M.L. 782530.
4. Bronze band.Width 5 mm.; total length 7 cm.
   Layer 806.
   A.M.L. 782531.

5. Two pieces of iron stylus or styli, ornamented with brass hoops. The spatulate end has three hoops around its neck, the point a single hoop. Cf. Atkinson (1942, 221 and Pl. 54, nos. B50–B79); Bushe-Fox (1949, 153 and Pl. LIX, nos. 304–316). For a spatula inlaid with bands of copper cf. *L.M.M.C.*, no. 3, p. 58 and Pl. XXIV, no. 2.
   Layer 8005.
   A.M.L. 782360A.
6. Piece of iron sheet, possibly part of a small tumbler lock case. Cf. Manning (1972, 181, and Fig. 67, no. 66, though the Verulamium example is rather larger).
   Layer 5160.
   A.M.L. 782334.

Anglo-Saxon (Fig. 63)

1. Gold *cloisonné* plate, square 11 x 11 mm.; thickness 1.25 mm. (Fig. 63; Col. Plate 3). The centre is a four-lobed device in yellow in a light blue surround. This comprises an inner square with a white enamel at each corner; an outer border is dark blue in colour with each side punctuated by a semi-circular yellow enamel.

   A copper alloy disc, also enamelled, from St. Augustine's is not closely similar but deserves citation: it is probably of the tenth century (Rigold 1970, 345 ff., no. 1; Evison 1977, 8 and Fig. 3C). A finger ring with enamelling from Wincheap dated to the eighth or ninth century carries the motif of a bird's head (British Museum, Inv. no. 1951, 2–5, 1; Evison 1977, 8, Pl. 1c). Another Anglo-Saxon ring with enamelled setting was found in Ireland (Oman 1974, 17 and 90, Pl. 7b). However, the closest parallel is the enamelled plate in the Minster Lovell

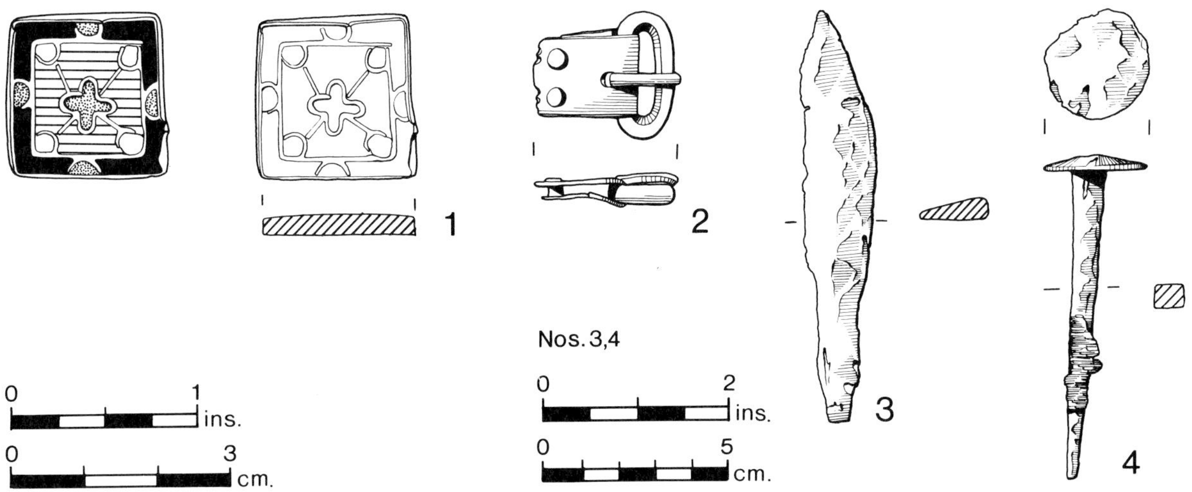

Fig. 63. Small Finds, 1976–78, Anglo-Saxon.

jewel (Hinton 1974, 27 ff., no. 22, Pl. IX), which has a central cruciform motif and employs white, light blue, dark blue and green enamel, all except the last found on the St. Augustine's plate. This is no later than the ninth century; and (*ibid.*, 47) probably made in Wessex. Cf. Evison (1977) for a discussion of Anglo-Saxon enamelling in connection with the discovery of an enamelled disc somewhat similar to the St. Augustine's find at Great Saxham.

A sample was taken from beneath the *cloisonné* plate and analysed by Justine Bayley of the Ancient Monuments Laboratory who writes: 'The sample was taken from directly beneath the plate. In among the earth were a few small pieces of what was apparently corroded metal. All the pieces were very powdery and pale lilac in colour – a typical form for silver to decay to. On the largest of these powdery lumps was a tiny metallic-looking flake. This was probably the remaining surface of what was once a gold-plated silver object to which the enamelled mount was fixed.'
Layer 764.
A.M.L. 777597.

2. Copper alloy buckle, somewhat ovoid 'kidney' shape with simple plate pierced by two rivets. 19 mm. For the type cf. Myres and Green (1973, 212, Fig. 62 Gr 17, B and Fig. 63, 13, sixth or seventh century).
Layer 5066.
A.M.L. 782518.
3. Iron knife of scramasax form with pronounced triangular blade. 105 mm. Cf. Durham (1977, 142 ff. no. 6, eighth century).
Layer 8003.
A.M.L. 782332.
4. Iron coffin nail with flat broad head and rounded shank. Length 8.6 cm. Found with four similar nails and two smaller ones. Eleventh century.
Layer 803.
A.M.L. 782344.

Later Medieval (Fig. 64, nos. 1–7)

Silver, Ecclesiastical

1. Silver strip, segmented, 15 mm.; width 1.5 mm. Probably from shrine decoration rather than independent object such as a finger ring.
Layer 758.
A.M.L. 777553.

Gilt Copper Alloy, Ecclesiastical

2. Gilt copper alloy ornamented strip, with wire decoration, imitating filigree standing proudly above surface of the plate. Note curving scroll. Length 10 mm.; width 14 mm.
Layer 764.
A.M.L. 777561.

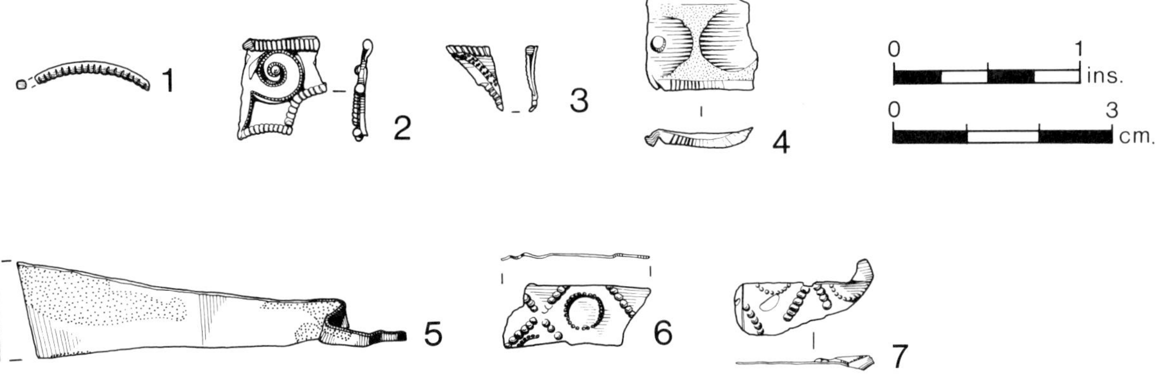

Fig. 64. Small Finds, 1976–78, Medieval, Silver and Gilt Copper Alloy.

3. Very small fragment of gilt copper alloy, with imitation filigree decoration, 8 mm. x 5 mm. From same or similar object.
   Layer 727.
   A.M.L. 777544.
4. Gilt copper alloy strip. The gilding provides a background, but there are plain reserved circular areas where jewelled (?) settings were affixed. Length 15 mm.; width 13 mm.
   Layer 513.
   A.M.L. 765740.
5. Fragment of copper alloy sheet with indication of gilded patterns or devices. Length 55 mm.
   Layer 5071.
   A.M.L. 782515.
6. Gilt copper alloy strip with *repoussé* criss-cross and circular ornament. Length 20 mm.; width 8 mm.
   Layer 754.
   A.M.L. 777557.
7. Gilt copper alloy strip with similar *repoussé* criss-cross and circular ornament. Length 20 mm.; width 7 mm.
   Layer 765.
   A.M.L. 777562.
8. Gilt copper alloy sheet, with silver rivets through it. Length 42 mm. Not illustrated.
   Layer 15.
   A.M.L. 765828.
9. Fragments of gilt copper alloy sheet. Not illustrated.
   Layer 15.
   A.M.L. 765713.

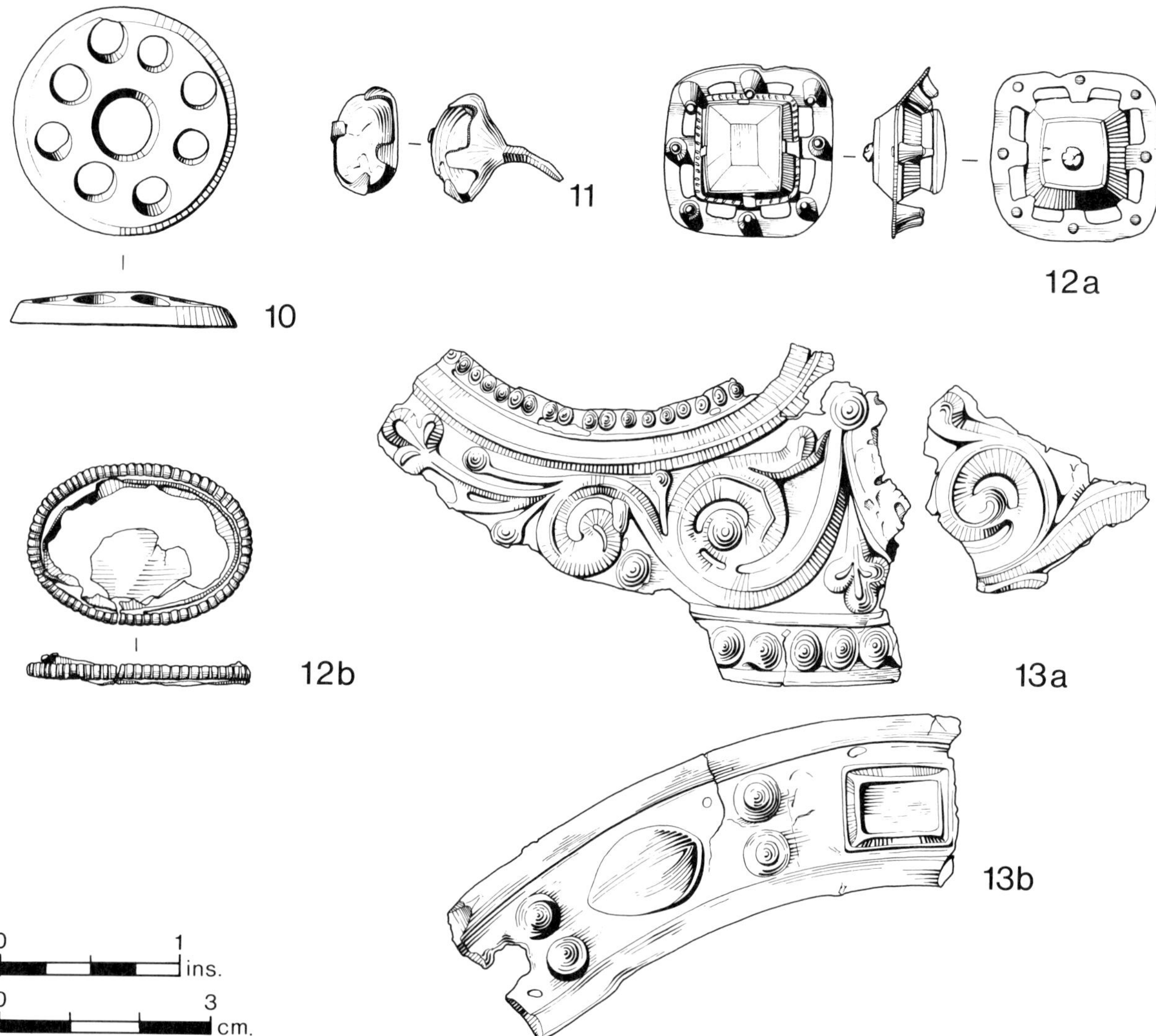

Fig. 65. Small Finds, 1976–78, Medieval, Gilt and silvered Copper Alloy with Gems and Gilt Lead.

Fig. 65, nos. 10–13b

10. Circular copper alloy plate, coated with lead/tin. Convex, with large central hole and eight surrounding smaller holes. Diam. 31 mm.; central hole 8 mm.; other holes 5 mm. The holes were perhaps filled with jewels or enamel and the object is best interpreted as coming from a shrine or reliquary.
Layer 500.
A.M.L. 777525.

11. Gilt copper alloy stud; the head contains a paste, completely decayed with a black upper face; 13 × 8 × 4 mm. Total length of stud 16 mm. The object was almost certainly affixed to a shrine or reliquary.
Layer 25.
A.M.L. 765735.

12a. Rectangular ornament of gilt copper alloy. The central mount contains a 'jewel' of rock crystal in two parts – the lower a truncated pyramid and the upper a curving plate of the mineral. There is a foil-backing and the jewel is held in place by means of four claws. Surrounding this is a metal rim attached by means of eight bridges and ornamented with eight cones topped by a glass *cabochon*. Length 22 mm. Rock crystal 11 × 95 mm. Lower section is 5 mm. in height; the upper section is 2 mm. thick.

The object is clearly of the same workmanship as no. 15, (p. 208, below) and may well, like it, be a bezel from an ecclesiastical ring – probably primarily intended for burial. The hoop of the ring is lost, but it is clear from the back of the object that there was some such attachment. It is, however, possible that, although dating from the same time and comming from the same workshop, that this object was employed rather differently in the abbey. See also textile report (p. 235, below).
Layer 513.
A.M.L. 765753.

12b. Setting for a gem. An oval of gilded beaded wire surrounds a curved sheet of copper alloy. The sheet is gilded on the outside and would have held the gem in place, but has become bent and torn when the gem was ripped out, so that the shape of its original curve is now impossible to reconstruct. This gilded curved sheet is itself attached to a fragment of flat sheet gilded on both sides. The flat sheet extends beyond the beaded wire and is here broken, so it would appear that the gem setting was attached to a larger object, with a flat surface, such as a box. Unstratified find by workmen excavating the concrete foundations of the hospital mortuary after its demolition in 1980.
A.M.L. 810690.

Gilt Lead, Ecclesiastical

13a. Gilded lead strip ornamented with stylised running scroll, between two rows of raised pellets. Length 100 mm. Part of the ornamental surround from a shrine.
Layer 540.
A.M.L. 765884.

13b. Strip with raised bosses, one rectangular and the other almond-shaped, the latter set between four raised pellets. Length 73 mm. This is skeuomorphic. The bosses certainly represent engraved gems.
Layer 540.
A.M.L. 765884.

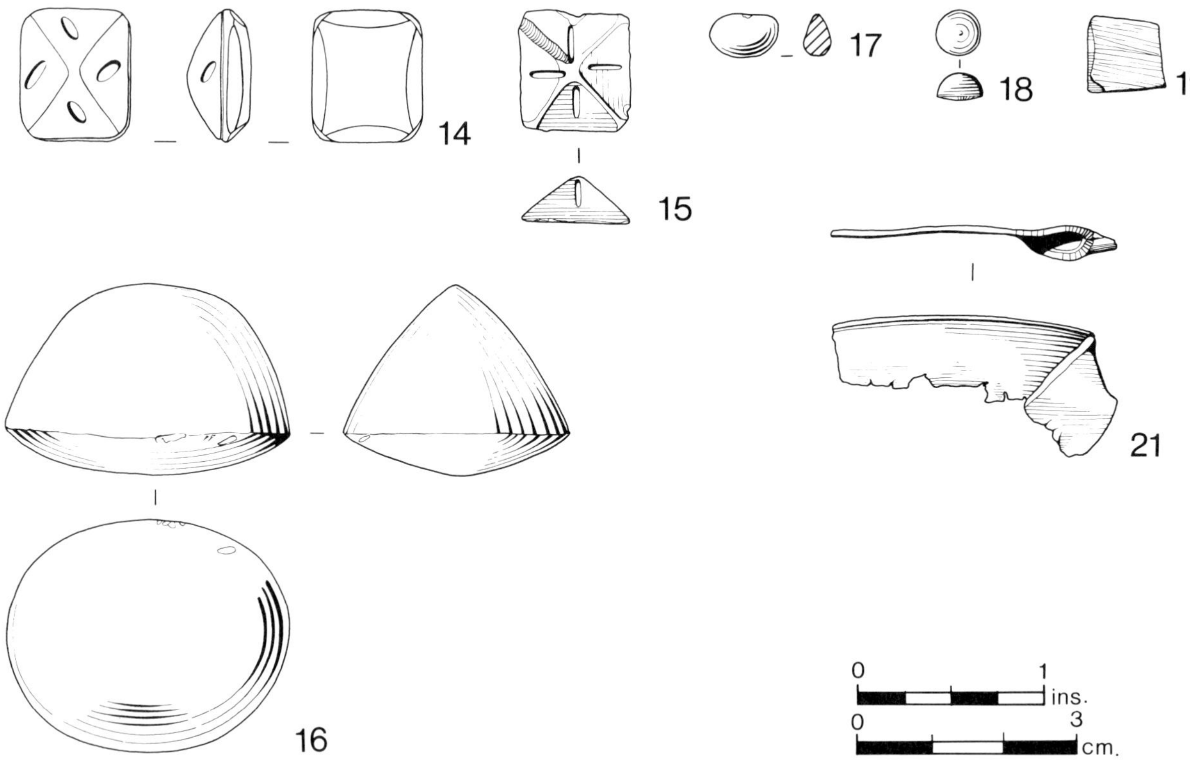

Fig. 66. Small Finds, 1976–78, Medieval, Gems and Church Plate.

Gems, Ecclesiastical Fig. 66, nos. 14–19

14. Rock crystal jewel in two parts as no. 12a; one part is a pyramid with all sides rounded; wheel-cut on each exposed face. The other part also has bevelled edges and is slightly convex. The two parts are bound together with a white adhesive. 18 × 15 mm.; pyramid 6 mm. thick; other part 3 mm. thick.
    Layer 764.
    A.M.L. 777615.
15. Rock crystal jewel; pyramidal, with wheel cut on each of four exposed faces. 16 × 16 × 5 mm. Type as last. Cf. rock crystal pendant from St. Mary's Priory, Coventry (Hobley 1970, 121 ff., Fig. 17, 5).
    Layer 25.
    A.M.L. 767482.
16. Rock crystal jewel, large, highly convex, ovoid profile at waist – jewel narrows towards apex. Lower part of jewel is convex. Length 38 mm.; maximum width 30 mm.; height 25 mm. Crystals of this shape and size are often found mounted in ecclesiastical metalwork. Cf.

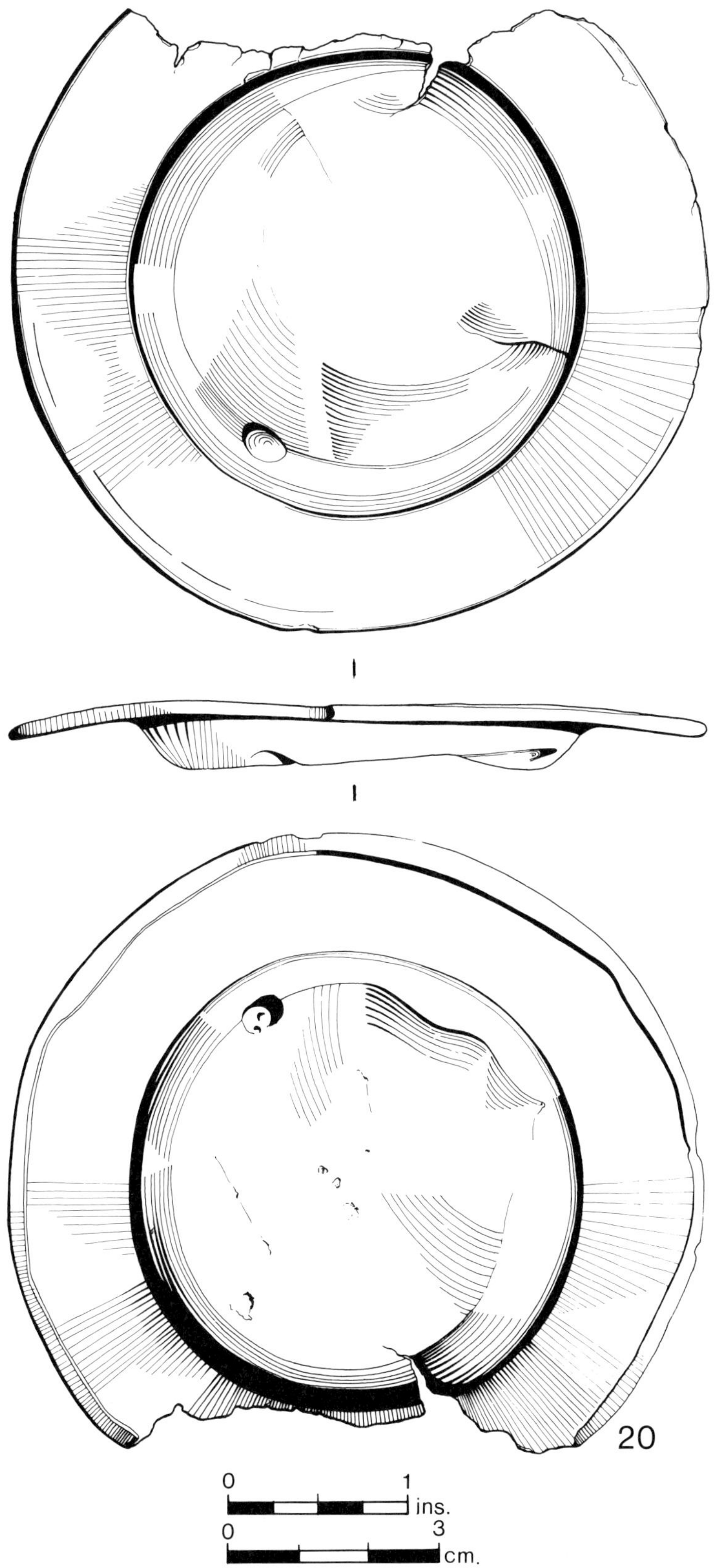

Fig. 67. Small Find, 1976–78, Medieval, Church Plate.

Henry 1970 (96 ff., Pl. 22) shrine of St. Patrick's bell – late eleventh century but the settings are later, (116, Pl. 48) Cumdach of Book of Dimma – twelfth century, but again jewel is later; Taralon (1966, 289 and Pl. 189) casket of St. Stephen of Muret, Ambazac – twelfth or thirteenth century; the jewels here seem to belong to their settings.
Layer 516.
A.M.L. 767483.

17. Light green polished emerald; ovoid 9 x 5 mm. Probably from a setting on a piece of metalwork.
Layer 533.
A.M.L. 767481.
18. Light blue glass jewel. Convex. Diam. 66 mm.; height 3 mm.
Layer 1045.
A.M.L. 777616.
19. Piece of blue glass – perhaps, despite its lack of shape, set in ecclesiastical metalwork. Greatest width 12 mm.
Layer 763.
A.M.L. 777617.

Church Plate

Fig. 67.

20. Pewter paten. Cf. example from burial at Oxford Blackfriars (Lambrick and Woods 1976, 218 and Fig. 12, no. 36).
Unstratified surface find.
A.M.L. 777632.

Fig. 66.

21. Strip of copper alloy with moulded edge along its length – possibly part of a paten or chalice. Length 45 mm.
Layer 720.
A.M.L. 777552.

Miscellaneous Silver, Copper Alloy and Pewter

Fig. 68, nos. 22–49.

22. Silver pin, with ring-head, perhaps for attachment to a brooch. 16 mm.
Layer 763.
A.M.L. 777569.
23. Copper alloy strap-end buckle, U-shaped with sides overlapping plate which has an

ornamental roundel stamped on it. Buckle 17 mm. Plate 41 mm. For the form in general, see no. 18, p. 190 above.
Layer 1002.
A.M.L. 765773.

24. Copper alloy buckle, stirrup-shaped with pin attached to central bar. Length 29 mm.; width 38 mm. For the type see Fingerlin (1971, 191 ff., Figs. 321 and 334, no. 65) from Churburg – second half of fifteenth century.
Layer 764.
A.M.L. 777563.

25. Part of buckle, probably a spectacle buckle with one side largely missing. Width 24 mm. Compare Steane and Bryant (1975, 111, no. 37, Fig. 42); Drewett (1975, 143 ff., Fig. 29, no. 358).
Layer 503.
A.M.L. 765722.

26. Part of simple buckle, rectangular with rounded corners and bevelled edges. Length 25 mm. Compare Williams (1978, 149 and Fig. 22, no. CV 10) from Greyfriars, Northampton.
Layer 26.
A.M.L. 765744.

27. Simple rectangular buckle, length 16 mm.; width 14 mm.
Layer 1042.
A.M.L. 777583.

28. Copper alloy tongue from large buckle. Length 47 mm.
Layer 18.
A.M.L. 765730.

29. Copper alloy tongue, simple form with fragment of iron buckle; length of tongue 21 mm.
Not illustrated.
Area I, unstratified.
A.M.L. 782533.

30. Belt chape, with horizontal piercing at end and vertical piercing behind this (within ring-like moulding). The two chape-plates survive, with their rivet. Length 33 mm. Compare Hagen (1973, 119) from Bedford; Andrews (1977, 194 and Pl. XL, 34).
Layer 24.
A.M.L. 765747.

31. Belt chape, horizontal piercing at end; vertical piercing behind this (moulding more ovoid than last). Two chape plates, with rivet through concave back of the object. Length 25 mm.
Layer 700.
A.M.L. 777547.

32. Copper alloy strap-end; two plates fixed together by means of four rivets. Central hole. The upper plate is notched along the two short edges with criss-cross cuts to provide pattern (lower plate similar without cross-crosses). Remains of leather survive. Length 35 mm. Cf. Rahtz and Hirst (1976, 202, no. 35, Fig. 38, 25) from Bordesley Abbey.
Layer 3.
A.M.L. 765720.

33. Plate from strap-end with stud through it. On the plate an animal (? a dog with head turned

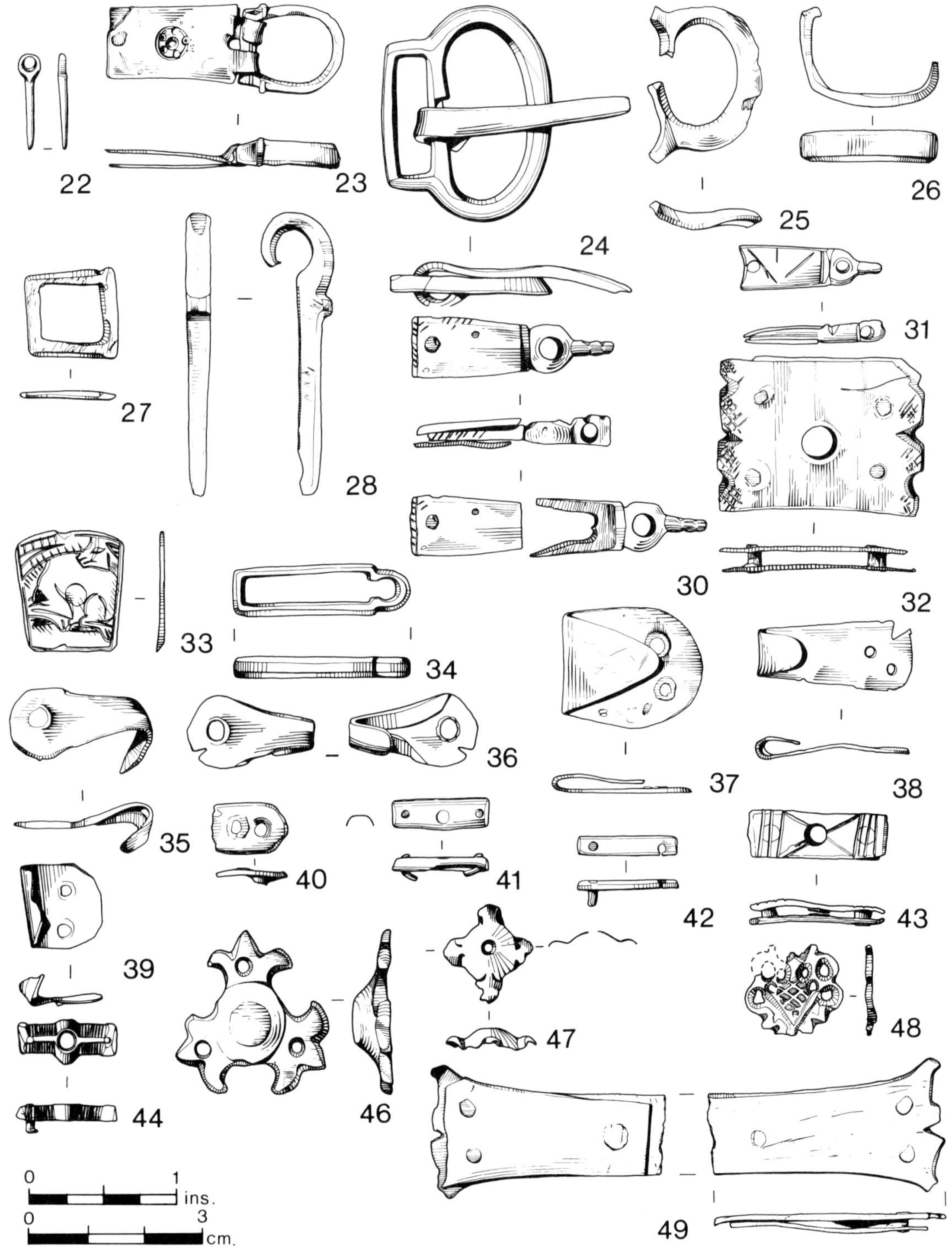

Fig. 68. Small Find, 1976–78, Medieval, Silver and Copper Alloy.

left) has been engraved. For similar ornament on strap-ends: Rahtz and Hirst (1976, 204, no. 54, Fig. 38, 24) from Bordesley Abbey, and Drury (1974, 56 and Fig. 8, 14) from the Dominican Priory, Chelmsford. Length of Plate 20 mm.
Layer 25.
A.M.L. 765751.

34. Elongated rectangle of metal, curved projection at end of one of the short sides. Perhaps part of strap-end (with the plates missing). Length 30 mm.; width 8 mm.
Layer 763.
A.M.L. 777589.

35. Copper alloy sheet, pear-shaped with piercing through wider end; probably a strap-end. Length 35 mm. Clarke and Carter (1977, 288 ff., Fig. 130, no. 27) from King's Lynn.
Layer 540.
A.M.L. 765764.

36. Tag-end, 34 mm. Type as last.
Layer 582.
A.M.L. 777538.

37. Tag-end, as last but with two piercings. Length 40 mm. Fingerlin (1971, 63, Fig. 50 and 353, no. 105).
Layer 561.
A.M.L. 765796.

38. Tag-end with three piercings. Length 32 mm.
Layer 500.
A.M.L. 765785.

39. Small piece of metal sheet, curved end with two piercings. Probably part of tag-end. Length 17 mm.
Layer 582.
A.M.L. 777540.

40. Piece of metal sheet with two piercings, perhaps part of tag-end. Length 12 mm.
Layer 727.
A.M.L. 777545.

41. Belt mounting, rectangular, convex. It is pierced by two rivets on either side of a larger central hole. Length 16 mm. Compare Fingerlin (1971, 322 ff., no. 47, dated early fifteenth century).
Layer 766.
A.M.L. 777575.

42. Rectangular belt mounting; type as last–only one rivet remains. Length 17 mm.
Unstratified.
A.M.L. 777524.

43. Belt mounting; type similar to last, but top of plate is flat. Both the rivets and the lower plate remain. Upper surface has simple incised decoration, three lines on each side and a 'St. Andrew's cross' scored across central portion. Length 24 mm.
Layer 3.
A.M.L. 765666.

44. Belt mounting, triangular section – expansion at centre point for piercing – rivet at each end

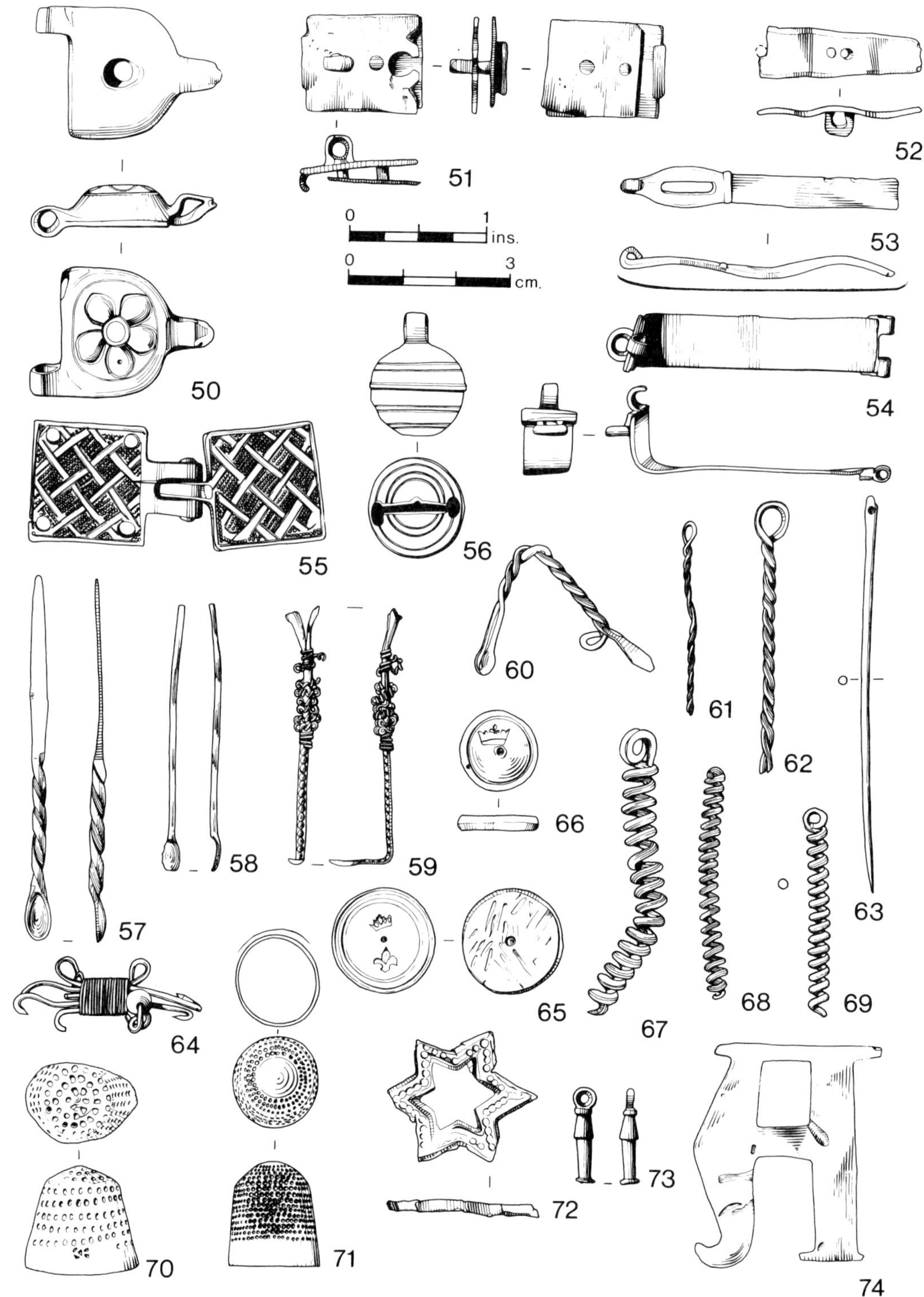

Fig. 69. Small Finds, 1976–78, Medieval, silvered Copper Alloy, Copper Alloy and Pewter.

(one remains). Decoration consists of striations on either side of central ridge. Length 16 mm. Compare Hall (1973, 113 and Fig. 4, no. 14) from Strixton, Northants. – thirteenth century.
Layer 582.
A.M.L. 777542.

45. Belt mounting, flat sheet, elongated oval with ring-shaped projection at each end for rivets (which are now lost). Much flimsier than nos. 41–44, but probably an object of the same type. Length 15 mm. Not illustrated. Compare Hall (1973, 113 and Fig. 4, no. 20) from Strixton, Northants. – thirteenth century.
Layer 557.
A.M.L. 765817.
46. Copper alloy boss with three trilobed extensions each pierced by a rivet-hole; almost certainly a belt-fitting. 26 mm.
Layer 503.
A.M.L. 765715.
47. Belt fitting. Sheet bronze boss with central rivet hole, and four raised extensions giving a quatrefoil shape. 12 mm. Cf. Fingerlin (1971, Figs. 85 and 103).
Layer 764.
A.M.L. 777559.
48. Copper alloy belt fitting in quatrefoil form. Back flat and plain. Broken; hook missing, 15 mm. For openwork hooked strap ends: Miles (1975, 96 ff. Fig. 66, 3) from Abingdon; Rigold (1970, 346 and Fig. 1 no. 5) St. Augustine's.
Layer 513.
A.M.L. 765739.
49. Copper alloy book-clasp or hinge-end. Two plates riveted together, the upper ending in a simple ogival moulding, and the lower a simple rectangle of bronze sheet. The upper plate is broken. Surviving length 40 mm.; width at moulding 23 mm. Compare Hobley (1970, 119, no. 2, Fig. 16) from St. Mary, Coventry, and especially Moorhouse (1971a, 59 and Fig. 25, no. 162 which has backing strip).
Layer 5025.
A.M.L. 782510.

Fig. 69, nos. 50–74

50. Gilt copper alloy hinged fitting. It is convex, ornamented on top with a five-petalled rosette pierced at the centre. In front is a loop. Probably the front portion of a two-part book clasp.
Layer 763.
A.M.L. 777590.
51. Copper alloy clasp – upper plate has an almost circular cut breaking the end of one of the short sides, and a curving extension at the end of the other; a transverse piercing runs through a small vertical attachment on it. Lower plate a simple rectangle – two rivets. Length 22 mm.; width 18 mm. Compare Williams (1978, 149 and Fig. 22, no. CV 12) from Greyfriars, Northampton, for a more simply made version.
Layer 513.
A.M.L. 765729.

52. Copper alloy clasp, with similar vertical attachment; broken but with part of hole for stud at one of the breaks. Surviving length 30 mm.; width 9 mm.
Layer 18.
A.M.L. 765731.
53. Copper alloy strip, slightly convex, with ovoid head open in the centre and simple curved termination beyond it. It may be part of a box fitting or a book-clasp. Length 51.5 mm.
Layer 1.
A.M.L. 765714.
54. Copper alloy strip with raised loop and hook at one end and hinge at the other end. Probably a book-clasp. Length 60 mm.
Unstratified.
A.M.L. 777612.
55. Hinged harness-pendant of silvered copper alloy, decorated with a strap-work pattern. The plate with the two outer hinge tongues is pierced by a hole at each corner. For the type, see Biddle (1961–62, 172 and Fig. 28 no. 25) from Seacourt; Drewett (1975, 142 and Fig. 28, no. 345) from Hadleigh Castle, Essex – both are examples of plate with single, central hinge-tongue. Fourteenth century.
Layer 766.
A.M.L. 777593.
56. Rumbler-bell, moulding around waist, contains small pea-sized ball. Height 19 mm. Platt and Coleman-Smith (1975, 255 ff., Fig. 240, no. 1726; Pl. 120, late thirteenth century).
Layer 721.
A.M.L. 777539.
57. Cosmetic spoon, small ovoid bowl, twisted neck and simple elongated handle, perhaps for use in manicure. Length 66 mm. Cf. Platt and Coleman-Smith (1975, 269 and Fig. 246, no. 1901, fourteenth-century pewter example, with arrow-headed manicure terminal).
Layer 20.
A.M.L. 765726.
58. Cosmetic spoon, small ovoid bowl and simple straight handle. Length 48 mm.
Layer 31.
A.M.L. 765763.
59. Cosmetic spoon hammered out of sheet (flat section), simple blob ornamentation along it; wire waist, and spatula projecting from the other end (now broken). Surviving length 57 mm.
Unstratified.
A.M.L. 782511.
60. Cosmetic spoon made by bending a piece of wire and hammering out a spoon; the stem is of twisted wire and terminates in a rhomboidal spatulate end. Length 55 mm. Compare Neal (1973, 53 ff. and Fig. XIV, no. 46); Platt and Coleman-Smith (1975, 264 and Fig. 244, no. 1851); Andrews (1977, 196 and Pl. XLI, 54).
Layer 763.
A.M.L. 777587.
61. Coiled wire with loop at end; conceivably a stage in the manufacture of cosmetic implements like the above. 34 mm. long. Compare Neal (1973, 51 ff. and Fig. XIII, no. 36) from King's Langley.

Layer 763.
A.M.L. 777588.

62. Another example of the same.
Layer 715.
A.M.L. 777604.

63. Pointed probe from a manicure set. Its head is somewhat wider and includes a depression, perhaps for attaching to other toilet implements. Length 72 mm.
Layer 774.
A.M.L. 777594.

64. Dress fastening; ten projections one of which still has a bead (? of bone) on it – possibly ornamental. Greatest length 35 mm. Compare Woods (1982b, 256 and Fig. 26, nos. 12, 13) from Eltham Palace; Geddes (1985, Fig. 51, no. 62) from Battle Abbey.
Layer 763.
A.M.L. 777560.

65. Cylindrical weight with crown and fleur-de-lys stamped on it. Slight depression between them; diameter 19 mm.; thickness 2.5 mm. It weighs 6.89 grammes.
Layer 24.
A.M.L. 765758.

66. Cylindrical weight with crown stamped on it; slight depression below; diameter 14 mm.; thickness 2.5 mm. It weighs 3.63 grammes. Compare Drury (1974, 56, Fig. 8, 13) from Chelmsford Blackfriars.
Layer 39.
A.M.L. 765783.

67. Copper alloy spring, length 51 mm. Compare Lambrick and Woods (1976, 216 and Fig. 12, no. 21) from Oxford Blackfriars; Williams (1978, 151 and Fig. 22, no. 26) from Northampton Greyfriars.
Layer 18.
A.M.L. 765728.

68. Copper alloy spring, length 41 mm.
Layer 26.
A.M.L. 765745.

69. Copper alloy spring, length 37 mm.
Unstratified.
A.M.L. 782539.

70. Thimble; apart from a plain area near the base, it is covered with small depressions which spiral round to the apex. Height 19 mm. Compare Biddle *et al.* (1959, 182 f, Fig. 19, no. 13).
Layer 3.
A.M.L. 765718.

71. Thimble, plain areas near base and at top; depressions around body. Height 20 mm.
Layer 720.
A.M.L. 777603.

72. Ornament of pewter in form of six-pointed star, openwork. Star is decorated with small blobs. Diam. 27 mm.

Layer 574.
A.M.L. 765886.

73. Small copper alloy object suspended from a loop – probably a pendant. Length 17 mm.
Layer 1040.
A.M.L. 777580.

74. Copper alloy letter A. (See note by John Blair, below, p. 231).
Layer 515.
A.M.L. 765733.

75. Copper alloy object, partly of rectangular section and partly cylindrical. Use uncertain. Length 10.5 mm. Not illustrated.
Layer 1002.
A.M.L. 765780.

Fig. 70, nos. 76–105.

76. Length of tubing, flattened and pierced at one end. 73 mm.
Layer 754.
A.M.L. 777554.

77. Simple copper alloy hook. 18 mm. Not illustrated.
Area III, unstratified.
A.M.L. 765807.

78. Copper alloy rod, rectangular section. Not illustrated. 48 mm.
Layer 522.
A.M.L. 765725.

79. Copper alloy rod, rectangular section and pointed end. Probably a nail. 37 mm.
Layer 720.
A.M.L. 777549.

80. Copper alloy stud, domed; with pin of rectangular section. Height 21 mm.; diam. 20 mm.
Layer 540.
A.M.L. 765756.

81. Stud, domed. Pin missing. Diam. 20 mm.
Layer 1002.
A.M.L. 765790.

82. Stud, pin missing. Hole in centre of head. Diam. 11 mm.
Layer 35.
A.M.L. 765778.

83. Stud or tack, head gilded. Height 10 mm.; diam. 8 mm. Not illustrated.
Layer 31.
A.M.L. 765767.

84. Bronze pin with lentoid head, the upper part ridged in a flower or star-shaped motif. Length 55 mm. A similar pin in the site museum, S.A.M. 59; also for the ornamentation, Farley (1976, 241 and Fig. 35, 8) late Anglo-Saxon from Walton, Aylesbury.
Layer 513.
A.M.L. 765765.

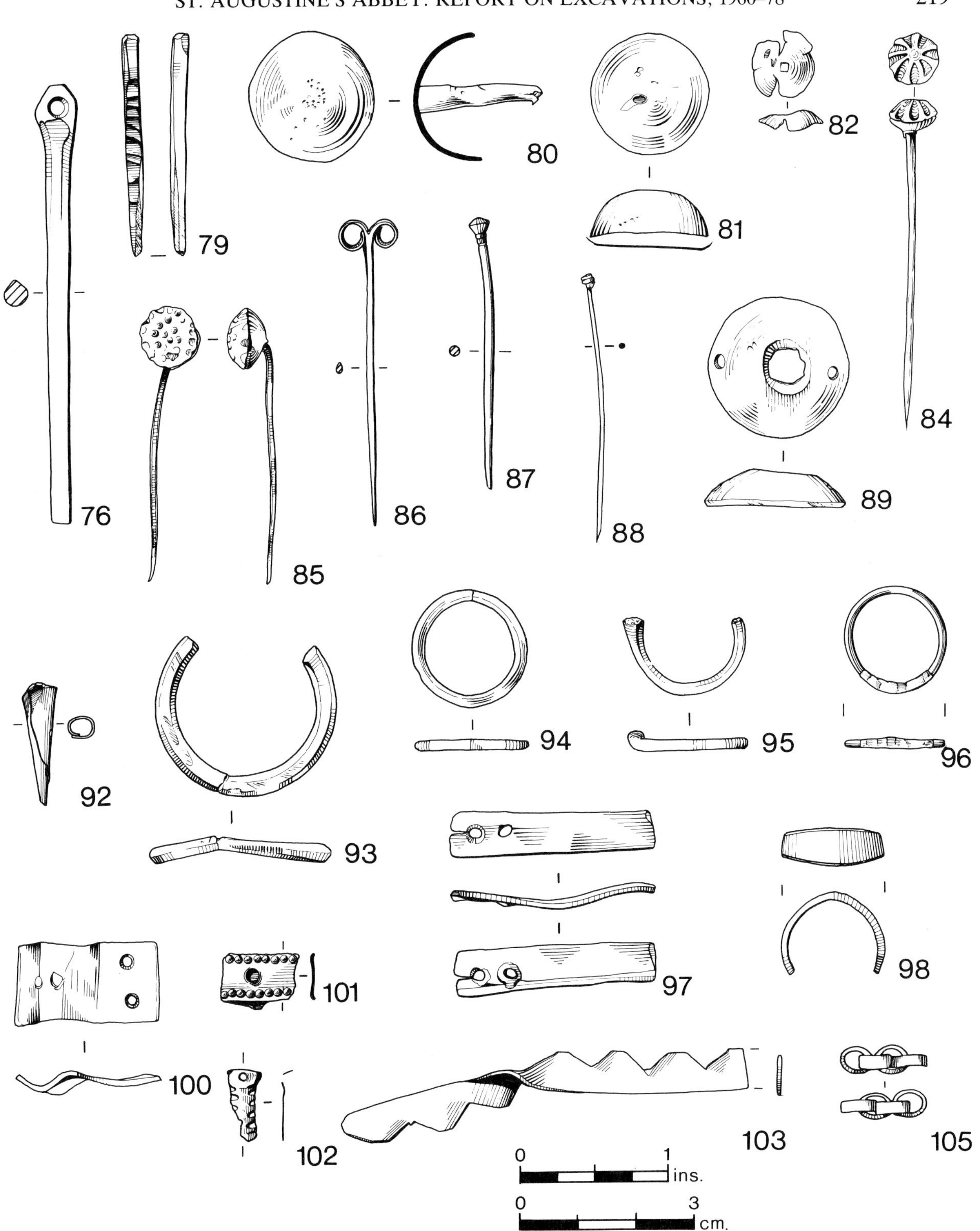

Fig. 70. Small Finds, 1976–78, Medieval, Copper Alloy.

85. Pin with lentoid head, which is hollow and filled with lead. Length 46 mm. Cf. Fig. 60, no. 27, above.
Layer 513.
A.M.L. 765723.
86. Pin with head made by splitting metal and bending it over on each side. Length 51 mm. Compare Steane and Bryant (1971, 53 and Fig. 12t); Dunning (1965, 62 and Fig. 10).
Layer 766.
A.M.L. 777570.
87. Pin with convex head and simple moulding on neck. Length 45 mm.
Layer 748.
A.M.L. 777555.
88. Pin with drawn stem, head of coiled wire. Length 45 mm. 117 others from this part of the site. Compare also, p. 194, nos. 34–35.
Layer 540.
A.M.L. 765755.
89. Boss of copper alloy, convex; central hole and two rivet holes one on each side. Diam. 24mm.
Layer 560.
A.M.L. 765795.
90. Boss of copper alloy, as last but no rivet holes. ? washer. Diam. 12 mm. Not illustrated.
Layer 513.
A.M.L. 765750.
91. 'Boot-lace tag' containing remains of leather. 30 mm. Not illustrated. See also, no. 40, p. 195, above.
Layer 509.
A.M.L. 765719.
92. Curled piece of bronze, now conical in shape. Probably a tag-end.
Layer 5161.
A.M.L. 782547.
93. Ring, circular section but slightly flattened at one point. Diam. 31 mm.
Layer 515.
A.M.L. 765732.
94. Ring, complete, diam. 19 mm.
Layer 533.
A.M.L. 765757.
95. Half ring, diam. 21 mm.
Layer 503.
A.M.L. 765717.
Not illustrated: part of ring, length 23 mm. Layer 513. A.M.L. 765749; half harness ring, diam. 33 mm. Layer 8. A.M.L. 765827; fragment of ring, length 14 mm. Layer 513. A.M.L. 765737; fragment of ring, length 15 mm. Layer 503. A.M.L. 765727.
96. Simple ring, type similar to last but hoop is thickened at one point and seems to be ornamented with striations. Diam. 15 mm.
Layer 709.
A.M.L. 777543.

97. Strip of bronze pierced by two holes.
Layer 763.
A.M.L. 777573.
98. Strip of metal, flange along edge, probably an off-cut from sheet. Length 17 mm.
Unstratified.
A.M.L. 782500.
99. Strip of metal pierced by a rivet hole at each end. Length 35 mm. Not illustrated.
Layer 545.
A.M.L. 765761.
100. Rectangular strip of metal pierced by two rivet holes at one end, and one at the other; possibly a strap-end plate. Length 25 mm.
Layer 503.
A.M.L. 765716.
101. Strip of metal with beading around the edge. Length 20 mm. Compare Addyman and Priestley (1977, 142 and 145, Fig. 11, no. 83) from Baile Hill, York.
Layer 5089.
A.M.L. 782540.
102. Small piece of sheet with transverse ridges and rivet hole through one end – possibly a belt mounting like 45 above. Length 12 mm.
Layer 53.
A.M.L. 777551.
103. Strip of metal with wave-like cuts along its length. Length 70 mm.
Layer 720.
A.M.L. 777550.
104. Two lengths of wire twisted together into simple chain. Length 120 mm. Not illustrated.
Layer 5012.
A.M.L. 782504.
105. Length of chain, four links. 15 mm.
Layer 588.
A.M.L. 765816.
106. Heavy piece of metal, in the form of a segment of a cylinder. Perhaps an ingot formed by the melting down of scrap. Length 80 mm. Not illustrated.
Layer 5071.
A.M.L. 782513.

Lead

Fig. 71. Nos. 110–137

110. Perforated lead object. Cf. Lambrick and Woods 1976, 216, no. 32, Fig. 12.
Layer 18.
A.M.L. 765879.
111. Lead pencil, circular section – one end rounded and the other pointed. Length 138 mm.

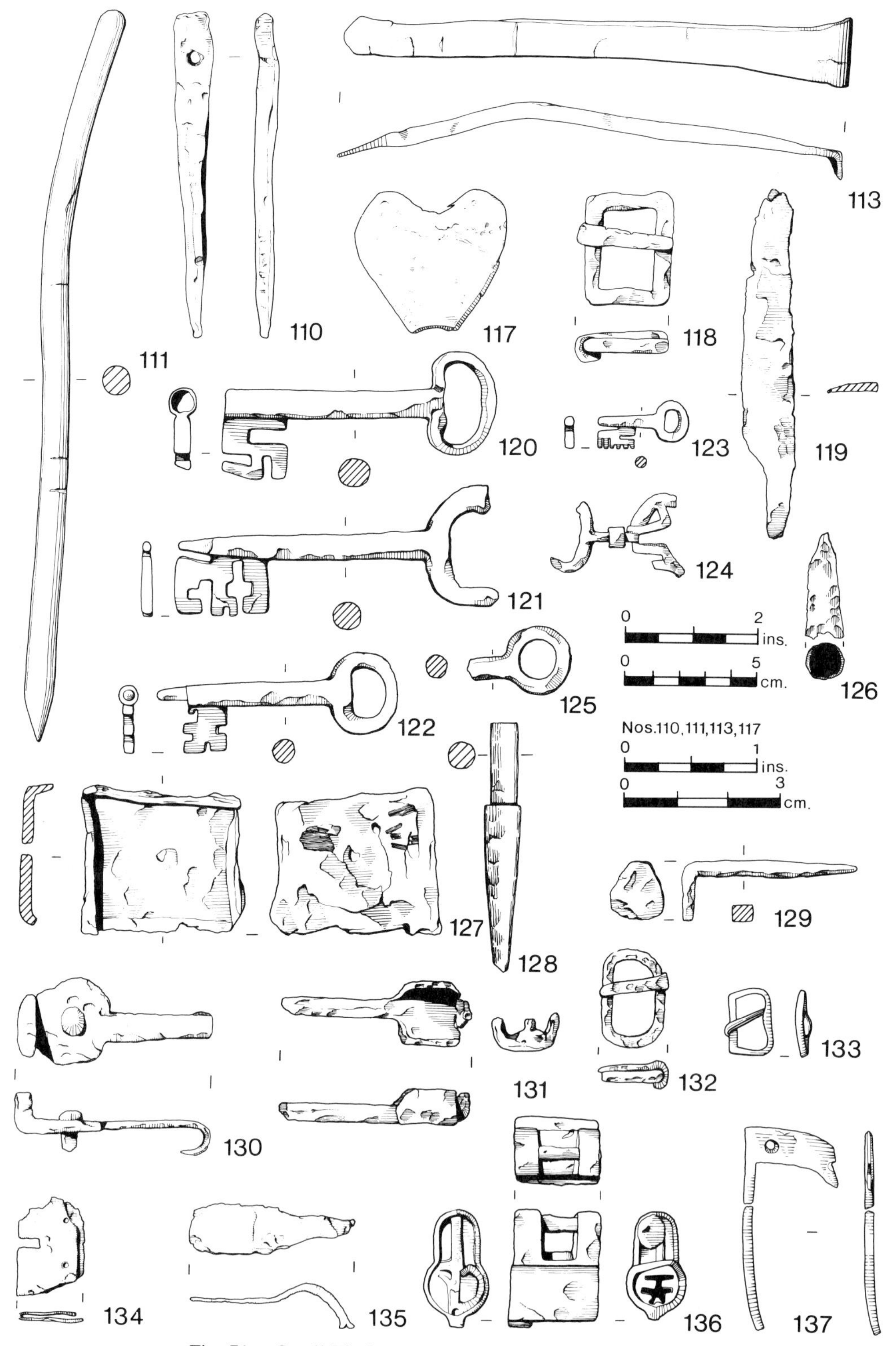

Fig. 71. Small Finds, 1976–78, Medieval, Lead and Iron.

Compare Lambrick and Woods (1976, 216 no. 29, Fig. 12); also Poulton and Woods (1984, Fig. 46, no. 44) from Guildford Dominican Friary.
Layer 5071.
A.M.L. 782415.

112. Lead pencil, type as last. 50 mm. Not illustrated.
Layer 763.
(No A.M.L. no.).

113. Flat strip of lead, slightly pointed at one end; bent at the other. Length 100 mm. Layer 5069. A.M.L. 782414.

114. Lead bar, flattened at one end, and rectangular in section at the other. Length 68 mm. Not illustrated.
Layer 1000.
A.M.L. 765885.

115. Strip of lead with a projection at each end. Length 140 mm. Not illustrated.
Layer 1002.
A.M.L. 765883.

116. Piece of lead partly lapped around an iron bar. Not illustrated.
Layer 1002.
A.M.L. 765882.

117. Piece of lead sheet, heart shaped (with bottom of heart broken away). Length 2.7 mm.
Layer 540.
A.M.L. 765880.

Iron

118. Buckle, rectangular with rounded corners, 42 mm. x 36 mm. Simple pin. Compare Beresford (1977, 276, Fig. 46, 85); Cunliffe (1977, 201 and Fig. 108, no. 53).
Layer 5001.
A.M.L. 782369.

119. Knife blade, back slightly convex. 130 mm. Compare Platt and Coleman Smith (1975, 285 and Fig. 255, no. 2071).
Layer 715.
A.M.L. 777470.

120. Key with kidney-shaped bow, tubular shank, non-symmetrical wards. Length 104 mm. *L.M.M.C.*, 136 ff., type III.
Layer 701.
A.M.L. 777489.

121. Key with circular or ovoid bow, solid shank. Length 125 mm. *L.M.M.C.*, 139, type IV.
Layer 720.
A.M.L. 777492.

122. Key with circular bow, solid shank. Length 93 mm. *L.M.M.C.*, type IV. Cf. Biddle (1961/2, 182 and Fig. 31, no. 10).
Layer 582.
A.M.L. 777521.

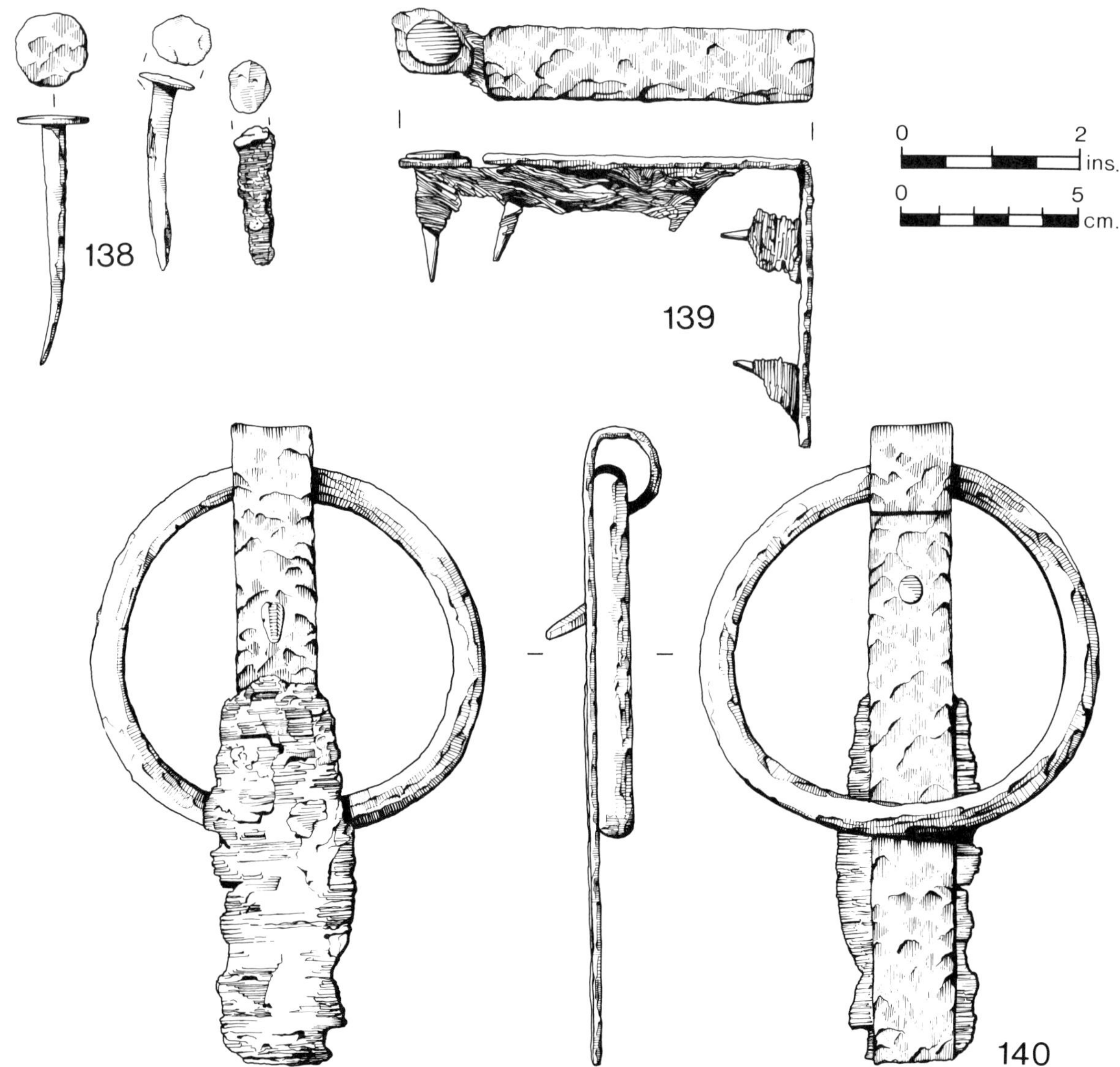

Fig. 72. Small Finds, 1976–78, Medieval, Iron.

123. Small key with circular bow and toothing along bit. Length 33 mm. *L.M.M.C.*, 139 and Pl. XXX, no. 27.
Layer 763.
A.M.L. 777466.

124. Iron object, probably a casket key. Bow and bit both incomplete. Surviving length 47 mm. *L.M.M.C.*, 143, type IX.
Layer 5089.
A.M.L. 782381.

125. Loop of casket key. Steane and Bryant (1975, 132 and Fig. 49, 160).
Layer 754.
A.M.L. 777458A.
126. Arrow-head. *L.M.M.C.*, type 5, for use in cross bow, cf. p. 71, no. A3825 (Pl. XV, 20) and p. 72 no. A27394 (Pl. XV, 19).
Layer 5028.
A.M.L. 782375A.
127. Iron 'box', rectangular with hole in centre of base. Some wood adheres to bottom; 60 x 50 x 12 mm.
Layer 762.
A.M.L. 777496.
128. Iron tool, perhaps bolster, made from a square sectioned bar with circular hammer end. Length 90 mm. Moorhouse (1971a, 44 and Fig. 20, no. 62).
Layer 5065.
A.M.L. 782377.
129. Iron bracket. Length 62 mm.
Layer 5154.
A.M.L. 782390.
130. Iron object expanded into leaf-form at one end and tapering at the other. Length 78 mm.
Layer 5016.
A.M.L. 782373.
131. Iron bar with socket at end, rushlight holder or candle holder. Cf. Steane and Bryant (1975, 119, no. 15. Fig. 45); and Beresford (1977, 258 and Fig. 46, nos. 69, 70).
Layer 761.
A.M.L. 777462.
132. Simple D-shaped buckle. Tongue now on wrong side of buckle. Cf. Beresford (1977, 258 and Fig. 46, no. 86).
Layer 720.
A.M.L. 777451A.
133. Simple D-shaped buckle; central thickening. Type characteristic of the fifteenth century. Cf. Fingerlin (1971, 197, no. 332 and 385, no. 213) – but the St. Augustine's example is much smaller.
Layer 574.
A.M.L. 765867.
134. Plate from strap-end buckle. Cf. Biddle (1961/2 168 and Fig. 28) from Seacourt.
Layer 766.
A.M.L. 777469A.
135. Fragment of a barrel – padlock key. Cf. *L.M.M.C.*, 146 ff., Figs. 44, 45.
Layer 766.
A.M.L. 777469B.
136. Barrel lock. Length 3.5 cm.
Layer 763.
A.M.L. 777500.
137. Part of an iron object pierced by two holes. Could be part of a simple latch mechanism.

Layer 502.
A.M.L. 765847.

Fig. 72. Nos. 138–140

138. Coffin nails.
Grave 1013.
A.M.L. 777510.
139. Corner bracket from coffin. One of a set of twelve (three at each corner). One example illustrated with wood adhering, and nails.
Grave 53.
A.M.L. 777522.
140. Support ring from coffin. One of a pair (one at each end). One example illustrated with wood adhering.
Grave 53.
A.M.L. 777515.

Stone

Fig. 73. Nos. 141–145

141. Whetstone, broken at one end.
Layer 5087.
A.M.L. 782417.
142. Whetstone, similar to last, also broken at one end.
Layer 5001.
A.M.L. 782418.
143. Fragment of whetstone.
Layer 5089.
A.M.L. 782419.
144. Fragment of a Caen-stone cresset lamp. The interior is fire-blackened.
Layer 766.
145. Base of Purbeck marble mortar with handle extending to base on one side (illustrated from underside).
Layer 771.

Painted Plaster

Fig. 73.

146. Wall-plaster with decoration in red and yellow paint, over a white wash.
Layer 1054.
A.M.L. 782309.

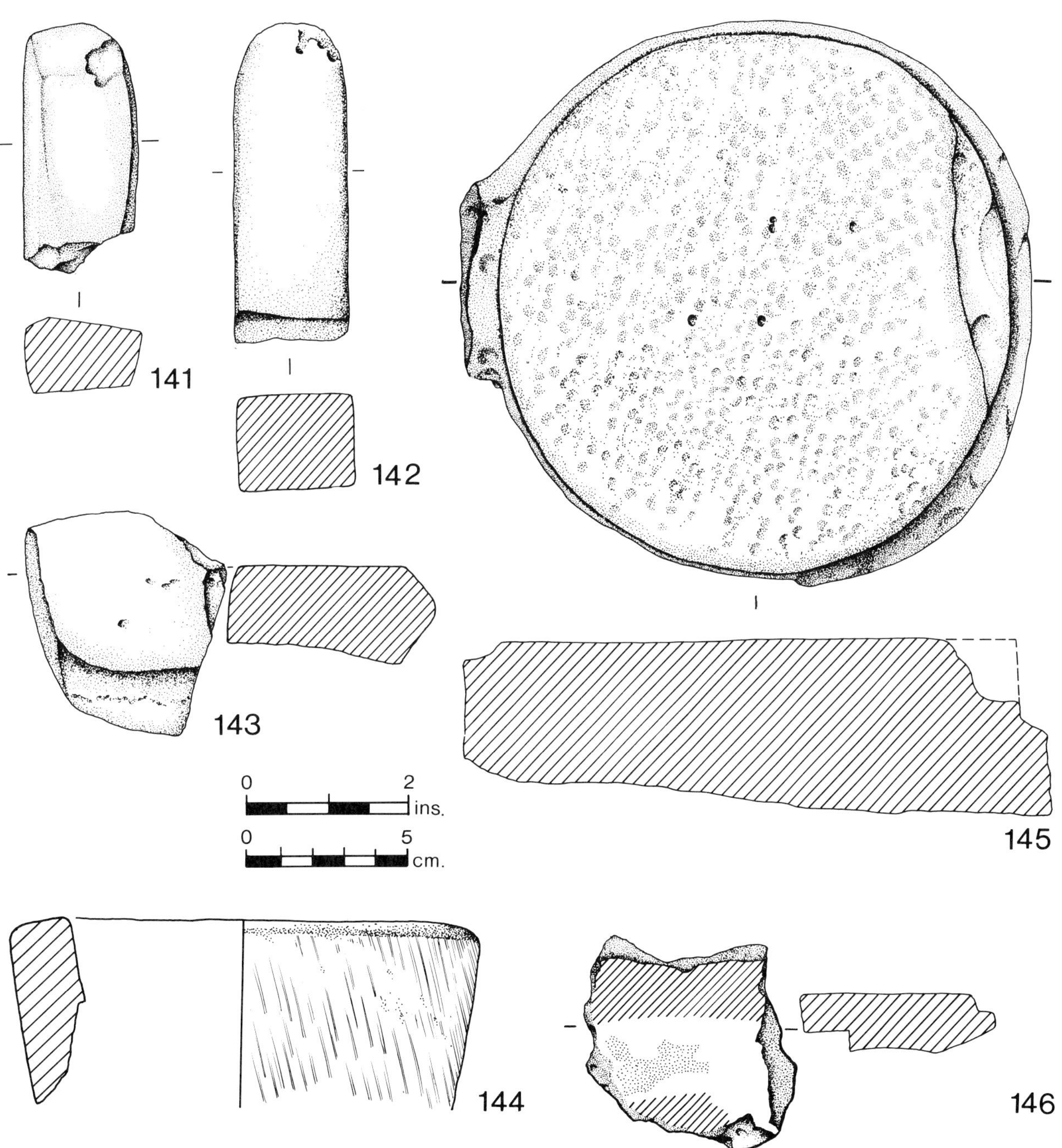

Fig. 73. Small Finds, 1976–78, Medieval, Stone and Plaster.

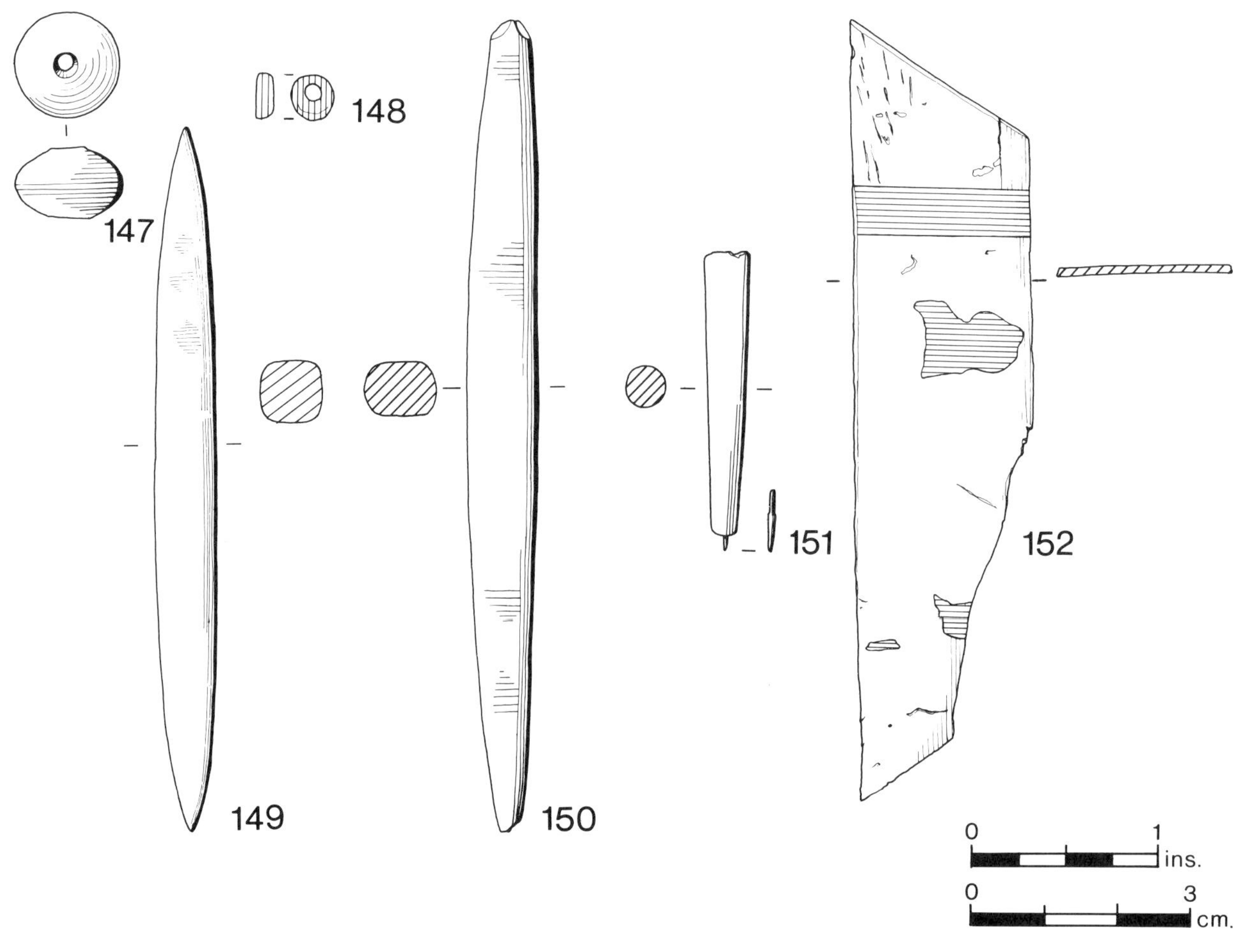

Fig. 74. Small Finds, 1976–78, Medieval Amber and Bone.

Beads

Fig. 74. Nos. 147–152

147. Amber rosary bead, ovoid section. Length 14 mm.; width 9 mm. See Mead (1977 for the industry in London, esp. Pl. 5); Platt and Coleman-Smith (1975, 276 and Fig. 249, no. 1956); Dunning (1965, 61 and Fig. 91).
    Layer 733.
    A.M.L. 777614.
148. Small bead of green glass. Diam. 5 mm.
    Unstratified.
    A.M.L. 782423.

Bone

149. Bone object, tapering at each end; very smoothly polished. Length 94 mm. Usually described as a 'thread picker' or 'pin-beater' (and the discovery of similar objects on simple occupation sites does suggest some such domestic use although the piece would have been ideal for applying gold-leaf to manuscripts, and it is by no means impossible that it had this function here). Addyman and Hill (1969, 76 and Fig. 29); Leeds (1923, 182 ff., Pl. XXVIII, Fig. 2); Jope and Pantin (1958, 73 and Fig. 25c); Farley (1976, 216 and Fig. 25, no. 2). Cf. Cook (1978, 228, Burial 10 and 233). Pin-beaters do not appear in Saxon times before the seventh century.
Layer 5066.
A.M.L. 782420.
150. Bone object of 'thread picker' type, similar to last. Length 107 mm.
Layer 763.
A.M.L. 777619.
151. Bone bodkin with small bronze pin inserted at the point; the head is broken. Length 38 mm. This is an object of the type usually described as a 'bodkin' but, following P.D.C. Brown's suggestion, most likely to have been used in pricking out lines in manuscripts. Cf. Durham (1977, 163 and Fig. 38, 15); Tebbutt (1966, 52 and Fig. 4e). Prickers of the same general form are used for both pricking out patterns on parchment, and for lace-making.
Layer 766.
A.M.L. 777598.
152. Strip of bone ornamented with stripe of blue paint. Possibly from a shrine or casket; the survival of paint is unusual though box-mountings with engraved ornament are not unusual.
Layer 1034.
A.M.L. 777618.

Post-Medieval

Iron and bone

Fig. 75. Nos. 1–8

1. Knife, iron blade is broken but the flat tang together with bone plates affixed by three rivets on each side remains. Surviving length 130 mm. (plates 95 mm.). Cf. Neal (1973, 53 and Fig. XIV, no. 56) King's Langley.
Layer 5001.
A.M.L. 782314.
2. Knife. Type as last but blade is almost completely lost. The bone plates are affixed by four rivets. Length of handle 113 mm.
Layer 5001.
A.M.L. 782313.

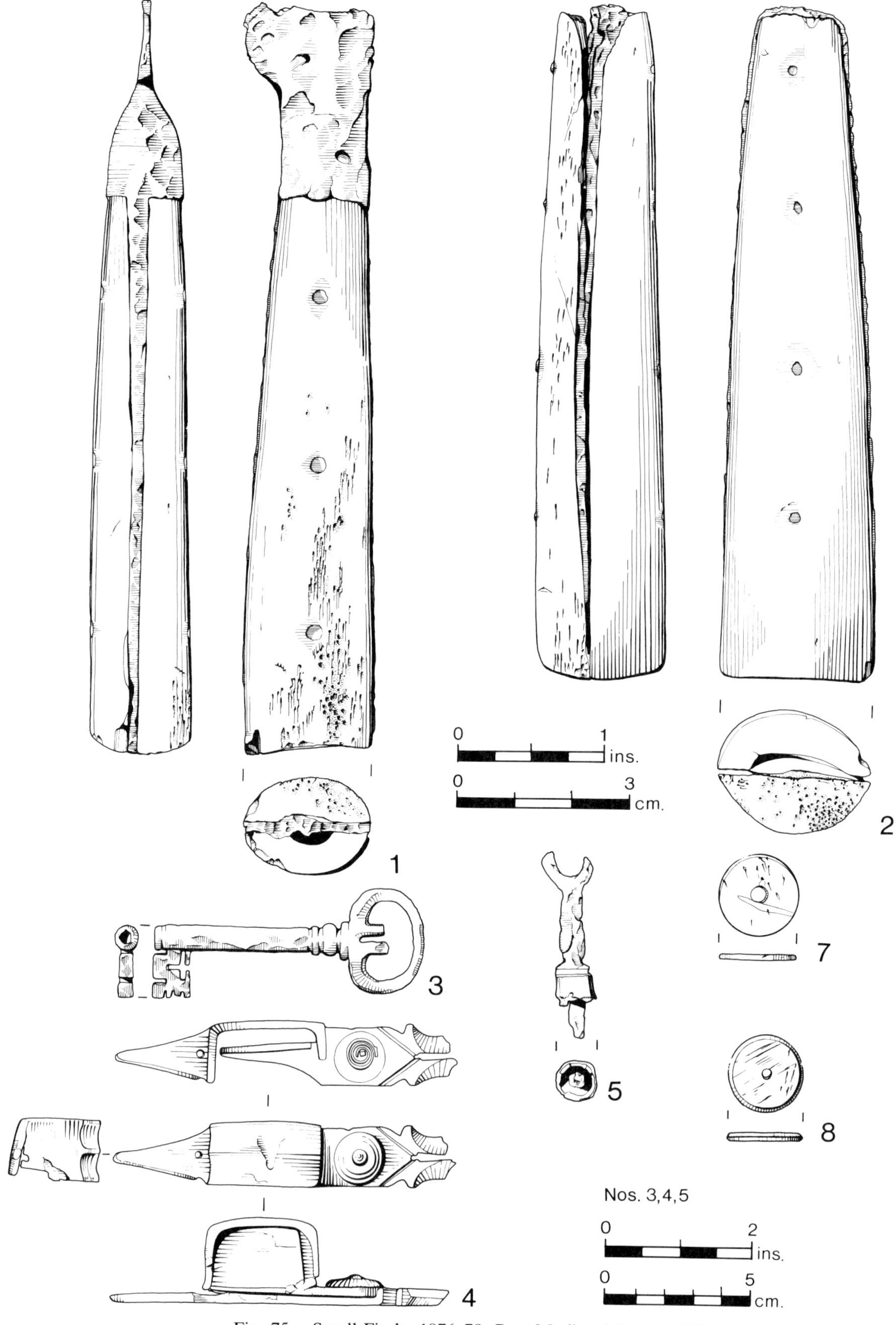

Fig. 75. Small Finds, 1976–78, Post-Medieval Iron and Bone.

3. Key with kidney-shaped bow and two central projections. Moulding around the neck below the bow. Tubular shank, non-symmetrical wards. Length 95 mm. *L.M.M.C.*, type III. Type as Ashmolean Museum 1887, 2941 from Stanton Harcourt, said to be sixteenth or seventeenth century. Cf. *L.M.M.C.*, 137, and Pl. XXXI, no. 42, which is simpler and less elegant than the St. Augustine's specimen, and probably medieval.
   Layer 5001.
   A.M.L. 782368.
4. Candle snuffers, with spike in front. The handles are lost. Eighteenth-century type. Cf. Lindsay (1964, 57 and Fig. 344).
   Layer 551.
   A.M.L. 765864.
5. Tanged two-pronged fork (the prongs are broken). Seventeenth or eighteenth century.
   Layer 5001.
   A.M.L. 777474.
6. Bone disc with hole in centre, probably a button, diam. of disc 23 mm. Platt and Coleman-Smith (1975, 274 and Fig. 249, no. 1948, (dated, probably, to seventeenth century); Durham (1977, 163 and Fig. 38, nos. 23–25). Not illustrated.
   Unstratified.
   A.M.L. 782421.
7. Bone disc with central piercing; type as last. Diam. 13 mm. Eighteenth century.
   Layer 5017.
   A.M.L. 782422.
8. Bone disc with central piercing; as last. Diam. 12 mm. Eighteenth century.
   Layer 503.
   A.M.L. 765665.

MONUMENTAL BRASS FRAGMENTS John Blair

Six additional fragments of monumental brasses, from a private source and now in the Victoria and Albert Museum, are known to have been found on the site of St. Augustine's Abbey (Fig. 76).

1. Portion of an open octofoil crosshead, 9.8 cm. long and 0.3 cm. thick. Two foliate terminals remain, and the band between is decorated with pellets-within-circles of which one serves as a rivet hole (the rivet remaining in position). One end was originally a joint between two plates, bevelled on the rear face and bearing traces of solder; the other is snapped off. The back remains rough from the casting of the plate. This fragment was undoubtedly engraved from the same pattern as the brass to Robert de Tring (1351) in Merton College chapel, Oxford (Blair 1981, Fig. 62, 63). It is virtually identical with the surviving half of the top right-hand foil of Tring's cross, and the plates were joined in the same position. Like the Oxford example, the brass at St. Augustine's probably had a small figure enclosed within the crosshead. The fragment provides an interesting early example of the exact reduplication of designs.

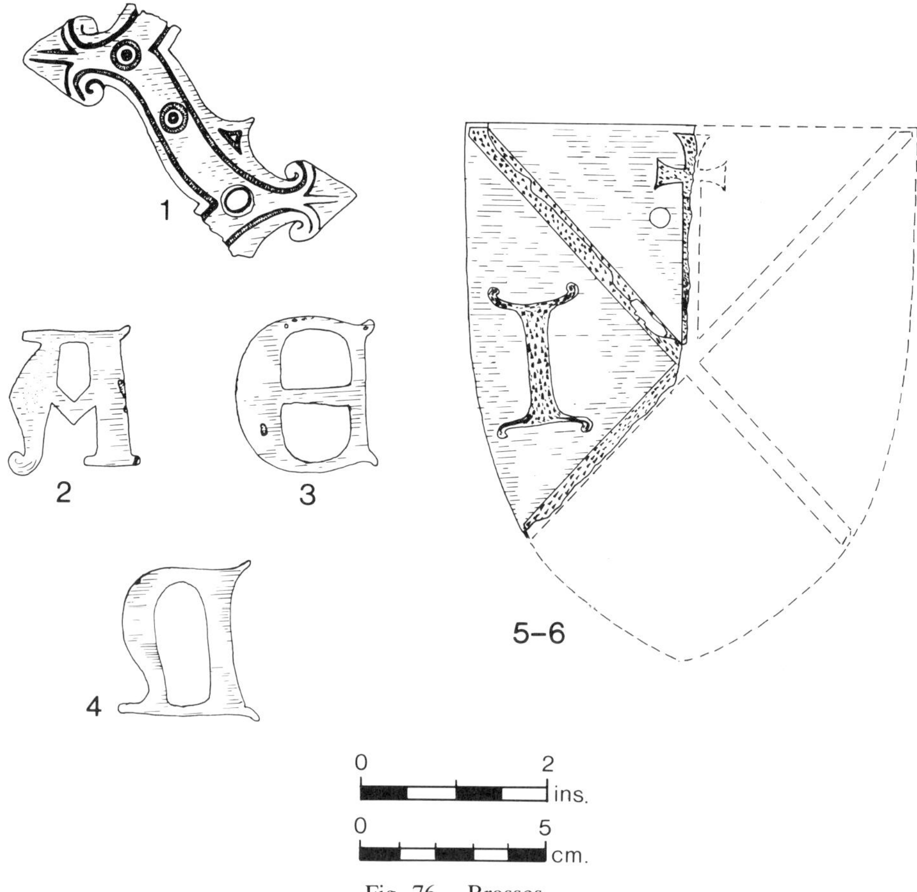

Fig. 76. Brasses.

2. Individual-inlay Lombardick letter A, Main Group size III. (Blair 1981, Fig. 57; Blair, forthcoming). Height 3.6 cm. thickness 0.2 cm.
3. Individual-inlay Lombardick letter E, Main Group size II. Height 4.1 cm., thickness 0.2 cm. For technical analysis see below, p. 233.
4. Individual-inlay Lombardick back-to-front letter N, Main Group size II. Height 4.0 cm., thickness 0.2 cm.
5–6. Two contiguous fragments of a brass shield, representing about one-third of its total area. The plate is 0.2 cm. thick, and when complete would have measured about 14.3 × 12.2 cm. The edges are filed on a slight bevel and one rivet hole is present. The shield was apparently divided in four by a saltire, the upper quarter containing a cross on a long stem and the dexter quarter a Lombardick letter I; presumably it was either a merchant's mark or an 'IHS' religious device. The incisions are broad and flat-bottomed, with their inner surface roughened by stabs of the graving tool; they must have been filled with colouring composition.

TECHNICAL ANALYSIS OF THE EARLY FOURTEENTH-CENTURY BRASS LETTERS
Peter Northover and John Blair

Five letters – two As, two Es and an N – are available from the site. One of the Es (Fig. 76, no. 3) was examined to determine the method of manufacture. A serif was sawn off, mounted in a conducting resin, and ground and polished to obtain a cross-section. This was etched in acidified ferric chloride solution and examined in the optical microscope. The structure is that of an as-cast $\propto$ brass, and the grain size is relatively small (as would be expected in such a small casting where cooling rates would be high). No obvious sign of surface working was observed, suggesting that the letter had been cast virtually in its final form, nor was there any indication that it had been cut from a cast sheet.

This supports the conclusion, already drawn on typological grounds, that brass letters were made in moulds, not cut out (Brownsword, forthcoming). The letters were evidently cast in moulds made by stamping wooden patterns into clay. The production of multiple letters from the same mould or stamp is illustrated by four identical Es found on the site of the London Greyfriars (now in the Department of Medieval and Later Antiquities, British Museum).

The major element content of the same specimen was determined by electron probe microanalysis, and two other letters were analysed by nondispersal X-ray fluorescence in the British Museum Research Laboratory. We are grateful to Dr Paul Craddock for two of the analyses. The results were as follows (to the nearest 1%):

	Cu(%)	*Zn(%)*	*Sn(%)*	*Pb(%)*
Fig. 76, no. 3	*c.* 80	*c.* 17	1	*c.* 2
A.M.L. 743695	78	12	4	6
A.M.L. 765733	83	8	4	5

These are consistent with Dr H.K. Cameron's analyses of early figure brasses and another brass letter (Cameron 1975, 10; Cameron, 1974, 229).

The back-to-front N (above, Fig. 76, no. 4) was apparently cast in a reversed mould, not reversed as part of a finishing process: the back is rough from the underside of the casting in the usual way. A letter R found on the site of the Oxford Greyfriars provides another instance of this peculiarity (report in *Oxoniensia*, forthcoming).

THE TEXTILES Elisabeth Crowfoot

1. Fragment of Silk

One fragment of embroidered silk, 4.0 × 1.5 cm. overall, with 0.5–0.6 cm. folded underneath on one long side of a roughly triangular piece, and 0.3 cm. folded under on the adjoining edge

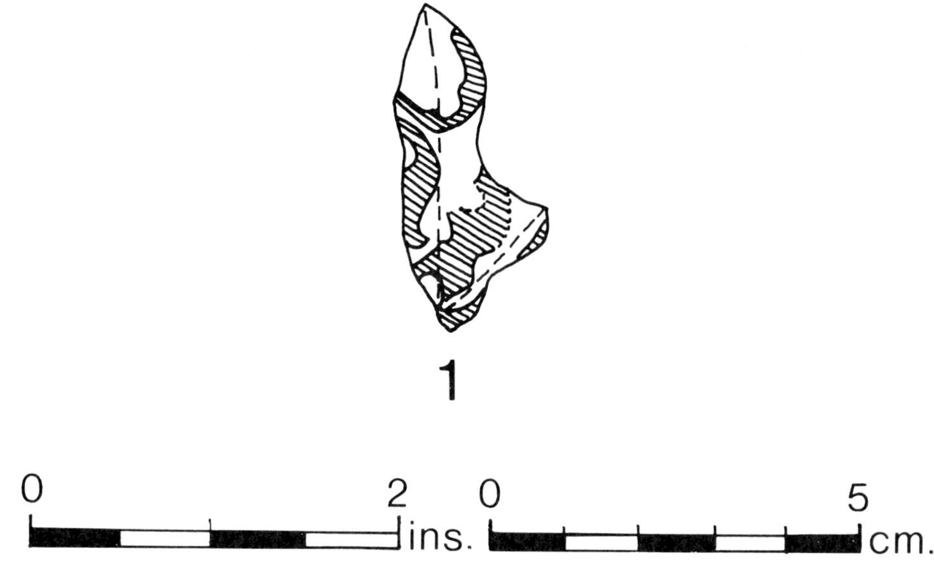

Fig. 77, a. Textile.

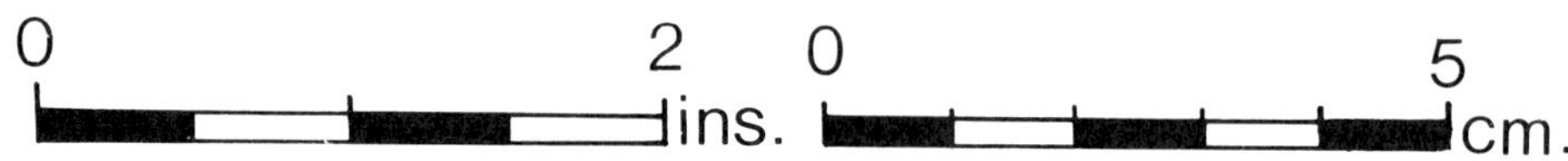

Fig. 77, b. Textile.

(Fig. 77, a). Both yarns are of silk, one system is slightly Z spun (?warp), the other unspun; the weave is tabby, the count *c.* 52/26 threads per cm., taken as 26/13 on 5 mm.; the colour is now dark brownish but was perhaps originally purple. There are remains of a surface pattern, all that can be seen suggesting a scroll with leaves; this is embroidered in couching, with a spun-gold (silver-gilt) thread, held down with rather coarse light-coloured unspun silk, perhaps originally yellow; the core of the laid thread has completely disappeared, suggesting that this may not have been of silk, but of some vegetable fibre such as flax. The couching threads are broken in many places, but can be seen here and there on the back of the fragment.

The shape of the fragment suggests the mitred corner of the border to a vestment or altar frontal; the couching continues under the turned-up edge, as would be natural in an embroidered ribbon, or strip cut from a larger area of embroidery used for this purpose. The surface couching used here is the method seen on embroideries in England from the early tenth century onwards – for example the stole and maniples among the relics of St. Cuthbert at Durham (Battiscombe 1956, 381–94, Pls. XXVI–XXXII). From the twelfth to the fourteenth century underside couching (*point couché rentré* or *retiré*), in which no stitches can be seen on the surface of the gold threads (Christie 1948, 135–41; Battiscombe 1956, 387), was used for fine ecclesiastical embroideries, but surface couching continued in general use on furnishings and vestments, as in the coarse fragments preserved at St. Augustine's from the woollen chasuble of Abbot Dygon (*d.* 1510) (Crowfoot 1981, 81–2). Late medieval.
Layer 513, post Dissolution deposit in Area III Chapel.
A.M.L. 765664.

2. Copper alloy gilt mount from ring.
   Underneath glass jewel was gold leaf (too delicate to remove), and showing beneath it, a white fragment of weave used as bedding, Z, Z, probably tabby, count 6/7 on 5 mm.; its threads were very well preserved. The fibre identified by H.M. Appleyard, F.T.I., was well-preserved flax. (See above, 12a, p. 207).
   Layer 513.
   A.M.L. 765753
3. Textiles from lead coffin in vault 1051. All from layer 1056.
   (a) With hair and organic substance from lower left side of skull and neck, some replaced fragments and impressions of fine Z spun twill; see (c) below.
   (b) On some pieces, impression of fabric, areas 2.4 × 1.1 and 3.0 × 1.4 cm. at widest parts, ?Z spun, tabby weave, count 10/9 on 5 mm.; one fragment of grave filling has a rough impression all over the 4.0 × 4.0 cm. surface. Probably shroud material, see (d) below.
   (c) The sample was extremely deteriorated, mostly an impression, but in some areas there were a few replaced threads, of which the largest patch was 3.0 × 3.0 cm. The spinning was Z, Z, four-shed diamond twill (Fig. 77, b), very regular and fine, with a count estimated at *c.* 22/19 threads per cm. This weave, which would almost certainly have been of wool, lay in folds, one piece being in a curve.
   (d) Fragments possibly from shroud, most impregnated with gypsum and ?lead, some still slightly flexible, largest clear patch (i) 2.2 × 2.0 cm. (ii) 2.5 × 1.6 cm. in two layers; fine variable Z thread both systems, tabby weave, count 18–20/16–17 threads per cm. Fragment (i) has a neatly rolled hem (?) along one edge, 2.5 mm. deep, one stitch, and tuft of thread

broken on other side, visible. Threads identified by H.M. Appleyard as of animal fibre, very poor condition and very friable, i.e. the fabric was probably woollen.
(e) Many fragments of similar material to (d), Z spun tabby, in clear folds; largest fragment 3.5 × 2.0 cm., lying in long curve, suggesting a piece wrapped round the head.

These two fabrics must have been good quality wools of types commonly used for upper garments; the twill was perhaps only round the head, a cap or hood, while the tabby weave was wrapped all round the corpse. Apart from ecclesiastical robes or monks' habits, fabrics preserved in late-medieval burials normally come from shrouds. Though these are often of flax, the medieval use of the word shroud for garments such as cloaks for the living probably indicates that wool was also commonly used for shrouding burials.

COINS AND JETONS FROM EXCAVATIONS IN 1960 S.E. Rigold

Ancient British

1. Dubnovellaunus (in Cantium) Æ. 14 mm. Horse/dog over name. *Rev.* Horse. Mack 290. Other east Kent finds known. *c.* 5 B.C. Fresh, fairly soon lost.
   Surface of cemetery north-east of quire.
   A.M.L. 858508.

Roman

1. Vespasian, *denarius*. *RIC* 90. *Pax* seated, COS VI. A.D. 75. Worn, but not excessively. Lost early second century.
   Bank north of quire.
   A.M.L. 858509.
2. Marius, base *antoninianus*. *RIC* 7. CONCORDIA MILITVM, clasped hands. A.D. 268. Fresh, lost 270s.
   East of north transept.
   A.M.L. 858510.

Medieval

1. Alfred Penny, *BMC* type 1 ('Burgred type'), lunettes broken and crooked at angles. + AELBRED REX, HVBEAR/HTMO/NETA Hubearht. *c.* 871–75. Corroded. Lost 870s.
   1964 surface find, from make-up over east range (1920s excavation spoil).
   No A.M.L. number.
2. Henry VI Penny, York; probably Group VIII of Archbishop William Booth; local dies, no leaf on breast, broken pellet beside crown and in quatrefoil on reverse. *c.* 1452–57. Worn and pierced. Lost end of fifteenth century.
   Pit below clay seam east of north transept (=F.6).
   A.M.L. 858512.

3. Edward IV Penny, Durham, local dies. No D in centre, no marks beside crown, DVNO/L. . . extra pellet in two quarters. 1473–76. Clipped but not very worn. Lost end of fifteenth century.
   Pit below clay seam east of north transept, as no. 2 (=F.6).
   A.M.L. 858513.
4. Richard III, groat, London. i.m. rose and sun dimidiated; reverse perhaps boar's head. 1483–84. Wear noticeable for a groat. Lost early sixteenth century.
   Above clay seam east of north transept (= layer 7).
   A.M.L. 858514.
5. Genoa, billon Quattrino. Stylised gateway (device of Genoa), . . . DV(X)/long cross, CO/NR/AD/I, commemorating the Emperor Conrad II and 'immobile'. Fifteenth century. Worn. Lost early sixteenth century.
   East of north transept under Dissolution mortar spread (= layer 7 or 12).
   A.M.L. 858511.

Miscellaneous Late Coins

1. Seventeenth-century ¼*d*. token. *Obv*. Unicorn; IOHN.SHALLCROSS. *Rev*. IES; EAST.GREENEWICH.Williamson's Boyne, Kent 336 (John Shalcross).
   Cloister bank.
   A.M.L. 858524.
2. Zeeland doit, 1709?
   Slype bank.
   A.M.L. 858523.
3. George III ½*d*. 1806.
   Cloister bank.
   A.M.L. 858525.

Medieval Jetons

1. English Sterling series, 21 mm. Crowned Sterling head, Fox class XIV (1318–20) but punches worn/long cross patonce (Berry 6b), cinquefoils or rosettes of six pellets in quarters. Border of pellets each side (Berry D/D). 1320s. A little worn. Lost 1330s.
   Topsoil near St. Pancras' Chapel.
   A.M.L. 858516.
2. French Official, late, 28 mm. Shield of France modern, crown over, MI and Lys between pellets, left and right, IOIE. DESIR. ALAMOVREV:S, crosslet stops/plain three strand cross flory in quadrilobe, as in angles, rosettes in spandrels. Fifteenth century (second quarter?). Slight wear.
   Topsoil.
   A.M.L. 858520.
3. French 'Derivative' (on fabric) or very late official, 27 mm. Four lys and four pierced

cinquefoils in field, AVE. MARIA. GRACIA, pierced cinquefoil stops/as previous, Ds in angles, pierced cinquefoils between pellets in spandrels. Fifteenth century (third or even fourth quarter). Some wear. Unusual in context.
East of north transept, Dissolution debris (= layer 7 or 12).
A.M.L. 858517.

4. 'Late Tournai' 27 mm., very thick (over 2 mm.). Shield (two lys canted, three quatrefoils in chief)/short cross paty, slipped quatrefoils in quarters, garbled legends, no stops. *c.* 1500. Somewhat worn.
East of north transept, Dissolution debris (= layer 7 or 12).
A.M.L. 858515.
5. 'Early–Middle' Nuremburg, 22 mm., 'normal' type (Reichsapfel in trilobe/three crowns and three lys). Large orb, nothing in spandrels, lys terminals. Garbled Lombardic legend. 1510s. Worn.
Under Dissolution debris.
A.M.L. 858521.
6. 'Early–Middle' Nuremburg, 30 mm. Field of France quartering Dauphiné, and of Lys. Garbled Lombardic legend. 1520s? Worn and battered.
Dissolution debris.
A.M.L. 858518.
7. 'Early–Middle' Nuremburg, 30 mm., ship/lozenge of lys trefoils between annulets at sides. Garbled Lombardic legend. Rough execution for the type. 1530s. Pierced but not worn.
Dissolution debris.
A.M.L. 858519.

COINS AND JETONS FROM EXCAVATIONS 1972–75. S.E. Rigold

Roman

1. *Dupondius?* brass. Very worn. Lost any time from second century onwards.
From Area 2, layer 35.
A.M.L. 756290.
2. Tetricus II (270–73). Radiate *antoninianus*. Regular issue. *Rev.* uncertain.
From Trench III, layer 18.
A.M.L. 743708.
3. Constantine II as Caesar (IVN NOB C), PROVIDEN/TIAE CAESS. Camp Gate, Trier, STRU (*LRBC*, 33); unworn, well centred and very well preserved. A.D. 324–30, lost then.
From Trench III, layer 27.
A.M.L. 743709.
4. Constantine I (CONSTANTINVSMAXAVG), GLOR/IAEXERC/ITVS, two standards, Trier, TRP (*LRBC* 48), unworn and well preserved. A.D. 330–35, lost then.
From Trench III, layer 18.
A.M.L. 743707.
5. Constantine I. Head of 320s, but legends look irregular. Wreath, legend around ends RVM;

could be (CAESARVM NOSTRO) RVM. Mint just TΛ. Not worn, but corroded in places: probably lost *c.* 330.
From Area 2, unstratified.
A.M.L. 756285.

6. Small (13 mm.) barbarous imitation of Magnentius type of two Victories holding votive shield (reads OV/IOT/X) with head not like him. Good condition: after 353 (*c.* A.D. 360?).
From Area II, layer 38.
A.M.L. 756291.

Medieval

1. Base silver ½ denier tournois (obol), accepted as equivalent of ⅛ stg. SANCTVS MARTINVS (not royal name). TVRONVS CIVIS. Considerably worn. End of twelfth or early thirteenth century.
From Trench III, layer 8.
A.M.L. 743704.
2. Edward I, farthing, London, Early (LON/DON/IEN/SIS) but heavily worn. Lost *c.* 1300 or later.
From Trench III, unstratified.
A.M.L. 743705.
3. Edward (later Edward I or II), farthing, London (probably class X), reads EDWARDVS(?) REXAN, 1302–20, little wear, soon lost.
From Area 1, layer 1.
A.M.L. 743651.
4. Henry VI, Cross-pellet coinage; York (pellet on light cross in reverse quatrefoil, small extra pellet in two quarters), pellet and trefoil (?) beside neck. Fairly heavily worn. 1454–60, lost 1480s?
From Trench III, unstratified.
A.M.L. 743706.
5. Henry VI, leaf-pellet issue, halfpenny, London. Leaf on breast, pellets flanking crown and in two rev. quarters. 1443–54. Some wear. Lost 1450s or '60s.
Stray find.
A.M.L. 775155.

Jetons, etc.

1. Nuremburg, 'normal' (Reichsapfel/three crowns). Diam. 24 mm. Garbled Lombardic legend. Crown initial mark. On orb side annulets in spandrels and annulets to crowns on other side.
From Trench III, layer 12.
A.M.L. 743703.

2. Nuremburg, early 'normal' type. Diam. 21 mm. A third missing. Large orb. Garbled Lombardic legend of above average quality, with double annulet stops, *c.* 1500s.
   From Area 1, layer 4.
   A.M.L. 743653.
3. Nuremburg, 'lady watering flowers'. Diam. 29 mm. Better than usual; 1520s or 1530s.
   From Area 2, layer 69.
   A.M.L. 756301.
4. Nuremburg, 'ship' type. Diam. 25 mm. Garbled Lombardic inscription. Late and careless, 1530s or 1540s.
   From Area 1, layer 1.
   A.M.L. 743652.
5. Rostock, 3 copper pfennig. Date: 173? Arms of Rostock.
   From Area 2, unstratified.
   A.M.L. 756286.

COINS AND JETONS FROM EXCAVATIONS 1976–78. S.E. Rigold

Roman

1. Constantine I, Æ 20 mm. MARTI CONSERVATORI, Mars standing, MLL in ex., SM in field. A.D. 313–16. Very fresh, lost immediately.
   Area V, layer 5156.
   A.M.L. 782397.
2. Constantine II, as Caesar, Æ 13 mm., GLORIA EXERCITVS, two standards; looks imitative, mm. unclear. A.D. 330–35. Fresh, soon lost.
   Area IV, layer 809.
   A.M.L. 782395.
3. Valens, Æ 18 mm. SECVRITAS REIPVBLICAE, LVG- (Lyon) in ex., OF I in field A.D. 364–75. Fresh but broken, soon lost.
   Area V, layer 5161.
   A.M.L. 782398.
4. Æ 19 mm. Might be a base radiate, totally corroded.
   Area III, layer 1058.
   A.M.L. 781635.

Medieval, English first

1. Harold I, Penny, *BMC* i, Hild. A (Jewel cross), Dover Cinstan. CINSTAN ON DOFR. 1036–37. Slightly worn and bent. Lost late 1030s.
   Area I, layer 24.
   A.M.L. 765640.

2. Edward the Confessor, *BMC* xiii, Hild. Ac. (Facing bust), Canterbury, probably Aelfric. . . . C ON CA. Cut halfpenny. 1062–65. Slightly worn and bent. Lost later 1060s.
Area IV, layer 790.
A.M.L. 781853.
3. Short-cross, cut halfpenny, Class 5b. prob. London, Wilhelm? WILL. . . .N . 1205–10. Moderate wear, lost 1210s or 1220s.
Area V, layer 5087.
A.M.L. 781853.
4. Short-cross, cut halfpenny, Class 7, early-ish. Mint and moneyer illegible. 1218–1220s. Badly struck, quite worn. Lost 1230s, poss. 1240s.
Area I, layer 34.
A.M.L. 765644.
5. Henry III, long-cross, Class 3b, cut halfpenny. Canterbury, Nicole. . . .OLE ON C. . . 1248–50. A little worn. Lost *c.* 1260, anyway by 1280.
Area II, layer 593.
A.M.L. 777639.
6. 'Edwardian', penny, Fox class Xe. London. *c.* 1307. Moderate wear. Lost 1310s or '20s.
Area II, layer 523.
A.M.L. 765638.
7. 'Edwardian', halfpenny, London; probably Edward III pre-'Florin', and late at that. Rough dies, apparently EDWA. . .ANG and 8-pointed star. Roman Ns. *c.* 1340? Very worn. Not lost before 1350s?
Area II, grave 549.
A.M.L. 765643.
8. 'Edwardian', farthing, London; probably Fox class X. 1300–10. Little wear. Lost 1310s.
Area II, layer 540.
A.M.L. 765642.
9. 'Edwardian', farthing, London; general correspondence with Fox classes XI–XV, perhaps XIII. Ends REX A. *c.* 1310–30. Some wear. Lost 1330s or '40s.
Area II, layer 503.
A.M.L. 765635.
10. Edward III, farthing, London, Florin issue, Lombardic Ns. 1344–51. Little wear. Lost 1340s or 50s.
Area II, layer 509.
A.M.L. 765634.
11. Edward III, penny, Treaty period, double annulet stops, EDWARD ANGL R. London. 1363–69. Much worn and clipped. Rejected *c.* 1390?
Area II, layer 500.
A.M.L. 765633.
12. Edward III, groat, London, Pre-Treaty period, C; stops broken annulets (*obv.*) and annulets (*rev.*). 1351–52. Wear quite heavy for a groat. Lost 1370s?
Area IV, layer 760.
A.M.L. 777644.
13. Richard II, or perhaps late Edward III; penny, York. Such pennies often linger in this

condition, *c*. 1380. Extremely worn; quatrefoil just visible at centre. Lost second quarter of fifteenth century?
Area I, layer 18.
A.M.L. 777637.

14. Richard II, penny, York, local dies. Two pellets by shoulders and two by hair curls, *c*. 1380–90. Moderate wear. Perhaps lost *c*. 1400.
Area IV, layer 772.
A.M.L. 777592.

15. Henry V, Class A (rare coinage, not clearly distinct from last issues ascribed to Henry IV), half-groat, London. Pellet l., annulet r. of crown, single saltire after first word of each otherwise double saltire stops; no clear pellet in initial cross. 1413–14. Some wear. Lost 1420s.
Area IV, layer 757.
A.M.L. 777642.

16. Henry V, Class C, groat, London. Mullet on shoulder, stops single saltires (*obv*.), double saltires (*rev*.), crosslet after POSVI. 1415–20. This and the two following, all almost unworn, and perhaps no. 15, seem to form a small scattered hoard from 1420 or soon after.
Area IV, layer 720.
A.M.L. 777649.

17. As previous.
Area IV, layer 720.
A.M.L. 777641.

18. As previous, but no crosslet after POSVI.
Area IV, layer 720.
A.M.L. 777646.

19. Edward IV, penny, Durham. London dies. Bishop L. Booth, B and trefoil beside bust. 1471–73. Very worn and clipped. Lost early sixteenth century.
Area I, layer 24.
A.M.L. 765639.

20. Henry VIII, Sov. penny, Durham, Bp. T Ruthall, TD over shield, i. m. lis. 1509–23. Fresh. Lost at least a decade before Dissolution.
Area I, layer 13.
A.M.L. 765636.

21. Alexander III of Scots, half-penny. Two mullets of six points. 1280–86. Some wear. Lost or rejected by 1300.
Area II, layer 515.
A.M.L. 765641.

22. Robert III of Scots (?), penny passing as halfpenny? Legend appears to begin ROB. RT; if not, must be the wreck of an early Edwardian halfpenny. Looks fair AR. *c*. 1393–1405? Chipped, extremely worn, has been bent.
Area II, layer 500.
A.M.L. 765977.

23. Salerno, Æ Follaro, diam. 24–27 mm.; temp. Robert Guiscard, overstruck. The more

prominent type (Sambon 1912, 148, Pl. XII, no. 845; Grierson, 1956, 37–59, Fig. 2, no. 53) is found in a hoard ascribed by Grierson to 1077 and is overstruck at latest by *c.* 1112; it shows, *obv.*, head of Christ between A and Ω, rev. (D)VX/(IT)A S A/LERNO. The weaker type is probably the *under*type and reads ..DI. .SAL. ., which appears to be Sambon no. 880 (HOC CI/DI.DVX/SALER/NO);this is assigned, without good reason to Roger II, after 1102. Both the coin itself and the circumstances of finding are against it. The general series presents a succession of rapid overstrikes; Grierson lists many combinations but not this one. Robert took Salerno from Gisulf, Princeps, not Dux, in 1076–77 and it may be a campaign striking.
1076–77 (?). Little worn; pierced. Lost soon after.
Area IV, layer 794.
A.M.L. 781854.

24. Venice, AR Soldino. Doge with banner, MI. .STEN'DVX, (Michele Steno), star over D in field/lion of St. Mark, (S) MARCVS VEN (ETI). Such coins, the typical 'Galley halfpence' are quite common in England over a long period, while those of Genoa, as above, are not. 1400–13. Not very worn. Lost early fifteenth century.
Area IV, layer 763.
A.M.L. 777643.

Medieval Jetons

1. Perhaps an English jeton-substitute. 13 mm.; blank, thin, pierced at centre, such things are commom in the fourteenth century, especially after *c.* 1340, when sterling jettons get scarce, but this one is very small.
Area II, layer 553.
A.M.L. 765653
2. French Official, 25 mm. Agnus Dei, MOVTON SVI: DE BERI, double annulet stop/ elaborate cross flory in quadrilobe, + A V E between annulets in spandrels. 1360s–'80s. Fresh. Lost later fourteenth century.
Area I, layer 3.
A.M.L. 765645
3. French Official, 25 mm. Crown, crosslets on band, AVE MARIA:GRACIA:PL, double crosslet stops/as previous, AVEG between crosslets in spandrels. 1360s–'80s. Fresh. Lost later fourteenth century.
Area I, layer 18.
A.M.L. 765647
4. French Official, relatively late and unusual (English régime?), 25 mm., thin fabric. Dolphin, AVE.MARIA.GRASIA.PLENA in late-ish lettering, single saltire stops/bowed cross flory, sixfoil in centre, in quadrilobe, ships (?), rather than crowns, in spandrels. (Paris?). 1420–35? Considerably worn. Lost mid–late fiftenth century.
Area IV, layer 766.
A.M.L. 777645

5. French Official, under English régime, at Rouen (?), 26 mm. Annunciation with two shields below, as on gold salutes (shields are: (i) three covered cups and three cinqfoils; (ii) St. George's cross cut over three lions rampant (or squirrels?), (SC) A:MARIA: ORA:PRO:AIABVS:EORV, pierced cinqfoils at ends, double saltire stops/as previous but trefoils in spandrels and AVE MARIA GRASIA PLENA (no stops), suggesting a like origin. Early fifteenth century. (1422–48). Fairly fresh. Soon lost.
Area I, layer 25.
A.M.L. 765651.
6. French Official, late, 26 mm. Shield of France modern, garbled Lombardic legend/plain three strand cross flory in quadrilobe, spandrels unclear. Fifteenth century. (Second quarter?). Some wear. Lost later fifteenth century.
Area I, layer 25.
A.M.L. 765648.

The next two are both of 'late Tournai' fabric on lettering, etc., but not identical in execution.

7. 25 mm., thin fabric. Shield (unclear)/short cross, garbled legends. *c.* 1500? Fragmentary (about half).
Area I, layer 24.
A.M.L. 765652.
8. 28 mm., normal fabric. Crowned shield (France modern)/short cross paty, lys at ends, crowned lys in quarters, garbled legends, no stops. *c.* 1500. Fairly fresh.
Area I, layer 18.
A.M.L. 765646.

The next four are all 'early–middle' Nuremburg, with garbled Lombardic legends.

9. 25 mm., 'normal' type (Reichsapfel in trilobe/three crowns and three lys). Medium orb, annulets in spandrels and as terminals to crowns. Badly made. 1520s or '30s. Bent and worn.
Area V, layer 5002.
A.M.L. 781633.
10. 25 mm., same types. Medium orb, pellets in spandrels, lys terminals to crowns. Well-spaced letters. 1530s or '40s.
Stray find.
A.M.L. 775154.
11. 25 mm., Ship/lozenge of lys, trefoils between annulets at sides. Rough execution. 1530s. Broken and corroded.
Area II, layer 513.
A.M.L. 765650.
12. 29 mm., 'The lady with the marguerites and watering-pot'/garbled shield of Burgundy-Flanders, briquet over. A type deriving from ducal jettons of the 1490s. Not the worst of its kind; big bold letters and colon stops. 1510s or '20s. Pierced but little worn.
Area II, layer 513.
A.M.L. 765649.

Lead Tokens, Méreaux, etc.

1. 19 mm., *c.* 1 mm. thick; wavy pattern/penny-like short-cross, with three or four pellets in quarters. Could be thirteenth century.
   Area V, layer 5087.
   A.M.L. 781852.
2. 14–15 mm., *c.* 1 mm. thick. Crude shield with bend and other ordinaries/web-footed creature(?), might be fourteenth–fifteenth century.
   Area IV, layer 1053.
   A.M.L. 781634.
3. 14 mm., thin, Fish/Agnus Dei, crude borders of strokes ? fourteenth century, if a poor relation of those found at Dublin.
   Area V, unstratified.
   A.M.L. 782396.

VIII. THE POTTERY

LYN BLACKMORE

INTRODUCTION

The excavations at St. Augustine's Abbey 1960–78 produced a total of some 12,000 sherds of Belgic, Roman, Saxon, medieval and post-medieval pottery, which have been studied over a number of years. The material from the excavations of 1976–78 was processed in 1979–80, the 1972 and 1974–75 assemblages were examined in 1982, the 1960 collection was studied in 1984. The following is arranged in a number of sub-sections which attempt to correlate the general characteristics of the entire assemblage with the specific aspects of each area. A description of the wares and local pottery industry is followed by a detailed analysis of the finds by site.

This work was completed in March 1985 and no account has been taken of any publications since that date. Since the excavations were concerned with the Anglo-Saxon and medieval history of the site, the Belgic and Roman pottery is only summarised here. The post-Roman material falls into three main groups: eleventh to twelfth century, thirteenth to fourteenth century, and fifteenth to seventeenth century, corresponding with major phases of construction, use and demolition of the abbey. The Anglo-Saxon and early medieval pottery is limited, but includes some important stratified sherds from the construction levels excavated in 1976–78 (see p. 293). The late medieval and post-medieval material, which includes a number of reconstructible vessels, greatly outnumbers that from the earlier contexts, although the demolition levels contained a quantity of residual sherds. Non-local wares are rare in all stratified medieval contexts, and are more common in the 1960 post-medieval assemblage than elsewhere on the site. These wares derive mainly from the Surrey-Hampshire border or from unknown kilns, probably in the Weald. Fifteenth - to sixteenth-century stonewares (Langerwehe, Raeren, Cologne) are common in the 1960 and 1974–75 groups, but less so in the other asssemblages. Sieburg and Westerwald are virtually absent in all groups, and other Continental imports are rare. A few sherds of Chinese porcelain, English tin-glazed ware and stoneware and a large amount of red earthenwares were found in the levels associated with the hospital and school on the south side of the church.

The catalogues are presented in tables which incorporate full references to external parallels quoted in the text; internal parallels are also noted, firstly by year of excavation, then Group/layer or Figure/sherd number. Details of internal and external glazing are coded as follows: C=clear, Y=yellow, G=green, B=brown, or combinations thereof. The suffix S indicates the use of underglaze slip.

Unabridged pottery reports and catalogues of published material are available for consultation in the site archive, together with the original finds books and pottery analysis sheets.

THE WARES

The pottery was classified as far as possible by eye into fabric groups. The original fabric codes have been retained here, but where possible the codes now employed by the Canterbury Archaeological Trust are included (in brackets) for the benefit of future workers. The samian from 1972–75 was studied by Joanna Bird; the samian stamps were all examined by B.R. Hartley. A small number of Anglo-Saxon and early medieval sherds from the 1976–78 excavations were studied in thin-section by Ailsa Mainman, while the stonewares were examined by Pamela Clarke. Their comments are incorporated in inverted commas below, or are available in the archive.

The distribution of the fabric types by phases is summarised in Tables 5–11, 13 and 14. These present sherd counts only; the bulk of the stratified medieval material consists of small body sherds which preclude any meaningful study of vessel equivalents, while sherds from the late- and post-medieval vessels which have been reconstructed were in most cases scattered throughout more than one context. The totals should, therefore, be taken as a quantitative approximation only, particularly as there are several sherds which represent an intermediate of two fabric types (mainly B/LB, C/D and LM/F). Further research may prove that these are groups in their own right, particularly for LB and F. For simplicity, however, the categories LB and F embrace all the late medieval/post-medieval coarse and fine red wares, respectively.

The fabric-types are discussed as follows: Belgic and Roman (Fabrics 1–3); Anglo-Saxon, medieval and post-medieval local wares (Fabrics 4–13); non-local wares (Fabrics 14–28); imported wares (Fabrics 29–45). In each group the sequence is as far as possible both chronological and geographical. The codes given below for each fabric are in some cases quoted in the discussions of the various assemblages in place of the full fabric name. The local pottery industry is discussed below (pp. 261–3).

Belgic and Roman Wares

1. *Belgic*: BE (B).

The Belgic pottery is quite typical of the Canterbury area, and presumably derives from the Belgic settlement which preceded the Roman city. Parallels for most sherds may be found in the material from the Belgic occupation and ditch just to the south of Rose Lane in Canterbury, which, together with the Belgic pottery tradition in Kent, has been discussed elsewhere (Frere 1954, 104–14). Other sites providing parallels include Burgate and Watling Street (Williams 1947, Figs. 7, 14), Butchery Lane (Frere 1948, Figs. 9, 12, 14, 16), Gravel Walk (Williams 1975, 110–43), North Lane (Macpherson-Grant 1978, Figs. 15, 16) and Canterbury Castle (Macpherson-Grant 1982, 97–150). Three grades of coarse-ware are present at St. Augustine's, mostly grog-tempered, and of a lumpy texture, but developing from a dark grey, crudely made ware with heavy forms and combed surfaces, to a much harder, denser ware with a silver-grey core and grey or reddish surfaces, which continue the Belgic tradition after the Roman conquest (see also Macpherson-Grant 1980a, 279–89; 1980b, 293). One sherd of possible Belgic/early Roman chaff-tempered ware (Macpherson-Grant 1980c, 2–4) was recovered (1976–78, Group 1, Fig. 89, no. 4).

The grog-tempered pottery from various sites within Canterbury has been discussed by Thompson (1982, 13, 20, 24, 659–67). For a catalogue of all Belgic fabric types found in Canterbury, see Macpherson-Grant and Green (1983, 22–3).

2. *Roman*: RO (R).

The Roman pottery from the midden deposits ranges from the first to the fourth century, but is predominantly of first- to second-century date. The group includes a range of samian, colour-coated wares, Castor ware, Oxfordshire ware, amphorae, mortaria and other oxidised wares. Exotic or decorated forms are rare, and little of the samian bears any decoration. The proportion of fine to coarse wares is approximately equal. Most forms find numerous parallels from stratified contexts within the Roman town of *Durovernum*, e.g. at Watling Street and Burgate (Williams 1947, Fig. 7), Butchery Lane (Frere 1948, Figs. 9 and 14, Rose Lane (Frere 1954, Figs. 7–8), Gravel Walk (Williams 1975, Fig. 9), Canterbury Castle (Bennet *et al.* 1982) and various sites in the St. George's Street and Burgate Street areas (Frere and Stow 1983). Much of the coarse pottery is of the smooth Upchurch-type (North Kent), but some at least of the sandy wares may be locally produced. A late first- or second-century kiln was located just outside the city walls of Canterbury (Bennett 1978, 166–8; Macpherson-Grant 1978, 174–6), and other kilns have been found within the city itself (Jenkins 1956, 40–56). To the south of Canterbury a further mid to late first-century kiln(s) has been excavated in advance of the Canterbury by-pass at Stuppington Lane (Bennett 1980a, 267–73; Macpherson-Grant 1980a, 281–9).

The samian from the 1960 excavations (Trench B, layers 26, 27) is mainly from Central Gaul, and of second-century date; one sherd is from East Gaul. The samian from the 1972 and 1974–75 excavations is predominantly of second- to third-century date, also mostly from Central Gaul. Six stamped bases, mainly from Lezoux, are discussed (pp. 277–8, 286, 293). Of these one (1974–75) is of mid to late first-century date, two are early to mid second century (1972, Trench 1), and three (1976–78) are mid to late second century. These are of interest in that one stamp (Cocillus) is a previously unknown type, and two (Icctiama and Pinna) are only the fourth of their kind to be recorded. The 1976–78 samian also includes Argonne roller-stamped ware (Group 4b, layer 779).

For a catalogue of the Roman wares found within Canterbury see Macpherson-Grant and Green (1983, 23–5).

3. *Late Roman*: LR (LR).

One heavily burnished rim sherd and one body sherd (1974–75, layers 1 and 2), are in a crudely made fabric which resembles the local 'Belgic' ware but which is rather harder, with more angular grit inclusions. Also one base from 1960 (P8), one body sherd from 1972 Trench 2, two rims and two body sherds from 1976–78. Similar sherds have been noted within Canterbury, and are thought to be of fourth- to fifth-century date (Frere 1966, 90–3); the source of these wares is unknown, but they are probably local. See also Macpherson-Grant and Green (1983, 25–6).

Saxon, Medieval and Post-medieval Local Wares

4. *Anglo-Saxon organically-tempered Ware*. (SOT = EMS 4; MLS 4/5)

Nine sherds from the Anglo-Saxon graveyard or contexts deriving from this level (1976–78, Groups 2, 3 and 4) and only three residual sherds (1974–75, layers 71, 37). Surface colouring varies from brown to buff, and some sherds appear to have been burnished. Thin-section analysis of five sherds shows two fabric types. The first (EMS 4, layers 803, 5145, 5158, 5158) contains 'a dense scatter of quartz sand grains, so small as to suggest that they are a composite part of the clay matrix'; the second (MLS 4/5, layer 5157) has 'larger quartz sand grains, this time presumably added as temper together with the chaff' (Mainman, pers. comm.). A second, more heavily sand-tempered sherd was found in layer 5156. Sand-and-organically-tempered ware was also found in the 1955–58 excavations at St. Augustine's (Ames 1978, Fig. 13, no. 5). The temper of the 1976–78 sherds 'is believed to be of non-cereal grasses, but no further comment may be made due to the carbonised nature of the organic material' (Mainman, pers. comm.). Organically-tempered wares are common in Canterbury. Evidence from recently excavated sites wihin the city suggests that this fabric-type first appears in the late sixth century; it is predominant by the seventh century, but dies out with the introduction of the first hand-made coarse sandy or sandy-gritty wares in the later seventh or eighth century (Mainman, pers. comm.; Macpherson-Grant, pers. comm.). How long the two traditions co-existed remains unclear, but it is possible that the sand-and-organically-tempered ware may represent an experimental or transitional phase *c.* 650 –*c.* 750/800 (Macpherson-Grant, pers. comm.). In Canterbury this more sandy fabric has been stratigraphically shown to post-date the pure organically tempered wares, but to be contemporary with Ipswich ware, which was imported after *c.* 650 (see below). One small sherd from St. Augustine's (1976–78, Group 9) is problematical, having apparently some grog, some ?organic content, moderate sand, and a burnished outer surface. This sherd has some late-Roman characteristics, but is probably of early or mid-Saxon date.

5. *Late Saxon and early medieval sandy Wares*: SS/EMS (LS1, EM1).

Eight sherds from the Anglo-Saxon graveyard and late eleventh- to twelfth-century contexts (layers 5161, 5161; 798; 796, 8002; 5153, 5153) were studied in thin section and found to be 'tempered with variable amounts of quartz sand which occurs in grains of uniform size and roundness. Grog also occurs in small quantities and as small rounded inclusions'. Both oxidised and reduced wares are represented. The former are generally low fired, slightly micaceous, and characterised by the presence of occasional haematite or ironstone inclusions (up to 3 × 5 mm.); the latter are similar, but appear to lack the additional grog and ironstone, and are more highly fired. Some sherds in both groups have sparse grits or rounded chalk inclusions and a tendency to laminate. These wares are almost certainly locally made, probably in the Tyler Hill area (Bennett 1980c, 293–95; Macpherson-Grant 1980d, 295–97; see section 2 below). They are closely related to the late Saxon and early medieval wares from Rosemary Lane (Macpherson-Grant 1982, 165–8; Mainman, pers. comm. and C.A.T. archive) and the Marlowe Car Park site (Blockley and Blockley forthcoming), while the collected late Saxon and early medieval wares from St. Augustine's 1960–78 include examples of most forms in the three typological groups first identified by Frere (Frere 1954, 128–32; Bennett *et al.* 1982, 66–9; Wilson 1983, 193).

Frere Group 1 (975–1025): 1960, no. 6; 1972, no. 1; 1974–75, no. 21; 1976–78, no. 69.
Frere Group 2 (1050–1100): 1972, nos. 2, 7; 1976–78, nos. 4, 8, 68, 70.
Frere Group 3 (1080–1150): 1972, nos. 3, 6, 8.

Most sherds date to the period 1050–1100, and presumably derive from levels associated with the construction of the abbey. A sequence from the late ninth or tenth century to the later twelfth century is, however, illustrated. The earliest sand-tempered pots are small and are entirely hand-made, but those from the later ninth century onwards were often finished on a turn-table and knife-trimmed. Knife-trimming may have begun as early as the late eighth century, but is particularly common in the tenth century (Frere 1954, 128, 130), when there was also an increase both in the size, range and decoration of vessels produced (Macpherson-Grant, pers. comm.). The unusual late tenth-century decorated rim (1960, Fig. 78, no. 6) reflects all these trends. Burnished sherds occur sporadically throughout late ninth- and tenth-century contexts in Canterbury, pitchers sometimes having a lattice burnish which copies imported wares from northern France or Ipswich (e.g. Wilson 1983, fig. 97, no. 325). The development from the knife-trimmed wares of the ninth and tenth centuries to the well-formed pots of the period 1050–1080 is shown by two early-mid eleventh-century sherds from the excavations of 1955–58 (Ames 1978, fig. 13, nos. 10 and 12, conversely numbered in the text), of which no. 12, from the Anglo-Saxon graveyard soil within the south-west tower, has early medieval characteristics but is heavily knife-trimmed internally in the late tenth-century style. A rim found in 1976–78 (Fig. 92, no. 68, internally knife-trimmed) also belongs to this transitional period. In the mid-later eleventh century a further increase in the size and standardisation of vessel forms is illustrated by a number of cooking-pot rims (1972, Fig. 83, nos. 1–6; 1976–78; Fig. 89, no. 6) and the large flat-based bowl (1976–78, Group 3a, Fig. 89, no. 8), which was apparently made on a turn-table and then knife-trimmed. Internal knife-trimming became largely redundant with the introduction of true wheel-made wares in the late eleventh or early twelfth century, but external knife-trimming (basal areas only) continued fairly consistently throughout the medieval period and later. The introduction of the wheel allowed a still greater variety in vessel size and form; spouted pitchers become more common in Canterbury (1976–78, Fig. 90, no. 9), while cooking-pot rims such as the finger-tipped rim (1960, P6) or the clubbed rim (1976–78, Fig. 92, no. 70) illustrate a new experimentation with established vessel types, which was interextended to glazing. Two early twelfth-century sherds (1960, P5, P18), both similar to no. 2 from the 1972 excavations (Fig. 83), bear a patchy green glaze.

6. *Late Saxon/Early Medieval Shell-tempered Ware* SH (= LS2, EM2).

Technically speaking all the shell-tempered wares are probably of non-local origin, but they form such a large part of the medieval pottery represented in Canterbury, if not at St. Augustine's, that they are included with the local wares. One reduced rim-sherd of twelfth-century date (1976–78, Fig. 92, no. 72) was analysed in thin section and shown to contain a mixture of coarsely crushed shelly-limestone with a little organic tempering. No. 71 (1976–78, Fig. 92), would appear to be purely shell-tempered.

7. *Late Saxon/Medieval Sand-and-shell-tempered Ware*: SHS (=LS3, EM3).

These wares show a considerable variety in the size and proportions of the three main inclusions, quartz sand, shell and grog, and some sherds contain only a minimal amount of shell. Analysis of shell-tempered wares from Rosemary Lane (Mainman pers. comm., C.A.T. archive) shows that this is quite typical; the sand and shell content were there found to vary between 9–17 per cent and 9–20 per cent, respectively, while grog never exceeded 4.6 per cent. One oxidised rim-sherd from St. Augustine's (1976–78, Fig. 89, no. 7), was studied in thin section and found to contain a mixture of finely crushed shelly limestone and quartz sand accounting for 30 per cent and 10 per cent of the fabric respectively; a fossil shell inclusion was identified by Dr Gilbertson of Sheffield University as a Tertiary planorbid. This may derive from the Upper Cretaceous chalk pockets which occur within one mile of Canterbury. A late twelfth- or early thirteenth-century rim found in 1960 (Fig. 78, no. 1) contains sand, shell and frequent fine, ill-sorted flint grits; a hand-made sherd of probable late Saxon date (1972, Trench 2) and several sherds from 1960 contain sand, coarsely crushed shell, occasional flint grits and clay pellets. Other sherds include nos. 32, 42 and 43 from the 1974–75 excavations (Figs. 86, 87).

Shell-tempered wares are found widely throughout southern England from the late tenth to the late thirteenth century, but the origins and development of the tradition in east Kent are unclear. While shell-tempered wares appear to have been in the minority throughout the medieval period (Rigold 1967, 112; 1968, 54–5), the tradition is long-lived. In 1954, a tentative seventh- or eighth-century date was given for a few sherds from Rosemary Lane (Frere 1954, 125, Fig. 12, nos. 114–5), and recent publications and excavations confirm that a small amount of shell-tempered ware was used from the eighth century on, becoming more popular in the tenth to eleventh century (Wilson 1983, nos. 124, 314, 329a, 329b, 371, 760; Macpherson-Grant forthcoming). A small pot, probably of early ninth-century date, was found over a late Saxon floor to the east of Canterbury Lane (Frere and Stow 1983, 89; Wilson 1983, Fig. 95, no. 314), while two stratified pre-Conquest sherds were found in the 1955–58 and 1976–78 excavations at St. Augustine's, from the Anglo-Saxon graveyard soil inside the south-west tower (Ames 1978, 61), and from the graveyard soil displaced *c.* 1070 by the construction of the south-aisle wall (1976–78, Fig. 89, no. 7, ninth to tenth century). In the cathedral precincts, a shell-tempered rim of probable pre-Conquest date was sealed by the *c.* 1080 foundations for Lanfranc's dormitory (Bennett *et al.*, forthcoming) while a large group of both shell- and sand-and-shell-tempered wares sealed by the foundations for the Aula Nova (Norman Staircase: Driver *et al.* forthcoming) is dated to pre-*c.* 1165, but may be considerably earlier than this. Both shell- and sand-and-shell-tempered wares were at their peak from the mid-twelfth to the early thirteenth century (Macpherson-Grant 1981a, 11–14; forthcoming and pers. comm.), dying out in the thirteenth century. Most sherds from St. Augustine's are typical of the later twelfth to early thirteenth century, the clubbed (1974–75, Fig. 87, no. 42) and flanged forms (1960, Fig. 78, no. 1; 1974–75, Fig. 86, no. 32; Fig. 87, no. 43; 1976–78, Fig. 92, nos. 71, 72) developing into the bevelled, or squared rim forms of the thirteenth-century shell-dusted and sandy wares. The presence of mica-dust in both the medieval shell- and sand-and-shell-tempered wares from Canterbury suggests a clay source east of the Medway, mica being generally absent from shell-tempered wares in west Kent (Streeten forthcoming). The shell itself is probably coastal in origin, possibly from the Whitstable area (Macpherson-Grant 1981a, 11–13; forthcoming). Some of the more sandy, less shelly wares, however, may prove to have been more locally produced, using imported shell (Macpherson-Grant 1981a, 14–17).

8. *Medieval Shell-on-surface Ware*: SOS.

Represented by only a few sherds of probable thirteenth-century date (1960, Fig. 78, no. 4; 1972, Fig. 83, nos. 9, 10; 1974–5, Fig. 86, no. 33; 1976–8, Fig. 90, nos. 10, 33). Finds from Canterbury suggest that the tradition starts within the early medieval period and continues until the mid to later thirteenth century, with a peak *c.* 1160–1225 (Macpherson-Grant 1981b, 6; forthcoming). It appears to derive from the formally more advanced shell-tempered wares. The latter may have prompted an 'up-dating' of the forms available in the sandy wares, with the SOS wares acting as a linking factor between the two traditions (Macpherson-Grant pers. comm.). The fairly hard fabric is similar both to the early sand-tempered ware and to the true medieval sand-tempered wares from Tyler Hill, and is likely to be of local origin. Analysis of sherds from Rosemary Lane shows that quartz sand accounts for over one-third of the fabric (35 per cent); other inclusions comprise fine black sand; mica; sparse chalk, grit and clay pellets. Grog also occurs, but only rarely (Mainman, pers. comm. and C.A.T. archive). Organic traces are quite common (see also medieval wares, Fabric A). The shell element is limited to a superficial dusting, mainly over and just inside the rim, and over the shoulder, perhaps as an economy of both shell and labour; the import of shell for this purpose alone would be uneconomical and waste oyster-shell or similar shell-fish may have been recycled by the potters. For a discussion of this ware and the forms produced, see Macpherson-Grant (1981a, 20–3; 1981b).

9. *Medieval Sandy Wares from Tyler Hill*

Two fabrics are apparent in the local medieval pottery, which was classified in four groups (A, B, C, D, see below) according to firing conditions. The first fabric contains a fine admixture of impure sand with occasional grit and grog; the second is densely tempered with rounded white quartz sand grains. Clay pellets and rounded chalk inclusions also occur sporadically in all groups, the latter more commonly in the later medieval period. It has been noted that the firing quality of Tyler Hill wares improves throughout the fourteenth century, becoming increasingly hard; this appears to be related to the use of grog or poorly refined clay (Macpherson-Grant 1980d, 295; 1983, 31; forthcoming). The predominance of Fabrics C and LB in the 1960–78 assemblages may indicate that most of the medieval wares are of fourteenth-century date, but as in Canterbury, less highly fired wares (Fabrics A and B) seem to continue, with Fabric B linking the medieval and late medieval traditions in Fabric LB. See also pp. 261–2 and p. 296 and Macpherson-Grant (1981a, 24–42). For detailed analyses of these wares, see Streeten 1979, 1982a, 1982b, and forthcoming.

Rough Medieval Red-ware: A.

A slightly micaceous, sandy fabric, low fired with a pale grey core and dull reddish-orange surfaces which may be knife-trimmed or wiped. A similar ware was found at Dover (Rigold 1967, 113–4). The amount of sand-tempering varies from fine to coarse, the earlier sherds (1976–78, Group 5, layers 594, 599) being characterised by the presence of blue-black flecks of burnt-out organic inclusions in the core of the sherd. Stratigraphically later sherds vary greatly from fine, with a slightly soapy texture, to a very coarse friable sandy ware. The latter types were found only in the demolition deposits (1960; 1976–78, Group 15), but may be residual.

Cooking-pots (1965, Fig. 82, nos. 44, 45; 1976–8, Fig. 90, nos. 31–2), bowls (1974–75, Fig. 86, nos. 34, 35) and jugs (1965, Fig. 82, nos. 41, 42; 1976–8, Fig. 90, nos. 11–14, 24, 26; Fig. 91, nos. 37–9, 41, 45, 66), are represented, some with incised decoration.

Medieval Red-ware: B.

Similar to the above but fired to a higher temperature, with a grey core, orange margins and orange or orange–grey surfaces. The amount of sand tempering, which appears to be whiter and purer than that in Fabric A, varies from fine to coarse; no organic inclusions are apparent. The surfaces may be knife-trimmed, but are rarely wiped, and are often rough to the touch. Mainly jug sherds, some decorated (1965, Fig. 82, nos. 42, 43).

Hard Medieval Ware: C.

A highly fired, very hard ware, often with thin walls distorted in the kiln; this appears to correspond with the 'dominant coarseware' at Dover (Rigold 1967, 91, 94), there dated to the late thirteenth century, but here continuing throughout the fourteenth century. Mainly reduced, with in some cases an orange margin and surfaces ranging from orange through buff to grey; later sherds often bear an orange slip externally. One lid (1974–75, Fig. 86, no. 40), cooking-pots (1976–78, Fig. 90, nos. 33–6; Fig. 91, no. 44), and jugs (1976–78, Fig. 90, nos. 15–9; 27–8; Fig. 91, nos. 62–3), the most striking being an anthropomorphic jug (1965, Fig. 82, no. 40).

Medieval Grey-ware: D.

Essentially the same as Fabric B but fully reduced, with grey or purplish-grey surfaces. Hardness varies from friable to very hard, but rarely attains the 'ringing' quality of Fabric C. Represented by both jugs and cooking-pots, and heavily stabbed lip of a ?dripping pan (1960, P10).

10. *Late Medieval Coarse Red-ware*: LB.

Sherds in this group have the characteristic colouring of Fabric B. Earlier wares usually have a grey core and orange surfaces; later wares are generally oxidised throughout, although some have streaky orange–grey surfaces. Both are densely tempered with white quartz sand, occasionally having additional quartz, calcite or calcareous grit inclusions (e.g. 1974–75, Fig. 85, no. 11). Wall thickness is greater than in Fabric B, and vessels are frequently knife-trimmed around the base angle (e.g. 1976–78, Fig. 91, no. 46), a feature also noted at Dover (Mynard 1969, Fig. 14, nos. 49, 50). Possibly as early as the late thirteenth or early fourteenth century (1976–78, Group 5), but only occasional sherds until the demolition levels. A wider range of forms than in the other fabrics, with jugs (1960, Fig. 78, no. 11; 1974–75, Fig. 84, no. 1), cooking-pots, bowls (1960, Fig. 80, no. 20; 1976–78, Fig. 92, nos. 73, 74), a lid (1960, Fig. 80, no. 21), a costrel (1974–75, Fig. 87, no. 47), a possible watering-can (1960, Fig. 79, no. 18) and a chafing dish (1974–75, Fig. 87, no. 56). A small pipkin (1960, Fig. 79, no. 14) of fourteenth- or fifteenth-century date is a rare example of reduced LB ware.

A small group of sherds (mainly 1974–75, Group 2, soakaway), in a similar, but rather darker, pink ware with occasional large chalk grits (3 x 5 mm.), also appears to belong to this group, but may be non-local. A similar ware was found in a group dated to *c.* 1375 at the latest at Pivington (Rigold 1964, 61).

A few sherds from the 1960 excavation with internal slip and glaze (Fig. 80, nos. 26, 27) show a possible Dutch influence, and may be the work of an immigrant potter. The forms may also be paralleled at Woolwich (Pryor and Blockley 1978). See also Imports: no. 34, North Holland slipware (NHS, below).

11. *Late Medieval 'Fine' Ware*: LM.

A hard sandy ware, distinctly finer than the above, but not as fine as Fabric F. The transition from the medieval Tyler Hill wares to the true post-medieval fine wares appears to have been gradual (Macpherson-Grant and Green 1983, 31), but a new fabric with a noticeably lower sand content was in use by the later fifteenth century, if not earlier

(Macpherson-Grant 1980d, 297; see also pp. 262–3). At St. Augustine's the ware first appears in the late fourteenth or early fifteenth century (1976–78, Group 8, two small sherds with a pale grey core and dull orange surfaces). Later sherds have a pale orange body and dull, sometimes streaky surfaces resembling Fabric H. The jug sherds frequently display striations inside the neck (1960, Fig. 78, no. 12), a feature which also occurs on the earlier fine wares (e.g. 1972, Fig. 83, no. 19; 1974–75, Fig. 86, no. 29). Fabric LM carries the medieval tradition of slipped decoration into the fifteenth century (1974–5, Fig. 84, no. 8; Fig. 86, no. 24), when cooking-pots, influenced by metal cauldrons, have rims seated for lids, and two opposing handles, sometimes very angular (1960, Fig. 79, nos. 13, 15, 17; 1974–75, Fig. 86, no. 24). Glazes tend to have a 'metallic' sheen, perhaps also imitating metal vessels, or imported stonewares. An unusual jug with incised decoration (1976–78, Fig. 93, no. 75) appears to be copying a leather bottle. Strap handles on jugs develop a characteristic triple thumbing at the base (1972, Fig. 92, no. 18).

12. *Fine Late Medieval/Early Post-medieval Red-ware*: F.

A fine very slightly sandy red ware possibly developing from Fabric LM. By far the most common ware in all the demolition groups, although only one sherd was found in a pre-Dissolution context (1976–78, Group 13, Grave 581). Four sub-groups were identified:

(a) Very fine, evenly fired, orange throughout, sometimes with 'powdery' surfaces (common);
(b) Slightly coarser and pinker, with fused surfaces (common);
(c) As above but with grey surfaces (e.g. 1960, Fig. 79, no. 19; 1976–78, Fig. 93, no. 79). Noted at Pivington (Rigold 1962, 42). Rare;
(d) Evenly fired pinkish-orange ware with small white, ?grog, inclusions, also found at Pivington. Possibly non-local (rare).

A wide range of fifteenth- and sixteenth-century forms is represented, including a bird-pot (1976–78, Fig. 93, no. 80), a panelled vessel of unknown function (1972, Fig. 83, no. 22), and two almost identical chafing dishes (1960, Fig. 80, no. 23; one not illustrated). Jars (1974–75, Fig. 86, nos. 36, 37), bowls (1974–75, Fig. 85, no. 14, Fig. 86, nos. 38, 41), and dishes (1960, Fig. 80, nos. 24, 25; 1972, Fig. 83, no. 23) are all more common; jugs are more varied (1960, Fig. 78, no. 10; 1974–75, Fig. 84, nos. 3, 5, Fig. 86, no. 29; Fig. 87, no. 48; 1976–78, Fig. 93, nos. 76, 77, 79). Handles are mainly oval in section, although rod-and-strap handles are also present. Like the jugs, the cooking-pots are generally flat-based with equally-spaced single or multiple thumbings around the base angle, which is often knife-trimmed and roughly wiped (1972, Fig. 83, no. 14; 1974–75, Fig. 85, nos. 15–17; Fig. 86, no. 39). The cooking-pot rims are everted and seated for lids (1960, Fig. 79, no. 16; 1974–75, Fig. 85, no. 13). Both cooking-pots and bowls generally bear a patchy rich green or brown glaze over one or both surfaces; jugs are less well glazed. As with Fabric LM, glazes tend to be rather 'metallic'. The hospital levels produced a large amount of seventeenth- to nineteenth-century pottery in both a finer and a coarser version of this ware. Production centres are as yet unknown (see pp. 261–2).

13. *Hard Late Medieval/Post-medieval Fine ware*: H.

A small group of sherds (1960 and 1974–75 excavations) are in a highly fired fine ware, possibly overfired LM ware, but perhaps trying to compete with imported stonewares. The fabric is slightly micaceous, tempered with quartz sand and grog, with distinctive streaky reddish-grey surfaces reminiscent of Martincamp or early Siegburg stoneware. The forms (1974–75, Fig. 84, nos. 6, 7; Fig. 87, no. 49), however, appear to be local. Wasters of similarly streaky wares have also been found in association with kilns at Hareplain, in Kent (Kelly 1972), and at Lower Parrock (Freke and Craddock 1979) and Boreham Street in East Sussex (A. Streeten, pers. comm.). The ware is also know within Canterbury.

Non-Local Wares.

14. *East Anglian/Saxon*: EAS. *c.* 600–850.

One sherd from the Anglo-Saxon graveyard (1976–78, Group 2, layer 5160) may be of East Anglian or possibly North French origin. The micaceous fabric is densely tempered with fine black and red inclusions, with occasional angular, fine white flint grits. Pale pink throughout, with black, apparently burnished surfaces and moulded decoration. Probably of seventh- to ninth-century date.

15. *Ipswich Ware*: IPS. *c.* 650–850.

One wheel-made base sherd with string marks underneath and a second base of probable Ipswich ware, from the Anglo-Saxon graveyard (1976–78, Group 2, Fig. 89, no. 5); two sherds from the redeposited graveyard soil (1976–78, Group 3c), and a few residual fragments, all dating to *c.* 650–850 (West 1963, 233–87). One sherd of decorated Ipswich ware was also recovered from the 1959 excavations (Ames 1978, Fig. 13, no. 2), and a ninth-century pit discovered during recent excavations in the outer court of St. Augustine's (Bennett 1984, 25–6) produced local pottery together with both fine and coarse Ipswich wares and a coin of 855–66 (Macpherson-Grant 1984, 28). Further finds of Ipswich ware in Canterbury, notably on the Marlowe Theatre site (Blockley and Blockley, forthcoming), at Yewden's Court in Dover (Dunning 1957, 36) and at Richborough all indicate strong connections with East Anglia in the Middle Saxon period (Macpherson-Grant 1984, 28).

16. *London*: LON. *c.* 1150–1250.

Fine, slightly micaceous sandy ware, mainly with orange surfaces and a grey core, less micaceous than the formally similar Mill Green wares. Finds include a few body sherds with cream slip and green glaze over applied rouletted strips (1972, Fig. 83, no. 20; 1974–5, Fig. 86, no. 30), and a handle from a copy of a 'Rouen' jug (1976–78, Fig. 91, no. 50), all of thirteenth-century date.

17. *Scarborough*: SCAR. *c.* 1225–1325.

Fine, pale pink fabric with pale green glaze: one sherd only (1976–78, Group 5, Fig. 90, no. 30), which is typical of the phase II wares, *c.* 1225–1325 (Farmer 1979, 2, 28, pers. comm.). Scarborough wares, possibly traded by sea, are known in Kent in Canterbury, at Dartford (Mynard 1973, 195–8) and on the south coast (Streeten ;1982a, 94).

18. *Probable Wealden Ware*: WEA. *c.* 1350–1500.

This group includes a wide range of fabrics, some possibly from Surrey or Rye. Three main wares are present (see also Streeten 1982a, 93):

(a) A coarse sandy ware with occasional quartz and flint inclusions, generally having a pale grey core and surfaces ranging from pinkish-yellow to yellow–grey;

(b) Harder, densely tempered with fine grey–black sand and lacking the grit inclusions. Colouring may be as the above (1960, Fig. 81, nos. 28, 29; 1976–78, Fig. 91, no. 58) or more orange (1976–78, Fig. 93, nos. 81, 82). No. 28 (1960) is virtually identical to a sherd from Rye in the British Museum reference collection, although the form appears to be too late for Rye; two sherds (1974–75) have a near parallel at the Hospital of Sts. Stephen and Thomas, New Romney (where pottery from Rye has also been found), from a context dated to *c.* 1300 (Rigold 1964, 61, 63–4);

(c) Contains moderate rose quartz inclusions, and is generally oxidised throughout.

Most identifiable forms appear to be of late fourteenth- or fifteenth-century date, including two jugs (1960, Fig. 81, nos. 28, 29), a pipkin with distinctive 'feet' (1960, Fig. 81, no. 30) and a cistern with splashed green glaze (1976–78, Fig. 93, no. 81). Other sherds include large internally glazed bowls, and a small two-handled strainer (1960, P15).

19. *Rye*: RYE. *c.* 1300–1450.

Part of an early fourteenth-century vessel with *repoussé* decoration and a rich green glaze was found in 1976–78, (Groups 6, 13–15, Fig. 91, no. 40). This is an unusually fine ware for the Rye kilns, evenly fired to a pale pinkish-buff colour throughout, with occasional silt-stone inclusions. Some of the 'Wealden' ware (e.g. 1960, Fig. 81, no. 28) may also derive from Rye, which was producing a variety of sandy red, white and intermediate wares with painted slip decoration (Vidler 1932, 83–101; 1933, 44–64). A small sherd of fine oxidised ware decorated with a *repoussé* ?fleur-de-lys (1972, Fig. 82, no. 21) is also probably from Rye. Rye pottery, including a sherd with rosette decoration similar to that from St. Augustine's, has also been found at New Romney (Rigold 1964, Fig. 11 no. 7), but Canterbury appears to have been outside the normal area of distribution of the Rye kilns. Coastal transport has been suggested (Streeten 1982a, 94).

20. *Surrey Wares. Kingston-type*: KING. *c.* 1270–1350.

Very little medieval white ware was found, but two jug sherds (1972 Trench 3, layer 12; 1976–78, Group 13, Grave 581) are in the 'Kingston variant' fabric, with abundant rounded orange quartz inclusions (Orton 1977, 82). Mid-Surrey white wares (for a general discussion, see Orton 1982a, 92–9) were common at Eynsford Castle (Rigold 1971, 168), but they do not appear to have reached east Kent in any significant quantity until the later fourteenth century (Streeten 1982a, 94; Macpherson-Grant pers. comm.). Pre-Dissolution white wares were rare at the moated site of Leigh (Parfitt 1976, 197) and at the Maison Dieu, Ospringe (Thorn 1979, 182). For forms and fabrics at Kingston, see Hinton (1980, 377–83), and Vince (1985, 34–9); production commenced in the mid thirteenth century, but the 1976–78 sherds appear to be of fourteenth-century date.

21. *Surrey Wares. Cheam*: CHEA. *c.* 1380–1450.

Cheam white wares are limited to a few sherds from small biconical drinking vessels found in the demolition deposits. The fourteenth- to fifteenth-century white-ware industry at Cheam has been discussed by Orton (1979a, 1982b). Of the sixteenth-century Cheam red-wares no definite examples were found, although one jug (1974–75, Fig. 84, no. 2) and one bowl (1974–75, Fig. 87, no. 50) are not dissimilar to these later Cheam products (Orton 1979b, 1982b and pers. comm.).

22. *Surrey Wares: Tudor Green:* TUDG. *c.* 1400–1500.

Although this industry was well-established by the mid-fifteenth century (Moorhouse 1979, 53–61), only two stratified sherds were found (1976–78, Group 9) and only isolated fragments occurred in the demolition levels. Fragments of lobed cups are present in the 1960 and 1976–78 (Group 14) assemblages.

23. *Surrey–Hampshire Fine 'Border Ware':* BORD. *c.* 1550–1700.

No medieval 'Coarse Border' ware was found, but sixteenth- to eighteenth-century fine white wares are present in the demolition and later groups (1974–75, Fig. 87, nos. 51–52). These include fragments from a large pitcher with a narrow neck and strap handle (1960) and two internally glazed bowls found in the 1972 excavations (Trench 2). Similar wares are known from Faversham Abbey (Hurst 1968, 57), Dover Castle (Mynard 1969, 38–40) and in Canterbury. Some of the finer Wealden ware may in fact be of 'Border' origin.

24. *Cistercian-type Ware:* CSTN. *c.* 1500–1600.

Only six sherds of sixteenth-century date, including one rim (1974–75, Fig. 86, no. 28), from demolition or landscaping levels.

25. *Metropolitan-type Slipware:* METS. *c.* 1550–1700.

One small rim, possibly from a copy of a North Holland slipware bowl, with dashes around the rim (1974–75, Group 2), and a dish (1960, Fig. 81, no. 32), are possibly Kentish products of sixteenth- to seventeenth-century date.

26. *London Tin-glazed Ware:* TGW. *c.* 1700–1800.

A few scattered sherds, probably from Lambeth, in the demolition levels; fragments of drug jars (1974–75, Fig. 87, nos. 54–56; 1976–78, Fig. 94, no. 84), dishes (1976–78, Fig. 94, nos. 83, 85) and chamber-pots in the features associated with the hospital period.

27. *English Stoneware:* ENGS. *c.* 1750–1900.

A few sherds of London and Nottingham stoneware were found in the uppermost deposits and features associated with the hospital.

28. *Eighteenth- and nineteenth-century 'China':* CHI. *c.* 1750–1900.

A few intrusive sherds from demolition and landscaping levels, and a large group of Staffordshire white wares from the area of the hospital excavated 1976–78.

Imported Wares.

29. *Germany: Pingsdorf-type Ware:* PING. *c.* 950–1150.

One body sherd only (1976–78, Group 6, Grave 5137), in a very hard, finely granular, buff ware with a pale grey core; possibly from a red-painted vessel (Vince pers. comm.). For discussion of a red-painted Pingsdorf-type pot found in Dover, see Dunning (1951, 148–9).

30. *North French?*: NFR (=possibly EM5). *c.* 1000–1100.

One sherd in a very hard, wheel-made fabric (1976–78, Group 3b/c, layer 8001). Fine pale grey ware with ill-sorted sub-angular inclusions of black iron ore, white flint, shelly-limestone, milky quartz and iron oxide. Flint-tempered wares predominate in twelfth-century groups in Sussex, and are known in Kent at Aldington and at Caesar's Camp, Folkestone (Streeten 1982a, 91–2). The origin of the St. Augustine's sherd is thus debatable at present, but the fabric is not dissimilar to that of North French wares from Canterbury (Macpherson-Grant, pers. comm.). Three pitcher handles thought to be of North French origin were found at Canterbury Lane (Wilson 1983, Fig. 97, no. 325).

31. *France: Rouen:* ROU. *c.* 1150–1300.

Fine pale pink ware. Three sherds only, two from a thirteenth-century jug with applied rouletted decoration in red slip on white slip, with a green glaze (1972, Trench 3, Group 4; 1974–75, Group 4, Fig. 84, no. 10). See also Barton (1965).

32. *South-west France: Saintonge*: STGE. *c.* 1250–1650.

Fine pinkish-white slightly micaceous ware with green glaze. One sherd from a pre-Dissolution context (1976–78, Group 13, grave 581), and a dozen or so sherds from fifteenth- to sixteenth-century deposits, including part of a horizontal strap-handle (1974–5, Group 2, layers 71, 76; Group 5, layer 1; same vessel as 1976–78, Group 16). One unstratified sherd from a polychrome jug was found in 1960 (Me.440, C.S.A.8, no P. number). Saintonge polychrome ware of thirteenth- or fourteenth-century date has been found in Dover (Dunning 1951, 147, Fig. 12, no. 35; Dunning 1955, 138–40), and in Rochester (Dunning 1970, 110–11); plain Saintonge ware has been found at the Maison Dieu, Ospringe (Thorn 1979, 160), amongst other sites in Kent. See also Hurst (1974).

33. *Low Countries: 'Aardenburg'-type Ware:* AARD. *c.* 1250–1400.

Three stratified thirteenth-century sherds (1976–78, Groups 5, 13, including Fig. 90, no. 29) and a dozen or so residual medieval sherds. Medium coarse sandy red ware with rilling or rouletted decoration, cream slip and green glaze. Jug sherds have internally bevelled rims (1960, Fig. 81, no. 33; 1974–75, Fig. 84, no. 4). Finds in Kent include some highly decorated jugs from a garderobe pit in Dover Castle, dated to *c.* 1300 or a little later (Cook *et al.* 1969, 91, 96, 98, Fig. 18).

34. *North Holland Slip-ware*: NHS. *c.* 1500–1600.

One sixteenth-century bowl (1960, Fig. 80, no. 22) with plain slip and glaze internally, and a small fragment of rim and part of a loop handle from a similar bowl with slip decoration in green and yellow (1972 Trench 3, layer 1), both in a fine, sandy, red ware. A dish (1974–75, Fig. 87, no. 53) is also possibly of Low Countries origin, but a bowl (1960, Fig. 80, no. 27) may be a local copy of a Dutch form. For a discussion of North Holland slip-wares, see Hurst *et al.* (1975, 47–66).

35. *Low Countries Red-ware:* LOW. *c.* 1350–1500.

Fine, slightly sandy, pale orange ware. Only two stratified late medieval sherds (1976–78, Group 13, one with internal glaze), but a few fifteenth- and sixteenth-century sherds from Dissolution deposits, including cooking-pots (1960, Fig. 81, no. 32 and one similar with handle scar), a skillet handle (1972, Trench 3, layer 1), and a jug (1976–78, Fig. 93, no. 78).

36. *South Netherlands Maiolica:* SNM. *c.* 1480–1550.

One base from a polychrome dish (1960, P18); one base and two body sherds, from altar or flower vases (1974–75, Fig. 86, no. 31, Fig. 87, no. 58; 1976–78, Group 16). A similar base was found at the Maison Dieu, Ospringe (Thorn 1979, Fig. 43, no. 97). These vases, usually decorated in blue and white, and often bearing the IHS monogram, are mainly found in late fifteenth- and sixteenth-century contexts, and are almost as much a type fossil as the Raeren stoneware mugs. A dish from Faversham Abbey, decorated with the elements of the Passion, was dated to pre-1539 (Hurst 1968, 58, no. 157).

37. *Germany: Werra Ware:* WER. *c.* 1575–1625.

Formerly known as Wanfried, this sandy red ware with trailed slip decoration was produced *c.* 1575–1625 at Wanfried-an-der-Werra and at Witzenhausen on the flood-plain of the River Werra near Kassel, West Germany (for full discussion, see Stephan 1981). The products of these kilns (which were frequently dated) were widely exported in Germany, and to the Low Countries and Great Britain; finds from Norwich have been discussed by Jennings (1981, 78–9). The distribution of this ware in England, which is predominantly found on sites along or near the eastern coast, has been discussed by Hurst (1972, 259–62). Find-spots in Kent include Dover Castle (Mynard 1969, 42) and Faversham Abbey (Hurst 1968, 58, Fig. 18, no. 155). One dish base only was found at St. Augustine's (1974–75, Fig. 87, no. 57), with internal *sgraffito* decoration, under trailed cream slip and a thin greenish glaze.

38. *France: Martincamp Stoneware:* MART. *c.* 1550–1650.

Martincamp, which is situated approximately half-way between Dieppe and Beauvais in Normandy, France, was from the late fifteenth to the seventeenth century the production centre for a distinctive form of flask with a long neck and a globular body which was convex on one side and flattened on the other. While the form itself changed little, study by Hurst (1977a, 156–7) has shown three distinct fabrics: Type 1, a hard off-white earthenware (late fifteenth to early sixteenth century); Type 2, a buff-grey to dark grey stoneware (sixteenth century), and Type 3, a very hard streaky orange-grey fabric similar to Fabric H (p. 254 above), dating to *c.* 1550–1650. The three sherds from the demolition levels at St. Augustine's (1972, Trench 3; 1974–75 Group 1) are all of Type 3. Martincamp flasks have been found in Kent at Dover Castle (Mynard 1969, 36, Fig. 11, no. 13) and in Canterbury: one flask recently published (Wilson 1983, Fig. 132, no. 887) together with another not identified to source (Fig. 92, no. 239).

39. *Italian/Mediterranean:* IT (=PM 23). *c.* 1500–1650.

Three sherds, probably from a small *albarello*, found in 1960 (P25). Very fine pale pink fabric with occasional iron-stone grits and dense very fine white 'chalky' inclusions, with a green glaze over a cream slip externally. A similar fabric (PM23) has been found in Canterbury at North Lane (Macpherson-Grant 1978, 190, Fig. 23, no. 63) and on the

Marlow site III (Macpherson-Grant pers. comm.) and tentatively identified as deriving from 'Mediterranean mercury jars' of probable sixteenth-century date. The exact provenance of these wares is unknown; this example may derive from North Africa or Spain, but is most probably from northern Italy.

40. *Chinese Porcelain:* CHPO. *c.* 1650–1900.

A few sherds of seventeenth- or eighteenth-century tea-bowl were found in features associated with the hospital period.

Rhenish Stoneware.

The original report on the stoneware from the excavations of 1972 and 1974–75 was prepared by Pamela Clarke; parts of this have been incorporated into the relevant sections below. Unfortunately, none of the wares from St. Augustine's were usefully stratified, but the assemblage as a whole is typical of the mid-sixteenth century, being scattered throughout the Dissolution and later deposits. For a useful general discussion of the wide range of forms and fabrics found at Norwich, see Jennings (1981, 109–27).

41. *Rhenish Stoneware. Siegburg:* SIEG. *c.* 1300–1550.

The few sherds recovered are mainly from jugs or beakers but include a base sherd (1976–78, Group 16, layer 3) from a shallow cup similar to Beckmann Group VIII, nos. 161–4 (Beckmann 1974, Fig. 19, 220). See also Reineking-von Bock (1971, 30–35).

42. *Rhenish Stoneware. Langerwehe:* LANG. *c.* 1350–1500.

Thirty-five sherds, mainly from the excavations of 1960, including two jugs, one with rouletted decoration (1960, Fig. 81, nos. 34, 35), and two jars (1974–75, Fig. 87, nos. 59, 60). Pamela Clarke comments: 'These have been classified according to the system used for the material from Edinburgh High Street (Clarke 1975, 206–11). Because of the extreme variability of the surface colouration of Langerwehe material, and its similarity to Raeren in appearance (though not usually in vessel form), it is often impossible to tell the origin of a vessel from single sherds. Taking into account such factors as the combination of surface appearance, fabric and general colouration, and the fact that heavy rilling is more usually a feature of Langerwehe than Raeren, while a very high glaze is more usually a feature of Raeren than Langerwehe, a further fifty-one sherds have been divided into two sub-groups, probable Langerwehe and probable Raeren'. See also Reineking-von Bock (1971, 39–40) and Hurst (1977b).

43. *Rhenish Stoneware. Raeren:* RAER. *c.* 1480–1550.

Fifty-eight sherds, mainly from the excavations of 1960, of which the most interesting piece is an anthropomorphic jug (Fig. 81, no. 38; see p. 266). The bulk of the group comprises fragments of drinking mug (1960, Fig. 81, nos. 36, 37; 1974–75, Fig. 87, nos. 61–64), which, as noted above, are common in Dissolution contexts, and are regarded as a type fossil for the period 1480–1550. See also Reintking-von Bock (1971, 40–3).

44. *Rhenish Stoneware. Cologne/Frechen:* COL/F. *c.* 1550–1700.

Seventy-five sherds, including two from an inscribed band jug, one from a small bellarmine (1972, Fig. 83, nos. 15, 16, see p. 277), and thirty-three from an oak-leaf jug (1974–75, Fig. 87, no. 65; see p. 282, and Reineking-von Bock (1971, 35–9) and Thwaite (1973).

45. *Rhenish Stoneware. Aachen:* AACH.

One fragment only, from the neck of a bottle with a glossy, mid-brown glaze (1960, Fig. 81, no. 39).

46. *Rhenish Stoneware. Westerwald:* WEST. *c* 1600–1800.

Only ten sherds from the excavations of 1974–75 (Fig. 87, nos. 66, 67), and 1976–78 (Groups 15, 16), all in a pale greyish-white fabric with decoration in cobalt and manganese. See also Reineking-von Bock (1971, 44–48).

THE LOCAL POTTERY INDUSTRY

Early Medieval and Medieval

The source of the local medieval pottery has long been recognised as being in the Tyler Hill or Blean Forest areas, on the London Clays which lie approximately one mile to the north-east of Canterbury. The first pottery wasters in this area were discovered by chance in a bomb crater in 1942 (Spillett *et al.* 1942). Since then field surveys have located numerous dumps of pottery wasters and thirteenth-/fourteenth-century kilns (Lyle 1965, 34; Cramp 1969, 14; Tatton-Brown 1983, 128), yet forty years later much of the pottery remains unpublished, and the origins and duration of the industry are only now beginning to become clear. Five excavated kilns have been published (Philp and Swale 1967, 15–16; Cramp 1970a, 26–8; Cramp 1970b, 11–12; Harrington 1971, 149–51; Philp 1974, 175–81), all of which were producing roof- and floor-tiles. Small amounts of pottery were associated with the kilns, or mixed with roof-tiles in nearby pits, but as yet no kiln has been discovered the sole function of which was to produce domestic pottery. Similarly no kiln has been found which may be dated with confidence to pre-1200, and until recently the source of the large quantities of late Anglo-Saxon and early medieval pottery found in Canterbury could only be surmised. In 1980, however, research using thin-section and textural analysis (Streeten 1982a, 91–2; forthcoming) showed that the same London clay sources were being exploited for the early medieval pottery sealed by the *c.* 1165 foundations of the *Aula Nova* (Driver *et al.* forthcoming) as were used for the thirteenth to fourteenth-century wares. The very high proportion of fine quartz grains in these wares was thought to result from the addition of brickearth to the London clay (Streeten 1982a, 91–2; 1982b, 131). It was also confirmed (Streeten 1982a, 91) that identical wares had been found on a number of twelfth-century sites up to twenty miles away, at Folkestone (Pitt-Rivers 1883, 456–60), Dover (Rigold 1967, 111; Cook *et al.* 1969, 89), Faversham (Rigold 1968, 56) and Rochester

(Tester 1972, 144). Pottery manufacture at Tyler Hill was thus seen to be well established and marketing on a fairly large scale by the mid-twelfth century, if not earlier (Streeten 1982b, 92). This hypothesis has now been confirmed by the recent discovery near Brittancourt Farm of a waster dump containing kiln debris and pottery almost identical to that found in the large *Aula Nova* group (Tatton-Brown 1983, 127–30; Macpherson-Grant 1983, 130–1). A date of *c.* 1150–65 has been proposed for this kiln, and it can only be a matter of time before further early kiln groups are located. Thin-section analysis of the Saxon wares from Canterbury (Mainman 1982, 93–100; forthcoming) has shown that the late Anglo-Saxon sandy wares are also virtually identical to the early medieval and medieval Tyler Hill wares. If so, pottery may have been produced in the Blean Forest area for some 600 years although, due to the insubstantial nature of Anglo-Saxon kilns, this may never be proven beyond doubt. Mention should perhaps be made here, however, of two 'kilns' discovered in early excavations in the cloisters at St. Augustine's Abbey. Nothing is known of these structures other than their existence on a plan of 1934. Potts (1928, 65) refers to the excavations then in progress in the cloister, which 'may throw some light on the early buildings adjoining the North Porticus and the extension of that porticus', but frustratingly omits any mention of the 'kilns' in the discussion of the cloister (Potts 1934, 191–4) which accompanies the full plan of the abbey. This shows a small oval 'kiln' just cut by the east wall of the west walk of the cloister, and a larger, circular 'kiln' which extends under the west wall of the west walk. The latter, which has an east–west division and possible flue on the eastern side, appears to be associated with the remains of walls on the north and south sides which, according to the key, should be of eighth- to tenth-century date. If this is so then, given its proximity to the Anglo-Saxon church, the structure is perhaps more likely to have been an oven rather than a kiln. The tantalising possibility of an early Anglo-Saxon kiln, pre-dating the church should not, however, be discounted, although the feature could equally be of Roman date.

Later Medieval and Post-medieval

The peak of the Tyler Hill industry appears to have been in the later thirteenth and fourteenth centuries, when the wares were widely marketed (Dunning 1955, 148–50; Streeten 1982a, 92), presumably through Canterbury itself. Sherds from the 1942 collection analysed by Streeten (1982a, 90 and Fig. 38a; forthcoming) were found to produce remarkably consistent patterns of grain size frequency, the great majority of quartz grains being less than 0.1 mm. (mainly *c.* 0.05 mm. or less). The range of wares produced is being studied by the Canterbury Archaeological Trust, and has been discussed elsewhere (Macpherson-Grant 1980b, 296–7; 1981a, 24–35). Two groups of jugs have been discovered in medieval wells at Canterbury Lane (Wilson 1983, 240–52) and at Worth (Gaunt 1978, 94–8).

The continuation of pottery manufacture in the fifteenth century was not proven until 1980, although documentary evidence showed that tile kilns were certainly in operation. Of these one (?possibly two) was in the parish of St. Stephen's, Hackington, where there are references (Harrington 1971, 150–1) to a 'tylhost' in 1363 and 1465 to a 'tyleoste' and workshops at 'tylernehelde' (?Tyler Hill). The possibility of further kilns is suggested in the Treasurer's Accounts of 1468–69 for St. Augustine's Abbey, where it is recorded that in addition to paying for the transport of fuel from various local woods for a tile furnace of which Brothers John

Ashmynton and William Mongeham were the wardens (Cotton 1939, 95–6, 104), the abbey not only contributed £6 12*s*. 7*d*. to the maintenance of a brick kiln (Cotton 1939, 101), but in the same year also purchased 6000 plain tiles (probably roof-tiles) from one Nicholas Alleyn. This may have been a specific order for the building works in progress at this time, but nonetheless confirms the existence of at least one local tilery in the later fifteenth century. The layout of the credit accounts, wherein the profits from a tile oven (£3 12*s*. 2*d*.) directly follow those for the sale of wood from Penwyngwode, and immediately precede those for the sale of wood from Dengrove and Rickerwood, suggests the existence of another kiln, owned by the abbey, but perhaps manned by a lay potter, at Penwyngwode or Dengrove.

In 1980, a group of wasters was discovered at Cane Wood, Tyler Hill (Bennett 1980c, 293). These were originally dated to *c*. 1325–75 (Macpherson-Grant 1980d, 295–7), although a single sherd, at the time considered a stray, was in a much finer ware, comparable to fifteenth- and sixteenth-century wares from Canterbury. The group is now thought to date to *c*. 1375–1450/75 (Macpherson-Grant forthcoming). The pottery industry is thus shown to continue into the later fifteenth century, and possibly into the sixteenth century, but the transition from the medieval sandy wares to the true fine wares is not fully understood. It appears to have been a gradual evolution; finer wares were appearing in Canterbury by the later fifteenth century (Macpherson-Grant 1983, 31), but the process may have begun earlier than this (see Fabrics LM, F, p. 254).

At present the only known early post-medieval kiln (*c*. 1600) in Kent is that at Hareplain, near Biddenden, some 30 miles away (Kelly 1972). At Dover it was suggested (Mynard 1969, 43) that a group of seventeenth-/eighteenth-century coarse lead-glazed wares might be the products of the High Halden kilns, also near Biddenden. This may be true of the coarser earthenwares recovered in 1976–78 from levels associated with the hospital at St. Augustine's, but it appears that there is no definite evidence for the High Halden industry before the nineteenth century. At Linacre Gardens, Canterbury, eight post-medieval fine-ware fabrics were identified (Macpherson-Grant 1983, 32), of which seven were thought to be of Kentish origin, possibly from High Halden or perhaps more locally produced. The products of the Hareplain kiln are characterised by a relatively high proportion of large quartz grains (Streeten 1982a, 90, Fig. 3; 1982b, 127 and Fig. 14), and it may be that some of the coarser early post-medieval fine wares from St. Augustine's and from Canterbury derive from this source.

THE POTTERY FROM THE EXCAVATIONS OF 1960

Introduction

The excavations and consolidation undertaken in 1960 produced a total of 1467 sherds of pottery from a number of contexts across a wide area, of which only the pottery from Trenches A–E is discussed here (1248 sherds). The pottery was stored by the excavator in bags marked with 'P' (Pottery) numbers and general layer descriptions, not all of which may be related with confidence to the layers recorded in the section drawings. For this reason the P numbers have been retained in this report; a correlation of the P numbers, original layer descriptions on the finds bags and the layers shown in Figs. 3, a–c or referred to in the text is presented in Table 4. Most of the pottery appears to have come from the Dissolution contexts in Trenches A, B, and

C, and is of mid to late sixteenth-century date. Although there are many similarities between this group and the 1972–78 assemblages, there appears to be a higher proportion of late medieval and early post-medieval non-local white wares and imported stonewares in the 1960 assemblage than elsewhere. The pottery was studied in three groups (see Tables 5 and 6).

Group 1. Roman/redeposited Roman deposits. P4, P8 (layer 27); P12, P14 (F7, layer 26).
Group 2. Late Medieval deposits. P2, P11, P16 (layers 16, ?25); P29 (layer 24), P5.
Group 3. Dissolution deposits. Trench A: P1, P3, P22, P24 (layer 7); P10 (layer 12); P25, P30 (layer 6); Trench B: P23, P28 (layer 22); P9 (layer 7), ?P13; ?Trench C: P6, P17; Trenches A/B/C: P18. Also P7.

The Belgic and Roman pottery is noted in the excavation report; the post-Roman pottery (Figs. 78–81 is presented by period as far as is possible. The pottery from the shaft (Fig. 82) is discussed as a separate group, although the figure numbers run on from Figs. 78–81. For fabric codes see above; for parallels for published sherds see the catalogues.

'Roman', Anglo-Saxon and Early Medieval.

The dating of the 'Roman' deposits is open to doubt since P8 includes late Roman, early medieval and medieval pottery and two sherds of fifteenth-century date, although these may be derived from layer 25. Some of the medieval sherds are paralleled in P16 (layer 16) and in P23 (layer 22).

No early or middle Anglo-Saxon wares are present in any of the 1960 pottery groups, and only one early medieval sherd (P29), a hand-made sand-and-shell-tempered ware of probable eleventh-century date) was found in the trench for the footing of the quire (F8, layer 24; see p. 25, pp. 28–9). P8 includes two rim sherds of early medieval sandy ware (no. 6 and one similar to 1972 Trench 3, Fig. 83, no. 3). A further thirty-one sherds of late Saxon/early medieval pottery were recovered from the Dissolution deposits. These presumably derive from the construction levels for the crypt and quire, which were disturbed in the medieval period. Most sherds date to the late eleventh century and are well matched in other groups from Canterbury, but the decorated rim with knife-trimmed surfaces (no. 5) is probably of tenth-century date. No parallels are known for this form. No. 7 may be a form of drain-pipe, although the fabric is rather porous for this purpose. It appears to be in a local early-medieval fabric, but could be an unusual late-medieval ware. Very little shell-tempered ware was found other than no. 1 (rim in P18, body sherd in P16), and no. 4, a cooking-pot rim. P16 (layer 16) also contains one jug rim with green glaze over cream slip (no. 2, possibly non-local grey sandy ware). No. 1 is late twelfth- or early thirteenth-century, nos. 2 and 4 are probably thirteenth-century; on the evidence of no. 3, however, layer 16 is of late fourteenth- or fifteenth-century date.

The medieval pottery from the Dissolution deposits consists mainly of small body sherds in Fabrics B/LB and C/D. No. 8, from the bank adjacent to the south-east side of the cloister, is one of the largest fragments found apart from the group from the shaft. The pottery from below the wall F10 (P5), consists of only two sherds of Roman and one sherd of early-medieval pottery.

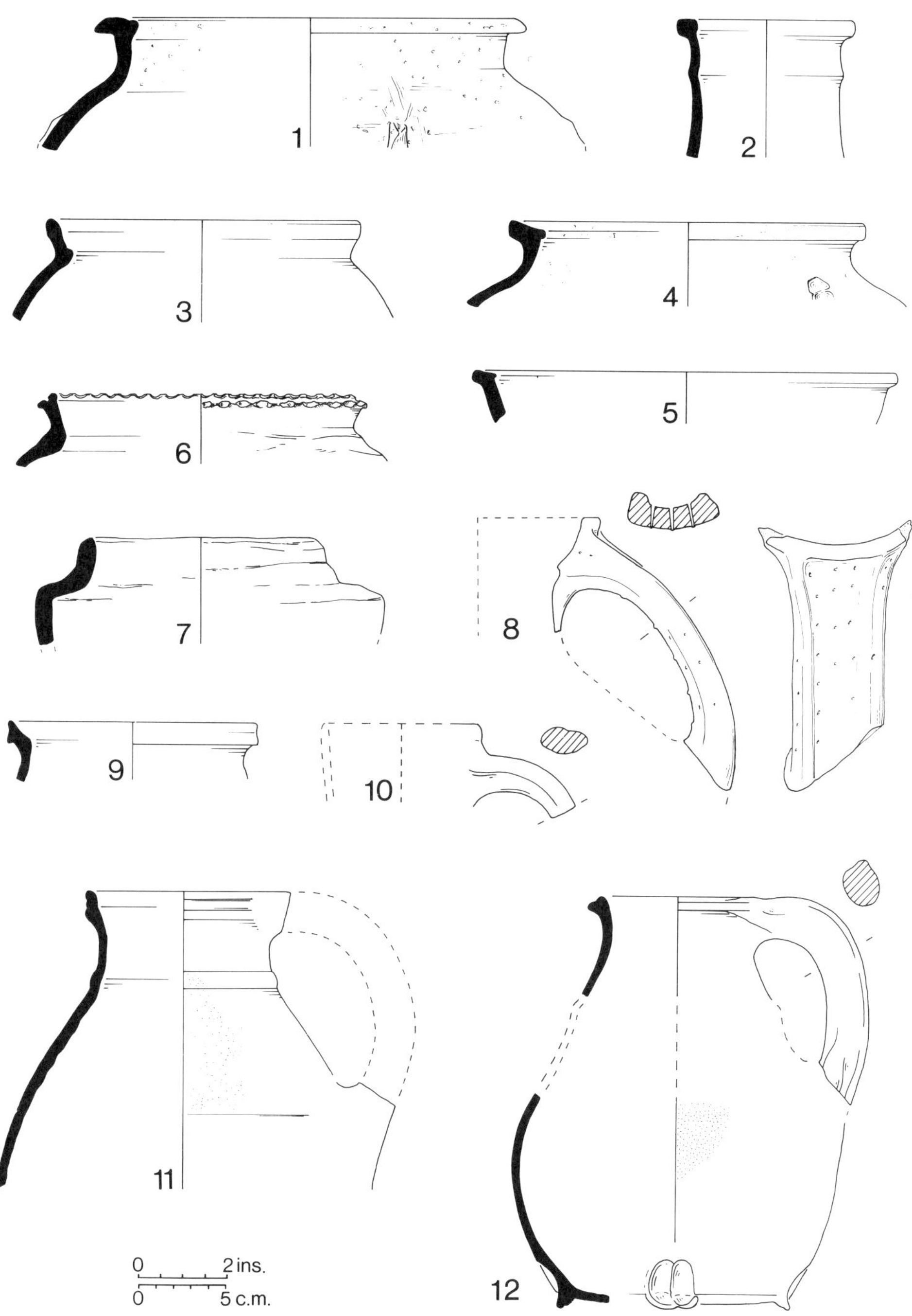

Fig. 78. Medieval and late medieval local Pottery, 1960. Groups 2 and 3. (Scale: ¼)

Late Medieval and Early Post-medieval.

The demolition layers produced a quantity of late medieval and post-medieval sherds, with a number of largely complete vessels. The group includes a wider range of cooking pots (nos. 9, 13, 15, 16), pipkins (nos. 14, 17), and bowls (nos. 20, 22, 24–7) than was found in the excavations to the south of the church, but fewer jugs; nos. 11, 12, and 28 are the only examples capable of reconstruction. Also present are some more unusual forms such as nos. 18, 21, 23, 26 and 27. No. 18, the head of a watering can, and the bowls nos. 26 and 27 appear to be local wares, but have close parallels in the seventeenth-century assemblage from Woolwich (Pryor and Blockley 1978). No. 27 is of interest as a copy, possibly by an immigrant potter, of a Dutch 'foot'. No. 17, the spiggot of a bung-hole pitcher is in a fine red ware with reduced, fused surfaces, similar to a jug from the demolition levels excavated in 1976–78 (Fig. 93, no. 79). The chafing dish, which has a facetted base in the shape of a ten-pointed 'star', and a large applied rosette pad in the bowl, has a lustrous green-brown glaze over both surfaces, but not over the base. A second base from a similar dish is also present in P3. A similar form from Ospringe was described as Flemish (Thorn 1979, 180), but this example appears to be in a local fabric. No. 21 is a lid from a storage jar.

Non-local white wares comprise a small group of Tudor Green ware, a range of probable Wealden wares, and a number of post-medieval fine Surrey–Hants. Border wares, mainly bowls and dishes. The 'Wealden' wares include an elegant green-glazed jug (no. 28, possibly Rye) with a slender body and a frilled foot, probably copying a metal or stoneware form (cf. 1974–75, Fig. 84, no. 4), a green-glazed jug in a similar fabric (no. 29), and the base of a late fourteenth-century pipkin (no. 30) with applied feet, which has deep thumb and fore-finger impressions on both the underside and the outer wall of the body. A few examples of this form are known in Canterbury (Macpherson-Grant pers. comm.). No. 32, a dish with slip decoration is probably a Kentish product in the Metropolitan-slipware tradition.

Imported wares consist almost entirely of German stonewares. Other imports are limited to two sherds of Aardenburg-type ware, including no. 33; a North Holland slipware bowl (no. 22) in a sandy red fabric with internal slip and clear glaze (see above p. 258), a bowl or cooking pot (no. 31) and a few sherds of Low Countries redware; two sherds of Saintonge ware, and two sherds from an *albarello*-type vessel (P25), of North Italian origin (see above, pp. 259–60). The stonewares fall into more or less equal groups: Langerwehe (twenty-four sherds=fourteen vessels, including nos. 34, 35) with a further seven sherds (seven vessels) of possible Langerwehe; Raeren (thirty-six sherds=sixteen vessels, including nos. 36–38); Cologne (seventeen sherds=sixteen vessels), and one sherd of Aachen ware (no. 39). No Siegburg or Westerwald wares were present, but these were rare in all other parts of the site. Plain Raeren mugs such as nos. 36–7 are frequently found in late fifteenth-century contexts, but decorated examples such as no. 38 are unusual, although quite common on the Continent. The decoration on the earlier anthropomorphic forms is incised, but later is mainly applied. No. 38, from pit F4 and adjacent deposits, is of interest as a rare example of a virtually complete anthropomorphic jug with applied, incised and stamped decoration, which probably dates to *c.* 1500–50. The decoration on the earlier anthropomorphic forms is incised, but later is mainly applied. The fabric is paler than usual, being a yellowish-grey colour, but the streaky-grey brown glaze over the rilled outer surface is typical of Raeren wares; the unglazed inner surface is yellow-brown in

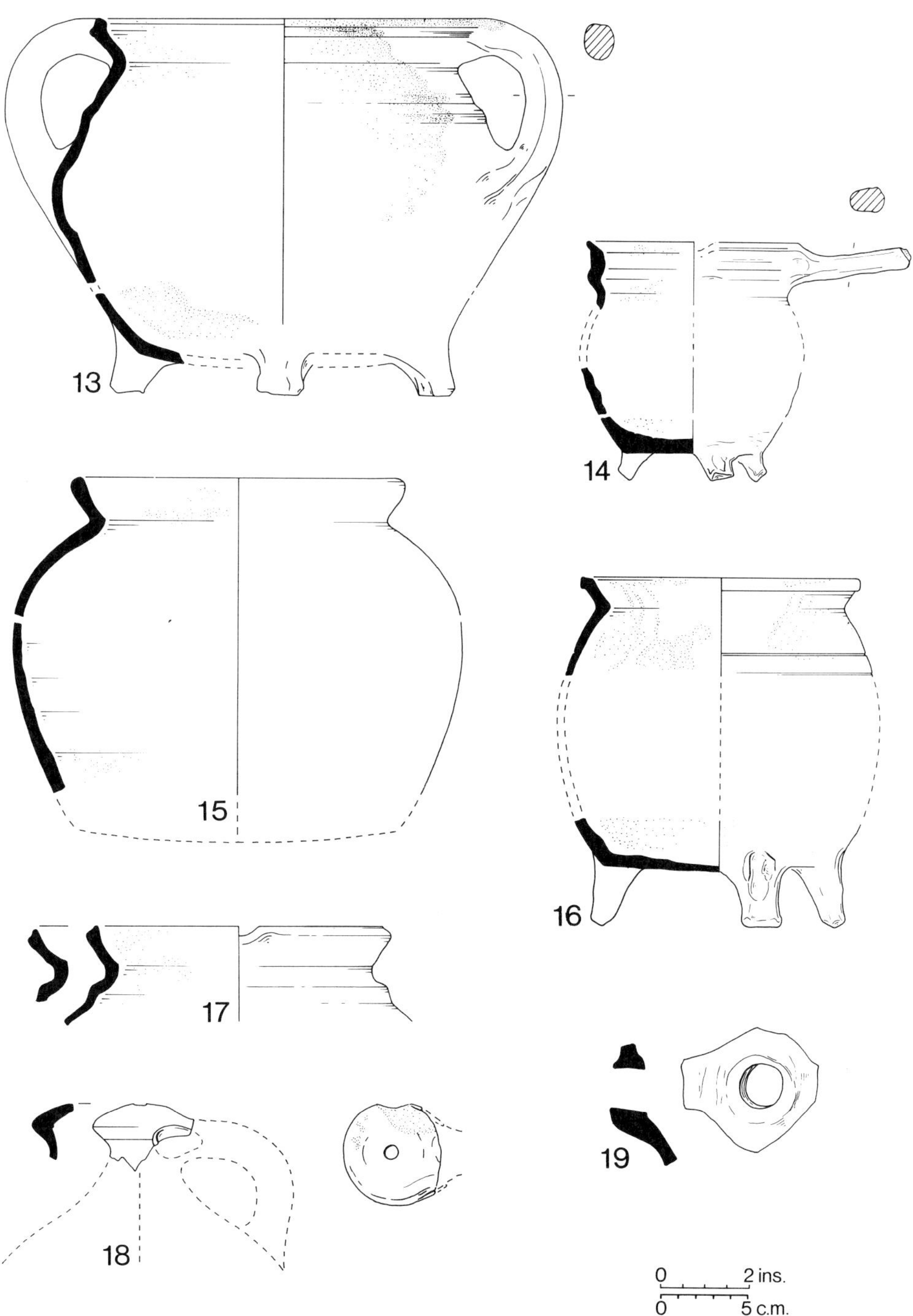

Fig. 79. Late medieval local Pottery, 1960. Group 3. (Scale: ¼)

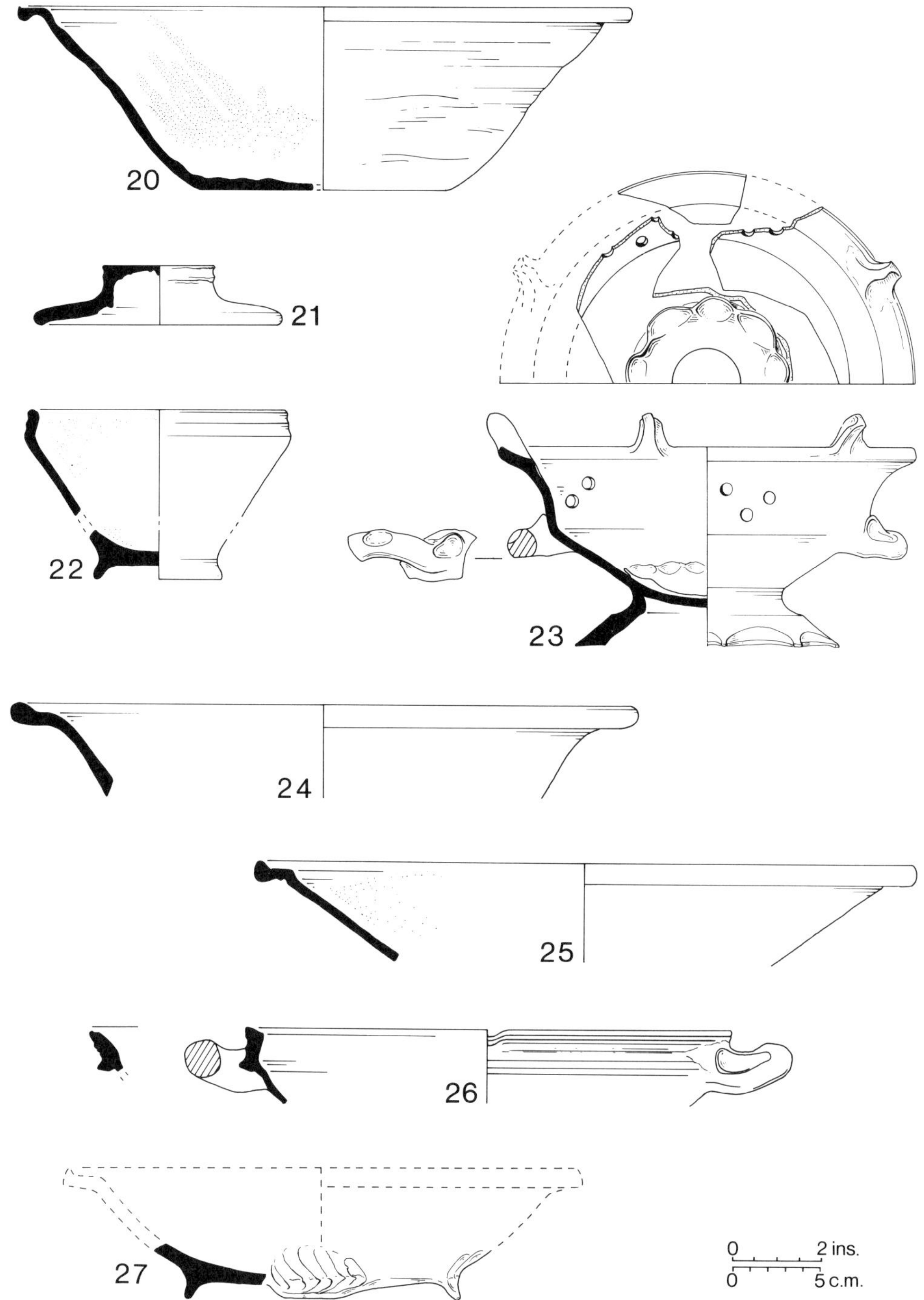

Fig. 80. Late medieval Pottery and North Holland Slipware (no. 22), 1960. Group 3. (Scale: ¼)

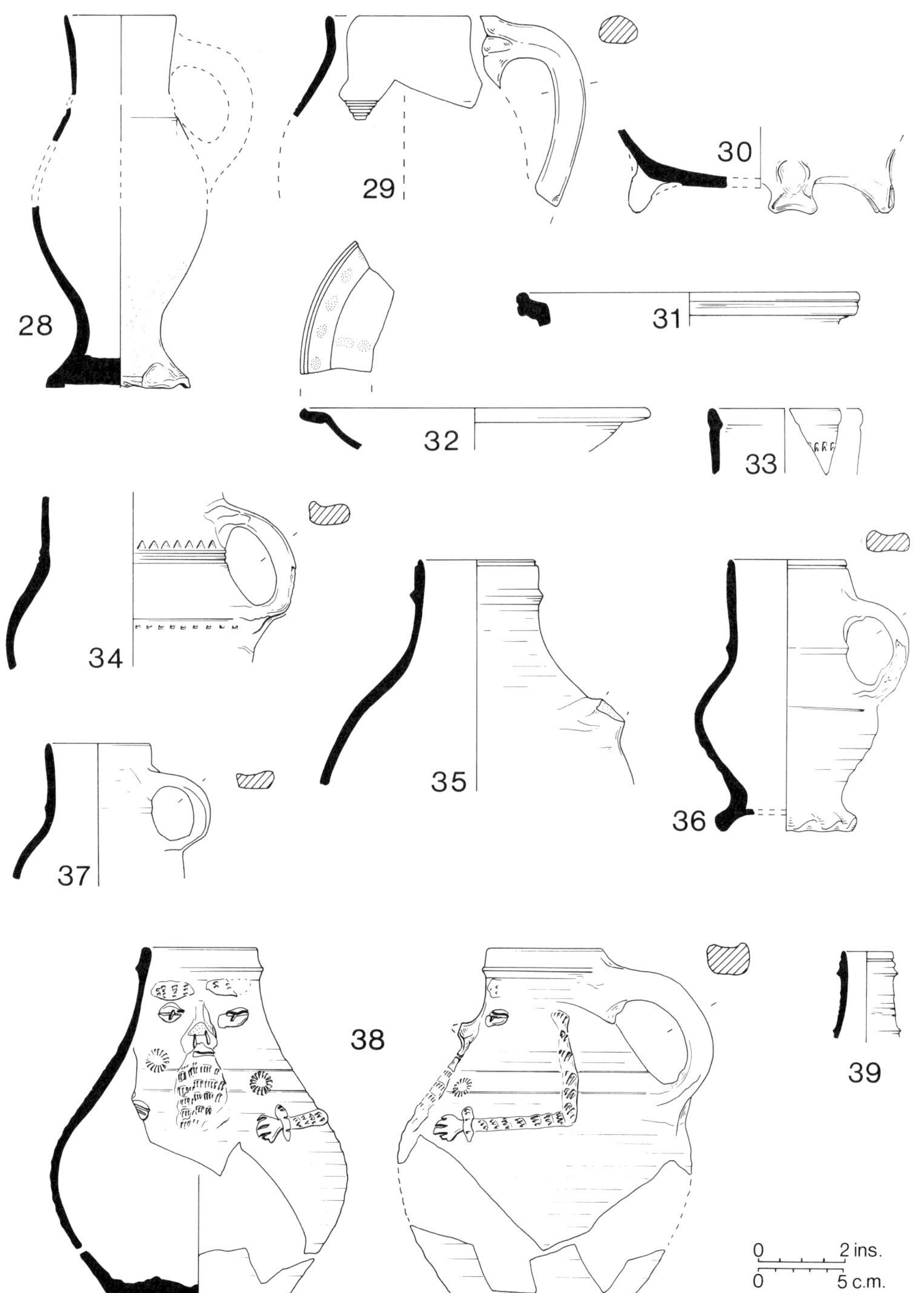

Fig. 81. Non-local (nos. 28–31) and imported (nos. 32–9) late medieval and early post-medieval Pottery, 1960. Group 3. (Scale: ¼)

colour. A large collection of mugs and jugs with both anthropomorphic and abstract decoration is displayed in the Van Beuningen Collection in Rotterdam; similar jugs and mugs in the Kunstgewerbe Museum at Cologne have been discussed by Reineking-von Bock (1971, 41).

TABLE 4

Excavations 1960. Correlation of pottery codes and layers (as described by S. E. Rigold)

Pot Code	*Description*	*Probable Layer/Trench*
P1	'St. Pancras' trench east of north transept apse under post-Dissolution floor.	7 (A/B)
P2	East–west trench. Old soil level below narrow N–S sleeper wall (F10).	16 (C)
P3	Trench east of north transept apse, demolition debris below mortar.	7 (A/B)
P4	N–S trench north of quire. Roman or over.	27 (B)
P5	Grave (F12 or F16).	?34/43
P6	East–west trench cemetery area.	? (C)
P7	South–east bank, cloister.	
P8	North of quire, Roman layer 2.10 m. below.	26/27 (B)
P9	North of quire below Dissolution period 'floor'.	7 (B)
P10	Trench east of north transept apse below intermediate clay.	12 (A)
P11	Trench east of north transept apse, east end, 0.90–1.20 m. below clay with medieval debris and tiles, sealed under clean clay.	16(A)
P12	'Roman pit' north–east of end of apse, 1.80 m.	26 (B)
P13	Trench north of quire, north–east end.	? (B)
P14	Trench north of quire, north corner, Roman.	26 (B)
P16	Trench east of north transept apse below Dissolution building debris, probably sealed beneath clean clay.	16 (A) or 25 (B)
P17	East–west trench east end, beyond cemetery wall.	? (C)
P18	Dissolution building debris.	7/12 (A/B)
P22	Trench east of north transept apse above intermediate clay.	7/12 (A/B)
P23	Trench east of north transept apse, pit with shell and coins.	22 (B)
P24	East of north transept below Dissolution mortar.	7 (A/B)
P25	East of north transept, sealed pit under Dissolution mortar (=F4).	6 (A)
P26	Weight pit (Shaft in north aisle).	
P27	Unstratified.	
P28	North of quire, medieval rubbish pit at north end 2.10 m. from surface (=F6).	22 (B)
P29	Footing trench of quire.	24 (B)
P30	East of north transept sealed pit under Dissolution mortar (=F4).	6 (A)

TABLE 5

Excavations 1960. The distribution of the stratified local pottery types

Group.	BE	RO	SS	EMS	SHS	SOS	A	B	C	D	LB	LM	F
1.	42	112		3	2		4		1			2	2
2.	2	6		2	2	1	2	1	1	3		1	1
3.	26	66	1	29	7	7	45	56	52	56	143	151	244
TOTAL	70	114	1	34	11	8	51	57	54	59	143	154	247

TABLE 6

Excavations 1960. The distribution of the stratified non-local and imported pottery

Group.	LON	CHEA	WEA	TUDG	BORD	CSTN	METS	ENGS	CHI	STGE	AARD	LOW	NHS	SNM	IT	LANG	L/R	RAER	COL/F	AACH
1.																				
2.	2	2	80	19	24	4	1	4	2	1	2	12	3	1	3	24	7	36	17	1
3.																				
TOTAL	2	2	80	19	24	4	1	4	2	1	2	12	3	1	3	24	7	36	17	1

Excavations 1960. Catalogue. Figs. 1–4.

N.B. No internal parallels for published material.

No.	*P. nos.*	*Fabric*	*Total Sherds*	*Glaze Int.*	*Glaze Ext.*	*External Parallels*
	Fig. 78					
1.	P.18,16	SHS	2			
2.	P.16	B?	1		SG	
3.	P.16	C	1		G	
4.	P.16	SOS	1			
5.	P.8	SN	1			
6.	P.18	SN	1			
7.	P.24	SN/A	1			
8.	P.7	C	1		SG	Macpherson-Grant 1978, Fig. 21, no. 46
9.	P.13	F/LM	1	G		
10.	P.18	F	1		G	
11.	P.18,22,24	LB	20		G	
12.	P.9,18,22,24, 25,28	LM/LB	30		G	

Excavations 1960. Catalogue (contd.).

No.	P. nos.	Fabric	Total Sherds	Glaze Int.	Glaze Ext.	External Parallels
	Fig. 79					
13.	P.18,24,25	LM	50	G	G	
14.	P.24,25	D/LB	6	G		Wilson 1983, Fig. 92, nos. 235–6
15.	P.18,22,24,25	LM	8	G		
16.	P.10,25 (P9,23,24)	LM/H	3+?19	G	G	
17.	P.18	F/?LOW	1	G		
18.	P.25	LB	1		Y	Pryor and Blockley 1978, Fig. 10, no. 31
19.	P.22	F	1			
	Fig. 80					
20.	P.3,10,22,24,25	LB	14	G		
21.	P.24	LB	3			
22.	P.24,25	NHS	3	SC		
23.	P.3,18,22,24	F	10	G	G	Thorn 1975, Fig. 43, no. 100
24.	P.24	F	3			
25.	P.6,24	F	2	C		
26.	P.18	LB	5	SG		Pryor and Blockley 1978, Fig. 7, nos. 8, 9 Dawson 1979, Fig. 10, nos. 144–6
27.	P.18,24	LB/NHS	10	SG		Pryor and Blockley 1978, Fig. 7, no. 6; Fig. 8, no. 17 Hurst *et al.* 1975, Fig. 10, nos. 1–4
	Fig. 81					
28.	P.10	WEA	9		G	
29.	P.24,25	WEA	5		G	
30.	P.18	WEA	2	G		
31.	P.18	LOW	1	G		
32.	P.18	METS	1	SC		
33.	P.18	AARD	1			
34.	P.18	LANG	1			
35.	P.18,24	LANG	6			
36.	P.10,17,24	RAER	8			
37.	P.24,25	RAER	3			
38.	P.24,25,30	RAER	14			Reineking-von Bock 1971, 234, no. 339; 236, no. 346
39.	P.27	AACH	1			Dawson 1979, Fig. 11, no. 175

THE POTTERY FROM THE SHAFT, EXCAVATIONS 1965 (Fig. 82).

The shaft contained 229 sherds of thirteenth- to fourteenth-century pottery from Tyler Hill (see Table 7). A minimum of twelve jugs and five cooking-pots are represented, and the group as a whole compares closely with the pottery from North Lane (Bennett 1978, 165–91) and from a fourteenth-century well in Canterbury Lane (Frere and Stow 1983, 92–9). The jug sherds are

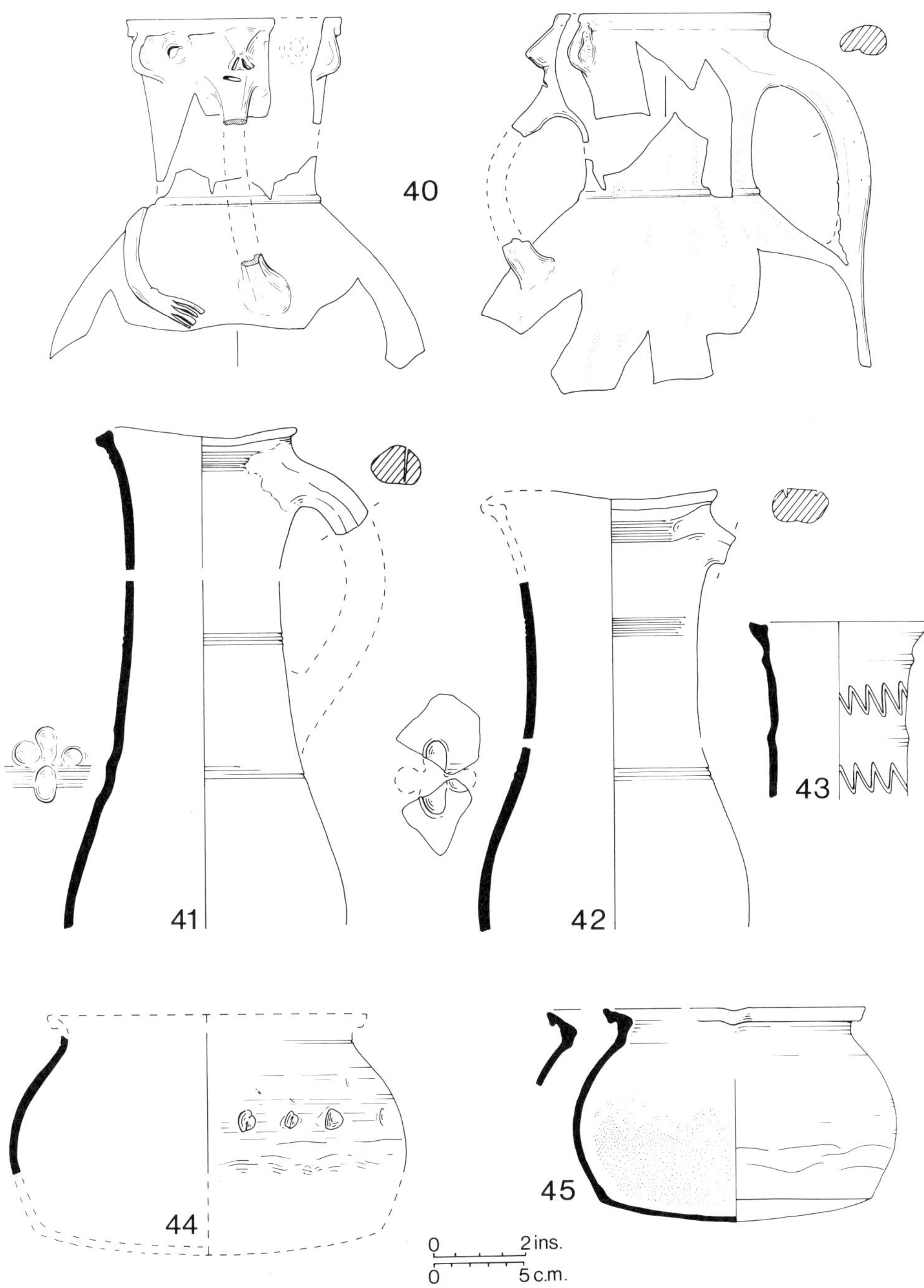

Fig. 82. Medieval Pottery from the Shaft, 1965. (Scale: ¼)

mainly derived from baluster jugs decorated with horizontal rilling, of which two (nos. 41, 42) have an impressed 'rosette' over the rilling on the girth of the jug, below the lip. This motif was also found in the 1976–78 assemblage (Group 14, layer 540). Another jug is decorated with bands of incised zig-zag lines (no. 43). Fragments of two large cooking-pots decorated with applied thumbed strips were found, and also a small skillet (no. 44) with finger impressions around the girth. A second, largely complete skillet with external knife trimming around the base angle and internal green glaze (no. 45) has a lip and may have had a ladle-type handle. A few sherds of sand-and-shell-tempered cooking-pot are also present.

The most interesting piece is a late thirteenth- or fourteenth-century anthropomorphic jug (no. 40) with a patchy green glaze over vertical stripes of cream slip. The glaze is mainly confined to a bib over the front of the vessel, but extends unevenly over the rest of the pot. This style of jug is not unknown in Canterbury, but such a substantial portion is unusual, most examples being restricted to the mask alone. Three examples of face masks from anthropomorphic jugs from Canterbury have recently been published (Wilson 1983), from the Bus Station,

TABLE 7

Excavations 1965. The distribution of the local pottery from the shaft

	BE	RO	SHS	SOS	A	B	C	D	LM
	1	1	4	4	58	88	63	9	1
TOTAL	1	1	4	4	58	88	63	9	1

Excavations 1965. The pottery from the Shaft

Catalogue. Fig. 82.

No.	*P. no.*	*Fabric*	*Total Sherds*	*Glaze Int.*	*Glaze Ext.*	*External Parallels*
40.	P275 (A.M.L.78203082)	C	27		SG	Macpherson-Grant 1978, Fig. 23, no. 60 Wilson 1983, Fig. 85, no. 140; Wilson 1983, Fig. 101, no. 397; Wilson 1983, Fig. 125, no. 773
41.	P275 (A.M.L.78203079)	A	15		G	Wilson 1983, Fig. 119, no. 666
42.	P275	B	20		G	
43.	P275	B	6		G	
44.	P275	A	1			
45.	P275 (A.M.L.78203080)	A/B	16	G		Wilson 1983, Fig. 106, no. 428

St. George's Street, and from the well in Canterbury Lane. Of these the Bus Station example compares most closely with the St. Augustine's jug in having a beard. Beards are common on the thirteenth-century Scarborough and Grimston face jugs, and this is clearly a local copy of the tradition. Of the two other examples that from St. George's Street resembles the St. Augustine's jug in having applied arms, but does not have a beard. A small squat jug from North Lane, dated to the late thirteenth century, has two applied arms and a collar, but the mask is missing (Bennett 1978, 165; Macpherson-Grant 1978, Fig. 23, no. 60). Two sherds from a second jug decorated with stripes of slip and a green glaze were also recovered from the shaft.

THE POTTERY FROM TRENCH III, 1972

Introduction

Excluding unstratified material, Trench III produced a total of 613 sherds of pottery, of which Belgic and Roman comprise 264 sherds. The pottery was studied in five groups according to stratigraphic location:

Group 1. Pre-dating F19; ?Roman, early medieval. Layers 35, 42, 43.
Group 2. Apparently pre-dating F19; medieval. Layers 27, 30, 33, 40.
Group 3. Post-dating F19. Layers 23, 24, 26, 34.
Group 4. Post-Dissolution build-up. Layers 15, 18.
Group 5. Demolition layers and modern deposits. Layers 8, 10, 12.

The distribution of the fabric types is illustrated in Tables 8 and 9. The Roman pottery includes eleven sherds of samian, with two stamps (Group 5). Of the medieval wares type C is predominant (fifty-seven sherds), superseded by Fabric LB in the late medieval period and Fabric F in the post-medieval period. As noted in the other assemblages there is a high proportion of residual pottery in the Dissolution and later groups, but late- and post-medieval wares are limited. Non-local and imported wares total only twenty-six sherds. For fabric codes see above; parallels for published sherds are listed in the catalogue.

Groups 1 and 2 (Fig. 83)

Layers 42 and 43, the early-medieval bank, produced two and twenty-three sherds of early medieval pottery, respectively; Group 2 yielded a further seventeen sherds of residual early medieval ware. Of the illustrated examples, nos. 2, 3, and 4 are oxidised, nos. 1, 5, 6, and 8 are reduced. Group 1, which includes both the simplest rounded rim form (no. 2) and the later flat-topped form (nos. 4 and 5), may be dated to *c.* 1100 (see also p. 250). Group 2 also contained some thirteenth- to fourteenth-century material (see Table 8), including a rim sherd in SOS ware (no. 9), similar to a rim from the interface of layers 26 and 42 (no. 10), which is presumed to derive from the later deposit. One sherd of London ware was found in layer 40.

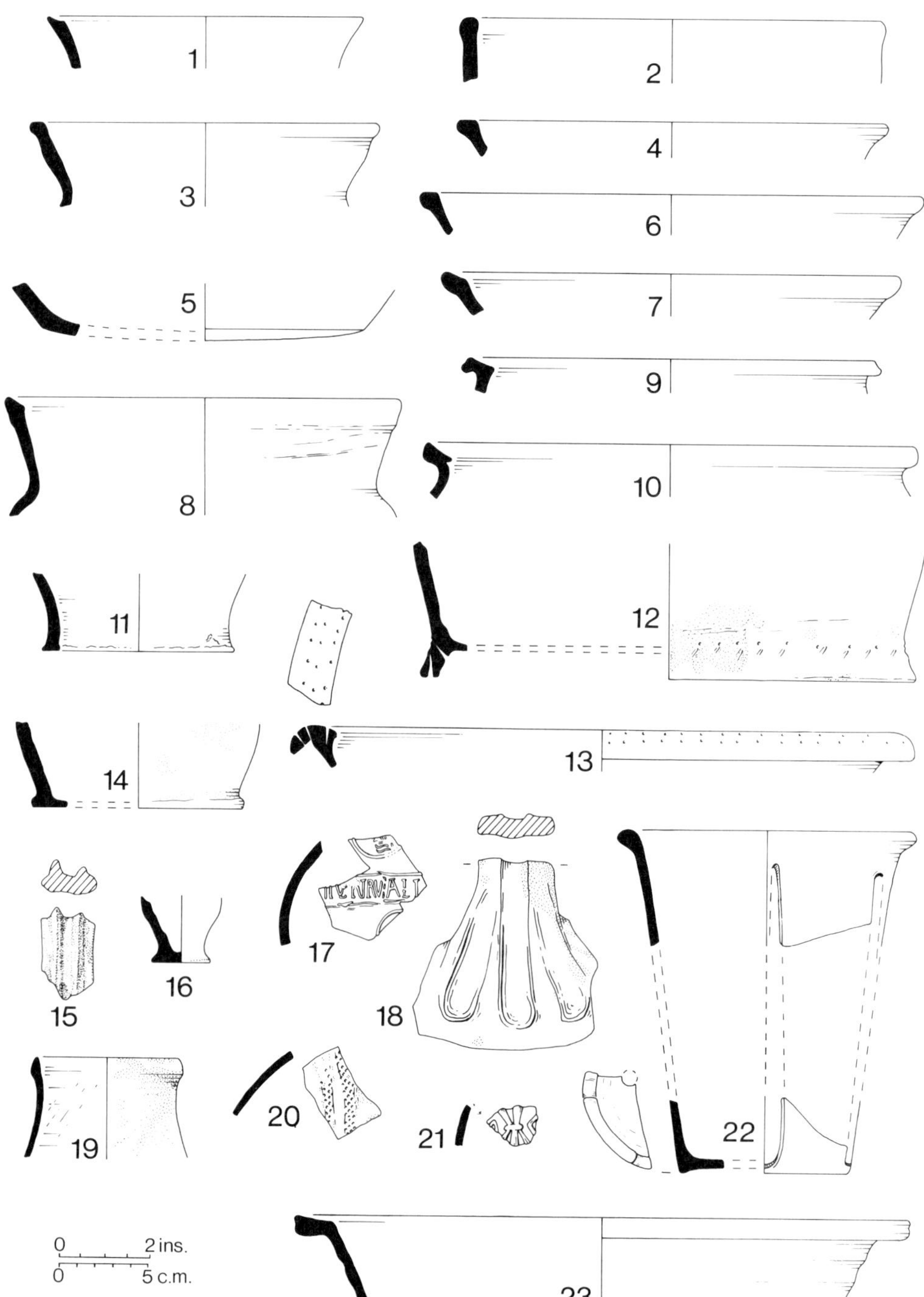

Fig. 83. Early medieval to post-medieval Pottery, Trench III, 1972. (Scale: ¼)

Group 3 (Fig. 83)

Although few in number, post-Roman sherds include four sherds in Fabric LB and one in Fabric F, which suggest that the group probably dates to the later fifteenth century. Residual medieval sherds include a large thirteenth-/fourteenth-century base (no. 12, cf. 1974–75, Fig. 87, no. 44, but here doubly stabbed), and a large bowl (no. 13) typical of the early fourteenth-century Tyler Hill wares. No. 11 is problematical in that the rim is very roughly finished, and the sherd may derive from the base of a chafing dish or cover of some sort. One sherd of London ware was found in layer 26/42.

The group is dominated by Belgic and Roman wares, which include a sherd (no. 354) of stamped samian from layer 46/24. This has been examined by B.R. Hartley, who comments: '[ICT]TIAMA on Form 31. Although the stamp may not be literate, it can be read tolerably clearly and it is possible to conjecture that the potter's name was Icttius or something similar. Stamps from this die are known from Lezoux (in a mid-Antonine context) and in Britain three have been noted from forts re-occupied about A.D. 160 after some decades of disuse. A date in the range A.D. 155–190 is clear.'

Group 4 (Fig. 84)

The post-Dissolution build-up produced a number of late fifteenth- to early sixteenth-century sherds, including the base of a bowl in Fabric F (no. 14), and Cologne/Frechen stoneware: a small base sherd (no. 16) with dark brown mottled glaze, and one sherd from an inscribed band jug (no. 17) which joins with a sherd from Group 5. Pamela Clarke comments: 'These jugs are usually decorated with a bellarmine mask, acanthus leaves or medallions containing heads and a band around the girth of the pot, often inscribed with a popular motto. A similar example was found in excavations at Chichester (Down 1974, 95, no. 51; Fig. 7.14, no. 55, incorrectly numbered). This example bears parts of two medallions, one of which appears to contain the neck/shoulders of a warrior. The motto cannot be interpreted'. As in all the demolition groups there is also a number of residual sherds; these include a strap handle with pronounced parallel ridges and a deep central groove, cream slip and green glaze (no. 15), and rilled body sherd in a fine buff fabric with a lemon glaze, probably from the neck of a Rouen jug.

Group 5 (Fig. 85)

The demolition and later deposits contained a mixed assemblage, with a number of non-local wares. These include six sherds of London ware, four with applied rouletted strips (as no. 20), and one oxidised sherd of probable Rye ware with part of an applied stamp, possibly a fleur-de-lys (no. 21). Imports include a skillet handle of probable Low Countries origin, and one small rim of North Holland Slipware (see p. 258).

Local wares include the base of a large strap handle (no. 18) in Fabric LM, of probable late fifteenth- or early sixteenth-century date. The distinctive thumbing is reminiscent of the Tudor forms from Hareplain (Kelly 1972). A jug rim (no. 19) and a large bowl (no. 23), both in Fabric

F, are probably of sixteenth-century date. No. 19 has diagonal striations inside the neck and a metallic brown glaze. The most unusual find consists of a rim and a base (no. 22), possibly from a chafing dish or similar object, with alternating solid panels which taper from 5.3 to 4.5 cm. and vertical slits incised at leather hard stage. The base, which has a small splash of yellow glaze on the underside, is also perforated.

Residual sherds in this group include an unusual samian stamp (no. 236) from layer 12. B.R. Hartley comments: 'COCILLIM on Form 33. This is a stamp of Coc(c)illus who worked both at Banassac (Lozère) and Lezoux (Puy-de-Dôme) in the middle of the second century. It is from a die hitherto unknown, but clearly one in use at Banassac, as the fabric shows. The forms used and the distribution of Coccillus's work on dated sites points to the period A.D. 130–160 and four of his stamped dishes, impressed with a die used both at Banassac and Lezoux, occurred in a grave-group at Riempst (Belgium) with stamped vessels of potters belonging to the two centres, all the datable ones being of the early-Antonine period (Schaetzen 1949–50, 41).'

TABLE 8

Excavations 1972. Trench III. The distribution of the stratified local pottery fabrics

Group.	BE	RO	EMS	SHS	SOS	A	B	C	D	LB	LM	F	H
1.	3	23	25										
2.	25	71	17	2	4	5	7	12	1				
3.	8	31	4	1	1	1		6		4		1	
4.	7	69	20	2	2	7	10	17	18	26	7	12	1
5.	6	21	6	1	1	19	8	22	22	8	4	16	3
TOTAL	49	215	72	6	8	32	25	57	41	38	11	29	4

TABLE 9

Excavations 1972. Trench III. The distribution of the stratified non-local and imported pottery

Group.	LON	RYE	WEA	KING	TUDG	BORD	ROU	NHS	LOW	COL/F
1.										
2.	1									
3.	1									
4.			1	1		1	1		1	2
5.	6	1	1	2	1			1	4	1
TOTAL	8	1	2	3	1	1	1	1	5	3

Excavations 1972, Trench III Catalogue. Fig. 83.

No.	Layer	Group	Fabric	Total Sherds	Glaze Int.	Glaze Ext.	Internal Parallels	External Parallels
1.	43	1	EM	1				Ames 1978, Fig. 13, no. 12
2.	43	1	EM	1				Frere 1954, Fig. 16, no. 11
3.	43	1	EM	1				Frere 1954, Fig. 17, no. 14 Wilson 1982, Fig. 35, no. 4
4.	43	1	EM	1				Frere 1954, Fig. 17, no. 16
5.	43	1	EM	1				
6.	43	1	EM	1				Frere 1954, Fig. 17, no. 14
7.	42	1	EM	1				
8.	40	2	EM	1				Frere 1954, Fig. 16, no. 13 Fig. 17, no. 23
9.	27	2	SOS	1				Frere 1954, Fig. 18, no. 29
10.	26/42	2	SOS	1				Frere 1954, Fig. 19, no. 33
11.	26	2	LB	1		C		
12.	26	2	A/C	1	G	G	1974–5, no. 44	
13.	34	3	A	1				Dunning 1942, 62, Fig. 2, no. 18 Macpherson-Grant 1980c, Fig. 10, no. 27
14.	18	4	F	1		GB		
15.	18	4	D	1		SG		
16.	18	4	COL/F	1		B		
17.	18 12	4 5	COL/F	2		Clear		
18.	12	5	LM	1		G		Kelly 1972, Fig. 2, no. 15
19.	12	5	F	1	B	B		
20.	12	5	LON	1+2		SG	1974–75, no. 30	
21.	12	5	RYE	1		SG		Barton 1979, 241, no. 8; 242, no. 10–o
22.	12	5	F	2			1976–78, 16/747	
23.	12	5	F	1		C		Hurst 1968, 57, Fig. 18, nos. 135, 145

THE MEDIEVAL AND POST-MEDIEVAL POTTERY FROM EXCAVATIONS 1974–75

Introduction

The excavations of 1974–75 produced a total of *c.* 2020 sherds of pottery ranging in date from Belgic to the twentieth century. The assemblage falls into two approximately equal groups of late medieval/early post-medieval pottery and residual medieval and earlier material. The former includes 107 sherds (thirty-six vessels) of Rhenish stoneware; the latter includes 588 sherds of Belgic and Roman date. A small but varied group of seventeenth- to twentieth-century pottery was also recovered. The fifteenth- and sixteenth-century pottery finds numerous local parallels in the material from the Dissolution contexts at Faversham Abbey (Philp 1968) and the Hospital of St. Mary at Ospringe (Smith 1979, 81–185). The pottery was studied in five groups according to stratigraphic location:

Group 1.	The earliest levels, layers 6, 39, 45.	pre-1540
Group 2a.	The soakaway (lower fill), layers 71, 76.	post-1542
Group 2b.	The soakaway (upper fill), layers 68, 69, 4/69 and other features, layers 5, 14, 54, 56.	
Group 3.	The post-Dissolution build-up, layers 4, 37, 38, 61.	post-1542
Group 4.	The mortar and rubble deposits, layers 2, 3, 19, 34, 35, 36, 47, 63.	post-1550
Group 5.	Eighteenth–Twentieth century, layers 1, 50, 59, 64, 66, unstratified.	

The most interesting find consists of the group from the soakaway, which contained a number of fifteenth- and sixteenth-century vessels (Figs. 84, 85). Little difference was noted between the pottery in groups 2–5, and sherds from several vessels appear in two or more groups, reflecting the considerable amount of disturbance on the site after the Dissolution. Group 1 contained only four sherds of pottery. For fabric codes, see above; for parallels for illustrated sherds, see the catalogue.

Group 2. The Pottery from the Western Soakaway and Other Drainage Features (Figs. 84, 85).

The pottery from the soakaway is of interest as a sealed group dateable to *c.* 1550 and for the variety of forms, fabrics and decorative techniques represented. Analysis of the groups from the lower and upper fills showed that the initial deposits contained mainly jug sherds, with very few cooking-pots, whereas in the later layers this pattern was reversed. A minimum of eight late-medieval or early post-medieval jugs are represented, of which four (nos. 1, 2, 5, 8) are either complete or near complete. These all have a squat form with a short neck and collar. A fifth jug (no. 10), although unmarked and dissassociated from its original finds bag, is included in this group both because of its similarity in form to the above, and because the soakaway is the most likely place on the site for a vessel to survive virtually intact. No. 2 is probably the local LM ware, but bears a resemblance to the late-medieval red wares from Cheam (C. Orton, pers. comm., and 1979b, 355). No. 8, in Fabric LM, with a double bib of white slip and green glaze, is of interest as the only example in the 1960–78 collection of a jug with thumbing underneath as opposed to on the outer wall (Hurst 1962, 295 and Fig. 93, no. 1). No. 10, in Fabric F, has a bib of green glaze only. The most elaborate form is no. 1, which has a twisted double rod handle, an applied thumbed cordon around the girth of the body, and a rich green glaze. No. 5, however, is perhaps of greater interest. Crudely made, with open blisters on the inner wall, the piece appears to be a copy of a maiolica or stoneware form. The outer wall has been roughly wiped, and handled while still wet, causing a patchy orange-grey surface. The upper portion of the pot is covered with a thick, unevenly applied yellow-green glaze which has run in some places, crazed in others, and in one area has dribbled through the blistered wall to accumulate in the inner angle of the body. Although unusual, similar forms have been found at North Lane, Canterbury (dated to the late fourteenth or fifteenth century) and at Faversham.

The upper levels of the soakaway produced sherds from a minimum of seven late-medieval or early post-medieval kitchen wares, ranging from small bowls or pipkins (nos. 15–17) to large cooking-pots with seated rims (no. 13) and applied decoration (no. 19, paralleled in the 1960 and 1976–78 assemblages), and a cistern (no. 20, cf. 1960, Fig. 79, no. 19). No. 13 was probably a handled vessel (cf. 1960, Fig. 79, no. 13). The dominant fabric is type F, but there is also a number of chalk-gritted sherds in Fabric type LB from layer 68 (see above p. 253). Glazing is present on sherds from all groups, but is generally patchy; nos. 14–16 are glazed internally.

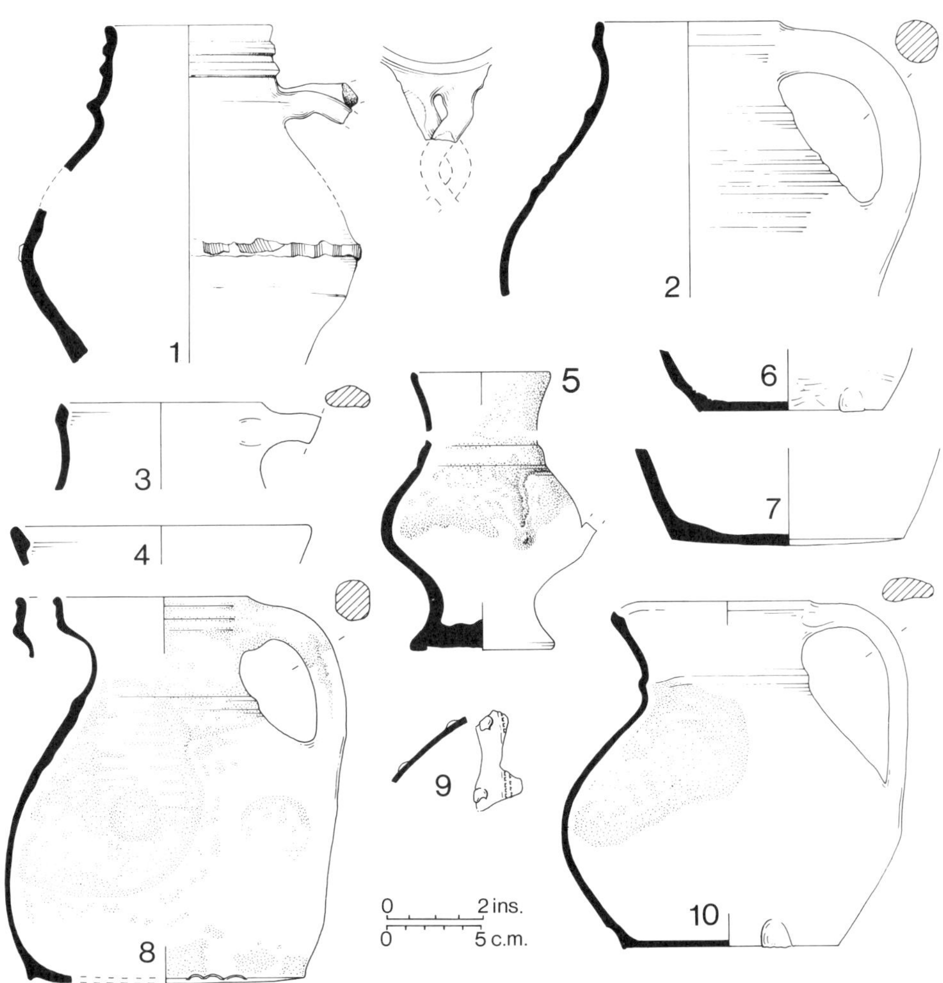

Fig. 84. Jug sherds from the late medieval Soakaway, 1974–75. Group 2a. (Scale: ¼)

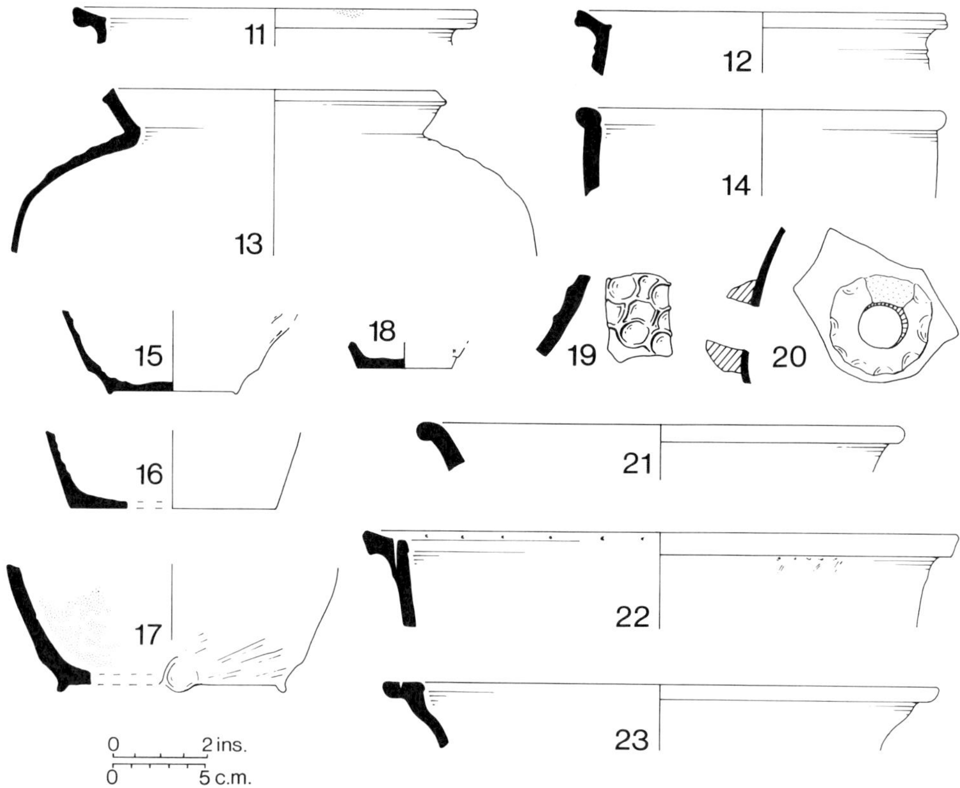

Fig. 85. Cooking-pots from the late medieval Soakaway, 1974–75. Group 2b. (Scale: ¼)

Isolated sherds from a number of these pots were also found in the adjacent drainage features (layers 10, 14, 5), in the trench against the west wall of the south transept (layers 54, 56) and scattered across the rest of the site. Residual sherds from all these deposits include nos. 11, 12, 21–23.

Non-local English wares comprise one sherd each of London, Cheam and Wealden ware, and one small rim-sherd of Metropolitan-type slipware. Imported medieval wares, found only in the lower levels, comprise one sherd of 'Aardenburg' ware (no. 4), three sherds of green-glazed Saintonge ware (paralleled in the 1976–78 assemblage, Group 15), and possibly also three small sherds from a decorated Rouen jug (no. 9), which were stored in the same finds box as no. 10. Fifteenth- and sixteenth-century imports, found only in the upper levels, consist of thirty-two sherds of Rhenish stoneware, and two sherds of Martincamp stoneware. The Raeren stonewares include no. 62, a plain jug with three intersecting lines, forming an 'A' or a '4', perhaps a potter's mark, inscribed on the body prior to firing and no. 64, from a Siegburg-type drinking vessel (cf. Beckmann 1974, Fig. 13, no. 79), the form of which was copied at Raeren. The Cologne wares include no. 65, an oak-leaf jug, sherds of which were also scattered through layers 19, 63, 4 and 3 (see Table 11b). Pamela Clarke comments: 'This type is not as common as the Raeren plain jug, which can be regarded as a type fossil for the first half of the sixteenth

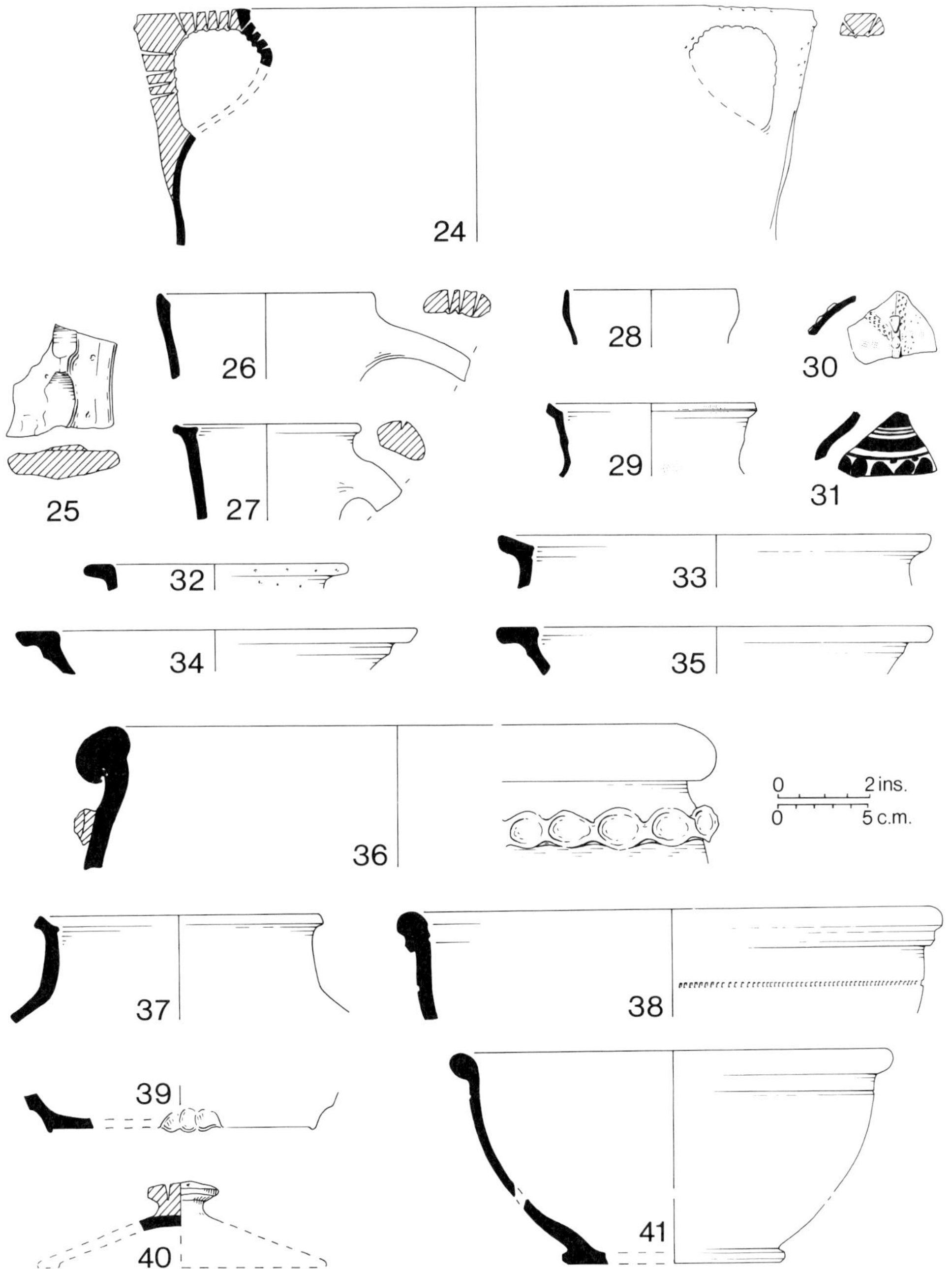

Fig. 86. Medieval, late medieval and early post-medieval Pottery, 1974–75. Group 3. (Scale: ¼)

century, but examples of oak-leaf jugs are known from Norton Priory (Green 1974, 32, frontispiece), Finchale Priory (Jarrett and Edwards 1961, no. 143), Farnham Castle (Moorhouse 1971b, Fig. 1, no. 26), and in Kent at the Bewl Valley Ironworks (Crossley 1975, Fig. 22, no. 4) and at Faversham Abbey (Hurst 1968, Fig. 18, nos. 153, 154). Evidence from Wharram Percy (Hurst 1971, 46) would suggest that this form may have been in use by *c.* 1500, but it would seem that the main production period was *c.* 1520–1540. This example is therefore by no means out of place in a demolition context of *c.* 1550'.

Group 3. The Late Medieval Ground Surface (Fig. 86).

There is little difference in the pottery from the soakaway and that from layer 4, which extended from the east end of the lady chapel to the former hospital basement. The bulk of the pottery is of fifteenth- and sixteenth-century date (nos. 36–39, 41), with several sherds from vessels noted above; a number of thirteenth- and fourteenth-century sherds, including no. 24, were, however, found in the area of Tomb F5. The angular form of no. 24, which bears a cream slip and green glaze, imitates a metal cauldron; a similar form was found at Leadenhall Market, London. No. 32, in Fabric SHS, is probably of late twelfth- or early thirteenth-century date. No. 27 is fourteenth-century, no. 29, a jug in Fabric F, with diagonal striations inside the neck (cf. no. 3), is late fourteenth- or fifteenth-century. Layer 37, the equivalent of layer 4 to the west of the chantry chapel, also produced a number of fifteenth- and sixteenth-century wares but contained a much higher proportion of residual material (cf. Group 14, 1976–78), including nos. 25 and 26, and one sherd from 1976–78 jug no. 75 (Fig. 93).

Non-local wares in this group include one sherd of thirteenth-century London ware (no. 30) with applied decoration of scales and rouletted strips (cf. 1972, Fig. 83, no. 20), and one sherd of Cistercian ware (no. 28). Continental imports consist of one sherd of South Netherlands maiolica (no. 31), and eleven sherds of Rhenish stoneware, all from layer 4 (see Table 11b). These include Raeren: nos. 61, and 63 (possibly from the same vessel as no. 62), and Cologne: no. 65. No stoneware was found in layer 37. No. 31 has possible parallels in Southampton and London; the continuous bands of decoration suggest that this vessel had no handle (J.G. Hurst, pers. comm.; see also above p. 259).

Group 4. The Mortar and Rubble Deposits (Fig. 87).

These layers produced pottery ranging in date from Belgic to the later seventeenth century, including a body sherd of late Roman ware. There is an overall predominance of early post-medieval brown-glazed cooking-pots in Fabric F, but also some jug sherds (no. 48). No. 50, a bowl, is unusual in having traces of a thin red slip externally, and a yellow-green glaze over the rim and inner wall. Sixteenth- and seventeenth-century non-local wares include green- or yellow-glazed Surrey ware (nos. 51, 52), plain white tin-glazed ware (nos. 54, 55, probably Lambeth), and one sherd of English stoneware. Imported wares comprise a dish rim with a scroll design in cream slip, possibly from North Holland (no. 53), and thirty-four sherds of Rhenish stoneware. These include no. 60 (Langerwehe), from a large jug, probably of Hurst type III (Hurst 1977b, 229–30, Fig. 4; Clarke, pers. comm.), nos. 62–63 (Raeren), no. 65 (Cologne), and nos. 66, 67 (Westerwald), the latter being found only in layer 35. Residual wares

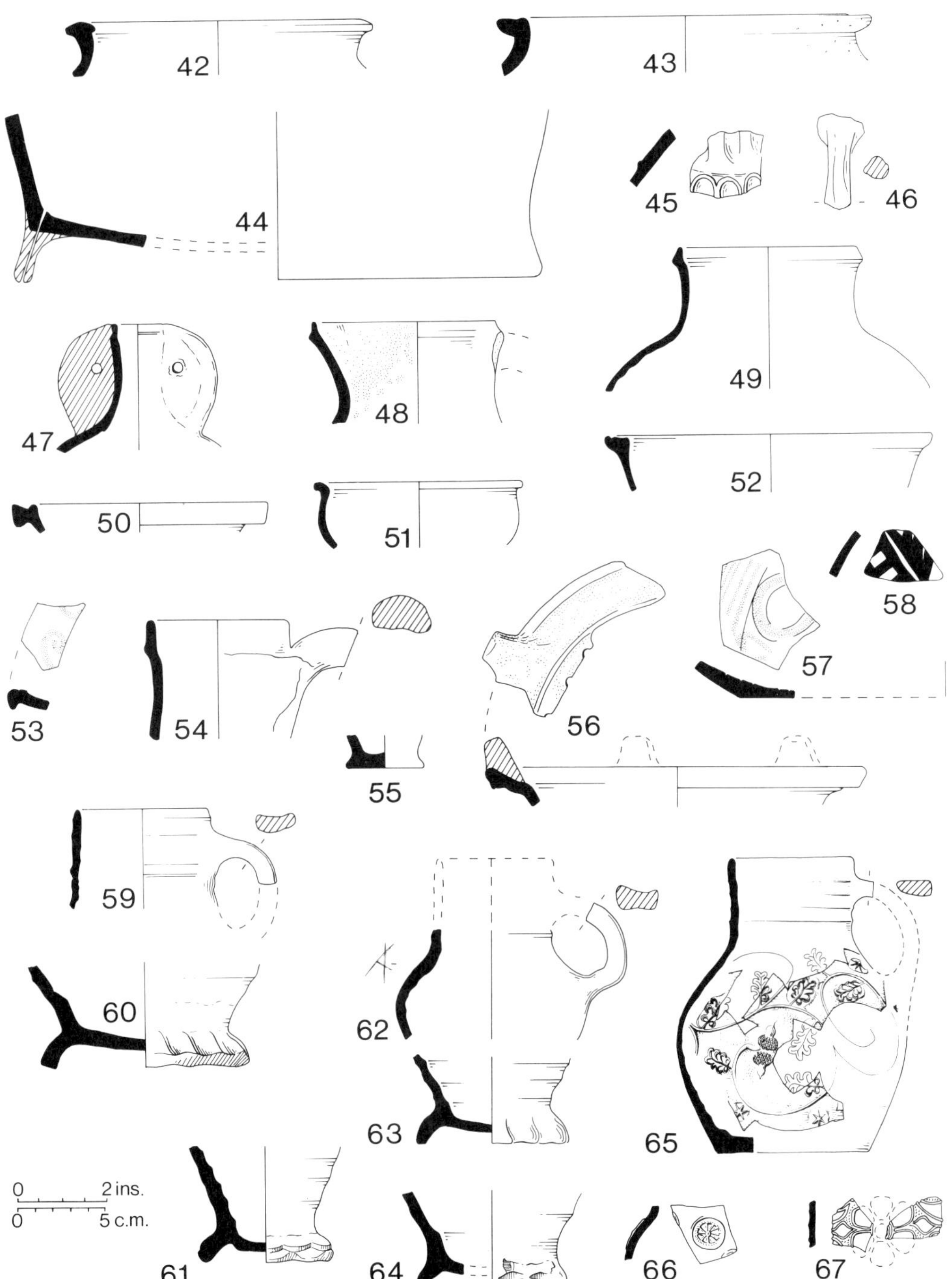

Fig. 87. Eleventh to eighteenth century Pottery, 1974–75. Groups 4 and 5. (Scale: ¼)

include a green-glazed decorated body sherd (no. 45, cf. 1976–78, Fig. 91, no. 63), probably of thirteenth- or fourteenth-century date. Fourteenth-and fifteenth-century wares include a few small sherds of Tudor Green, and a small rod handle (no. 46) in Fabric LB, probably from a two- or three-handled cup or tyg; similar handles were found elsewhere in the demolition deposits (1976–78, groups 14 and 15).

Group 5. Eighteenth- to Twentieth-century Deposits (Fig. 87).

These layers produced a similarly mixed group of finds, including a rim of fourth- or fifth-century date (see p. 248), one base sherd of Middle Saxon Ipswich-type ware, one rim of early medieval SHS ware (no. 42), one rim of late twelfth- or early thirteenth-century SHS ware (no. 43), and a large base sherd (no. 44) of probable thirteenth-century date, with a stabbed ring foot (cf. 1972, Fig. 83, no. 12). Splashes of cream slip and green glaze on the outer wall and underside of the vessel suggest that it may have been fired upside down. Late medieval and early post-medieval wares include the upper part of a jug in Fabric H (no. 49), a chafing dish (no. 56) in a coarse sandy ware similar to Fabric LB, with a cream slip both internally and over the rim, and the mouth of a lugged costrel (no. 47), in Fabric LB with a patchy green glaze. A similar, shorter-necked example with a brown glaze was found at Faversham Abbey, but a closer parallel is perhaps a green-glazed costrel from Hareplain, although this has a slightly wider mouth.

Continental imports comprise a few sherds of Rhenish stoneware, including no. 59 (Langerwehe), probably from a jar of Hurst type IV (Hurst 1977b, 231–3, Fig. 5; Clarke, pers. comm.), and no. 64 (Raeren), one sherd of South Netherlands maiolica (no. 58), possibly from an altar or flower vase, and a flat base sherd from a dish in Werra-type ware (no. 57) with *sgraffito* decoration combined with rings of cream slip under a thin greenish glaze (see p. 259).

Also in this group is one sherd of stamped samian, unstratified, but found in Area 1. This has been examined by B.R. Hartley, who comments: 'OFRVFI retrograde on Form 33. A stamp of the well-known Rufus of La Graufesenque. This occurs several times at sites founded under the Flavians (e.g. the Nijmegen fortress, Brough-under-Stainmore, Chester and York). The possible range seems to be A.D. 65–90 with A.D. 70–85 as the likely date of production'.

TABLE 10

Excavations 1974–75. The distribution of the local pottery fabrics.

Group	BE	RO	LR	SOT	EMS	SH	SHS	SOS	A	B	C	D	LB	LM	F	H
1.		4														
2a.	6	29		1					5		9	1	12	113	126	
2b.	12	80			4				8	1	12	16	61	12	183	15
3.	59	153		2	20	1	1	3	16	7	48	9	31	13	80	
4.	15	68	1		6				9	8	16	9	22	3	112	13
5.	38	122	1		6		2	1	23	12	29	12	35	26	98	15
TOTAL	130	456	2	3	36	1	3	4	61	28	114	47	161	167	599	43

TABLE 11a

Excavations 1974–75. The distribution of the non-local and imported pottery (excluding Rhenish stoneware).

Group.	IPS	LON	WEA	KING	CHEA	TUDG	BORD	CSTN	METS	TGW	ENGS	CH	ROU	STGE	AARD	NHS	SNM	WER	MART
2a.													3	3	1				
2b.		1	1		1				1										2
3.		2	2		1			1									1		
4.			5	2		3	4			3	1					1			
5.	1	1		1		1	2			2	3	1		2			1	1	
TOTAL	1	4	8	3	2	4	6	1	1	5	4	1	3	5	1	1	2	1	2

TABLE 11b

Excavations 1974–75. The distribution of the stoneware.

Group	*Layer*	LANG	EVE	*Fig. No.*	?LANG	EVE	*Fig. No.*	?RAER	EVE	*Fig. No.*	RAER	EVE	*Fig. No.*	COL/F	EVE	*Fig. No.*	WEST	EVE	*Fig. No.*	*Total*
2b.	68				1	1					1	1	64	2	1	65				4
	4/69				2			2	2		5	2	62	14	1	65				23
	5	1	1		1			3	1											5
3.	4	2	2		2	2		1	1		4	3	61 63 64	3	1	65				12
4.	2													1	1	65				1
	3	3	2	60							1	1		1	1	65				5
	19				2	2					1	1	63							3
	35										1	1		21	3		5	4	66 67	27
	63				1	1					2	2	62 63	7	1	65				10
5.	1	1	1	59				3	3					1	1					5
	U/S				2	2		1	1		1	1	64	7	2	65	1	1		12
Total sherds		7			11			10			16			57		6				107
Total vessels			6			7			7			6			5			5		36

Excavations 1974–75. Catalogue.

No.	Layer	Group	Fabric	Total Sherds	Glaze Int.	Glaze Ext.	Internal Parallels	External Parallels
	Fig.84							
1.	71	2a	LB	14		G		
	68	2b						
	69	2b						
	4/69	2b						
	1	5						
2.	71	2a	LM	22		G		
	68	2b						
	4	3						
3.	4/69	2b	F	1				
4.	71	2a	AARD	1	S	SG		
5.	76	2a	F	10		SYG		Macpherson-Grant 1978, 190, Fig. 23, no. 63
	71	2a						Hurst 1968, 57, Fig. 18, nos. 138, 149
6.	4/69	2b	H	8+?31			1974–75 no. 7	
	63	3					no. 49	
7.	4/69	2b	H	5			1974–75 no. 6	
	63	3					no. 49	
8.	76	2a	LM	102		SG		Hurst 1962, 295, Fig. 293, no. 1
	71	2a						
	69	2b						
	68	2b						
9.	U/S	2a?	ROU	3		SG		Dunning 1954, 138, Pl. 3, no. 2 Thorn 1979, 163, Fig. 34, nos. 21–22
10.	U/S	2a?	F	116		G		
	5	2b						
	Fig. 85							
11.	71	2a	LB	1		YG		
12.	4/69	2b	C	1		G		
13.	4/69	2b	F	21+?1			1960, no.13	Rigold 1967, Fig. 14, IV1, IV4
	68	2b						
	4	3						
14.	71	2a	F	1	Y			
15.	4/69	2b	F	2	G			
16.	4/69	2b	F	2	G			Rigold 1967, Fig. 14, IV3
17.	4	3	F	52	G			
	63	4						
18.	4/69	2b	F	1	B			
19.	68	2b	F	1	B		1960, P24 1976–78, 16/9	Macpherson-Grant 1980c, Fig. 10, no. 28.

No.	Layer	Group	Fabric	Total Sherds	Glaze Int.	Glaze Ext.	Internal Parallels	External Parallels
20.	68	2b	F	1				
21.	5	2b	EM	2				
22.	5	2b	A	1		G		
23.	14	2b	A	1	G			
	Fig. 86							
24	4	3	LM	4	SG	S		L.M.M.C. 1940, 255, Fig. 74
25.	37	3	D	1				
26.	37	3	A	1				
27.	4	3	LB	1				
28.	4	3	CIST	1	B	B		
29.	4	3	F	3		GB		
30.	4	3	LON	1		SG	1972, No.20	Rigold 1971, 158, Fig. 24. D57 Mynard 1973, 190, Fig. 1, nos. 9, 10 Thorn 1979, 157, Fig. 34, no. 16
31.	4	3	SNM	1		W/blue		Rackham 1939, 285–9, Pl.2 Platt and Coleman-Smith 1975, Fig. 196, no. 1175
32.	4	3	SHS	1				
33.	4	3	SOS	1				
34.	4	3	A	1				
35.	4	3	A	1	G	G		
36.	4	3	F	1	G	G		
37.	4	3	F	1				
38.	4	3	F	1	G			
39.	4	3	F	2	B			
40.	4	3	C	1		G		
41.	4	3	F	3	B			
	Fig. 87							
42.	U/S	5	SHS	1				
43.	1	5	SHS	1				
44.	1	5	A	1		SG	1972 no.12	
45.	34	4	C	1		G	1976–78 no.63	
46.	35	4	LB	1			1976–78, 14/1006, 14/1007	
47.	U/S	5	LB	1		G		Hurst 1968, 57, Fig. 18, no. 142 Dunning 1975, 175, Fig. 6, no. 65
48.	2	4	F	5		Y		
49.	1	5	H	3			1974–75 Nos. 6,7	
50.	2/3	4	F	1	YG			
51.	35	4	BORD	1	C/Y			
52.	U/S	5	BORD	1	Y			

No.	*Layer*	*Group*	*Fabric*	*Total Sherds*	*Glaze Int.*	*Glaze Ext.*	*Internal Parallels*	*External Parallels*
53.	35	4	NHS?	1	SC			Hurst *et. al* 1975, Fig. 8, no. 2
54.	3	4	TGW	1	W	W		
55.	35	4	TGW	1	W	W		
56.	1	5	LB?	1	SC			
57.	U/S	5	WER	1	SG			Hurst 1968, 58, Fig. 18, no. 155
58.	1	5	SNM	1		W/Blue		
59.	1	5	LANG	1				
60.	3	4	LANG	1				Hurst 1977, 231–33, Fig. 5
61.	4	3	RAER	1				Hurst 1977, 229–30, Fig. 4
62.	4/69	2b	RAER	5				
	63	3						
63.	4	3	RAER	4				
	19, 63	4						
64.	69	2	RAER	4				Beckmann 1974, Fig. 13, no. 79
65.	69	2	COL/F	33				Green 1974, 32, Frontispiece
	4	3						Jarrett and Edwards, 1961, no. 143
	3	4						Moorhouse 1971b, Fig. 1, no. 26
	2	4						Crossley 1975, Fig. 22, no. 4
								Hurst 1968, Fig. 18, nos. 153, 154
66.	35	4	WEST	1				
67.	35	4	WEST	2				

THE SAXON, MEDIEVAL AND POST-MEDIEVAL POTTERY FROM EXCAVATIONS 1976–78

Introduction

The excavations of 1976–78 produced a total of *c.* 7,800 sherds ranging in date from Belgic to the twentieth century. Belgic and Roman sherds were present in almost every context. Stratified medieval wares were few, but a large amount of residual medieval pottery was found in the demolition and later groups, which also contained a number of fifteenth- and sixteenth-century jugs and fifty sherds of Rhenish stoneware. A large amount of nineteenth-century earthenware was found in the levels associated with the hospital, but seventeenth- and eighteenth-century pottery was not common. The most important finds were the stratified late Anglo-Saxon and early medieval sherds from the levels associated with the construction of the south aisle wall: Group 3a, *c.* 1060–70; Groups 3b and 3c, *c.* 1070–1099 (discussed below). The pottery was studied in sixteen groups based on stratigraphic location and ceramic content (see Table 12). Many of these groups contained very little pottery, and some groups have therefore been amalgamated in this report. For fabric codes see above; parallels for published sherds are listed in the catalogue.

TABLE 12

Excavations 1976–78. The pottery groups.

Group 1. The Roman midden and burial.
Layers 804, 805, 806, 8004, 8005, 8006; Grave 8011.

Group 2. The Anglo-Saxon graveyard. *c.* 600–1070.
Layers 803, 1058, 5160, 5161, 8003, 8007.

Group 3a. Layers pre-dating the south aisle wall: Area 4. *c.* 1060–1070.
Layers 795, 798, 799.

Group 3b. The construction phase: Areas 4, 8. *c.* 1070–1099.
Layers 796, 807, 809, 8001, 8002, 8009, 8012.

Group 3c. Post-construction build-up: Areas 4, 5. *c.* 1099–1124.
Layers 790, 793, 794, 797, 5156, 5157, 5158.

Group 4. The early medieval deposits and cemetery: Areas 4, 5. Twelfth–thirteenth century.
Layers 779, 786, 788, 789, 792, 5151; Graves 5133, 5145, 5154.

Group 5. The medieval deposits: Areas 1, 2, 5. Thirteenth–fourteenth century.
Layers 594, 599, 601, 602, 548, 566, 578, 582, 5147, 5149.

Group 6. The medieval cemetery: Areas 1, 2, 5. Fourteenth century.
Graves 57, 53/66, 557, 580, 5135, 5137, 5139, 5146, 5148.

Group 7. The construction of the chantry chapel: Areas 2, 3. Late fourteenth century.
Layers 545, 561, 575, 1046.

Group 8. The medieval cemetery: Area 3. Late fourteenth–fifteenth century.
Graves 1013, 1059, 1060.

Group 9. The construction of the vault: Area 3. Mid-fifteenth century.
Layers 1045, 1047, 1050, 1054, 1055, 1056.

Group 10. The late medieval deposits and construction of the buttresses: Areas 4, 5.
Fourteenth–fifteenth century.
Layers 784, 787, 5124, 5127, 5144, 5150.

Group 11. The late medieval ground surface: Area 5. Fifteenth century.
Layers 5101, 5125.

Group 12. The late medieval cemetery: Area 5. Fifteenth–sixteenth century.
Graves 5090, 5102, 5110, 5111, 5116, 5128.

Group 13. The late medieval cemetery: Areas 2, 4. Fifteenth century.
Graves 549, 560, 574, 581, 587, 589, 595, 603, 787. Layers 784, 552.

Group 14. The demolition features and post-demolition deposits: Areas 2, 4, 5. Sixteenth century.
Features 783, 5075, 5078, 5079, 5086, 5129; Layers 532, 533, 537, 539, 540, 542, 547, 550, 558, 763, 764, 766, 780, 781, 5056, 5071, 5072, 5074, 5081, 5087, 5088.

Group 15. The demolition features and post-demolition deposits: Areas 1, 2, 3, 4. Sixteenth century.
Features 541, 579, 1034; Layers 16, 19, 24, 31, 513, 515, 524, 529, 704, 715, 719, 720, 732, 1000, 1002, 1003, 1005, 1007.

Group 16. The post-demolition deposits. Sixteenth–nineteenth century.
All remaining contexts.

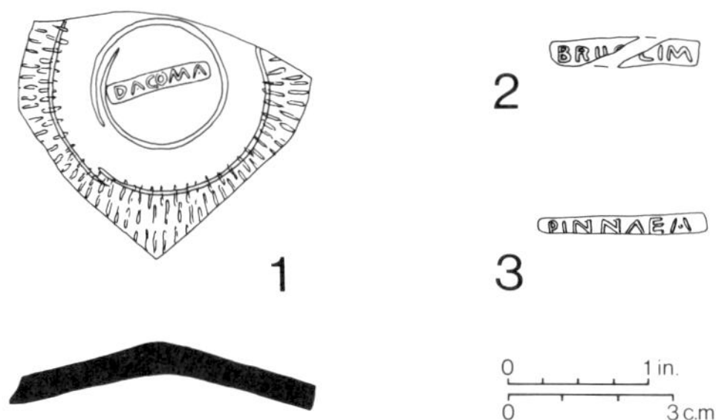

Fig. 88. Samian Stamps (nos. 1–3), 1976–78. Group 1. (Scale: ½)

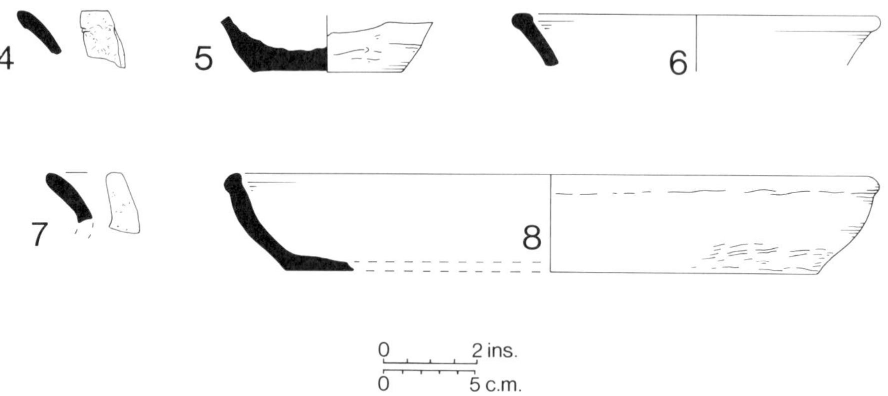

Fig. 89. Belgic (no. 4), Ipswich Ware (no. 5), Anglo-Saxon/early medieval Pottery (nos. 6–8), 1976–78. Groups 1–3. (Scale: ¼)

Group 1. The Roman Midden and Burial

A total of 276 sherds of Belgic and 799 sherds of Roman pottery was recovered from these layers. These include one rim of possible Belgic chaff-tempered ware (Macpherson-Grant 1980b, 2–4) from layer 804, and 178 sherds of samian, mortaria, flagons, and other oxidised or colour coated wares. Three stamped bases (Fig. 88, nos. 1–3) have been examined by B.R. Hartley, who reports as follows: 'No. 1. Dagomarus of Lezoux and Les Martres-de-Veyre, Die 13a on form 18/31R. Dagomarus worked at Les Martres before migrating to Lezoux. This particualr stamp turns up on Hadrian's Wall in Period 1a and may be dated to *c.* A.D. 125–140. No. 2. Briccus of Lezoux, die 31 BR(IC)CI.M on form 31. Briccus was not a very prolific potter and this particular stamp has been recorded only three times before. The range of forms, and the sites on which the stamps occur, point to manufacture *c.* A.D. 150–180.

No. 3. Pinna, assigned to Lezoux on distribution/fabric. Die 1A PINNΛEΛ on form 31. Presumably Pinna m(anu) was intended. There is little evidence for the date of stamps from this die, but Pinna's general record implies activity *c.* A.D. 150–180.'

Group 2. The Anglo-Saxon Cemetery

The excavated areas of the graveyard produced only nine sherds of probable Anglo-Saxon date: one sherd of possible East Anglian origin (see p. 255); one organically-tempered body sherd; a wheel-thrown base sherd (no. 5) and a similar base sherd of Ipswich fine ware, and one body sherd of Ipswich 'pimply' ware (Middle Saxon). Four sherds of late Anglo-Saxon/early medieval sandy ware may have been trampled in from Group 3.

Groups 3a, 3b, 3c. The Construction Phase

The most important finds in this group, and possibly from this excavation, are a large shallow dish (Fig. 89, no. 8) from a layer pre-dating the construction of the south aisle wall (Group 3a, layer 798), and a rim sherd (Fig. 89, no. 7) from the construction trench (Group 3b, layer 796). The former may be dated to pre- *c.* 1070, the latter to *c.* 1070–1099. Groups 3b and 3c contained a further six sherds of late Anglo-Saxon/early medieval sandy ware. At the time of excavation only three groups of eleventh-century pottery had been recovered from sites in Canterbury with supporting documentary dating evidence. The first was sealed by and associated with the foundations of Lanfranc's dormitory at Christchurch, which was constructed between 1070 and 1099 (Frere forthcoming). The second was from the Anglo-Saxon graveyard and layers within the Anglo-Saxon chapel at the west end of the post-Conquest church of St. Augustine's Abbey (Saunders 1978, contexts dateable to pre-Conquest, pre-1070 and pre-1091). The third group, loosely dateable to pre- *c.* 1086 was from excavations at Canterbury Castle (Bennett *et al.* 1982), which also produced another group dating to *c.* 1100–1150. Since 1978 two further groups have been found, one sealed by the *c.* 1096 foundations for St. Gabriel's Chapel in the cathedral (Driver *et al.* forthcoming), the second sealed by the *c.* 1165 foundations for the *Aula Nova* of the cathedral priory (Bennett *et al.* forthcoming). It is to be regretted that the two stratified groups from St. Augustine's are not richer in diagnostic forms (a re-examiniation of the published material from the excavations of 1955–58 showed that some of this is in fact of Belgic date). Nonetheless, the dish is of importance as the first published example of this form from Canterbury. Apparently made on a turn-table and then knife-trimmed, it is in a coarse sandy fabric with occasional large grit and siltstone inclusions which give a lumpy appearance; the base diameter is 288 mm., rim diameter 338 mm., depth 52 mm. The bevelling of the rim has caused a slight internal bead (see also pp. 250–1).

Residual sherds in the group include one fragment of daub (layer 809), six sherds of Anglo-Saxon organically-tempered ware, two sherds of Ipswich-type ware, and a shell-tempered rim-sherd of probable ninth-/tenth-century date from the redeposited graveyard soil (no. 7, see above p. 251).

Layer 8001, the mortar raft for the south-east tower, contained a single sherd of possible North French ware (see above p. 258).

Groups 4a and 4b. The Medieval Cemetery and Build-up: Areas 4 and 5

With the exception of two sherds of Anglo-Saxon organically-tempered ware from Grave 5145, pottery from the early graves in Area 5 (Group 4a) was entirely Belgic and Roman in date. It would appear that these features were cut fairly soon after the completion of the south-west tower in *c.* 1124. Layers 5151 and 5153, which sealed these graves, and layers 779, 788, 789, and 792 (Group 4b) were similarly lacking in dating evidence, containing only two sherds of late Anglo-Saxon/early medieval sandy ware. Residual sherds include one fragment of Argonne ware from layer 779. Layer 786, which sealed all these deposits, yielded a single internally glazed sherd of early to mid thirteenth-century date.

Group 5. The Medieval Levels: Areas 1, 2, and 5. (Fig. 90)

The earliest layers excavated in Area 2 produced little pottery, but layer 601 contained three small joining sherds from a spouted pitcher with an applied thumbed strip (no. 9). Similar twelfth-/thirteenth-century pitchers have been found in Canterbury at Butchery Lane and Rose Lane, at Dover Castle, and at Rochester.

The homogeneous nature of the pottery from the subsequent deposits suggests that layers 599, 594 and 582 within the chalk building are contemporary with layers 548, 578 and 566 in the trench between this building and the east wall of the chantry chapel. The presence of joining sherds in layers 602/594, 599/594 and 548/566 (nos. 11, 22, 23) suggests that these deposits probably built up rapidly in the late thirteenth or early fourteenth century. This date is supported by the absence of shell-tempered wares, which begin to die out *c.* 1225, the minimal presence of shell-dusted ware (no. 10 and possibly no. 33), which disappears by *c.* 1250, and the number of stabbed rims, rod handles and thumbed bases. These forms were all declining in popularity after *c.* 1250 (Macpherson-Grant 1981, 24–7). Six sherds, moreover, are in an intermediate of fabrics B and LB; the latter appears to be emerging *c.* 1275–1300. Layer 47 (Area 1) and layer 5149 (Area 5), which contained a single sherd in Fabric LB (early fourteenth-century), may also be contemporary with these deposits.

This group, which formed the basis for the initial classification of the local medieval pottery (pp. 252–3) contains a typical range of thirteenth- and fourteenth-century Tyler Hill wares. Of the four fabric sub-groups, types A and C are predominant. Visually, Fabric A appears to be earlier than Fabric C, but there is obviously a considerable overlap. The baluster jugs and thumbed bases in all fabrics date to the mid/late thirteenth century, but the 'tulip' rim (no. 17) is unusual, and may be of fourteenth-century date. Nos. 11, 16 and 18 have formal parallels at North Lane, Canterbury, and at Dover Castle; the average height for these jugs is *c.* 35–40 cm. The bowls (nos. 31, 32, Fabric A) are probably of early or mid thirteenth-century date, whereas no. 34 (Fabric C unstabbed rim) may be of mid to late thirteenth-century date. No. 31, which had a thin green glaze internally, and no. 32 have mid thirteenth-century formal parallels at Dover Castle. No. 33 resembles finds from Rose Lane, Canterbury, which has two small fragments of shell on the rim, but would otherwise be classified as Fabric C; this probably dates to *c.* 1250. The quality of Fabric A is not good, but it is fairly consistent. Fabric C varies considerably and many sherds are roughly finished or are distorted as a result of overfiring. Decoration in all fabrics consists mainly if incised zig-zag (nos. 12, 13, 21), vertical (no. 23) or

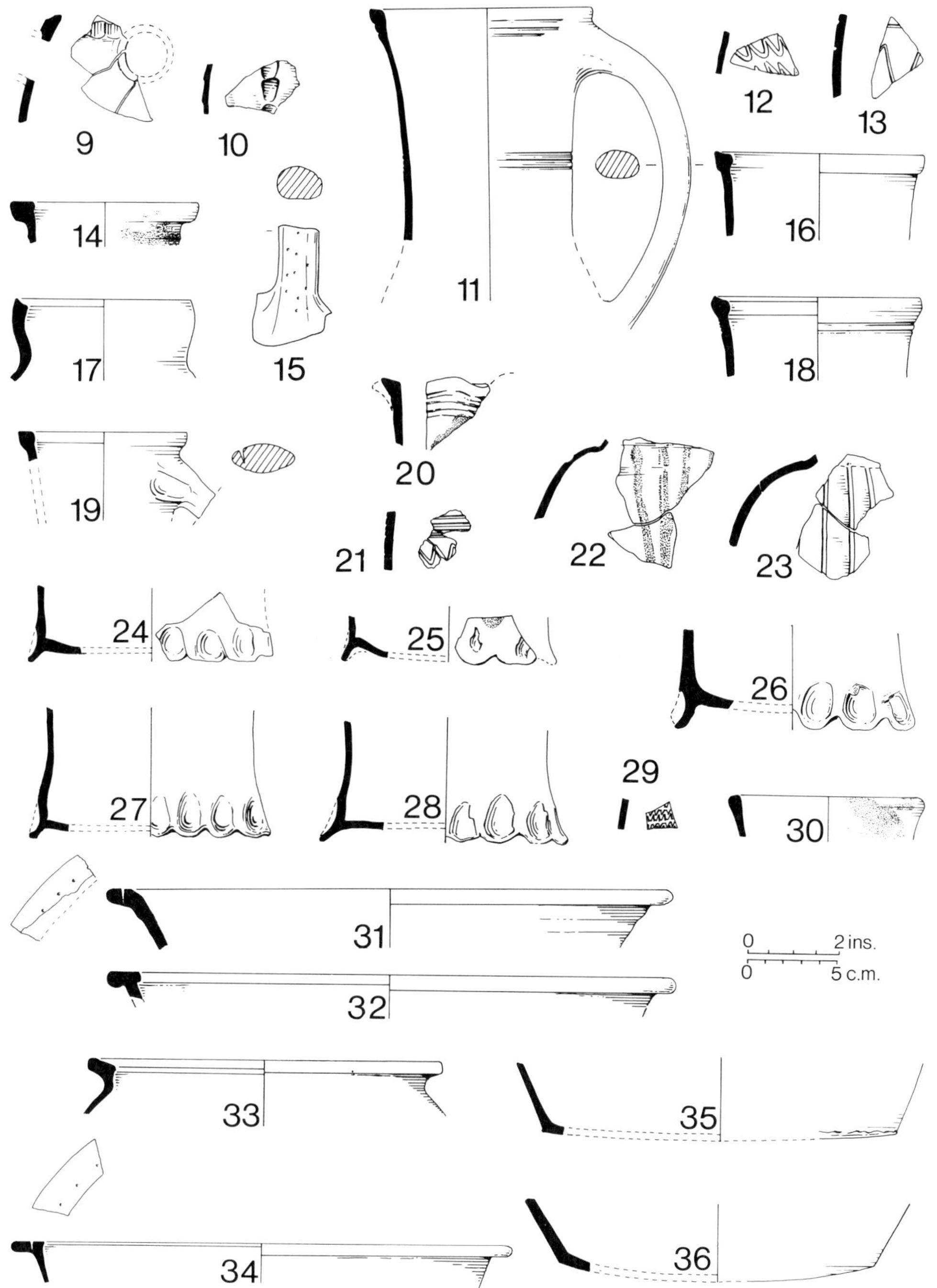

Fig. 90. Medieval local, non-local (no. 30) and imported Pottery (no. 29) 1976–78. Group 5. (Scale: ¼)

horizontal lines; a few sherds bear a painted slip decoration (no. 22), while a number of sherds in Fabric C (particularly in layer 47) carry an overall orange slip; this appears to be a fourteenth-century trait. Glazing is patchy, exceptions being nos. 16 and 22.

Non-local wares comprise one sherd of Aardenburg-type ware (no. 29) with notched rouletting under a cream slip and a green glaze, one sherd of London ware, and one rim of Scarborough ware (no. 30). The fabric of no. 30 is typical of the Phase 2 Scarborough products (*c.* 1225–1325), but the rim form suggests that it is probably fairly early within this period (P.G. Farmer, pers. comm.).

Group 6. The Medieval Cemetery: Areas 1, 2 and 5

The pottery from the earliest graves excavated in Areas 1 and 2 (pre-dating the construction of the chantry chapel) consists largely of residual Roman material, and thirteenth/early fourteenth-century pottery in Fabric A (Fig. 91, nos. 37, 38, 39). A few sherds, however, appear to be of mid fourteenth-century date; one strap handle from grave 557 is in Fabric B/LB, while a body sherd from grave 580 is in Fabric C/LB (cf. Group 5, layer 5149). Sherds in Fabric C are slightly finer than those in Group 5, with a thinner wall and a distinctive pale orange-grey mottled inner surface. The developed rim of no. 42 also suggests a mid fourteenth-century date. The pottery from the early graves in Area 5 is entirely residual, suggesting that there was little activity in this area in the later twelfth and thirteenth centuries.

The most interesting finds in this group are one sherd of eleventh-/twelfth-century Pingsdorf-type ware (Grave 5137, possibly from a red-painted vessel), and a sherd from a Rye jug, (no. 40; for fabric, see p. 256), from grave 580; a further seventeen sherds from this jug were recovered from the subsequent deposits. The jug, which has a sub-rectangular stabbed strap handle, is decorated with at least two bands of *repoussé* rosettes at intervals of *c.* 35 mm. across the shoulder, and a glossy olive glaze with brown streaks. Numerous parallels for the *repoussé* raspberry stamp were found in the excavation of one of the Rye kilns (Vidler 1933, 45–64; Barton 1979, 240, 242), which produced vessels bearing a variety of stamped motifs. These, and other highly decorated wares, constitute the early output of the kiln, which Barton (1979, 218–21) considers to have been *c.* 1300–75, overlapping slightly with the second period of production *c.* 1350–1400 to 1425. A date of 1325–50 is thus suggested for the St. Augustine's jug, although the quality of the piece raises the possibility of longer preservation and a depositional date approaching 1400. In addition to no. 40, sherds from two other jugs were also found in several later contexts (no. 39, and a jug in Fabric C; grave 580, Groups 7, 14).

Group 7. The Construction of the Chantry Chapel: Areas 2 and 3

Layers 561 and 575 appear to represent the soil displaced by the construction trenches for the chantry chapel; this may account for the similarity of Groups 6 and 7, and for the presence of sherds from vessels noted above. Two bases (Fig. 91, no. 44, Fabric C; no. 45, Fabric B/LB), however, may be of late thirteenth- or fourteenth-century date.

Groups 8 and 9. The Later Medieval Cemetery and Vault: Area 3

As the surrounding ground surfaces were not excavated, the relationship of graves 1059 and 1060 with the later graves in Areas 1 and 2 is unclear. Grave 1060, however, contained the first sherds in Fabric LM, a few sherds in Fabric LB, and four sherds (possibly from a vessel noted in grave 580), which are heavily covered in mortar. If the mortar is derived from the construction of the chantry chapel, then both graves post-date the chapel, but pre-date the vault, which may be dated by two sherds of Tudor Green ware found in the rebedding cut for the grave slab over grave 1059. Although as yet little is known about the origins of this late medieval fine ware, it was certainly well established by *c.* 1430 (Moorhouse 1979, 54). As the rebedding of the grave slab must have taken place immediately prior to the excavation of the vault, a date of *c.* 1440–50 seems appropriate for this structure. Grave 1013 (within the chapel), Grave 1059, Layer 1046 (from which the vault was cut), and the vault all contained mainly residual material, but layer 1054 in the vault contained two sherds in Fabric LB, including no. 46 (Fig. 14). Grave 1060 produced a green-glazed London ware rod handle.

Groups 10–12. The Late Medieval Levels and Cemetery: Areas 4 and 5 (Fig. 91)

The medieval levels excavated in Area 5 are remarkable for their consistent paucity of post-Roman material. Virtually no pottery was recovered from the layers either pre-dating or associated with the construction of the buttress 5140/702, although their fourteenth-century date is suggested by a sherd from layer 5149 (Group 5). Features post-dating the buttress but pre-dating the refacing of the south-west tower, and even the late fifteenth- and sixteenth-century deposits were similarly lacking in pottery. Layer 5101 held one sherd (no. 47); layer 5125 contained nine sherds, including a splash-glazed strap handle (no. 48) and a body sherd in Fabric LB. The most productive feature was Grave 5116 (forty sherds). A further thirty-two sherds were found in the five other late medieval graves excavated. The bulk of these is residual, including a battered London ware rod handle with applied spurs (no. 50, mid-thirteenth century copy of a Rouen jug). Sherds in Fabric LB (nos. 49, 51) were, however, found in all features, while one sherd in Fabric LM and two sherds of Tudor Green ware were found in Grave 5111.

Group 13. The Late Medieval Cemetery: Areas 2 and 4. (Fig. 91)

As in Area 5, most of the pottery from these late-medieval graves is residual (mainly Fabrics C and D). Also present, however, are one sherd in Fabric F (Grave 587), which joins a sherd in Group 14, layer 540); eleven in Fabric LB (including no. 56 Fabric LB/H), and a few non-local wares. These comprise one sherd of Surrey white ware (Grave 581, Kingston variant type), three sherds from the Rye jug (no. 40), one small sherd of Saintonge ware (Grave 581), two sherds of Aardenburg-type ware (Graves 587, 603), and three sherds of fine oxidised ware, probably of Low Countries origin (Grave 574, two sherds externally glazed, similar to Fig. 93, no. 78; Grave 581, internally glazed). The most productive grave was 581, with forty-one sherds (nos. 51–3, 56).

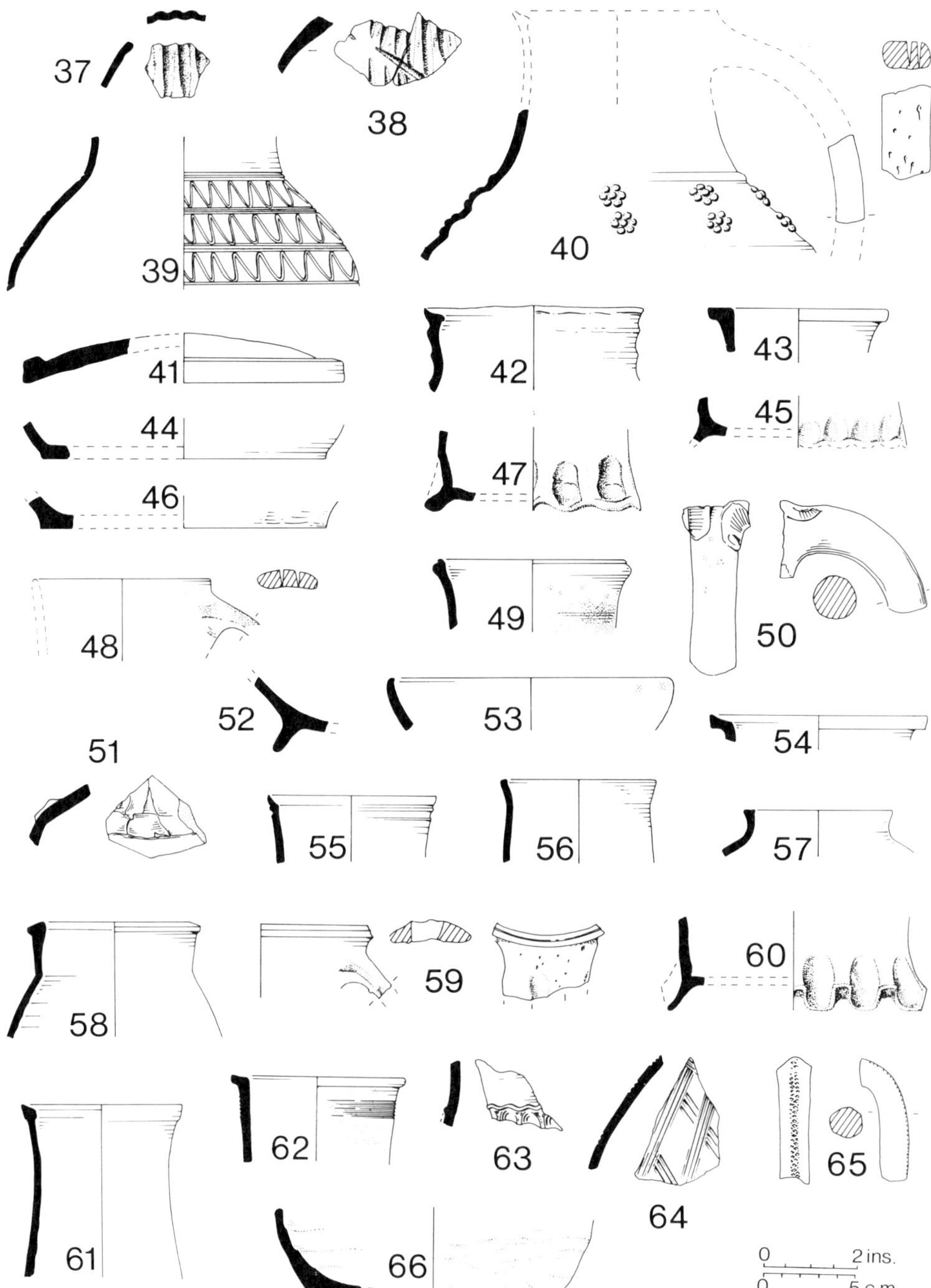

Fig. 91. Medieval local and imported Pottery (no. 65), 1976–78. Groups 6–15. (Scale: ¼).

TABLE 13

Excavations 1976–78

The distribution of the local pottery fabrics in the pre-Dissolution deposits.

Group	BE	RO	LR	SOT	SS	EMS	SHS	SOS	A	B	C	D	LB	LM	F
1.	276	799													
2.	53	227	1	1		4									
3a.	1	2				30									
3b.	26	114				3									
3c.	32	97	1	6	4	1	1								
4.	11	63		2	1	1			1						
5.	3	8	1			4		11	184	28	51	22	7		
6.	5	28				1		1	6	5	8	1	2		
7.	3	4				1		2		4	10	1	1		
8.	5	28						5	3	10	2	4	2		
9.	5	13			1	1			2		2		4		
10.	3	7							1						
11.						3					4		3		
12.		6			1				8	5	27	6	14	1	
13.	3	11					3		7	6	14	15	11		1
TOTAL	426	1407	3	9	7	49	4		19	58	119	49	44	1	1

TABLE 14

Excavations 1976–78. The distribution of the non-local and imported pottery in the pre-Dissolution deposits.

Group	EAS	IPS	LON	SCAR	RYE	KING	TUDG	NFR	PING	SAIN	AARD	LOW
2.	1	3										
3.		2						1				
4.												
5.			1	1							1	
6.					1				1			
7.												
8.		1										
9.							2					
10.												
11.												
12.			1				2					
13.					3	1				1	2	3
TOTAL	1	6	2	1	4	1	4	1	1	1	3	3

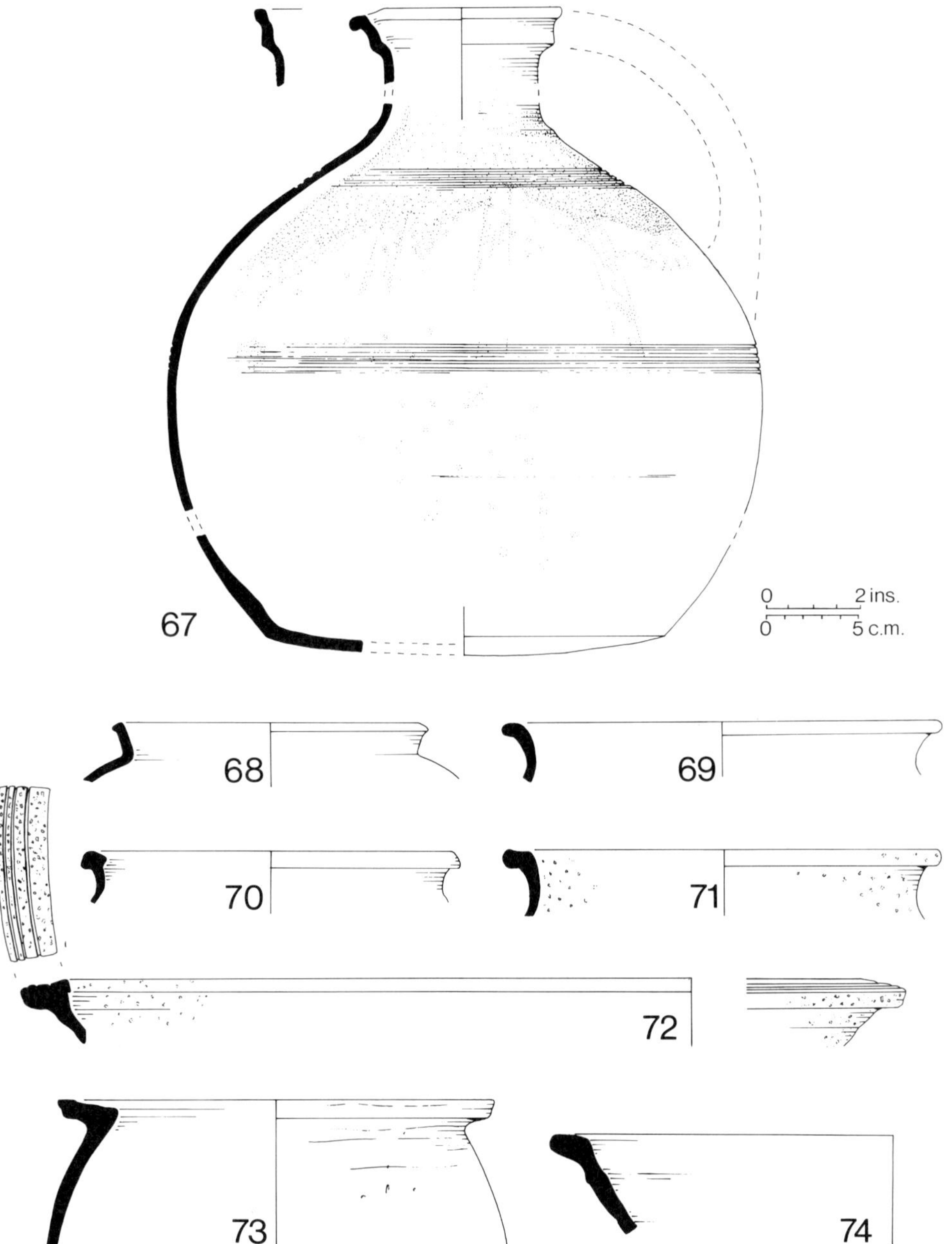

Fig. 92. Anglo-Saxon, medieval and late medieval Pottery, 1976–78. Groups 14–16. (Scale: ¼)

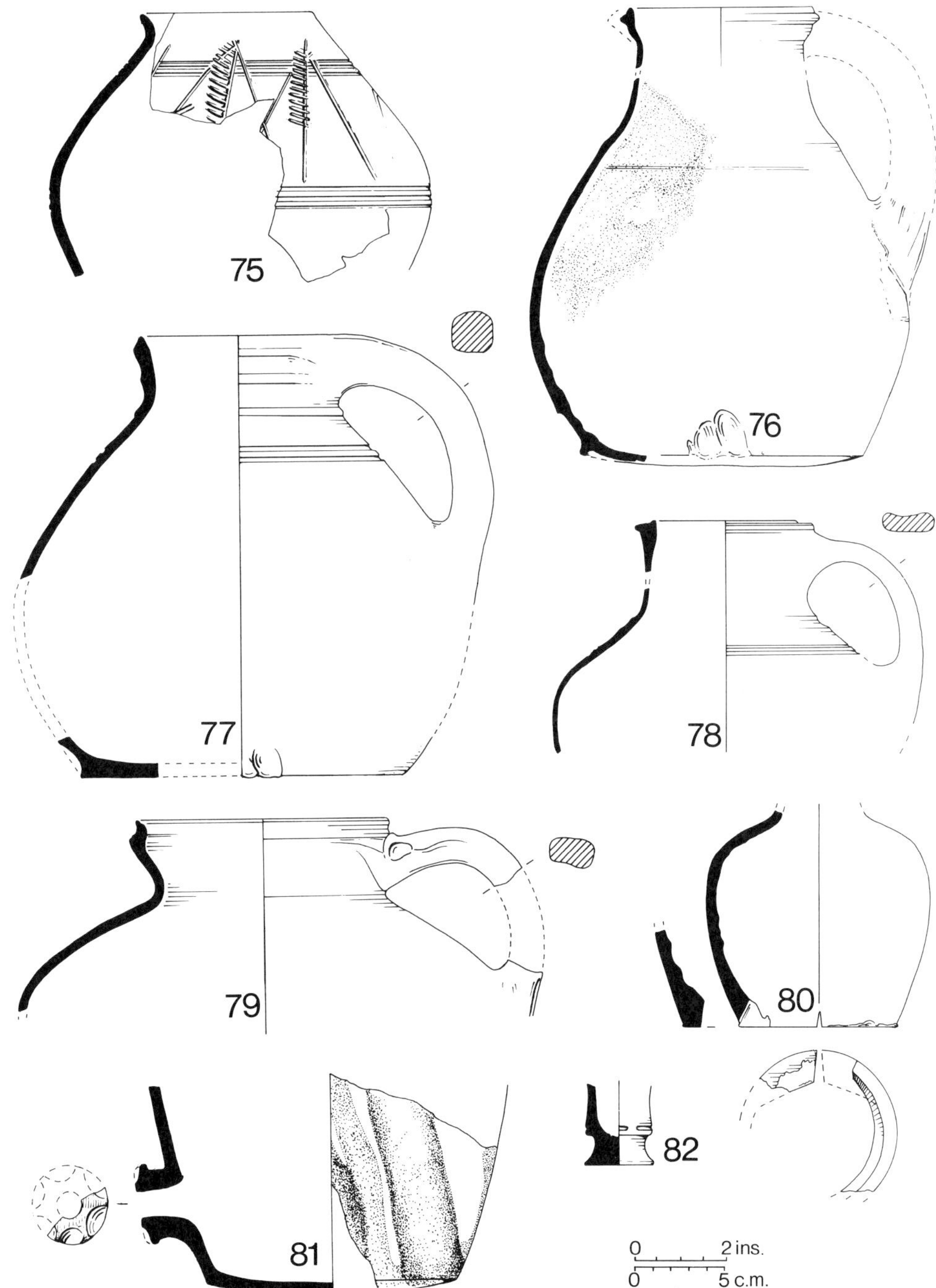

Fig. 93. Late medieval and early post-medieval local and non-local (nos. 81–2) Pottery, 1976–78. Groups 14–16. (Scale: ¼)

Group 14. The Demolition Features and Post-demolition Build-up: Areas 2, 4, and 4

Following the demolition of the church, the area to the south and east of the south-east tower was levelled with a series of tips containing a quantity of medieval and late-medieval pottery, especially layers 766 and 763. These layers sealed some scaffold bases and demolition deposits in Areas 4 and 5, and were cut and sealed by later features and deposits in Area 2. The relationship of this deposit to the chalk building in Area 2 was not clear, but the pottery suggests that the layers in Group 14 correspond with those in 1974–75 Group 4. Both the chalk building and these tips were sealed by a second phase of demolition material (Group 15) which also filled and covered the remains of the chapel; this would seem to equate with 1974–75 Group 3. The pottery in Group 14 (Fig. 91, nos. 57–65; Fig. 92, nos. 66–71) is clearly earlier than that in the subsequent groups, containing only ten sherds in Fabric F, and only one sherd of Langerwehe stoneware (layer 540). Other non-local sherds include probable Wealden ware (no. 48), Aardenburg-type ware (no. 65), and seven sherds of Tudor Green ware lobed cup.

Residual post-Roman material ranges from the early eleventh century (no. 68) to the fifteenth century. Nos. 70 and 71 are probably of twelfth-century and late twelfth- early thirteenth-century date, respectively. Amongst the thirteenth- and fourteenth-century wares are decorated body sherds (nos. 63, 64), a variety of jug rims, and the greater part of a large globular jug with a rod handle and sagging base (no. 67, from inside the chalk building). Fourteenth- and fifteenth-century wares include a few reduced jug sherds with white painted slip decoration, and a number of rims from large jugs in Fabric LB, with rim diameters up to 120 mm. and strap handles up to 68 mm. wide. The handle of no. 59 divides at the point of fracture, and was possibly originally twisted or plaited like that from the excavations of 1974–75 (Fig. 84, no. 1).

Groups 15 and 16. Later Demolition Features and all Post-demolition Groups

These groups constitute a very mixed assemblage. Excluding the mass of seventeenth- to nineteenth-century pottery associated with the hospital period, residual medieval and post-medieval wares appear in approximately equal numbers. Group 15 contains a number of substantially complete late-medieval and early post-medieval jugs (Fig. 93, nos. 76–79, 81), but non-local and imported pottery is limited to no. 78 (possible Low Countries origin), no. 81 (Wealden ware) and six sherds of Langerwehe and Raeren stoneware. Group 16, by contrast, contains a disparate collection of single sherds, with a wide range of non-local and imported wares. The latter include one sherd of Saintonge ware from a jug noted in the 1974–75 assemblage, Groups 2, 4; a few sherds of Aardenburg-type ware; a base from a South Netherlands maiolica altar vase, and forty-three sherds of Rhenish stoneware. Later wares include English tin-glazed ware (nos. 83–5, probably Lambeth), Staffordshire marbled ware, English stoneware, a small amount of Chinese porcelain and a quantity of English china.

Residual post-Roman material includes an unusual shell-tempered bowl with reeded rim of probable twelfth-century date (see Fig. 92, 72); late medieval wares include an intriguing jug in Fabric LM (no. 75), with incised decoration which recalls the *sgraffito* decoration found on some of the more individual products of the Rye kilns (Vidler 1933, 53–5, PL. VII; PL. VIII). The forms of nos. 79 and 80 are also unusual; no. 80, a bird pot, appears to be in Fabric F, but may prove to be an import from the Low Countries.

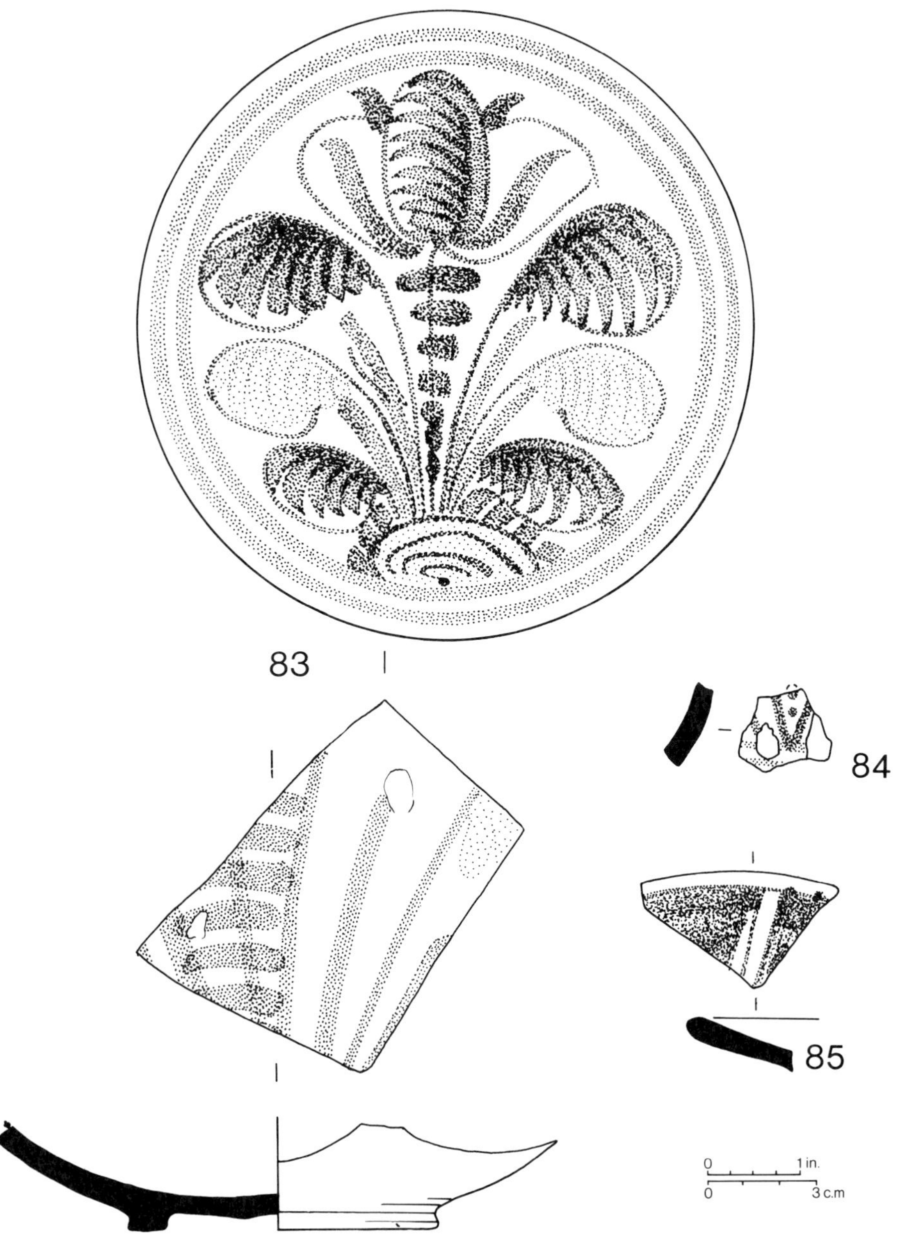

Fig. 94. English tin-glazed Pottery, 1976–78. Group 15. (Scale: ½)

Excavations 1976–78. Catalogue.

No.	*Layer*	*Group*	*Fabric*	*Total Sherds*	*Glaze Int.*	*Glaze Ext.*	*Internal Parallels*	*External Parallels*
Fig. 88								
1.	805/6	1	Samian	1				
2.	804	1	Samian	1				
3.	805/6	1	Samian	1				
Fig. 89								
4.	804	1	BE	1				
5.	5160	2	IPS	1				
6.	796	3b	SS/EM	1				
7.	5157	3b	SHS	1				
8.	798	3a	SS/EM	30				
Fig. 90								
9.	601	5	EM	3				Williams and Frere 1948, Fig. 7, no. 2 Frere 1954, Fig. 18, no. 12 Rigold 1967, Fig. 18, A30 Tester 1972, Fig. 16, no. 25; Fig. 17, no. 43
10.	599	5	SOS	1				
11.	594 602	5 5	A	106		SG		Macpherson-Grant 1978, 188, Fig. 22, no. 59 Cook *et al.* 1969, 91–4, Fig. 16, no. iiiYBI
12.	599	5	A	1		G	1976–78, no. 24	
13	594	5	A	1			1976–78, no. 24	
14.	599	5	A/C	1		G		
15.	594	5	D	2				
16.	594	5	D	1+?5	G	G	1976–78, no. 22	
17	599	5	C	1		G		
18	599	5	C/D	1		G		Spillett *et al* 1942, 58–9, Fig. 1, no. 4
19.	594	5	D	1				
20.	578	5	D	1		G		
21.	548	5	D	3		G		
22.	594 599	5 5	C/D	2+?5		SG	1976–78, no. 16	
23.	548 566	5 5	D	2+?1		G		Rigold 1967, 112, Fig. 12, no. IIB3 Macpherson-Grant 1978, 180, Fig. 17, no. 36
24.	594	5	A	26		G	1976–78, no. 13	
25.	594 599	5 5	B	3+?11		G		
26.	594	5	A/C	1				

No.	*Layer*	*Group*	*Fabric*	*Total Sherds*	*Glaze Int.*	*Glaze Ext.*	*Internal Parallels*	*External Parallels*
27.	594	5	C	4				
	599	5						
28.	594	5	C	1		G		
29.	594	5	AARD	1		SG		
30.	594	5	SCAR	1		G		Farmer 1979, 28–31
31.	599	5	A	2+?6	G	G	1976–78, 5/594	Cook *et al.* 1969, 91, 94, Fig. 14, no. iiiXA9
32.	594	5	A	3				Rigold 1967, 112–3, Fig. 11, no. IIAZ
33.	594	5	SOS/C	1			1976–78, no. 36	Frere 1954, Figs. 18, 19
34.	594	5	C	2				
35.	599	5	A/C	2				
36.	594	5	C	1			1976–78, no. 33	
Fig. 91								
37.	53	6	A	2+?5		G	1976–78, 6/66	
38.	53	6	A	2		G	1976–78, no. 75	
39.	557	6	A	4	G			
	540	14						
40.	580	6	RYE	18		G		Vidler 1933, 49, Pl. II; Pl. XII, no. 6
	574	13						Barton 1979, 201–5, Fig. 8, nos. 1, 5; Fig. 11, no. 8
	560	13						
	540	14						
	529	15						
41.	577	6	A	1		S		
42.	577	6	D	1				
43.	561	7	D	1	G			
44.	575	7	C	1				
45.	545	7	B/LB	1				
46.	1054	9	LB	1				
47.	5101	11	B/LB	1		S		
48.	5125	11	LB	1		C		
49.	5128	12	LB	1				
50.	5128	12	LON	1		C		
51.	5110	12	LB	1				
52.	581	13	D	1				
53.	581	13	C	1		SG		
54.	589	13	A	1				
55.	589	13	A	1				
56.	581	13	LB/H	1				
57.	537	14	LB/H	1		S		
58.	766	14	WEA	1		G		
59.	763	14	LB	1			1976–78, no. 60	
60.	763	14	LB	1			1976–78, no. 59	
61.	532	14	B	3		G		
	18	15						
62.	533	14	C	1+?4		SG		

Excavations 1976–78. Catalogue (contd.).

No.	*Layer*	*Group*	*Fabric*	*Total Sherds*	*Glaze Int.*	*Glaze Ext.*	*Internal Parallels*	*External Parallels*
63.	539	14	C	1		G	1974–75, no. 45	
64.	533	14	D	1		G		Rigold 1967, Fig. 13, no. IIB14
65.	540	14	?AARD	2		SG		
66.	533	14	A	2+?66			1976–78, 14/532; 15/539; 15/763	
Fig. 92								
67.	537	14	A	175		SG		
	540	14						
	547	14						
	558	14						
	555	16						
68.	550	14	SS/EM	1				Frere 1954, 125, Fig. 13, no. 122
69.	540	14	SS/EM	1				Frere 1954, Fig. 12, no. 118 Wilson 1982, Fig. 35, no. 22
70.	511	14	EM	1				
71.	1027	14	SH	1				Williams and Frere 1948, Fig. 18, no. 14
72.	U/S	15	SH	1				
73.	726	15	LB	1				
74.	24	15	LB	3	G			
	31	15						
Fig. 93								
75.	726	14	LM	13		G	1974–75, 3/37	
	763	15						
76.	513	15	LM	33		YG		
	1002							
77.	503	15	F	58		B		
	513	15						
	1002	15						
	1003	15						
78.	720	15	?LOW	31		G	1976–78, 13/574	
	726	15						
79.	720	15	F	57				
	726	15						
80.	715	15	F	25				Pryor and Blockley 1978, 77, Fig. 19, no. 104
	704	16						
81.	16	15	WEA	14		G	1974–75, 4/35	
	24	15						
	29	15						
	31	15						
82.	U/S	15	WEA	1		C		

No.	*Layer*	*Group*	*Fabric*	*Total Sherds*	*Glaze Int.*	*Glaze Ext.*	*Internal Parallels*	*External Parallels*
Fig. 94								
83.	704	15	TGW	1		Y, Blue		Bloice 1971, 131, Fig. 56, no. 17 Sotheby and Co. 1965, 47, no. 167
84.	6	15	TGW	1		Blue		
85.	13	15	TGW	1		Blue		

ACKNOWLEDGEMENTS

The author wishes to thank all those who contributed to this report, or commented on specific sherds or aspects of the text, and particularly: Joanna Bird and Brian Hartley for their reports on the samian wares; Ailsa Mainman for the thin-section analyses of and assistance with the reports on the Anglo-Saxon and early medieval wares; and Pamela Clarke for her contribution to and assistance with the reports on the stoneware. Pam Broady, Peter Farmer, John Hurst, Stephen Moorhouse, Clive Orton, the late S.E. Rigold, Anthony Streeten, and Alan Vince all advised on the medieval and post-medieval wares, while Jim Thorn (A.M.D.O., H.B.M.C.) offered invaluable assistance with the illustrations, and drew Fig. 84, no. 1, and Fig. 87, nos. 59–65. I am also indebted to Andrew Saunders (H.B.M.C.), D. Kelly (Maidstone Museum), G.S. Bagley (Ypres Tower Museum, Rye), and the Canterbury Archaeological Trust for making available the material in their collection. The greatest debt is owed to Nigel Macpherson-Grant, for his contribution to the study of Kentish pottery, and for his assistance throughtout the project and comments on the many drafts of this report.

IX. APPENDIX

BONES

FISH BONES Alison Locker

The following bones from the shaft dug in 1965 were identified:

Blue-fin tunny (*Thunnus thynnus*), one vertebral centrum.

Conger eel (*Conger conger*), two coalesced vertebral centra, four vertebral centra.

Ling (*Molva molva*), one vertebral centrum.

Small gadoid ?whiting (*Merlangius merlangus*), one vertebral centrum.

Plaice/flounder (*Pleuronectes platessa/Platichthys flesus*), seven vertebral centra, one anal pterygiophore.

The blue-fin tunny is the only common large tunny in north European waters, where it is mainly a summer-time visitor appearing in July and August. It is a surface-living schooling fish rarely found deeper than 100 m.

The conger eel is mainly found on rocky shores and off-shore and can be caught on lines or in traps.

Ling are deep-water fish, in 300 to 400 m. on rocky grounds in the northern part of the North Sea, so this specimen must have been brought down to Canterbury from a more northerly port probably in a salted or dried state. They are usually caught on lines.

Whiting are shallow in-shore fish from 30 to 100 m., often caught in nets.

Plaice and flounders are found from the shoreline to 200 m. in the case of the former, the latter only being found at a maximum depth of 30 m. Both species may have been fished or caught in shoreline traps (Wheeler 1978).

SUMMARY OF BURIALS Justine Bayley

Only a small proportion of the graveyard associated with the abbey church was excavated and not all of the burials that were found were examined osteologically. The data collected cannot, therefore, be taken as representative of the whole population that was buried in the graveyard as it is only a very small and non-random sub-sample. Data was collected by Justine Bayley, Janet Henderson and Faye Powell from those skeletons that were examined and is available in A.M.L. Reports 2175, 2883, 2884, 4939 and 2901. A summary of their findings appears in the Table of Burials.

Three distinct types of bone deposits were identified among the material examined. First were the articulated burials which exhibited varying degrees of preservation and completeness. Second were the disarticulated burials that had been disturbed in antiquity, probably by later grave digging, in which all parts of the skeleton were represented. Finally, there were mixed deposits of only large bones which had been re-interred after medieval building works had disturbed parts of the Anglo-Saxon graveyard. These are described as charnel deposits.

Table 15. Burials from St. Augustine's 1960, 1976–78.

*indicates description in A.M.L. report.

No.	*Body*	*Type of Burial*	*Finds*	*Location*
		1960, TRENCH D		
No number	Well preserved, Male 35–45	Stone coffin made of ten stone slabs.		F16.
No number	Not excavated.	Part of stone coffin found in section.		F17.
		1976–78, AREA I		
32.		Tomb base of flint chalk and mortar.		Above grave 57.
37.		Tomb base of greensand ashlar.		Under E baulk.
53.	Badly preserved skeleton.	Oak coffin, iron brackets at top, middle and bottom of each corner. Iron rings for lowering. Greensand block under skull. Skeleton lying on bed of charcoal. Fig. 72, nos. 139–140.		West of tomb base 37.
57.	Articulated skeleton, arms straight. Not lifted.	Loam, no coffin.		Grave under 32.
67.		Flint base for tomb.		Consolidated on surface.
		AREA II		
549.*	Juvenile, 11–12 years.		Halfpenny of Edward III, lost *c.* 1350s.	Under grave 581.
557.*	Adult, probably female, 35–45 years.	Traces of wooden coffin, iron nails.		Cut from 582, containing Henry III halfpenny, *c.* 1260–80.
560.*	Adult skull, possibly male. 17–20 years.			Under grave 595.
574.*	Juvenile, *c.* 7–12 years.		Pilgrim badge Fig. 69, no. 72.	Under building X.
577.*	Juvenile, 3–5 years.	Coffin nails.		Cut from 582.
580.*	Infant, 0–2 months.	Stain of wooden coffin, iron nails.		Cut from 582.
581.*	Immature adult, probably male, 17–20 years.		Copper alloy shroud pin.	Cut into 552.
589.	Infant, partly destroyed by 581.			Under graves 549 and 581.

No.	*Body*	*Type of Burial*	*Finds*	*Location*
592.	Obliterated by 581. No bones found.			
595.*	Juvenile, 6–7 years.			Under wall 520, cut into 552.
603.	Adult, very poor condition.			Under building X, cut into 552.
		AREA IV		
758.*	Young adult, possibly male.	Wooden coffin, nails.		Below 720.
772.	Two articulated skeletons. West end of one body in 5148.			In bottom of hole 772. Hole dug for looting.
773.	Disarticulated bones.			773 and 775 in same grave below hospital drain.
775.*	Juvenile, *c.* 7–15 years.			
87.*	Adult male, 17–25 years.	Charnel in backfill. No trace of coffin.		Cut from 784.
790.*	Charnel, minimum of 47 individuals, including males, females and juveniles.			Under 792. Cut halfpenny of Edward the Confessor in layer 790.
792.*	Charnel. Only one mature adult, probably male, skull examined.			Anglo-Saxon burials re-deposited beside 741A.
803A–M.*	Twelve individuals.	Intersecting graves, Plate XXXIX.		Anglo-Saxon graveyard.
803A.	Adult, probably male, 19–23 years.			
803B.	Adult, probably male.			
803C.	Skull only, possibly male, 25–35 years.	Skull on cushion of flints.		
803D.	Adult, lower body only.			
803E.	Adult, 17–25 years			
803F.	Adult, male, over 19 years.			
803G.	Adult, probably male, 17–25 years.			
803H.	Skull only, probably male.			
803J.	Adult, probably male.			
803K.	Adult, probably male, possibly mature.			
803L.	Adult.			
803M.	Elderly adult, probably male.			

No.	*Body*	*Type of Burial*	*Finds*	*Location*
803 misc.	Parts of at least four adults, both male and female, and an infant. Some may be further parts of individuals 803A–803M.			
		AREA III		
405.		Purbeck tomb slab, not lifted. Plate XXXV.		South of chapel.
406.		Purbeck tomb slab, over 1059. Plate XXXV.		South of chapel.
407.		Purbeck slab over 1060. Plate XXXV.		South of chapel.
1009.	Not excavated.			Floor of chapel.
1005 and 1010.	Not excavated.	Purbeck fragments. Fig. 37, no. 39 (s.f. nos. 187, 188, 189, 190).		Demolition layer and floor of chapel.
1011.	Not excavated.	Bedding for tomb slab, plain fragment of Purbeck.		Floor of chapel.
1012.	Not excavated.	Bedding for tomb slab, painted mouldings.		Floor of chapel.
1013.	Skeleton.	Bedding for tomb slab, of mortar, shells, Purbeck slivers. Elm coffin. All nails *in situ*.		Floor of chapel.
1014.	Not excavated.	Mortar and chalk bedding for tomb slab.		Floor of chapel.
1039.	Not excavated.	Cut for grave.		Sealed by 1009.
1054.*	Mature adult male.	Wooden coffin, nails.	Shroud pin.	Second burial in vault 1051.
1056.*	Adult, 18–25 years. Some head hair was preserved.	Lead coffin encased in oak, coffin nails.	Woollen shroud, head in bandage. (See p. 00).	Primary burial in vault 1051.
1059.		Grave partially cut away for construction of vault 1051.		Partially covered by 406.
1060.	Skeleton not lifted.	Wooden coffin, nails.		Below 407.
1058.	Anglo-Saxon charnel.			Below vault 1051.
		AREA V		
5061.*	Elderly male, plus skull of juvenile, 10–11 years.			Post-monastic.
5090.*	Adolescent.			Below 5074.
5102.*	Adult, probably female, 17–25 years.			Sealed by 5089.
5110.*	Juvenile, under 15 years.			Sealed by 5089.

No.	*Body*	*Type of Burial*	*Finds*	*Location*
5111.*	Elderly adult, probably male.			Sealed by 5074.
5116.*	Immature adult, probably female, 18–20 years.			Sealed by 5089.
5127.*	Juvenile, 5–7 years.			Below 5125.
5128.*	Juvenile, *c.* 6 years.			Sealed by 5089.
5133.*	Adolescent, possibly female, 12–15 years.			Cuts 5157.
5137.	Under baulk, not lifted.	See section L–M, fig. 22		Below 5136.
5138.*	Infant, 0–6 months.			Below 5125.
5139.	No skeleton.			Cut by 5140.
5145.*	Adult male, 17–25 years.			Cut by 5110, 5128, 5133.
5146.*	Infant, 12–24 months.			Sealed by 5144.
5148=772.	Loose fragments from bodies in 772.			Sealed by 5144 and cut by 5140.
5150.	Under baulk, not lifted.	See section P–Q, fig. 23		Below 5125.
5154.*	Adult, probably female, 35–45 years.	Wooden coffin.		Under 5135.
5160A.*	Juvenile, under 6 years.			Anglo-Saxon graveyard.
5160B.*	Adult, probably female, 35–45 years.			
5160C.*	Adult, male, 17–25 years.	Skull on pillow of Roman tiles and chalk.		
5160D.	Not lifted.			
		AREA VIII		
8003A.*	Adult, possibly female, 25–35 plus parts of another, young adult.	On pillow of Roman brick and flints. Plate XLVII.		In 8003.
8011.*	Immature adult, possibly male.			Under 8004.

PLATES

Plan of the East End of St. Augustine's Abbey, from a copy of Thomas of Elmham's Chronicle, early fifteenth century. (Cambridge, Trinity Hall MS 1, f. 77R).

Names of the Altars (reading clockwise):

Sanctus Lambertus
Sanctus Northelmus
Sancta Mildreda virgo. Istud altare dedicatum in honore sanctorum Innocencium Anno Domini mcclxx^{0} *et corpus sancte Mildrede reconditum fuit in novo monumento vij*^{0} *kal. Junii.*
Sanctus Deusdedit
Sanctus Iustus
Sanctus Laurencius
Sanctus Augustinus
Beneath St Augustine: *Istud altare dedicatum de sancta Trinitate Anno Domini mccxl, viij kal. Octobris.*
Sanctus Mellitus
Sanctus Honorius
Sanctus Theodorus
Sanctus Adrianus abbas. Istud altare dedicatum in honore Sancti Stephani Prothomartiris, sancti Laurencii et Sancti Vincencii Anno Domini mccxl, viij kal. Octobris.
Sanctus Brithuvaldus
Sanctus Tatwinus

In the Centre:

Antiqua ecclesia presentis monasterii dedicata fuit a sancto Laurencio archiepiscopo anno domini dcxiij^{0} *anno xvj*^{0} *ab adventu sancti Augustini in Angliam; quo anno translatum fuit corpus sancti Augustini a loco quo prius iacuit per vij*^{tem} *annos foras iuxta ecclesiam nondum perfectam in eamdem ecclesiam iam consecratam, ac revereter in porticu aquilonali ubi modo est ecclesia sancte Marie tumulatum fuit; ubi iacuit per cccc*^{t0s} *lxxviij annos usque ad annum Domini mxcj.*
Anno domini mxcj, pontificatus Urbani pape secundi tercio, Willelmi ij regis Anglie post conquestum quinto, anno v^{0} *Wydonis abbis, et tempore vacationis archiepiscopatus cantuariensis post obitum Lanfranci anno tercio, nova ecclesia per Scotlandum abbem incepta per Widonem perfecta. Translatum est corpus sancti Augustini cum corporibus aliorum sanctorum a loco quo prius in prima ecclesia iacuit usque ad locum ubi modo iacet per Gundulfum episcopum rofensem.*

Over the Nave Altar:
Sanctus Letardus *Reliquiae*
Libri missi a Gregorio ad Augustinum
Sanctus Ethelbertus

Left and Right of Altar:
Ostium in parte aquilonali ad corpora sanctorum
Ostium in parte australi ad corpora sanctorum

Along the Bottom:
Anno Domini mccxl^{0} *istud altare dedicatum in honore apostolorum Petri et Pauli et sancti Augustini v*^{o} *kal. Novembris.*
Anno Domini mccccxxv^{o} *istud altare dedicatum fuit in honore apostolorum Petri et Pauli sancti Augustini Anglorum apostoli et sancti Aethelberti regis, kal. Martii a petro episcopo corbaniensi.*

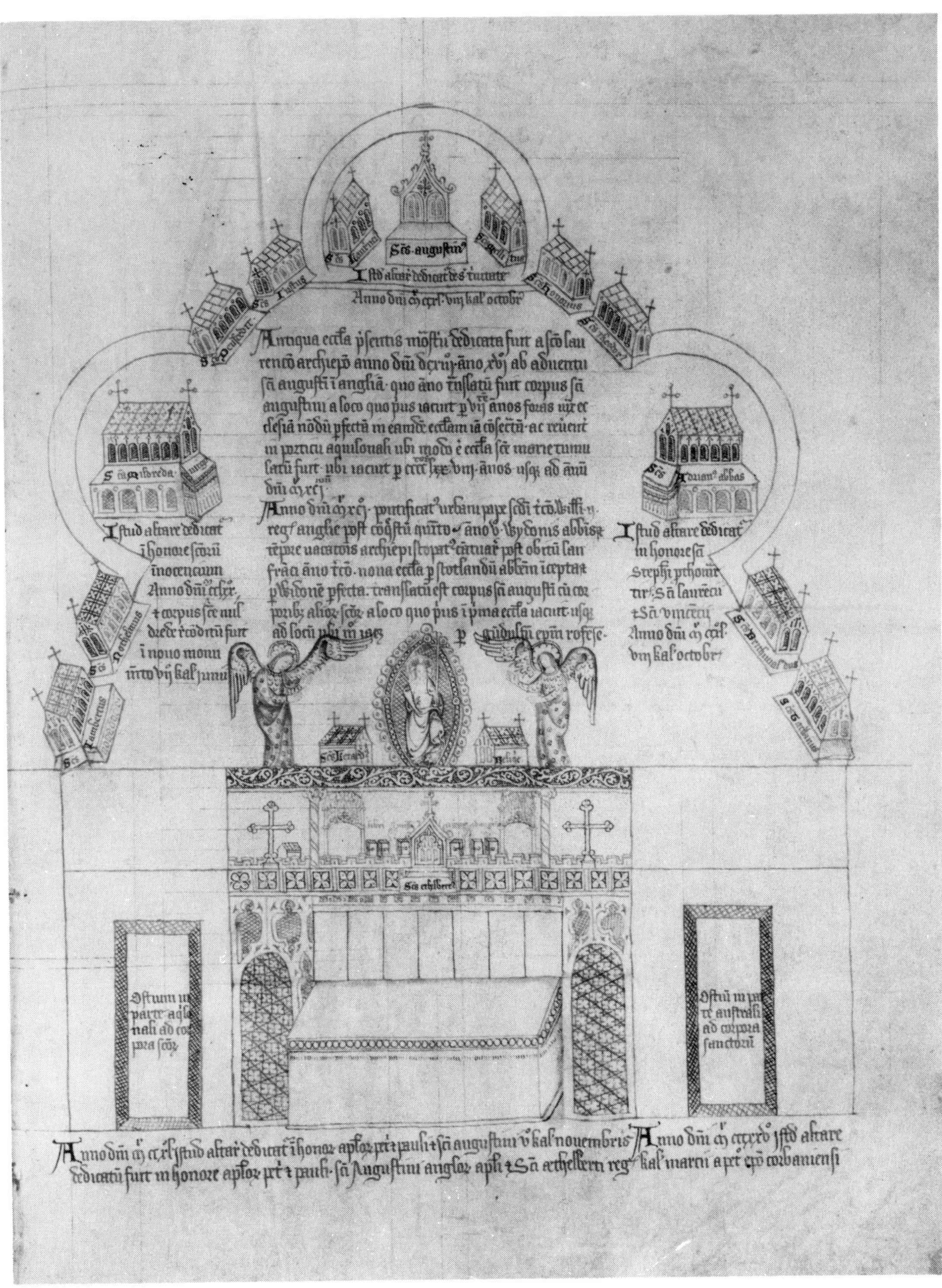

Canterbury Pilgrims outside a City, by an English artist *c.* 1460 (B.L. Royal MS 18D, f 148). The western towers of the abbey church may be represented in the top left-hand corner.

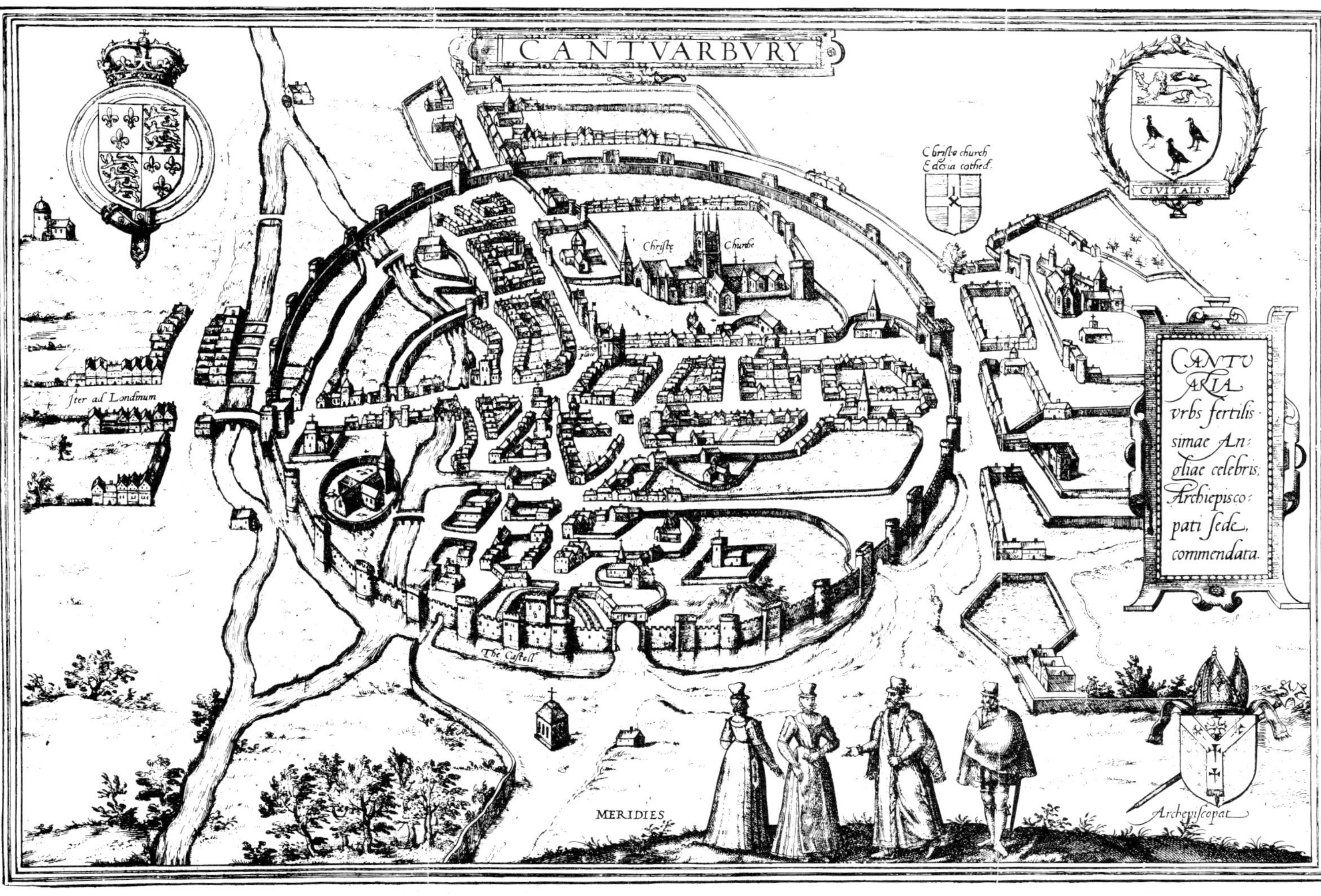

Part of Braun and Hoggenburg's Map of *c.* 1560.

Part of a Map of Canterbury, *c.* 1580, showing the buildings of the royal residence. (Canterbury Cathedral Library, Map 49).

Part of a Map of *c.* 1620, showing the royal residence and formal gardens. (Canterbury Cathedral Library, Map 123).

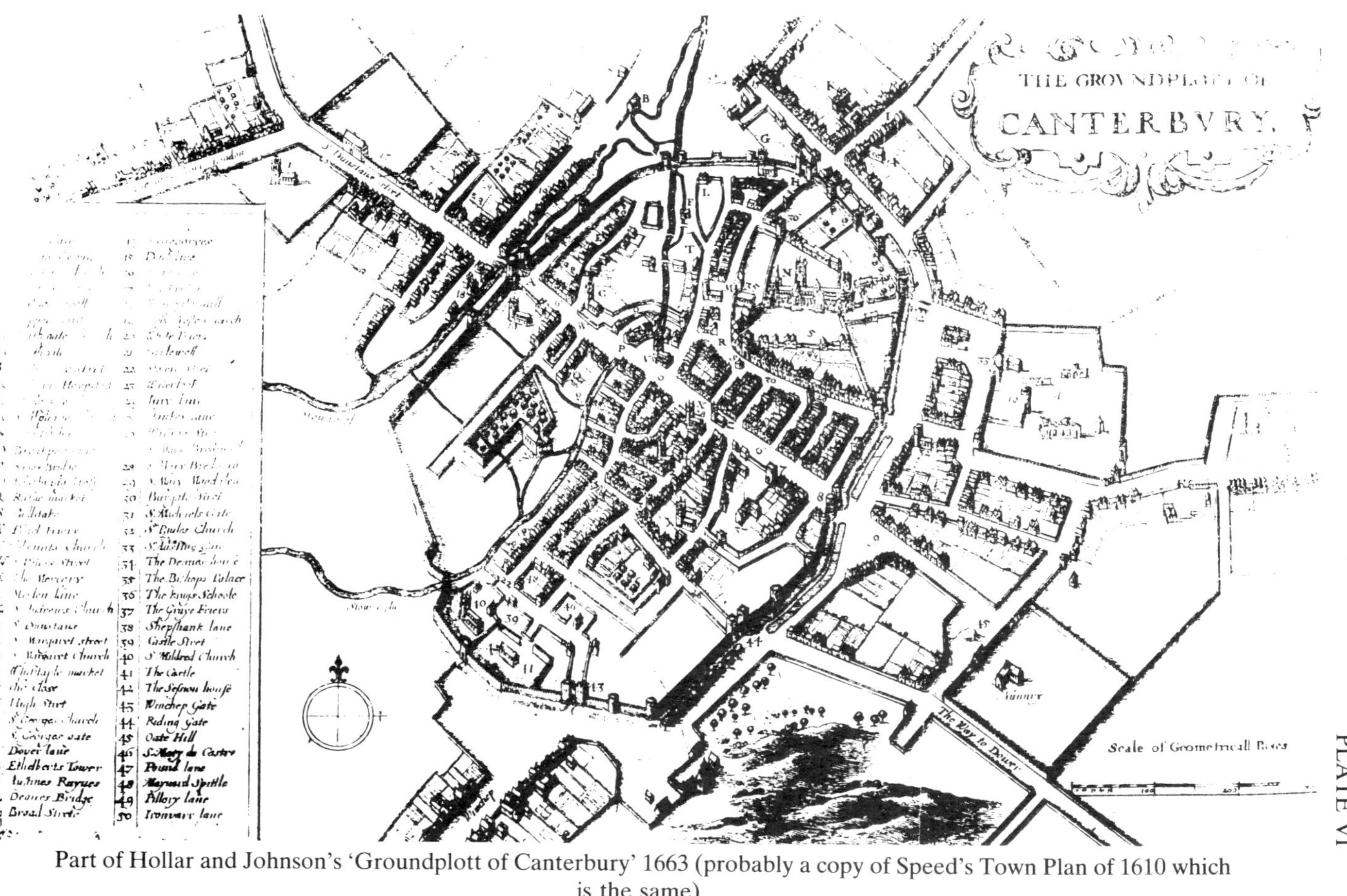

Part of Hollar and Johnson's 'Groundplott of Canterbury' 1663 (probably a copy of Speed's Town Plan of 1610 which is the same).

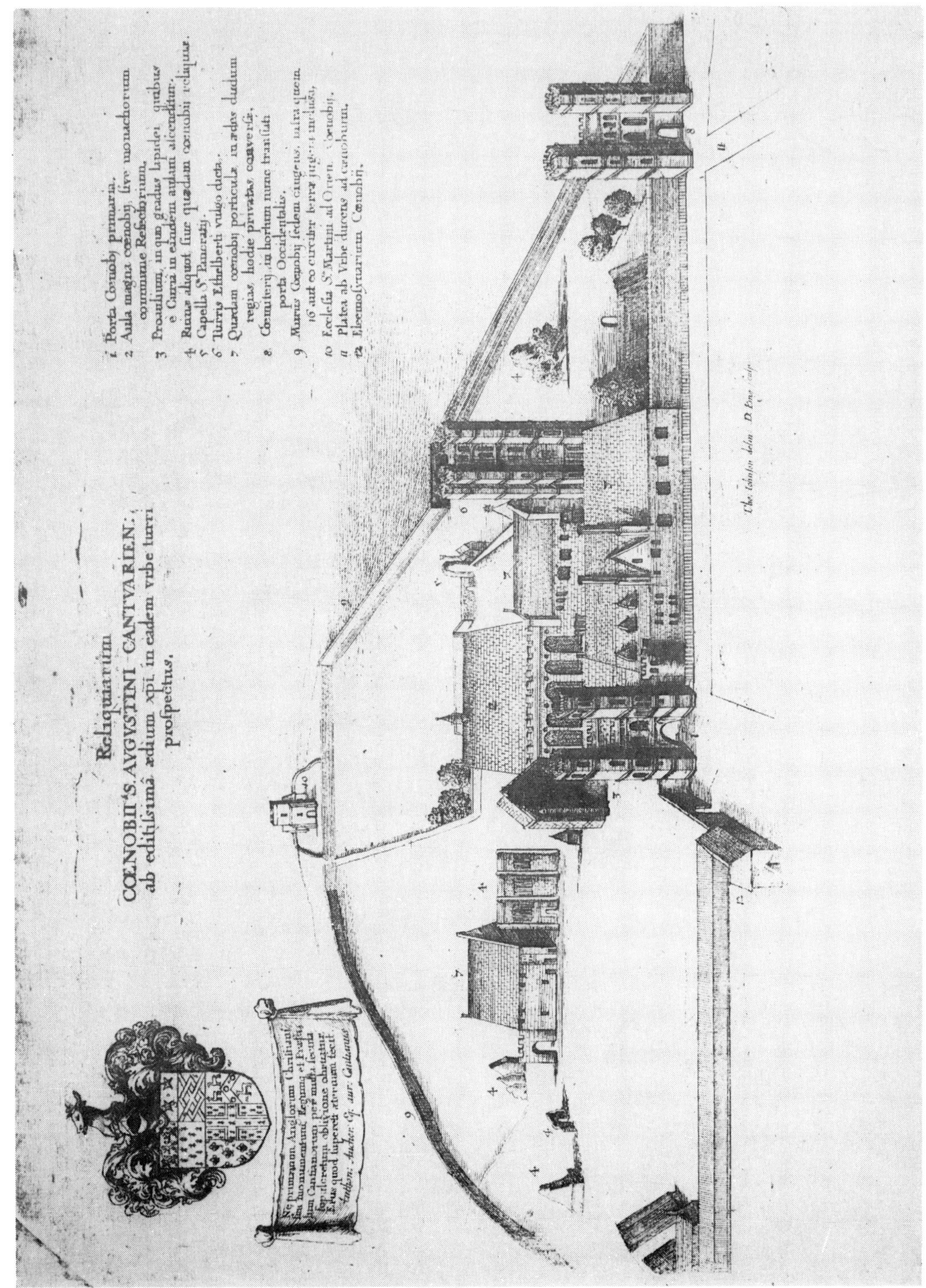

Daniel King's Engraving of *c.* 1640.

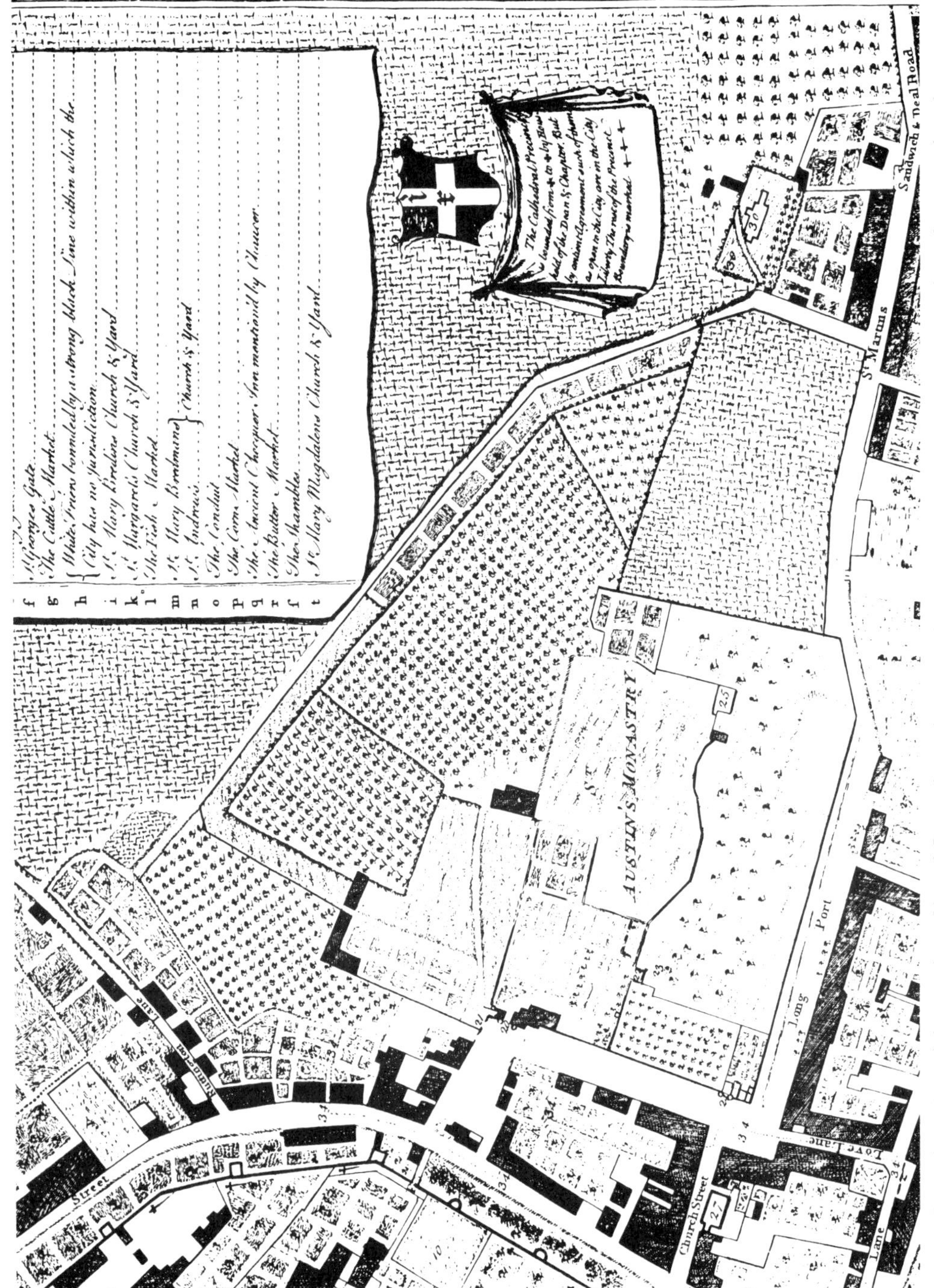

Part of 'A plan of the Ancient City of Canterbury' by W. and H. Doidge, 1752. Note the suggestion of a mound to the south of St. Pancras'.

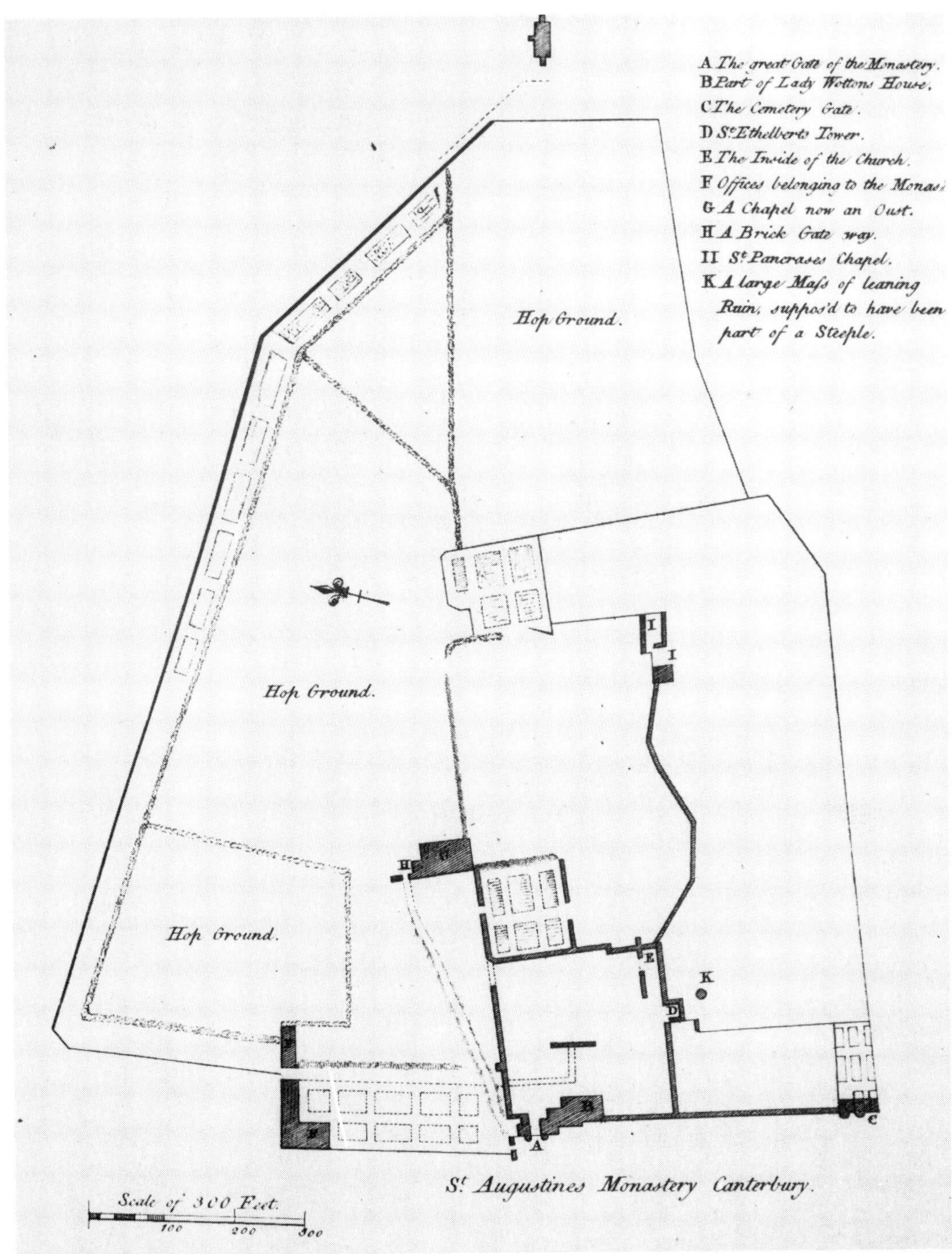

Plan of St. Augustine's engraved by Thornton, from Francis Grose, *Antiquities of England and Wales* (1797).

PLATE X

The Kent and Canterbury Hospital, built 1793. (Maidstone Record Office).

Aerial View of St. Augustine's Remains with the Hospital and Technical College Buildings, 1954.

PLATE XII

(*Crown Copyright*).

St. Augustine's Abbey, looking East with the Technical College Buildings just visible beyond the Boundary Wall, 1953.

PLATE XIII

The Site, viewed from the South-West, 1980.

PLATE XIV

Trench A, 1960. West End of Trench showing Footings of Apse in North Transept.

PLATE XV

Trench B, 1960. South End of Trench showing North Side of Crypt.

Cemetery Area, 1960, showing Wall (F10) and Grave (F13).

PLATE XVIIa

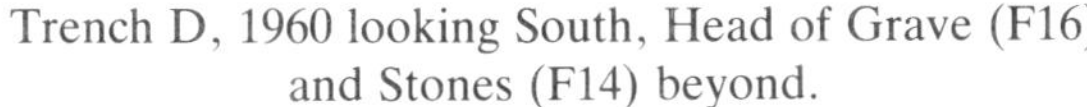

Trench D, 1960 looking South, Head of Grave (F16) and Stones (F14) beyond.

PLATE XVIIb

Trench D, 1960. Grave (F16) looking West after total Excavation.

PLATE XVIII

Trench III, 1972, looking South before Start of Excavation.

PLATE XIX

The Ground immediately to the North of Trench III, April 1972.

PLATE XX

Trench III, 1972, *a*. northern Buttress; *b*. southern Buttress (2 m. scales).

Trench II, 1972, *a*. northern Masonry Footings; *b*. southern Masonry Footings (metre scale).

PLATE XXII

Trench III, 1972, Road Surface (metre scale).

PLATE XXIII

Trench III, 1972, southern End, Hearth (metre scale).

PLATE XXIV

Trench II, 1972, looking South at Chalk Wall Footings in Front of modern Wall on Longport (metre scale).

PLATE XXV

Trench II, 1972, looking North showing Portions of fallen Masonry. The flint boundary wall was demolished in 1974.

PLATE XXVI

Lady Chapel, South Side, looking West showing earlier and later Buttresses, 1974.

PLATE XXVII

East Side of fallen Wall, 1974.

PLATE XXVIII

The fallen Wall, looking North after the Removal of the Core, 1975.

PLATE XXIX

(a)

(b)

The fallen Wall Face up (a), as reassembled (metre scale); (b) Detail showing Plaster and Offset.

PLATE XXX

Looking West after Excavation of fallen Wall, 1975.

PLATE XXXI, a

Tomb 8, View of North Side from Lady Chapel Buttress, 1975.

PLATE XXXI, b

Tomb 13, half excavated, looking West (metre scales in both), 1975.

(*Photo.: N. James.*)

The post-monastic Workshop, Building X, sealing the final phases of burials in the lay cemetery of the monastery. The robbing cut for buttress 519 (right) has partly cut away wall 520.

(*Photo.: N. James.*)

The Chantry Chapel viewed from the South Aisle during the 1976 Season, showing the floor bedding of re-used Roman tiles and robber trench 1007 excavated.

(*Photo.: J. Woods*)

Vault 1051 during Excavation (with North Wall dismantled). The rope groove for lowering the coffin is visible at its head.

(*Photo.: J. Woods*)

The Chantry Chapel viewed from the South Side during the 1977 Season, with the floor of Roman tile removed and showing tomb slabs 405, 406 and 407.

(*Photo.: J. Woods*)

Structure 702 from the East during the 1977 Season, showing the secondary facing and the impressions of robbed facing stones in the flint core.

(*Photo.: J. Woods*)

View from the West during the 1977 Season of Foundation 750 supporting Feature 741, the Footing for the South Aisle Wall. The core of the footing has been robbed.

(*Photo.: J. Woods*)

Feature 741, the Footing for the South Aisle Wall, from the South, with its Construction Trench, Feature 796 (before Excavation) cutting Layer 795. On the left is structure 702, and on the right, butted up against footing 741, buttress 740.

(*Photo.: J. Woods*)

The Anglo-Saxon Cemetery in Area IV, showing Burials 803 F, G, H, J and K. Burial 803 F is cut by structure 702 (background).

(*Photo.: J. Woods*)

Overall View from the South of the 1978 Excavation. The secondary stairbase, feature 5108, can be seen at the south-west corner of structure 702/5140.

(*Photo.: J. Woods*)

View of Saxon Tower, Feature 5105 (left), Foundation 5165 under Wall 5106 (centre) and Footing 5107 and 5107A (right). Foundation 5165 has been keyed into 5105. Footing 5107A cuts foundation 5165 and butts up against 5106. Footing 5107 overrides 5106.

(*Photo.: J. Woods*)

View from the North of Layer 8001 supporting Fragments of the robbed Norman Tower, Features 8013 and 8016 in the background, abutted by Structure 5140, and Features 8015 and 8017 in the Foreground, abutted by Structure 8014.

PLATE XLIII

(*Photo.: H. Woods*)

Detail (from North) of Feature 8013, abutted by Structure 5140.

PLATE XLIV

(*Photo.: J. Woods*)

View from the North of Feature 8010, the Foundation for the Norman South-West Tower, cutting Feature 8019, the Foundation for the South Aisle Wall, with Layer 8001, which seals both, unexcavated on the right of the picture.

(*Photo.: H. Woods*)

View from the East showing how Feature 8010, the Foundation for the Norman South-West Tower, cuts Feature 8019 (right), the Foundation for the South Aisle Footing. Both are sealed by layer 8001.

PLATE XLVI

(*Photo.: J. Woods*)

The foundation for the South Aisle Footing viewed from the South-West, showing the Stone Revetment, Feature 8018 (three courses have been removed) retaining Layer 8019, and Layers 8009 and 8012 excavated to expose Layer 8020.

PLATE XLVII

(*Photo.: J. Woods*)

Anglo-Saxon Burial 8003A in Area VIII, sealed under Structure 702. The skull is cushioned on a nest of flints and pieces of Roman brick.

Painted Arch from the Area of the Tumble. (Stone Cat. 1972, no. 84).

Plain Arch and Lead Flashing from the Area of the Tumble (Stone Cat. 1974, no. 96; Lead no. 19).

Stiff-leaf Stone Capital. (Stone Cat. 1974, no. 97).

Part of Corinthian Capital. (Stone Cat. 1976–78, no. 2).

Tile Floor in Position, East Walk of the Cloister.

Tile Mosaic Floor at Western End of the Nave.

GENERAL INDEX

Compiled by Mrs. L. Merrifield

Numerals in italics refer to figure numbers, e.g. *27*
Roman numerals refer to Plates, e.g. XIV
Numerals in bold type refer to Colour Plates, e.g. **2**